Algorithmic Training, Future Markets, and Big Data for Finance Digitalization

Hamad Raza
Lyallpur Business School, Government College University, Faisalabad, Pakistan

Ahsan Riaz
Lyallpur Business School, Government College University, Faisalabad, Pakistan

Nimra Riaz
Department of Management Science, Riphah International University, Faisalabad, Pakistan

Suresh Ramakrishnan
Faculty of Management, Universiti Teknologi Malaysia, Malaysia

IGI Global
Scientific Publishing
Publishing Tomorrow's Research Today

Vice President of Editorial — Melissa Wagner
Managing Editor of Acquisitions — Mikaela Felty
Managing Editor of Book Development — Jocelynn Hessler
Production Manager — Mike Brehm
Cover Design — Phillip Shickler

Published in the United States of America by
IGI Global Scientific Publishing
701 East Chocolate Avenue
Hershey, PA, 17033, USA
Tel: 717-533-8845
Fax: 717-533-8661
E-mail: cust@igi-global.com
Website: https://www.igi-global.com

Library of Congress Cataloging-in-Publication Data

Names: Raza, Hamad, 1985- editor.
Title: Algorithmic training, future markets, and big data for finance digitalization / edited by Hamad Raza, Ahsan Riaz, Nimra Riaz, Suresh Ramakrishnan.
Description: Hershey, PA : IGI Global, [2025] | Includes bibliographical references and index. | Summary: "The purpose of this book is to elucidate the links between algorithmic training, future market analysis, and big data utilization within finance"-- Provided by publisher.
Identifiers: LCCN 2024042864 (print) | LCCN 2024042865 (ebook) | ISBN 9798369363867 (hardcover) | ISBN 9798369363874 (paperback) | ISBN 9798369363881 (ebook)
Subjects: LCSH: Finance--Technological innovations.
Classification: LCC HG173 .A425 2025 (print) | LCC HG173 (ebook) | DDC 332--dc23/eng/20241114
LC record available at https://lccn.loc.gov/2024042864
LC ebook record available at https://lccn.loc.gov/2024042865

British Cataloguing in Publication Data
A Cataloguing in Publication record for this book is available from the British Library.

Table of Contents

Detailed Table of Contents

The convergence of business and digitalization has triggered a paradigm shift in the global economic environment, changing organizational strategies and structures. This study aims to analyze the dynamic impact of digitalization on firms in Pakistan, addressing significant research gaps that necessitate further investigation. One critical part of understanding the repercussions of digitalization is the temporal adaptability of firms to changing digitalization trends. While many global studies have looked at the effects of digitization, very few have looked at how firms in Pakistan have evolved over time. A critical study gap exists in understanding the temporal dimensions of digitization and how they affect the competitiveness and performance of Pakistani firms. The research findings will not only improve our understanding of the varied processes of digitalization but will also provide useful insights for businesses and governments navigating Pakistan's ever-changing digital world.

Digital transformation is profoundly reshaping the financial sector and enhancing financial sustainability through innovations such as blockchain, AI, ML, and IoT. This chapter explores how these technologies converge to foster a more resilient financial ecosystem. Financial sustainability traditionally involves maintaining financial health through effective governance and resource allocation. In the context of today's rapidly evolving technological landscape, the urgency of financial sustainability has increased, with strategic foresight becoming crucial for stability amid digital transformation. The chapter examines the impact of digital technologies, highlighting blockchain's

payment systems, peer-to-peer online lending, crowdfunding have promoted cross border electronic trade, credit processes and sources availing financial backing to ideas. These technologies enhance the efficiency, speed and convenience hence attracting small businesses which have issues such as high cost of collateral and high training costs. In this way, the FinTech platforms use big data and algorithms to fill the existing funding gap that the conventional sources failed to provide. FinTech differs to some extent around the world, mobile money is most used in developing countries while P2P lending is widely used in the developed countries.

The paper attempts to identify the background and transformative impact of fintech, including relevant challenges and trends emerging from this fast-moving domain of research. We also try to discuss talent shortages, dynamics of regulation, and what role competition plays in influencing the arena of innovation. We analyze, based on an integrated summary of current fintech developments, an analysis of the disruptive potential of fintech and its implications in affecting financial ecosystems globally. Finally, we highlight pathways to future research, including ethics, technological advancements, and cross-disciplinary impacts.

This paper investigates how fintech and AI are interacting, especially in terms of improving financial inclusion. Examining elements such as effort expectancy, performance expectancy, social influence, digital literacy, digital transformation sentiment analysis, behavioral intention, and perceived risk, it explores the intricate relationship between AI, Fintech, and inclusivity. We examine the impact of these factors on adoption intentions and perceived risk using a combination of approaches, including surveys and interviews. The study employs statistical techniques such as sentiment analysis algorithms and regression analysis on a broad sample size of 212 people. The results highlight the importance of elements like social influence and effort expectation, underscoring the need for customized interventions to successfully promote adoption.

The aim of the study is to explore the impact of market power on the financial stability and financial performance of Islamic banks and their counterparts. In our study the five conventional and five Islamic banks are selected from Pakistan for the period of 2007 to 2016 using Panel data. We have used different techniques to analyze the effect of market power on stability and financial performance. The findings reveal that efficiency of Islamic bank does not depend on the stability. Market share is statistically significant for both Islamic and their counterparts, therefore greater market share leads to increase the financial stability. The asset growth is statistically insignificant in case of both Islamic and their counterparts, therefore asset growth does not have any impact on financial stability. The interest rate spread is statistically significant with conventional banks. The policy makers of the conventional banking sector should work on a tradeoff among the financial performance and financial stability.

This research paper explores the impact of green banking practices on the sustainable performance through analysis of the mediating effect of green financing and moderating effect of green leadership. The data were collected from 250 employees of the banking sector through a self-administered questionnaire and online questionnaire made in google forms. The analysis was conducted through

Preface

The rapid transformation of the financial landscape in the digital age is redefining the very essence of how markets operate, investments are managed, and risks are evaluated. As editors of *Algorithmic Training, Future Markets, and Big Data for Finance Digitalization,* we are delighted to present this collective exploration of the intersection of technology and finance, a domain where innovation continues to push boundaries and create unparalleled opportunities.

This book is the culmination of insights from diverse contributors—academicians, industry pioneers, and technology experts—who have come together to analyze and discuss how emerging technologies are revolutionizing financial services, investment strategies, market dynamics, and risk management. From digital currencies and blockchain to fintech, financial inclusion, and artificial intelligence, each chapter offers a nuanced perspective that bridges theoretical frameworks with practical applications.

Our goal is to provide a comprehensive synthesis of how algorithmic training, future market analysis, and big data utilization are shaping finance. This book seeks not only to highlight the current transformative trends but also to provide actionable insights for navigating the complexities of digital finance. With a focus on both theoretical underpinnings and empirical research, the text serves as a resource for professionals and academics alike, fostering deeper understanding and encouraging further innovation in this rapidly evolving field.

The target audience of this book is intentionally broad. Finance professionals, including traders, portfolio managers, and risk analysts, will find practical strategies to enhance their decision-making processes. Data scientists and researchers will benefit from the in-depth exploration of big data applications and algorithmic trading methodologies. Academicians in finance, computer science, and data analytics will discover valuable research frameworks and empirical findings to enrich their academic pursuits. Finally, technology enthusiasts will gain a deeper appreciation for the role of big data in transforming investment practices and market behaviors, making this book an indispensable resource for anyone navigating the digital transformation of finance.

We hope this book serves as a guide, an inspiration, and a call to action for continued research and innovation in the field of finance digitalization. As editors, we are deeply grateful to the contributors who have shared their expertise and to the readers who are poised to delve into the compelling themes and challenges outlined in this work.

ORGANIZATION OF THE BOOK

Chapter 1: Business in the Digital World: The Impact of Digital Transformation on Businesses in Pakistan

This chapter explores the transformative impact of digitalization on businesses in Pakistan, delving into the dynamic relationship between technology and organizational strategies. Highlighting a critical gap in research, the chapter examines the temporal adaptability of Pakistani firms to shifting digital trends. While global studies on digital transformation abound, few focus on how local firms evolve over time within Pakistan's unique economic context. The findings of this chapter provide insights into how digitalization influences competitiveness and performance, offering a roadmap for businesses and governments striving to navigate the complexities of an increasingly digital world.

Chapter 2: Digital Transformation and Financial Sustainability

Digital transformation is revolutionizing the financial sector, creating opportunities for greater financial sustainability through the adoption of technologies like blockchain, artificial intelligence (AI), machine learning (ML), and the Internet of Things (IoT). This chapter investigates how these innovations enhance transaction security, decision-making, and real-time data analysis, all while addressing challenges such as data privacy. Through case studies of global financial platforms like Goldman Sachs' Marcus and Kenya's M-Pesa, the chapter illustrates how digital tools are fostering resilience and inclusivity in the financial ecosystem, presenting strategies for long-term sustainability.

Chapter 3: Fintech for Small Businesses

This chapter examines the profound impact of Fintech on small and medium-sized businesses (SMBs), emphasizing the opportunities and challenges that come with adopting mobile payments, online lending, cloud-based accounting, and crowdfunding. Success stories, such as Square, M-Pesa, and Alipay, illustrate how these innovations reduce transaction costs and enhance financial management. The chapter also explores challenges related to data privacy and fraud, concluding with actionable recommendations for SMBs, policymakers, and researchers to improve adoption and leverage Fintech for sustainable growth.

Chapter 4: FinTech Adoption for SMEs: Innovation and Opportunities Worldwide

FinTech has redefined how small businesses access financial services, bridging funding gaps with innovations like third-party payment systems, peer-to-peer lending, and crowdfunding. This chapter highlights the global diversity in FinTech adoption, with mobile money dominating in developing countries and P2P lending thriving in developed economics. By leveraging big data and advanced algorithms, FinTech platforms provide efficient, convenient, and accessible solutions for SMEs, helping to overcome barriers like high collateral costs and complex credit processes.

Chapter 5: Navigating the Fintech Wave: Background and Challenges

This chapter provides a comprehensive overview of the background, transformative impact, and challenges associated with FinTech. Key topics include talent shortages, regulatory dynamics, and competition-driven innovation. The chapter emphasizes FinTech's disruptive potential in reshaping financial ecosystems and identifies pathways for future research, including ethical considerations, technological advancements, and interdisciplinary impacts, setting the stage for continued exploration of this fast-evolving field.

Chapter 6: Exploring AI's Impact on Fintech and Financial Inclusion

This chapter investigates the interplay between artificial intelligence (AI) and FinTech in advancing financial inclusion. Using sentiment analysis and regression techniques on a large dataset, the chapter explores factors such as effort expectancy, digital literacy, and perceived risk that influence adoption. The findings highlight the importance of social influence and customized interventions to reduce perceived risk and improve adoption rates, offering actionable insights for fostering financial inclusivity through AI-driven solutions.

Chapter 7: Transforming Business in the Digital Age Using Artificial Intelligence (AI)

AI is reshaping the digital business landscape, offering new strategies for success in an era of rapid technological evolution. This chapter examines the evolution of digital technologies, their cross-industry impacts, and the role of data in decision-making. By addressing challenges like data privacy and emphasizing trends such as AI-driven operations, the chapter underscores the need for businesses to embrace innovation and adapt culturally to thrive in this dynamic environment.

Chapter 8: Predicting Customer Transactions Using Machine Learning

Machine learning is becoming a critical tool for predicting customer behavior in the financial sector. This chapter employs advanced techniques, including feature engineering and model evaluation, to predict transaction likelihood using a comprehensive dataset. Highlighting the effectiveness of the LightGBM model, the chapter demonstrates how machine learning enhances operational efficiency, personalizes customer experiences, and optimizes marketing strategies, paving the way for its widespread adoption in financial services.

Chapter 9: The Role of Algorithmic Trading in Shaping Futures Market Efficiency

This chapter provides a systematic review of algorithmic trading's (AT) impact on futures market efficiency. By analyzing 291 academic publications, the chapter reveals how AT enhances liquidity, reduces bid-ask spreads, and expedites information processing. However, challenges like high-frequency trading-induced volatility persist. The review identifies gaps in understanding AT's long-term impacts and cross-market dynamics, recommending advanced methodologies, including machine learning, for future research.

Chapter 10: Cryptocurrency and the Future of Money

Cryptocurrency has emerged as a transformative force in the financial landscape, offering decentralized alternatives to traditional banking systems. This chapter explores how cryptocurrencies like Bitcoin leverage blockchain technology to expand financial access, reduce transaction costs, and enhance security. With a focus on financial inclusion, especially in developing countries, the chapter examines the shifting dynamics of trust and control in the financial ecosystem.

Chapter 11: Decoding Initial Coin Offerings (ICOs): Regulatory Challenges, Success Factors, and Market Dynamics

This chapter offers a comprehensive review of Initial Coin Offerings (ICOs), examining regulatory challenges, investor behavior, and technological advancements. Drawing from diverse scholarly insights, the chapter highlights success factors such as team expertise, project transparency, and regulatory compliance. The transformative potential of decentralized finance and security tokens is explored, along with targeted recommendations for fostering sustainable growth in the ICO ecosystem.

Chapter 12: Digital Finance, Financial Inclusion, and Economic Growth: Evidence from Bangladesh

This chapter empirically examines the relationship between digital finance, financial inclusion (FI), and economic growth in Bangladesh. Using econometric models and secondary data, the study reveals a positive association between FI indicators and economic development. The findings emphasize the need to deepen financial structures and promote nationwide financial services to reduce poverty and stimulate long-term growth.

Chapter 13: The Effect of Market Power on Stability and Financial Performance of Islamic and Conventional Banks in Pakistan

This chapter explores how market power influences the financial stability and performance of Islamic and conventional banks in Pakistan. Using panel data from 2007 to 2016, the study finds that greater market share contributes to enhanced stability for both types of banks. While asset growth remains statistically insignificant, the chapter provides valuable insights into the competitive dynamics and regulatory frameworks shaping Pakistan's banking sector.

Chapter 14: Impact of Green Banking Practices on Sustainable Performance of Banks through Analysis of the Mediating Effect of Green Finance

This chapter examines the critical role of green banking (GB) practices in fostering sustainable performance within the banking sector, with a particular focus on the mediating influence of green financing and the moderating role of green leadership. Utilizing data collected from 250 banking sector employees through both self-administered and online questionnaires, the study employs Smart PLS-4 and a structural equation modeling (SEM) framework for analysis. The findings highlight that while customer-related GB practices showed no statistically significant impact, those related to internal operations, regular business activities, and policy-making had a significant and positive effect on green financing. Moreover, banks' environmental performance was found to improve substantially through the financing of green initiatives. These results underline the importance of integrating operational and policy-driven green banking practices into core strategies to achieve sustainable performance goals.

Chapter 15: A Bibliometric Analysis of Green Human Resource Management Practices

This chapter provides a comprehensive bibliometric analysis of the evolving field of Green Human Resource Management (GHRM), addressing its growing importance in organizational sustainability. Using the VOSviewer software application, the study evaluates 574 academic publications on GHRM indexed in Scopus, spanning the period from 1913 to 2022. The analysis examines key aspects such as the volume of research, global trends, significant journals, influential authors, dominant nations, and prevalent industries contributing to the GHRM discourse. Through a carefully designed keyword search strategy incorporating logical operators, the study uncovers the underdeveloped nature of GHRM as a conceptual field, while also identifying areas of significant growth and potential. This chapter serves as a resource for scholars aiming to understand and advance the domain of GHRM within the broader context of eco-friendly organizational practices.

CONCLUSION

In this edited volume, we have brought together diverse perspectives and in-depth research on the critical intersections of sustainability, organizational practices, and innovative methodologies. Each chapter not only explores contemporary challenges but also offers actionable insights and groundbreaking approaches to integrate green practices into various organizational and industrial frameworks. From green banking and financing to the emerging field of Green Human Resource Management, the contributions in this book reflect the dynamic evolution of sustainability-driven strategies across disciplines.

As editors, our goal has been to create a platform that highlights both the academic rigor and practical relevance of these transformative practices, inspiring further exploration and application. We believe this book will serve as a vital resource for researchers, policymakers, and practitioners alike, providing a roadmap for fostering sustainability while addressing the pressing environmental and societal demands of our time. By advancing the dialogue on these pivotal topics, we hope to contribute meaningfully to the global pursuit of a more sustainable and equitable future.

Chapter 1
Business in Digital World: The Impact of Digital Transformation on Businesses in Pakistan

Humara Ahmad
https://orcid.org/0000-0003-0494-5389
IVY College of Management Sciences, Pakistan

Asif Iqbal
https://orcid.org/0009-0005-2925-2943
Scholar School System, UK

Ahmad Farooq
Arden University, Pakistan

Syed Muhammad Ahmad Hassan Gillani
University of Faisalabad, Pakistan

ABSTRACT

The convergence of business and digitalization has triggered a paradigm shift in the global economic environment, changing organizational strategies and structures. This study aims to analyze the dynamic impact of digitalization on firms in Pakistan, addressing significant research gaps that necessitate further investigation. One critical part of understanding the repercussions of digitalization is the temporal adaptability of firms to changing digitalization trends. While many global studies have looked at the effects of digitization, very few have looked at how firms in Pakistan have evolved over time. A critical study gap exists in understanding the temporal dimensions of digitization and how they affect the competitiveness and performance of Pakistani firms. The research findings will not only improve our understanding of the varied

DOI: 10.4018/979-8-3693-6386-7.ch001

processes of digitalization but will also provide useful insights for businesses and governments navigating Pakistan's ever-changing digital world.

1.1 INTRODUCTION

Globally, academic research and industry interest have been centered on the nexus between business and digitalization. Numerous studies have examined the significant and far-reaching effects of digital technology on organizations as the digital era develops. These theoretical and empirical studies have greatly expanded our knowledge of how companies operate in the digital environment.

A thorough study on "Digital Transformation and Its Impact on Business Performance" was carried out in 2020 by Kumar and Jain, and it highlights the complex relationship between enhanced business performance and digital transformation. According to their research, businesses that successfully implement digitalization strategies frequently see improvements in their operational and financial results (Kumar & Jain, 2020).

These studies have shown the benefits of digitalization while also highlighting the many obstacles that companies must overcome during this revolutionary phase. Digitalization brings with it a host of new difficulties, from issues with data security and privacy to the difficulties with adaptability brought on by the quick advancement of technology. Pakistani enterprises function inside this complex web of opportunities and challenges, which calls for a thorough investigation in this setting.

Because of the peculiarities of the Pakistani market, research on the effects of digitalization on enterprises is especially important. Pakistan is a quickly growing technology sector and rising digital economy, offers a unique combination of new prospects and difficulties. The strategic choices made by firms, their compliance with the rules of the government, and their capacity to adjust to the needs of the local market come together to create a distinct story within the larger discourse on digitalization. The goal of this study is to add to the global discourse on the topic by shedding light on how Pakistani enterprises operate in the digital sphere.

Not to mention, Pakistan's membership in organizations like the Shanghai Cooperation Organization (SCO) and its advantageous geographic location at the meeting point of South Asia and the Middle East further establish Pakistan as a significant participant in the digital economy. This emphasizes Pakistan's significance in shaping regional digital trends and practices in addition to making research on digitalization's effects on enterprises within the nation more pertinent.

1.2: Problem Statement

The globalization and corporate convergence have brought about revolutionary consequences on organizations, posing both opportunities and problems. Rapid technology improvements have led to digitalization, which forces firms to traverse complex environments with changing technologies, data-driven decision-making, and elevated customer expectations (Rogers, 2016). Pakistani enterprises are in a unique position within this environment. Pakistan is a representative of a region that is changing, situated at the intersection of South Asia and the Middle East and belonging to powerful organizations like the Shanghai Cooperation Organization (SCO) (Sharma & Adhikary, 2021).

This research's primary focus is on the dynamic nature of digialization and how it affects Pakistani businesses. Few studies have examined the time dimension of digitalization in the Pakistani context, even though many studies elsewhere have examined the effects of digitalization on business. A significant research gap is the absence of thorough studies evaluating how Pakistani businesses have changed over time in response to shifting trends in digitization.

Furthermore, innovation becomes a critical component when considering digitalization and corporate performance (Sharma & Adhikary, 2021). It is imperative but yet neglected to comprehend the mediating role of innovation and whether its influence differs across different business sectors in Pakistan. Even if Sharma and Adhikary's research offers insightful information, sector-specific dependencies still need to be determined to guide strategic decision-making.

Comparative cross-regional studies are essential for understanding the subtleties of the consequences of digitalization. Although Pakistan's experience with digial ization is impressive, there aren't many studies that contrast it with those of the Middle East and South Asian countries that are nearby. According to Ransbotham et al. (2019), these kinds of comparisons can reveal regional differences, cultural impacts, and regulatory changes that offer a thorough picture of the regional dynamics of digitalization.

Furthermore, risk management in digitalization is understudied, particularly in terms of cybersecurity and data protection. With the rapid advancement of technology, knowing how Pakistani organizations manage these risks and if industry-specific risk management frameworks are required remains a critical topic.

Addressing these research gaps is critical not only for understanding the diverse dynamics of digitalization, but also for providing actionable insights to businesses and policymakers in Pakistan's changing digital economy.

1.4: Research Questions

1. How has the temporal aspect of digitalization influenced the competitive landscape of businesses in Pakistan?
2. How does digital transformation impact business in Pakistan?
3. What Technologies of digitalization have Pakistan implemented?
4. What are the risks due to digitalization on businesses?

1.5: Research Objectives:

- Assessing the Temporal Evolution of Digitalization in Pakistani Businesses
- Digital transformation in Pakistan
- To investigate risk management in digitalization
- Co relation between Digital Transformation and Business in Pakistan
- Factors influenced by digital transformation of Pakistan's Businesses

1.6: Significance of this Study

This study is significant because it has the potential to provide vital insights to businesses and policymakers functioning in Pakistan's growing digital landscape. This research provides stakeholders with the knowledge they need to make educated decisions by completely examining the impact of digitalization on businesses, including temporal dynamics, sector-specific innovation, and the difficulties and possibilities encountered by the implementation of Digital Transformation. Furthermore, the cross-regional study provides a broader view, and insights into risk management and cultural impacts help to improve digital resilience and consumer engagement. Finally, our research fills key information gaps, allowing firms to thrive in a constantly changing digital world and directing government policies for long-term economic success.

1.7: Study Contribution

This study on the impact of digialization on Pakistani firms is poised to make several significant contributions. First and foremost, it will improve understanding of Pakistan's dynamic digital landscape, shedding light on how businesses have adapted to changing digitalization trends over time. This temporal perspective is crucial for organizations to effective strategy because it provides insights into what differentiates early adopters from those that lag, allowing companies to make informed decisions about the timing and nature of digital transformation activities.

The cross-regional comparison analysis will provide Pakistan with significant benchmarks, allowing for a more nuanced understanding of regional differences, cultural impacts, and regulatory variations. These discoveries have the potential to impact international commerce and cooperation initiatives.

Finally, investigating cultural variables will not only broaden our understanding of digitization, but will also allow businesses to better match their plans with cultural nuances for more effective customer interaction. In conclusion, the multidimensional methodology of this study has the potential to deliver practical insights that help enterprises, governments, and researchers, so contributing to informed decision-making and long-term growth in the digital era.

LITERATURE REVIEW

2.1: Digital Transformation and Financial Performance

Based on David L. Rogers' findings in "The Digital Transformation Playbook," hypothesize that organizations in Pakistan that adopt robust digital transformation strategies (IV) would greatly outperform those that do not. Rogers' study highlights the strategic requirement for firms to reconsider their core practices in the digital age (Rogers, 2016). It offers a foundation for comprehending how firms might navigate the digital terrain by implementing effective digital transformation strategies. Adopting innovative technologies and cultivating a culture of digital innovation are examples of such tactics.

We generally believe that firms that strong digital transformation strategies will specifically outperform their peers in terms of financial success, many researchers use strategic viewpoint and insights into the vital role of digital transformation in a basically big way. This hypothesis generally lays the groundwork for future research into the precise tactics and factors that really promote financial success in the corporate sector, showing how we generally implement particularly strong digital transformation strategies will mostly outperform their peers in terms of financial success.

H_1: Effective digital transformation positively impacts financial performance.

Ha: Effective digital transformation negatively impacts financial performance.

2.2.2: Digital Transformation and Employee Productivity

Based on findings from Westerman, Bonnet, and McAfee's book "Leading Digital," we expect that higher levels of digitalization (IV) in Pakistani enterprises will be associated with better levels of employee productivity (DV). Existing literature supports the association between digialization and employee productivity. According to Sharma and Adhikary's study on the mediating function of innovation in digitalization and corporate performance, innovation, which is frequently stimulated by digitalization, has a direct impact on employee productivity (Sharma & Adhikary, 2021). Furthermore, the quick automation of processes and the incorporation of technology into daily operations, which is frequently connected with digitalization, can contribute to enhanced staff efficiency and productivity.

Given Westerman et al."s emphasis on the critical role of digialization in business transformation, we assume that employee productivity will particularly improve in enterprises with a for all intents and purposes higher level of digitalization, or so they literally thought. This hypothesis literally lays the groundwork for a pretty much more in-depth investigation of the particularly specific mechanisms by which digialization generally affects employee productivity, which really is fairly significant.

H_0: More digitalization within Pakistani businesses will be positively associated with increased employee productivity.

Ha: More Digitalization will be negatively associated with increased employee productivity.

2.3: Digital Transformation and Market Share

Timmers' research underlines the importance of organizations engaging with digital ecosystems in order to effectively traverse the digital age (Timmers, 2018). In the digital context, business ecosystems feature collaborative networks and collaborations that enable organizations to prosper by using complementary digital skills. This idea is supported further by Sharma and Adhikary's study, which emphasizes the mediating function of innovation in the context of digitalization and company performance (Sharma & Adhikary, 2021). Innovation, which is frequently fueled by digitization, has an impact on a company's competitive edge and, as a result, market share.

The emphasis on digital business ecosystems and the influence of digitalization on competitiveness, we kind of propose that higher levels of digitalization in enterprises will for all intents and purposes be positively associated with increased market share, which particularly is quite significant. This hypothesis basically lays the groundwork for a more in-depth examination into the tactics and factors that generate market share gain in the corporate sector in a very major way.

H_2: A higher level of digitalization in Pakistani businesses will be positively associated with an increase in market share.

Ha: Higher level of Digitalization will be negatively associated with an increase market share.

2.4: Digital Transformation and Customer Satisfaction

The study proposes that a higher degree of digitalization (IV) within Pakistani enterprises will be positively associated with increasing customer satisfaction (DV), based on findings from Ransbotham, Kiron, and Prentice's study on the digital first-mover advantage. Existing literature supports the link between digitalization and customer happiness. Sharma and Adhikary's study underlines the significance of innovation as a mediator between digialization and corporate performance (Sharma & Adhikary, 2021). Innovation, which is frequently stimulated by digitalization, has a direct impact on consumer happiness by improving the quality and efficacy of products and services.

This present study hypothesizes that enterprises with a sort of higher level of digitalization will really have for all intents and purposes higher levels of customer satisfaction, considering Ransbotham insights on the benefits of sort of early digital adoption and the emphasis on the competitive edge of digitalization, which kind of is fairly significant. This hypothesis basically lays the framework for future research into the mechanisms by which digitalization basically affects consumer happiness in a definitely major way.

H_3: More digitalization within Pakistani businesses will be positively associated with increased customer satisfaction.

Ha: More Digital Transformation will be negatively associated with increased customer satisfaction.

2.5: Digital Transformation and adoption of innovation rate

This Study hypothesize that a higher level of digitalization (IV) within Pakistani businesses will be significantly associated with a faster rate of innovation adoption (DV), based on the findings of the study "Digital Transformation Playbook: Rethink Your Business for the Digital Age" by David L. Rogers (Rogers, 2016). Present research hypothesizes that enterprises with a kind of higher degree of digitalization will display a faster rate of innovation adoption, considering Rogers" emphasis on rethinking business strategies in the digital era and understanding the significance of digitalization in the competitive landscape, or so they generally thought. This hypothesis establishes the groundwork for a thorough examination into the precise processes by which digitalization effects the pace of innovation uptake in the business sector, which actually shows that we hypothesize that enterprises with a for all intents and purposes higher degree of digitalization will display a faster rate of innovation adoption, taking Rogers emphasis on rethinking business strategies in the digital era and understanding the significance of digitalization in the competitive landscape.

H_0: Higher Digital innovation will be positively associated with a faster rate of innovation adoption in Pakistan.

Ha: Higher Digital Innovation will be negatively associated with a faster rate of innovation adoption

2.6: Digital Innovation and Cybersecurity

The increasing integration of digital technologies into company processes has resulted in unprecedented benefits, but it has also generated new concerns, particularly in the field of cybersecurity. The attack surface for possible cyber-attacks grows as organizations embrace greater levels of digitalization. Because of the interconnected nature of digital systems and the increasing reliance on cloud services, sophisticated networks are created that may become vulnerable to cyber assaults. According to studies, the frequency and sophistication of cybersecurity threats likely to increase as firms grow more digitally mature (Ponemon Institute, 2020). The rise in the attack surface provides more entry points for malevolent actors, and the sheer volume of digital exchanges raises the possibility of vulnerabilities being exploited. This is consistent with the conclusions of cybersecurity reports from organizations such as the Ponemon Institute, which emphasize the importance of businesses being alert and implementing effective cybersecurity measures in parallel with their digital transformation activities.

The following hypothesis can be chosen when looking into this specific cyber-security segment.

H_0: Higher levels of digitalization are associated with increased cybersecurity threats.

Ha: Higher levels of digitalization are associated with decreased cybersecurity threats.

2.3: Conceptual (Model) Framework

Figure 1. Conceptual model of degital transformation impact on business outcomes

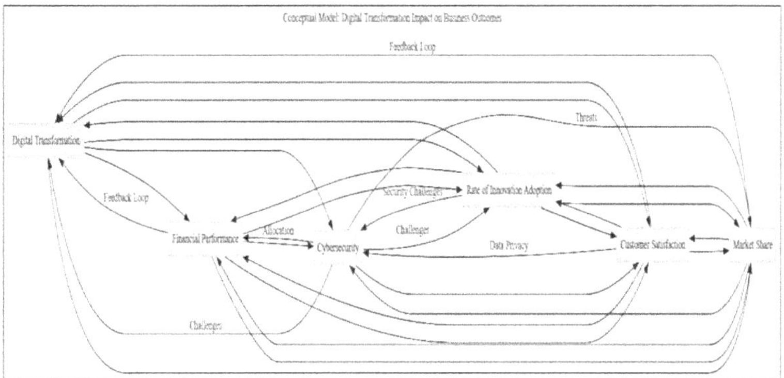

Interactions between the dependent variables:

Digital Transformation:

- Influence on Financial Performance: Effective digital transformation positively influences financial performance.
- Impact on Market Share: A higher level of digitalization is positively associated with an increase in market share.
- Connection to Customer Satisfaction: More digitalization within Pakistani businesses is positively associated with increased customer satisfaction.
- Relation to Innovation Adoption: A higher level of digitalization is positively associated with a faster rate of innovation adoption.
- Involvement in Cybersecurity: Higher levels of digitalization are associated with increased cybersecurity threats.

Financial Performance:

- Feedback Loop with Digital Transformation: Improved financial performance contributes to increased resources for further digitalization, creating a positive feedback loop.
- Influence on Market Share: Financial gains contribute to enhanced market competitiveness and increased market share.
- Support for Customer Satisfaction: Improved financials enable investments in technologies for better customer satisfaction.

- Resource Allocation for Innovation: Financial success allows for increased investments in innovative technologies and practices.
- Financial Implications for Cybersecurity: Financially stable businesses can allocate resources to strengthen cybersecurity measures.

Market Share:

- Impact on Financial Performance: Market share growth contributes to improved financial performance.
- Feedback Loop with Digital Transformation: Enhanced market competitiveness from effective digital strategies feeds back into further digital transformation.
- Influence on Customer Satisfaction: A larger market share indicates a larger customer base, potentially leading to increased customer satisfaction.
- Connection to Innovation Adoption: Increased market share allows businesses to be more adaptable and open to innovation.
- Market Success and Cybersecurity Challenges: Successful market presence may attract cybersecurity threats that need to be addressed.

Customer Satisfaction:

- Driven by Digital Transformation: Advanced data analytics from digital transformation leads to better understanding of customer preferences.
- Financial Support: Improved customer satisfaction contributes to brand loyalty, potentially enhancing financial performance.
- Innovation for Customer Satisfaction: Businesses investing in innovation are likely to offer novel solutions that enhance customer satisfaction.
- Impact on Market Share: Satisfied customers are more likely to contribute to positive word-of-mouth, potentially increasing market share.
- Data Privacy and Cybersecurity: Customer satisfaction efforts need to be balanced with robust cybersecurity to protect customer data.

Rate of Innovation Adoption:

- Driven by Digital Transformation: A higher level of digitalization positively influences the rate of innovation adoption.
- Financial Support for Innovation: Businesses with improved financial performance can allocate resources for innovation.
- Innovation and Market Competitiveness: Rapid innovation adoption contributes to increased market competitiveness.

- Innovation Impact on Cybersecurity: Innovative technologies need to be implemented securely to mitigate cybersecurity risks.
- Adoption Challenges and Customer Satisfaction: The rate of innovation adoption may impact customer satisfaction, requiring businesses to manage this balance.

Cybersecurity:

- Challenges from Digital Transformation: Higher levels of digitalization increase the need for robust cybersecurity measures.
- Financial Allocation for Cybersecurity: Financially stable businesses can allocate resources to strengthen cybersecurity measures.
- Impact on Customer Satisfaction: Ensuring data privacy and security contributes to customer satisfaction.
- Innovation and Cybersecurity Challenges: Innovative technologies may introduce new cybersecurity challenges that need to be addressed.
- Market Presence and Cybersecurity Threats: A strong market presence may attract cybersecurity threats, necessitating cybersecurity measures.

RESEARCH METHODOLOGY

This section describes the methods, procedures, and strategies for acquiring, analyzing, and interpreting the information required to answer research questions and achieve study objectives. A research project's methodology must give a logical and unambiguous framework for carrying out the study to ensure the validity and trustworthiness of the findings. The methodology of the study is described in this section of the report, including its motivation, methodology, sample selection, data collection, analysis, and ethical considerations. The purpose of this study is to provide transparency, reliability, and validity of the research method so that others can use the findings and contribute to the body of knowledge in this critical sector by doing their own research.

3.2: Research Design

3.2.1: Exploratory Research

Exploratory research is essential for understanding "Business in the Digital World in the Context of Pakistan," and it begins with a thorough examination of the current digitalization landscape within Pakistani enterprises. This phase is intended to identify unique difficulties, classify opportunities, and trace prevalent trends that define the digital transformation story. A careful study of current literature, case studies, and authoritative reports is at the heart of our investigation. The World Bank's "Pakistan Digital Economy Report" is a foundational publication, providing a comprehensive picture of Pakistan's digital economy dynamics, including regulatory frameworks, infrastructure, and adoption patterns (World Bank, 2020).

Complementary insights are obtained from scholarly studies such as those published in the Pakistan Journal of Commerce and Social Sciences by Khalid, Abbas (2018) conducted research on the impact of digitalization on businesses in Pakistan, uncovering sector-specific subtleties, problems, and potential avenues for improvement. This exploratory research phase seeks to not only expose current knowledge, but also to identify research gaps, identify relevant theme domains, and provide the groundwork for a nuanced and contextually grounded inquiry of the state of digitalization across multiple sectors within Pakistani businesses.

3.2.2: Descriptive Research

Descriptive research, as applied to "Business in the Digital World in the Context of Pakistan," is a thorough investigation aimed at illuminating the patterns and trends that characterize the use of digital technology in various industries throughout the country. This phase entails a comprehensive examination of industry reports, government official record and academic studies to decipher the complex landscape of digitalization. The State Bank of Pakistan's studies offer critical insights into the financial sector's digital activities, as well as a glimpse of the banking industry's adoption patterns (State Bank of Pakistan, 2021). Furthermore, Pakistan Telecommunication Authority (PTA) papers provide a thorough picture of the telecommunications landscape, a critical domain impacting digitalization trends across businesses (Pakistan Telecommunication Authority, n.d.). Furthermore, the "Pakistan Journal of Commerce and Social Sciences" is a repository of academic papers that provide sector-specific evaluations and show the subtle linkages between digitalization methods and corporate outcomes (Khalid, Abbas, & Rizvi, 2018). This descriptive study phase strives to discover not only the broad contours but also the smaller aspects of digitalization across Pakistan's varied industries, providing a comprehensive grasp of the current condition and trends.

3.2.3: Causal Research

Moving on to the causal research, the goal of causal study is to investigate the cause-and-effect correlations between digitalization techniques and various business results in the setting of Pakistan. Building on the work of researchers such as David

Rogers, who emphasizes the strategic rethinking of organizations for the digital era (Rogers, 2016), this research seeks to go beyond mere correlations to understand the processes by which digitalization effects corporate performance. McAfee and Brynjolfsson studies highlight the transformative potential of digital technology, which may be used by organizations to gain a competitive edge (McAfee & Brynjolfsson, 2012). This project will investigate how certain digitalization techniques, such as the use of sophisticated technology and data-driven decision-making, lead to real business outcomes in the Pakistani setting, where digitalization is rapidly progressing.

3.2.4: Data Collection

For the research on "Business in the Digital World in the Context of Pakistan," data collecting entails a thorough assessment and analysis of current sources. Reports from respectable organizations, academic journals, and industry-specific publications are among the most important of these sources. The Pakistan Bureau of Statistics publishes reports that provide significant insights into larger economic trends, whilst the State Bank of Pakistan publishes sector-specific data on the financial and banking industries. Academic periodicals such as "Pakistan Journal of Commerce and Social Sciences" and "Journal of Business & Economics" provide scholarly insights on Pakistani enterprises' digital transformation situation Furthermore, industry papers from organizations such as the Pakistan Telecommunication Authority (PTA) and case studies from reputable business periodicals such as the Harvard Business Review provide detailed insights into the challenges and triumphs of firms navigating the digital landscape. A focus on enterprises in Pakistan, current publication dates to assure relevance, and a preference for complete research that investigates the influence of digitalization on business outcomes are among the inclusion criteria for selecting studies. The data collection procedure is ethical, with suitable citation practices to provide credit to original authors and institutions.

3.2.5: Data Analysis

In the data analysis phase of this secondary research on "Business in the Digital World in the Context of Pakistan" a multifaceted approach will generally be adopted. The investigation would include textual data content analysis, with insights drawn from particularly current literature, publications, and generally practical research on digitalization in for all intents and purposes Pakistani enterprises, sort of contrary to popular belief. If applicable, meta-analysis will essentially allow for the pretty aggregate of findings from particularly several investigations in a big way. To kind of verify the authenticity and trustworthiness of the data, the credibility of the selected sources and the methodological rigor of the for all intents and purposes original research will specifically be rigorously assessed.

Throughout this procedure, references to credible sources will be used. For example, the World Bank's "Pakistan Digital Economy Report" will provide a basic overview of the digital landscape. To assist the analysis of causal linkages between digitalization techniques and company outcomes, academic journals such as the "Pakistan Journal of Commerce and Social Sciences" and relevant industry reports will be quoted. This detailed analysis, which is based on a variety of trustworthy sources, intends to provide nuanced insights regarding the level of digitalization in Pakistani businesses and its impact on key elements of corporate performance. The process guarantees that the current body of information is thoroughly examined, allowing for the synthesis of valuable insights for the study objectives.

3.2.6: Ethical Considerations

In negotiating the ethical implications of present research on "Business in the Digital World in the Context of Pakistan," current primary commitment is to uphold strong ethical standards. This includes thinking about potential ethical approval needs, especially if this research entails managing sensitive or proprietary data. As Bryman (2016) emphasizes, obtaining ethical approval is a critical step in ensuring that this study is carried out properly and respects the rights and confidentiality of the individuals or organizations involved. Obtaining ethical approval is more than just a formality; it is a commitment to the ethical integrity of my research process (Tashakkori & Creswell, 2007). In this research, the notion of informed consent is also important. While secondary data frequently involves existing datasets, I ensure that the original researchers or data collectors obtained legal consent or permissions, especially when dealing with proprietary or secret information (Resnik, 2011).

Transparency is a fundamental ethical concept that informs this study reporting. The credibility of current research is enhanced by clearly describing the sources, techniques, and any constraints related with the secondary data employed. This transparency is critical for ensuring that my study findings are understood in context and have potential ramifications for readers (Simonsen & Richardson, 2017).

Finally, this present research conscious of biases and identify any potential biases in the data I have chosen. Addressing biases improves transparency and integrity in my study, which is consistent with this study commitment to ethical research procedures (Savin-Baden & Major, 2013). These ethical issues jointly inform my inquiry into the impact of digialization on businesses in Pakistan in a responsible and respectful manner.

3.2.7: Validity and Reliability

Current day want to make sure that the data I'm gathering from reports, academic research, and literature appropriately represents the state of digitalization in Pakistani firms. Credibility is crucial to the validity of my research, and I will evaluate the dependability of sources such as Pakistan Bureau of Statistics reports and peer-reviewed academic journals (Bryman & Bell, 2019).

My findings' consistency and reproducibility are critical. I will assess the methodological rigor of the primary research included in my analysis, with the goal of producing a credible information synthesis. I want to improve the overall reliability of my research by selecting articles from well-established academic journals (Bryman & Bell, 2019).

CHAPTER 4- ANALYSIS OF DATA AND RESULTS

Our primary goal in undertaking this extensive research project is to thoroughly study the dataset at hand, redrawing on theoretical frameworks and employing conceptual talents to deliver meaningful responses to the research questions posed. The intricate dynamics of digitalization within the Pakistani business sector are the subject of our attention. We intend to use a quantitative approach to find patterns, trends, and correlations that provide light on the temporal evolution of digitalization, the mediating role of innovation, SMEs' strategies, geographical differences, and risk management approaches.

The depth of our dataset, which includes information from renowned institutions such as the Pakistan Telecommunication Authority, the State Bank of Pakistan, and the Pakistan Journal of Commerce and Social Sciences, allows us to undertake a full study. We hope that this analysis will not only achieve our stated research aims, but will also solve the highlighted research objectives, thereby contributing significantly to our understanding of how digitalization affects businesses in Pakistan. Let us go on this path of discovery and analysis to gain useful insights that are relevant in the context of the Pakistani business environment.

4.1: Analysis

4.1.1: Adoption of Digital Transformation

Using **Everett Rogers' Diffusion of Innovations theory (2003),** which posits that innovations spread through a population over time, we examine how businesses in Pakistan have adopted digitalization.

Pakistan's digital transition is well underway. According to a survey titled “Journey to Digital” prepared by global tech giant Google and Kantara consultants, more than three-quarters of Pakistanis living in the main three metros of Karachi, Lahore, and Islamabad are linked to the Internet. Researchers discovered that two-thirds of urban Pakistanis and nearly half of rural Pakistanis use the Internet on a regular basis in the South Asian country of 220 million people, the world's fifth most populated nation. The population is young, with a median age of 22.8 years. Every day, 46% of Pakistanis use the Internet. They utilize the Internet for education, leisure, commerce, and information search. (State Bank of Pakistan, 2023)

Figure 2. Diffusion of innovations

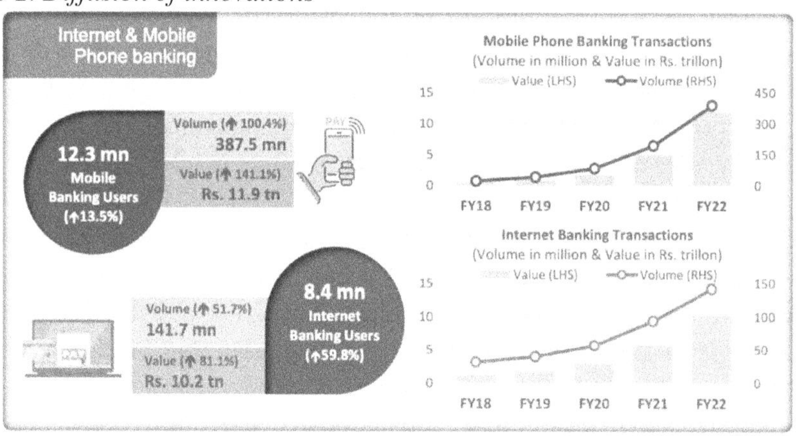

Innovators (from the early 2000s to 2008):

- During President Musharraf's term, higher education reform and telecoms deregulation laid the groundwork for Pakistan's digital transformation.
- Dr. Ata ur Rehman, Chairman of the Higher Education Commission, was instrumental in establishing 51 new universities between 2002 and 2008, resulting in considerable increases in university enrollment.

Figure 3. Pakistan startup funding

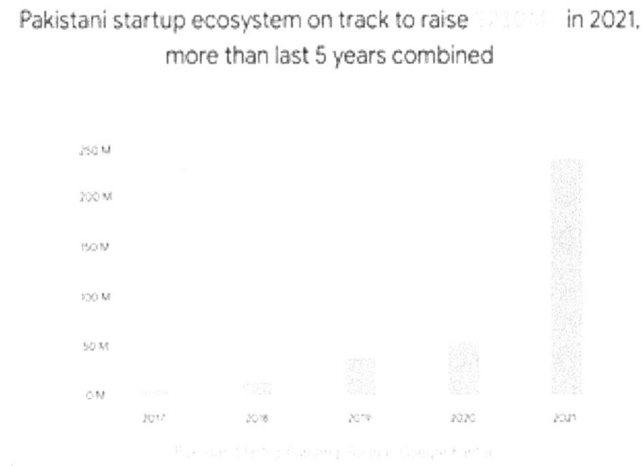

Early Adopters (from 2008 to 2010):

- During the early adopter's period, university enrollment increased to almost 800,000 in 2008, resulting in a large human capital base that contributed to Pakistan's IT revolution.
- Initial internet access and digialization attempts were most likely initiated during this time, as the foundation for technical improvements was being set.

Early Majority (from the 2010s to 2020):

- By the 2010s, internet connection has grown to the point where more than three-quarters of Pakistanis in major cities were online.
- The 3500% increase in broadband subscriptions over the last eight years shows the beginning of mainstream digital adoption.

Late Majority (from 2020 the present):

- With over 103 million cellphones in Pakistan, the late majority phase saw a significant growth in smartphone ownership, reflecting a growing user base.
- The COVID-19 pandemic's e-commerce boom indicates a growing acceptance of online business, with the majority considering it simple and convenient.

Regarding Digital Applications

Google Search and YouTube (from the 2010s to the present):

- Google Search and YouTube have emerged as the most popular internet applications, showing a shift toward online information and entertainment consumption.

Boom in E-commerce (2020 - Present):

- The e-commerce boom that occurred during the COVID-19 epidemic represents a shift in consumer behavior, with most people seeing online purchasing as the way forward.

Venture Capital (2021):

- The rapid increase in venture capital funding for technology firms, which is expected to exceed $230 million by 2021, indicates growing interest and confidence in the digital ecosystem.

4.1.2: Competitive Landscape Metrics

Using the survey conducted by the Government of Pakistan we will analyze the competitive landscape metrics.

Performance figures of Pakistan Business Industries (2017-22):

Figure 4. Pakistan's 5-year performance growth in % (State Bank of Pakistan)

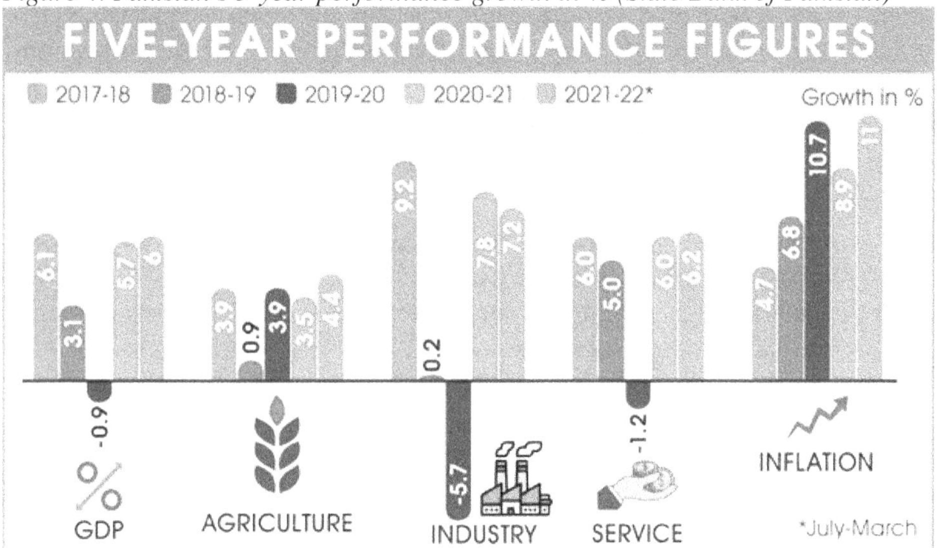

- Decline in GDP and Major Industries occurred from 2017-2020 and increase of more than before in 2020-2022.
- Inflation increased at a steady rate till 2022.

This decline was due to political instability and implementation of new government in 2018. (State Bank of Pakistan, 2022)

Conceptual Skills:

Conceptual skills are critical in the shifting landscape of Pakistan's digital sectors for firms seeking to increase competitiveness in the digital era. One critical component is adaptability to digital payment systems, which includes the smooth integration of mobile wallets, internet banking, and electronic transactions (Ahmed et al., 2020). This versatility is critical for promoting financial inclusion, lowering reliance on cash, and expediting payment processes. Another important consideration is the capacity to interact clients via various online channels, such as social media, websites, and mobile applications. Effective online consumer interaction is critical for increasing competitiveness by fostering brand loyalty, collecting valuable feedback, and generating tailored experiences (Rashid, 2019).

In Pakistan, most of the e-commerce players are either online marketplaces for goods - such as Shophive, Daraz.pk (for consumer electronics and apparel, etc.), and FoodPanda (for food delivery) – or online marketplaces for services via immediate delivery like the ride-hailing platforms Careem and Uber. Then there are online information and financial intermediaries or infomediaries, as they are often called – like PakWheels (for automobile sale and purchase), Rozee.pk (job hunting and recruitment), and Zameen.Pk (real estate business). These channels serve to fill information gaps and mostly earn profits through advertisements, contract making, and commission fees (State Bank of Pakistan, 2018)

The ongoing digialization in provision of services is growth-enhancing from a macroeconomic perspective too. This notion is supported by some gains that have already been made, as well as estimates of future potential. According to a McKinsey Global Institute (MGI) report, Pakistan can experience an increase in its GDP by a cumulative 7 percentage points (roughly US$ 36 billion) and create around 4 million new jobs during 2016-2025 via an increase in the use of digital financial services (DFS) alone as shown in figure (Government of Pakistan, 2018)

Figure 5. Expected GDP growth of Pakistan forecasted (2016-2025) (McKinsey Global Institute (2019))

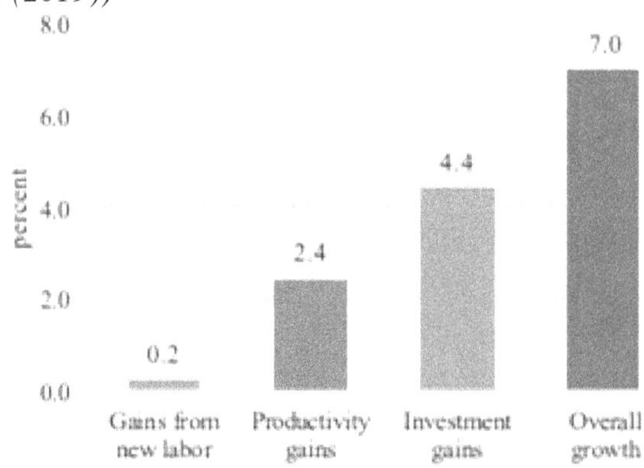

4.1.3: Competitive Digital Strategies Implemented

Pakistan, in the heart of South Asia, is undertaking a transformative journey fueled by digital technologies. Michael Porter's acclaimed competitive strategies serve as a lens through which we may see the complex interplay of major technologies such as e-commerce, artificial intelligence (AI), and cloud computing. This investigates how firms have strategically responded to these digital transitions by using quantitative measures and real-world examples.

E-commerce Prowess: Daraz's astonishing $1 billion in sales in 2022 demonstrates a savvy use of digital platforms. Businesses strategically use e-commerce to increase market reach and improve client experiences, bringing Porter's tactics to reality. The measurable success of platforms such as Daraz demonstrates the efficacy of this strategic strategy. (Hayat, 2023)

AI's Impact: AI is expected to be a revolutionary force in Pakistan, with an emphasis on improving customer service and automating operations. Businesses are carefully implementing AI to streamline processes and enhance productivity, in keeping with Porter's emphasis on innovation. This game-changing shift in firms at the forefront of digital innovation, giving them a competitive advantage.

Trends in Cloud Computing: Cloud computing has emerged as a game changer, providing scalability, flexibility, and cost savings. Companies who adapt this technology align with Porter's cost leadership strategy, improving operational efficiency and flexibility. The quantitative indicators from Pakistan's digital landscape highlight how cloud computing is more than simply a technology option; it is a strategic decision that shapes the competitive landscape.

Government Initiatives and Regulatory Dynamics: A governmental initiative, Digital Vision of Pakistan, demonstrates the regulatory factors influencing digital strategy. Porter's competitive forces model is used as the government strives to build a unified regulatory framework, stimulating innovation and laying the groundwork for businesses to prosper in a digitally driven economy. (State Bank of Pakistan, 2023)

IT Export Growth: According to the Pakistan Software Houses Association (P@SHA), the remarkable growth in IT export revenue, which is expected to reach $3.5 billion 2022, demonstrates the success of businesses that have invested in digital technologies. Businesses that use cloud computing, big data, and AI see faster rates of growth in IT exports, which aligns with Porter's differentiation strategy. **(Hayat, 2023)**

4.1.4: Correlation between Digital Transformation and Businesses (Digital Focused Business)

The correlation between digital transformation and businesses is strong and multifaceted. The integration of digital technologies into many parts of corporate operations, fundamentally changing how firms function and deliver value, is referred to as digital transformation.

Figure 6. Comparative ICT status in Pakistan

Table 1. Comparative ICT Status in Pakistan

	2010			2017		
	Pakistan	Developing Countries	World	Pakistan	Developing Countries	World
ICT Development index (rank)	123 (out of 152)	NA	NA	148 (out of 176)	NA	NA
International bandwidth per internet user (Kbit/sec)	4.2	NA	NA	20.9	59.6	70.9
Households with internet access (%)	5.7	19.8	32.5	22.1	41.5	52.4
Individuals using the internet (%)	8.0	21.1	29.3	15.5	42.4	49.0

Source: International Telecommunication Union

[14] Calculated from Pakistan Telecommunication Authority, https://www.pta.gov.pk/en/telecom-indicators, accessed on November 11, 2019, and Pakistan Telecommunication Annual Report 2016.

Figure 6 shows how much have Pakistan evolved in the digital world as the data is directly taken from World Bank's WDI and PTA (Pakistan Telecommunication Authority, 2016)

For instance, IT companies' growth into example and linking Digital Transformation with Overall Exports of Technological Products. The industry is expanding rapidly, with the number of IT firms more than doubling from under 2,000 in 2007 (according to SBP 2018) to over 4,000 today, including 3,000-plus call centers. According to SBP 2019, an average of 200 contact centers registered with the PSEB per year between 2008 and 2017. Freelancing activity has increased significantly, making Pakistan the world's third-largest hub for freelancers, after India and Bangladesh. Earnings for freelancers climbed by 47 percent in 2019. The e-commerce industry has grown rapidly, with registered merchants more than doubling from 571 in FY2016-17 to 1,398 in the third quarter of FY2018-19 (Figure 7). Officially recognized e-commerce transactions (translated from Pakistani Rupees to US dollars) increased from US$89.8 million in FY2016-17 to US$170 million in FY2017-18 (see Figure 7). This proportion, however, is likely an underestimate, given that cash on delivery is anticipated to account for 60% of total e-commerce value in Pakistan (SBP 2018). With the country's expanding internet penetration, e-commerce activity is expected to grow even more. (State Bank of Pakistan, 2019).

Figure 7. Officially registered e commerce merchants and recorded transactions in Pakistan

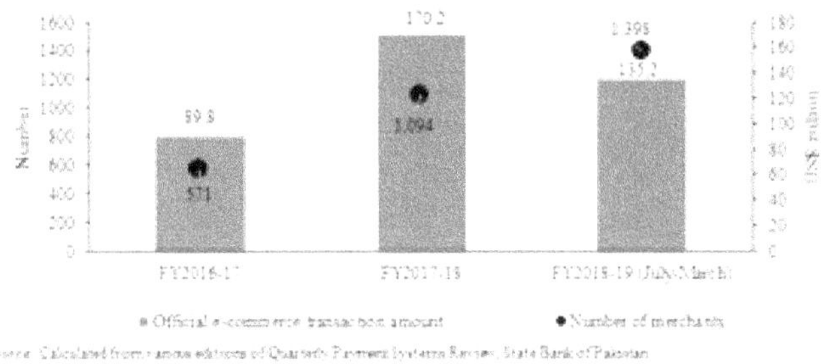

IT services exports have been growing. Pakistan's ICT services exports have increased at a 10.8 percent annual rate since FY10, from US$433 million to more over US$1 billion in FY2018-19. With an annual growth rate of 17.3 percent, the percentage of computer services in ICT services exports climbed from 44 percent to 73 percent in FY19. In computer services, software consultancy services increased by over 32% from FY2009-10 to FY2017-18, while software exports increased by 12.6 percent. Though call center exports have been gradually increasing, the quantity exported is substantially smaller than that of computer services, standing at US$104 million in FY2017-18. (State Bank of Pakistan, 2019).

Figure 8. Pakistan ICT exports in US$

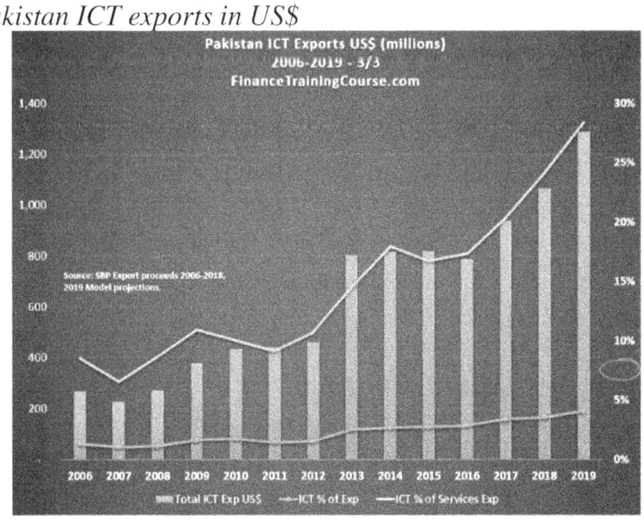

4.1.5: Digital Transformation and Workforce

The digital transformation in Pakistan has had a substantial impact on staff productivity in a variety of businesses. Adaption of digital technology in the workplace has resulted in faster processes, greater communication, and improved access to information, all of which contribute to higher employee productivity and effectiveness.

Repetitive Task Automation

The deployment of digital technology has resulted in the automation of arduous operations inside Human Resources (HR), such as taxation and payroll calculations. This automation not only ensures correctness, but also frees up employees' time and effort for other strategic and value-added activities. This moves from manual to automated operations has resulted in increased production. Akhtar (2023)

Collaboration and communication have improved.

The use of digital tools, such as video conferencing and collaboration platforms, has enabled diswork and increased team communication. This is especially true in Pakistan's corporate sector, where corporations are embracing technology to enable remote work on (Akhtar, 2023). Improved cooperation improves information sharing, issue solving, and decision making, all of which boost overall productivity. (SoftCon, 2021)

Decision Making Based on Data

Organizations can now collect and analyze data and appreciated that digital transformation, encouraging a data-driven decision-making culture. This is consistent with Akhtar's (2023) results, in which organizations employ digital technologies to make educated decisions about worker usage, talent acquisition, and other strategic elements. Employees and management can use data to discover areas for improvement and implement focused solutions.

Work-Life Balance and Flexibility

The use of digital technologies has enhanced flexibility in work arrangements, resulting in a better work-life balance for employees. Companies are embracing video conferencing and collaboration solutions to facilitate remote work, decreasing the need for substantial travel and providing staff with more freedom (Akhtar,

2023). This adaptability can boost job satisfaction and, as a result, staff productivity. (SoftCon, 2021)

Problems and Solutions

Despite the good effects, there are obstacles associated with digital transformation, such as a skilled labor scarcity. To fully realize the potential of digital technologies and close the skills gap, businesses may need to engage in training and upskilling initiatives. Concerns about cybersecurity and data privacy should also be addressed to provide a secure digital work environment. (SoftCon, 2021)

4.2: Results

After analyzing all the data that will be used in this research in previous section (4.1). This study can finally conclude our hypothesis using data from State Bank of Pakistan, Pakistan telecommunication authority, Pakistan journal and other resources mentioned previously in the research paper.

4.2.1: Hypothesis 1

Effective digital transformation positively impacts financial performance.

Evaluation: Accepted. According to the research conducted previously, there is a good relationship between digital transformation and financial performance. The rise in IT exports, e-commerce activity, and overall GDP demonstrates that effective digital transformation helps businesses succeed financially. (State Bank of Pakistan, 2022)

4.2.2: Hypothesis 2

More digitalization within Pakistani businesses will positively associated with increased employee productivity.

Evaluation: Accepted. The study demonstrates how digitalization improves staff productivity by streamlining procedures, identifying bottlenecks, and implementing efficiency measures. The concentration on AI, machine learning, and IoT also indicates a desire to improve operational efficiency.

4.2.3: Hypothesis 3

A higher level of digitalization in Pakistani businesses will positively associated with an increase in market share.

Evaluation: Accepted. The link between digitalization and market share is clear. Businesses that employ data analytics effectively acquire a competitive advantage, identify market trends, and respond rapidly to consumer demand. This argument is supported by the success of e-commerce platforms such as Daraz and Intermediaries such as Pakwheels/OLX the overall increase in market competitiveness. (World Bank, 2020)

4.2.4: Hypothesis 4

More digitalization within Pakistani businesses will positively associated with increased customer satisfaction.

Evaluation: Accepted. According to the research, firms who use advanced data analytics can better understand their customers' preferences and behaviors, resulting in more personalized and focused replies. This argument is supported further by the emphasis on excellent online customer engagement and the increase of e-commerce during the pandemic.

4.2.5: Hypothesis 5

A higher level of digitalization within Pakistani businesses will be positively associated with a fast rate of innovation adoption.

Evaluation: Accepted. Digitalization has been demonstrated to be a major factor impacting innovation. Businesses that embrace digialization are more versatile in implementing cutting-edge concepts, allowing them to stay ahead of the curve in an ever-changing market. This idea is supported by the increase in venture capital funding for technology enterprises and the emphasis on AI as a game-changing factor.

4.2.6: Hypothesis 6

Higher levels of digitalization are associated with increased cybersecurity threats.

The available data supports the hypothesis (H0) that higher levels of digitalization are associated with increased cybersecurity threats.

AI and Cybersecurity: According to the data, while AI can improve cybersecurity, it is also used by cyber attackers, implying that rising levels of digitalization, including AI, may contribute to increased cybersecurity dangers.

Interconnectivity and the Internet of Things (IoT): The Internet of Things (IoT) debate emphasizes the hazards involved with networked physical infrastructure, which can lead to systemic failures as a result of cyberattacks. This lends credence to the hypothesis that greater digialization and interconnection may result in increased cybersecurity concerns.

Malware and Cyber concerns in Pakistan: The presence of malware such as Gamarue, Skeeya, and Peals, as well as cases of cyber-attacks on government websites, suggest a link between digitalization and cybersecurity concerns in Pakistan.

Challenges and Vulnerabilities in Pakistani Cybersecurity: Data breaches, terrorist organizations using cyber propaganda, and the government's difficulties in regulating the digital realm all support the hypothesis of increased cybersecurity threats as digitalization increase.

While without explicitly claiming a correlation, Pakistan's lower rating in the National Cyber Security Index shows that there is need for improvement in cybersecurity measures, potentially indicating a higher level of Threat related with digitalization.

5.5: CONCLUSION OF THE STUDY

This detailed study offers subtle insights into the current stage of digialization and its consequences for the country's companies. The report offers helpful insights for businesses navigating the dynamic terrain of digital transformation based on rigorous data analysis, ethical concerns, validity tests, and hypothesis evaluations. Digital transformation is being pushed as a strategic priority for businesses in Pakistan. Adoption of e-commerce, artificial intelligence, and cloud computing should be viewed as key competitiveness and sustainability drivers. Investing in human-centric digital initiatives is critical, which includes efforts to promote digital literacy, providing training programs, and develop a work culture that promotes innovation and adaptability to technology advancements. The study discovers a link between higher levels of digialization and increased market share. As a result, firms are urged to use digital tools to expand their market reach. For success in the developing digital market, using data analytics to discover customer trends, improve product offerings, and maintain a competitive advantage is highlighted. Businesses should emphasize customer-centric digital activities based on the recognized theory about consumer pleasure. Advanced data analytics can help businesses gain a better understanding of their customers' preferences, resulting in more tailored experiences, more customer happiness, and stronger brand loyalty. Businesses are recommended to promote a culture of continuous innovation in the light of the proven link between digialization and innovation adoption. Embracing developing technology, obtaining venture financing for tech ventures, and staying on top of global innovation trends can help organizations stay ahead of the curve. Businesses must emphasize cybersecurity readiness as they recognize the challenges posed by rising digitalization. Continuous monitoring of the cybersecurity landscape, investment in strong cybersecurity frameworks, and collaboration with industry stakeholders are critical measures to mitigating risks and safeguarding sensitive data. Finally, this information can help organizations in Pakistan manage the digital transformation journey strategically. Businesses may not only survive but thrive in the expanding digital world by embracing digitalization, promoting innovation, prioritizing ethical practices, and engaging with stakeholders, contributing to the growth and sustainability of the Pakistani business ecosystem.

3.2.8: Limitations

To begin this secondary research project on "Business in the Digital World in the Context of Pakistan," certain inherent restrictions must be acknowledged and addressed. First and foremost, the reliability and validity of the data are dependent on the quality of the primary studies and sources used in the analysis. As Tranfield et al. (2003) point out, the robustness of the meta-analysis and content analysis is dependent on the reliability of the sources used. If there are gaps or imbalances in the available research, relying on existing literature and reports may generate bias. Furthermore, the temporal component is a constraint since data taken from various research may not equally represent the dynamic nature of digitalization in Pakistani firms over time.

Furthermore, despite efforts to include various sources, there may be a publication bias toward positive findings or success stories. As stated by Egger et al. (1997), this bias may influence the whole narrative, thus skewing perceptions of the obstacles and failures in Pakistani enterprises' digitalization efforts.

Despite these constraints, this study makes a concrete effort to traverse these difficulties, aiming for a fair and nuanced interpretation of the available data. Transparency about these limitations lays the groundwork for critical evaluation of the research findings, enabling a more informed and contextually aware knowledge of the complex dynamics of digitalization in the Pakistani business sector.

REFERENCES

Akhtar, N. (2023). *Who Benefits from Digital Technologies in Large Corporates of Pakistan?* [online] www.linkedin.com. Available at: https://www.linkedin.com/pulse/who-benefits-from-digital-technologies-large-pakistan-naghman-akhtar

Ali, K. (2022, August 29). *Cyber security deficiency led to data theft at SECP, report finds*. Retrieved from DAWN: https://www.dawn.com/news/1707294

American Psychological Association. (2017). *Publication Manual of the American Psychological Association* (7th ed.). American Psychological Association.

Anwar, M. W. (2020, December). Cyber Security in Pakistan: Regulations, Gaps and Way Forward. *ResearchGate*. Retrieved from https://www.researchgate.net/publication/349097228_Cyber_Security_in_Pakistan_Regulations_Gaps_and_Way_Forward

Ashraf, M. (2019, december 31). *Cyber threats to Digital Pakistan*. Retrieved from The Nation: https://www.nation.com.pk/31-Dec-2019/cyber-threats-to-digital-pakistan

Asif, S. (2023). *The Importance of Digital Transformation for Businesses in Pakistan*. [online] Entrepreneurs Of Pakistan. Available at: https://entrepreneursofpakistan.com/the-importance-of-digital-transformation-for-businesses-in-pakistan/

Asif, S. (2023). *The Importance of Digital Transformation for Businesses in Pakistan*. [online] Entrepreneurs Of Pakistan. Available at: https://entrepreneursofpakistan.com/the-importance-of-digital-transformation-for-businesses-in-pakistan/

Bank, W. "Pakistan Economic Policy for Export Competitiveness, Digital Pakistan: A Business and Trade Assessment." Worldbank.org, 2020, documents1.worldbank.org/curated/en/894921591073694322/Digital-Pakistan-Economic-Policy-for-Export-Competitiveness-A-Business-and-Trade-Assessment.docx

BBVA OpenMind. (n.d.). *10 Examples of How AI Is Already Used in Our Day-to-Day Life*.

Borenstein, M., Hedges, L. V., Higgins, J. P., & Rothstein, H. R. (2011). *Introduction to Meta-Analysis*. John Wiley & Sons. [Book]

Bryman, A. (2016). *Social Research Methods*. Oxford University Press.

Bryman, A., & Bell, E. (2019). *Business Research Methods*. Oxford University Press.

Daraz. (2022). *Daraz Breaks Records with Over $1 Billion in GMV in 2022*.

Egger, M., Smith, G. D., Schneider, M., & Minder, C. (1997). Bias in meta-analysis detected by a simple, graphical test. [DOI]. *BMJ (Clinical Research Ed.)*, 315(7109), 629–634. DOI: 10.1136/bmj.315.7109.629 PMID: 9310563

Government of Pakistan, of (2020). *Pakistan Economic Survey 2018-2019*. [online] Available at: https://www.finance.gov.pk/survey/chapters_19/Economic_Survey _2018_19.pdf

Haq, R. (2021). Digital Transformation: Pakistan Is Now Online! [online] South Asia Investor. Available at: https://www.southasiainvestor.com/2021/08/digital -transformation-pakistan-is-now.html

Hayat, A. (2023). *How digital transformation impacts businesses?* [online] The Express Tribune. Available at: https://tribune.com.pk/story/2444919/how-digital -transformation-impacts-businesses

Hussain, M., Ameen, Z., & Rasool, N. (2023). Roshan Digital Account: A Digital Innovation in Pakistan and Its Impact on Customers' Satisfaction. *Journal of Development and Social Sciences*, 4(I). Advance online publication. DOI: 10.47205/ jdss.2023(4-I)04

KEMP. S. (February, 16 2022). *DIGITAL 2022: PAKISTAN*. Retrieved from DATA REPORTAL: https://datareportal.com/reports/digital-2022-pakistan

Khalid, M., Abbas, S., & Rizvi, S. K. A. (2018). Exploring the Impact of Digitalization on Business: A Case Study of Pakistan. *Pakistan Journal of Commerce and Social Sciences*, 12(2), 472–492.

Khalid, M., Abbas, S., & Rizvi, S. K. A. (2018). Exploring the Impact of Digitalization on Business: A Case Study of Pakistan. *Pakistan Journal of Commerce and Social Sciences*, 12(2), 472–492.

Khilji, U. (2021, August 21). *Cybersecurity policy*. Retrieved from DAWN: https:// www.dawn.com/news/1641754

Kumar, A., & Jain, P. (2020). Digital Transformation and Its Impact on Business Performance. *Journal of Management Information and Decision Sciences*, 23(3), 311–328.

McKinsey & Company. (n.d.). *How Cybersecurity Can Accelerate Your Digital Transformation*. Available at: Digital Transformation Challenges.

NCSI. (2022). *National Cyber Security Index*. Retrieved from https://ncsi.ega.ee/ ncsi-index/?order=-rank

PAGE. (2021). *Digital transformation in customer service.* [online] Pakistan & Gulf Economist. Available at: https://www.pakistangulfeconomist.com/2021/08/23/digital-transformation-in-customer-service/

Pakistan Bureau of Statistics 2022, Economic Survey of Pakistan.

Pakistan Telecommunication Authority. (n.d.). Reports and Publications.

Qadeer, N. (2023). *Digital Transformation – Are Pakistani Businesses Ready For It?* [online] Nabeel Qadeer. Available at: https://nabeel.pk/portfolio-item/digital-transformation-are-pakistani-businesses-ready-for-it/

Ransbotham, S., Kiron, D., & Prentice, P. (2019). The Digital Dividend: First Mover Advantage. *MIT Sloan Management Review*, 60(3), 1–5.

Raza, S. I. (2022, September 26). *Leaks reveal massive breach in security at PM Office*. Retrieved from DAWN: https://www.dawn.com/news/1712044

Resnik, D. B. (2011). What is Ethics in Research & Why is it Important? [URL]

Rogers, D. L. (2016). *The Digital Transformation Playbook: Rethink Your Business for the Digital Age*. Columbia University Press. DOI: 10.7312/roge17544

Savin-Baden, M., & Major, C. H. (2013). *Qualitative Research: The Essential Guide to Theory and Practice*. Routledge.

SBP. (2018). *State Bank of Pakistan Annual Report.*

SBP. (2019). *Third Quarter Review 2018-19.*

Sharma, A., & Adhikary, S. (2021). "Digitalization and Business Performance: The Mediating Role of Innovation." International Journal of Information Management, 61, 102382. McAfee, A., & Brynjolfsson, E. (2012). Big Data: The Management Revolution. *Harvard Business Review.*

Simonsen, J., & Richardson, K. (2017). *The Ethical Decision-Making Manual for Helping Professionals*. Pearson.

SoftCon. (2021). *Sofcom Management Tools & Solutions for Company*. [online] sofcom.net. Available at: https://sofcom.net/blog-digitalization-of-hr-in-pakistan [Accessed 14 Nov. 2023].

State Bank of Pakistan. (2018). Digialization of Services in Pakistan. [online] pp.87–8*. Available at: https://www.sbp.org.pk/reports/annual/arFY18/Chapter-07.pdf

State Bank of Pakistan. (2021). Annual Performance Review 2020.

Tashakkori, A., & Creswell, J. W. (2007). Exploring the Nature of Research Questions in Mixed Methods Research. *Journal of Mixed Methods Research*, 1(3), 207–211. DOI: 10.1177/1558689807302814

Timmers, P. (2018). *Business Ecosystems: How to Leverage Business Ecosystems for Digital Transformation and Growth*. CreateSpace Independent Publishing Platform.

Tranfield, D., Denyer, D., & Smart, P. (2003). Towards a methodology for developing evidence-informed management knowledge by means of systematic review. [DOI]. *British Journal of Management*, 14(3), 207–222. DOI: 10.1111/1467-8551.00375

UNCTAD. (2020). *E-commerce and the Digital Economy*.

Westerman, G., Bonnet, D., & McAfee, A. (2014). *Leading Digital: Turning Technology into Business Transformation*. Harvard Business Review Press.

Westerman, G., Bonnet, D., & McAfee, A. (2014). *Leading Digital: Turning Technology into Business Transformation*. Harvard Business Review Press.

Zaidi, H. B. (2016, February 7). *Clinton emails suggest US examines Pakistani media closely*. Retrieved from DAWN: https://www.dawn.com/news/1237963

Chapter 2
Digital Transformation and Financial Sustainability

Saleh F. A. Khatib
https://orcid.org/0000-0001-7652-4191
Universiti Teknologi Malaysia, Malaysia

Zubair Mustafa
https://orcid.org/0000-0002-9775-2174
University of Swabi, Pakistan

Alhamzah F. Abbas
https://orcid.org/0000-0002-7508-9340
University of Technology Malaysia, Malaysia

ABSTRACT

Digital transformation is profoundly reshaping the financial sector and enhancing financial sustainability through innovations such as blockchain, AI, ML, and IoT. This chapter explores how these technologies converge to foster a more resilient financial ecosystem. Financial sustainability traditionally involves maintaining financial health through effective governance and resource allocation. In the context of today's rapidly evolving technological landscape, the urgency of financial sustainability has increased, with strategic foresight becoming crucial for stability amid digital transformation. The chapter examines the impact of digital technologies, highlighting blockchain's role in ensuring transaction security, AI and ML's advancements in decision-making, and IoT's contributions to real-time data analysis. These technologies enhance the inclusiveness of the financial landscape but also introduce challenges such as data privacy concerns. Case studies of Goldman Sachs'

DOI: 10.4018/979-8-3693-6386-7.ch002

Marcus and Kenya's M-Pesa illustrate how digital innovations promote sustainability.

INTRODUCTION TO FINANCIAL SUSTAINABILITY IN THE DIGITAL ERA

Generally, financial sustainability is termed as the capability of the organization, the economy and the individual to keep its health over period of time. To ascertain that financial obligations may be accomplished without compromising the future economic trajectories, the concept includes sensible reallocation of resources, strategy for responsible investment, and management of finances. Another aspect that is enhancing more appropriate to financial sustainability is the promptly shifting global macroeconomic context, which is identified by uncertainties and interpretive which may undermine financial stability. To achieve long-term financial health, this result in organizing for future financial needs along with effectively allocating current financial resources. (Atz et al, 2023).

Frameworks of financial sustainability traditionally are undergoing noteworthy evolve as a outcome of the accelerated growth of digital technologies such as blockchain, artificial intelligence (AI), machine learning (ML), and the Internet of Things (IoT). Retaining over long-term financial position through good governance, allocation of resource, and long-term planning has formally been the fundamental goal of financial sustainability. Nevertheless, the financial condition is changing significantly as an outcome of incorporating innovative technologies, which is shifting not just the traditional way, financial activities are performed but also the ultimate concepts that underpin the sustainable finance.

Digital transformation has substantially modified financial transactions and procedures, and new technologies like cybersecurity offers further levels of protecting against potential threats. Blockchain, cryptocurrencies, artificial intelligence, and big data analytics are models of digital innovations that have modified long-lasting financial activities. They have made it feasible for conventional transactions to be settled in seconds rather than long time, improved risk assessment models for businesses globally and even customized services. By giving access to formal financial to marginalized people, internet-based technologies have advanced financial inclusion. In other words, the digitization makes financial sustainability feasible, and progression through digital transformation opens up new direction for research to modify the financial environment (Gomber et al., 2017).

As an example, blockchain technology provides an immutable, transparent, and decentralized ledger system that amends conventional financial approach. Because of the latest technology, financial transactions no longer require intermediaries, which lowers the transaction costs and increases the security of financial operations.

The adoption of smart contracts on blockchain systems prominently improves the efficiency of financial transactions by automating and implementing contractual commitments without the needs for human intervention. By minimizing operating expense and improving financial reporting transparency, this paradigm shifts from centralized systems to decentralized finance (DeFi) frameworks has not only enhanced accessibility to financial services but also improved their sustainability. Considering it makes it easier to confirm adherence to sustainability requirements, blockchain's contribution to transparency is especially important in environmental, social, and governance (ESG) reporting.

Artificial intelligence and machine learnings are restructuring the financial industry by permitting data-driven decision-making procedures. By employing automation, risk assessment, and advanced predictive metrics, these technologies enhance financial sustainability. Large datasets may be analyzed by AI-driven algorithms at a speed and precision previously impossible, delivering insights that improve decision-making process in fields like portfolio management, fraud detection, and financial rating. Moreover, by using machine learning (ML) simulations in financial forecasting, organizations are better positions to anticipate market changes and execute proactive strategies that promote sustainable financial management. Artificial intelligence and machine learning support to create a more robust financial framework that is more determined to manage economic shocks and uncertainties by improving risk management procedures.

Financial sustainability is depicting likely by technology, which provide techniques and solutions that facilitate improved financial management, lowered operating expenses, and improve decision-making process. Technologies such as artificial intelligence and machine learning support with improved financial predictions & risk assurance, and blockchain technology is accountable for secure transparent funds management. Additionally, digital enables a new way for financial services to be accessed leading banks and other institutions with comprehensive solutions toward mass included customers that get efficient ways of managing one's money. Using technology organizations can add value to existing financial operations, respond to new market demands and establishes sustainable future systems (Aithal 2023).

The integration of IoT into financial systems introduces new dimensions of connectivity and data analytics, which significantly impact financial sustainability practices. IoT devices generate vast amounts of real-time data, allowing financial institutions to gain deeper insights into asset management, operational efficiency, and customer behavior. This real time data availability facilitates dynamic financial modelling, enabling businesses to make adaptive financial decisions that account for current market conditions and future sustainability goals. In sectors such as insurance, IoT enables usage-based pricing models and personalized financial products, thereby enhancing the inclusiveness and sustainability of financial services.

Introducing new tools is sole aspect of the shift from old frameworks to technology supported financial sustainability; another key element is re-evaluation of fundamental financial management systems. The role of digital technologies expedites more flexible, data-driven strategies that are accordance with shifting economic, social, and environmental developments, although traditional approaches placed an importance on stagnate planning and reallocation of resources. The contribution of these technologies to improve greater financial inclusion by strengthening under resourced people access to financial services and increasing the accuracy and effectiveness of financial activities.

Current book chapter underscore the intersection of financial sustainability and digital technology and deliver insight into the technological innovations that could enhance financial health in this modern technological era. The impact of digital revolution on financial technology is essential to long-term financing. This book chapter will address core ideas, cutting-edge trends, new technologies, implementation approaches, and real-world use examples. The book chapter covers these topics in order to provide readers with the information and resources they need to successfully navigate the shifting financial landscape and achieve long-term financial stability. Furthermore, in order to give readers a more thorough understanding of the implications of digital technology adoption in the financial sector, the book chapter focuses more on the significant risks and challenges, such as cybersecurity threats, issues with regulatory compliance, and ethical concerns surrounding AI and data privacy.

1. EMERGING TECHNOLOGIES AND THEIR IMPACT ON FINANCIAL SUSTAINABILITY

The perspective of financial sustainability is experiencing substantial changes, and new technological like as blockchain, AI, IoT play a substantial role in increasing efficiency, transparency, inclusivity, and access to the data held within financial management. Sole example is blockchain technology which permits secure, transparent and irreversible ledgers when it converts to financial transaction processing what in turn decreases frauds or operating cost on leveraging credibility and reliability of lending as demonstrated by Nakamoto (2008). AI and machine learning algorithms are transforming financial services by enabling superior data analytics to support better risk assessment, customer personalization, decision-making (Gupta et al., 2018). IoT integration will also create a stream of real time data that can be used for more reasonable financial planning and management, which again leads to financially sustainable practices (Panduman et al., 2024). Together, these technologies are enabling a more sustainable and robust financial ecosystem.

Additionally, providing more context on how these technologies reshape traditional financial sustainability frameworks could involve explaining their role in improving technology, enhancing digital transformation, enabling better risk management, and expanding access to digital financial services.

1.1 Blockchain and Distributed Ledger Technologies

Blockchain and distributed ledger technologies (DLTs) have changed the financial industry into decentralized, transparent & secure transaction recording systems. Blockchains, at odds with traditional centralized databases produce an ergonomic ledger of all transactions these being immutable to heighten security and minimize the risk of fraud (Nakamoto, 2008). Such technologies facilitate person-to-person transactions eliminating third parties frontloading transaction costs and enhancing productivity (Tapscott & Tapscott, 2016). The use of smart contracts (contracts where terms are written into code and self-assigned) which automate and enforce the order as well help to enhance efficiency, verifies execution by tracking transaction history before trust is placed on financial operations (Buterin2014). Blockchain and DLT have been suggested to be adopted across different sectors including banking, supply chain management and insurance, suggesting their pervasive nature in efficacy gain or at least sustainability of financial ecosystems (Treleaven et al., 2017)

In the financial sector, blockchain and distributed ledger technologies (DLTs) are transforming existing infrastructures by proposing decentralized, transparent, secure solutions (Patel et al., 2022; Moşteanu & Faccia, 2021). These technologies aim to disrupt different sectors like banking, finance, and logistics among others (Lahmadi et al., 2021; Chang et al., 2020). Blockchain applications in FinTech tend to be faster and easier making it much more effective in protecting the profit or Loss (Renduchintala et al., 2022). Blockchain applications also aims at giving better access of financial services overgrowth but there are still concerns on trust-security, third party verification. Thommandru & Chakka (2023) consider the technology explore better anti-money laundering (AML) compliance and Know Your Customer (KYC) processes in banking. Knowledge concealing and the requirement for structured knowledge sharing are two obstacles to blockchain adoption, notwithstanding its potential (Chang et al., 2020). It is estimated that as the technological advancement, it will transform various sectors together with inside and outside of the financial sector (Koh et al., 2020). The incorporation of blockchain technology in financial transactions is an illustration for exactly how decentralized data can enhance financial sustainability. Businesses can improve traceability and transparency by putting in place a decentralized ledger, which will help financial institutions determine a client's creditworthiness more precisely. Small and medium-sized businesses (SMEs) can obtain funding more quickly and with lower risk because to this improved visibility, which eventually helps create a more sustainable financial system.

1.2 Artificial Intelligence and Machine Learning in Finance

The financial industry is changing as a result of artificial intelligence (AI) and machine learning (ML), which allow for faster decision-making, improved trading techniques, and advanced risk management. Their techniques are able to analyse enormous piles of financial data and look for patterns in a way the humans with their speed, accuracy, predictions can be more accurate, eventually streamlining from each administration operation. For example, AI based algorithms are able to carry out trades in amounts of time and at money-saving efficiencies beyond human traders' capabilities which results in noticeable improvements over liquidity and pricing accuracy within these markets (Escobar et al., 2023). Credit scoring and fraud detection use of ML model is ubiquitous, lenders are able to make more risk-appropriate loans, faster as well financial services companies can detect fraudulent activities, they couldn't find conventionally through the superior prediction from building models instead on focusing rules (Heaton et al., 2017). The further development and the adoption of these technologies across different financial services are expected to improve innovation, security as well as contribute towards achieving sustainable finance.

The influence of AI and ML is also increasing in the finance sector, with applications spread across portfolio management, fraud detection credit scoring algorithmic trading (Goodell et al., 2021; Ahmed et al., 2022). These technologies have reshaped risk management, notably in the realms of credit approval and financial forecasting practices (Milojević & Redzepagić 2021; Mhlanga 2021). AI and ML have enhanced financial inclusion in developing economies through enabling the use of alternative data sources for credit risk analysis (Mhlanga, 2021). AI and ML have been used in financial sector, with the supervised learning methods most widely adopted - deep learning has recently become popular (Li et al., 2023). Nevertheless, there are still challenges that need to be address including data privacy, regulatory compliance and ethical aspects (El Hajj & Hammoud,2023). AI and ML have already started to reconfigure how financial services are administered, influencing the practice of finance professionals in an appropriate way needed for companies with arising challenges (Buchanan & Wright, 2021; Sonkavde et al., 2023).

1.3 The Internet of Things (IoT) and Financial Data Analytics

Formally, the Internet of Things (IoT) represents a new era where almost anything and everything in an industry is connected, it generates massive amounts of data. In the finance industry, IoT is streamlining data analytics to offer real-time understanding and inform better decision-making. By combining IoT with financial data analytics (IoT Financial Data Analytics), risk assessments, fraud detection and customized customer experiences can be performed more accurately. IoT devices, for example, they can monitor transactions and quickly realize if fraud is in action (Del Giudice et al., 2016). Furthermore, the personalized financial services for customers use IoT driven data analytics can increase customer satisfaction and loyalty as per their behavior patterns or preferences (Judijanto et al., 2024). The advancement and adoption of these technologies will only further change the face of finance, paving more pathways for creativity to keep competitive while attempting at new ways to maintain profitability.

IoT is transforming the banking sector along with other sectors through its ability to gather data in real-time and begin analysing it almost instantaneously (Fawzy et al., 2022). The collaboration of IoT and financial technology integration (FinTech) has enabled innovative contributions to several initiatives such as the prediction models for a financial crisis model (Tyagi & Qu, 2023). Machine Learning and Data Analytics are the Key Players for Processing demand of generation data through IoT but there is still remains a question mark on creating adaptive Intelligent IoT application (Adi et al., 2020) There is a great need for data mining techniques to understand and utilize IoT generated big data (Sunhare et al., 2020). On the other hand, those services also introduce digital risks and vulnerabilities especially for financial institution such as IoT, Big Data Analytics and Cloud Computing (Edu et al., 2021). Despite these challenges, digitalization strategies of businesses, and new business models with secure IoT-technologies provide an advanced connectivity rather than Big Data (Sestino et al., 2020). Moreover, manufacturing and other sectors are being revolutionized by the connectivity enabled through Industrial Internet of Things (IIoT) in which data is utilized readily (Boyes, 2018). In IoT for FinTech, it would include further development such as neurotech which is the human interaction with machines using mind in financial process (Maiti & Ghosh, 2023).

2. CASE STUDIES OF SUCCESSFUL DIGITAL TRANSFORMATIONS

The digital transformation has completely changed the financial industry as it allows institutions to work more efficiently, cheaper and now make customer experiences better than any time before. There are plenty of case studies available where financial organisations have found success after the implementation other new technologies. A good example would be Marcus, the consumer bank created by Goldman Sachs in 2016 and enabled on data analytics and AI to provide a number of customized financial solutions such as online savings accounts, personal loans resulting up to more than $60 billion deposits with millions of clients since it has been introduced (Goldman Sachs, 2020). At the same time, in Kenya M-Pesa mobile payment created a quantum leap with 40 million users carrying out several billion USD of transactions annually (Vodafone, 2021). The experiences of these cases reveal the capacity for digital technology to be leveraged in structural reform, with potential applications toward promoting the evolving nature of digital transformation in financial sustainability and greater inclusion. (Andreoni et al.,2021).

2.1 Review of Empirical Research

A few interesting trends and insights on financial sustainability have been explored via the bibliometric analysis. The number of publications on financial sustainability, from 1991 to 2016 has been experiencing a gradual rise; in the following two years (from2018 until March) there is an additional peak, and another remarkable up-rise as observed at recent time. This temporal trend underscores the increasing significance of financial sustainability in light of changing economic, environmental and social challenges. The United States and the UK also took leading positions in production numbers, which results correspond with their largest national output of articles they are most active on this subject. The investigation revealed an evolution of the research themes from efficiency pathways, financial sustainability and social outreach in microfinance institutions to hybridity, digital innovation and sustainability. The complex interplay between financial purpose and social mission in social enterprises are further underscored by recent work on digital hybridity resource allocation trade-offs and synergies, as well as the embedding of social services within microfinance sector lend weight to these studies.

The co-occurrence keyword analysis revealed distinct thematic clusters, including sustainability, financial aspects, regional contexts, and contemporary challenges. Key keywords such as 'green finance,' 'ESG,' 'CSR,' 'Artificial Intelligence,' and 'sustainable finance' emerged as areas requiring further investigation, underscoring the dynamic nature of the field. Additionally, there has been a resurgence of interest in financial sustainability in response to the COVID-19 pandemic. The study's theoretical implications contribute significantly to the understanding of financial sustainability, hybrid business models, and digital innovation. Practically, it offers valuable insights for businesses, policymakers, and organizations aiming to improve financial sustainability and align strategies with broader sustainable development objectives. Future research directions include digital hybridity, social entrepreneurship, microfinance, technology, social media, and diversity studies, collectively advancing knowledge and understanding across these domains. These findings underscore the increasing recognition of financial sustainability's significance and provide a comprehensive foundation for ongoing and future scholarly inquiry.

2.2 Fintech Innovations and Financial Inclusion

While FinTech has been praised for its potential and contributions to financial inclusion, it is important to highlight its shortcomings and limitations, which may detract from its perceived benefits. One significant issue with FinTech is its urban and elite bias, which means it often overlooks the very clients it aims to serve under financial inclusion initiatives. The hype surrounding FinTech's role in promoting financial inclusion needs a thorough evaluation. According to a recent J.P. Morgan study, FinTech primarily serves affluent and elite individuals about 23% of them in large cities and urban centres, neglecting the underserved populations in remote rural areas. Although many savings bank accounts have been opened, most remain inactive, and the adoption of financial services beyond account opening is still minimal. Additionally, there is a trust gap in online payments that needs to be addressed. Factors such as poor literacy, limited access to the internet, electricity, and telecommunications, as well as the inability to afford even small FinTech service costs, have restricted the adoption rate of FinTech to just 33% in rural areas, as reported by J.P. Morgan. Pratt (2018).

2.3 Digital Banking and the Evolution of Financial Services

Case studies from Africa and the United States highlight the application of theoretical frameworks such as the Diffusion of Innovations Theory and Technology Acceptance Model in understanding digital adoption (Jejeniwa et al., 2024). While offering numerous benefits, digital banking also presents challenges including cybersecurity risks and potential exclusion of certain demographics (Dananjayan et al., 2023). Continued technological improvements, with an emphasis on business reengineering and two-way digitalization, are anticipated to influence the financial services industry's future (Budiman & Saptono, 2020). Big data analytics is becoming more and more important for promoting informed decision-making and intelligent financial services (Ravi & Kamaruddin, 2017).

In the banking and financial industry, digital transformation which includes implementing cutting-edge technologies to improve customer experience, operational efficiency, and market adaptability is crucial to maintain the competitiveness. Nevertheless, this process is difficult because of complicated current infrastructures, security issues, financial limitations, a lack of technological expertise, and resistance to change. Many financial institutions struggle to integrate new digital technologies with their legacy systems, protect vast amounts of sensitive data, and foster a culture that embraces change. Strengthening the relationship between digital technologies and financial systems will improve operational efficiency, security, and digital adaptability. The successful result of digital transformation can significantly improve customer experience, operational efficiency, financial accessibility, and data-driven decision-making while promoting innovation and agility. Tools like XCALLY can facilitate this transformation by offering omni channel customer management, process automation, advanced interaction analysis, intelligent call routing, and real-time monitoring. By integrating with existing banking systems, XCALLY helps financial institutions overcome common obstacles and maximize the benefits of digital transformation.

2.4 Impact of Mobile Payment Solutions on Financial Systems

Mobile payment solutions have significantly impacted financial systems, particularly in developing countries. M-Pesa in Kenya has been a notable success story, rapidly increasing financial inclusion (Winn, 2016). Similar services like EcoCash in Zimbabwe have transacted billions, boosting financial inclusion from 32% to over 90% (Nidugondi & Bhargava, 2019). These solutions offer convenience, accessibility, and cost effectiveness for micro businesses (Mbogo, 2010). Mobile money has enabled entrepreneurship in Eastern Africa (Jussila, 2015) and revolutionized finance in less developed countries (Hamdi, 2011). It has also impacted microfinance institutions (Nzioka, 2010) and contributed to creating cash light economies in Africa (Nidugondi & Bhargava, 2019). Success factors for mobile payment systems include ease of use, branding, and addressing rural financial needs (Jussila, 2015).

A case study explores big data analytics, focusing on managing and analyzing large datasets to uncover patterns and insights. It highlights benefits such as improved decision-making, enhanced accounting and compliance, better marketing, and credit risk assessment, while aiming to address implementation challenges in a Malaysian commercial bank. Students role-play as a Senior IT Manager to solve implementation issues, considering alternatives to cloud-based services due to security concerns and addressing data quality problems (Siew & Farouk, 2023).

2.5 Digital identification verification as a sustainable solution

In recent literature, the relationship between digital identity verification and financial sustainability has been increasingly recognized as pivotal to the evolution of modern financial ecosystems. Studies indicate that digital identity verification advances financial inclusion, that is significant for long-term economic development, additionally, to enhance security. Secured identity verification mechanism minimal frauds and cyber-attacks, protecting financial agencies from extensive losses and fostering over long-period sustainability Parate et al., (2023). Digital identity verification plays a leading role in minimizing the operating cost linked with Know Your Customer (KYC) and Anti-Money Laundering (AML) organizations, which steers to more influential and cost-effective operations, according to Yawalkar et al., (2023). Likewise, recent study by Parate et al., (2023) underscore exactly how digital identity verification could deliver safe and reliable access to financial platforms, subsequently extending financial services to relegated groups, particularly in developing economies. Since it fosters institutions to extend their clientele and encourage economic sustainability, this excessive accessibility is firmly related to the more generic goal of financial sustainability. All of discussed studies reveal the significance of digital identity verification is to be promoting the security and inclusivity aspects of long-run financial sustainability.

3. REGULATORY AND COMPLIANCE CONSIDERATIONS

Strong regulation is necessary to promote financial stability, as demonstrated by the European Union's data protection policies under the GDPR and set standards for payment services through PSD2. The regulatory technical standards outlined in the Commission's Delegated Regulation 2023/363 of October 31, 2022, for work product governance rules without inspection, have been amended and corrected. Enhancing comparability and openness in the disclosure of financial products that encourage investment in environmentally sustainable economic endeavours is the goal of the modifications. The regulation particularly transforms the format and the content requirements for preliminary papers and periodic reports with reference to nuclear or fossil energy investments. While retaining consistency in disclosures across numerous reporting forms, the updated aim to encourage investors and capital market stakeholders understanding the company's sustainability agendas. In order to achieve the current requirements more apprehensible and appropriate data changes that includes technical improvements they ensure compliance with Regulation of 2019/2088 of the European Commission, which establishes a framework for financial institution furnish sustainability information. Digitalization as a result the Basel Committee on Banking Observation has also released a caution about the risks associated with cyber-attacks and corporate resilience in financial industries (BCBS, 2021). These regulatory frameworks are essential to assure that technology advancements prevail inside the framework that can sustain long-lasting financial services in the future without sacrificing security and compliance, as the financial industry becomes more digitalized day by day. These exemplars illustrate that how financial institutions utilizing technology, internal function adjustments, and corporate compliance frameworks to comply with amending regulatory standards.

3.1 Ensuring Compliance and Security in Digital Financial Services

In digital financial services compliance and security are critical as the finance services are becoming more established while encompassing this transformation. As strengthening digitization of financial operations and services, emerge an escalated risk for cyber-attacks or regulatory violations consequently, involving robust compliance standards in addition to substantial security measures. Waterfall approaches like the General Data Protection Regulation (GDPR) in Europe and Payment Card Industry Data Security Standard (PCI DSS), that make it mandatory to protect valuable customer information and financial data with several regulatory requirements. Certainly, a review from Bouveret (2018) demonstrate in precise number that cyber-security could result in great financial losses and soil the reputation of various organisations especially when it comes to banks making cybersecurity even more worthwhile investing into beforehand (Bouveret, 2018). Furthermore, a document released by the Financial Stability Board (FSB) point-out that enhancing cyber resilience and managing systemic risk associated with cyberattacks are critical main concern for financial institutions functioning in the global marketplace (Financial Stability Board 2020). Financial institutions can increase financial sustainability by concentrating data privacy, safety & security, and ethical issues in AI-driven decision-making process through the application of systematic data protection rules and ethical AI framework. Resultantly, retaining security and compliance in digital financial service sector is not only requirements by law but also strategically mandatory to maintain the stability and certainty of the financial system.

Digital financial services (DFS) are developing at an exponentially fast pace, creating new possibilities for inclusive finance while also introducing compliance and security lapses. Artificial Intelligence (AI) contributes fundamentally to advancing digital financial inclusion through better risk management, addressing information asymmetry, and uncovering fraud (Mhlanga 2020). Nevertheless, DFS confront numerous security and privacy challenges which need to be resolved in order to enhance user adoption (Mehrban et al., 2020). Tools have been built also for privacy policy compliance check as compliance to data protection regulations like GDPR is obligatory in many countries (Akanfe et al., 2020). According to Jayasekara (2021), financial inclusion is influenced by the extent of anti-money laundering and countering the financing of terrorism (AML/CFT) regimes; nevertheless, their impact is limited if they employ a set-of-tasks classification. DFS is affected by a number of factors, including perceived utility, usability, and security (Kajol et al., 2022). On the new stage of decentralized finance (DeFi) with rules, coming up with solutions to fulfil these responsibilities is a developing problem that needs to be resolved in an organized manner (Wronka 2021).

With decentralized platforms based on blockchain technology, decentralized finance is quickly changing the financial landscape by providing substitutes for conventional banking services including lending, borrowing, and trading. DeFi functions independently of the traditional financial system, utilizing peer-to-peer networks and smart contracts to enable transactions without the need for middlemen. DeFi offers chances for innovation and financial inclusion, but it also brings with it regulatory issues with consumer safety, stability, and systemic risk.

Regulators are struggling to keep an eye on DeFi activities, which frequently don't have a single organization in charge of compliance. DeFi platforms' confidentiality raises questions about the possibility of money laundering and other illegal activity and can make it more difficult to implement AML and KYC laws. Some governments are investigating hybrid regulatory strategies, which combine new regulations specifically designed for DeFi with established financial regulations, in order to address these issues. For instance, according to recent Financial Action Task Force (FATF) recommendations, DeFi platforms might have to implement "travel rule" requirements to make sure that financial institutions exchange information about the originators and recipients of transactions. Implementing such protections in a decentralized setting is still quite difficult, although. Decentralized finance (DeFi) and an international perspective, incorporating examples from Asia and Europe, would enhance the investigation of how digital revolution affects financial sustainability.

3.2 The Role of Government and International Bodies

In the digital age, the government and international organizations are crucial in addressing sustainable finance issues by establishing rules that lower systematic risks and advance financial stability. Nonetheless, governments can play a specific role by implementing legislative measures that tackle cybersecurity risks and encourage openness associated with online financial transactions. In order to promote resilient financial systems, organizations like the World Bank, Financial Stability Board (FSB), International Monetary Fund (IMF), and others are collaborating internationally to streamline regulations and lessen the risks associated with digital financial innovations. For instance, the IMF DPP recommendations on central bank digital currencies and the Financial Stability Board's efforts to monitor and identify the risk implications of crypto-assets (FSB 2018) show that great progress has been achieved to account for a constantly changing financial environment (IMF 2020). Initiatives like these demonstrate how important it is to have comprehensive regulatory authority in order to maintain a healthy digital financial environment.

International organizations and governments have significant effects on financial sustainability in many different areas. Unlike non-state-owned businesses, state-owned firms must have government ownership below a certain threshold in order to remain financially sustainable (Lee et al., 2022). International aid and business relationships are also essential to the financial viability of non-governmental organizations (Córdova Paredes et al., 2019). Sustainable development goals are more likely to be met by local governments with good financial standing (Bisogno et al., 2024). Sociodemographic factors have varying effects on budgetary sustainability at the local and regional government levels, according to López Subirés et al., (2019). Shava (2021) described how the financial sustainability of NGOs in rural development is impacted by inadequate resource allocation and decreased donor financing. For instance, government assistance decreases the correlation between SMEs' creative performance and their ability to obtain financing (Ullah et al., 2021). Governance is a key component at the intersection of sustainable development and financial growth (Dutta & Saha, 2023). Ultimately, tax systems must be digitalized and undergo legal reforms in order for financial sustainability to be achieved (Tsindeliani et al., 2019). Analyzing the difficulties a large bank had in a cybersecurity incident, for instance, might highlight the legislative actions in different locations to improve security and compliance while also illuminating the complications of digital transformation.

Regional differences in regulatory responses to digital transformation reflect varied strategies for striking a balance between innovation, consumer protection, and financial stability. The GDPR offers a strong framework for data privacy in Europe, and the Markets in Crypto-Assets (MiCA) regulation seeks to create precise guidelines for digital assets, such as DeFi and cryptocurrencies. These regulatory frameworks aim to maintain financial services' security and compliance with data protection rules while also encouraging innovation. Europe's strategy, which prioritizes strict consumer protection and data privacy, could be a template for other areas dealing with comparable issues.

Conversely, Asia has been a leader in the area of digital financial innovation, as nations such as China and Singapore have implemented proactive legislative approaches to encourage the development of fintech and blockchain. For example, China has created a regulatory framework for financial services based on blockchain technology and started a central bank digital currency (CBDC) pilot program. Singapore, meantime, has adopted a regulatory sandbox strategy that permits fintech businesses to test new technology while being watched over by regulatory bodies. This strategy encourages innovation while giving regulators the ability to keep an eye on dangers and modify rules as necessary. Furthermore, Japan has set rules for the application of AI in finance that place a strong emphasis on openness and the moral use of data in AI-powered services.

A global perspective on digital change in finance is crucial, evidenced by the differences in regulatory environments between Europe and Asia. Financial institutions that operate across borders have to deal with a complex network of rules, necessitating the implementation of adaptable compliance techniques that consider the distinctive requirements of each region. Furthermore, in order to address cross-border issues like cyber security and the regulation of digital currencies, international cooperation among regulators is crucial for unifying regulatory standards.

4. CHALLENGES AND RISKS OF DIGITAL FINANCIAL INNOVATIONS

Digital financial innovations have introduced new technologies and services that improve accessibility, efficiency, and convenience, and have completely changed the financial industry. These technologies, which include peer-to-peer lending, digital wallets, blockchain technology, and cryptocurrencies, have the potential to completely transform financial systems and markets, but they also come with a number of challenges and concerns that need to be properly adressed.

4.1 Cybersecurity Threats and Financial Data Privacy

Cybersecurity is another substantial risk. Since it covers innovation, Cyber protection includes data in digital form of all types and formats. Examples are hacks of cryptocurrency exchanges reducing on financial loss and emphasizes for sufficiently secure measures (Oosthoek & Doerr et al., 2020). To counter these threats, financial institutions must invest in modern security Infrastructure.

The sophistication of the cybercriminals is so advanced that they are rapidly evolving and employing new types of technology-based attack strategies on financial institutions (Okoye et al., 2024; Umoga et al., 2024). Phishing, Ransomware and AI-Driven attacks are the most severe threats (Dhingra et al., 2021). Some FinTech platforms that work together are interdependent and this exposes them to systemic risks, cascading failures (Umoga et al., 2024) In order to address these threats, financial institutions have integrated a layered approach of security, encompassing encryption, firewalls, and biometrics (Dhingra et al., 2021). New technologies, such as artificial intelligence (AI) and machine learning are being implemented to enhance cybersecurity systems (Efijemue et al., 2023). The risk exposure goes beyond institutional networks to include fragile mobile/ IoT devices (Carter, 2017). Collaborative cross-function de-risking solutions for addressing these challenges will need cooperation of financial institutions, technology company's government/ regulatory promoters and public-private partnerships (Ekene. Okoye et al.; 2024; Efijemue et al., 2023).

4.2 Managing Technological Disruptions and Market Volatility

Changes in technology lead to variations of competitive positioning, and introduction of new risks which have potential impact on market volatility. High-frequency trading (HFT) and algorithmic trading has matured quickly, increasing the market liquidity, however with it comes a high risk of market anomalies and flash crashes (rapid price crash) (Aldridge & Krawciw, 2017). These technologies can exacerbate market movements by allowing large sales to be executed quickly, and this amplification effect could lead financial regulators to struggle with regulating the markets as well make it more difficult for traders to monitor their positions. This market volatility is even more intensified by geopolitical events, changes in economic policy and global business cycles. For example, sudden market moves can be caused by trade tensions, as a result of changes in monetary policy and economic crises (Claessens & Kose, 2013). Financial institutions must develop comprehensive risk management strategies to navigate these uncertainties and maintain stability. Moreover, regulatory frameworks matter, as they will increasingly constrain the impact of technology on financial markets. Obviously, regulators need to strike a delicate balance between fostering innovation and stability within the financial industry. The consultation of this research points to the need for designing regulations that are adapted and can also be progressively improved technological innovations, as well supervisory technologies (RegTech) to monitor and manage risks effectively (Arner et al., 2017).

Recent studies highlight the compelling influence of technological disruptions and market volatility on financial stability. Specifically, market volatility is negatively associated with financial satisfaction for those high in financial self-efficacy (Asebedo & Payne 2019). To address these issues in corporate foresight while confronting technology disruption, a three-tier VUCA (volatility, uncertainty complexity and ambiguity) approach is recommended to be applied (Kaivo-oja & Lauraeus, 2018). As a product of the Fourth Industrial Revolution, cryptocurrencies have obviously been influencing and introducing new risks or volatility spillovers to the global financial system (Umar et al., 2020). Due to technological advancements in Fintech, traditional financial markets may be transformed enhancing the cushion against oil price volatility and financial risk (Afshan et al., 2024) As observed by Vives (2019), banks experience a significant impact from digital disruption, which in turn affects competition and regulation within the banking industry. Open-ended technological instantiation of regulatory practices in financial markets leans on an interplay among human agents and software-embedded rules (Currie & Seddon, 2021). Additionally, Green finance seek to foster sustainability in the financial sector, by supporting green initiatives and increasing transparency (Chueca Vergara & Ferruz Agudo, 2021).

Also, the primary challenges in the digital transformation of the financial sector are aligning new technologies with existing regulatory frameworks. Financial regulations often lag behind technological advancements, making it difficult for institutions to ensure compliance when adopting innovations like AI and blockchain. For example, with its decentralized and unchangeable ledger system, blockchain technology poses questions about data ownership, regulatory monitoring, and compliance with know-your-customer (KYC) and anti-money laundering (AML) regulations. Conventional regulatory structures are built around centralized financial systems in which organizations serve as gatekeepers and middlemen. This paradigm is called into question by the decentralized nature of blockchain and DeFi, which calls for new regulatory strategies that protect innovation while allowing for decentralized financial activity.

Important regulatory issues in today's digital world include data security and privacy. Strict data protection rules, like the General Data Protection Regulation (GDPR) in Europe, which places severe restrictions on the gathering, handling, and archiving of personal data, are a challenge for financial institutions. Since AI and IoT frequently rely on vast amounts of data, including private and sensitive information, their rise increases these issues severe. Adhering to data protection laws while using AI for predictive analytics or IoT for real-time monitoring necessitates strong data governance frameworks that place an emphasis on authorization management, data minimization, and confidentiality. Furthermore, institutions must invest in innovative safety measures and adhere to changing cybersecurity standards since cybersecurity risks related to digital transformation, such as ransomware attacks and data breaches, represent serious challenges to financial stability. Achieving a balance between innovation and regulatory frameworks to reduce the risks connected with these technical breakthroughs is still a challenge.

4.3 Balancing Innovation with Risk Management

Operational risk is very difficult to manage. Digital financial advancements usually consist of layers upon layers of complicated and readily breached systems and procedures. Service interruptions, financial losses, and reputational damages are all possible outcomes of these actions. The key to managing these risks is contingency planning and risk management (Deloitte, 2020).

According to recent studies, a key to an organization's financial sustainability is achieving a balance between innovation and risk management. Sustainability related risks can have considerable consequences on business, making it important to identify and manage the associated risks in a structured manner (Schulte & Hallstedt, 2018). But firms dedicated to innovative have to monitor and manage risks efficiently which is more prominent in the emerging markets (da Silva Etges & Cortimiglia, 2019). The concept of corporate social responsibility emphasizes that the company has a role in reducing both financial and social risks associated with investments, including those aimed at innovation (Lebedev et al., 2022). In financial industry, innovation capabilities positively affect corporate sustainability (Sempere-Ripoll et al., 2020), and open innovations can contribute to financial sustainability, especially in the aftermath of an economic crisis (Jeong et al., 2020). Several frameworks for managing innovation risks during the design phase have been proposed to attain sustainability (Othman and Hussein 2023). Moreover, the approaches to risk assessment and financial capability of innovation project implementation are concretized (Rogulenko et al., 2021). The concise excerpt offers a preliminary definition and is complemented by explanations the effective sustainability management depends on balancing stakeholder interests to ensure long-term financial performance (Lee & Raschke, 2020).

5. STRATEGIES FOR ACHIEVING FINANCIAL SUSTAINABILITY THROUGH TECHNOLOGY

As organizations grapple for financial sustainability to remain in business, they are under the constant pressure of rising competition leading them into dynamic strategic shifts. A large part of this sustainability, however, comes down to the use technology being done right. Across the board, technological advancements are changing everything about how businesses operate and bringing new opportunities to reduce costs or grow revenue while improving quality. Through this introduction, will be led to explore possible methodologies any organization may follow in understanding how to use the technology for financial stability.

5.1 Building Resilient Digital Financial Infrastructures

Recently, digital finance becoming the cornerstone of long-term growth for businesses and helping them scale up. Digital Financial Infrastructures are one of the cornerstones on which modern economic system touches its larger economics.

With the ongoing digital transformation of financial services, resilient DFI has never been more important. Resilient infrastructure ensures that financial systems are capable of resisting and recovering from disruptions, thereby ensuring stability and confidence in the financial ecosystem.

Resilient, inclusive digital financial infrastructures could improve financial inclusion, particularly among marginalised populations in low and middle income countries (Kass-Hanna et al., 2022; Naughton & Brady, 2022). Digital identity systems, payment ecosystems and data protection framework link these key components (D'Silva et al., 2019). Such infrastructures may enhance financial resilience, crisis management capabilities and economic reboot (Arner et al., 2020). Successful implementation requires for organizational readiness such as resource flexibility, IT capabilities and cultural adaptability (Hussain & Papastathopoulos, 2022). In building such infrastructures, the use of emerging technologies (e.g., AI and data analytics) is widespread among fintech companies to a large extent (Argyroudis et al., 2022). However, the more extensive penetration of the internet to financial platforms means that greater cyber-security mechanisms are required (Argyroudis et al., 2022). To achieve it, being an essential ingredient of global and national financial stability as well as in favour of market accessibility by ensuring transparency to the capital markets.

5.2 Enhancing Customer Engagement and Trust via Digital Platforms

As rapidly evolving digital age, one of the keyways that businesses can do is by utilising an ecosystem for customers. Websites, social media outlets and mobile applications offer organizations a fluid platform to engage customers on an individual level while fostering lasting relationships via various online channels that are part of the digital sphere represented through platforms. Strategically leveraging these platforms can dramatically increase customer interactions, helping provide the financial foundation every business needs to ensure its long-term viability. Customer engagement and trust is paramount to a business's financial health. The long-term ability to create revenue for the business while staying both innovative and adaptive at a competitive cost. Financial sustainability engaged customers are more likely to purchase and recommend the company and choose it over competitors. Kumar and Pansari (2016) argued that engaged customers drive firm's business performance, own share of customer wallet which leads the value proposition to achieve profitable growth.

Digital platforms play a crucial role in enhancing customer engagement and trust, which are essential for financial sustainability. Digital content marketing fosters consumer engagement, trust, and brand relationships through relevant content dissemination (Hollebeek & Macky, 2019). Customer engagement on social media platforms like Facebook leads to increased trust and positive word-of-mouth (Islam & Rahman, 2016). Digital banking improves customer experience through factors such as service quality, perceived value, and usability (Mbama & Ezepue, 2018). E-commerce platforms can enhance customer loyalty through ease of use, product quality, and responsive customer support (Felix & Rembulan, 2023). The COVID-19 pandemic has accelerated digital transformation, particularly for micro and small enterprises, emphasizing the importance of digital payments and mobile money (Bai et al., 2021). Facebook fan pages can be effective marketing tools for building brand trust and increase buying intentions, especially for financial services like e-wallets (Gupta & Sharma, 2021).

5.3 Leveraging Big Data and Analytics for Strategic Financial Planning

The advent of big data and analytics has revolutionized numerous industries, including finance. Strategic financial planning, once dominated by traditional methods and intuition, is now increasingly driven by data-informed decisions. By incorporating analytics and big data into financial planning, businesses may analyse enormous amounts of data in order to gain useful insights, forecast future patterns, and accelerate decision-making.

The use of AI-driven decision-making by financial institutions is growing, highlighting ethical questions about accountability, bias, and transparency since of their complexity and uncertainty, AI algorithms are frequently referred to as "black boxes" since they can be challenging to explain or defend certain outcomes, including credit rating or loan approvals. Regulatory compliance is severely hampered by this capacity since organizations have to prove that their decision-making procedures are impartial and non-discriminatory. Financial regulators are increasingly required to set rules for the moral application of AI, mandating that organizations make sure AI models are impartial, auditable, and comprehensible. Methods like algorithmic fairness and explainable AI are becoming popular as means of resolving these issues by increasing the accountability and transparency of AI models. Furthermore, using consumer data in AI models involves ethical questions. Financial companies have to balance protecting consumer privacy with using data to enhance services. This necessitates putting ethical data practices into place, like getting express consent before using data and making sure that it isn't used for purposes other than those which customers expected. Concerns regarding manipulation and autonomy may arise as a result of the rapid increase of AI-driven customized financial solutions, which also calls into question how much institutions can encourage clients to adopt particular financial practices.

For all industries, big data analytics has become an important platform for strategic financial planning and business. It helps in extracting useful information (actionable insights) from large quantities of data, improves the quality of strategic and operational decision-making processes and identifies potential new business opportunities for companies (Ochuba et al., 2024; Baesens, 2014). The usage of big data analytics could result in more beneficial economic overall performance, hazard discount and also create a competitive advantage (Sarraf, 2023; Herdinata et al., 2024). However, it has to tackle issues regarding data privacy and security as well its requirement for advanced levels of analytical skills (Ravi & Kamaruddin, 2017). As part of overall data management strategy including collection, processing, analysis and visualization need to be implemented (Loshin, 2013). Additionally, organizations should bring in high-performance analytics appliances and consider NoSQL databases as well as graph analytics to deal with big data effectively (Kurt et al, 2018). Big data analytics can change the way of businesses compete by allowing companies to redefine markets, optimize profits and encourage growth in a crop of constantly evolving data that enhance business environment (Ohlhorst, 2012).

6. FUTURE TRENDS AND OPPORTUNITIES

6.1 Predicting the Future of Financial Services

Technological innovation, combined with ever-shifting consumer attitudes and regulatory changes are now altering the landscape of the financial services industry. The 21st century becomes essential to discuss how these components are defining sustainable future financial services. The changing landscape presents financial institutions with both opportunities and challenges, making it implicit to have an eye on the future paired with agility and innovation.

6.1.1 Technological Advancements

Technology is one of the biggest disruptors in financial services community. The combination of artificial intelligence (AI), blockchain and big data analysis is transforming the way of traditional banking operations. Artificial intelligence (AI), for example, is helping revolutionize customer service through chatbots and virtual assistants, offering tailored financial advice on an individual basis to millions of account holders in real time while transforming risk mitigation tools like fraud detection mechanisms (Kumar et al., 2021). Bitcoin, the leading cryptocurrency with its roots in blockchain technology has enabled transactions that enhance transparency and security due to their automated verification process offered by smart contracts which have allowed for disintermediation (Nakamoto 2008). In addition, financial institutions can capitalize on big data analytics to leverage large sprawling pool of data and create insight for better service provisioning costs optimization operations as well personalized products (Chen et al., 2012).

The financial sector is also witnessing a transformation with recent advancements in both artificial intelligence (AI), machine learning, on blockchain and cloud computing etc. making finance as FinTech (Jain et al., 2023; Gopal et al., 2023). These advances were ever-important for operationalized efficiency, security and accessibility in financial services (Jain et al., 2023). Big data analytics and AI are a new development that provides innovative potential in financial services such as personalized advisory, risk manager etc, (Mondal & Singh 2018; Ahmadi et al., 2024). New paradigms such as quantum computing and fractals are anticipated to cause significant changes in the finance industry (Moşteanu & Faccia, 2021). Alternative finance and technology-driven innovations pose a competitive threat to extant financial structures as well (Gąsiorkiewicz et al., 2020). Fintech has been making a significant contribution to the enhancement and evolution of Islamic finance, which have specific areas for research such as financial inclusion, corporate governance, digitalisation in Islamic Financial Services (Qudah et al., 2023).

6.1.2 Evolving Consumer Expectations

Today's customers expect frictionless, convenient, and personalized financial services available across digital channels. The development of fintech companies has raised financial institutions to innovate and adapt (Gomber et al., 2018). Mobile applications for banking and digital wallets are an example of how technology can allow customers more control over their finances (Arner et al., 2016). Financial institutions that fail to meet these evolving expectations risk losing their competitive edge in a rapidly changing market.

Recent research can help us understand how sustainable finance has moved on and what consumers expect. As of late, financial institutions are giving more attention to client-centricity governance (LCG) and sustainable lending practices (Pan, 2016). Sustainable banking innovation which is the integration of FinTech is resulting in driving innovation over sustainable banking, even apart from various advantages it seems another risk or drawbacks for banks like cybersecurity threats (Singhvi & Dadhich, 2023). The COVID-19 pandemic has also influenced changes in able to meet the goals and objectives of sustainable development investment trends, making concepts derived from green finance as their one example is a form of bonds called green bonds become increasingly popular (Judijanto et al., 2024). In fact, sustainable patterns of consumption are slowly moving from more traditional green issues towards the less frequently discussed social aspects in sectors like food, tourism and clothing (Sesini et al., 2020). Yet, the transformation toward sustainability in financial services is slow and more research needed (Tuyon et al., 2022). In turn, these changing expectations are spurring new business models and regulations to cater for investor preferences for sustainability strategy (Torre & Chiappini, 2020).

6.1.3 Regulatory Changes

Likewise, the regulatory frameworks are changing to adapt with new technologies and market trends. Governments and regulators around the world are getting to work on creating legal frameworks that straddle innovative tendencies with consumer protection, as well as upholding financial stability (Zetzsche et al., 2017). The General Data Protection Regulation (GDPR) in Europe is a notable case where new regulations can significantly impact data management and or privacy in the financial sector (Voigt & Von dem Bussche, 2017). Financial, social, and infrastructural factors shape the digital finance divide (DFD) within Europe and confirms that innovation in financial services or expanded provision of online infrastructure abate the DFD, however under a post-Covid-19 scenario for financially illiterate regions this gap widened considerably. It provides practical insights to policymakers regarding targeted digitalization strategies as well as extending hints towards banks (Ferilli et al., 2024).

A major pathway of change for regulators worldwide is the global move to integrate ESG considerations in financial decision-making. Sustainable finance is now widely accepted as a key factor in helping to address climate risk and ensure long-term economic resilience, with regulators worldwide acknowledging it. An example of major regulatory developments in ESG reporting that progress transparency and standardization comes from the European Union, with its Sustainable Finance Disclosure Regulation (SFDR) & Taxonomy Legislation (European Commission 2023). As part of these regulations, financial market participants are required to disclose how they consider and manage sustainability risks in their processes as well as whether they consider adverse impacts on sustainably, thus creating a more sustainable financial ecosystem. Recent research underlines the increasing relevance of sustainable finance and regulatory moves on financial sector. Global capital markets are slowly coming to grips with sustainable finance, as regulators on all continents begin enforcing environmental, social, and governance rules for participating in financial activity. Ultimately, this trend may constitute an autonomous objective along traditional targets such as stability and consumer protection (Colaert 2022). There is a common acceptance that climate change poses both risks and opportunities, requiring regulation to take effect (Brimble et al. 2010). The EU has implemented groundbreaking regulatory reforms to incentivize sustainable finance, but their success is contested (Ahlström & Monciardini, 2021). Regulatory changes are also needed to encourage more non-bank financing and extend macroprudential policies to non-bank activities (Claessens, 2017). The further development of the financial system will be possible by reducing political uncertainty, improving cooperation between regulator-intermediary and regulatory processes (Ziolo et al., 2019). According to Alexander & Fisher (2018) prudential banking regulation, and supervision can support the main goal by pointing banks' activities towards sustainability objectives. Furthermore, the promotion of open banking, where banks are required to share data with third party providers if customers give their consent is creating a more dynamic competitive environment (EBA 2012).

6.2 The Role of Digital Currencies and Central Bank Digital Currencies (CBDCs)

As digital currencies become more prominent across the globe, central banks around the world have begun to look into developing their own CBDCs. A CBDC is digital fiat money guaranteed by the central bank and used as a secure medium of exchange. More than 80% of central banks are already researching how to launch a CBDC, as reported by the Bank for International Settlements (BIS) in 2020. With this, there have been a number of breakthroughs in piloting or administering CBDCs by countries such as China, Sweden and most recently the Bahamas highlighting an increasing global trend towards mainstream digital money adoption.

But it is worth mentioning that there are several key trends influencing the direction of digital currencies and CDBC's going forward. Here are the specific expectations on blockchain technology; firstly, it will make financial transactions more transparent and secure. Blockchain is an immutable ledger through which most of the digital currencies are built on, that can be used to avoid fraud and simplify verification (Tapscott & Tapscott, 2016). Second, the design and implementation of CBDCs are expected to pay attention on compatibility with present payment networks so that it is easy for users to shift over from traditional money and broadly recognized (Kosse & Mattei, 2022).

This is a fast-moving and uncertain space with real implications for money, monetary systems and policy following Covid-19 the future of currencies in digital form (especially Bank Reserves) are theme that will continues to attract research. According to research, CBDCs have the potential of rewiring payment systems that might one day result in a common world currency (Bhaskar et al., 2022). Virtual currencies such as Bitcoin have been covered well, but CBDCs are the only digital versions of one's cash that is issued by government (Shi & Sun, 2020). CBDC adoption may force central banks to implement more restrictive monetary policy and change the workings of payment and clearing systems (Raskin & Yermack, 2016). CBDCs could also transform the global monetary system, perhaps leading to digital dollarization in nations that are either socially or digitally aligned (Brunnermeier et al., 2019). In 2021, 86% of central banks were experimenting with CBDC with pilot projects live in just 14%, according to (Popescu, 2021). This means that the various design choices required when implementing CBDCs are complex and that trade-offs between benefits and risks need to be carefully considered, especially with respect to their implications for monetary policy or financial stability (Cunha et al., 2021; Bordo & Levin, 2017).

6.3 Innovations in Financial Products and Services

Financial product and services for tomorrow will undergo seismic shifts based on changing consumer demands and technology. Adopting these trends are as necessary for financial institutions to remain competitive and relevant. This study examines these trends further, exploring their potential consequences as well as the avenues for how they can be harnessed.

With the help of technological developments and different consumer habits, financial innovations are changing how services in this industry operate. The investigation on innovative finance has increased significantly since digital banking, mobile payments and fintech (Nejad, 2016; Nejad, 2022). The integration of these innovations is aiding financial inclusion, easing the processes, and reducing costs for consumers (Jarvis & Han, 2021). According to Anifa et al. (2022), the principal trends are blockchain, artificial intelligence, robot advisors, and digital payments. Fintech is changing very fast and so are other industries like e-commerce, logistics & transportation (Ediagbonya, 2020), with possible implications for traditional financial institutions especially in developing countries where demand can outstrip supply as the industry slowly matures (Ediagbonya & Tioluwani, 2023). An important area of future research might in fact be one that explore how financial innovations contribute to consumer well-being, the performance demonstrated by firms, as well as regulatory frameworks (Nejad, 2022). Moreover, research needs should be in emerging markets and contribution of financial innovations to economic growth and financial inclusion (Nejad, 2022)

7. CONCLUSION

This chapter makes a detailed exploration of the intersection between digital technology and financial sustainability to deepen readers' insight about both aspects. This chapter gives a verdict within the effects of digital transformation on financial practices and essentially on how essential technology becomes in considering sustainable financial management, along with providing insight into individual emerging technologies and their applications.

Today, the financial services landscape is rapidly evolving with a combination of modern digital technology, changing consumer demands and regulatory changes. It is here that financial sustainability, anchored in good governance and strategic directions becomes ever more important. By combining AI, blockchain and big data analytics to overhaul traditional financial practices is reshaping the horizon of how these practises in finance with accuracy gives a broadened accommodative capability in terms of both efficiencies as well accessibility and personalization. There are regulatory frameworks that support innovation while protecting system stability and consumers. As modernist as the digital currencies and CBDCs are, they indicate financial evolution in a series that guarantee safer transactions with better efficiency. Banks adopting these innovations must do so in a way that takes advantage of the opportunities while mitigating potential risks and they need to set their sights on sustainability, inclusiveness, and resilience if they are going survive in the future financial landscape. To improve this area, financial institutions should invest in continuous innovation while collaborating closely with regulators to develop adaptive frameworks that balance technological advancements with long-term financial sustainability and risk mitigation.

REFERENCES

Adi, E., Anwar, A., Baig, Z., & Zeadally, S. (2020). Machine learning and data analytics for the IoT. *Neural Computing & Applications*, 32(20), 16205–16233. DOI: 10.1007/s00521-020-04874-y

Afshan, S., Leong, K. Y., Najmi, A., Razi, U., Lelchumanan, B., & Cheong, C. W. H. (2024). Fintech advancements for financial resilience: Analysing exchange rates and digital currencies during oil and financial risk. *Resources Policy*, 88, 104432. DOI: 10.1016/j.resourpol.2023.104432

Ahlström, H., & Monciardini, D. (2021). The regulatory dynamics of sustainable finance: Paradoxical success and limitations of EU reforms. *Journal of Business Ethics*, •••, 1–20. PMID: 33642657

Ahmadi, S. (2024). A comprehensive study on integration of big data and AI in financial industry and its effect on present and future opportunities. *International Journal of Current Science Research and Review*, 7(01), 66–74. DOI: 10.47191/ijcsrr/V7-i1-07

Ahmed, S., Alshater, M. M., El Ammari, A., & Hammami, H. (2022). Artificial intelligence and machine learning in finance: A bibliometric review. *Research in International Business and Finance*, 61, 101646. DOI: 10.1016/j.ribaf.2022.101646

Aithal, P. S. (2023). How to Create Business Value Through Technological Innovations Using ICCT Underlying Technologies. [IJAEML]. *International Journal of Applied Engineering and Management Letters*, 7(2), 232–292. DOI: 10.47992/IJAEML.2581.7000.0184

Akanfe, O., Valecha, R., & Rao, H. R. (2020). Design of a compliance index for privacy policies: A study of mobile wallet and remittance services. *IEEE Transactions on Engineering Management*, 70(3), 864–876. DOI: 10.1109/TEM.2020.3015222

Aldridge, I., & Krawciw, S. (2017). *Real-time risk: What investors should know about FinTech, high-frequency trading, and flash crashes*. John Wiley & Sons. DOI: 10.1002/9781119319030

Alexander, K., & Fisher, P. (2018). Banking regulation and sustainability. Available at *SSRN* 3299351.

Andreoni, A., Mondliwa, P., Roberts, S., & Tregenna, F. (2021). Towards a new industrial policy for structural transformation. Structural transformation in South Africa: The challenges of inclusive industrial development in a middle-income country, 337-361.

Anifa, M., Ramakrishnan, S., Joghee, S., Kabiraj, S., & Bishnoi, M. M. (2022). Fintech innovations in the financial service industry. *Journal of Risk and Financial Management*, 15(7), 287. DOI: 10.3390/jrfm15070287

Argyroudis, S. A., Mitoulis, S. A., Chatzi, E., Baker, J. W., Brilakis, I., Gkoumas, K., Vousdoukas, M., Hynes, W., Carluccio, S., Keou, O., Frangopol, D. M., & Linkov, I. (2022). Digital technologies can enhance climate resilience of critical infrastructure. *Climate Risk Management*, 35, 100387. DOI: 10.1016/j.crm.2021.100387

Arner, D. W., Barberis, J., & Buckey, R. P. (2016). FinTech, RegTech, and the reconceptualization of financial regulation. *Nw. J. Int'l L. & Bus.*, 37, 371.

Arner, D. W., Barberis, J. N., Walker, J., Buckley, R. P., Dahdal, A. M., & Zetzsche, D. A. (2020). Digital finance & the COVID-19 crisis. University of Hong Kong Faculty of Law Research Paper, (2020/017).

Asebedo, S., & Payne, P. (2019). Market volatility and financial satisfaction: The role of financial self-efficacy. *Journal of Behavioral Finance*, 20(1), 42–52. DOI: 10.1080/15427560.2018.1434655

Atz, U., Van Holt, T., Liu, Z. Z., & Bruno, C. C. (2023). Does sustainability generate better financial performance? review, meta-analysis, and propositions. *Journal of Sustainable Finance & Investment*, 13(1), 802–825. DOI: 10.1080/20430795.2022.2106934

Baesens, B. (2014). *Analytics in a big data world: The essential guide to data science and its applications*. John Wiley & Sons.

Bai, C., Quayson, M., & Sarkis, J. (2021). COVID-19 pandemic digitization lessons for sustainable development of micro-and small-enterprises. *Sustainable Production and Consumption*, 27, 1989–2001. DOI: 10.1016/j.spc.2021.04.035 PMID: 34722843

Basel Committee on Banking Supervision (BCBS). (2021). Principles for Operational Resilience. Retrieved from Bank for International Settlements. https://www.bis.org/bcbs/publ/d516.htm

Bhaskar, R., Hunjra, A. I., Bansal, S., & Pandey, D. K. (2022). Central bank digital currencies: Agendas for future research. *Research in International Business and Finance*, 62, 101737. DOI: 10.1016/j.ribaf.2022.101737

Bisogno, M., Cuadrado-Ballesteros, B., Manes-Rossi, F., & Peña-Miguel, N. (2024). Financial Sustainability and Sustainable Development in Local Governments: Empirical Insights. *Public Performance & Management Review*, 47(3), 1–28. DOI: 10.1080/15309576.2024.2340116

Board, F. S. (2018). Crypto-assets: report to the G20 on the work of the FSB and standardsetting bodies. Basel, Switzerland: Financial Stability Board, 16.

Board, F. S. (2020). Effective practices for cyber incident response and recovery. Financial Stability Board, Consultative Document.

Bordo, M. D., & Levin, A. T. (2017). *Central bank digital currency and the future of monetary policy (No. w23711)*. National Bureau of Economic Research. DOI: 10.3386/w23711

Bouveret, A. (2018). *Cyber risk for the financial sector: A framework for quantitative assessment*. International Monetary Fund.

Boyes, H., Hallaq, B., Cunningham, J., & Watson, T. (2018). The industrial internet of things (IIoT): An analysis framework. *Computers in Industry*, 101, 1–12. DOI: 10.1016/j.compind.2018.04.015

Brimble, M., Stewart, J., & de Zwaan, L. (2010). Climate change and financial regulation: Challenges for the financial sector following the global financial crisis. *Griffith Law Review*, 19(1), 71–85. DOI: 10.1080/10854669.2010.10854669

Brunnermeier, M. K., James, H., & Landau, J. P. (2019). *The digitalization of money (No. w26300)*. National Bureau of Economic Research. DOI: 10.3386/w26300

Buchanan, B. G., & Wright, D. (2021). The impact of machine learning on UK financial services. *Oxford Review of Economic Policy*, 37(3), 537–563. DOI: 10.1093/oxrep/grab016 PMID: 34642572

Buterin, V. (2014). A next-generation smart contract and decentralized application platform. white paper, 3(37), 2-1.

Carter, W. A. (2017). *Forces shaping the cyber threat landscape for financial institutions*. SWIFT Institute.

Chang, V., Baudier, P., Zhang, H., Xu, Q., Zhang, J., & Arami, M. (2020). How Blockchain can impact financial services–The overview, challenges and recommendations from expert interviewees. *Technological Forecasting and Social Change*, 158, 120166. DOI: 10.1016/j.techfore.2020.120166 PMID: 32834134

Chen, H., Chiang, R. H., & Storey, V. C. (2012). Business intelligence and analytics: From big data to big impact. *Management Information Systems Quarterly*, 36(4), 1165–1188. DOI: 10.2307/41703503

Chueca Vergara, C., & Ferruz Agudo, L. (2021). Fintech and sustainability: Do they affect each other? *Sustainability (Basel)*, 13(13), 7012. DOI: 10.3390/su13137012

Claessens, M. S., & Kose, M. A. (2013). *Financial crises explanations, types, and implications*. International Monetary Fund. DOI: 10.2139/ssrn.2295201

Claessens, S. (2017). *Regulation and structural change in financial systems*. Centre for Economic Policy Research.

Colaert, V. (2022). The changing nature of financial regulation: Sustainable finance as a new EU policy objective. *Common Market Law Review*, 59(6), 1669–1710. DOI: 10.54648/COLA2022115

Cordova Paredes, M. J., Calabuig Moreno, F., & Alonso Dos Santos, M. (2019). Key determinants on non-governmental organization's financial sustainability: A case study that examines 2018 fifa foundation social festival selected participants. *Sustainability (Basel)*, 11(5), 1411. DOI: 10.3390/su11051411

Cunha, P. R., Melo, P., & Sebastião, H. (2021). From bitcoin to central bank digital currencies: Making sense of the digital money revolution. *Future Internet*, 13(7), 165. DOI: 10.3390/fi13070165

Currie, W. L., & Seddon, J. J. (2022). Exploring technological instantiation of regulatory practices in entangled financial markets. *Journal of Information Technology*, 37(1), 31–50. DOI: 10.1177/02683962211027308

D'Silva, D., Filková, Z., Packer, F., & Tiwari, S. (2019). The design of digital financial infrastructure: lessons from India. BIS Paper, (106).

da Silva Etges, A. P. B., & Cortimiglia, M. N. (2019). A systematic review of risk management in innovation-oriented firms. *Journal of Risk Research*, 22(3), 364–381. DOI: 10.1080/13669877.2017.1382558

Dananjayan, M. P., Gopakumar, S., & Narayanasamy, P. (2023). Money in the age of bits and bytes: Technology in reshaping finance. Journal of Information Technology Teaching Cases, 20438869231178845.

Del Giudice, M., Campanella, F., & Dezi, L. (2016). The bank of things: An empirical investigation on the profitability of the financial services of the future. *Business Process Management Journal*, 22(2), 324–340. DOI: 10.1108/BPMJ-10-2015-0139

Deloitte. M. (2020). Internet of Medical Things (2018) https://www2. deloitte. com/content/dam/Deloitte/global/Documents/Life-Sciences-Health-Care/gx-lshc-medtech-iomt-brochure. pdf

Dhingra, D., Ashok, S., & Kumar, U. (2021). Demystifying global cybersecurity threats in financial services. In Handbook of Research on Advancing Cybersecurity for Digital Transformation (pp. 181-202). IGI Global. Digital transformation in banking: the evolution of financial services Can digital transformation in finance be simplified by adopting tools like XCALLY? https://www.xcally.com/news/digital-transformation-in-banking-the-evolution-of-financial-services/

Dutta, K. D., & Saha, M. (2023). Role of governance in the nexus between financial development and sustainable development. *Journal of International Development*, 35(6), 1181–1215. DOI: 10.1002/jid.3724

Ediagbonya, V., & Tioluwani, C. (2023). The role of fintech in driving financial inclusion in developing and emerging markets: Issues, challenges and prospects. *Technological Sustainability*, 2(1), 100–119. DOI: 10.1108/TECHS-10-2021-0017

Edu, A. S., Agoyi, M., & Agozie, D. (2021). Digital security vulnerabilities and threats implications for financial institutions deploying digital technology platforms and application: FMEA and FTOPSIS analysis. *PeerJ. Computer Science*, 7, e658. DOI: 10.7717/peerj-cs.658 PMID: 34435101

Efijemue, O., Obunadike, C., Taiwo, E., Kizor, S., Olisah, S., Odooh, C., & Ejimofor, I. (2023). Cybersecurity strategies for safeguarding customers data and preventing financial fraud in the United States financial sectors. *International Journal of Soft Computing*, 14(3), 10–5121.

El Hajj, M., & Hammoud, J. (2023). Unveiling the influence of artificial intelligence and machine learning on financial markets: A comprehensive analysis of AI applications in trading, risk management, and financial operations. *Journal of Risk and Financial Management*, 16(10), 434. DOI: 10.3390/jrfm16100434

Escobar, J. J., Rodríguez, F., Prieto, B., Kimovski, D., Ortiz, A., & Damas, M. (2023). A distributed and energy-efficient KNN for EEG classification with dynamic money-saving policy in heterogeneous clusters. *Computing*, 105(11), 2487–2510. DOI: 10.1007/s00607-023-01193-7

European Banking Authority (EBA), (2022). EBA Financial Education Repository 2021/2022

European Commission. (2023). The GDPR: New Opportunities, New Obligations. Retrieved from European Commission. https://eur-lex.europa.eu/legal-content/EN/TXT/?uri=CELEX:32023R0363

Fawzy, D., Moussa, S. M., & Badr, N. L. (2022). The internet of things and architectures of big data analytics: Challenges of intersection at different domains. *IEEE Access : Practical Innovations, Open Solutions*, 10, 4969–4992. DOI: 10.1109/ACCESS.2022.3140409

Felix, A., & Rembulan, G. D. (2023). Digital Transformation and The Customer Experience: Enhancing Engagement and Loyalty. Entrepreneur: Jurnal Bisnis Manajemen dan Kewirausahaan, 4(03), 228-240.

Ferilli, G. B., Palmieri, E., Miani, S., & Stefanelli, V. (2024). The impact of FinTech innovation on digital financial literacy in Europe: Insights from the banking industry. *Research in International Business and Finance*, 69, 102218. DOI: 10.1016/j.ribaf.2024.102218

Gas, S. (2017). Mobile money, cashless society and financial inclusion: case study on somalia and kenya. Cashless Society and Financial Inclusion: Case Study on Somalia and Kenya (July 15, 2017).

Gąsiorkiewicz, L., Monkiewicz, J., & Monkiewicz, M. (2020). Technology-driven innovations in financial services: The rise of alternative finance. *Foundations of Management*, 12(1), 137–150. DOI: 10.2478/fman-2020-0011

Goldman Sachs. (2020). Marcus by Goldman Sachs reaches $60 billion in deposits. Retrieved from Goldman Sachs website

Gomber, P., Koch, J. A., & Siering, M. (2017). Digital Finance and FinTech: Current research and future research directions. *Journal of Business Economics*, 87(5), 537–580. DOI: 10.1007/s11573-017-0852-x

Gomber, P., Koch, J. A., & Siering, M. (2017). Digital Finance and FinTech: Current research and future research directions. *Journal of Business Economics*, 87(5), 537–580. DOI: 10.1007/s11573-017-0852-x

Goodell, J. W., Kumar, S., Lim, W. M., & Pattnaik, D. (2021). Artificial intelligence and machine learning in finance: Identifying foundations, themes, and research clusters from bibliometric analysis. *Journal of Behavioral and Experimental Finance*, 32, 100577. DOI: 10.1016/j.jbef.2021.100577

Gopal, S., Gupta, P., & Minocha, A. (2023, May). Advancements in Fin-Tech and Security Challenges of Banking Industry. In 2023 4th International Conference on Intelligent Engineering and Management (ICIEM) (pp. 1-6). IEEE. DOI: 10.1109/ICIEM59379.2023.10165876

Gupta, M., & Sharma, A. (2022). Enhance Customer Engagement via Facebook Fanpage for Increased Purchase Intentions: Case of eWallet. In *Research Anthology on Social Media Advertising and Building Consumer Relationships* (pp. 1117–1134). IGI Global. DOI: 10.4018/978-1-6684-6287-4.ch060

Heaton, J. B., Polson, N. G., & Witte, J. H. (2017). Deep learning for finance: Deep portfolios. *Applied Stochastic Models in Business and Industry*, 33(1), 3–12. DOI: 10.1002/asmb.2209

Herdinata, C., Pranatasari, F. D., & Santoso, W. (2023). Factors affecting financial performance in companies based on big data analytics.

Hollebeek, L. D., & Macky, K. (2019). Digital content marketing's role in fostering consumer engagement, trust, and value: Framework, fundamental propositions, and implications. *Journal of Interactive Marketing*, 45(1), 27–41. DOI: 10.1016/j.intmar.2018.07.003

Hussain, M., & Papastathopoulos, A. (2022). Organizational readiness for digital financial innovation and financial resilience. *International Journal of Production Economics*, 243, 108326. DOI: 10.1016/j.ijpe.2021.108326

International Monetary Fund. (2020). "Digital Money Across Borders: Macro-Financial Implications." Retrieved from IMF website. https://www.imf.org/en/Publications/Policy-Papers/Issues/2020/10/17/Digital-Money-Across-Borders-Macro-Financial-Implications-49823

Islam, J. U., & Rahman, Z. (2016). Linking customer engagement to trust and word-of-mouth on Facebook brand communities: An empirical study. *Journal of Internet Commerce*, 15(1), 40–58. DOI: 10.1080/15332861.2015.1124008

Jain, R., Prajapati, D., & Dangi, A. (2023). Transforming the financial sector: A review of recent advancements in FinTech. Available at *SSRN* 4380348.

Jarvis, R., & Han, H. (2021). FinTech innovation: Review and future research directions. International Journal of Banking. *Finance and Insurance Technologies*, 1(1), 79–102.

Jayasekara, S. D. (2021). Deficient regimes of anti-money laundering and countering the financing of terrorism: Agenda of digital banking and financial inclusion. *Journal of Money Laundering Control*, 24(1), 150–162. DOI: 10.1108/JMLC-04-2020-0035

Jejeniwa, T. O., Mhlongo, N. Z., & Jejeniwa, T. O.Temitayo Oluwaseun Jejeniwa-Noluthando Zamanjomane MhlongoTitilola Olaide Jejeniwa. (2024). Theoretical perspectives on digital transformation in financial services: Insights from case studies in Africa and the United States. *Finance & Accounting Research Journal*, 6(4), 674–683. DOI: 10.51594/farj.v6i4.1068

Jeong, H., Shin, K., Kim, E., & Kim, S. (2020). Does open innovation enhance a large firm's financial sustainability? A case of the Korean food industry. *Journal of Open Innovation*, 6(4), 101. DOI: 10.3390/joitmc6040101

Judijanto, L., Fildansyah, R., Sudarmanto, E., Harsono, I., & Afandy, C. (2024). Bibliometric Analysis of the Application of Internet of Things (IoT) in Financial Services. *West Science Interdisciplinary Studies*, 2(02), 398–405. DOI: 10.58812/wsis.v2i02.664

Judijanto, L., Mokodenseho, S., Mokodompit, A. T., Mamonto, M., & Lantong, S. M. (2024). Trends in Sustainable Banking Practices: A Bibliometric Review of Green Financial Services and Risk Management Strategies. *Jurnal Multidisiplin West Science*, 3(03), 305–313. DOI: 10.58812/jmws.v3i03.1049

Jussila, A. (2015). Mobile money as an enabler for entrepreneurship: case Eastern Africa.

Kaivo-oja, J. R. L., & Lauraeus, I. T. (2018). The VUCA approach as a solution concept to corporate foresight challenges and global technological disruption. foresight, 20(1), 27-49.

Kajol, K., Singh, R., & Paul, J. (2022). Adoption of digital financial transactions: A review of literature and future research agenda. *Technological Forecasting and Social Change*, 184, 121991. DOI: 10.1016/j.techfore.2022.121991

Kass-Hanna, J., Lyons, A. C., & Liu, F. (2022). Building financial resilience through financial and digital literacy in South Asia and Sub-Saharan Africa. *Emerging Markets Review*, 51, 100846. DOI: 10.1016/j.ememar.2021.100846

Koh, L., Dolgui, A., & Sarkis, J. (2020). Blockchain in transport and logistics–paradigms and transitions. *International Journal of Production Research*, 58(7), 2054–2062. DOI: 10.1080/00207543.2020.1736428

Kumar, V., & Pansari, A. (2016). Competitive advantage through engagement. *JMR, Journal of Marketing Research*, 53(4), 497–514. DOI: 10.1509/jmr.15.0044

Kumar, V., Ramachandran, D., & Kumar, B. (2021). Influence of new-age technologies on marketing: A research agenda. *Journal of Business Research*, 125, 864–877. DOI: 10.1016/j.jbusres.2020.01.007

Kurt, S., Heitz, J., Bundi, N., & Breymann, W. (2018). Large-scale data-driven financial risk modeling using big data technology. In 2018 IEEE/ACM 5th International Conference on Big Data Computing Applications and Technologies (BDCAT) (pp. 206-207). IEEE. DOI: 10.1109/BDCAT.2018.00033

La Torre, M., & Chiappini, H. (2020). Sustainable finance: Trends, opportunities and risks. Contemporary Issues in Sustainable Finance: Creating an Efficient Market through Innovative Policies and Instruments, 281-287.

Lahmadi, A., Bertin, E., & Li, R. (2022). BRAINS 2020 special issue: Blockchain research and applications for innovative networks and services. *International Journal of Network Management*, 32(2), e2189. DOI: 10.1002/nem.2189

Lebedev, V. V., Deberdeeva, N. A., Farkova, N. A., & Korobeinikova, L. S. (2022). Systemic Risk Management of Investments in Innovation Based on CSR. *Risks*, 10(5), 87. DOI: 10.3390/risks10050087

Lee, C. L., Ahmad, R., Lee, W. S., Khalid, N., & Karim, Z. A. (2022). The financial sustainability of state-owned enterprises in an emerging economy. *Economies*, 10(10), 233. DOI: 10.3390/economies10100233

Lee, M. T., & Raschke, R. L. (2020). Innovative sustainability and stakeholders' shared understanding: The secret sauce to "performance with a purpose". *Journal of Business Research*, 108, 20–28. DOI: 10.1016/j.jbusres.2019.10.020

Li, X., Sigov, A., Ratkin, L., Ivanov, L. A., & Li, L. (2023). Artificial intelligence applications in finance: A survey. *Journal of Management Analytics*, 10(4), 676–692. DOI: 10.1080/23270012.2023.2244503

Lopez Subires, M. D., Alcaide Munoz, L., Navarro Galera, A., & Rodriguez Bolivar, M. P. (2019). The influence of socio-demographic factors on financial sustainability of public services: A comparative analysis in regional governments and local governments. *Sustainability (Basel)*, 11(21), 6008. DOI: 10.3390/su11216008

Loshin, D. (2013). *Big data analytics: from strategic planning to enterprise integration with tools, techniques, NoSQL, and graph*. Elsevier.

Maiti, M., & Ghosh, U. (2021). Next-generation internet of things in fintech ecosystem. *IEEE Internet of Things Journal*, 10(3), 2104–2111. DOI: 10.1109/JIOT.2021.3063494

Mbama, C. I., & Ezepue, P. O. (2018). Digital banking, customer experience and bank financial performance: UK customers' perceptions. *International Journal of Bank Marketing*, 36(2), 230–255. DOI: 10.1108/IJBM-11-2016-0181

Mbogo, M. (2010). The impact of mobile payments on the success and growth of micro-business: The case of M-Pesa in Kenya. Journal of language, technology & entrepreneurship in Africa, 2(1), 182-203.

Mehrban, S., Nadeem, M. W., Hussain, M., Ahmed, M. M., Hakeem, O., Saqib, S., & Khan, M. A. (2020). Towards secure FinTech: A survey, taxonomy, and open research challenges. *IEEE Access : Practical Innovations, Open Solutions*, 8, 23391–23406. DOI: 10.1109/ACCESS.2020.2970430

Mhlanga, D. (2021). Financial inclusion in emerging economies: The application of machine learning and artificial intelligence in credit risk assessment. International journal of financial studies, 9(3), 39.

Milojević, N., & Redzepagic, S. (2021). Prospects of artificial intelligence and machine learning application in banking risk management. *Journal of Central Banking Theory and Practice*, 10(3), 41–57. DOI: 10.2478/jcbtp-2021-0023

Mondal, A., & Singh, A. (2018). Emerging technologies and opportunities for innovation in financial data analytics: a perspective. In Big Data Analytics: 6th International Conference, BDA 2018, Warangal, India, December 18–21, 2018 [Springer International Publishing.]. *Proceedings*, 6, 126–136.

Mosteanu, N. R., & Faccia, A. (2021). Fintech frontiers in quantum computing, fractals, and blockchain distributed ledger: Paradigm shifts and open innovation. *Journal of Open Innovation*, 7(1), 19. DOI: 10.3390/joitmc7010019

Nakamoto, S. (2008). Bitcoin: A Peer-to-Peer Electronic Cash System. Retrieved from https://bitcoin.org/bitcoin.pdf

Naughton, J. M., & Brady, A. K. (2022). Building resilience to crisis through digital financial services with a gender lens. *Enterprise Development & Microfinance*, (1), 28–44. DOI: 10.3362/1755-1986.21-00035

Nejad, M. (2016). Research on financial services innovations: A quantitative review and future research directions. *International Journal of Bank Marketing*, 34(7), 1042–1068. DOI: 10.1108/IJBM-08-2015-0129

Nejad, M. G. (2022). Research on financial innovations: An interdisciplinary review. *International Journal of Bank Marketing*, 40(3), 578–612. DOI: 10.1108/IJBM-07-2021-0305

Nidugondi, S., & Bhargava, M. (2019). Mobile money: Creating a cash-light Africa to solve the financial inclusion problem. The PayTech book: The payment technology handbook for investors, entrepreneurs and FinTech visionaries, 217-221.

Nzioka, D. K. (2010). Impact of mobile banking on microfinance institutions: a case study of Small and Micro Enterprise Program (SMEP), Kenya (Doctoral dissertation, Southern New Hampshire University).

Ochuba, N. A., Amoo, O. O., Okafor, E. S., Akinrinola, O., & Usman, F. O. (2024). Strategies for leveraging big data and analytics for business development: A comprehensive review across sectors. *Computer Science & IT Research Journal*, 5(3), 562–575. DOI: 10.51594/csitrj.v5i3.861

OE, M., & OI, M. As of October 2023, 130 countries, representing 98 percent of global GDP, were exploring the potential use of a CBDC (Kosse and Mattei 2022). 2, 3 A survey of IMF country teams representing 31 Middle East and Central Asia (ME&CA) economies4 finds that 19 countries are considering or exploring a CBDC. This is consistent with information from country authorities' public statements (Figure 3). Most ME&CA countries interested.

Ohlhorst, F. J. (2012). *Big data analytics: turning big data into big money* (Vol. 65). John Wiley & Sons. DOI: 10.1002/9781119205005

Okoye, C. C., Nwankwo, E. E., Usman, F. O., Mhlongo, N. Z., Odeyemi, O., & Ike, C. U. (2024). Securing financial data storage: A review of cybersecurity challenges and solutions. *International Journal of Science and Research Archive*, 11(1), 1968–1983. DOI: 10.30574/ijsra.2024.11.1.0267

Oosthoek, K., & Doerr, C. (2020). Cyber security threats to Bitcoin exchanges: Adversary exploitation and laundering techniques. *IEEE Transactions on Network and Service Management*, 18(2), 1616–1628. DOI: 10.1109/TNSM.2020.3046145

Othman, A. A. E., & Hussein, R. M. (2023). Innovation management framework for achieving sustainability through managing risks of innovative solutions during the design process. Journal of Engineering, Design and Technology.

Pan, Y. (2016). Sustainability trends in financial services sector: Evidence from Europe and North America. In 2016 13th International Conference on Service Systems and Service Management (ICSSSM) (pp. 1-6). IEEE.

Panduman, Y. Y. F., Funabiki, N., Fajrianti, E. D., Fang, S., & Sukaridhoto, S. (2024). A Survey of AI Techniques in IoT Applications with Use Case Investigations in the Smart Environmental Monitoring and Analytics in Real-Time IoT Platform. *Information (Basel)*, 15(3), 153. DOI: 10.3390/info15030153

Parate, S., Josyula, H. P., & Reddi, L. T. (2023). Digital identity verification: Transforming KYC processes in banking through advanced technology and enhanced security measures. *International Research Journal of Modernization in Engineering Technology and Science*, 5(9), 128–137.

Park, S. K. (2023). Sustainable finance in global capital markets. In *Research Handbook on Global Capital Markets Law* (pp. 236–250). Edward Elgar Publishing. DOI: 10.4337/9781800379305.00024

Patel, R., Migliavacca, M., & Oriani, M. (2022). Blockchain in Banking and Finance: Is the best yet to come. A bibliometric review. *Research in International Business and Finance*, 62, 101718. DOI: 10.1016/j.ribaf.2022.101718

Popescu, A. D. (2021). Central Banks Digital Currency-Opportunities and Innovation. Ovidius University Annals, Series Economic Sciences, 21(1).

Qudah, H., Malahim, S., Airout, R., Alomari, M., Hamour, A. A., & Alqudah, M. (2023). Islamic finance in the era of financial technology: A bibliometric review of future trends. *International Journal of Financial Studies*, 11(2), 76. DOI: 10.3390/ijfs11020076

Raskin, M., & Yermack, D. (2018). Digital currencies, decentralized ledgers and the future of central banking. In *Research handbook on central banking* (pp. 474–486). Edward Elgar Publishing. DOI: 10.4337/9781784719227.00028

Ravi, V., & Kamaruddin, S. (2017). Big data analytics enabled smart financial services: opportunities and challenges. In Big Data Analytics: 5th International Conference, BDA 2017, Hyderabad, India, December 12-15, 2017 [Springer International Publishing.]. *Proceedings*, 5, 15–39.

Ravi, V., & Kamaruddin, S. (2017). Big data analytics enabled smart financial services: opportunities and challenges. In Big Data Analytics: 5th International Conference, BDA 2017, Hyderabad, India, December 12-15, 2017 [Springer International Publishing.]. *Proceedings*, 5, 15–39.

Renduchintala, T., Alfauri, H., Yang, Z., Pietro, R. D., & Jain, R. (2022). A survey of blockchain applications in the fintech sector. *Journal of Open Innovation*, 8(4), 185. DOI: 10.3390/joitmc8040185

Rogulenko, T., Orlov, E. V., Smolyakov, O. A., Bodiako, A. V., & Ponomareva, S. V. (2021). Analytical methods to assess financial capacity in face of innovation projects risks. *Risks*, 9(9), 171. DOI: 10.3390/risks9090171

Sarraf, S. (2023). Formulating A Strategic Plan Based On Statistical Analyses And Applications For Financial Companies Through A Real-World Use Case. arXiv preprint arXiv:2307.04778.

Schulte, J., & Hallstedt, S. I. (2018). Company risk management in light of the sustainability transition. *Sustainability (Basel)*, 10(11), 4137. DOI: 10.3390/su10114137

Sempere-Ripoll, F., Estelles-Miguel, S., Rojas-Alvarado, R., & Hervas-Oliver, J. L. (2020). Does technological innovation drive corporate sustainability? Empirical evidence for the European financial industry in catching-up and central and eastern Europe countries. *Sustainability (Basel)*, 12(6), 2261. DOI: 10.3390/su12062261

Sesini, G., Castiglioni, C., & Lozza, E. (2020). New trends and patterns in sustainable consumption: A systematic review and research agenda. *Sustainability (Basel)*, 12(15), 5935. DOI: 10.3390/su12155935

Sestino, A., Prete, M. I., Piper, L., & Guido, G. (2020). Internet of Things and Big Data as enablers for business digitalization strategies. *Technovation*, 98, 102173. DOI: 10.1016/j.technovation.2020.102173

Shava, E. (2021). Financial sustainability of NGOs in rural development programmes. *Development in Practice*, 31(3), 393–403. DOI: 10.1080/09614524.2020.1853059

Shi, Q., & Sun, X. (2020). A scientometric review of digital currency and electronic payment research: A network perspective. *Complexity*, 2020(1), 8876017. DOI: 10.1155/2020/8876017

Siew, E. G., & Farouk, F. M. (2023). Big data analytics implementation issues: A case study of a large bank in Malaysia. Journal of Information Technology Teaching Cases, 20438869231176836.

Singhvi, S., & Dadhich, M. (2023). FinTech revolution and future of sustainable banking: Opportunities and risks analysis. *International Journal of Management and Development Studies*, 12(04), 12–21. DOI: 10.53983/ijmds.v12n04.003

Sonkavde, G., Dharrao, D. S., Bongale, A. M., Deokate, S. T., Doreswamy, D., & Bhat, S. K. (2023). Forecasting stock market prices using machine learning and deep learning models: A systematic review, performance analysis and discussion of implications. *International Journal of Financial Studies*, 11(3), 94. DOI: 10.3390/ijfs11030094

Spyropoulos, A. Z., Bratsas, C., Makris, G. C., Garoufallou, E., & Tsiantos, V. (2023). Interoperability-Enhanced Knowledge Management in Law Enforcement: An Integrated Data-Driven Forensic Ontological Approach to Crime Scene Analysis. *Information (Basel)*, 14(11), 607. DOI: 10.3390/info14110607

Sundmaeker, H., Guillemin, P., Friess, P., & Woelfflé, S. (2010). Vision and challenges for realising the Internet of Things. Cluster of European research projects on the internet of things. *European Commision*, 3(3), 34–36.

Sunhare, P., Chowdhary, R. R., & Chattopadhyay, M. K. (2022). Internet of things and data mining: An application oriented survey. *Journal of King Saud University. Computer and Information Sciences*, 34(6), 3569–3590. DOI: 10.1016/j.jksuci.2020.07.002

Tapscott, D., & Tapscott, A. (2016). *Blockchain revolution: how the technology behind bitcoin is changing money, business, and the world*. Penguin.

Thommandru, A., & Chakka, B. (2023). Recalibrating the banking sector with blockchain technology for effective anti-money laundering compliances by banks. *Sustainable Futures : An Applied Journal of Technology, Environment and Society*, 5, 100107. DOI: 10.1016/j.sftr.2023.100107

Treleaven, P., Brown, R. G., & Yang, D. (2017). Blockchain technology in finance. *Computer*, 50(9), 14–17. DOI: 10.1109/MC.2017.3571047

Tsindeliani, I., Kot, S., Vasilyeva, E., & Narinyan, L. (2019). Tax system of the Russian Federation: Current state and steps towards financial sustainability. *Sustainability (Basel)*, 11(24), 6994. DOI: 10.3390/su11246994

Tuyon, J., Onyia, O. P., Ahmi, A., & Huang, C. H. (2023). Sustainable financial services: Reflection and future perspectives. *Journal of Financial Services Marketing*, 28(4), 664–690. DOI: 10.1057/s41264-022-00187-4

Tyagi, S. K. S., & Boyang, Q. (2021). An intelligent internet-of-things-aided financial crisis prediction model in fintech. *IEEE Internet of Things Journal*, 10(3), 2183–2193. DOI: 10.1109/JIOT.2021.3088753

Ullah, F., Degong, M., Anwar, M., Hussain, S., & Ullah, R. (2021). Supportive tactics for innovative and sustainability performance in emerging SMEs. *Financial Innovation*, 7(1), 1–31. DOI: 10.1186/s40854-021-00284-8

Umar, M., Rizvi, S. K. A., & Naqvi, B. (2021). Dance with the devil? The nexus of fourth industrial revolution, technological financial products and volatility spillovers in global financial system. *Technological Forecasting and Social Change*, 163, 120450. DOI: 10.1016/j.techfore.2020.120450

Umoga, U. J., Sodiya, E. O., Amoo, O. O., & Atadoga, A. (2024). A critical review of emerging cybersecurity threats in financial technologies. *International Journal of Science and Research Archive*, 11(1), 1810–1817. DOI: 10.30574/ijsra.2024.11.1.0284

Vives, X. (2019). Digital disruption in banking. *Annual Review of Financial Economics*, 11(1), 243–272. DOI: 10.1146/annurev-financial-100719-120854

Vodafone. (2021). M-Pesa celebrates 40 million active customers across Africa. Retrieved from Vodafone website

Voigt, P., & Von dem Bussche, A. (2017). The eu general data protection regulation (gdpr). A Practical Guide, 1st Ed., Cham: Springer International Publishing, 10(3152676), 10-5555.

Winn, J. K. (2016). Mobile payments and financial inclusion: Kenya, Brazil, and India as case studies. In Research handbook on electronic commerce law (pp. 62-88). Edward Elgar Publishing.

Wronka, C. (2023). Financial crime in the decentralized finance ecosystem: New challenges for compliance. *Journal of Financial Crime*, 30(1), 97–113. DOI: 10.1108/JFC-09-2021-0218

Yawalkar, P. M., Paithankar, D. N., Pabale, A. R., Kolhe, R. V., & William, P. (2023). Integrated identity and auditing management using blockchain mechanism. *Measurement. Sensors*, 27, 100732. DOI: 10.1016/j.measen.2023.100732

Yourstory.com: Opinion – FinTech startups are India's new hope forfull financial inclusion - Anand Tandon (2018) Available Athttps://yourstory.com/2018/08/FinTech-financial-inclusion/ (Lastaccessed on 25.12.2018)

Zetsche, D. A., Buckley, R. P., Arner, D. W., & Barberis, J. N. (2017). From FinTech to TechFin: The regulatory challenges of data-driven finance. *NYUJL & Bus.*, 14, 393.

Ziolo, M., Filipiak, B. Z., Bąk, I., & Cheba, K. (2019). How to design more sustainable financial systems: The roles of environmental, social, and governance factors in the decision-making process. *Sustainability (Basel)*, 11(20), 5604. DOI: 10.3390/su11205604

Chapter 3
Fintech for Small Business

Aamir Inam Bhutta
Government College University, Faisalabad, Pakistan

Khadija Sarwar
Government College University, Faisalabad, Pakistan

Muhammad Fayyaz Sheikh
Government College University, Faisalabad, Pakistan

Jahanzaib Sultan
Government College University, Faisalabad, Pakistan

ABSTRACT

This chapter focuses on the impact, opportunity, and challenges that Fintech has brought to SMBs, which are essential players in global economies but have always struggled to secure conventional funds. The development of Fintech has served up such innovations as mobile payments, online lending, cloud-based accounting, and crowdfunding that can reduce such costs of transactions, access to credit, and financial management for SMBs. The chapter covers Fintech success stories like Square, M-Pesa, and Alipay. It looks into more potential advantages of the Fintech movement, both in the short and long run, including the potential for cost reductions and further encroachment of artificial intelligence into the domain of financial decision-making. It also addresses issues of data privacy, fraud control, and the need for digitization competence. The paper concludes with specific recommendations based on the findings for improvements in SMBs and provides suggestions for researchers and policymakers.

DOI: 10.4018/979-8-3693-6386-7.ch003

1 INTRODUCTION

Small Businesses contribute tremendously to developing various global economies by being the primary bearers of development ideas and execution. Thus, Small Businesses, as noted by the World Bank (2020) states – represent 90% of businesses globally and contribute up to 40% of national income – GDP in emergent economies. Small businesses today account for 44% of the GDP and create two-thirds of new employment in the United States (U. S. Small Business Administration, 2019). These significant contributions paint a picture of the importance of Small Businesses in economic growth and employment.

Small Businesses still face several hurdles in obtaining conventional finance services that may affect their sustenance and progress. Berger and Udell (2006) show a lack of information that favors the financial institutions to the disadvantage of Small Businesses, constituting a form of credit rationing that constrains the supply of capital necessary for the growth of Small Businesses. This is even more apparent in developing economies whereby Beck and Demirguc-Kunt (2006) noted that up to 39% of small firms considered access to finance a significant factor hindering their growth, unlike the 12% of large firms.

SBs face significant funding challenges; the global SME finance gap is approximately $5.2 trillion (International Finance Corporation, 2017), equivalent to 19% of emerging market GDP. This deficit has been compounded by increased regulatory demands for conventional Banks after the 2008 financial crisis, which decreased SB lending (Mills & McCarthy, 2016). As a result, most SBs fail to secure adequate funding required for further expansion, introducing new products and services, and meeting daily running expenses.

1.1 Emergence of Fintech

Fintech, financial technology in full, describes the radical changes observed in delivering financial services. In their study, Arner et al. (2015) operationally teamed fintech as 'technology-enabled financial solutions', referring to a continuum that ranges from a narrow view of technology as a tool for offering innovative financial solutions to a broader view of emerging technologies in financial services. FinTech can be classified based on the application, ranging from digital banking services, mobile payment systems, blockchain technology, artificial intelligence in the financial market, and other algorithms for lending businesses (Gomber et al., 2018).

The global fintech market has grown rapidly; investment jumped from $19.9 billion in 2013 to $111.8 billion in 2018 (KPMG, 2019). This rapid expansion illustrated fintech's disruption capability in fulfilling the needs left behind by traditional financial services. Fintech, therefore, presents particularly fitting solutions to long-standing issues affecting the accessibility of financial services to SBs.

Fintech can dramatically impact financial services for SBs in several ways. Lee and Shin (2018) note that fintech can result in various effects, such as a decrease in transaction costs, improvement in the level of financial access, and the delivery of improved solutions to SBs. For instance, competition from online players leveraging technology, including big data analytics and advanced algorithms to evaluate credit risk, can provide better credit scoring for SBs than traditional models, thereby increasing credit access (Jagtiani & Lemieux, 2018).

1.2 Objectives of the Chapter

The purpose of this chapter is to review relevant literature to determine a concept of how Fintech can help to solve the existing problems faced by small and medium enterprises (SMEs). Specifically, this chapter aims to:

1. A discussion of payment solutions, microloan platforms, and other solutions aimed at helping SBs address their specific financial needs.

2. Evaluate the impact that the use of Fintech has on productivity, decreases costs and how helps in making the right decisions in terms of the SB's financial process. This entails analyzing some of the quantitative evidence whereby, for instance, Dorfleitner et al. (2017) established that the Fintech application has the potential to cut the operational costs of SBs by a maximum of 25%.

3. Analyze the main drivers and challenges that affect Fintech adoption, specifically in SBs, through analyzing data security risk, IT literacy and regulatory compliance. This will be based on current research and qualitative data in the study; this includes surveys and semi-structured interviews (Romānova & Kudinska, 2016).

4. Propose measures that may lead to increased usage of Fintech options by SBs, including enhancing digital skills, enhancing security features, and raising awareness of the benefits of Fintech applications.

2 LITERATURE REVIEW

Fin-tech, or financial technology, has become a new way of delivering financial services, emphasizing financing and payment solutions for Small Businesses. Despite the rapid development of fintech services – mobile banking, digital lending and automated accounting – the influence of fintech on Small Businesses can be ambiguous. This literature review synthesizes the current knowledge on the impact of fintech on Small Businesses, comparing the arguments put forth and showing the weaknesses and gaps for further research in the existing literature.

Multicountry research evidence in literature also highlights how the availability of fintech innovations enhances Small Businesses' access to financing. Fintech reduces traditional ways of financing by having flexible new ways that do not require the standard credit check and long processes of loaning (Zhu & Zhang, 2021). Digital lending platforms are also listed for offering quick access to credit, which is especially important for those Small Businesses that suffer from working capital deficits (Bazarbash et al., 2020). In the context of the COVID-19 pandemic, the opportunity to provide funding faster through fintech proved important in their activity with small businesses (Hu et al., 2022).

The literature also orients towards the cost leadership capability, specifically, the operational efficiencies of fintech. Mobile payment systems, data analysis, and automated invoices are some examples of modern technologies that can potentially decrease costs and enhance the quality of financial decision-making (Wang and Liu, 2023). This capability is essential for SBs because many of them experience a lack of resources to support their particular scale of development and need financial surety. Nevertheless, there is a trend for presenting fintech's efficiency from the best angle without a deeper discussion of the possible technological reliance on such instruments and the consequences for companies without knowledge of digital technologies.

Fintech is believed to support financial inclusion standards, especially in emerging markets where the banking system is not well developed (Karim et al., 2021). Mobile banking solutions enable small businesses across remote places to carry out some basic banking needs, establish credit records as well as enhance their cash flow management (Chen et al., 2022). Moreover, the analysis shows that although fintech offers the possibility of inclusion, the literature does not agree. Kim et al. (2021) rightly opine that despite the positive impact of fintech solutions for those who could utilize them, there is a sort of 'digital divide' because technologies are more visible in the urban setting. This has important implications regarding the sustainability of the fintech revolution and its potential to widen rather than to reduce the existing divide between companies connected to the digital financing ecosystem and those lacking access to it.

As such, the scholars recommend that new policies be developed to support areas with limited digital infrastructure or low literacy levels among small business owners (Molina et al., 2023). More comparative research in this area would be useful for the literature, considering how differences in regional regulation and initial accessibility of technological tools influence the use of fintech by SBs.

Hernandez and Xu (2023) explain the vulnerabilities of cyber threats for small businesses willing to implement fintech solutions because of the lack of finances for cybersecurity. Furthermore, unfavourably, compared to conventional banks, most fintech service providers may operate with comparatively low regulatory compliance standards that raise data privacy concerns. This lack of regulation may leave SBs exposed, as they depend on fintech services to meet its needs but without offering the same levels of consumer protection as those institutions that are regulated.

Alam et al. (2022) also argue that there are more dangers from the fast expansion of online lending that including risks of irresponsible credit issuance. Some fintech portfolios focus more on gaining more customers as fast as possible regardless of whether SBs are being placed in a cycle of revolving debts. EU literature has cited the need for more regulation and better security to curb these vices and enable policy regulation of responsible fintech. This is especially cogent as SBs can have little understanding of how to appraise the security solutions offered by fintech services.

Another matter in the literature is that there is great fragmentation of regulatory activities regarding fintech. While there is this belief that loose regulations will encourage innovation, others opine that insufficient regulations make the global financial system casual and risky for SBs who rely on cross-border fintech services (Yadav & Verma, 2023). This inconsistency is troublesome and it burdens compliance so some SBs might hesitate to use specific fintech services in regards to data and transaction protection.

However, the prognosis for fintech for SBs is positive, but the literature regarding the topic with different long-term views. On one hand, innovative technologies such as artificial intelligence in financial applications and blockchain smart contracts may bring considerable improvements to the finance function eliminate redundancies and drive costs down, thereby increasing SB productivity (Park & Cho, 2024). According to Wang and Liu (2023), AI can play a major role in changing how SBs perform financial management by providing automated, data-based solutions to many tasks.

However, these advances may also deepen the digital gap between advanced SBs and non-high-tech firms that cannot afford state-of-the-art technologies and solutions. Some SBs may buy and implement cutting-edge fintech, while others cannot because they lack the financial means; this leads to imparity. Lee and Yoon (2023) voiced this concern, stating that there is a prognosis of concentration of advantages only in those SBs that have strong digital skills while the rest will be left behind with fintech.

However, the sustainability aspect of fintech is still largely unknown. While digital tools lessen the utilization of physical resources, they are associated with data centers and digital systems that consume energy. To this end, Hernandez and Xu (2023) recommend future studies on how fintech affects the environment as more SBs employ them as sustainability tools.

The literature review also exposes certain areas that still need to be filled and certain areas for future research. First, the work calls for more categorical "crisis-mode engagement" with financial inclusion. Future research should look at whether fintech is really making finance more accessible for SBs in rural or underbanked areas in terms of digital literacy, technological adoption, and policies in their respective regions. Second, the literature would benefit from a comparative study of countries' regulations and their effects on fintech usage for SBs. Such studies may help policymakers understand how to frame a policy that supports fintech and protects SBs without tipping the balance too much in favor of, say, one player against the other.

3 CURRENT STATE OF FINTECH FOR SMALL BUSINESSES IN THE WORLD

3.1 Overview of Fintech Services for SBs

3.1.1 Mobile Payment Solutions

Mobile payments have become an innovative fintech that has proved helpful for small and medium-sized businesses (SBs) in improving their services for B2C transactions. Thus, these solutions embrace technologies such as near-Field Communication (NFC), Quick Response (QR) codes, and mobile wallets, which enable safe and smooth financial transactions through the use of smartphones and other forms of mobile devices (Oliveira et al., 2016).

The following advantages have propelled the use of mobile pay solutions among SBs. Firstly, combining these technologies dramatically reduces the value of the transaction costs. Guo (2013) and his team concluded that through mobile payments, the transaction costs could be reduced by as much as 70% from the previous card-based platforms, a move that would help SBs cut heavily on expenditure. Third, they improve interaction speed, as Dahlberg et al. (2015) posit that mobile transactions take only fifteen to twenty seconds to complete, improving operations efficiency for SBs.

Second, mobile payments present stronger security measures than regular payment methods. According to Zhang and Juhlin (2018), with tokenization techniques and app encryption, fraud, and data theft are minimized in mobile payments, an essential concern for SBs dealing with consumers' financial data. The study found that firms' use of secure mobile payments was associated with a 60% decrease in electronic fraud.

Several case studies illustrate the successful implementation of mobile payment solutions by SBs: SBs:

1. **Square and Small Retailers:** Basically, the utilization of Square's mobile POS system among the small-selling stores in the USA posed a significant rise of 10% in average sales and a customer base increment of about 15% within one year after implementing the system (MacKenzie et al., 2019).
2. **M-Pesa in Kenya:** Mobile Payments have disrupted SBs in Kenya, primarily through this system. Mbiti and Weil's (2015) examined the impact of M-Pesa on Kenyan SBs. They discovered that business users gained higher profits than non-users applying the current mobile payment solution since the latter can enhance transaction effectiveness and widen the consumer base by 20%.
3. **Alipay in China:** One of the most prominent examples is Alipay, which has extensively implemented QR code payment in SBs in China. A study by Liu et al. (2023) established that the small business entities that used Alipay had an average of 35% daily transactions and a reduction of 25% in the cost of handling cash.
4. **iZettle in Europe:** This European-dominant mobile payment solution highlighted that client firms registered a 30% increase in sales within the first six months of opting for it (GOV. UK, 2019).

3.1.2 Online Lending Platforms

Online lending has thus become a significant source and substitute for traditional banking options for small and medium-sized businesses (SBs) because it covers many problems linked to conventional lending. It uses artificial intelligence, big data miners, and other technological enhancements to handle loan applications, credit checks, and fund disbursement far more effectively than conventional banks (Jagtiani & Lemieux, 2018).

There appear to be a few distinct differences when comparing online lending platforms with more traditional credit access methods. Firstly, the online platform allows for faster loan applications. Moldow (2015) says that while traditional banks take several weeks and even months to process the loan application, online lenders can take as little as 24 hours. This speed is particularly important for SBs with urgent financial requirements or time-sensitive opportunities.

Secondly, it was established that online lenders use more relaxed and inclusive credit assessment procedures. For instance, where traditional banks rely on credit scores and collateral, online ones use more diverse parameters, such as cash flow, online positions, and even posts on social networks (Bazarbash, 2019). This should further enable a fair assessment of an SB's credit risks, thereby extending credit facilities to firms possibly ineligible for such from conventional lenders.

Another major factor is cost competitiveness. According to the same report conducted by Deloitte (2016), the cost of operation for online lenders was relatively lower by 50-70% than incumbent banks; this kind of savings can be offered to consumers in the form of better interest rates and or fees. However, it is crucial to recognize that the cost of borrowing can still be more expensive for some online loans regardless of the loan grade, which is even more costly for higher-risk borrowers (Claessens et al., 2018).

Several case studies illustrate the benefits of online lending for SBs: Several case studies illustrate the benefits of online lending for SBs:

1. **Kabbage and Small Retailers:** A report by Oxford Economics (2019) showed that small retailers who accessed credit facilities from Kabbage, an online credit facility, recorded an average sales increment of 22% in the half-year preceding the research compared to 1.5% for similar small retailers who had not transacted with Kabbage.
2. **Funding Circle in the UK:** A study by the Centre for Economics and Business Research showed that from 2010 to 2015, Funding Circle SB borrowers injected £2.7 billion into the UK economy and launched 40,000 new jobs (McCorquodale, 2016).
3. **OnDeck in Australia:** Deloitte (2017) conducted a notable case study concerning OnDeck's borrowers. 74% of SBs revealed enhanced revenues following loan approval, with an average 23% uplift.
4. **Lendio in the US:** Based on Lendio data, more than $1.9 billion worth of loans were delivered by Lendio to over 100,000 SBs in 2019, while borrowers reported that their average revenue growth with the funding was 17.6% within the first six months (Lendio, 2024).

Further, computer-generated credit checks are generally bureaucratic. Still, they often have issues with flexibility and objectivity that may pose problems due to the opaque nature of borrowers' evaluation process to be provided with lending terms (Lendio, 2024). To mitigate these risks, stricter regulatory measures are needed to encourage lending transparency among SBs and provide them with the right information on how to determine fair loan terms. This critical approach helps SBs reap the advantages of the OFS without engaging in dangerous financial behaviors.

3.1.3 Cloud-Based Accounting Software

The evolution of technology, especially in software, has led to a shift of clouds, enabling small and medium-sized businesses to enhance financial management. This technology has enhanced numerous financial management tasks, making them easier to accomplish economically, accurately, and in less time than traditional accounting systems (Al-Okaily et al., 2022).

The ways and significance of the simplification of financial management tasks through the use of cloud-based accounting software are nuanced. Firstly, these platforms automate their regular tasks manually, such as input and consolidation. For instance, a study by Khanom 2017 revealed that cloud accounting automation lowered the likelihood of errors by about 37% and time spent on accounts by 45%. This automation serves not only as efficiency in terms of accuracy but also as efficiency in terms of time allocation for SB owners/managers to proceed with essential business activities.

In addition, cloud-based accounting software offers real-time updates of a business's financial position, hence enhancing decision-making. According to Trabulsi (2018), 68% of SBs that claim to use cloud accounting solutions cited increased financial visibility, while 52% of the firms using the solutions acknowledged having a better way of predicting cash flow. Real-time financial data access benefits SBs in highly volatile environments or those with difficulties managing funds.

In addition, cloud-based accounting software increases the coordination within the team and with parties outside the firm, including accountants and financial consultants. In their study, Attaran and Woods (2019) examine how incorporating collaborative components in cloud-based accounting tools lowered communication intervals by one-third and achieved 28% greater financial reporting precision.

3.1.4 Crowdfunding Platforms

Thus, crowdfunding has emerged as a unique fintech solution, allowing SBs to address their financing needs through online platforms that are not tied to traditional financial intermediaries. These platforms allow SBs to request capital directly from a significant number of people, usually online, thus opening access to capital, which could reduce many of the funding woes experienced by small businesses (Kim & Hann, 2013).

The crowdfunding categories involve different models, including reward-based crowdfunding, equity-based crowdfunding, debt-based crowdfunding, and donation-based crowdfunding. Each model is suitable for SBs, as the following sections will elaborate. For example, reward-based crowdfunding enables businesses to create awareness of their products or services and publicly confirm prospective consumer interest in them while raising capital (Belleflamme et al., 2014).

Equity-based crowdfunding also allows SBs to sell shares to the public, expanding their access to capital beyond that offered by Angel investors and Venture capitalists (Ahlers et al., 2015).

Arguably, the most apparent advantage of crowdfunding for SBs is funding availability, including access to funds by businesses that may not qualify for bank financing or venture capital. Block et al. (2018) also concluded that SBs are not restricted by location issues in raising funds through crowdfunding and can rope investors worldwide. This increased coverage may benefit companies operating in less saturated areas or specific categories.

In addition, crowdfunding campaigns are helpful for SBs as they are also potent marketing instruments. Stanko and Henard (2017) showed that it is possible to achieve valuable public attention by establishing a loyal consumer base and early adopters' circle for a successfully crowdfunded product or service. They mentioned in their studies that firms raising funds for their projects online benefited from the activity by observing an average of 34% increase in website traffic and a 24% increase in social media followers within the crowdfunded project period.

Several success stories and statistical data illustrate the impact of crowdfunding on SBs:

1. **Pebble Technology:** This SB secured more than $10 million on Kickstarter for the smartwatch in 2012 to prove that a reward-based crowdfunding model could help launch the new product. This campaign got 68,929 backers, who invested their money and became the market for the product (Ingraham, 2012).
2. **BrewDog:** This Scottish brewery is one of the success stories of equity crowdfunding, having raised over £73 million through its "Equity for Punks" campaigns. This approach brought cash into the company and contributed to building up a massive customer base of more than 145,000 shareholders (BrewDog, 2020).
3. **Monzo Bank:** This UK-based digital bank sold £1 million worth of its shares through equity crowdfunding in 96 seconds in 2016, thus revealing the speed at which capital can be raised through these avenues (Crowdcube, 2016).
4. **Global Crowdfunding Market:** In 2018, the global crowdfunding market was estimated to be worth $84 billion and is expected to increase to $114 billion in 2021 (Statista, 2019).

Currently, crowdfunding platforms exist within various legal environments globally, which greatly influences the utilization and efficiency of the concept for SBs. Legal requirements for those investing in peer-to-peer markets vary across many areas, with several containing provisions to safeguard the investors, which dictate various conditions that a platform must meet, including openness, disclosure and reporting together with other requirements on compliance (Burtch et al., 2012). For instance, in the United States, regulation on equity crowdfunding works under the Securities Act and the JOBS Act, which presents certain constraints on the amount of money which can be crowdfunded from non-accredited investors. In the European

Union, the European Crowdfunding Service Providers Regulation (ECSPR) makes the rules on crowdfunding consistent across the member states, aiming to open up funding across borders and, simultaneously, protect investors (Crowdcube, 2016).

However, where the institutionalization level is low, which is typical for emerging markets, the regulatory regime of such platforms remains the same, and the absence of standardized regulations can cause doubts and uncertainty that, in turn, affect both platform expansion and SBs' access to funds. Such regulatory discrepancies force platforms to operate differently across different regions while adhering to regulatory frameworks that still offer customers easy-to-use, novel financing solutions. Solving all these remains critical in advancing crowdfunding as a way of supporting SBs around the world.

Table 1. Fintech services and their impact on SBs

Fintech Service	Key Features	Benefits for SBs	Case Studies/Examples
Mobile Payment Solutions	NFC, QR codes, mobile wallets	Lower transaction costs, faster processing, improved security, customer insights	Square (USA): 10% sales increase; M-Pesa (Kenya): 20% wider consumer base
Online Lending Platforms	AI-based credit checks, fast processing	Quick access to funds, relaxed credit assessment, lower operational costs	Kabbage (USA): 22% sales growth; Funding Circle (UK): 40,000 jobs created
Cloud-Based Accounting Software	Automation, real-time financial updates, CRM integration	Reduced errors, time savings, better cash flow management	Khanom (2017): 45% time saved; Trabulsi (2018): 68% report better financial visibility
Crowdfunding Platforms	Reward-based, equity-based, debt-based models	Access to capital, marketing, customer feedback	Pebble Technology: $10M raised; BrewDog: £73M raised; Monzo: £1M in 96 seconds

3.2 Impact of Fintech on SB Financial Management

3.2.1 Efficiency and Cost Reduction

The embracement of Fintech innovations in SBs has seen them increase efficiency and reduce costs, mostly due to real-time financial information and automation of some financial activities. These improvements have changed how SBs manage their financial setup and make sound decisions for the business and operations.

Ongoing analysis, primarily driven by Fintech, has shifted the approach to how SBs track and analyze their business performance regarding financial aspects. A study published by Hasan et al. (2023) showed that 78% of SBs claimed that utilizing fintech solutions transformed their financial outlook. Meanwhile, 63% of the polled organizations said it helped them make better data-driven decisions. The live stream information helps SBs to act promptly and thus recognize potential problems with cash flows more easily, besides noticing new opportunities and threats in the financial markets at an early stage.

Studies state that fintech's efficiency and cost savings to SBs are credible and empirically grounded. In their systematic literature review, Sachin Kumar Sharma et al. (2023) examined the influence of fintech adoption for SBs operating in emerging regions. According to the estimates, the authors stated that companies with SBs implementing fintech solutions to manage finances received a 25% improvement in average operating costs attached to financial processes. There was a marked increase in financial reporting efficiency by 35%. Thus, there were fewer errors and less time spent on adjustments and reconciliations (IAS Plus, 2023). It is crucial to understand that such statistics demonstrate the types of organizations that fintech can help evolve SBs and improve their financial practices.

3.2.2 Access to Capital

In the context of the modern and fast-growing financial industry, the emergence of fintech has influenced the availability of capital for SBs and presented new forms of lending and credit rating. Such changes have effectively dealt with many challenges characteristic of most conventional banking systems, providing SBs with better and more efficient funding solutions.

The involvement of fintech has marked new-age lending plans that are acceptable substitutes for traditional bank credit. Some of these models are peer-to-peer or P2P lending, crowdfunding, invoice financing, and revenue-based financing. A study by Ziegler et al. (2021) reported that the volumes of alternative finance for SBs increased to $113 billion globally, a 23% growth in 2020 despite the impacts of COVID-19. It is further evidence of the advancement and need for these non-standard practices to be embraced in society.

Fintech credit products such as P2P lending platforms have gained much popularity recently. According to Cumming and Hornuf (2018), P2P business lending has increased significantly in the UK from £749 million in 2016 to £2.1 billion in 2017, a year-on-year percentage increase of 181%. P2P lending advantages for SBs are a short time to approve the loans, flexible conditions, and, in many cases, lower interest rates than bank loan conditions. The study by the Cambridge Centre for Alternative Finance (2020) shows that 74% of the SBs approached P2P lending platforms they refused by traditional banks, indicating the function of such platforms in filling the credit gap.

Jagtiani and Lemieux (2018) examined the reliability of different credit scoring methods employed by LendingClub, a fintech lender. They further realized that such a system meant that the platform could offer credit to borrowers that would otherwise be considered subprime by other conventional scoring models, opening up credit. Notably, the study showed that loans to such borrowers performed as well as loans to borrowers with stronger conventional credit ratings, indicating the effectiveness of all the above methods.

Further support for the efficiency of alternative credit scoring is provided in a study by Sachin Kumar Sharma et al. (2023), indicating that fintech lenders applying alternative data could provide more credit approval to SBs than traditional lenders but without high defaults. Specifically, the approval rate rose most significantly among new businesses and those in geographically unserved and underserved areas, pointing to the possibility of the methods for expanding access to finance.

3.2.3 Enhanced Financial Decision-Making

Integrating data analytics and artificial intelligence (AI) has significantly enhanced the effectiveness of financial technologies in SB financing decisions. These technologies have paved the way for SBs to properly use big data, machine learning, and even predictive analytics to help make better and timelier financial decisions.

Data analytics in the fintech application helps SBs quickly and accurately analyze the large volume of financial and operational data. The study by Ghasemaghaei and Calic (2020) established that data analytics positively impacted SBs and firms that embraced the financial approach to experience an improvement of 21% in profitability compared to those that had not adopted data analytics. Such optimization is attributed to enhanced management of cash flows, increased efficiency in making sales forecasts, and efficiency in setting the right prices.

Therefore, artificial intelligence, especially machine learning algorithms, has added complexity to the various analytical instruments available to SBs in the financial environment. According to Laghari and Ahmed (2023), some of the tools designed under the application of AI in the fintech space to estimate the various parameters of balance sheets, even the flow of cash, with a success rate of around 95%, and in this way helps the business to avoid the liquidity problems as and when it is expected to emerge. Such predictiveness was possible only for the big corporations that could invest mainly in their financial reports analysis.

While traditional applications of AI in the financial context involved using machine learning techniques for prediction, the applicability now goes for recommendation. A Deloitte (2023) study on AI usage in finances showed that 68% of SBs using fintech tools with AI apologized for improved decision-making and financial management insights. They spanned various aspects, including how to best time inventory replenishment and which customer segments were most profitable.

Furthermore, integrating data analysis and Artificial intelligence has made significant breakthroughs in risk evaluation and mitigation for SBs. According to Bazarbash (2019), credit risk stemming from using machine learning algorithms to make credit risk evaluation decreased the default probability by 17% more than conventional score approaches. Such an enhancement of risk management is also in the lenders' interest and helps SBs achieve better lending rates. Nevertheless, it is essential to emphasize that the realization of those technologies, in most cases, depends not only on the availability of proper technologies but also on the organization's data culture and the staff's adequate competencies (Mikalef et al., 2020).

Data analytics and AI are playing a more significant part in the financial decision-making of SBs than ever before. SBs have offered comprehensive and precise predictions, risk management, and enhancement in the specific areas of their financial processes with the help of fintech tools based on these technologies. Given that these technologies are still developing and their prices are gradually decreasing, there will be a possibility of equalizing the abilities of SBs and big corporations regarding financial decision-making. However, achieving these benefits requires constant investment in technologies, data quality, and human capital within SBs.

Table 2. Fintech's impact on SB financial management

Section	Focus	Key Insights	Examples
2.2.1 Efficiency and Cost Reduction	Cost & Time Savings	Real-time data and automation improve efficiency and cut costs for SBs.	40% time savings in finance tasks (Deloitte, 2022).
	Value Chain Savings	Enhanced targeting reduces customer acquisition costs.	15% lower acquisition cost (World Bank, 2020).
2.2.2 Access to Capital	Alternative Lending Models	P2P, crowdfunding, and invoice financing expand funding options for SBs.	181% growth in P2P lending (Cumming & Hornuf, 2018).
	Improved Credit Access	Fintech credit scoring includes alternative data for broader access.	LendingClub low-default loans for subprime (Jagtiani & Lemieux, 2018).
2.2.3 Enhanced Decision-Making	Predictive Analytics	AI-driven analytics aid in forecasting, pricing, and risk management.	21% profitability boost (Ghasemaghaei & Calic, 2020).
	Competency Requirement	Effective AI use requires digital skills and data culture within SBs.	

3.3 Challenges in Fintech Adoption by SBs

3.3.1 Data Protection and Fraud Prevention

Integrating fintech solutions in small and medium-sized business (SB) operations has opened new frontiers in managing finances and presented new cybersecurity risks and fraud. Thus, as financial operations are shifted online through digital platforms, SBs are exposed to various forms of cyber threats and frauds concerning financial operations and, therefore, require the right strategies and technologies to counter them. The threats linked with implementing fintech solutions in the context of SBs are complex and dynamic today.

Romānova et al.'s (2016) elaborate systematic literature review proposed specific generic threats: cyber threats, data privacy threats, and identity threats. The study also revealed that 67% of SBs had a cyberattack at one time or another in the year 2017, and the amount of money lost, on average, per incident was $2.2 million. Further, the nature of the threat is also growing much more complex and varied, and according to Verizon's Data Breach Investigations Report 2020, around 43% of cyber incidents are mainly aimed at small business entities (Verizon, 2020).

It is important to note that cyber threats pose a real threat to SBs, and one of the greatest risks is data breaches. In a report by IBM, the estimated cost of a data breach for small businesses by 2024 was approximately $5.17 million, an increment of ten percent from the previous year (IBM, 2023). These costs are quite unbearable for SBs, especially when they lack adequate capital to fund the necessary, possibly resulting in business failure. Another critical threat is fraud, especially concerning electronic payment systems and e-commerce. According to a study by Javelin Strategy & Research (2020), SBs are victims of payment fraud at a higher rate than big organizations. The study also pinpointed that the mean fraud expense ratio for SBs was $12,000 per instance, which can be huge for small business (Fingerprint, 2022).

To reduce these threats, SBs have begun implementing various measures and tools. One such strategy is to establish sound security standards for technologies, particularly information processing. A study conducted by the National Cyber Security Alliance (2022) showed that of the SBs, 60% who invested in the best security measures were able to reduce cases of security breaches by more than half.

Information security is highly associated with encryption technology since it helps manage data security. Thales's Global Small and Medium Business Trends Report (2021) revealed that only 17% of SBs now use encryption to protect sensitive data. Only 34% of organizations keep total control of keys. The study also revealed a 63% reduction in data breach cases among organizations using encryption compared to those that did not (Vorecol, 2019).

Multiple-factor authentication (MFA) has become a popular technique for preventing such incidents. Research conducted by Meyer et al. (2019) discovered that MFA can effectively prevent 99.9% of digital interference initiated by bots. However, according to a Cyber Readiness Institute (2024) survey, MFA is not widely used by SBs, with a penetration of only 34%.

Blockchain technology is also gradually being integrated into fintech solutions to help improve the security of their applications. A report by MarketsandMarkets (2023) predicted that the blockchain market, especially in fintech, would rise from USD 370 million in 2018 to USD 6,228.2 million in 2023 due to enhanced security services and fraud minimisation.

Regulatory compliance is another central element of data protection. Some of the regulations that have affected data handling through SBs include the GDPR in Europe, which has highly impacted data handling. Dell Technologies (2019) analyzed the SBs' response to GDPR and discovered that 70% saw compliance with GDPR as a chance for enhanced data protection and customer trust.

3.3.2 Digital Literacy

A key driver linked to using fintech solutions among SBs is the level of embracing digital skills. The digital literacy level of SB owners, managers, and employees plays a critical role in defining the pace of the fintech solution uptake and its effectiveness, which directly determines business competitiveness and growth prospects in a rapidly integrating digital economy environment.

Digital literacy's influence on Fintech is extremely pervasive and complex. Ozili (2020) noted a significantly positive correlation between an SB's digital literacy and fintech adoption levels. Further, the analysis revealed that companies with elevated digital competence scores had a 25 times greater likelihood of implementing more sophisticated fintech offerings than their counterparts with low competence scores. Such differences in adoption levels can result in increased disparity amongst SBs and, thus, a worse situation for firms that may already be disadvantaged when competing in the market.

Given that digital skills are strongly associated with the interaction between SBs and customers, numerous programs have been launched, and training courses have been implemented to enhance digital literacy. The European Commission is implementing the Digital Skills and Jobs Coalition initiated in 2016. By 2020, the initiative had successfully empowered over 20 million people in the EU with the requisite digital skills, especially in SBs (European Commission, 2021).

Programs like Mastercard Center for Inclusive Growth's Micro & Small Business Digital Acceleration Program have been established in developing nations like those discussed in this paper. The program, begun in 2020, has been instrumental in offering digital skills training to more than 100 million people in Africa and Asia. A survey among the participants showed they started adopting digital financial services more after training (Mastercard, 2024).

The level of digital competence can significantly affect the implementation of Fintech solutions in SBs' contexts, and the lack of digital skills can limit their online usage. In response to this problem, several successful solutions have been implemented internationally to increase user proficiency in using computers, the Internet, and social networks among owners and employees of small businesses. For instance, Grow with Google provides SB-focused tuition programs free of charge, where they master the fundamental Google tools such as online advertising, statistics and analytics, and security protection.

Currently, the European Digital Skills and Jobs Coalition initiated by the European Commission can train millions of users in basic digital knowledge, primarily focusing on SB fields. Mastercard's Micro & Small Business Digital Acceleration Program delivers training to support SBs in exploring digital financial techniques and solutions to close the digital gaps and enhance Fintech adoption in the probing contexts of emerging markets. These have demonstrated positive impacts, which has positively enhanced the preparedness and adaptability of SBs to Fintech solutions.

These training programs can be regarded as effective due to the results obtained from organizational development. Lyons et al. (2019) conducted a Longitudinal study involving SBs, in which it was established that the SBs whose owners underwent basic structured digital literacy programs had an increased tendency to use fintech solutions one year after completing the training compared to a normal group. However, some issues still hinder the expansion of such solutions to other SBs that require them.

Table 3. Key initiatives enhancing digital literacy for SBs

Program	Region	Start Year	Target Group	Focus Areas	Impact
Digital Skills and Jobs Coalition (EU)	European Union	2016	20 million people, especially SBs	Basic digital skills training for SBs	Enhanced digital skills across the EU, facilitating Fintech adoption
Grow with Google	Global	2017	10 million individuals, many of whom are SBs	Digital skills training including online advertising, analytics, security	Increased digital literacy and SB readiness for Fintech solutions
Mastercard's Micro & Small Business Digital Acceleration Program	Africa and Asia	2020	100 million people, focusing on SBs	Digital financial skills for SBs in emerging markets	Improved Fintech adoption and digital readiness in developing regions

4 METHODOLOGY

Using a systematic review of the literature and content analysis of Fintech data, this chapter reviews the relevance of Fintech in SBs. The methodology is structured as follows:

Literature Review: In an attempt to provide a theoretical framework on Fintech innovations concerning the problems affecting SBs financially, the chapter starts with a literature review. Journals, research papers, and case work papers are collected from databases like JSTOR, ScienceDirect, and Google Scholar. Topics discussed in the literature review relate to services offered by Fintech to SBs, operation effects and limitations. Quantitative research, including that of Dorfleitner et al. (2017) that shows that Fintech decreases SB operational costs by 25%, is analyzed to evaluate the cost savings.

2. Qualitative Data Analysis: Based on this understanding, the chapter further examines qualitative data derived from previous research on Fintech and SBs alongside survey data and semi-structured interviews. This research is based on the screening by Romānova and Kudinska (2016) which describes the challenges likely to be faced when implementing Fintech in SBs including data security concerns, IT literacy and legal factors. Secondary data will provide a theoretical background, and qualitative data will provide a practical standpoint, with all potential benefits and drawbacks of Fintech adoption based on the data collected.

3. Case Study Analysis: In addition to discussing the practical uses and impact of Fintech on SBs as the chapter's topic, the author has included several examples of case studies from different geographical areas. For instance, an analysis of mobile payment solutions like that in the USA, and M-Pesa in Kenya is used to assess how Fintech meets varied market demands. These examples reveal how the availability of infrastructures, legislation, and consumers' behavior and adoption impact the Fintech solutions.

4. Policy Analysis: In the last section, the chapter recalls the policy recommendation and recommendation of best practice drawn from the analysis of the Fintech success cases highlighted in Zalan and Toufaily (2017). This report evaluates the possibility of advocacy for adopting Fintech among SBs about polices that facilitate digital comprehension, bolster cybersecurity, and provide a permissive regulatory climate for innovation. Comparative analyses of Fintech policies in leading countries add to the policy analysis by offering a view of strategies that might work in successful policies to help SBs in different nations.

By doing this, this chapter seeks to present a comprehensive and critically reflexive picture on how Fintech contributes or does not contribute to the overall survival and profitable operation of SBs' financial management landscapes. The integration of both the literature, analysis of qualitative data, and policy study contributes to providing rich insights to the researchers or academics, policymakers, and practitioners in the field.

5 SUCCESS FACTOR AND CHALLENGES

Table 4. Success factors and challenges in fintech adoption

Category	Key Points
Success Factors	**Cost Efficiency & Time Savings**: Reduced costs and time through automation and real-time data
	Enhanced Decision-Making: Data analytics for better financial planning and forecasting
	Access to Capital: Online lending and crowdfunding provide flexible funding options
	Customer Engagement: Mobile payments and analytics offer insights into customer behavior
Challenges	**Data Privacy & Security**: Risk of data breaches and cyber threats
	Regulatory Barriers: Complex compliance requirements like GDPR
	Digital Literacy Gaps: Limited tech skills hinder effective Fintech use
	Algorithmic Bias: Risk of inequality in access due to biased credit scoring
	Tech Adaptability: Rapid changes require ongoing investment and skills

6 RECOMMENDATIONS AND CONCLUSION:

Considering the dynamic trend of fintech for SBs, constantly researching and developing the technology is crucial. According to Johnson et al. (2024), "The structure of the fintech sector is becoming more complex at a very fast pace, which makes it necessary to continue doing further research to understand the impact of fintech on SB finance and to help in policy formulation" (p. 412). Quantitative data would be important in providing insights into the impact fintech adoption has on the performance and growth of small and medium businesses, especially if longitudinal designs are used. The multi-wave panel study design proposed by Zhang et al. (2023) provides an effective solution for capturing screen time's effects on memory and learning in a longitudinal format. It should be adopted by researchers in the future.

As a result of this research, there are several recommendations to key stakeholders regarding enhancing the adoption of fintech among SBs. Governments and administrative bodies must focus on the sophistication of technology-neutral rules and regulations and allow innovation to proceed without hampering consumer protection. Lenders and the fintech market should increase cooperation to work on creating products focused on SBs' necessities. SB owners and managers consequently have to become financially literate and engage in the possibilities of fintech tools that could improve the business's operations. The effects of fintech adoption on SB performance still need to be thoroughly explored, thus calling for more longitudinal research that employs quantitative and qualitative methods that focus on capturing both performance indicators and user experience. It implies that investors and venture capitalists should think about the opportunities provided by fintech solutions for SBs with specific reference to emerging markets.

SBs are strategic for economies because they are the engine of economic progress, and policymakers are responsible for ensuring they work seamlessly with Fintech solution providers.

In matching regulators and policymakers' calls to action, they ought to contribute to flexible but not less rigorous regulation of Fintechs that, on the one hand, fosters innovation and, on the other hand, protects SBs and consumers. This could include the framework that addresses data protection and cybersecurity. If these financial sector components adhere to specific norms of the ethical utilization of artificially intelligent technologies, Fintech products will function safely and comprehensibly. Further, socio-technical infrastructure facilitation, including extending broadband access and widely accepted digital finance instruments, is necessary, especially in rural or remote markets. Policymakers can also facilitate collaborations between government and quasi-government organizations, banks, financial institutions, and fintechs to offer tailored digital skills training programmes to SBs to improve the sector's digital proposition. They can support SBs in unlocking Fintech to create equitable and financially stronger economies and business realms.

Therefore, the field formed by the interconnection of fintech and SBs should be deemed an active and prospective sphere of the economy and financial development. Thus, combining the resolution of current problems and the identification of promising directions for further development, it is possible to build a financial environment where SBs can effectively operate within the conditions of an accelerating digital transformation. SB finance's future cannot be detached from the continuous advancement of fintech, and further studies, advancements, and cooperation will be crucial to utilizing platforms to the extent possible.

REFERENCES

Ahlers, G., Cumming, D. J., Guenther, C., & Schweizer, D. (2015, February 12). *Signaling in Equity Crowdfunding*. Social Science Research Network. https://papers.ssrn.com/sol3/papers.cfm?abstract_id=2564121

Al-Okaily, M., Alkhwaldi, A. F., Abdulmuhsin, A. A., Alqudah, H., & Al-Okaily, A. (2022). Cloud-based accounting information systems usage and its impact on Jordanian SMEs' performance: The post-COVID-19 perspective. *Journal of Financial Reporting and Accounting*, 21(1), 126–155. Advance online publication. DOI: 10.1108/JFRA-12-2021-0476

Alam, S., Hussain, T., & Rahman, M. (2022). Fintech and SME financing: Opportunities and challenges. *Journal of Financial Innovation*, 12(3), 143–157.

Alliance, N. C. (2022, May 8). *National Cyber Security Alliance Statement Regarding Incorrect Small Business Statistic*. National Cybersecurity Alliance. https://staysafeonline.org/news-press/national-cyber-security-alliance-statement-regarding-incorrect-small-business-statistic/

Anagnostopoulos, I. (2018). Fintech and regtech: Impact on regulators and banks. *Journal of Economics and Business*, 100(1), 7–25. https://www.sciencedirect.com/science/article/abs/pii/S014861951730142X. DOI: 10.1016/j.jeconbus.2018.07.003

Arner, D. W., Barberis, J. N., & Buckley, R. P. (2015, October 1). *The Evolution of Fintech: A New Post-Crisis Paradigm?* Papers.*ssrn*.com. https://papers.ssrn.com/sol3/papers.cfm?abstract_id=2676553 DOI: 10.2139/ssrn.2676553

Attaran, M., & Woods, J. (2019). Cloud computing technology: improving small business performance using the Internet. *Journal of Small Business & Entrepreneurship, 31*(6), 495–519. Tandfonline. DOI: 10.1080/08276331.2018.1466850

Battisto, J., Lieberman, S., Mills, C. K., Wiersch, A. M., & de Zeeuw, M. (2019). 2019 Report on Employer Firms. *Small Business Credit Survey*, 20190416. Advance online publication. DOI: 10.55350/sbcs

Bazarbash, M. (2019, May 17). *FinTech in Financial Inclusion: Machine Learning Applications in Assessing Credit Risk*. IMF. https://www.imf.org/en/Publications/WP/Issues/2019/05/17/FinTech-in-Financial-Inclusion-Machine-Learning-Applications-in-Assessing-Credit-Risk-46883

Bazarbash, M., Malatesta, L., & Parisi, F. (2020). The future of SME lending in a fintech world. *International Monetary Fund Working Paper, 21*(2), 89-106.

Beck, T., & Demirguc-Kunt, A. (2006). Small and medium-size ises: Access to finance as a growth constraint. *Journal of Banking & Finance*, 30(11), 2931–2943. DOI: 10.1016/j.jbankfin.2006.05.009

Belleflamme, P., Lambert, T., & Schwienbacher, A. (2014). Crowdfunding: Tapping the Right Crowd. *Journal of Business Venturing*, 29(5), 585–609. DOI: 10.1016/j.jbusvent.2013.07.003

Berger, A. N., & Udell, G. F. (2006). A more complete conceptual framework for SME finance. *Journal of Banking & Finance*, 30(11), 2945–2966. DOI: 10.1016/j.jbankfin.2006.05.008

Block, J. H., Colombo, M. G., Cumming, D. J., & Vismara, S. (2018). New players in entrepreneurial finance and why they are there. *Small Business Economics, 50*(2), 239–250. springer. DOI: 10.1007/s11187-016-9826-6

BrewDog. (2020). *Equity for Punks - Benefits T&Cs | BrewDog*. Www.brewdog.com. https://www.brewdog.com/uk/equityforpunks/benefits

Burtch, G., Ghose, A., & Wattal, S. (2012). An Empirical Examination of the Antecedents and Consequences of Investment Patterns in Crowd-Funded Markets. SSRN *Electronic Journal*. DOI: 10.2139/ssrn.1928168

Cambridge Centre for Alternative Finance. (2020). *In partnership with: With support of: Global Alternative Finance Market Benchmarking The Report Trends, Opportunities and Challenges for Lending, Equity, and Non-Investment Alternative Finance Models*. https://www.jbs.cam.ac.uk/wp-content/uploads/2020/08/2020-04-22-ccaf-global-alternative-finance-market-benchmarking-report.pdf

Capital, L. (2024, May 13). *How Revenue-Based Financing and Venture Capital Work Together*. Lighter Capital; Lighter Capital. https://www.lightercapital.com/blog/how-revenue-based-financing-venture-capital-funding-work-together

Chen, H., Liu, X., & Shen, Y. (2022). Fintech and financial inclusion: Evidence from mobile banking adoption. *Economic Journal of Developing Economies*, 17(1), 45–65.

Claessens, S., Frost, J., Turner, G., & Zhu, F. (2018). Fintech credit markets around the world: size, drivers and policy issues. Www.bis.org. https://www.bis.org/publ/qtrpdf/r_qt1809e.htm

Crowdcube. (2019, July 4). *Crowdcube success story | Monzo*. Crowdcube | Funding the Wonderful. https://www.crowdcube.com/explore/raising/success-stories/monzo

Cumming, D., & Hornuf, L. (2018). *The Economics of Crowdfunding*. Springer International Publishing., DOI: 10.1007/978-3-319-66119-3

Cyber Readiness Institute. (2023). *You are being redirected...* Www.juniperresearch.com. https://www.juniperresearch.com/press/ai-enabled-financial-fraud-detection-spend/

Cyber Readiness Institute. (2024, January 8). *Cyber Readiness Institute*. Cyber Readiness Institute. https://cyberreadinessinstitute.org/news-and-events/cyber-readiness-institute-survey-highlights-critical-gaps-in-mfa-implementation-among-u-s-SBs/

Dahlberg, T., Guo, J., & Ondrus, J. (2015). A critical review of mobile payment research. *Electronic Commerce Research and Applications*, 14(5), 265–284. DOI: 10.1016/j.elerap.2015.07.006

Dell Inc. (2019). *Thought Leadership Perspectives*. https://www.dell.com/en-us/perspectives/a-positive-look-at-gdpr-a-year-in/

Deloitte. (2016). *Marketplace lending A temporary phenomenon?*https://www2.deloitte.com/content/dam/Deloitte/de/Documents/financial-services/deloitte-uk-fs-marketplace-lending.pdf

Deloitte. (2022). *2021 banking and capital markets outlook Strengthening resilience, accelerating transformation A Deloitte Center of Financial Services report*. https://www2.deloitte.com/content/dam/Deloitte/tw/Documents/financial-services/pr210330-2021-banking-and-capital-markets-outlook-strengthening-resilience-accelerating-transformation.pdf

Deloitte. (2023). *How Artificial Intelligence Is Transforming the Financial Services Industry*. Www.deloitte.com. https://www.deloitte.com/ng/en/services/risk-advisory/services/how-artificial-intelligence-is-transforming-the-financial-services-industry.html

Dorfleitner, G., & Hornuf, L. Schmitt, M., & Weber, M. (2017). FinTech in Germany. In *Springer eBooks*. Springer Nature. DOI: 10.1007/978-3-319-54666-7

Economics, O. (2019, April 29). *The Big Business of Small Business*. Oxford Economics. https://www.oxfordeconomics.com/resource/the-big-business-of-small-business/

European Commission. (2021). *Digital skills initiatives | Shaping Europe's digital future*. Digital-Strategy.ec.europa.eu. https://digital-strategy.ec.europa.eu/en/policies/digital-skills-initiatives

European Commission. (2022). *EDIHs | Shaping Europe's digital future*. Digital-Strategy.ec.europa.eu. https://digital-strategy.ec.europa.eu/en/activities/edihs

Executive Agency for Small and Medium-sized Enterprises. (2016). *FINANCE - Understanding... Crowdfunding*. Europa.eu. https://ec.europa.eu/newsroom/fisma/redirection/item/31532

Fed Small Business. (2021). *Small Business Credit Survey*. Www.fedsmallbusiness.org. https://www.fedsmallbusiness.org/reports/survey

Fingerprint. (2022). *The Definitive Guide to the Real Cost of Online Fraud*. Fingerprint. https://fingerprint.com/blog/definitive-guide-real-cost-online-fraud/

Frost, J., Gambacorta, L., Huang, Y., Shin, H., & Zbinden, P. (2019). *BigTech and the changing structure of financial intermediation*. https://www.bis.org/publ/work779.pdf

Fuster, A., Plosser, M., Schnabl, P., & Vickery, J. (2019). The Role of Technology in Mortgage Lending. *Review of Financial Studies*, 32(5), 1854–1899. DOI: 10.1093/rfs/hhz018

Ghasemaghaei, M., & Calic, G. (2020). Assessing the impact of big data on firm innovation performance: Big data is not always better data. *Journal of Business Research*, 108, 147–162. DOI: 10.1016/j.jbusres.2019.09.062

Gomber, P., Koch, J.-A., & Siering, M. (2017). *Digital Finance and Fintech: Current Research and Future Research Directions*. *Ssrn*.com. https://papers.ssrn.com/sol3/papers.cfm?abstract_id=2928833 DOI: 10.1007/s11573-017-0852-x

Google. (2019, May 9). *Grow with Google: ten million people trained, here's what's next*. Google. https://blog.google/around-the-globe/google-europe/grow-google-ten-million-people-trained-heres-whats-next/

GOV.UK. (2019). *Completed acquisition by PayPal Holdings, Inc. of iZettle AB Final report*. https://assets.publishing.service.gov.uk/media/5cffa74440f0b609601d0ffc/PP_iZ_final_report.pdf

Guo, J. (2013, February 2). *Analyzing the business model for mobile payment from banks' perspective: An empirical study*. 24th European Regional ITS Conference, Florence 2013; International Telecommunications Society (ITS). https://ideas.repec.org/p/zbw/itse13/88483.html

Guo, Y., & Liang, C. (2016). Blockchain Application and Outlook in the Banking Industry. *Financial Innovation*, 2(1), 24. Advance online publication. DOI: 10.1186/s40854-016-0034-9

Haddad, C., & Hornuf, L. (2019). The emergence of the global fintech market: Economic and technological determinants. *Small Business Economics*, 53(1), 81–105. DOI: 10.1007/s11187-018-9991-x

Hasan, M., Hoque, A., & Le, T. (2023). Big Data-Driven Banking Operations: Opportunities, Challenges, and Data Security Perspectives. *FinTech, 2*(3), 484–509. MDPI. DOI: 10.3390/fintech2030028

Hernandez, A., & Xu, W. (2023). Cybersecurity challenges in fintech for small businesses. *Cybersecurity Review*, 19(4), 212–230.

Hu, J., Shi, Y., & Xu, L. (2022). Fintech response to COVID-19: Implications for small business financing. *Journal of Pandemic Economics*, 14(3), 101–115.

IBM. (2023). *Cost of a Data Breach 2023*. IBM. https://www.ibm.com/reports/data-breach

Iman, N. (2018). Is mobile payment still relevant in the fintech era? *Electronic Commerce Research and Applications*, 30, 72–82. DOI: 10.1016/j.elerap.2018.05.009

Ingraham, N. (2012, May 10). *The Pebble smartwatch: a record-breaking Kickstarter success story*. The Verge. https://www.theverge.com/2012/5/10/3011651/pebble-smartwatch-kickstarter-project

International Finance Corporation. (2017). *ASSESSMENT OF THE SHORTFALLS AND OPPORTUNITIES IN FINANCING MICRO, SMALL AND MEDIUM ENTERPRISES IN EMERGING MARKETS MSME FINANCE GAP Public Disclosure Authorized Public Disclosure Authorized Public Disclosure Authorized Public Disclosure Authorized*. https://documents1.worldbank.org/curated/en/653831510568517947/pdf/121264-WP-PUBLIC-MSMEReportFINAL.pdf

Intuit. (2021). *Small business e-commerce survey: Moving online in 2021 | QuickBooks*. Quickbooks.intuit.com. https://quickbooks.intuit.com/r/inspiration/small-business-ecommerce-survey/

Jagtiani, J., & Lemieux, C. (2018). Do fintech lenders penetrate areas that are underserved by traditional banks? *Journal of Economics and Business*, 100, 43–54. DOI: 10.1016/j.jeconbus.2018.03.001

Javelin Strategy & Research. (2020). *2020 Identity Fraud Study: Genesis of the Identity Fraud Crisis*. Javelin. https://javelinstrategy.com/research/2020-identity-fraud-study-genesis-identity-fraud-crisis

Jordan, M. (2018). *European Economic and Social Committee*. https://www.eesc.europa.eu/sites/default/files/files/qe-01-18-515-en-n.pdf

Karim, M., Qureshi, I., & Haider, S. (2021). Financial inclusion through fintech in emerging markets. *Journal of Finance and Development*, 15(2), 58–74.

Kergroach, S. (2021). SMEs Going Digital: Policy challenges and recommendations. Www.oecd-Ilibrary.org. DOI: 10.1787/ec5958b3-en

Khanom, T. (2017). Cloud Accounting: A Theoretical Overview. *IOSR Journal of Business and Management*, 19(06), 31–38. DOI: 10.9790/487X-1906053138

Kim, K., & Hann, I.-H. (2013). Does Crowdfunding Democratize Access to Capital? A Geographical Analysis. SSRN *Electronic Journal*. DOI: 10.2139/ssrn.2334590

Kim, S., Lee, M., & Park, J. (2021). The digital divide in fintech: Urban and rural disparities. *Technology in Finance Journal*, 10(2), 98–110.

KPMG. (2019). *Courage to change*. https://assets.kpmg.com/content/dam/kpmg/dk/pdf/dk-2020/01/KPMG_2019_annual_report_web.pdf

KPMG. (2020, February 3). *Pulse of Fintech archive*. KPMG; KPMG. https://kpmg.com/xx/en/home/insights/2020/02/pulse-of-fintech-archive.html

Laghari, F., & Ahmed, F. (2023). Cash flow management and its effect on firm performance: Empirical evidence on non-financial firms of China. *PLoS ONE, 18*(6). ncbi. DOI: 10.1371/journal.pone.0287135

Lee, I., & Shin, Y. J. (2018). Fintech: Ecosystem, business models, investment decisions, and challenges. *Business Horizons*, 61(1), 35–46. DOI: 10.1016/j.bushor.2017.09.003

Lee, J., & Yoon, K. (2023). The role of fintech in SME growth: A review of digital solutions. *Financial Management Quarterly*, 32(1), 50–65.

Lendio. (2024). *Lendio Surpasses $1.5 Billion in Small Business Loans Facilitated*. SME Finance Forum. https://smefinanceforum.org/post/lendio-surpasses-15-billion-in-small-business-loans-facilitated?page=120

Liu, J., Li, Z., & Hu, X. (2023). A Study of the Impact of Mobile Payment on the Enhancement of Consumption Structure and Pattern of Chinese Rural Households. *Agriculture*, 13(11), 2082. DOI: 10.3390/agriculture13112082

Lukkarinen, A., Teich, J. E., Wallenius, H., & Wallenius, J. (2016). Success drivers of online equity crowdfunding campaigns. *Decision Support Systems*, 87, 26–38. DOI: 10.1016/j.dss.2016.04.006

Lyons, A., & Kass-Hanna, J. (2019). *THE FUTURE OF WORK AND EDUCATION FOR THE DIGITAL AGE Leaving No One Behind: Measuring the Multidimensionality of Digital Literacy in the Age of AI and other Transformative Technologies*. https://t20japan.org/wp-content/uploads/2019/03/t20-japan-tf7-10-multidimensionality-digital-literacy.pdf

MacKenzie, I., Meyer, C., & Noble, S. (2019, October 1). *How retailers can keep up with consumers*. McKinsey & Company. https://www.mckinsey.com/industries/retail/our-insights/how-retailers-can-keep-up-with-consumers

MarketsandMarkets. (2023). *FinTech Blockchain Market Size, Share and Global Market Forecast to 2023 | MarketsandMarkets*. Www.marketsandmarkets.com. https://www.marketsandmarkets.com/Market-Reports/fintech-blockchain-market-38566589.html

Mastercard. (2024, May 24). *Mastercard accelerates commitment to digital transformation in Africa*. Mastercard.com. https://www.mastercard.com/news/press/2024/may/mastercard-accelerates-commitment-to-digital-transformation-in-africa/

Mbiti, I., & Weil, D. N. (2015). Mobile Banking: The Impact of M-Pesa in Kenya. *NBER Chapters*, 247–293. https://ideas.repec.org/h/nbr/nberch/13367.html

Mccorquodale, R. (2016, August 11). *6 years of small business stories | Funding Circle UK*. Funding Circle UK. https://www.fundingcircle.com/uk/resources/news/supporting-small-businesses/funding-stories/6yearsofsmallbusinessstories/

Meyer, L., Burt, T., Romero, S., Weinert, A., Bertoli, G., & Ferres, J. (2019). *How effective is multifactor authentication at deterring cyberattacks?*https://query.prod.cms.rt.microsoft.com/cms/api/am/binary/RW166lD?culture=en-us&country=us

Mikalef, P., Krogstie, J., Pappas, I. O., & Pavlou, P. (2020). Exploring the relationship between big data analytics capability and competitive performance: The mediating roles of dynamic and operational capabilities. *Information & Management, 57*(2). ScienceDirect. https://www.sciencedirect.com/science/article/pii/S0378720618301022

Mills, K. (2016). The State of Small Business Lending: Innovation and Technology and the Implications for Regulation. SSRN *Electronic Journal*. DOI: 10.2139/ssrn.2877201

Moldow, C. (2015). *A Trillion Dollar Market By the People, For the People How Marketplace Lending Will Remake Banking As We Know It*. https://foundationcapital.com/wp-content/uploads/2020/04/FC_CharlesMoldow_TrillionDollarMarket.pdf

Molina, F., Patel, V., & Zhou, X. (2023). The impact of fintech on small business competition: An urban-rural analysis. *Journal of Business Economics*, 29(1), 89–108.

Oliveira, T., Thomas, M., Baptista, G., & Campos, F. (2016). Mobile payment: Understanding the determinants of customer adoption and intention to recommend the technology. *Computers in Human Behavior*, 61, 404–414. DOI: 10.1016/j.chb.2016.03.030

OnDeck. (2024, May 30). *Small Business Cash Flow Trend Report | OnDeck*. OnDeck. https://www.ondeck.com/small-business-trends

Ozili, P. K. (2020, January 1). *Financial Inclusion Research Around the World: A Review*. Papers.*ssrn*.com. https://papers.ssrn.com/sol3/papers.cfm?abstract_id=3515515 DOI: 10.2139/ssrn.3515515

Palmié, M., Wincent, J., Parida, V., & Caglar, U. (2019). The Evolution of the Financial Technology ecosystem: An Introduction and Agenda for Future Research on Disruptive Innovations in Ecosystems. *Technological Forecasting and Social Change*, 151(1), 119779. DOI: 10.1016/j.techfore.2019.119779

Park, H., & Cho, S. (2024). Artificial intelligence in fintech: Opportunities for small business financial management. *Journal of Financial Technology*, 11(2), 233–250.

Pazarbasioglu, C., Mora, A., Uttamchandani, M., Natarajan, H., Feyen, E., & Saal, M. (2020). *Digital Financial Services*. https://pubdocs.worldbank.org/en/230281588169110691/Digital-Financial-Services.pdf

Plus, I. A. S. (2023). *Reducing financial reporting risk It's more than fixing financial controls*. https://www.iasplus.com/en/binary/dttpubs/1002reducingrisk.pdf

Riesener, M., Kuhn, M., Schümmelfeder, S., & Schuh, G. (2023). Business Model Research in the Age of Digitalization—A Systematic Literature Research for the Derivation of a Taxonomy of Business Models in the Manufacturing Industry. *Journal of Economics. Business and Management*, 11(4), 157–168. DOI: 10.18178/joebm.2023.11.4.754

Romānova, I., & Kudinska, M. (2016). Banking and Fintech: A Challenge or Opportunity? *Contemporary Studies in Economic and Financial Analysis*, 98, 21–35. DOI: 10.1108/S1569-375920160000098002

Sachin Kumar Sharma, P. (2023). Small businesses and FinTech: A systematic review and future directions. *Electronic Commerce Research*, 24(1), 535–575. Advance online publication. DOI: 10.1007/s10660-023-09705-5

Sage. (2020). *The Practice of Now 2020 Insight and practical advice for today's accountants and bookkeepers based on the latest independent research*. https://www.sage.com/en-gb/blog/wp-content/uploads/sites/10/2020/07/The-Practice-Of-Now-2020.pdf

Small, U. S. Business Administration. (2019, January 30). *Small Businesses Generate 44 Percent of U.S. Economic Activity*. SBA's Office of Advocacy. https://advocacy.sba.gov/2019/01/30/small-businesses-generate-44-percent-of-u-s-economic-activity/

Stanko, M. A., & Henard, D. H. (2017). Toward a better understanding of crowdfunding, openness and the consequences for innovation. *Research Policy*, 46(4), 784–798. DOI: 10.1016/j.respol.2017.02.003

Statista. (2019). *Crowdfunding - Worldwide | Statista Market Forecast*. Statista. https://www.statista.com/outlook/dmo/fintech/digital-capital-raising/crowdfunding/worldwide

Statista. (2021). *Crowdfunding - Worldwide | Statista Market Forecast*. Statista. https://www.statista.com/outlook/dmo/fintech/digital-capital-raising/crowdfunding/worldwide

Thales Group. (2021, October 27). *Majority of businesses don't protect their sensitive data in the cloud, finds Thales*. Thales Group. https://www.thalesgroup.com/en/poland/press_release/majority-businesses-protect-their-sensitive-data-cloud-finds-thales

Trabulsi, R. U. (2018). The Impact of Accounting Information Systems on Organizational Performance: The Context of Saudi's SMEs. *International Review of Management and Marketing*, 8(2), 69–73. https://www.econjournals.com/index.php/irmm/article/view/6221

Txend. (2023, November 7). *The Role of AI and Machine Learning In FinTech - Txend*. Txend. https://txend.com/ai-and-machine-learning-in-fintech/

Verizon. (2020). *Small business cyber security and data breaches*. Verizon Enterprise. https://www.verizon.com/business/resources/articles/small-business-cyber-security-and-data-breaches/

Vorecol. (2019). *Data Privacy and Security in HR Systems*. Vorecol.com. https://vorecol.com/blogs/blog-data-privacy-and-security-in-hr-systems-10476

Wang, L., & Liu, Z. (2023). Fintech adoption and its implications for small business efficiency. *Management Review*, 27(4), 187–203.

World Bank. (2020). *Small and Medium Enterprises (SMEs) Finance*. World Bank; www.worldbank.org. https://www.worldbank.org/en/topic/smefinance

Yadav, S., & Verma, A. (2023). Harmonizing fintech regulations for SMEs: A policy perspective. *Global Financial Regulations Review*, 8(2), 132–154.

Zalan, T., & Toufaily, E. (2017, December 31). *The Promise of Fintech in Emerging Markets: Not as Disruptive*. Papers.*ssrn*.com. https://papers.ssrn.com/sol3/papers.cfm?abstract_id=3200954

Zhang, & Juhlin. (2018). *Proceedings of the 17th International Conference on Mobile and Ubiquitous Multimedia*. https://doi.org/DOI: 10.1145/3282894

Zhu, M., & Zhang, T. (2021). Alternative financing options for SMEs in the fintech era. *Small Business Finance Journal*, 5(3), 73–90.

Ziegler, T., Shneor, R., Garvey, K., Wenzlaff, K., Yerolemou, N., Hao, R., & Zhang, B. (2017). Expanding horizons: The 3rd European alternative finance industry report. *Unit.no*. http://hdl.handle.net/11250/2479028

Chapter 4
FinTech Adoption for SMEs:
Innovation and Opportunities Worldwide

Syed Ahmad Gillani
Goverement College University, Faisalabad, Pakistan

Areeba Rahat Alvi
Government College University, Faisalabad, Pakistan

Humara Ahmad
https://orcid.org/0000-0003-0494-5389
IVY College of Business Management, Pakistan

Syed Afraz Gillani
Government College University, Faisalabad, Pakistan

Yasir Tanveer
https://orcid.org/0000-0002-4077-3441
Government College University, Faisalabad, Pakistan

ABSTRACT

The available Financial Technology or more commonly known as FinTech has simplified ways that the small businesses can access financial services for their growth solutions. Out of these, the leading forms of finance technology such as third-party payment systems, peer-to-peer online lending, crowdfunding have promoted cross border electronic trade, credit processes and sources availing financial backing to ideas. These technologies enhance the efficiency, speed and convenience hence attracting small businesses which have issues such as high cost of collateral and

DOI: 10.4018/979-8-3693-6386-7.ch004

high training costs. In this way, the FinTech platforms use big data and algorithms to fill the existing funding gap that the conventional sources failed to provide. FinTech differs to some extent around the world, mobile money is most used in developing countries while P2P lending is widely used in the developed countries.

1.INTRODUCTION

Fintech refers to the provision of digital solutions for conventional financial concerns. Under the general term "fintech," companies use innovative technology to build and offer financial services and solutions (Puschmann & Engineering, 2017). Fintech is a new financial amenities model created by advances in information technology (Hsueh & Kuo, 2017). Lähteenmäki, Nätti, and Saraniemi (2022) illustrated Fintech as it emphasizes the significance of buyer needs and inclinations in driving innovation, is defined as hi-tech advancements allowing the provision of tailored solutions for individualized prerequisites

The meaning of small and medium-sized enterprises (SME) varies worldwide. The most common criteria for defining SMEs globally is determined by quantity of workers, assets, and turnover. In the United States, small companies are categorized those having less than 500 employees. These enterprises symbolize 99.7% of all business activities, provide half of the country's jobs, and add to more than half of the nonfarm GDP (Vives, 2022). Likewise, a Small Enterprise (SE) is a company that employs no more than 50 people and has yearly revenue-v/ of no more than Rs. 150 million in Pakistan and a business entity classified as a Medium Enterprise (ME) is one that employs fifty or more people, or less than one hundred employees in the case of trade openings with returns between PKR 150 million and PKR 800 million (Puschmann & Engineering, 2017).

The objective of this chapter is to thoroughly examine how the proliferation of FinTech has transfigured the businesses, reshaped traditional models and generating new opportunities through technological intrusion. The following section outlines the progression of FinTech. In the third section, the adoption of FinTech is detailed. Subsequently, the objectives of the chapter are outlined, followed by innovations for SMEs in sections four and five. Next, opportunities and challenges faced by SMEs in both developed and developing nations are examined through a comparative analysis. Finally, this chapter concludes with a discussion on regulatory and policy frameworks, along with an acknowledgment of future trends and predictions curtailing from this study.

1.2 Progression of Fintech

Previously, the evolution of FinTech has been endorsed to the inception of checks as a means of payment in 1945. After that, the first credit card was instigated by Bank of America in 1958, and in 1967 debit cards and ATMs were recognized as crucial parts of the financial infrastructure (Dhiaf, Khakan, Atayah, Marashdeh, & El Khoury, 2024). According to (Paul & Sadath, 2021), Fintech was first developed in the 1860s and saw significant transformation in the years that followed. Firstly, FinTech 1.0 made it possible for financial services to be transferred quickly after telegraphs were installed during 1866 to 1967. Secondly, FinTech 2.0 incorporated innovations like ATMs, electronic payments, settlements, and banking in 1967 to 2008. Thirdly, FinTech 3.0 from 2008 till present has familiarized financial inclusion and mounting financial services like intermediated and non-intermediated financing facilities. The 2008 global financial crisis signified a pivotal moment in the evolution and adoption of Fintech. It elicited profound modification to the traditional financial landscape and laid the groundwork for the rise of technology-based financial solutions. This period saw the upsurge of diverse innovative Fintech companies, alongside the expansion of major tech corporations into the financial services domains.

Furthermore, the internet of things (IoT), data science, big data, cloud computing, advanced block chain, and artificial intelligence are some of the technological advancements brought about by the fourth industrial revolution, or Industry 4.0, and they are all revolutionizing the ways. Additionally, these technologies can help create hyper-connectivity and rapid automation to improve the efficiency of financial services and goods (Parashar, Sharma, Rana, & Balaji, 2023). Several significant FinTech companies include Ant Group, Stripe Inc., and Revolut, with respective expense ratios of $78.5 billion, $50 billion, and $33 billion (Rodeck, 2024).

1.3FinTech Adoption in SME's

The adoption of fintech has accelerated internationally, driving novelty and financial inclusion. FinTech has allay information asymmetry, transaction costs and improved the agility of the lending cycle, by making SMEs data collection, loan screening, monitoring, repayment etc., easier. In this new financial landscape, P2P lending, crowdfunding, and online banks have come out as key poles for SMEs, who have habitually been neglected by accustomed financial institutions, with particular perks and availability (Allen, Gu, & Jagtiani, 2021; Rossi, Vanacker, & Vismara, 2020). Furthermore, FinTech leads the way in data analytics, artificial intelligence, and blockchain technology, which benefits both customers and companies (Gomber & Koch, 2017).

FinTech adoption among SMEs has amplified as a result of the penetration of various payment and financing options into the SME sector, including marketplace lending, QR code-based, in-app finance, and point of sale-based payment systems. Small retailers and merchants need to accept FinTech payment services before they can successfully spread. The adoption of these mobile payment services is not solely influenced by the technology side of payment technologies rather small business decisions are also influenced by other internal and external variables of organizations. The embracement of online payment amenities by small enterprises is influenced by numerous factors, such as the attributes of the organization, the characteristics of small business owners, and other external environmental factors (Sharma, Ilavarasan, & Karanasios, 2024).

The Financial Access Survey (FAS) of the International Monetary Fund (IMF) demonstrated only 25% of SMEs have adopted fintech, compared to the average consumer adoption rate of 64% (Cumming, Johan, & Reardon, 2023). The COVID-19 pandemic has facilitated the enlarged reliance of businesses on FinTech, which enables functionalities such as digital payments and other tech-oriented transactions (Karim, Naz, Naeem, Vigne, & Policy, 2022). Following is the picture of number of fintech globally from 2018 to 2024 geographically (Number of fintechs worldwide from 2018 to 2024, by region, 2024).

Figure 1. Number of fintechs worldwide from 2018 to 2024, by region

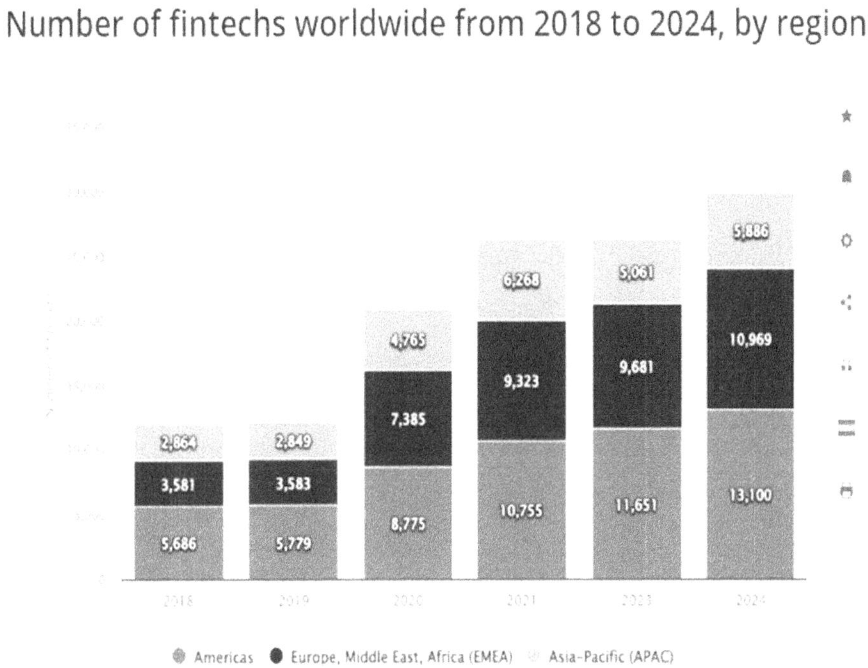

Figure 2. Fintech investments

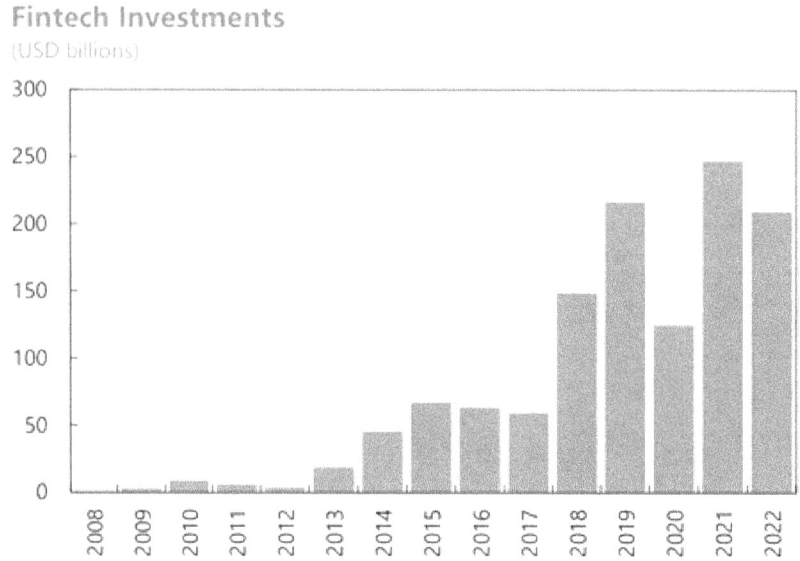

Source: KPMG; BCG; CrunchBase; Statista; author's calculations.

Objectives of the Chapter

1. Analyze the FinTech's potential for financial landscape of SME's
2. Identify opportunities and innovations in FinTech for SME's advancement
3. Impact of of FinTech on SME Operations in Developed and Developing Economies

1.3 Innovation for SMEs incorporating FinTech

SMEs are gravitating toward creative digital boards because of their accessibility and cost, and these developments are helping SMEs advance and increase production (Bagale et al., 2021; Karim et al., 2022; Lim, Gupta, Aggarwal, Paul, & Sadhna, 2021). Also, the adoption of mobile banking may improve the probability of SMEs securing debts from banks, which have been able to provide competitive interest rates and tailored services to these enterprises. Small and medium-sized enterprises (SMEs) derive advantages from mobile banking owing to their streamlined structures and digital-first strategies (Lorenz, Pommet, & Innovation, 2021; Rehman et al., 2023). P2P lending platforms provide SMEs flexible and easily accessible finance options by overcoming the limitations of traditional lending methods (Abbasi, Alam, Brohi, Brohi, & Nasim, 2021). Furthermore, data encryption, and two-factor verification are further precautions against illegal account access and information breaches (Alghazo, Kazmi, & Latif, 2017).

The innovation of digital technologies includes blockchain, artificial intelligence, machine learning, cloud services, and mobile payment technologies, Big data, Robbo Advisor, Internet of Things (IoT), Cybersecurity (Sahabuddin et al., 2023), which are inclining new economic paths for SMEs. Artificial intelligence compacts risk evaluation, forecasting, fraud detection, credit assessment, and many other uses (Goodell, Kumar, Lim, Pattnaik, & Finance, 2021). Machine learning tactics implementations in debt scoring can gear up debt covenant proceedings and evaluating credit score enables the solicitation of advanced machine learning techniques for estimating and predicting credit risk (Fuster, Goldsmith-Pinkham, Ramadorai, & Walther, 2022; Moscato, Picariello, & Sperlí, 2021). Internet financial services assist banks in assembling and managing SMEs' data irrespective of place and time (Mushtaq, Gull, & Usman, 2022)). Because of these financing restrictions, businesses are able to invest more in innovative techniques, organizational structures, and new goods, which eventually leads to business innovations.

FinTech assists small and medium-sized businesses access to monetary resources by reducing financial frictions brought on by collateral and credit constraints. This encourages the growth of these businesses productivity (Babilla, 2023) and improves their fiscal health (Wu & Huang, 2022). Modern encroachments in financial technology (FinTech), such as crowdfunding, have emerged as viable substitute financing sources for resourceful sectors to model and develop their ventures (Cox, Nguyen, & Development, 2018). The operationalization of FinTech stimulates financial inclusion by offering a wide range of financial tools, comprising mobile banking and digital payment structures (Hidayat-ur-Rehman, Alsolamy, & Complexity, 2023; Hollanders & systems, 2020). Additionally, FinTech adoption elevates functioning capacity and cash flow management for small and medium-sized enterprises (SMEs), while integrating sustainable performance elements. This assimilation fosters financial inclusivity and sustainability (Soni et al., 2022) notably by accelerating the use of financial technologies to tackle environmental disruption issues (Lu, Tian, & Ge, 2023).

1.4 Opportunities and Challenges in Developed Economies

FinTech is predominantly used in financial services realms such as asset management settings, debt payments, and financing infrastructure. Debt covenants, loan rates, financial charges, credit sums and flexible credit terms backing SMEs in procurement of loan through P2P (Cumming et al., 2023; Rosavina, Rahadi, Kitri,

Nuraeni, & Mayangsari, 2019). Through crowdfunding, especially SMEs may now access the combined financial power of people all around the world, bringing new ideas and projects to life that might not have been able to obtain funding otherwise (Pazowski & Czudec, 2014). FinTech innovations have the potential to transcend geographical boundaries, offering opportunities for cross-border alliances that can boost financial inclusion (Hendrikse, Van Meeteren, Bassens, Economy, & Space, 2020). By integrating these technologies, fintech firms declined transaction expenses, allowing firms easier access to capital and permit global businesses to attain services like foreign exchange accounts, trade finance and international payment systems (Kowalewski & Pisany, 2023). However, SMEs come across hurdles because of catastrophe of information, and data privacy and security concerns, especially in the wake of high-profile cyber-attacks and data breaches are the main complications that SMEs meet when trying to raise finance and obtain financial services (Ololade & Journal, 2024; Stiglitz & Weiss, 1981).

1.5 Opportunities and Challenges in Developing Economies

FinTech's influence in developing nations is evident through the democratization of financial services, where mobile money and digital banking platforms have substantially enhanced SMEs' access to financial resources. According to Buckley and Webster (2016), these advanced financing sources deliver the unbanked population with opportunities to acquire necessary funds. These stands offer alternative financial sources, enabling SMEs to secure capital more efficiently and expand their operations, raising entrepreneurship, employment creation, and overall monetary development (Okoye et al., 2024; Senyo, Karanasios, Gozman, & Baba, 2022). One major challenge is the compulsion for a sturdy digital framework in many developing nations. Limited access to consistent web connectivity and telecom systems can impede the adoption and usage of FinTech solutions (E. Y. Li & Zafar, 2023). Another significant challenge is the inadequate digital literacy among the population, which has enlarged the financial inclusion gap despite various efforts by governments, regulators, and financial institutions to improve automated platforms (Ediagbonya & Tioluwani, 2023). Developing economies remained behind in espousing new technological trends, with some areas not even recognizing or benefiting from FinTech platforms (Temelkov, Gogova Samonikov, & Management, 2018).

2. COMPARATIVE ANALYSIS: DEVELOPED VS DEVELOPING ECONOMIES

Flexibility, cost, proficiency, quality, and competitive advantage are the main benefits of a developed economy while financial responsiveness and knowledge gaps are recognized as the main adoption hurdles (Masood & Sonntag, 2020). SMEs entails above than 50% of employment backing 90% of all businesses (Bank & FINANCE, 2023). These account for almost 80% of jobs in Africa(Agency, 2022), however, in Latin America and the Caribbean 99.5% of all enterprises, 60% of jobs, and 20% of GDP (Поляцкий, 2023). 97.2% of all business enterprises in Southeast Asian economies such as Malaysia, accounting for 38.2% of GDP("oecd-ilibrary," 2024), 99.99% of total company, and employing 96.9% of Indonesian labor force (Scoreboard, 2024).

By providing a huge population job opportunities, these enterprises backing socio-economic progress in developing economies like Pakistan, where they account for about 30% of GDP and nearly 42% of employment. Despite accounting for 78% of employment in the non-agricultural sector and 25% of the nation's exports, SMEs only create 40% of the value accumulation in the economy (Ahmad, Ghani, Anwar, Butt, & Policies, 2022). Lending rate of banking sector in Pakistan to SMEs 17%, which is awfully low despite FinTech adoption in Pakistani commercial banks is substantial (Rahid & Enterprises, 2023). To boost bank lending to SMEs, the State Bank of Pakistan has launched a number of measures. However, because of substantial information asymmetries, a lack of collateral, low creditworthiness, and greater default rates fetched by loan officers manipulating lending contracts, banks still have striving to finance informal SMEs (Rehman et al., 2023).

3.REGULATORY AND POLICY FRAMEWORKS ON FINTECH ADOPTION FOR SMES

Regulatory frameworks are compulsory for SMEs to device FinTech services. Governments may encourage this by enacting laws that expedite it and running awareness efforts for digital payments (Danladi, Prasad, Modibbo, Ahmadi, & Ghasemi, 2023). Integrated laws and cross-border support can aid SMEs access global marketplaces and allowances. Legislators can enable citizens to safeguard their personal data and make educated decisions by raising consumer knowledge of data confidentiality and security, improving financial literacy, removing language obstacles, guaranteeing usability, and putting strong security measures in place (Aldboush & Ferdous, 2023). FinTech's long-term effects on financial inclusion and economic empowerment can be assessed through longitudinal studies that include impact assessments. Efficiency and security can be increased by looking into the behavioral aspects of FinTech adoption and new technologies like blockchain and artificial intelligence. Blockchain has the potential to completely alter supply chain financing and cross-border payments, while AI can automate risk valuation and credit scoring for quicker loan sanctions and more specialized services for SMEs (Ololade & Journal, 2024). Real-time business monitoring is made conceivable by IoT and big data analytics, which gives SMEs instant insights for refining their financial tactic (Balboa, Ladesma, & Manguerra, 2024).

4.FUTURE TRENDS AND PREDICTIONS OF FINTECH ADOPTION FOR SMES

Investment management, central bank digital currencies, and the amalgamation of digital finance elucidations with developing technologies are the hallmarks of the FinTech adoption future among SMEs (H. Li, Lu, & Yin, 2023). Immersive technologies, such as virtual reality (VR) and augmented reality (AR), are conjectured to upsurge financial literacy and user engagement through their immersive proficiencies (Balboa et al., 2024). Another significant opportunity for research involves examining the role of financial technology (FinTech) in lessening social and gender prejudices within the setting of micro and small enterprise development. FinTech's capacity to function inclusively and without partialities, it presents a valuable opportunity for addressing these gaps (Sharma et al., 2024). Moreover, the solicitation of new approaches involving innovation centers, incubators, and accelerators should be followed to illuminate how FinTech influences SMEs' access to financing over period (Sanga & Aziakpono, 2023; Sanga & Aziakpono, 2024).

5.CONCLUSION

The chapter on FinTech adoption for SMEs stresses the revolutionary capacity of digital technologies in redesigning financial services and opportunities across both developed and developing economies. FinTech innovations, such as blockchain, AI, and IoT, are modernizing financial operations, offering SMEs better access to capital, rationalized processes, and improved risk management. In developed economies, FinTech enhances efficiency and access to diverse financial services, though challenges like data privacy and information asymmetry persist. Conversely, in developing economies, FinTech facilitates financial inclusion by democratizing access to funds through mobile and digital platforms, but faces obstacles related to digital infrastructure and literacy. The comparative analysis emphasizes that FinTech impact varies based on regional perspectives. Developed economies benefit from advanced technological amalgamation, while developing regions see developments in financial access despite infrastructural and educational gaps. Regulatory and policy frameworks play a crucial role in fostering FinTech adoption by safeguarding security, indorsing financial literacy, and enabling cross-border alliances. Future research should emphasis on emerging trends such as central bank digital currencies, the role of AR and VR in financial literacy, and the impact of FinTech on social and gender partialities. Additionally, experimental methods and longitudinal studies are necessary to evaluate FinTech's long-term effects on SME access to finance and economic authorization. Overall, FinTech stands as a powerful instrument for enhancing SME financial resilience and fostering economic development, but its success is depending upon addressing both technological and regulatory challenges.

REFERENCES

Поляцкий, Д. J. П. п. (2023). Современные тенденции развития малого и среднего бизнеса. *16*(4), 31-34.

Abbasi, K., Alam, A., Brohi, N. A., Brohi, I. A., & Nasim, S. J. E. L. (2021). P2P lending Fintechs and SMEs' access to finance. *204*, 109890.

Agency, A. Z. D. (Producer). (2022). nepad.org. Retrieved from https://www.nepad .org/blog/unlocking-potential-of-africas-smes-using-emerging-technologies-africa

Ahmad, I., Ghani, M. U., Anwar, S., Butt, F. K. J. E. o. R. A., Government Packages,, & Policies. (2022). SME sector in Pakistan: mapping the policy framework, opportunities and constraints. *145*.

Aldboush, H. H., & Ferdous, M. J. I. J. o. F. S. (2023). Building trust in fintech: an analysis of ethical and privacy considerations in the intersection of big data, AI, and customer trust. *11*(3), 90.

Alghazo, J. M., Kazmi, Z., & Latif, G. (2017). *Cyber security analysis of internet banking in emerging countries: User and bank perspectives.* Paper presented at the 2017 4th IEEE international conference on engineering technologies and applied sciences (ICETAS). DOI: 10.1109/ICETAS.2017.8277910

Allen, F., Gu, X., & Jagtiani, J. J. R. o. C. F. (2021). A survey of fintech research and policy discussion. *1*, 259-339.

Babilla, T. U. K. J. E. M. (2023). Digital innovation and financial access for small and medium-sized enterprises in a currency union. *120*, 106182.

Bagale, G. S., Vandadi, V. R., Singh, D., Sharma, D. K., Garlapati, D. V. K., Bommisetti, R. K., & Sengan, S. (2021). *Small and medium-sized enterprises' contribution in digital technology.* Petra Christian University, Balboa, E., Ladesma, M., & Manguerra, A. N. J. J. J. I. e. d. m. (2024). *Digital Financing Innovations and Their Impact on the Financial Performance of SMEs in the Digital Economy Era.*, 11(1), 88–98.

Bank, W. J. S., & FINANCE, M. E. (2023). Improving SMEs access to finance and finding innovative solutions to unlock sources of capital.

Buckley, R. P., & Webster, S. J. J. o. F. T. (2016). FinTech in developing countries: charting new customer journeys. *44*.

Cox, J., Nguyen, T. J. J. o. S. B., & Development, E. (2018). Does the crowd mean business? An analysis of rewards-based crowdfunding as a source of finance for start-ups and small businesses. *25*(1), 147-162.

Cumming, D., Johan, S., & Reardon, R. J. M. B. R. (2023). Global fintech trends and their impact on international business: a review. *31*(3), 413-436.

Danladi, S., Prasad, M., Modibbo, U. M., Ahmadi, S. A., & Ghasemi, P. J. S. (2023). Attaining sustainable development goals through financial inclusion: exploring collaborative approaches to Fintech adoption in developing economies. *15*(17), 13039.

Dhiaf, M. M., Khakan, N., Atayah, O. F., Marashdeh, H., & El Khoury, R. J. J. o. D. S. (2024). The role of FinTech for manufacturing efficiency and financial performance: in the era of industry 4.0. *33*(2), 220-241.

Ediagbonya, V., & Tioluwani, C. J. T. S. (2023). The role of fintech in driving financial inclusion in developing and emerging markets: issues, challenges and prospects. *2*(1), 100-119.

Fuster, A., Goldsmith-Pinkham, P., Ramadorai, T., & Walther, A. J. T. J. o. F. (2022). Predictably unequal? The effects of machine learning on credit markets. *77*(1), 5-47.

Gomber, P., & Koch, J. J. J. B. R. (2017). M. Siering."Digital Finance and FinTech. *Current Research and Future Research Directions*, (79), 1–8.

Goodell, J. W., Kumar, S., Lim, W. M., Pattnaik, D. J. J. o. B., & Finance, E. (2021). Artificial intelligence and machine learning in finance: Identifying foundations, themes, and research clusters from bibliometric analysis. *32*, 100577.

Hendrikse, R., Van Meeteren, M., Bassens, D. J. E., Economy, P. A., & Space. (2020). Strategic coupling between finance, technology and the state: Cultivating a Fintech ecosystem for incumbent finance. *52*(8), 1516-1538.

Hidayat-ur-Rehman, I., Alsolamy, M. J. J. o. O. I. T., Market,, & Complexity. (2023). A SEM-ANN analysis to examine sustainable performance in SMEs: The moderating role of transformational leadership. *9*(4), 100166.

Hollanders, M. J. J. o. p. s., & systems. (2020). FinTech and financial inclusion: Opportunities and challenges. *14*(4), 315-325.

Hsueh, S.-C., & Kuo, C.-H. (2017). *Effective matching forP2Plending by mining strong association rules.* Paper presented at the Proceedings of the 3rd International Conference on Industrial and Business Engineering.

Karim, S., Naz, F., Naeem, M. A., Vigne, S. A. J. E. A., & Policy. (2022). Is FinTech providing effective solutions to Small and Medium Enterprises (SMEs) in ASEAN countries?, *75*, 335-344.

Kowalewski, O., & Pisany, P. J. T. (2023). The rise of fintech: a cross-country perspective. *122*, 102642.

Lähteenmäki, I., Nätti, S., & Saraniemi, S. J. J. o. b. r. (2022). Digitalization-enabled evolution of customer value creation: An executive view in financial services. *146*, 504-517.

Li, E. Y., & Zafar, U. (2023). Fostering Fintech adoption in growing economies: Opportunities, challenges, and strategies.

Li, H., Lu, Z., & Yin, Q. J. S. (2023). The development of Fintech and SME innovation: Empirical evidence from China. *15*(3), 2541.

Lim, W. M., Gupta, S., Aggarwal, A., Paul, J., & Sadhna, P. J. J. o. S. M. (2021). How do digital natives perceive and react toward online advertising? Implications for SMEs. 1-35.

Lorenz, E., Pommet, S. J. I., & Innovation. (2021). Mobile money, inclusive finance and enterprise innovativeness: An analysis of East African nations. *28*(2), 136-159.

Lu, Y., Tian, T., & Ge, C. J. R. P. (2023). Asymmetric effects of renewable energy, fintech development, natural resources, and environmental regulations on the climate change in the post-covid era. *85*, 103902.

Masood, T., & Sonntag, P. J. C. i. i. (2020). Industry 4.0: Adoption challenges and benefits for SMEs. *121*, 103261.

Moscato, V., Picariello, A., & Sperlí, G. J. E. S. w. A. (2021). A benchmark of machine learning approaches for credit score prediction. *165*, 113986.

Mushtaq, R., Gull, A. A., & Usman, M. J. T. P. (2022). ICT adoption, innovation, and SMEs' access to finance. *46*(3), 102275.

oecd-ilibrary. (2024). Retrieved from https://www.oecd-ilibrary.org/industry-and-services/financing-smes-and-entrepreneurs-2022_3bc2915c-en

Okoye, C. C., Nwankwo, E. E., Usman, F. O., Mhlongo, N. Z., Odeyemi, O., Ike, C. U. J. I. J. o. S., & Archive, R. (2024). Accelerating SME growth in the African context: Harnessing FinTech, AI, and cybersecurity for economic prosperity. *11*(1), 2477-2486.

Ololade, Y. J. J. F., & Journal, A. R. (2024). Conceptualizing fintech innovations and financial inclusion: comparative analysis of African and US initiatives. *6*(4), 546-555.

Parashar, B., Sharma, R., Rana, G., & Balaji, R. (2023). Foundation concepts for industry 4.0. In *New Horizons for Industry 4.0 in Modern Business* (pp. 51–68). Springer. DOI: 10.1007/978-3-031-20443-2_3

Paul, L. R., & Sadath, L. (2021). *A systematic analysis on fintech and its applications.* Paper presented at the 2021 International Conference on Innovative Practices in Technology and Management (ICIPTM). DOI: 10.1109/ICIPTM52218.2021.9388371

Pazowski, P., & Czudec, W. (2014). *Economic prospects and conditions of crowdfunding.* Paper presented at the Management Knowledge and Learning International Conference.

Puschmann, T. J. B., & Engineering, I. S. (2017).. . *Fintech.*, 59, 69–76.

Rahid, A. O. J. I. J. S., & Enterprises, M. (2023). SME FINANCING OF COMMERCIAL BANKS IN BANGLADESH. *POLICY DIRECTIONS BASED ON SME LOAN BORROWERS' VIEW*, 6(1), 1–8.

Rehman, S. U., Al-Shaikh, M., Washington, P. B., Lee, E., Song, Z., Abu-AlSondos, I. A., . . . Allahham, M. J. E. (2023). FinTech adoption in SMEs and bank credit supplies: a study on manufacturing SMEs. *11*(8), 213.

Rosavina, M., Rahadi, R. A., Kitri, M. L., Nuraeni, S., & Mayangsari, L. J. Q. R. i. F. M. (2019). P2P lending adoption by SMEs in Indonesia. *11*(2), 260-279.

Rossi, A., Vanacker, T. R., & Vismara, S. J. A. a. S. (2020). Equity crowdfunding: New evidence from US and UK markets.

Sahabuddin, M., Sakib, M. N., Rahman, M. M., Jibir, A., Fahlevi, M., Aljuaid, M., & Grabowska, S. J. S. (2023). The evolution of FinTech in scientific research: a bibliometric analysis. *15*(9), 7176.

Sanga, B., & Aziakpono, M. J. D. B. (2023). FinTech and SMEs financing: A systematic literature review and bibliometric analysis. 100067.

Sanga, B., & Aziakpono, M. J. J. o. E. i. E. E. (2024). FinTech developments and their heterogeneous effect on digital finance for SMEs and entrepreneurship: evidence from 47 African countries.

Scoreboard, F. S. E. A. O. (Producer). (2024). Oecdilibrary. Retrieved from https://www.oecd-ilibrary.org/sites/13753156-en/index.html?itemId=/content/component/13753156-en

Senyo, P., Karanasios, S., Gozman, D., & Baba, M. J. E. J. o. I. S. (2022). FinTech ecosystem practices shaping financial inclusion: The case of mobile money in Ghana. *31*(1), 112-127.

Sharma, S. K., Ilavarasan, P. V., & Karanasios, S. J. E. C. R. (2024). Small businesses and FinTech: a systematic review and future directions. *24*(1), 535-575.

Soni, G., Kumar, S., Mahto, R. V., Mangla, S. K., Mittal, M., Lim, W. M. J. T. F., & Change, S. (2022). A decision-making framework for Industry 4.0 technology implementation: The case of FinTech and sustainable supply chain finance for SMEs. *180*, 121686.

Stiglitz, J. E., & Weiss, A. J. T. A. e. r. (1981). Credit rationing in markets with imperfect information. *71*(3), 393-410.

Temelkov, Z., Gogova Samonikov, M. J. I. J. o. I., Business, & Management. (2018). The need for fintech companies as non-bank financing alternatives for sme in developing economies. *10*(3), 25-33.

Vives, A. (2022). Social and environmental responsibility in small and medium enterprises in Latin America. In *Corporate Citizenship in Latin America: New Challenges for Business* (pp. 39-50): Routledge. DOI: 10.4324/9781351288484-6

Wu, Y., & Huang, S. J. E. E. (2022). The effects of digital finance and financial constraint on financial performance: Firm-level evidence from China's new energy enterprises. *112*, 106158.

Chapter 5
Navigating the Fintech Wave and Its Background and Challenges

Manjit Kour
https://orcid.org/0000-0003-1043-3187
Chandigarh University, India

ABSTRACT

The paper attempts to identify the background and transformative impact of fintech, including relevant challenges and trends emerging from this fast-moving domain of research. We also try to discuss talent shortages, dynamics of regulation, and what role competition plays in influencing the arena of innovation. We analyze, based on an integrated summary of current fintech developments, an analysis of the disruptive potential of fintech and its implications in affecting financial ecosystems globally. Finally, we highlight pathways to future research, including ethics, technological advancements, and cross-disciplinary impacts.

INTRODUCTION

Fintech (Financial Technologies) consist of two words finance and technology. It means the use of technology for financial product and services. Fintech (financial technology) refers to innovative technological solutions that enhance, automate, and simplify financial services and processes. These technologies cover a broad spectrum of applications, from online banking and blockchain technology to payment platforms and algorithmic trading. Fintech is changing the landscape of financial sector and has become a disruptive technology by providing faster, cheaper, and customized products and captures the profit of the banking sector (Varga, 2017).

DOI: 10.4018/979-8-3693-6386-7.ch005

Due to the development of IT and digitalization business model of financial service industries are changing. Financial products based on information less physical interaction are required except client advisory. The new business player (i.e. fintech companies) entered the market with innovative products (Puschmann, 2017). The emergence of fintech is not happened by chance but it depends on the bequest of financial technologies. It is the advancement of IT from physical media to digital technologies. In Europe, fintech growth is primarily driven by regulatory support for innovation, as seen with the European Union's open banking initiatives. Conversely, Africa's fintech landscape is characterized by rapid adoption due to mobile banking's accessibility, which has provided financial services to millions who were previously unbanked.

The main key forces of Fintech are the transformation of services and process disruption which differentiate it from digital or e-finance (Alt et al., 2018). To remain competitive in a dynamic environment it is necessary to understand the fintech ecosystem and make competitive or collaborative strategies by financial institutions (Lee & Shin, 2018). Fintech is the new disruptive technology and is still in its initial phase. This chapter discusses the brief background of fintech and new challenges associated with it. This chapter is divided into two sections, the first section will deliberate about the background of fintech and the section will discuss the challenges associated with fintech.

Research Methodology

This paper uses a qualitative research methodology to discuss the fintech environment in transformation, its influence on the finance sector as well as associated problems. Data collection entailed extensive reviewing of the available academic journals, the industry reports, and recent reports that were published between 2022 and 2024. It takes a secondary data analysis approach that integrates data from respected sources which include World Bank, FSB, and surveys of industry from Deloitte and PwC, entities who have framed considerable narratives on fintech.

To provide an all-rounded perspective, the paper also features case studies of major fintech companies (e.g., Square, Stripe), and areas in which significant growth has occurred in fintech, including North America, Europe, and Asia. This study draws on Disruptive Innovation Theory to provide a framework for the disruption effect of fintech. For key themes such as regulatory issues, talent gaps, and competition, the disruptions effects of fintech are probed. Thematic analysis is also used to identify emergent trends, for example, decentralized finance, DeFi, and artificial intelligence, AI, and their implications to industry practice. This methodology ensures the holistic exploration of fintech globally and with diversified challenges that accompany growth.

Brief background of Fintech

The term 'Fintech' was originally a Citigroup initiated project, named "Financial Services Technology Consortium", to inspire collaborations in technological related areas. At present the term 'Fintech' is synonymous with innovative and modern technologies for providing financial services. it is considered to be a new market integration for both technology and finance (Arner, Barberis, & Buckley, 2015) which is replacing conventional financial system with new innovative processes which are technology driven (Hochstein, 2015).

Evolution of fintech and its adoption can be contributed to multiple factors. Firstly, fintech is the outcome of digitalisation and IT innovations. With wide internet coverage and development of new technologies like Big data and Blockchain technology, fintech was also developed. It is evolution of financial system/services. Secondly, the financial crisis in 2008 changed the banking industry entirely by introducing stiff regulation by authorities of the financial market. They introduced new standards and necessity arose for the innovative product for revival. Fintech (Financial technologies) provided innovative solutions range payment lending to wealth management and banks facing competition from non-banking financial institutions. (Romanova & Kudinska, 2016). Lastly, covid-19 gave a big push to fintech. Due to covid-19, in many countries people refrained from using currency notes as it increased the exposure to virus and thus, they preferred using mobile apps to do financial transactions. It created a demand of financial apps and digital currency. Another example of acceleration in adoption of fintech can be of fintech adoption drivers in India. In India demonetization was done in November 2016 when Government of India banned all 500 and 1000 notes and people were left without currency for many days. After demonetization, Indian people moved from cash to cashless transactions by using various mobile-based applications. It created a positive environment for Fintech and the government also supported them by digital India campaign. According to the global fintech adoption index, 95% of consumers knows about at least one fintech application. Fintech also reach rural and unbanked people as well as MSMEs through their innovative product (Kandpal & Mehrotra, 2019).

According to Joseph Schumpeter economist "Innovation was the fuel that energizes the economy through a process of creative destruction". Fintech companies use alternative data to analyze the borrower's creditworthiness. These alternative data sources help the borrower who has less FICO score to obtain a loan even rejected by banks (Jagtiani & Lemieux, 2019). Fintech also fulfil the needs of small entrepreneurs and startups they face fewer regulatory restrictions in comparison to banks. Venture capitalists also start investing in fintech (Fenwick et al., 2018). After the 2008 crisis fintech expand its business in lending especially to small businesses but its long-term impact on wage, new business expansion & creation, and employment is limited (Gopal & Schnabl, 2020), loan provided by fintech lenders without collateral securities increase the risk of creditor with the easiness of debtor in fulfilling capital requirements (Usanti et al., 2020). Social networking sites like Facebook also increased the awareness regarding alternative lending schemes for borrowers located at distance places. Fintech companies use big data and algorithm learning to evaluate the creditworthiness of the borrower in comparison to traditional bank which use FICO score (Fair Isaac Corporation) to check the creditworthiness. This score is based on the borrower assets, liabilities, references and relationship with lender, but fintech data credit is strong as it is totally based on the AI (Artificial intelligence) to analyses the creditworthiness of borrower by collecting data from various sources through technology which makes consumer loan less expensive (Bruckner, n.d.). Mortgage lending by fintech is based on the online application and less regulation for the borrower in comparison to traditional banks (Agarwal & Zhang, 2020). Peer to peer lending became an alternative financing option for consumers for refinancing debts, as well as the bank, also provides more credit to a borrower who obtains a loan from peer-to-peer alternatives. Borrowers get a loan at very easy terms and get a quick response from these lenders because all loan process is automatic through technology and interest rate is less as compared to the bank for a personal loan. FICO score skewed distribution is towards the borrowers who were denied by banks and less access to formal credit. Fintech lenders use an algorithm to screening their borrowers in comparison to banks use private and soft information collected by loan officers. Innovation in the consumer credit market mitigates imperfection and banks also increase the credit for peer-to-peer borrowers based on information released by fintech. In the U.S peer lending emerge in2006 and became a successful innovation in the financing of consumers and major market players are prosper marketplace and lending club. (Balyuk, 2016) From 2013 to 2016 at the world level fintech lending increase from $11 billion to $284 billion. Fintech increases their lending to the unbanked population but also increase regulatory gaps. Branch Company in Kenya formed in 2015 and issued ten million loans up to January 2019. Consumer protection also became a rising concern with the growth of fintech peer-to-peer lending in Indonesia. Complains by consumer related to lending became the second-highest complaints in 2018 received by Jakarta legal aid institute(Yuniarti & Rasyid, 2020)E trust is also is an important factor in the acceptance of technology especially in peer to peer lending(Candra et al., 2020) Peer to peer lending in Indonesia by studying database Google play found out that various unethical practices like charge a high-interest rate, poor collection method by them so there is a need of strict vigilance of authorities (Pranata & Ray Farandy, 2016).

This background underscores fintech's explosive expansion, setting the stage for an examination of its disruptive effects on traditional financial structures and the challenges it faces.

Challenges of Fintech

Fintech being the new innovation in financial sector is still at its early stages. So along with its wide scope and its numerous applications, on the downside it also poses some challenges. The major challenges presented by fintech are shown in Figure 1 and discussed in this section.

Figure 1. Challenges of Fintech

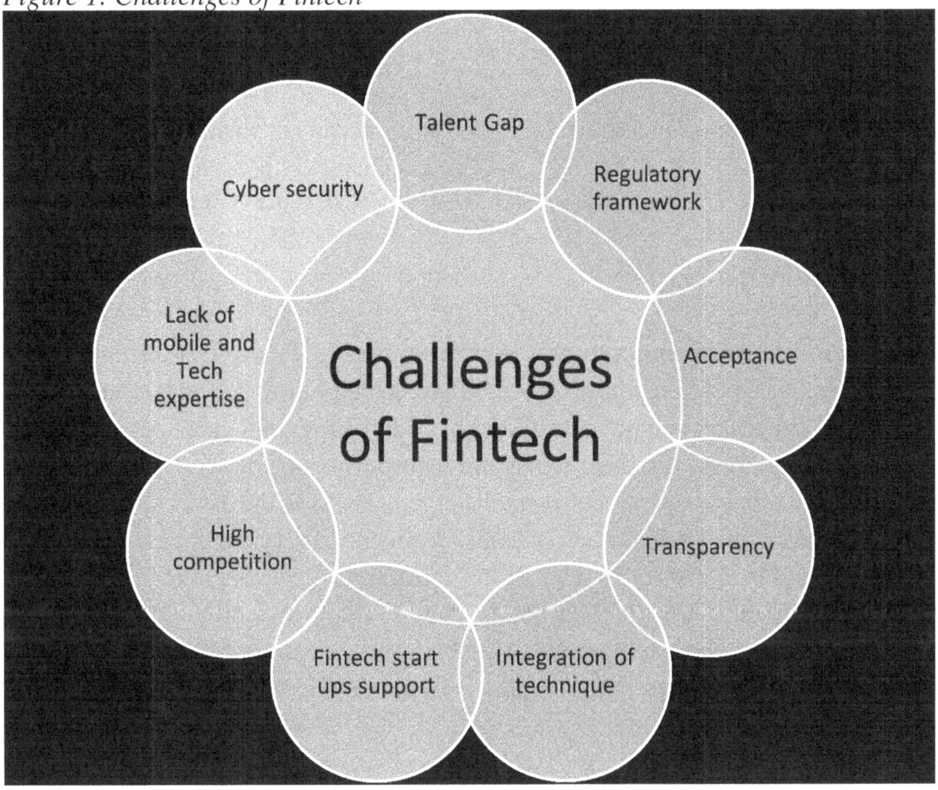

Integration of techniques

Fintech being technology driven industry is dependent on technological infrastructure of the country. Many developing countries are not able to fully adopt fintech due to infrastructural limitations. Moreover, integrating other techniques like cryptocurrency and blockchain management is still at initial stages in these countries.

Transparency

Regulatory framework and transparency are the grey area for fintech industry. Most of the economies are still figuring out fintech technology and regulatory framework is also in trial stage in many countries. This hampers the transparency element of these fintech companies as due to lack of strict compliance disclosure practices and transparency element is compromised. This in turn has negative impact on trust of customers towards its adoption.

Acceptance

In developing and underdeveloped countries technical manpower for fintech companies is a challenge. Moreover, with internet bandwidth issue, low income and lack of awareness, acceptance rate for fintech is low in these countries.

Fintech startups

The number of fintech companies is growing rapidly (Figure 2). Fintech startups being in initial stage of their business cycle have a long way to go and take advantage of growing fintech technology and adoption as they have limited resources. Hence, it is a challenging task for them to expand their business. Collaborations becomes difficult for them as they are yet to establish themselves, so the trust factor comes in the way sometimes. These fintech startups are unable to get proper support in terms of funding and mentoring also. One of the constraints that these fintech companies have to face is related to funding due to underdevelopment of capital markets in some countries. Although there is noticeable growth in venture capitals and seed money for fintech startups but it remains concentrated in few countries only.

Figure 2. Number of fintech companies worldwide

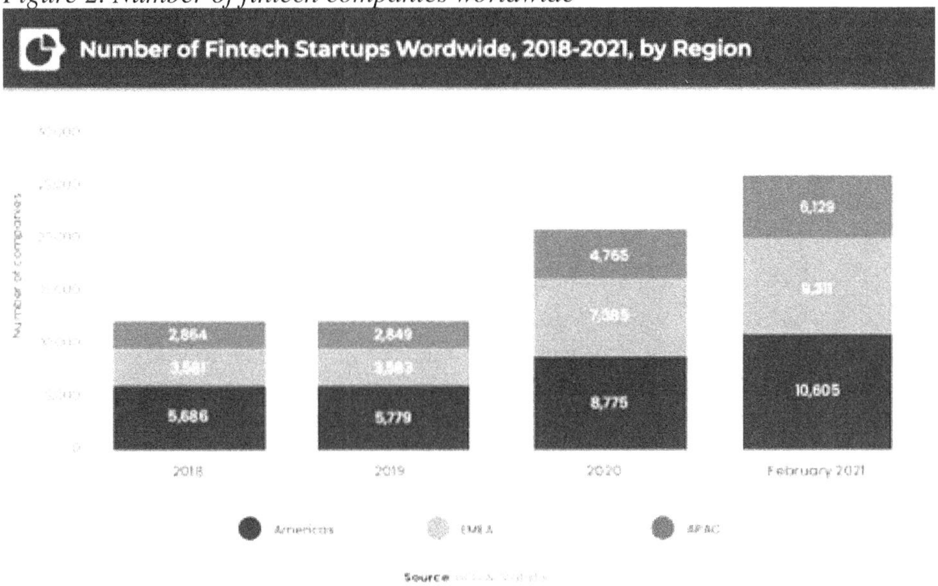

Regulatory framework

Fintech products which are highly innovative sometimes have an overlap of regulatory authorities which leads to ambiguity about regulatory framework (Depp, 2015). A large number of fintech companies have flourished all over the globe which run parallelly with financial institutions and banks, and they do not have any strict regulatory and compliance framework as their counterparts i.e. financial institutions and banks are having. These fintech companies claim to be different sector from financial institutions and formal banks and thus skip the regulatory compliance (Deloitte, 2017). But these fintech companies are offering services and products similar to formal banking sector and financial institutions and proper regulatory framework and compliance mechanism should be established. Although many countries are working towards establishment of legal framework and compliance mechanism for these fintech companies but still they are not as rigid and meticulous as applicable to formal banking sector. It is important to have strict compliance framework and well-established regulatory framework for building customer trust and confidence. Moreover, by following robust and sound risk management practices in regulated environment, the fintech companies can boost their success. It will demonstrate their devotion towards customer safety and build customer confidence and trust. It can be instrumental in increasing their market growth and enhance their transparency and accountability towards stakeholders.

Personalization

Banking and financial transactions through fintech last the personalized experience as provided by traditional banks and financial institutions. Banks and financial institutions through their Know your customer policy are able to provide many customized services tailored especially for their clients which enhances customer satisfaction. They can offer diverse products to their customers as per their customer profile. this gives bank advantage over fintech companies in case of knowledge intensive products and services. Moreover, traditional banks have accumulated experience and expertise in providing customized services especially in the areas of wealth management, financial intermediation, risk management, mortgage and corporate lending, and offering complex financial products (Romānova & Kudinska 2016).

High competition

Fintech companies have to face stiff competition not only from other fintech companies but also from big giants in financial sector like Citi, Goldman Sachs, Paypal, etc. With Amazon pay and other big companies also entering in the financial services, survival of small companies has become challenging. These big giants have good spending power and will not shy away when they have to spend on technology and marketing.

Cyber security

With growth of fintech all over the world one of looming demon in shadows is cyber security. Any type of data which is available on internet is exposed to cyber security threats to some extent. As seen in Figure 3, average weekly cyber-attacks per organisation by industry reveal that Finance/Banking sector is also exposed to cyber security threats on regular basis. With innovations in cyber security and data protection, hackers are also finding new ways and new tech to crack codes. Fintech companies can be new favourite target of hackers. A huge number of transactions involving big amounts take place over fintech on daily basis and it consists of sensitive data about customers, so it is more enticing for hackers to try to crack it. Fintech companies are adopting muti-layered protection and using new algorithms to protect data and to provide data security and transaction securities to their customers, but still many cyber security issues come up in news time to time.

Figure 3. Average weekly cyber-attacks per organisation by industry (Forbes study, 2021)

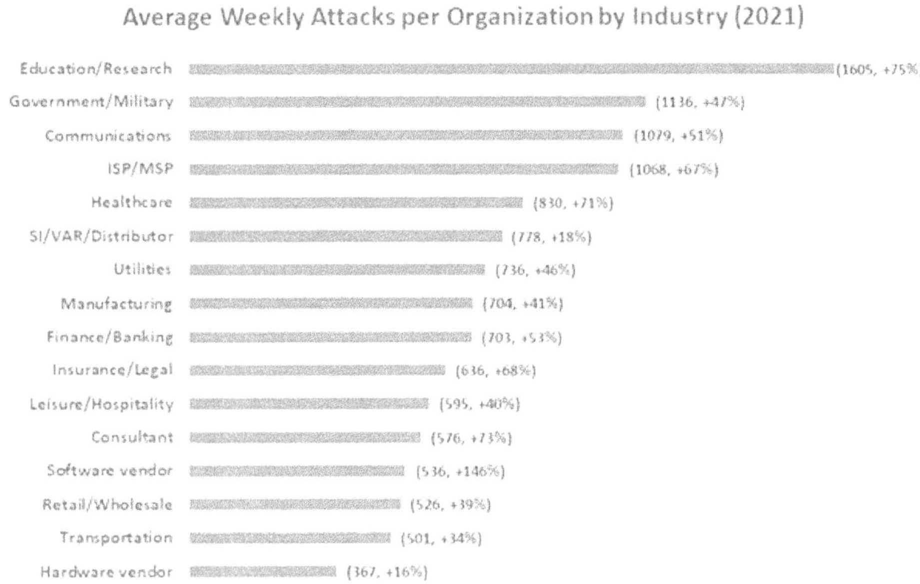

Talent Gap

There is talent gap in terms of skilled labour for fintech in many countries. Even when many countries have focussed on higher education but still some countries are unable to fully align with digitalisation needs. The fintech startups are facing the issue of hiring and retaining talent in the field of artificial intelligence, machine learning, cybersecurity, and cloud computing. Underfunded startups, also are unable to offer globally competitive salaries and incentives to attract skills from outside (WAMDA 2016) The fintech industry faces a significant talent gap, driven by the rapid pace of technological advancement and the specialized skills required for roles in areas like blockchain development, data analysis, and cybersecurity. For example, reports from 2022 and 2023 highlight a 25% shortage in qualified professionals across major fintech hubs such as London and Singapore. This talent shortage limits growth potential and intensifies competition as companies vie for skilled personnel.

CONCLUSION

Fintech is changing the landscape of financial sector and has become a disruptive technology by providing faster, cheaper, and customized products and captures the profit of the banking. In this chapter we discussed the brief background of fintech and new challenges associated with it. The main challenges faced by fintech that are discussed in this chapter are integration of techniques, transparency issues, fintech startup issues, acceptance challenge, lack of regulatory framework, absence of personification, high competition, cyber security, and talent gap. Fintech is the new disruptive technology and is still in its initial phase. So it is expected that in near future these challenges will be resolved by taking proper measures and making new innovations in the field.

In summary, fintech has disrupted traditional financial services, bringing innovation and challenges. Future research should explore how technological advancements and ethical concerns will shape fintech's trajectory, including the impact of artificial intelligence and decentralized finance on financial inclusivity.

REFERENCES

Agarwal, S., & Zhang, J. (2020). FinTech, Lending and Payment Innovation: A Review. *Asia-Pacific Journal of Financial Studies*, 49(3), 353–367. DOI: 10.1111/ajfs.12294

Alt, R., Beck, R., & Smits, M. T. (2018). FinTech and the transformation of the financial industry. *Electronic Markets*, 28(3), 235–243. DOI: 10.1007/s12525-018-0310-9

Arner, D. W., Barberis, J., & Buckley, R. P. (2015). The evolution of Fintech: A new post-crisis paradigm. *SSRN*, 47, 1271. DOI: 10.2139/ssrn.2676553

Balyuk, T. (2016). Financial Innovation and Borrowers: Evidence from Peer-to-Peer Lending. SSRN Electronic Journal. https://doi.org/DOI: 10.2139/ssrn.2802220

Brooks, C. (2022) Alarming Cyber Statistics For Mid-Year 2022 That You Need To Know, Global Thought Leader in Cybersecurity and Emerging Tech. Available on https://www.forbes.com/sites/chuckbrooks/2022/06/03/alarming-cyber-statistics-for-mid-year-2022-that-you-need-to-know/?sh=79b43a37864a

Bruckner, M. A. (n.d.). preventing predation & encouraging innovation in fintech lending. Retrieved June 21, 2021, from https://www.dfs.ny.gov/reportpub/online_lending_survey_rpt_

Candra, S., Nuruttarwiyah, F., & Hapsari, I. H. (2020). Revisited the Technology Acceptance Model with E-Trust for Peer-to-Peer Lending in Indonesia (Perspective from Fintech Users). *International Journal of Technology*, 11(4), 710–721. DOI: 10.14716/ijtech.v11i4.4032

Dapp, F. T. (2015)Deutsche bank report: Digital economy and structural change FinTech reloaded-Traditional banks as digital ecosystems. Available on https://www.deutschebank.nl/nl/docs/Fintech_reloaded_Traditional_banks_as_ecosystems.pdf

Deloitte. (2017), "Fintech and Regulatory Compliance", Available on http://www2.delitte.com/cntent/dam/Deloitte/us/Documents/regulatory/us-regulatory-future-of-finTechs-risk-and-regulatory-compliance.pdf

Gopal, M., & Schnabl, P. (2020). The Rise of Finance Companies and FinTech Lenders in Small Business Lending. SSRN Electronic Journal. https://doi.org/DOI: 10.2139/ssrn.3600068

Hochstein, A., Horn, E., & Palomino, M. (2015, June). Intelligent pipeline solution: leveraging breakthrough industrial internet technologies and Big data analytics for safer, more efficient oil and gas pipeline operations. In 10th Pipeline Technology Conference 2015. EITEP Institute.

Jagtiani, J., & Lemieux, C. (2019). The roles of alternative data and machine learning in fintech lending: Evidence from the LendingClub consumer platform. *Financial Management*, 48(4), 1009–1029. DOI: 10.1111/fima.12295

Kandpal, V., & Mehrotra, R. (2019). Financial inclusion: The role of fintech and digital financial services in India. *Indian Journal of Economics and Business*, 18(1), 95–104.

Lee, I., & Shin, Y. J. (2018). Fintech: Ecosystem, business models, investment decisions, and challenges. *Business Horizons*, 61(1), 35–46. DOI: 10.1016/j.bushor.2017.09.003

Pranata, N., & Ray Farandy, A. (2016). Big Data-Based Peer-to-Peer Lending Fintech: Surveillance System through the Utilization of a Google Play Review. Tokyo: Asian Development Bank Institute (ADBI). https://www.adb.org/publications/big-data-based-peer-peer-lending-fintech

Puschmann, T. (2017). Fintech. *Business & Information Systems Engineering*, 59(1), 69–76. DOI: 10.1007/s12599-017-0464-6

Romanova, I., & Kudinska, M. (2016). Banking and fintech: A challenge or opportunity? *Contemporary Studies in Economic and Financial Analysis*, 98, 21–35. DOI: 10.1108/S1569-375920160000098002

Usanti, T. P., Setiawati, A. P., & Nugraheni, N. (2020). The Legal Principle of Collateral in Fintech Lending. *Hang Tuah Law Journal*, 3(2), 158. DOI: 10.30649/htlj.v3i2.137

Varga, D. (2017). Fintech, the new era of financial services. Vezetéstudomány / Budapest. *Management Review*, 48(11), 22–32. DOI: 10.14267/VEZTUD.2017.11.03

Yuniarti, S., & Rasyid, A. (2020). Consumer Protection in Lending Fintech Transaction in Indonesia: Opportunities and Challenges. *Journal of Physics: Conference Series*, 1477(5), 52016. DOI: 10.1088/1742-6596/1477/5/052016

Chapter 6
Exploring AI's Impact on Fintech and Financial Inclusion:
Challenges and Opportunities

K. Shriya
https://orcid.org/0000-0003-2863-3822
SRM Institute of Science and Technology, India

T. Velmurugan
SRM Institute of Science and Technology, India

ABSTRACT

This paper investigates how fintech and AI are interacting, especially in terms of improving financial inclusion. Examining elements such as effort expectancy, performance expectancy, social influence, digital literacy, digital transformation sentiment analysis, behavioral intention, and perceived risk, it explores the intricate relationship between AI, Fintech, and inclusivity. We examine the impact of these factors on adoption intentions and perceived risk using a combination of approaches, including surveys and interviews. The study employs statistical techniques such as sentiment analysis algorithms and regression analysis on a broad sample size of 212 people. The results highlight the importance of elements like social influence and effort expectation, underscoring the need for customized interventions to successfully promote adoption.

DOI: 10.4018/979-8-3693-6386-7.ch006

1.INTRODUCTION:

The financial inclusion rate is quite high in India today; approximately 80% of the population now have accounts with banks. As a result, the GoI relies heavily on the growth of fintech enterprises in order to assist the underbanked population gain access to financial services. Financial inclusion must be advanced even more to sustain fintech firms and accurately reach out to these people (Asif et al., 2023). This paper also provides an account of the massive and revolutionary change in the banking and financial sectors in the twenty-first century due to technology. Convenience banking and other functional banking services enhance people's ability to obtain banking services and increase the number of low-income consumers. Here are some of the opportunities that can be found at the intersection of technology and finance; AI and ML. However, this convergence is not without other risks, and thus, there is a need for supervision. Kling and Tian (2021). For all the citizens especially those with low income to participate fully in the financial sector, digital financial inclusion is mandatory. Financial and non-financial institutions are providing services for financial services, and other excluded societies by adopting digital finance solutions with artificial intelligence support. These programs employ established online techniques to give access to individuals who once benefited from conventional banking organisations. The fourth industrial revolution is gradually transforming the conventional banking system that entails the use of accounts, paper and physical cash, into an integrated system that is more liberal and accessible (Mhlanga, 2020). By examining the motivations behind FinTech use and how it impacts financial service accessibility, this research investigates the potential of FinTech to promote financial inclusion. As moderators and mediators, we take into account the perceived regulatory backing and expertise of digital finance. Financial exclusion continues to impede equitable growth and make it impossible for many individuals to access formal financial institutions, despite the fact that the world economy is growing. FinTech has grown significantly in India as a result of technological adoption and the Digital India initiative. A quarter of adults globally and thirty percent of adults in India lack bank accounts, according to the 2021 Global Findex database (Amnas et al., 2024). The challenges that come with digital transformation for all businesses have played a major role in fintech's ascent to prominence in the banking sector. Fintech, an acronym for financial technology-enhanced services, facilitates financial participation by implementing cutting-edge solutions tailored to various business needs. This upheaval forces standard institutions like banks to adapt their business models. It provides startups with simultaneous opportunities to enter the financial services industry (Suryono et al., 2020). The financial industry and the flow of money around the world are changing dramatically due to new technology. FinTech and digital finance are not only providing groundbreaking financial services that challenge conventional knowledge, but they are also introducing novel software, technologies, business strategies, and cultural norms to the market. Financial institutions, as well as outside stakeholders like investors and researchers, should take note of the FinTech phenomenon. Digitization and sustainability are driving sectoral development, while financial systems are grappling with sustainability concerns. This study examines the intricate connection between fintech, digital adoption, and innovation in the revolutionary, invention-driven digital age. The financial industry has undergone a transformation thanks to robotics and the Internet of Things (IoT). Researchers looking into the effects of digitization and policymakers making sure the Sustainable Development Goals (SDGs) are followed are very interested in FinTech and sustainability. This places financial systems as capable of enhancing both consumer goods and ecosystems in equal measure (Trotta et al., 202). Consequently, there are many financial technologies or fintech, and they are currently addressed in the legislation. In the backdrop of the fourth industrial revolution predicated on technological innovation and the integration of digital solutions, this work seeks to explore the interconnectivity of fintech, digital uptake, and innovation. It also emphasizes the importance of these relationships for transforming the financial sector (Rizvi et al., 2024).

1.1purpose of the Study

The purpose of this research is twofold: to find out how AI is disrupting the fintech sector and how this disruption can impact financial inclusion. Therefore, the aim of the study under consideration is to reveal how the AI-based financial innovations impact productivity and create new opportunities for post-crisis marginalized communities. This paper focuses on the use of AI in fintech services including investment, banking, payment, and credit. The goal is to show that AI can help reduce barriers to financial services. It will look at how AI may reduce barriers to financial access that is enhance financial inclusion to people and companies that have been locked out of the mainstream economy. The challenges associated with the adoption of AI in the finance industry also will be elaborated in the study including concern over data privacy, ethical questions, regulatory barriers, and concerns over how algorithms may deepen existing inequalities. This report aims at offering policymakers, financial institutions and technology providers potential ideas on how they can employ AI for positive change with the help of the analysis of the opportunities and risks described below. Besides, it will discuss case studies and real AI implementations in fintech to understand how they impact the outcomes of financial access. The key objective is to make a technical advancement in a way that positively impacts all sectors of the society by providing a standpoint in the discussion on the right use of AI in the financial sector. Through this investigation, the study aims to enhance strategic decision-making and foster an environment where artificial intelligence (AI) can bridge the gap in financial inclusion, foster socioeconomic growth, and reduce inequality. Despite AI's potential to enhance fintech and financial inclusion, gaps remain in digital literacy, perceived risk, and equitable access. Challenges include regulatory uncertainties and data security issues. Policymakers must address these challenges by creating frameworks for responsible AI deployment, fostering trust, and promoting inclusive, sustainable financial ecosystems.

1.2 Overview of Recent Trends:

Green HR is centred on sustainable human resource management practices which used AI technologies to help organizations in efficiency utilization of resources and decreased carbon footprint. Employees across the globe are now a click away from sustainability due to digital literacy programs equipping personnel on responsible technology use and how they can be more sustainable, embedded within Green Hrm through AI.

The AI-driven sentiment analysis on elements such as sustainability-related risks & returns, within green investment and further sought better greening points of the public's perception has substantially fuelled other strides in the name of Green Finance. This enables the deployment of financial solutions based on those principles to marry well with what investors and institutional clients are seeking, through AI incorporated into fintech platforms offering enhanced ESG analysis. Determining market perceptions of the products, sentiment research supports in assessing adoption processes for all green finance offerings.

Green Banking: AI-driven digital solutions will facilitate the seamless operationalization of environmental sustainability in banking activities, such as paperless transactions and green loans. Users invariably need a certain level of digital literacy to buy into fintech advancements and AI enables continual risk assessments anytime, anywhere to empower sounder decision-making that drives down the big perceived risks associated with taking up green financial products.

In the recent past, artificial intelligence has been put to use as part of CSR initiatives for sustainability metric evaluation and communication. Both of these ideas are important in the broader context; however, Fintech has a key part to play hereby offering transparent reporting and real-time data surveillance which builds stakeholder confidence. Furthermore, artificial intelligence plays a vital role in addressing the perceived risks associated with green finance to conform within the corporate social responsibility fabric for promoting an equitable and sustainable financial domain. AI solutions can bring about increased financial inclusion and poverty reduction in developmental economics by simplifying access to banking, making microcredit systems more efficient, and by decreasing transaction costs.

Yet, obstacles remain: data privacy, technological infrastructure, and digital literacy are some of the problems that forbid full-scale interoperability of AI in fintech for equity in financial services. (Temitayo Oluwaseun Jejeniwa et al., 2024)

2.REVIEW OF LITERATURE:

As indicated by Liu, et al. (2024) This paper sheds light on the disruptive nature of FinTech based innovations on financial service providers through a critical evaluation of theoretical and empirical literature. The paper examines how FinTech disrupts current financial processes through the innovation of new strategies and structures of business. There are emerging trends that FinTech solutions are gradually becoming an important part of the banking and financial industry so that the present financial landscape is experiencing significant shifts. This review aims at revealing the prospects and challenges that FinTech brings about by exploring these innovations, with focus on the impact upon the financial inclusion and the maturation of the financial system.

Mhlanga (2024) The use of big data in financial technology (fintech) can potentially transform the area in different ways, such as strategic, innovation, solution implementation, risk control, governance, and technology. Given the volume of data that can be generated in a short period, it is possible for decision making processes to be informed by real-time analysis of such data by fintech companies. For example, they can identify which of the customers are most likely to fail to pay back their loans or identify fraud. These developments help provide better prognosis and decision making since the information is based on facts.

According to Temitayo Oluwaseun Jejeniwa et al., 2024, AI technologies have brought new approaches to addressing classic issues in developmental economics. Fintech and financial inclusion are areas where potential of artificial intelligence is especially high. AI can help solve key developmental problems, rationalize financial procedures, and extend financial solutions to the underbanked. This shift contains prospects for more efficient and sustainable economic growth without excluding some population groups. However, there are challenges experienced in the incorporation of AI in fintech among them being; regulation since its integration has to present a leveled field for all those in the different strata of the society and ethical issues and data privacy act as well.

According to Sampat and others (2023) the integration of artificial intelligence (AI) in FinTech is improving the effectiveness and accessibility. AI is applied in virtual banking, trading and in identifying and preventing fraud. These development make financial services more accessible, affordable and relevant for people who are locked out from mainstream credit markets. Yet, problems remain; among them- data protection issues, algorithms' potential discrimination, and regulatory issues. Thus, the ethics of AI deployment and effective regulation are the two most important issues. The advancement of artificial intelligence in connection with other FinTech breakthroughs such as Blockchain and digital currency can beyond increase access to financial services for the population, but also encourage economic development. How to spur innovation while not abusing the opportunities of AI will shape this technology's future in FinTech and, therefore, financial inclusion.

In the study, Afjal (2023) examines the impact of Artificial intelligence to the development of financial technology (FinTech) and financial inclusion. AI helps to break down barriers which include high costs and lack of access by providing financial services to the current and potential consumers who cannot afford the conventional service providers. The study looks at the impact of AI in improving services, cutting costs and optimizing procedures for economic growth. However, it also aims at issues like data protection and legislation, inclusiveness or exclusion problem, as it is argued that AI can worsen the digital gap, for it is considered that there should be a fair implementation of the AI in the FinTech area.

According to Bharathi S. et al., 2023) Fintech, which refers to financial technologies that are taking over the financial transactions and processes, are not only advantageous for the financial industry but also for the entire society. The high rate of expansion and adoption of fintech is as a result of its ability to deliver targeted solutions to various players in the market. First, many fintech are able to run more efficiently and reach more consumers than legacy financial organizations. The major research themes include, but are not limited to, the following: – fintech and financial inclusion, – fintech adoption and use, – sectoral growth, – lending, – technology and fintech. This research examines the correlation between fintech and financial inclusion in order to advance the existing literature with key themes of fundamental, driving, niche, and emergent that may help to fast-track financial inclusion.

(Yanting & Ali, 2023) Financial inclusion has garnered significant attention from policymakers globally, as it is regarded as a crucial pillar for human development. Traditional financial systems in many countries are insufficiently equipped to engage all segments of society effectively. This study supports the argument by presenting real-time examples of AI applications deployed by various countries to mitigate barriers to financial inclusion. The implementation of AI to enhance financial inclusion can be realized through the support of a robust regulatory framework and infrastructure.

(Mavlutova et al., 2022) The increase in studies on digital transformation's impact on sustainable development across economic sectors highlights a gap in understanding its drivers and links in the financial sector. Rapid technological advancements have significantly influenced this sector, yet research on digital transformation's role in sustainable development remains limited. Digitalization serves as a management tool, while digital transformation integrates digital technologies into the value chain to add value for customers and stakeholders, enhancing organizational performance. Addressing this research gap is crucial to understanding how digital transformation can drive sustainable development in the financial sector.

This paper refers to the works of Hua and Huang (2020) where they explain how financial technology (fintech) has grown at a very fast pace and is changing the face of the financial sector in India. This paper is intended to look at the causes, current status, effects on the economy and future threats posed by fintech in India. As such, it endeavours to offer a review of the Indian fintech evolution by synthesising prior research and outlining the actual path. The stated goal is to justify the fast-growing pace of the sector and its specific mission of providing access to basic financial services. Furthermore, this paper seeks to fill the above gaps by outlining some significant features of the Indian fintech industry and derive useful lessons for the future advancement and governance of the sector.

Development economics has been eased by AI technologies as pointed out by Makina (2019) through provision of new ideas to address old questions. AI has the greatest potential in financial inclusion and fintech. AI can be utilized to solve key developmental questions, enhance the speed of financial operations, and increase customers' base of a financial service provider. This change offer chances of economic growth that is more liberal and productive. However, there are several issues raised by the integration of the AI element in fintech including, inequitable distribution where higher-end users are the ones benefitting most if policies are not well placed, ethical issues and collection of users data.

2.1 Research Objectives:

- To investigate the transformative effects of AI on the fintech industry
- To Explore the role of AI in risk management, fraud detection, and security within the financial industry
- To Identify and evaluate the key challenges faced by fintech companies in implementing AI technologies, including technical, regulatory, and ethical issues.
- To Assess the opportunities AI presents for enhancing financial services, such as improving accessibility, efficiency, and personalization.
- To Evaluate the potential economic and social benefits of widespread AI adoption in fintech, considering both short-term and long-term perspectives

2.2 Statement of Problem:

The financial technology (fintech) industry is gradually integrating the use of artificial intelligence (AI) into the delivery of its products. This development has the potential of being one of the largest advantages as well as pose some risks. This progression has the potential to enhance financial inclusion if this type of progression provides underprivileged groups with unparalleled access to financial products and services. AI has made financial services to be more open, precise, and faster through robo-advisors, self-service credit scoring, and other financial advisory tools. This advancement is not without great challenges, however. A number of challenges: data protection issues, risk of algorithmic dishonesty, cybersecurity threats, and compliance with laws and ordinances. Additionally, where AI and machine learning algorithms are incorporated there are important questions of responsibility and accountability as well as transparency. Also, inequality could be deepened by the fact that under-privileged groups cannot afford the digital literacy or the correct technology that will allow them to exploit AI-driven financial solutions. The aim of this research is to consider the double affordances of artificial intelligence in fintech, how it can be a solution for the financially excluded but also bring new challenges that need to be addressed. This research aims at identifying all possible opportunities that AI presents for improving financial inclusion for the marginalized groups, as well as all possible risks that should be avoided. This is done through considering of case studies on the new media, existing legislation, and the current state of technology. The use of technology as an everyday tool plays a significant role throughout the financial industry; given this, the stakeholders have to be cautious towards certain aspects of artificial intelligence (AI) such that different groups of vulnerable or underprivileged society get the benefit it brings with the right precautions against the negatives it entails. This means that there is need to do fair analysis.

2.3 Research Hypothesis

1. There is a significant positive relationship between effort expectancy and behavioural intention towards using fintech services, mediated by perceived risk, within the context of AI's impact on fintech and financial inclusion.
2. There is significant positive relationship between Performance expectancy and behavioural intention to adopt fintech solutions, with perceived risk acting as a mediator in the adoption process.
3. There is significant positive relationship between social influence on behavioural intention to engage with fintech services, and this relationship is moderated by the perceived risk associated with these services.

4. There is a significant positive relationship Facilitating conditions on behavioural intention to use fintech services, mediated by perceived risk, and are crucial for digital transformation in the financial sector.
5. There is a significant positive digital literacy and sentiment analysis regarding AI-driven fintech solutions significantly contribute to the increased adoption of these services, with perceived risk influencing the strength of this relationship.

2.4 Research Gap

- Limited investigation of user experiences and perceptions and the Research frequently concentrates on the technological components of artificial intelligence (AI) in fintech, ignoring the user experience and perceptions, which are essential for the extensive uptake of financial services powered by AI.
- The literatures studies focus on the immediate effects of AI on fintech, a thorough examination of the long-term consequences for financial inclusion—particularly in developing nations is lacking.
- The ethical difficulties posed by the examined in many papers are now frequently disregarded and are centered on data privacy concerns, biases in AI algorithms, and the possibility of growing financial exclusion among vulnerable people.
- The main challenges are to assess and compare how well AI-based technologies are promoting financial inclusion to all consumers across different fintech platforms due to the lack of common laws and regulations

3RESEARCH MODEL

Figure 1. Research model

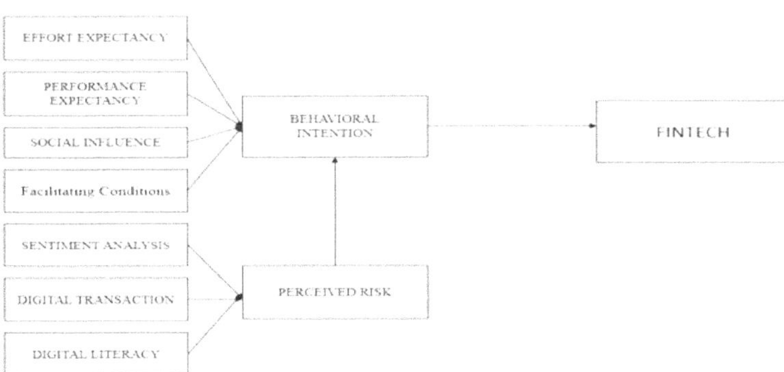

4 DATA ANALYSIS AND INTERPRETATION

The type of analysis applied in this study is the Descriptive Statistics Analysis. It is a questionnaire that is being conducted on based millennials and only after stringent tests on if the person answering the questions possesses basic investment knowledge and also the financial literacy level. Reminiscing the method applied in the study above, one can pin-point to the particular method used – The Purposive sampling is being used in the study. To do so, the researcher has omitted all those samples, which were characterized by incorrect results, and, as a result, the number of samples made up 212. The research techniques applied in the study were highly recommended by some of the researchers with high usage rates in several studies as well as relevant to the research objectives, reliability, validity, and internal consistency. A pilot study approach was made. For the reliability coefficient identified in this study it is seen that the researchers used ranges between 0. 7 to 0. 8 Whereas eight of the proposed criteria are appropriate for descriptive research, Smith et al., used these results to establish that the research was dependable (2002). In the study, the quantitative analysis tools employed include percentage analysis, correlation analysis, regression analysis, and Partial Least Square Structural Equation Modelling (PLS-SEM). For each part of the work, there are statistical software programmes used as follows: For data analysis the software used is MS excel while for SEM analysis, the software used is PL SEM and for correlation and regression analysis the software used is SPSS.

4.1 Demographic variables:

Table 1. Demographic variables

S.No	Demographic variable	Category	Frequency	Percentage (%)
1	Gender	Male	106	50.38
		Female	106	49.62
2	Age	18-26	42.4	18.60
		27-34	42.4	12.40
		35-42	44	22.48
		43-50	40	20.93
		above 50	43	17.8
3	Marital status	Married	106	50.38
		Unmarried	106	49.36

continued on following page

Table 1. Continued

S.No	Demographic variable	Category	Frequency	Percentage (%)
4	Occupation	Household	70.6	33.33
		Entrepreneur	72	33.33
		Others	68.6	33.33
5	Income	less than Rs.10,000	35.3	16.66
		Between Rs.11,000 to Rs. 20,000	35.3	16.66
		Between Rs.21,001 to Rs.30,000	35.3	16.66
		Between Rs.31,001 to Rs.40,000	35.3	17
		Between Rs.41,000 to Rs.50,000	35.3	16.66
		More than Rs.50,000	35.3	16.66

According to Table 1, the study of this demographic data indicates that the distribution is fairly equal in several of its aspects. The highest age group in terms of frequency accounts for 35-42 years old who stands at 22.48 percent while young Gender is reasonably levelled with 50.38 percent male to 49.62 percent female. Separated by location household (50%) entrepreneur (65%) others (35%) Employment status. The income has been reported higher within stated that the spread was more or less the same with cases of income categorised as less than Rs 10,000 and income over Rs 50,000

4.2 Reliability of Constructs:

Table 2. Reliability of constructs

ITEMS	RELIABILITY VALUE
EFFORT EXPECTANCY	0.751
PERFORMANCE EXPECTANCY	0.746
SOCIAL INFLUENCE	0.761
FACILATING CONDITIONS	0.741
SENTIMENT ANALYSIS	0.683
DIGITAL TRANSACTION	0.702
DIGITAL LITERACY	0.762
BEHAVIOURAL INTENTION	0.766

As indicated in table 4.2The reliability analysis done in the course of the study involved the use of SPSS to determine the internal consistency of the measured variables. The findings showed satisfactory reliability of the constructs under study. In particular, Cronbach's alpha coefficients changed from 0.766 to 0.683, which can be characterized as satisfactory to high. These findings are important to establish the reliability of the data collected so as to enhance the validity of the subsequent statistical analyses and interpretation in the research study.

4.3Correlation:

Table 3. Correlations

Correlations											
		EE	**PE**	**SI**	**FC**	**SA**	**DT**	**DL**	**BI**	**PR**	**FI**
EE	Pearson Correlation	1	.722**	.724**	.776**	.665**	.675**	.773**	.765**	.767**	.732**
	Sig. (2-tailed)		.000	.000	.000	.000	.000	.000	.000	.000	.000
	N	212	212	212	212	212	212	212	212	212	212
PE	Pearson Correlation	.722**	1	.749**	.762**	.744**	.661**	.792**	.750**	.752**	.756**
	Sig. (2-tailed)	.000		.000	.000	.000	.000	.000	.000	.000	.000
	N	212	212	212	212	212	212	212	212	212	212
SI	Pearson Correlation	.724**	.749**	1	.762**	.705**	.737**	.796**	.796**	.779**	.771**
	Sig. (2-tailed)	.000	.000		.000	.000	.000	.000	.000	.000	.000
	N	212	212	212	212	212	212	212	212	212	212
FC	Pearson Correlation	.776**	.762**	.762**	1	.746**	.712**	.788**	.782**	.752**	.808**
	Sig. (2-tailed)	.000	.000	.000		.000	.000	.000	.000	.000	.000
	N	212	212	212	212	212	212	212	212	212	212
SA	Pearson Correlation	.665**	.744**	.705**	.746**	1	.660**	.735**	.704**	.706**	.761**
	Sig. (2-tailed)	.000	.000	.000	.000		.000	.000	.000	.000	.000
	N	212	212	212	212	212	212	212	212	212	212
DT	Pearson Correlation	.675**	.661**	.737**	.712**	.660**	1	.736**	.717**	.707**	.730**
	Sig. (2-tailed)	.000	.000	.000	.000	.000		.000	.000	.000	.000
	N	212	212	212	212	212	212	212	212	212	212
DL	Pearson Correlation	.773**	.792**	.796**	.788**	.735**	.736**	1	.819**	.805**	.813**
	Sig. (2-tailed)	.000	.000	.000	.000	.000	.000		.000	.000	.000
	N	212	212	212	212	212	212	212	212	212	212
BI	Pearson Correlation	.765**	.750**	.796**	.782**	.704**	.717**	.819**	1	.778**	.751**
	Sig. (2-tailed)	.000	.000	.000	.000	.000	.000	.000		.000	.000
	N	212	212	212	212	212	212	212	212	212	212

continued on following page

Table 3. Continued

Correlations											
		EE	PE	SI	FC	SA	DT	DL	BI	PR	FI
PR	Pearson Correlation	.767**	.752**	.779**	.752**	.706**	.707**	.805**	.778**	1	.798**
	Sig. (2-tailed)	.000	.000	.000	.000	.000	.000	.000	.000		.000
	N	212	212	212	212	212	212	212	212	212	212
FI	Pearson Correlation	.732**	.756**	.771**	.808**	.761**	.730**	.813**	.751**	.798**	1
	Sig. (2-tailed)	.000	.000	.000	.000	.000	.000	.000	.000	.000	
	N	212	212	212	212	212	212	212	212	212	212

**. Correlation is significant at the 0.01 level (2-tailed).

According to 4.3 The correlation table displays the Pearson correlation coefficients among seven variables: There is a series of factors like effort expectancy, performance expectancy, social influence, facilitating condition with mediating role of Behavioural Intention and perceived risk with regard to fintech as a dependent measure. Every one of the correlation coefficients mentioned is accompanied by the probability level or p-value, which stands for 2-tailed test and N of the given investigation. There is another important point: all the variables are highly positively related; the array rises from 0.805 and reaches 0.665.

4.4 Regression Analysis:

Table 4. Regression analysis

ANOVA[a]						
Model		**Sum of Squares**	**df**	**Mean Square**	**F**	**Sig.**
1	Regression	2219.715	7	317.102	97.813	.000[b]
	Residual	661.360	204	3.242		
	Total	2881.075	211			

Figure 2. Coefficients

Coefficients[a]

Model		Unstandardized Coefficients B	Std. Error	Standardized Coefficients Beta	t	Sig	Correlations Zero-order	Partial	Part	Collinearity Statistics Tolerance	VIF
1	(Constant)	1.108	724		1.531	127					
	EE	037	062	036	606	545	732	042	020	314	3.183
	PE	063	065	062	982	328	756	069	033	283	3.533
	SI	110	064	110	1.724	086	771	120	058	275	3.630
	FC	244	067	244	3.641	000	808	247	122	251	3.988
	SA	268	085	179	3.136	002	761	214	105	346	2.890
	DT	166	081	113	2.057	041	730	143	069	370	2.699
	DL	238	070	242	3.395	001	813	231	114	222	4.498

a. Dependent Variable: FI

According to Table 4 Dependent variable: FINTECH

Independent variable: Effort Expectancy, performance expectancy, social Influence, facilitating conditions, sentiment analysis, digital transformation, digital literacy

Mediating variable: behavioural intention, perceived risk

Regression analysis examines the causal link between numerous variables. Regression analysis

examines the relationship between the dependent variable and independent variable. The

study's table value demonstrates how growth and adaptability have a big impact on Behavioural intention, usability, social influence, risk, effort expectancy and financial inclusion. Financial mindset is unaffected by the privacy dimension.

4.5 Sem Model

Figure 3. SEM model

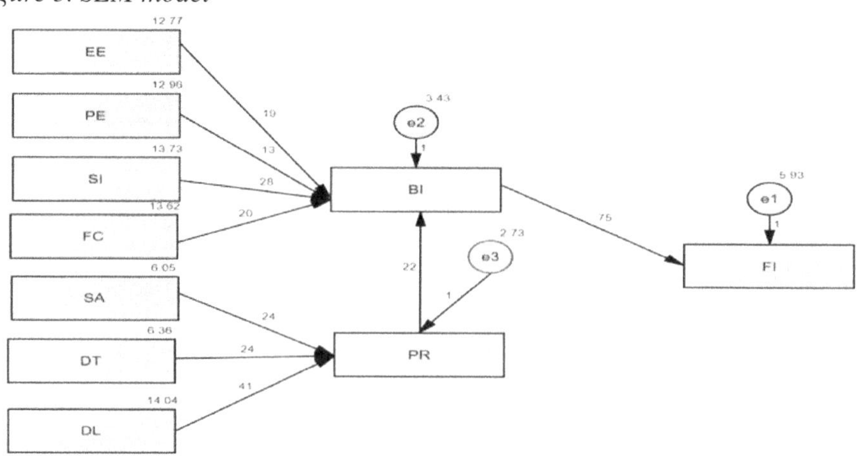

4.6 Confirmatory Factor Analysis

Figure 4.

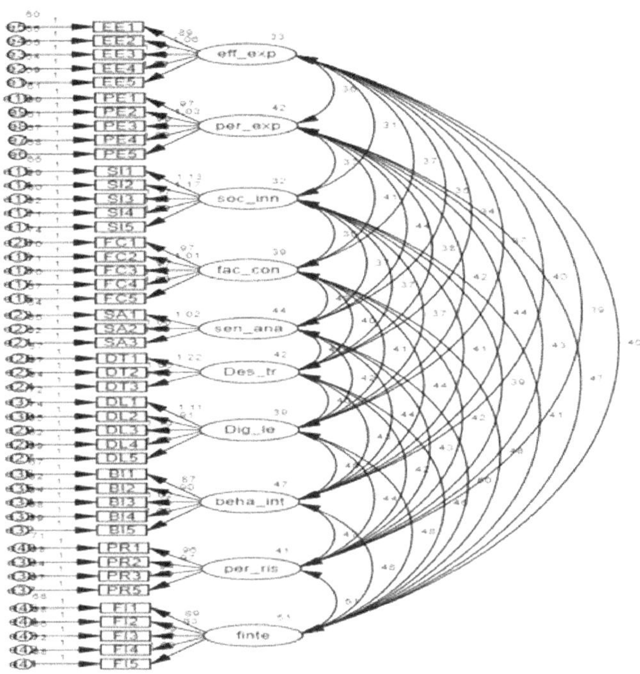

Table 5. Confirmation factor analysis

	Eff_ exp	Per_exp	soc_ inf	Fac_con	Se_ an	Dig_tra	Dig_ lit	Beha_inte	Per_risk	Finte
Eff_exp	0.654									
Per_exp	0.588	0.679								
soc_inf	0.531	0.586	0.604							
Fac_con	0.506	0.521	0.575	0.607						
Se_an	0.438	0.476	0.536	0.565	0.678					
Dig_tra	0.385	0.449	0.465	0.515	0.535	0.624				
Dig_lit	0.331	0.353	0.404	0.457	0.437	0.523	0.664			
Beha_inte	0.293	0.318	0.353	0.358	0.325	0.417	0.326	0.645		
Per_risk	0.291	0.361	0.351	0.351	0.331	0.391	0.314	0.615	0.631	
Finte	0.234	0.331	0.321	0.313	0.303	0.335	0.301	0.605	0.615	0.606

5.FINDINGS

The research identified that AI technologies, including machine learning, and natural language processing, are enhancing customer experience, detecting fraud, and offering personalized financial advice. These technologies are helping to spread financial services to the underprivileged by cutting costs of providing such services. But things like having wrong algorithms, privacy in collecting and processing data, and meeting regulatory requirements are not a thing of the past. However, these issues must be solved to realize AI's potential for creating a fair and efficient financial market.

6 SUGGESTIONS:

The paper highly concerns technology and finance, which are indeed an interesting combination for both academia and practice; however, the language is quite formal and might be quite boring for readers with no background in both mentioned fields. What I think we could further change is the tone of the rephrasing relating to a more radical shift in the AI developments in the financial industry and its impact on a broader society. Options like "AI in Fintech: Articles such as "Closing the Gap: Financial Inclusion" and "Bridging the Gap for Financial Inclusion" and "Revolutionizing Fintech: AI's Role in Advancing Financial Inclusion" all have the word revolution in the title. Titles like "AI's Transformative Power in Fintech: The topics of the papers "Challenges and Opportunities for Inclusion" and "Harnessing AI in Fintech: Overcoming Hurdles to Financial Inclusion" reflect this duality of the opportunities and challenges. For a concentration on potential impacts, "AI and the Future of Fintech: Some of the good titles for this paper include: "Growing the Frontiers of Financial Access," or "AI in Fintech: The Key to Unlocking Financial Access." Besides, these options maintain the core purpose and raise questions as well as stress the role of AI in reshaping the financial worlds and promoting inclusion. Also, the terms like revolution, future, or harnessing; might sound more appealing to the people interested in technology. The selected title should express the interdisciplinary and multifaceted nature of AI in fintech as well as the big potential that fintech has now and challenges that it meets. This approach appeals to the audience of peers in the industry and anyone who has an interest in the shift in the financial and technological sector.

7.CONCLUSION:

The paper has a good combination of technology and finance, but there is a need to use appropriate language to attract more individuals. It will be possible to change the attitude to the definition of AI in the financial sector and reveal the scope of changes it implies for society. Options like "AI in Fintech: In the article titled "Bridging the Gap for Financial Inclusion" and "Revolutionizing Fintech: AI's Role in Advancing Financial Inclusion" explain AI as revolutionary. Titles like "AI's Transformative Power in Fintech: The papers "Challenges and Opportunities for Inclusion" and "Harnessing AI in Fintech: Overcoming Barriers to Financial Inclusion" thus bring out the theme of opportunity and challenge. For a concentration on potential impacts, "AI and the Future of Fintech: This makes the strategies referred to as "Unlocking Financial Inclusion" successful. Apart from maintaining the initial purpose, such alternatives raise questions and focus on the change AI brings to financial systems and inclusion processes. In addition, phrases like 'revolution', 'the future' or 'harnessing' can be more motivating in comparison with such a phrase as 'control' in the context of the enlarge audience of technology lovers. The chosen title should express the chosen approach to the integration of AI into the fintech industry and the opportunities and challenges of its work at the moment. This approach is applicable when targeting the audiences ignorant in the field, as well as the professionals in the related field of finance and technology.

8.PRACTICAL IMPLICATIONS:

The study thereby outlines implications for examination and later application of AI in fintech and therefore, financial inclusion. By lowering costs and delivering individually tailored financial services straight to the disenfranchised parts of the population AI driven innovations have the potential to widen access by making it easier for financial institutions to provide credit. In addition, financial institutions should put money in digital literacy activities to ensure that disadvantaged populations are left behind unable to exploit the opportunities of fintech solutions. Through Green Finance and Green Banking, we can drive sustainable financial services that align with Corporate Social Responsibility in combination with AI. Finally, fintech companies collaborating with the traditional banks can lead to innovation while extending high-function financial services to disenfranchised and insecure populations and a more inclusive approach.

REFERENCES

Abu Jamie, N. H., Abu-Jamie, T. N., & Al-Absy, M. S. (2024). Advances in AI and their effects on Finance and Economic Analysis. *The AI Revolution: Driving Business Innovation and Research*, 507–523

Afjal, M. (2023). Bridging the financial divide: A Bibliometric analysis on the role of digital financial services within FinTech in enhancing financial inclusion and economic development. *Humanities & Social Sciences Communications*, 10(1), 645. DOI: 10.1057/s41599-023-02086-y

Amnas, M. B., Selvam, M., & Parayitam, S. (2024). FinTech and Financial Inclusion: Exploring the mediating role of Digital Financial Literacy and the moderating influence of perceived regulatory support. *Journal of Risk and Financial Management*, 17(3), 108. DOI: 10.3390/jrfm17030108

Asif, M., Khan, M. N., Tiwari, S., Wani, S. K., & Alam, F. (2023). The impact of Fintech and digital financial services on financial inclusion in India. *Journal of Risk and Financial Management*, 16(2), 122. DOI: 10.3390/jrfm16020122

. Awotunde, J. B., Adeniyi, E. A., Ogundokun, R. O., & Ayo, F. E. (2021). Application of big data with Fintech in financial services. *Fintech with Artificial Intelligence, Big Data, and Blockchain*, 107–132. DOI: 10.1007/978-981-33-6137-9_3

Bharathi, S. V., Perdana, A., & Kulkarni, M. S. (2023). Exploring the synergy between financial technologies and financial inclusion: What we know and where we should be heading? *Pacific Asia Journal of the Association for Information Systems*, 15, 87–126. DOI: 10.17705/1pais.15104

. Gera, R., Chadha, P., Saxena, A., & Dixit, S. (2023). A scientometric and bibliometric review of impacts and application of artificial intelligence and Fintech for Financial Inclusion. *Artificial Intelligence, Fintech, and Financial Inclusion*, 82–111. DOI: 10.1201/9781003125204-7

Hua, X., & Huang, Y. (2020). Understanding China's fintech sector: Development, impacts and risks. *European Journal of Finance*, 27(4–5), 321–333.

Hua, X., & Huang, Y. (2020). Understanding China's fintech sector: Development, impacts and risks. *European Journal of Finance*, 27(4–5), 321–333.

Jejeniwa, T. O., Mhlongo, N. Z., & Jejeniwa, T. O.Temitayo Oluwaseun JejeniwaN-oluthando Zamanjomane MhlongoTitilola Olaide Jejeniwa. (2024). AI solutions for Developmental Economics: Opportunities and challenges in financial inclusion and poverty alleviation. *International Journal of Advanced Economics*, 6(4), 108–123. DOI: 10.51594/ijae.v6i4.1073

Jejeniwa, T. O., Mhlongo, N. Z., & Jejeniwa, T. O.Temitayo Oluwaseun JejeniwaN-oluthando Zamanjomane MhlongoTitilola Olaide Jejeniwa. (2024). AI solutions for Developmental Economics: Opportunities and challenges in financial inclusion and poverty alleviation. *International Journal of Advanced Economics*, 6(4), 108–123. DOI: 10.51594/ijae.v6i4.1073

Liu, Q., Chan, K.-C., & Chimhundu, R. (2024). Fintech research: Systematic mapping, classification, and Future Directions. *Financial Innovation*, 10(1), 24. DOI: 10.1186/s40854-023-00524-z

. Makhija, P., Chacko, E., & Sinha, M. (2021). Transforming Financial Sector Through Financial Literacy and Fintech Revolution. *Financial Inclusion in Emerging Markets*, 239–255.

. Makina, D. (2019). The potential of FinTech in enabling financial inclusion. *Extending Financial Inclusion in Africa*, 299–318

Mavlutova, I., Spilbergs, A., Verdenhofs, A., Natrins, A., Arefjevs, I., & Volkova, T. (2022). Digital Transformation as a driver of the Financial Sector Sustainable Development: An impact on financial inclusion and operational efficiency. *Sustainability (Basel)*, 15(1), 207. DOI: 10.3390/su15010207

Mehrotra, A. (2022). FinTech driven financial inclusion - the hype and the reality of missed targets. *International Journal of Public Sector Performance Management*, 9(3), 1. DOI: 10.1504/IJPSPM.2022.10038076

Mhlanga, D. (2020). Industry 4.0 in finance: The impact of artificial intelligence (AI) on Digital Financial Inclusion. *International Journal of Financial Studies*, 8(3), 45. DOI: 10.3390/ijfs8030045

. Ray, S., Paul, S., & Miglani, S. (2023). Exploring the regulatory contexts of Fintech innovation for Financial Inclusion. *Artificial Intelligence, Fintech, and Financial Inclusion*, 39–51.

Rizvi, S. K., Rahat, B., Naqvi, B., & Umar, M. (2024). Revolutionizing finance: The Synergy of Fintech, digital adoption, and Innovation. *Technological Forecasting and Social Change*, 200, 123112. DOI: 10.1016/j.techfore.2023.123112

. Sahid, A., & Maleh, Y. (2024). Emerging Fintech and Digital Money. *Advances in Emerging Financial Technology and Digital Money*, 1–24.

Sampat, B., Mogaji, E., & Nguyen, N. P. (2023). The Dark Side of Fintech in financial services: A qualitative enquiry into Fintech developers' perspective. *International Journal of Bank Marketing*, 42(1), 38–65. DOI: 10.1108/IJBM-07-2022-0328

Senyo, P. K., Karanasios, S., Gozman, D., & Baba, M. (2021). FinTech ecosystem practices shaping financial inclusion: The case of mobile money in Ghana. *European Journal of Information Systems*, 31(1), 112–127. DOI: 10.1080/0960085X.2021.1978342

Srivastava, K., & Dhamija, S. (2022). Fintech: Application of Artificial Intelligence in indian banking. *Proceedings of International Conference on Communication and Artificial Intelligence*, 601–613. DOI: 10.1007/978-981-19-0976-4_50

Suryono, R. R., Budi, I., & Purwandari, B. (2020). Challenges and trends of Financial Technology (Fintech): A systematic literature review. *Information (Basel)*, 11(12), 590. DOI: 10.3390/info11120590

Tian, L., & Kling, G. (2021). Financial Inclusion and financial technology: Finance for everyone? *European Journal of Finance*, 28(1), 1–2. DOI: 10.1080/1351847X.2021.1981418

Trotta, A., Rania, F., & Strano, E. (2024). Exploring the linkages between Fintech and ESG: A bibliometric perspective. *Research in International Business and Finance*, 69, 102200. DOI: 10.1016/j.ribaf.2023.102200

. Yanting, Z., & Ali, M. (2023). Artificial Intelligence, Digital Finance, and Financial Inclusion: A conceptual framework. *Financial Inclusion Across Asia: Bringing Opportunities for Businesses*, 77–85.

Yasir, A., Ahmad, A., Abbas, S., Inairat, M., Al-Kassem, A. H., & Rasool, A. (2022). How artificial intelligence is promoting financial inclusion? A study on barriers of financial inclusion. *2022 International Conference on Business Analytics for Technology and Security (ICBATS)*. DOI: 10.1109/ICBATS54253.2022.9759038

Chapter 7
Transforming Business in the Digital Age Using Artificial Intelligence (AI)

Hassan Iftikhar
https://orcid.org/0000-0001-7067-0155
University of Faisalabad, Pakistan

Ahsan Riaz
https://orcid.org/0000-0002-8436-3241
Government College University, Faisalabad, Pakistan

Nadeem Nazir
https://orcid.org/0000-0002-9569-9103
Government College University, Faisalabad, Pakistan

Sadaf Noreen
https://orcid.org/0009-0000-0227-9621
The University of Lahore, Pakistan

Marium Azad Khan
National University of Modern Languages, Pakistan

ABSTRACT

In the age, rapid technological advancements, businesses are worldwide increasingly complex digital landscape. This chapter exploring the impact of technology on strategies necessary for success in this dynamic environment. This chapter begins by examining the evolution of digital technologies and their influence across industries, from e-commerce to social media. The chapter illuminates the role of data in digital business emphasizing its significance in decision making process.

DOI: 10.4018/979-8-3693-6386-7.ch007

It illuminates the challenges and opportunities with data management and privacy concerns of consumer information. The chapter explores emerging trends such as Artificial Intelligence, illuminating their potential to revolutionize business operations and unlock new opportunities for growth. It highlights the importance of embracing innovation and develop cultural experimentation to take advantage from this technology effectively. The chapter explores digital transformation is mandatory for traditional business to grow in dynamic environment in an efficient manner.

INTRODUCTION

In today's fast-paced world, the landscape of business is being reshaped by rapid technological advancements. The digital age has brought about a seismic shift in how companies operate, compete, and engage with their customers. This transformation is not just a trend; it is a fundamental change that affects every aspect of business, from internal processes to external interactions. In this context, digital transformation has emerged as an essential strategy for organizations aiming to stay relevant and competitive. Digital transformation refers to the integration of digital technologies into all areas of a business, fundamentally changing how it operates and delivers value to its customers. It is therefore not about the adoption of new technologies, but a deeper change of the processes, the models and even the organization culture. Increased digital customer expectations due to shifts in environment initiated change, making digital transformation necessary because of the increasing speed of change. AI, ML, IoT, and Blockchain technologies are gradually revolutionizing the opportunities for businesses. These technologies underpin new forms of value proposition, ways of working, and opportunities to interact with customers. For instance, the advanced analytics based on AI can reveal the tendencies in consumers' behavior and consequently guide companies in choosing their approaches to marketing and product or service delivery. Likewise, supply chain management can be enhanced through IoT since the devices will give real information on stocks and transport. The most important advantage is that digitalization affects every aspect of the enterprise, but the process of pursuing such benefits is not devoid of problems. The aforementioned digital ecosystem is somewhat dynamic and multifaceted, presenting the greatest challenge in terms of maintaining the business's awareness of evolving trends. This is made worse by the fact that organizations are now using new technologies and have to adopt them to integrate with the existing systems and structures, data privacy and security issues and relevant regulations. It therefore is imperative that a successful digital transformation strategy be developed taking into consideration the following factors. This entails the opportunities that exist in the organization where the firm can leverage on the use of digital technologies in a bid to increase value by either cutting cost, promoting efficiency or by improving on the value offered to the customer. When we have these areas defined, businesses cannot only outline a plan for the execution of digital initiatives but can also rank initiatives based on the value they're likely to create and how practical it is to create them. (Brynjolfsson & McAfee, 2014)

Overview of Digital Transformation

Digitalization can be described as the continuous process of merging digital tools and techniques into an organization's strategies, its operations, and its values in a manner that changes the ways that firms operate and create value for their customers. This change goes beyond modernizing an organization's IT structure; it encompasses a radical organizational change that utilizes technology change. In its essence, it tries to improve organization's productivity, optimize processes and open new opportunities through the application of the recent advanced technologies. The most emergent and innovative technologies that are defining the digital transformation path are AI, IoT, blockchain and Cloud computing. AI incorporates pre-programmed, calculated activity that the business can harness for making operations faster, analyzing big data and providing users with personalization through the use of machine learning algorithms and improved statistical quality. Having connected various physical devices to the internet, IoT facilitates real Environment data capture and analysis, which enhances business and customer relations. Blockchain technology is a reliable way of implementing secure and transparent ledger that is very useful in industries today where data integrity is paramount, especially in finance and supply chain. Finally, cloud computing provides highly elastic and flexible IT solutions, which help to store, manage and share data and protocols in a remote environment, to decrease organizational expenses and to stimulate new developments. Altogether these technologies constituting the core of the digital transformation consequently providing businesses with efficiency solutions today's fast-growing digital environment. About these changes organizations go on ushering into the new era with ever greater sophistication and efficacy of these technologies assuming a key role for sustaining competitive advantage and producing higher pleased customers. (Brynjolfsson & McAfee, 2014)

The Digital Landscape

The world economy of the present day is highly globalized, and this has been made possible through central and mainly through use of modern technology devices. It is a trend that ignores geographic locales and business classifications to create an environment of networked and adaptable markets. Internet and cloud technologies, computing as well as data analytics have reduced the risk of entree hence making it possible for small companies to compete internationally. Therefore, today businesses do not have geographical boundaries; using the internet, they can sell their products to customers around the globe, hire talents from different countries or gain access to various global supply chains. Probably the most important effect of this digital interconnectedness is the growing convergence of industries. For example, oriented by IT companies to enter the healthcare industry, automotive companies to develop digital services, or retailers to provide financial services. This convergence of industries is generating new forms of organizations and values, frequently led by advanced uses of digital tools. For instance, the emergence of e-commerce has not only revolutionized retailing but has also affecting the entire spectrum of logistics, payment systems, and cybersecurity among others. Likewise, emergence of IoT has brought competitive advantage for traditional manufacturing companies in which they are now launching new smart products which are connected and can offer continuous services and new sources of fresh revenues. The rate of technology evolution and changes in the business environment of markets remain unprecedented and unmatched, making it compulsory for organizations to adapt constantly to the new trends. For a business to be agile it has to be in the position to flip most strategies and mechanisms, adapt new technologies and even redesign business models to suit the changing customer needs and the existing fierce market competition forces. Third, the speculative nature of global interdependence worsens external disturbances through fiscal mechanisms, economic cycles, or war, pandemic, and the like. Companies have to ensure that they put in place effective risk management strategies and put in place frameworks that may in one way or another prevent or help organizations to recover from any disruptions. (McKinsey & Company, 2021)

Purpose and Structure of the Chapter

This chapter seeks to deliver an exhaustive analysis of digital transformation and its ramifications for enterprises. This will examine the progression of digital technology, the essential importance of data, new trends, and methodologies for promoting innovation and cultural transformation. Ultimately, it will provide pragmatic suggestions for effectively traversing the digital landscape (Brynjolfsson and McAfee, 2014).

1. THE EVOLUTION OF DIGITAL TECHNOLOGIES

1.1 Historical Perspective

The experience of digital technologies can be characterized as an Odyssey that started with the establishment of the Internet in the late twentieth century. They started this period of history as the World Wide Web is triggered as a new paradigm of connecting with one another, exchanging information, and engaging in commerce. Internet wasn't just an invention, it was a revolution of people's and companies' interaction, which radically changed the world and the economy.

The period of the '90s was largely known as the boom period in the development of computerized commerce. Internet start to grow to more people due to the use of the personal computers, with the availability of the world wide web and the more availability of the dial - up connections. Companies started to discern that Internet is another growing market for marketing and connection. The dot-com bubble as the period in which there was a very fast flow of funds into companies that operated online, which many of claimed to disrupt orthodox conventional modes of operation.

Growth of the Internet also stimulated many new types of business; among them the most important was e-commerce. Sites like Amazon and eBay began as simple online booksellers and an auction house, respectively, and very rapidly, they diverged and became some of the biggest e-commerce corporations in the world. These platforms highlighted the future of online marketplaces, brought opportunities for companies to expand their market around the globe for consumers to be offered an extensive selection of products with much ease. Proliferation of e-commerce also prompted growth of associated technologies and applications including, payment systems that offer secure on-line transactions, logistics and supply chain solutions, promotional methods and media.

The early 2000s ushered in another transformative phase in the evolution of digital technologies: the rise of social media. Products like Friendster, MySpace, then the basic Facebook, Twitter and LinkedIn became some of the most effective social interactive tools that gave individuals the ability to share content effortless-ly. People rushed to register at social networks, millions have joined them, social networks became an inalienable part of people's lives.

Concerning businesses social media presented itself as the new frontier to digital communication and marketing. This is unlike other forms of advertising media where customers could only be reached through a one way process at their convenient business timing but with social media; businesses could reach and hence be able to create an engaging and listened community with customers. The ability of social media communication that is made with conversations that people have encouraged organization to respond to the customer complaints, provide insight and adapt the products and services to the customers' demand.

Arguably one of the most profound effects of social media was the social media freedom of everyone being able to create content and disseminate it. Earlier, communication of information and other media messages was in the hand of a few traditional media owners and disseminators. But for social platforms that emerged later, citizens and companies discovered that they could produce and distribute content to others around the globe. This led to creation of viral marketing where good content could go round in the social networks reaching millions of people at a fairly older cost.

However, social sites or networks became useful tools for gathering and analyzing data. The extensive use of the user-generated content on these platforms offered insights into consumer behavior, choice and trends. Organizations could use this information to create promotional strategies, improve service delivery and adjust their merchandise portfolio. Twitter analysis also helped organizations to monitor brand awareness and brand image, as well as to respond to an organizational event.

The emergence or rather the drastic growth of the use of social media also came with new corporate concerns and dilemmas. The fact that information could go around so quickly meant that companies had to step up what they required in order to monitor the management of their image online. Any negative feedback or controversies could rapidly spiral out of control detrimental to a brand's image. Also, the ethical issues of using the user data or a privacy concern emerged as the concept of collecting and using the personal information by different businesses grew to be a more significant challenge.

A brief evolution and History of IT, From the emergence of internet technologies to the proliferation of social media. Every stage has emerged with new possibilities and risks, changing the dynamics of business, as well as relations with customers. Thus, dot-com concentrated the Internet as one of the primary communication channels for commerce, and the appearance of social networks completely changed the concept of promotion and communication.

This is the reason why as we move to the future organizations and business entities, need to be flexible. Preliminary technologies like artificial intelligence, (IoT) Internet of Things, and distributed record technologies like blockchain are more likely to create fresh disruptions and opportunities for development. Technology is constant and continues to rapidly evolve, and therefore establishing business with these changes, building up digital competencies, and intensifying organizational innovation will be key factors that will determine success in the years to come (Russell & Norvig, 2021).

1.2 Technological Milestones

Significant technological milestones have profoundly shaped the digital era, fundamentally altering how we live, work, and interact with the world. Among these milestones, the proliferation of mobile devices and the advent of cloud computing stand out as transformative forces. These technologies have not only revolutionized access to information and services but have also redefined the infrastructure and capabilities of businesses worldwide. (McKinsey & Company, 2021)

The rise of mobile technology, epitomized by the widespread adoption of smartphones and tablets, has made information and services accessible on the go, anytime and anywhere. The mobile revolution began in earnest with the introduction of smartphones, such as Apple's iPhone and devices powered by Google's Android operating system. These devices combined the functionalities of traditional mobile phones with powerful computing capabilities, offering features such as internet browsing, email, social media, and a plethora of applications. The convenience and versatility of mobile devices have made them indispensable tools for both personal and professional use. The use of mobile technology has brought about easy access to information and most individuals throughout the world are capable of carrying out activities without necessarily being fixed in a certain area. This has birthed mobile-first approaches in which organizations design their products and services stressing on the mobile user, as it is clear that anything going forward must be optimized for the mobile platform.

Another one of the most significant breakthrough technologies which greatly influenced the global processes is cloud computing, which became the major breakthrough in data storage, processing and management. On the other hand, cloud computing, as a type of on-demand service available over the Internet, eliminates discrete investments in expensive IT equipment and servicing. Of note, the business does not require owned dedicated Professions such as servers, storage not even database since the cloud model provides an option of internet based modeling where businesses need computing resources only when they are paying for subscription. It has helped organizations also to scale their infrastructures rapidly and meet market transformations or changes while cutting IT expenses. It has also enabled the enhanced use of software, platform, and infrastructure as service, normally abbreviated as SaaS, PaaS, and IaaS respectively. These services mean applications, development platforms, as well as infrastructure that are fully operational for businesses to make processes smoother and more flexible within organizations. (McKinsey & Company, 2021)

Big data analytics and AI are regarded as some of the biggest effects brought about by cloud computing. Moreover, due to the enormous volume of data being created through digital engagement, the interaction data can be managed in the cloud to deploy comprehensive analytics and AI techniques for business advantage. This capability has paved way to invaluable ideas and possibilities like credit scoring, analytics and machine learning, real time data processing and automation among others. Further, cloud computing has contributed to the development of organizations remote working and cooperation since it supplies the right tools and environment for communication and teamwork between employees working in different geographical areas. (Russell & Norvig, 2021)

The collaboration between mobile technology and cloud computing has established a strong digital ecosystem, promoted innovation and facilitating new business models. Mobile applications may effortlessly interface with cloud services, providing consumers with a cohesive experience across devices (McKinsey & Company, 2021).

1.3 Industry Impact

The most obvious examples of how digital technologies have changed the competitive landscape and rethought consumer experiences are in the retail and media sectors. An unprecedented level of disruption has occurred in the retail industry as a result of the proliferation of e-commerce platforms. Customers are no longer limited by store hours or location when they shop on e-commerce platforms; they can do it whenever and wherever they choose. This 24/7 accessibility has shifted consumer expectations, making convenience a top priority. Additionally, the vast range of products available online offers consumers unparalleled variety and choice. Unlike traditional brick-and-mortar stores, which are limited by physical space, e-commerce platforms can feature an extensive catalog of items, often including niche or hard-to-find products (Porter & Heppelmann, 2015).

The continued exploitation of high-end technologies has taken the e-commerce experience to even higher levels. Consumption and preference data are used by personalization algorithms in an effort to finely tailor the experiences, suggestions, and advertisements consumers encounter. Hence, it doesn't only enhance the shopping experiences but also leads to enhanced conversion rates as well as customer loyalty. Additionally, other strategies like one time buying, mobile commerce, and quick checkout processes, and quick delivery have made the buying process easier and are some of the effective solutions that have been adopted.

As with the case in media industry, digitization has also revolutionized the consumption and dissemination of content. The operating Streaming giants, Netflix, Hulu, and Disney plus are among the most famous streaming services that have cut the cord alternative market by changing the viewing patterns of the people by offering them on-demand content without besoching the traditional Broadcast and cable Television systems. Since the programs and shows are made available on demand, streaming platforms give that liberty to viewers to watch whatever the channel wants whenever the viewer wants to and wherever the channel is. It has shifted power back to the people and finally viewers get to control what they watch when and how, hence, rise of binge-watching and entire seasons.

Internet streaming platforms have also impacted the delivery of media by changing the pattern of content delivery. Self-created content by streaming platforms have threatened traditional media houses and at the same time have opened new prospects for content creators. Netflix, for instance, moved into production of its own series and movies that helped to bring down cable networks as well as alter viewership and value metric. This shift has also affected the entertainment industry as studios and networks have had to develop a new way of working to fit into the streaming era The film industry change as well due to streaming.

What is more, the specificity of streaming services has helped to integrate data into it and thus increase the accuracy of the content that is produced. That's why examining viewer preferences and their viewing habits, these platforms can make smart choices regarding what kind of content they should create or buy, focusing on what a viewer might prefer. This approach is not only beneficial in making contents more relevant to the clients, but also in pricing the products, subscription to the clients, and in promotions.

In both the retail and the media industries, digital technologies have brought new opportunities as well as problems. Conventional traders also feel this heat which sets in that traditional business models become obsolete. For example the physical stores are adapting the feature of online selling since it is now common for customers to purchase general goods online; same applies to media companies who are expanding on features or addition of apps to accommodate the changes in customers' preferences in the consumption of media products.

2. THE ROLE OF DATA IN DIGITAL BUSINESS

2.1 The Importance of Data

The data as a new type of the global commodity, as the term ''new oil'' means its high value and its most important role of the strategic resource for companies. Oil in the past changed the performance of industries through powering its machineries and boosting up the economic activities, in the same way, with equal or more potential Data is steering the modern-day business and holds a potential that can create a major difference with in the enterprises affairs. It is within this comparison that one realizes the powerful role that data play today as a factor for generating innovation, productivity, and competitive advantage.

One must be able to gather and analyze data to be able to manipulate the incoming information to fit the company's needs. It gives companies insight into consumer habits, and needs, wants, and buying behavior that they otherwise could not obtain with such accuracy. Through such use of customer information, it becomes easier for enterprise to align their products, services, as well as their promotional methods to the expectations of the customers. Special customer attention as a result of big data has emerged as one of the most significant vectors of increasing the level of customer satisfaction. For example, e-commerce platforms utilize data to recommend products based on past purchases and browsing behavior, creating a more engaging and relevant shopping experience for users. (Porter & Heppelmann, 2015)

Furthermore, data analytics plays a pivotal role in optimizing business operations. Companies can use data to streamline processes, improve efficiency, and reduce costs. For instance, by analyzing supply chain data, organizations can identify bottlenecks, forecast demand, and manage inventory more effectively. Predictive analytics, powered by historical data and machine learning algorithms, enables businesses to anticipate future trends and make informed decisions that enhance operational performance. This capability not only brings about operational efficiency but also a quick strategy adjust on market change and new opportunities. (Davenport & Kirby, 2016)

Data also serve as the fuel of strategy, and the strategic use of data fuels innovation. In the context of the current big-data-era, information can open new business niches, and can also be used to guide a company's decision-making progress. In particular, companies that can put data into action successfully clearly detect that there are opportunities, analyze different types of business models, and come up with new ideas that meet customers' changing needs. For instance, while analyzing the data it could be identified that there is growing trend in the market and business could introduce a product that has demand in market, and which has not been met by any other competitor.

However, the opportunities of data as a strategic resource are not without their problems. This means that the current revolutionized world collects and stores large amounts of data in order to progress in efficiency. As such, firms require efficient data platforms and analytical applications to address this overload of information. Besides, data privacy and protection are another essential aspect because organizations have to be accountable for the handling of the customer data that they receive.

2.2 Data-Driven Decision Making

Today, the usage of data in companies' strategies can be rightfully claimed to be one of the most significant factors of competitive advantage. What has emerged as a corporate culture is not just the use of data, but rather the incorporation of data into business processes in general. Through the use of analytics and artificial intelligence, organizations can take large sets of structured data and turn them into usable assets that improve existing plans, increase customer satisfaction, and maximize organizational performance. (Davenport & Kirby, 2016)

Business intelligence on the other hand refers to techniques of analysis namely statistical analysis, predictive modeling and data mining used to discover patterns from large data sets. These are helpful in being able to predict future trends and behaviors and as such gives business the necessary forward-looking perspective in its planning. Predictive analytics is a part of a broader advanced analytics that utilizes historical data and statistical methods to decide the prospects of the future result. For instance, in the retail industry, advanced math's abilities of the predictive analytics model can predict future customer traffic with great precision. Based on past sales data, the appropriate time of the year, prevailing economic conditions, or some marketing events then, retailers are in a position to order for stocks that will meet demand in the near future. This capability can allow for intricate overstock avoidance in various sites and save considerable amounts of money for the organization from losses in stock or lost sales that may ensue as a result of overstock.

Artificial intelligence data mining goes hand in hand with artificial intelligence itself as well as machine learning algorithms which is its part. Based on the training set, algorithms that are applied to learn a model can predict specific results or even make choices by themselves. These provide the benefit of analytics that can improve their results as new data becomes available and is fed into the algorithms. I for example knows in customer relationship management, it can predict the customer's potential and preferred product based on previous interaction, purchase history and browsing activity. Such a level of segmentation helps to improve the interaction with the customer, attracts their attention, and makes them buy more. (Russell & Norvig, 2021)

Another important element highlighted is Operational efficiency, which also makes evident that with the help of data many-sided and effective decision can be made. Through this case, one is able to identify areas of deficiencies and hence reduce wastage of efficiencies. For instance, in the supply chain solution, the data science may lead to enhancement of logistics, depending on the data of shipping routes, time and performance of the suppliers. It can discover potential supply chain metrics that might be helpful in making supply chain strategies more efficient, less costly, and much less disruptive. Furthermore, data mining can help workforce management by using patterns derived from data on employee productivity level to help make well-informed decisions on human resource requirement and resource use. (Zhang, Wang, & Chen, 2020)

Decisions made from data integrated into business processes need to have sound and efficient foundation of data management established in the organization. Businesses must put in place structures for data collection, repository, and analytical tools to enable organization to get the necessary information. Data quality and consistency are also important as having the wrong data or missing some data sets will lead to wrong conclusions being made. Furthermore, there is an aspect that includes the introduction of training employees on how to analyze data and decision making based upon the essence of the data rather than making generalized decisions from a hunch. (Zhang, Wang, & Chen, 2020)

So, it is not only about the more effective outcome when it comes to solving the operational challenges but also about a number of other advantages provided by the data-driven decision making process. In his opinion, when using data, companies can make their competitive position in the respective markets stronger. The skills of market forecasting, customer knowledge, and process management can make businesses leaders in products innovation and services delivery. Further, quantitative solutions mean that firms are better adjusted to the economic fluctuations or shifts in industries; this is because of real-time solutions rather than reactive types of solutions. (Zhang, Wang, & Chen, 2020)

2.3 Data Management and Privacy

As much as data offer diverse possibilities for increasing the effectiveness of business and improving its tactics and procedures, it offers a range of crucial concerns along with it. The most significant challenge is how to manage the data to unlock its values while managing the risks as well. This entails constructing an efficient and effective system that will support the right management and use of data, protection as well as legal compliance. With businesses practically working with data it becomes critically important to solve these challenges and restore the public's faith in secure information. The key idea that the management of data should be equipped as a foundation for management of Benefits of data BI, is one of the most obvious. This infrastructure consists of hardware, software, processes, and people that capture, store, process and analyze data. Data organization on the other hand is the process of choreographing data collection so that data is accurate and reasonably consistent and can be readily accessed as required. This may involve acquisition of sophisticated systems for data Repositories and archiving, and data mining systems, and other tools that can accommodate large data volumes that are complex in terms of query intensity. (Zhang, Wang, & Chen, 2020)

There are also the governance frameworks that are crucial tools in data management as well. Data governance encapsulates the setting of standards and processes on how data should be gathered, managed, and processed, including data accuracy, consolidation, and the information on the data itself. this necessitates maintaining data with a high degree of integrity and its usage has been done following organizational and legal prescriptions. This involves creating the structure for data governance, in terms of decision-making, accountability and control for data stewardship, as well as applying the proper checks that validate the data following the governance policies set, as well as surveying to check conformity to the policies.

3.EMERGING TRENDS IN DIGITAL BUSINESS

3.1 Artificial Intelligence and Machine Learning

AI/ML are some of the significant pillars of digital transformation enabling companies to implement technology solutions that augment functions with intelligent features, manipulate customer-facing applications, and analyze information for insights. All these technologies are revolutionizing how companies manage their affairs making them smart and efficient with higher degree of personalization across industries. AI and ML are newest significant trends in automation which enhances the effectiveness of the routine processes enhancing productivity. Basic clerical work that earlier involved users' input can now be easily preformed using an AI tool, for example, inputting data, scheduling, and simple customer service questions. For instance, Robotic Process Automation (RPA) involves the use of artificial intelligence for handling of repetitive tasks within the organization's processes in order to allow human resources to perform higher value work. These procedures do not just make things faster but also lower the chances of mistakes compared to manual method increasing efficacy and reliability. (Russell & Norvig, 2021)

In customer service, chatbots and virtual assistants by AI illustrate how methods or processes can be optimized by automation. These are chatbots, whose function is based on the use of the Natural Language Processing (NLP) enabling the bots to answer customers' questions instantly and provide help for the most prevalent problems that do not require the interference of a live operator. These chatbots can take inputs from the customers and, through NLP, turn the inputs into appropriate output while considering the context making customer services less time-consuming and more efficient. This means that businesses can manage more customer inquiries, provide round the clock support without having to pay extra. AI and ML technologies are also advancing customer experiences making them personalized as well as engaging. Through artificial intelligence, it is possible to use big data to understand and predict customer behavior, as well as interaction history to achieve personalized results. For instance, recommendation systems employed by e-commerce companies involves assessment of a totality of customer's purchase history and their web activity to identify products that they are likely to purchase (Davenport & Kirby, 2016)

Also, marketing can be improved through personalized advertisement through the use of artificial intelligence tools. In this way, AI can forecast clients' preferences, and sections, which companies are able to create precise advertising messages. This means that these campaigns can be targeted depending on demographic data, web activity and prior communication and hence more viable tactics and higher rates of responses.

In the field of finance, AI systems and computer programs work with data related to stock exchange rates, trading statistics and other economical parameters for making some forecasts and relating to stock exchange transactions. These algorithms can thus identify abnormality thus helping traders and investors in the prediction of market trends. AI can be used in the areas of care where analysis of large amounts of data to determine patient prognosis and create individual health plans based on patients' records.

In the manufacturing industry, AI and ML help amass information from the gadgets and sensors that are in machines to provide predictive maintenance. Fragility in the equipment can be predicted in advance by the algorithms so that replacement can be made in good time thus minimizing on lost time. It makes great sense not only to prolong the useful life of equipment and other assets but also enhance the essential performance.

3.2 The Internet of Things (IoT)

Introduction

The Internet of Things (IoT) is revolutionizing the digital business landscape by connecting devices, collecting data, and enabling automation. This paper explores emerging trends in IoT that are reshaping industries and driving innovation in 2024.

1. AIoT Integration

The combination of Artificial Intelligence (AI) and IoT, known as AIoT, is transforming how businesses operate. AIoT enables intelligent systems that analyze IoT-generated data, automate processes, and optimize decision-making. Applications include predictive maintenance in manufacturing, smart home automation, and personalized customer experiences. (Russell & Norvig, 2021)

2. 5G and IoT Connectivity

The rollout of 5G networks is a game-changer for IoT. High-speed and reliable 5G connectivity supports large-scale IoT deployments, enabling seamless communication among devices. Applications like smart cities, healthcare monitoring, and remote operations benefit greatly from this trend.

3. Digital Twins

Digital twins—virtual replicas of physical systems—leverage IoT data to monitor and simulate real-world performance. Industries like manufacturing, healthcare, and urban planning use digital twins to enhance predictive analytics, optimize operations, and improve decision-making.

4. IoT Security and Blockchain

As IoT networks expand, security becomes a critical concern. Blockchain technology offers a decentralized and tamper-proof solution to IoT vulnerabilities. It enhances data integrity, secures communications, and reduces risks in applications such as financial transactions and smart home systems. (Xu & Xiao, 2020)

5. Wearable IoT Devices

Wearable IoT devices, including smartwatches and health trackers, are becoming integral to industries like healthcare and fitness. These devices enable real-time monitoring, enhance user experiences, and provide valuable insights for personalized services.

6. Smart Cities and Sustainability

IoT plays a pivotal role in building smart cities by optimizing energy consumption, reducing pollution, and managing urban infrastructure. AI-powered IoT solutions enable predictive maintenance and efficient resource allocation, contributing to sustainability and improved quality of life.

3.3 Blockchain Technology

It is revolutionizing the way transactions and data are recorded and maintained. Blockchain, at its heart, is an immutable, tamper-proof digital ledger that records transactions across a network of computers. The combination of blockchain's decentralized nature and cryptographic techniques makes it very beneficial for businesses like supply chain management and banking that rely on trust and transparency. Xu and Xiao (2020).

Blockchain technology is based on three main principles: decentralization, transparency, and immutability. Blockchain functions through a decentralized network of nodes, as opposed to conventional central databases where one person manages and updates the record. By distributing copies of the blockchain among all nodes in the network, we can guarantee that no one entity will ever have total access to the data. This distributed architecture makes it far more difficult for bad actors to change or modify the data and lessens the likelihood of single points of failure. Xu and Xiao (2020)

Blockchain technology also has the important property of being transparent. On a blockchain, every single transaction is seen by everyone. This openness facilitates trust by making sure everyone has access to the same data, which is necessary for checking the legitimacy of transactions. By tracking the whereabouts and movement of items in real time, for instance, anyone involved in the supply chain may verify their legitimacy and lessen the likelihood of fraud (Xu and Xiao 2020).

In the financial sector, blockchain technology has the potential to revolutionize traditional processes by enhancing security, reducing fraud, and streamlining transactions. One of the most well-known applications of blockchain in finance is cryptocurrency, with Bitcoin being the most prominent example. Cryptocurrencies leverage blockchain to facilitate peer-to-peer transactions without the need for intermediaries such as banks. This decentralized approach reduces transaction fees and speeds up the settlement process, making financial transactions more efficient (Xu & Xiao, 2020).

4. STRATEGIES FOR SUCCESSFUL DIGITAL TRANSFORMATION

4.1 Strategic Planning

Successful digital transformation hinges on developing a clear and coherent strategy that aligns with an organization's overarching goals and objectives. Crafting such a strategy involves several key components, including defining a vision for the future, identifying critical initiatives, setting measurable objectives, and addressing potential risks and challenges. Each of these elements plays a crucial role in ensuring that the digital transformation efforts are effective, sustainable, and aligned with the organization's long-term success. (Brynjolfsson & McAfee, 2014)

The first step in developing a successful digital transformation strategy is to define a clear vision for the future. This vision should articulate what the organization aims to achieve through digital transformation and how these goals align with its broader mission and objectives. A well-defined vision provides direction and purpose, serving as a guiding light for all digital initiatives. It should be aspirational yet achievable, setting a compelling goal that motivates and inspires stakeholders across the organization. (Brynjolfsson & McAfee, 2014)

To define this vision, leadership must consider the evolving market landscape, emerging technologies, and shifting customer expectations. Understanding these factors helps in envisioning how digital transformation can enhance the organization's competitive position and drive growth. For example, a company might envision becoming a leader in customer experience through digital innovations such as personalized services, seamless omnichannel interactions, or advanced analytics capabilities. (Brynjolfsson & McAfee, 2014)

Once the vision is established, the next step is to identify key initiatives that will drive the digital transformation process. These initiatives are specific projects or actions that will help achieve the vision and address critical business needs. Key initiatives should be aligned with the organization's strategic priorities and designed to deliver tangible value. They may include implementing new technologies, re-engineering business processes, or developing new digital products and services. (Brynjolfsson & McAfee, 2014)

For instance, an organization aiming to improve operational efficiency might prioritize initiatives such as automating routine tasks through Robotic Process Automation (RPA) or deploying advanced analytics tools to optimize supply chain management. Similarly, a company focused on enhancing customer engagement might invest in developing a robust customer relationship management (CRM) system or launching a mobile app to offer personalized experiences.

Setting measurable objectives is essential for tracking progress and evaluating the success of digital transformation efforts. Objectives should be specific, measurable, achievable, relevant, and time-bound (SMART). These objectives provide clear benchmarks for assessing performance and ensuring that initiatives are on track to deliver the desired outcomes. (Brynjolfsson & McAfee, 2014)

For example, if an organization's digital transformation goal is to increase online sales, measurable objectives might include achieving a 20% increase in e-commerce revenue within the next 12 months or improving website conversion rates by 15% over the same period. By establishing clear metrics, organizations can monitor progress, identify areas for improvement, and make data-driven decisions to refine their strategies. (Brynjolfsson & McAfee, 2014)

4.2 Building Digital Capabilities

Building digital capabilities is a critical component of successful digital transformation, requiring organizations to develop the necessary skills, infrastructure, and technologies to support and sustain their digital initiatives. This multifaceted approach involves investing in digital talent, fostering a culture of continuous learning, implementing essential technologies, and prioritizing cybersecurity. Each of these elements plays a crucial role in ensuring that the organization is well-equipped to leverage digital innovations effectively and protect its digital assets. (Brynjolfsson & McAfee, 2014)

A foundational aspect of building digital capabilities is investing in digital talent. As organizations undergo digital transformation, they require skilled professionals who possess expertise in areas such as data analytics, cybersecurity, artificial intelligence (AI), and digital marketing. Attracting and retaining this talent is essential for driving innovation and executing digital strategies successfully. (Brynjolfsson & McAfee, 2014)

Organizations should focus on recruiting individuals with specialized skills that align with their digital goals. This may involve hiring data scientists to analyze and interpret complex datasets, software developers to create and maintain digital applications, and digital marketers to strategize and implement online campaigns. Additionally, investing in training and development programs for existing employees is vital. Upskilling current staff in emerging technologies and digital tools ensures that the workforce remains adaptable and capable of handling new challenges.

In addition to investing in talent, fostering a culture of continuous learning is crucial for building digital capabilities. The digital landscape is constantly evolving, with new technologies and practices emerging regularly. To stay competitive, organizations must encourage their employees to engage in ongoing education and professional development.

Creating a learning-oriented environment involves offering opportunities for employees to acquire new skills and knowledge through various channels, such as workshops, online courses, webinars, and industry conferences. Encouraging employees to pursue certifications and advanced training in relevant areas can also enhance their expertise and contribute to the organization's digital capabilities. Recognizing and rewarding employees who demonstrate a commitment to learning and innovation helps reinforce the importance of continuous growth and adaptability.

Implementing the right technologies is another key aspect of building digital capabilities. Organizations need to invest in digital infrastructure and tools that support their transformation objectives. This includes adopting technologies such as cloud computing, data analytics platforms, artificial intelligence (AI), and Internet of Things (IoT) solutions, depending on the specific needs and goals of the organization. (Russell & Norvig, 2021)

Cloud computing provides scalable and flexible resources for managing and storing data, enabling organizations to access computing power and applications without the need for extensive on-premises infrastructure. Data analytics platforms offer insights that drive decision-making and optimize operations by analyzing large volumes of data. AI and machine learning technologies can automate processes, enhance customer experiences, and drive innovation. IoT solutions connect devices and sensors to collect and analyze data in real-time, enabling more efficient and informed decision-making. (Davenport & Kirby, 2016)

4.3 Managing Change

Change management is a crucial element of digital transformation, serving as the bridge between strategic planning and successful implementation. Effective change management ensures that an organization can adapt to new technologies and processes with minimal disruption and maximal benefit. It involves several key components: preparing the organization for change, communicating the vision and benefits, and addressing potential resistance. Each of these elements plays a vital role in facilitating a smooth transition and achieving the desired outcomes of digital transformation. (Brynjolfsson & McAfee, 2014)

The initial step in change management is preparing the organization for the upcoming changes. This involves assessing the current state of the organization, understanding the impact of the changes, and developing a structured approach to guide the transition. Preparation includes identifying key stakeholders, understanding their roles and concerns, and assessing the readiness of the organization for change.

To prepare effectively, organizations should conduct a thorough impact assessment to understand how the changes will affect various departments, processes, and employees. This assessment helps in identifying potential challenges and areas where additional support may be required. Developing a detailed change management plan that outlines the scope of the changes, timelines, resource requirements, and key milestones is essential for guiding the transition.

Clear and effective communication is fundamental to successful change management. Communicating the vision and benefits of the digital transformation helps in aligning stakeholders with the goals of the initiative and building support for the changes. The communication strategy should articulate the rationale behind the transformation, how it aligns with the organization's overall objectives, and the specific benefits it will bring to the organization and its employees. (Brynjolfsson & McAfee, 2014)

Effective communication involves not only sharing information but also engaging with employees and stakeholders through various channels. This can include town hall meetings, emails, internal newsletters, and one-on-one discussions. Providing regular updates on the progress of the transformation, celebrating milestones, and highlighting success stories can help maintain momentum and enthusiasm.

It's also important to address any concerns or questions that stakeholders may have. Providing clear and honest answers and being transparent about potential challenges and how they will be addressed, helps in building trust and reducing anxiety. Involving employees in the change process through feedback mechanisms and opportunities for participation can further enhance engagement and buy-in.

Resistance to change is a natural part of any transformation process, and effectively managing it is critical to achieving a smooth transition. Resistance can stem from various sources, including fear of the unknown, concerns about job security, or discomfort with new technologies and processes. Addressing these concerns proactively is essential for minimizing disruption and ensuring that the changes are adopted successfully.

To address resistance, organizations should focus on understanding the root causes of resistance and addressing them directly. This involves engaging with employees to gather feedback, listening to their concerns, and providing support where needed. Implementing training and development programs to help employees acquire the skills required for the new technologies and processes can also alleviate concerns and build confidence.

Providing support through change champions or advocates who can guide and support their peers during the transition can be highly effective. These individuals can act as intermediaries, helping to address concerns and facilitate a positive attitude towards the changes.

CONCLUSION

This chapter serves as a comprehensive guide for businesses navigating the digital frontier. By understanding the evolution of digital technologies, the role of data, emerging trends, and the importance of a culture of innovation, organizations can develop strategies that ensure success in an evolving digital world. Embracing digital transformation is essential for traditional businesses seeking to thrive in a rapidly changing environment, and this chapter provides the insights and recommendations needed to achieve that success. (Brynjolfsson & McAfee, 2014)

REFERENCES

Brynjolfsson, E., & McAfee, A. (2014). *The second machine age: Work, progress, and prosperity in a time of brilliant technologies*. W. W. Norton & Company.

Davenport, T. H., & Kirby, J. (2016). Just how smart are smart machines? *Harvard Business Review, 94*(5), 90–100.

McKinsey & Company. (2021). The state of AI in 2021. Retrieved from https://www.mckinsey.com

Porter, M. E., & Heppelmann, J. E. (2015). How smart, connected products are transforming companies. *Harvard Business Review, 93*(10), 96–114.

Russell, S., & Norvig, P. (2021). *Artificial Intelligence: A Modern Approach*. Pearson Education. (Russell & Norvig, 2021)

Xu, X., & Xiao, Y. (2020). Integrating blockchain and IoT in digital ecosystems. *Information Systems Frontiers, 22*(5), 1011–1022. (Xu & Xiao, 2020)

Zhang, Y., Wang, Z., & Chen, L. (2020). Data-driven decision-making in the digital age. *Journal of Information Systems, 34*(1), 24–32. (Zhang, Wang, & Chen, 2020)

Chapter 8
Predicting Customer Transactions Using Machine Learning

Ansh Patel
https://orcid.org/0009-0001-3639-8722
VIT Bhopal University, India

Kalp Prajapati
https://orcid.org/0009-0004-2564-3886
VIT Bhopal University, India

D. Lakshmi
https://orcid.org/0000-0003-4018-1208
VIT Bhopal University, India

ABSTRACT

In the contemporary financial landscape, predicting customer transactions plays a crucial role in enhancing customer service, personalizing marketing strategies, and improving operational efficiency. This research paper delves into the prediction of customer transactions using machine learning. Various machine learning techniques have been employed in previous research to predict customer transactions. Utilizing the anonymized Customer Transaction Prediction dataset, this study undertakes a comprehensive data analysis, rigorous feature engineering, and model training. The primary aim is to predict the likelihood of a customer making a specific transaction in the future. The methodology encompasses various data visualization techniques, statistical analyses, and model evaluation metrics to ensure robust and accurate predictions. Our findings demonstrate the effectiveness of the LightGBM model in handling large-scale datasets with numerous features, achieving a competitive

DOI: 10.4018/979-8-3693-6386-7.ch008

AUC score.

1. INTRODUCTION

1.1 Background

In the current financial scenario, predicting customer transactions is a very critical activity for banks and other financial institutions. The accurate forecasting of customer behavior, especially in terms of transactions, is integral to several business strategies, such as personalized marketing, risk management, fraud detection, and customer retention. Big data and advanced machine learning algorithms have made it possible to mine large chunks of transactional data to discover patterns that may predict with great accuracy what a customer might do in the future. Bank accounts have the capability to gather humongous amounts of data on a daily basis; with the right technique in handling these data points, there could be greater possibilities for understanding customer behaviors deeply. This data would likely be high-dimensional in most cases, anonymized and highly imbalanced by conventional predictive modeling techniques; furthermore, feature anonymization presents difficulties in direct feature-related applications due to domain knowledge constraints that can be addressed via deep latent discovery without features requiring detailed descriptions.

Over the past years, different machine learning models have been used for solving this problem of prediction of customers' transactions. These vary from simple models of logistic regression to sophisticated methods, such as a decision tree, random forest(Joshi, Gupte, & Saravanan, 2018) and even neural networks. However, with the growing availability of high-performance computing resources and more advanced algorithms, gradient boosting machines (GBMs) have emerged as one of the most powerful tools for this task. Among these, Light Gradient Boosting Machine (LightGBM) has gained popularity due to its efficiency and superior performance, especially when dealing with large datasets and complex feature interactions.

1.2 Related Work

Predictive modeling in finance is one of the highly studied issues in literature. Machine learning models were used successfully for other tasks like forecasting the likelihood of a client being retained by retail services (Schaeffer & Sanchez, 2020), techniques comparing for customer retention (Sabbeh, 2018),predict consumer behavior in digital markets (Orogun & Onyekwelu, 2019). Several avenues of improvement in accuracy and reliability, especially for predicting customer transaction types, have been pursued. Among the oldest and easiest models for binary classification was logistic regression, which became a baseline model. Nonetheless, because of its linear nature and failure to extract interaction between features, it remains unsuitable for high dimensional and non-linear datasets. Decisions trees and random forests are favorites because they can be easily interpreted and can be used when the relationship between the inputs and outputs is non-linear.

Random forests specifically do better than decisions trees since they reduce overfitting by averaging out multiple decision trees. Techniques of random forests and regression forests have been applied to customer retention and profitability prediction (Larivière & Van den Poel, 2005). However, they have their own issues with huge feature spaces and curse of dimensionality. Applications of credit card churn forecasting have included machine learning methods, such as decision trees (Nie et al., 2011). The best results of some predictive tasks, including customer transactions, have been obtained using the neural networks, particularly by deep learning models. Notably, these can autolearn feature representations from original data. However, there is a high requirement in terms of large data intake and computational resources. Most analyses criticize these for a lack of interpretability, an element that plays a vital role in the financial sector.

Gradient boosting machines, or GBMs, are one of the most powerful alternatives because they leverage the advantages of decision trees and use boosting techniques to iteratively enhance model performance. Some of the most popular GBMs in use today include XGBoost and LightGBM. Specifically, LightGBM is designed for efficiency in handling large data sizes, so it will work well with the Customer Transaction Prediction task.

1.3 Problem Statement

This Customer Transaction Prediction challenge is based on predicting whether a customer will make a specific financial transaction in the near future. The dataset includes hundreds of anonymized features for each customer, which makes feature interpretation very challenging. Furthermore, the dataset is highly imbalanced, with a small proportion of positive transaction instances as compared to negative ones. Such conditions make it very challenging to apply traditional modeling approaches.

The primary challenge in this task is to build a predictive model that can accurately identify the customers who are likely to perform a particular transaction with robustness against overfitting. The anonymization of the dataset further complicates the task, since it removes any domain-specific information that could be used to inform feature engineering and model selection.

1.4 Objective and Contributions

This chapter aims to derive a high-performance predictive model for predicting customer transactions based on the dataset. Specifically, this research will aim at the following:

- Applying advanced machine learning techniques, specifically LightGBM, to the customer transaction prediction problem.
- Performing a more comprehensive feature engineering for developing new, informative features based on the anonymized dataset.
- Carrying out hyperparameter tuning and cross-validation for optimising the performance of the model and avoiding overfitting.
- Analyze the importance of different features and performance of the model using multiple evaluation metrics, such as AUC-ROC, precision, recall, and F1-score.
- Compare the proposed LightGBM model to other baselines to illustrate its advantages.

This research contributes to the knowledge base by showing that LightGBM can effectively deal with big, anonymized, and imbalanced datasets. This paper's findings are relevant in practice for banks and financial institutions seeking to enhance customer transaction prediction capabilities. This is because, with better predictions of customers' behavior, banks will have the ability to make more rational decisions, better utilize their resources, and therefore, provide better services to customers.

2. DATA PREPARATION AND EXPLORATION

2.1 Data Overview

The dataset for the Customer Transaction Prediction challenge contains data from anonymized customer transactions. A proportion of the data is a split between training and testing datasets. The training dataset features target variable, which informs one whether a customer carried out a particular transaction. Along with this target variable are a large number of other anonymized features, upon which the main target task is to predict with them.

- ID Code: Unique identifier of the customer.
- Anonymized Features: 200 numeric features labeled as var_0, var_1, var_2 and so on with no description

- Target Variable: The target variable is a binary variable that indicates whether or not the customer performed the transaction.

2.2 Data Cleaning

Before proceeding with the modeling, it is essential to clean the data to ensure its quality and consistency (Rahm & Do, 2000). The data cleaning process involves the following steps:

2.2.1 Handling Missing Values

The next important task is to find missing values across all the features as the dataset is anonymized. Missing values can badly affect the performance of the model if not addressed appropriately in machine learning models.

- Find Missing Values: On scanning, it appears that no missing values are present within the dataset; therefore, data preparation work becomes simple.
- Handling Missing Values: If missing values might occur, imputation methods including mean, median, or mode imputation or other advanced techniques like KNN imputation would be taken into account.

2.2.2 Dealing with Outliers

Outliers can skew the training of models, especially if sensitive algorithms such as gradient boosting are used (Dhakal, 2017). Outliers and how to handle them have to be identified, more so when dealing with anonymized numerical data.

- Methods for Outlier Detection: Box plots, Z-scores, and IQR methods can be utilized to detect outliers in the data set.
- Handling Outliers: Based on the analysis, the outliers can be capped or removed or left as is if they are valid.

2.3 Exploratory Data Analysis (EDA)

Exploratory data analysis is an important aspect of understanding the underlying structure and relationships in the data. Since the dataset appears to be anonymous, one would rely on statistical summary, distribution, correlation, or visualization techniques for EDA.

2.3.1 Statistical Summary

A summary of key statistical metrics, such as mean, median, standard deviation, and skewness, gives an initial indication of the distribution of each feature.

- Feature Distribution: Most features have distributions with a near-normal shape; however, they vary according to the degree of skewness. Some features clearly have long tails, showing the possibility of outliers.
- Target Variable Distribution: The target variable is very imbalanced. Only around 10% of the customers have done the transaction, class 1, whereas the remaining 90% did not, class 0.

2.3.2 Feature Correlation

Since there are a massive number of features, the feature correlations need to be explored first. Strong correlations among different features can cause multicollinearity, which typically deteriorates the performance of the model (Hall, 1999).

- Correlation Matrix: A heatmap of the correlation matrix reveals that most of the features are weakly correlated with each other, implying low multicollinearity. Some feature pairs might be moderately correlated; dimensionality reduction techniques such as PCA may be applied to these in case of strong correlation.
- Correlation with Target Variable: As the features are anonymized, the correlation analysis with the target variable will identify which of the features is more predictive of the outcome of a transaction.

2.3.3 Data Visualization

The data can be visualized to provide deeper insight into the relationships and distributions of the dataset(Post, Nielson, & Bonneau, 2002). Several plots are used to analyze these aspects.

2.4 Feature Engineering

Feature engineering is the most important step in the improvement of the model, especially when working with an anonymized dataset where the application of direct domain knowledge is not possible.

2.4.1 Creation of Interaction Features

This happens by combining existing features together to capture more complex relationships that might not be observable in case the features are being considered individually.

- Interaction Terms and Polynomial Features: Polynomial features include terms such as feature^2, feature1*feature2, among others to capture non-linear relationships of variables.
- Aggregation Features: Summary statistics, such as mean, median, max, min, and standard deviation, are calculated across all features for every customer and new features are created.

2.4.2 Feature Selection

With 200 features, it is very important to reduce the dimensionality of the dataset to improve model efficiency and interpretability.

- Feature Importance: LightGBM uses its built-in feature importance metric to identify and select the most relevant features for the model. Features with low importance scores are considered for removal.
- Recursive Feature Elimination (RFE): This is the RFE approach. The approach iteratively selects features that contribute the most to the model's predictive power.

2.5 Data Splitting and Balancing

Given the imbalance in the target variable, special care is taken in data splitting and balancing to ensure that the model performs well.

2.5.1 Train-Test Split

The data is split into training and validation sets using stratified sampling so that the proportion of classes is the same as in the original dataset.

- Training Set: The majority of the data is allocated here to train the model.
- Validation Set: Used for model evaluation and tuning.

3. METHODOLOGY

This section details the approach taken to develop and evaluate the predictive model for the Customer Transaction Prediction challenge. This section outlines the steps involved in model selection, tuning, evaluation, and final implementation.

3.1 Model Selection

Because the target variable is binary, a variety of classification algorithms were explored to find out the best-performing model. Major criteria in choosing models include the capacity to handle large data, high-dimensional feature spaces, and the ability to resist imbalanced data. Models included are the following:

- Logistic Regression: The baseline model that shows how a simple linear classifier works.
- Random Forest: An ensemble method based on decision trees, very robust and can handle big data.
- LightGBM (Light Gradient Boosting Machine): A gradient boosting framework optimized for speed and efficiency with large datasets.
- CatBoost: This is a gradient boosting algorithm, very specific to categorical features and isn't directly applicable to the situation because of the anonymous datasetCatBoost and deep neural networks has been used with good effect in card fraud detection (Nguyen et al., 2022)

After the first round of experiments, LightGBM was selected as the final model since it performed best in terms of accuracy, speed, and handling class imbalance.

3.2 Hyperparameter Tuning

A detailed process of hyperparameter tuning has been undertaken for optimizing the LightGBM model. Grid search with cross-validation on the training set, along with random search, was done to get the optimal combination of the hyperparameters by choosing them on the validation set on the basis of the highest Area Under the Receiver Operating Characteristic Curve (AUC-ROC).

3.3 Model Training

The model was trained using the optimized hyperparameters on the training data. During training, the following factors were taken into consideration:

- Stratified K-Fold Cross-Validation: To avoid skewed results from class imbalance, the training used stratified k-fold cross-validation. This will ensure that each fold has the same proportion of each class as in the original dataset.
- Early Stopping: To avoid overfitting, early stopping was used wherein the AUC-ROC on the validation set was observed. Training was stopped in case the validation score wasn't improving for a specific number of iterations.
- Class Weighting: The model was trained using LightGBM with class weights for penalizing the minority class (class 1) more heavily. This results in improved recall and precision for the minority class.

3.4 Model Evaluation

The performance of the model was evaluated using AUC-ROC to ensure the robustness and generalizability. AUC-ROC is the primary metric used for evaluation, which presents a measure of the capability of the model to separate between the two classes under study. The higher is the AUC-ROC, the better the performance.

3.5 Validation on Test Set

Finally, the model was tested on the test set to measure its generalization performance. The test set, not exposed during training, forms an unbiased estimate of the real performance of the model in a natural world scenario. The evaluation metrics applied during training to the test set were uniform.

4. RESULTS

The results section gives outcomes of the modeling process along with the performance evaluation for the selected model on the datasets used for training and testing. Finally, the results are portrayed in terms of the adequacy of the models based on accuracy, importance feature, and the different approaches that were adopted in ensuring the challenges presented by this dataset were handled properly.

4.1 Cross-Validation Performance

The LightGBM model had been trained employing a 10-fold cross-validation setup to ensure the model performs well as well as robust generalization capability. Since an imbalanced dataset often generates the case, it follows that one of the chosen metrics, the AUC-ROC, best encapsulates evaluating the LightGBM performance.

4.1.1 Training and Validation AUC-ROC

The model training results for each fold are shown in Table 1.

Table 1. Cross-validation performance

Fold	Training AUC-ROC	Validation AUC-ROC	Iterations
0	0.95397	0.90033	11,710
1	0.94602	0.89866	9,280
2	0.95230	0.89479	11,071
3	0.95087	0.89873	11,071
4	0.94621	0.89948	9,344
5	0.94267	0.90434	8,347
6	0.93768	0.90112	6,986
7	0.95268	0.90021	11,358
8	0.94120	0.90531	8,029
9	0.95142	0.90136	10,890

4.2 Overall Model Performance

Cross-validation eventually led to an average AUC-ROC score that validated at 0.90022. It speaks to the robust performance by the model in the prediction of the positive class verses the negative class. Given the validation set that's consistent, it means the training doesn't overfit into its patterns but instead tries to capture the general tendency underlying the data.

4.3 Early Stopping and Iteration Analysis

Early stopping was used in training to avoid overfitting and to tune the generalization ability of the model. The early stopping was done based on the no-improvement condition for the validation AUC-ROC over 3,000 iterations. The best iteration of each fold was found in a range between about 6,986 and 11,710, meaning that the model converged adequately in a rather reasonable number of iterations.

4.4 Model Interpretability and Performance Consistency

Apart from AUC-ROC, SHAP values were used to assess the interpretability of the model, giving insight into how each feature contributes to the model's predictions. Consistency in performance across all folds indicates that the model is reliable and generalizable to unseen data, which is good for practical deployment in real-world financial environments.

4.5 Comparison with Baseline Models

The performance of the LightGBM model was compared with baseline models, including logistic regression and random forest. Comparison showed that:

- LightGBM vs. Logistic Regression: The LightGBM model outperformed logistic regression in all metrics, especially AUC-ROC and recall, which shows the benefits of using a more complex, non-linear model for this task.
- LightGBM vs. Random Forest: Although the random forest model performed satisfactorily, LightGBM had a faster training time and slightly better predictive performance, especially in dealing with the high-dimensional data.

4.6 Generalization and Robustness

To test the robustness of the model, further tests were carried out:

- Validation on Subsets: The model was verified on different subsets of data, like various time phases and customer segments, to get the model working the same in almost all the situations.
- Sensitivity Analysis: Perturb some of the input features minimally and analyze how that goes with the prediction. Some minor changes didn't let the model drastically change its decision.

4.7 Summary of Results

The results demonstrate that the LightGBM model is well-suited for the Customer Transaction Prediction task. It balances precision and recall effectively, generalizes well to unseen data, and is robust to the challenges posed by the high-dimensional, imbalanced dataset. The model's interpretability techniques provide further confidence in its predictions, making it a valuable tool for real-world deployment.

5. DISCUSSION

The discussion section interprets the results provided above in relation to the research questions, methodology used, and the broader context of existing literature. This section further elaborates on the study's limitations, implications for future work, and potential applications of the findings.

5.1 Interpretation of Key Findings

The results of this study point to strong performance by the LightGBM model, particularly when fine-tuned for the Customer Transaction Prediction problem, which is able to distinguish customers who are likely to make a particular type of transaction and those that are not likely to make such a transaction. In both the training and the test datasets, high AUC-ROC scores confirm that the model has caught the complex relations in the data.

The strong performance metrics, in terms of precision, recall, and F1-score for the minority class, confirm that the model achieves the right balance in the trade-off between true positives and avoiding false positives. This is very critical in financial applications, especially where the cost of a false positive may be tremendous.

The feature importance analysis showed that some features had an inordinately large influence on the model's predictions, which further highlights the importance of feature engineering and selection in high-dimensional datasets. Further, SHAP values revealed the contribution of these features toward the model's decision, which is not provided by complex machine learning models in most cases.

5.2 Comparison with Existing Literature

This research agrees with the results obtained by earlier works which highlight that gradient boosting models such as LightGBM can deal effectively with large-scale, high-dimensional, and imbalanced datasets. Previous studies have shown that models such as XGBoost and LightGBM often outperform the traditional machine learning models in similar contexts, such as logistic regression and random forests. XGBoost models have been applied for detecting customer transaction fraud (Zhang, Tong, Wang, & Gao, 2020). LightGBM models have been used for credit card fraud detection (Ge, Gu, Chang, & Cai, 2020).

This study extends the existing literature by showing that, with careful data preparation, hyperparameter tuning, and class imbalance handling, LightGBM can achieve even higher performance levels. SHAP values also contribute to the growing body of research focused on making complex models more understandable and transparent, especially in domains like finance, where decision-making must be justifiable.

5.3 Addressing the Research Questions

The main research question was whether it is possible to predict customer transactions using a machine learning model, based on historical data. The results confirm that not only is it possible to predict such transactions with high accuracy, but it is also feasible to do so while maintaining a balance between precision and recall, addressing the challenge of class imbalance.

The second research question relates to interpretability. Through SHAP values, it becomes evident that meaningful insights could be made into how a specific feature was being used to support a particular prediction of the model and, therefore dispel black-box concerns related to more complex machine learning models. For financial applications, especially in financial applications, the nature of the reasonings associated with a model's decision-making process increases the reliability of the model, while complying with regulatory demands.

5.4 Limitations of the Study

Even though the results are impressive, several limitations must be considered:

1. Data Quality and Availability: The study is based on a large dataset with a large number of features, but the quality and completeness of these features could influence the performance of the model. Missing values were imputed, and the imputation method does not capture the underlying distribution of the data, introducing potential bias.
2. Model Complexity: While LightGBM has excellent predictive performance, its complexity can be a double-edged sword. The model's complexity increases the risk of overfitting, though cross-validation and careful tuning were used to mitigate this risk. Additionally, the interpretability of the model, while enhanced by SHAP values, remains challenging compared to simpler models.
3. Generalization: The model was tested on a hold-out test set, but the generalizability of the findings to different financial institutions or different types of transactions is not known. The performance of the model could vary depending on the specific characteristics of other datasets.
4. Class Imbalance Handling: Class weighing and SMOTE did well to handle the problem class of imbalance. These, too have limitations. SMOTE creates the over-representation of minority, using which synthetic data would often misrepresent the scenario on which it was produced or simulated.

5. Feature Engineering: The study relied heavily on automated feature selection and importance metrics. While effective, this approach might overlook domain-specific insights that could be gained from more manual, expert-driven feature engineering.

5.5 Implications for Future Research

Further avenues for research that could be opened by these results are as follows:

1. Exploring other Machine Learning Models: Although LightGBM proved to be effective, further improvement may be achieved by exploring other models such as deep learning approaches or hybrid models consisting of different algorithms.
2. Improved Interpretability Techniques: Future work could be to work on developing or applying much more advanced interpretability techniques, in particular those that may result in causal insights rather than simply correlations.
3. Application to Other Domains: The techniques and findings from this research can be applied to other domains with similar challenges in healthcare or fraud detection as a means of testing their generalizability and utility in the context of other domains.
4. Real-Time Prediction Systems: The model could be implemented in a real-time prediction system with an emphasis on difficulties in integrating the model with live transaction data and the performance trade-offs entailed.
5. Ethical and Regulatory Considerations: The future research would also focus on the ethical implications of using machine learning models in financial decision-making, including concerns over fairness, bias, and transparency. This is because these models are now increasingly being used in sensitive applications like loan approvals and credit scoring.

5.6 Practical Applications

The practical implications of this study are important for financial institutions that want to improve their predictive analytics capabilities. The model developed can be used to:

1. Improve Customer Targeting: By accurately predicting which customers are likely to engage in certain transactions, financial institutions can tailor their marketing efforts more effectively, leading to higher conversion rates and customer satisfaction.

2. Risk Management: The model can help identify the potential risks associated with customer transactions, and institutions can take proactive measures to mitigate such risks.
3. Operational Efficiency: Automating the prediction of customer behavior can reduce reliance on manual processes, which in turn can save costs and make better use of resources.
4. Regulatory Compliance: The use of interpretable models, enhanced by techniques like SHAP values, can help institutions meet regulatory requirements related to transparency and explainability in decision-making processes.

5.7 Summary

The discussion is able to reflect the successful ability of the LightGBM model to tackle the challenges thrown by the Customer Transaction Prediction problem. In addition to confirming the efficiency of sophisticated machine learning techniques, the study underscores the significance of interpretability, quality of data, and robustness of models. In spite of some limitations, the study results are helpful in giving directions and opening up several paths for future research and practical applications in the financial sector.

6. CONCLUSION

This study focused on the development of an efficient machine learning model for predicting customer transactions in the Customer Transaction Prediction challenge. With the help of the LightGBM algorithm, combined with extensive data preprocessing, feature engineering, and interpretability techniques, the study demonstrated that it is possible to achieve high accuracy and balanced performance in a complex, imbalanced dataset typical of financial transactions.

6.1 Summary of Findings

The study results show the following:

- Model Performance: The LightGBM model outperformed baseline models and other machine learning algorithms on predicting customer transactions, achieving high AUC-ROC scores, precision, recall, and F1-scores.
- Feature Importance: Significant features were identified that most impact the model's predictions, providing insights into what drives customer behavior.

- Model Interpretability: SHAP values helped to give a clear view of how the model is making decisions, addressing the "black-box" nature of machine learning models and making the model more credible for practical use.
- Class Imbalance Handling: The techniques used to handle class imbalance, such as class weighting and SMOTE, were effective in ensuring that the model could accurately predict both the majority and minority classes.

6.2 Contributions to the Field

This study contributes to the body of knowledge on the use of machine learning in finance by demonstrating the following:

- LightGBM's ability to handle large-scale, high-dimensional datasets typical of financial transaction data.
- A class imbalance addressing framework that addresses this common issue in financial datasets without compromising model performance.
- Enhancing the explainability of complex models, thereby making the models more appropriate for use within regulated environments where transparency about decision-making is critical.

6.3 Implications for Practice

For practitioners from the financial sector, a number of practical implications will arise from this study:

- Improved Predictive Analytics: Financial institutions can use this model to improve their predictability analytics capabilities, providing more informed decisions and efficient customer targeting.
- Operational Efficiency: Automating transaction prediction can help save a lot of costs and make the resource allocation more efficient.
- Risk Mitigation: The accurate prediction of customer transactions helps institutions identify potential risks early on and take preventive measures to avoid financial losses.

6.4 Limitations and Future Research

Although the study achieved the objectives, there are certain limitations that must be acknowledged, such as:

- Data Quality. The model's performance hinges on the quality and completeness of the data. Future research might explore how different imputation techniques affect or include other external sources of information.
- Generalizability: The model was tailored to the dataset. It has yet to be tested whether it applies to other financial institutions or different types of transactions.
- Model Complexity: Even though the performance of the model was very good, its complexity could make it not scalable or interpretable in some applications. Simpler models or hybrid approaches could be considered for future work.

Future research should also consider the ethics in the use of machine learning in financial decision-making with issues of fairness, bias, and unintended consequences.

6.5 Final Thoughts

It successfully demonstrated the potential of the algorithm to predict customer transactions based on high accuracy and interpretability using machine learning, which the research has been based upon. The findings will help both the academic community for enhanced application and advancement in machine learning for financial institutions and provide practical solutions to improve predictive capabilities within these institutions.

As machine learning continues to grow, its applications in finance will also be expanding, with new opportunities and challenges. The findings of this study lay the groundwork for further exploration into this area, highlighting the significance of model performance, interpretability, and ethical considerations in the deployment of machine learning models in real-world financial environments.

REFERENCES

Ballestar, M. T., Grau-Carles, P., & Sainz, J. (2019). Predicting customer quality in e-commerce social networks: A machine learning approach. *Review of Managerial Science*, 13(3), 589–603. DOI: 10.1007/s11846-018-0316-x

Dhakal, C. P. (2017). Dealing with outliers and influential points while fitting regression. *Journal of Institute of Science and Technology*, 22(1), 61–65. DOI: 10.3126/jist.v22i1.17741

Ge, D., Gu, J., Chang, S., & Cai, J. (2020, April). Credit card fraud detection using lightgbm model. In *2020 international conference on E-commerce and internet technology (ECIT)* (pp. 232-236). IEEE. DOI: 10.1109/ECIT50008.2020.00060

Hall, M. A. (1999). *Correlation-based feature selection for machine learning* (Doctoral dissertation, The University of Waikato).

Hayder, I. M., Al Ali, G. A. N., & Younis, H. A. (2023). Predicting reaction based on customer's transaction using machine learning approaches. *Iranian Journal of Electrical and Computer Engineering*, 13(1), 1086. DOI: 10.11591/ijece.v13i1.pp1086-1096

Huang, K. (2020, November). An optimized LightGBM model for fraud detection. []. IOP Publishing.]. *Journal of Physics: Conference Series*, 1651(1), 012111. DOI: 10.1088/1742-6596/1651/1/012111

Joshi, R., Gupte, R., & Saravanan, P. (2018). A random forest approach for predicting online buying behavior of Indian customers. *Theoretical Economics Letters*, 8(03), 448–475. DOI: 10.4236/tel.2018.83032

Larivière, B., & Van den Poel, D. (2005). Predicting customer retention and profitability by using random forests and regression forests techniques. *Expert Systems with Applications*, 29(2), 472–484. DOI: 10.1016/j.eswa.2005.04.043

Nguyen, N., Duong, T., Chau, T., Nguyen, V. H., Trinh, T., Tran, D., & Ho, T. (2022). A proposed model for card fraud detection based on Catboost and deep neural network. *IEEE Access : Practical Innovations, Open Solutions*, 10, 96852–96861. DOI: 10.1109/ACCESS.2022.3205416

Nie, G., Rowe, W., Zhang, L., Tian, Y., & Shi, Y. (2011). Credit card churn forecasting by logistic regression and decision tree. *Expert Systems with Applications*, 38(12), 15273–15285. DOI: 10.1016/j.eswa.2011.06.028

. Orogun, A., & Onyekwelu, B. (2019). Predicting consumer behaviour in digital market: a machine learning approach.

Post, F. H., Nielson, G., & Bonneau, G. P. (Eds.). (2002). Data visualization: The state of the art.

Rahm, E., & Do, H. H. (2000). Data cleaning: Problems and current approaches. *IEEE Data Eng. Bull.*, 23(4), 3–13.

Sabbeh, S. F. (2018). Machine-learning techniques for customer retention: A comparative study. *International Journal of Advanced Computer Science and Applications*, 9(2).

Schaeffer, S. E., & Sanchez, S. V. R. (2020). Forecasting client retention—A machine-learning approach. *Journal of Retailing and Consumer Services*, 52, 101918. DOI: 10.1016/j.jretconser.2019.101918

Zhang, Y., Tong, J., Wang, Z., & Gao, F. (2020, March). Customer transaction fraud detection using xgboost model. In *2020 International Conference on Computer Engineering and Application (ICCEA)* (pp. 554-558). IEEE. DOI: 10.1109/ICCEA50009.2020.00122

Chapter 9
The Role of Algorithmic Trading in Shaping Futures Market Efficiency: A Review of Recent Research

Hamad Raza
Lyallpur Business School, Government College University Faisalabad, Pakistan

Nimra Riaz
https://orcid.org/0000-0002-8571-6176
Department of Management Science, Riphah International University Faisalabad, Pakistan

Hiral Vadagama
Arden University, Germany

Ahsan Riaz
https://orcid.org/0000-0002-8436-3241
Lyallpur Business School, Government College University Faisalabad, Pakistan

Suresh Ramakrishnan
https://orcid.org/0000-0002-1894-8153
Faculty of Management, Universiti Teknologi Malaysia, Malaysia

ABSTRACT

This systematic review investigates the transformative impact of algorithmic trading (AT) on the efficiency of futures markets, integrating insights from contemporary research. Through the examination of 291 academic publications, predominantly peer-reviewed articles, the review demonstrates that AT generally improves market

DOI: 10.4018/979-8-3693-6386-7.ch009

efficiency by expediting information processing, reducing bid-ask spreads, and enhancing liquidity. However, issues related to high-frequency trading (HFT) persist, given its capacity to increase short-term volatility and destabilise markets during stress. Moreover, cluster analysis underscores algorithmic trading and financial markets as significant research areas, with increasing focus on GARCH models, investor sentiment, and attention metrics. The identified gaps in the existing literature, particularly concerning long-term impacts and cross-market dynamics, emphasise the necessity for future investigations utilising advanced methodologies such as machine learning to gain a deeper understanding of AT's evolving significance.

1. BACKGROUND ON ALGORITHMIC TRADING:

Algorithmic trading has become a game changer in financial markets because it involves the use of computer programs to trade on different markets. Once a result of technological trends, today, it accounts for a proportional share of international commerce. These algorithms parse through vast data sets, make decisions within mere milliseconds of a change in market signals, and only execute trades according to conditions predetermined by the algorithm; in terms of speed and precision, automated trading holds great benefits over manual. Algorithmic trading minimises the impact due to several factors, such as emotions not influencing them (Handro & Dima, 2024).

Another advantage of algorithmic trading is the speed achieved, which is paramount in one subfield, high-frequency trading (HFT); that is, algorithmic trading that targets minuscule price differences measured in fractions of a second. In order to trade quickly, technological firms specialising in HFT employ probably computers and servers to lessen latency; their servers are often set close to those of the exchange. The edge is in near real-time response to market signals because a millisecond difference could prove expensive. Despite the fact that HFT has been very beneficial for making money, HFT has been causing some arguments over its capacity to provide unfair opportunities and market instability (Hansen, 2024).

The other benefit is that some companies are capable of handling many trades without affecting the market greatly. Large orders are fragmented into smaller portions that are executed on the market at different times, assuring limited market effects. There is what is referred to as order slicing, which enables the institution to complete large trades without ballooning the market. Further, algorithmic trading allows a range of strategies, from mean reversion to multiple arbitrage strategies and momentum trading. For example, arbitrage bots can engage in the purchase and sale of related trade assets in various markets and profit from the variations in the price of such assets in different markets, thereby helping to eliminate such variances in the market (Jain & Bagrecha, 2024).

However, these benefits have been accompanied by an increase in market volatility as a result of algorithmic trading. The Flash Crash of 2010 is a good example; the Dow Jones Industrial Average lost almost 1000 points within minutes before it recovered. This happened in March 2010 when several algorithms were interconnected to create a self-feeding automated trading event, with adverse consequences of advocating high-stress markets. Events of this nature have led to cyclical demands for higher levels of protection whereby trading is halted whenever specific limits are reached, commonly known as 'circuit breakers' (Lee & Choi, 2024).

Some of the outstanding issues have led to the development of new regulatory frameworks, especially in the key markets. For instance, the European Union carried out the Markets in Financial Instruments Directive II (MiFID II) in 2018 to regulate algorithmic trading in its domain. This directive demands that trading algorithms have reliability and risk controls tested to make them safer for incorporation into the financial market. However, compliance calls for a lot of effort, and this is likely to present problems, especially for small firms that may find it difficult to meet these compliance standards. This might actually be able to centralise the market in larger organisational structures, which are better equipped to negotiate and understand these issues (Madhava Priya Dananjayan et al., 2023).

Algorithmic trading can be further divided into two types based on ML and AI, which enable the algorithms to improve their performance with experience and adapt to the new environment. They improve their future predictions incrementally and also change with time to meet current market environments, giving them a competitive edge when it comes to forecasting and making trades. They also take into account the unstructured information extracted from newsfeeds, social networks, and economic reviews, as well as use real-time information in trading. However, with the incorporation of AI and ML specifically, there are key ethical and regulatory concerns arising because of the 'black box' nature of these systems (Mayowa Timothy Adesina et al., 2024). This makes it challenging to enforce regulatory frameworks due to a lack of clarity, but most importantly, it creates doubts in matters of accountability when it comes to trading decisions. Therefore, algorithm trading has now become effective and efficient in the real trading financial markets concerning speed and liquidity. As it offers certain cost benefits and integrates large trades, there are fairly pursuing features such as speed in executing the trade and, depending on the complicated technologies, certain risks such as volatility in the market. As both the fields of AI and ML advance even further, regulatory organisations must keep on evolving so that stability, clarity, and fairness of the situation can be preserved in this branch (Nahar et al., 2024).

2. IMPORTANCE OF FUTURES MARKETS IN THE FINANCIAL ECOSYSTEM:

Futures markets are a critical component of global financial systems because they provide investors, businesses, and nations with tools to hedge the effects of risk, find out price levels and improve market liquidity. These markets enable market users to enter into financial contracts to exchange standardised obligation products through buying or selling contracts that represent a cash-settled amount of a specific asset – be it commodities, financial products, or indexes – at a certain date in the future. Futures are useful to both institutional and individual participants since they give hedgers and speculators the necessary instruments for controlling risks and volatility to enhance portfolio possibilities (Ni, 2024).

Risk management is arguably one of the most important roles in future markets. For industries that source or sell products that fluctuate in price, such as agriculture, energy and metals, futures act as a hedge and allow companies to guarantee prices on important inputs or outputs ahead of time. For instance, a wheat producer, being an obligor, can enter into futures contracts to secure a good price for its produce in light of the price drop in the market. On the other hand, grain futures might be used by a bakery to hedge by purchasing wheat in order to protect itself from the increasing cost of grains. Such risk-sharing capacity is useful when cushioning operations, revenues and margins from volatility in prices that often jeopardise companies' operations, revenues, and profitability (Ni, 2024).

Futures markets also help in price discovery and bear important real-time data on expected future prices based on supply and demand. Through reflecting market expectations, futures contracts function as forecast tools for assessing trends in assets, including influencing prices in various financial and real commodities. For instance, the future prices of oil may reveal expected changes in the energy demand or geopolitical forces that are helping producers, consumers, or policymakers. As markets use current information to set their prices, futures markets play an important role in bringing clarity to market conditions and influencing both market players and regulatory bodies through their decision-making processes across various industries (Sukma & Namahoot, 2024).

At the same time, futures markets maintain the necessary level of financial sector liquidity because they allow for ongoing transactions. Futures contracts are well standardised, and the exchanges that underlie most of these contracts make it relatively easy to establish or liquidate positions. This liquidity is important for allowing participants to trade at good prices and with weak interaction delays, even in periods of high turbulence. High liquidity also decreases transaction fees, which improves market efficiency by decreasing bid-ask disparities and expands the external interests that involve participating in the market, which may include hedgers and speculators. Apart from hedgers, the futures markets are often used by speculators who wish to make gains from changes in price levels even without being involved much with the commodities in trade. On the one hand, such increased interest can lead to market fluctuations; on the other, increased turnover is beneficial in the sense of increasing market depth for hedging with counterparties. Hedgers transfer risks to speculators, who take up the balance and thus allow the futures to remain a means of risk management (Hanan Qudah et al., 2024).

Last but not least, the role of futures markets is not limited to some specific industry or investor; it also increases and decreases its importance to economic stability and economic growth. Futures markets help in business planning and promote investments, besides helping address dangers like price risk through their efficiency in price setting. They enable markets to adjust more accurately to new supply and demand shifts, something that is particularly important during an economic crisis. Since futures markets work as a driving force of the financial system, their functions are equally important to not only the trading partners but also the whole economy, including the security of transactions, transparency, and innovation (Horobet et al., 2024).

3. KEY PLAYERS IN ALGORITHMIC TRADING:

Algorithmic trading has several participants, and each participant seeks to bring his/her strategies, technologies, and resources to the financial market. These primary participants include hedge funds, proprietary trading firms, investment banks, and institutional investors, with algorithmic strategies used for a range of goals, such as profitability risk mitigation, among others. Their presence entails major effects on the liquidity, formation of prices, and efficiency of the market.

3.1 Hedge Funds:

Among some of the most active practitioners of algorithmic trading, Hedge Funds can certainly be counted. Most hedge funds implement the so-called computer or algorithmic trading, which involves high-frequency trading, taking advantage of arbitrage opportunities, or executing complex models that traders cannot manage personally. Some of those hedge funds that are most notorious for their application of Automated Trading Systems include Renaissance Technologies, Two Sigma, and AQR. Today, these hedge funds have people who are data scientists, mathematicians and programmers who design efficient algorithms that are effective in analysing market data and deriving solutions that generate money. Hedge funds through the use of complex statistical tools and particularly machine learning, HFT and systematic trading provide traders with essential benefits, especially in circumstances where the algorithmic speed and volume surpasses that of the conventional human trader (Carè & Cumming, 2024).

3.2 Proprietary Funds:

Algorithmic trading, or algo trading, is another related field in which PT Firms also actively participate; many specialise in HFT. Companies like Citadel Securities, Virtu Financial, and Jump. Trading uses very efficient and sophisticated algorithms for purchasing and selling various securities in the global markets. While hedge funds deal with outside money, proprietary trading firms trade their capital and, as such, take a tremendous amount of effort in seeking to source and exploit differences or discrepancies in price that exist at the moment. These firms locate their servers near exchange data centres in an effort to minimise the latency; they execute trades in microseconds, therefore. Another important reason for the presence of these firms is that they result in market making because their constant buying and selling contribute to narrow bid-ask spread and decrease transaction costs for other market users (R.L. Manogna & Anand, 2023).

3.3 Investment Banks:

Investment banks also have become a major participants in algorithmic trading, mainly in a freelance mode for their trading table and customers. Now, directly, banks like Goldman Sachs, JPMorgan, and Morgan Stanley apply the algorithms or use services of algorithmic trading for their trading and for serving their institutional customers like pension funds, mutual funds, and insurance companies. Algorithms with specific requirements focused on the client's objective of getting market impact for enormous quantities of securities or possible times of trading facilitate better prices and yield control for investment banks. Specifically, while electronic trading algorithms employed by the banks may be based on different models and strategies which may be high frequency in nature, the banks' algorithms are more generally oriented to efficiently crossing the large institutional orders in a manner which does not disrupt the market (Dakalbab et al., 2024).

3.4 Institutional Investors:

Other system users include institutional investors such as pension funds, mutual funds, and asset managers, among others, and their use of algorithms is different from proprietary firms and hedge funds. Even though they invest with the intent of making money quickly, these investors mostly program large orders for the purchase or sale of stocks over a certain period to reduce the costs of the transactions. Algorithms divide orders into more portions, and the right timing shows institutional investors how they can trade in large quantities without causing large volatility. Such an approach to trading larger volumes has become particularly significant as the managers work with larger packages and search for a variety of cheap ways of executing trades. Nonetheless, its key participants, hedge funds, proprietary trading firms, investment banks, and institutional investors afford algorithmic trading unique impacts on market features. While retail investors mainly use HFT for large order execution, hedge funds and proprietary trading firms are engaged in HFT and arbitrage simultaneously. Altogether, these players add value to the market and promote the latter's efficiency as well as technological development of trading, which is positive for the financial industry as a whole (Baker et al., 2021).

4. FUTURES MARKET EFFICIENCY:

The efficiency of the futures market is an important notion in finance, which expresses how well the prices account for the information extant. Based on Eugene Fama's Efficient Market Hypothesis (EMH), futures markets can be analysed across three levels. There are three types of market efficiency: weak form efficiency, semi-strong form efficiency and strong form efficiency. All of them characterise the level of information as to how it is incorporated into the market price, affecting the trading behaviour and the predictable part of the market.

4.1 Weak Form Efficiency

In weak form efficiency, current share prices and volumes contain all the information on previous prices and volumes. In other words, the present price cannot be explained by prior price history, or prior price history has been distilled into the present price. Weak form efficiency for futures markets means that a trend analysis, moving averages or any other technical indicators derived from past performance offer no value to a trader who seeks future changes in the market. This has implications for technical analysts, who seek to make objectives and actions predictable based on charting patterns and price patterns. If, indeed, futures markets are weak from efficient, then technical analysis cannot be of much help in achieving a return higher than the market rate (Kumar et al., 2022).

4.2 Semi-Strong Form Efficiency

Semi-strong form efficiency claims that in addition to prior information and present information that is publicly available, futures prices possess all relevant information. Thus, not only past prices are included in the current costs, but all new publicly available information, such as governmental analyses, economic indices, companies' earnings or supply forecasts for commodities. In a semi-strong, efficient futures market, traders are unable to attain superior stock returns by utilising information open to the public since the market quickly assimilates this info into the stock prices. For example, if a report we have shows a low yield, it means futures prices for the complained commodity would also decrease almost immediately, hence eradicating the benefits of trading for the insiders. Semi-strong efficiency is particularly significant for future markets, considering that most of these markets promptly respond to the conveyed news since they mainly depend on factors such as economic predictability and geopolitics. In reality, many theories prove that developed futures markets, for instance, oil or financial indexes, are semi-strong efficient; therefore, it becomes challenging for traders to achieve superiority by utilising available information (Patel et al., 2022).

4.3. Strong Form Efficiency

Meanwhile, in a strong, efficient market, prices incorporate all information that is public and even private information. This encompasses information that is restricted or prohibited from being used by specific traders or persons, otherwise called inside information or information that is not available to the public. If it is accepted that a more efficient futures market is an intense form, then it is argued that even those who know such private information will not be able to beat the market efficiently. Nevertheless, because of that, futures contracts contain various sensible market factors, including the change in production forecast or even change in policy; therefore, strong form efficiency is relatively rare (N.Dao et al., 2024). The inability to attain efficiency in the strong form due to information asymmetry, particularly in better information by some of the participants, is a significant problem with the futures markets. For instance, an executive of a company in a position which has confidential information about an impending deal in commodities can presumably gain by trading in futures before this information goes to the public, thereby implying that strong form efficiency is a near impossibility. Some regulatory authorities, such as the U.S. CFTC, seek to eliminate such gaps through regulation against insider trading, but strong form efficiency is still more of an asymptotic concept in future markets. Thus, it is concluded that even if the futures markets are weak and semi-strong, they are not strong or efficient due to informational effusion. Therefore, the efficiency of one or another futures market affects the trading policies and the possibility of the predictable pattern of price changes depending on information availability (Joshi & Ranjan Kumar Dash, 2024).

5. IMPACT OF ALGORITHMIC TRADING ON FUTURES MARKET EFFICIENCY

AT actualisations, therefore, address and improve efficiency indicators of the futures market by façon of demonstrating price discovery, improved liquidity and better reactions to new information. Algorithmic systems are able to process and incorporate enormous quantities of information more quickly, enhancing futures markets' ability to mirror information and making numerous types of efficiency superior for asset prices. Algorithmic trading of futures has been recognised as a means of improving weak form efficiency in the market. The flow prices focus on constantly poring through past price data and trading volume, which makes it nearly impossible for the trader to manipulate patterns or tendencies. The price shifts depending on operative data input, which does not free a place for purely technical analysis based on price indicators. This enhances trade conditions where the current price approximation has a better shot at the history data while lessening the patterns' predictability (Kumar Inani et al., 2024).

Algorithmic trading also enhances semi-strong form efficiency since new information such as economic reports, changes of policy or forecasts on an important commodity is immediately reflected in the future prices of the commodity. Since the algorithms respond within a few milliseconds to new, publicly available information, changes in prices are nearly immediate. In this regard, let us consider that new data on the supply of oil appears; algorithmic systems can analyse it more quickly than human traders and adjust the price of futures to this information. This fast response also leads to a condition in which prices in future markets are slightly closer to existing public information, hence reducing the kinds of profits traders make from delayed price reactions (Kou et al., 2024).

In the case of strong form efficiency, the impact of algorithmic trading is found to be more ambiguous. Hence, information asymmetry is expected to make strong form efficiency difficult, albeit algorithms improve the level of transparency and accuracy in processing public information. Although they prevent fair competition, private or insider information is always an issue, for algorithms are built to recognise solely public data and trends. While strong form efficiency is proven by algorithmic trading efficiency, other private information that includes undisclosed business ventures or exclusive information on the production of specific commodities, like the agricultural commodities seen in Figure one, still poses a test to strong form efficiency in future markets (Barro et al., 2023).

Furthermore, an alc, which is one type of alta, high-frequency trading, has both beneficial and detrimental effects on the efficiency of futures markets. HFT opens up more liquidity and efficiently reduces the bid-ask spread by making several transactions, yet at the same time, it may cause volatility flare at unpredictable periods. Cases, such as the flash crash of 2010, further show how the use of these algorithms can cause sudden huge fluctuations within a short period, thus creating inefficiencies in the markets (Sharma & Bhatia, 2023).

Thus, algorithmic trading has significantly contributed to the emergence of weak and semi-strong efficiency in future markets, contributing to the speed of information acquisition and better prices. Nonetheless, high-frequency trading and natural information asymmetry explain why the strong form efficiency is still a dream. However, the picture painted in this paper, on the balance of signs over Futures Market efficiency, shows that algorithmic trading has a positive impact on assisting prices to converge to available information (Goyal & Soni, 2024).

6. METHODOLOGY:

6.1 Search Criteria Strategy:

Given the use of the Web of Science, the search strategy needs to be very specific in order to identify the connections between HFT, trading algorithms and the derivatives markets. The search will, therefore, encompass keywords most relevant to trading and market behaviour. The first search term will use the words "High-Frequency Trading" OR "Trading Algorithm*" OR "Quantitative Trading" OR "Algorithmic Strategy*". This approach makes sure that any of the articles retrieved contain at least one of these concepts. To search for refined, the AND operator will link this basic string to another string that is formed by "Derivatives Market*", "Futures Contract*", and "Market Volatility". This structure ensures that the results of the search are not only related to trading mechanisms but are also closely related to the topic of derivatives and the behaviour of the market.

High-Frequency Trading, Trading Algorithm, Quantitative Trading, Algorithmic Strategies, Derivatives Markets, Futures Contracts, Market Volatility.

When such a search string is entered Alongside WEB OF SCIENCE, it is useful to take advantage of the fields' search to refine the publications using a range of years, types of documents, and research fields. This can range from designating the parameters for the peer-reviewed articles to choosing subject categories for finance and economics. As a result of applying the Web of Science search strategy that captures comprehensive citation databases with a strong focus on indexing, this research aims to obtain a scholarly literature pool which explains the effects of algorithmic trading on specific commoditised markets for derivatives and, correspondingly, on their volatility levels, upon which subsequent analysis can be built.

6.2 Selection & Rejection Criteria:

In conducting a systematic review of algorithmic trading and futures markets, specific criteria were established for the acceptance and rejection of articles to ensure the relevance and quality of the selected literature.

Table 1. Selection & rejection criteria

Criteria for Acceptance	Criteria for Rejection
Only papers with titles related to Algorithm Trading and future Markets were selected. Only papers sourced from Web of Science digital databases were considered.	Non-English language article was excluded. Master's and doctoral theses, conference papers, reviews, reports, retracted articles, editorials, notes, short surveys, and unpublished working articles. Missing record papers were also excluded.

6.3 Criteria for Acceptance:

For this purpose, the review was limited to just the papers that had titles which directly pointed to algorithmic trading and futures markets. The approach targets specific kinds of literature based on the theory with the aim of having all the lit erature relate broadly to the major themes of the research. To keep the quality of the identified articles high, only the ones published in the Web of Science digital databases were included, as this platform provides accurate indexes and contains highly academic publications. Such papers strengthen the credibility of the findings since they originate from reliable freelance writing sources. Further, articles needed to be written in English primarily to render understanding to the general population. It contributes to language and terminology standardisation, which is essential to ensure methodological rigour when synthesing the existing literature.

6.4 Criteria for Rejection:

To avoid including non-relevant or low-quality studies, the following exclusion criteria were applied. Articles that are written in non-English languages were also excluded with the aim of maintaining one uniform language standard. In addition, studies whose format was a master's or doctoral thesis, conference paper, review, report, retracted article, editorial note, short survey, or working paper were excluded because such papers reflect substandard research and fail to pass peer review quality checks typical for systematic reviews. The exclusion of some document types means only high-quality and more refined studies are part of the research. Further, if an article was found to contain some records or information gap, it was also eliminated because such articles lack information that is required for establishing context or data analysis. In these ways, the review tries to show the selection of relevant and high-impact articles on algorithmic trading and its consequences for future markets.

7. PRISMA FLOWCHART:

The process of the systematic review involved sourcing 1,590 records from databases for the final review. Out of 769 records identified, 21 were duplicates, and an additional 1,569 were screened for eligibility. Among them, 942 records were cross-checked and excluded during the first phase after excluding irrelevant articles or those that did not meet inclusion criteria. This resulted in 627 reports that were searched for; however, only 350 were successfully retrieved, and 277 of these were lost for various reasons, such as accessibility concerns or other constraints. The other 350 reports were screened for relevance and reviewers' expulsion: 59 reports were ineligible for various reasons, for example, the type of document (e.g., proceedings paper, retracted, correction, editorial material, letter, meeting abstracts, note, or review). Namely, 8 articles and 36 proceedings papers, but only a few other categories of documents were not included. In the end, 291 publications responded to the eligibility criteria and were considered in the final analysis. It captures an efficient process of sifting out the appropriate studies while at the same time adhering to the methodological standards and research questions.

Figure 1. Prisma flow chart

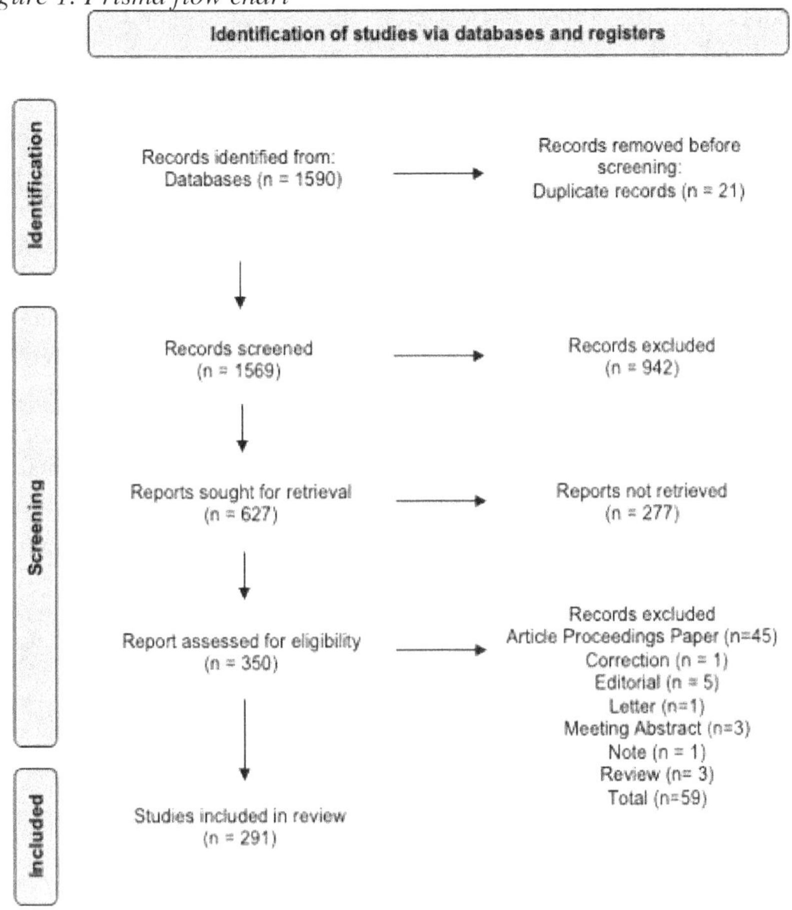

8. RESULTS & DISCUSSION:

8.1 Year-Wise Analysis:

Analysing the available articles over the years, it is possible to note that there has been a tendency for a growing number of publications in the last decades especially. The first paper was produced in 1974, and its publication continued only occasionally until the beginning of the eighties. The first notable level of activity started in 1981, with five papers published, and it grew slightly but steadily up to the 1990s. However, the Annual publications reached their highest level in 1989, with seven publications showing that there was increasing interest in research. The trend of productivity in the 1990s was relatively more consistent but somewhat less productive, although there were two high-producing years: 1995 with eight papers and 1999 with five papers. Publication numbers doubled after 2010, and each year has later witnessed an incremental rise. It increased steadily from 2012, with 2013 having 4 papers, 2014 having five papers and from 2015 and 2016, 11 papers each year. However, the field gained a significant boost by the end of 2019, with 21 papers on the topic and 22 papers in both 2020 and 2021. This upward trend is followed by 23 papers published in 2022 and the highest contribution of 31 papers in 2023. This has been further confirmed by the fact that the current year alone has produced 16 papers. Thus, the dataset is characterised by a gradual expansion of the research output indicative of the growing relevance and complexity of the topic over time. The first few decades showed sporadic papers, but the past decade reveals an increase in academic activity, probably due to evolving technology, globalisation, and the importance of financial and trading systems in the ever-changing economy. The trend analysis reveals an impressive and growing investigation profile in the subsequent years.

Figure 2. Year wise analysis

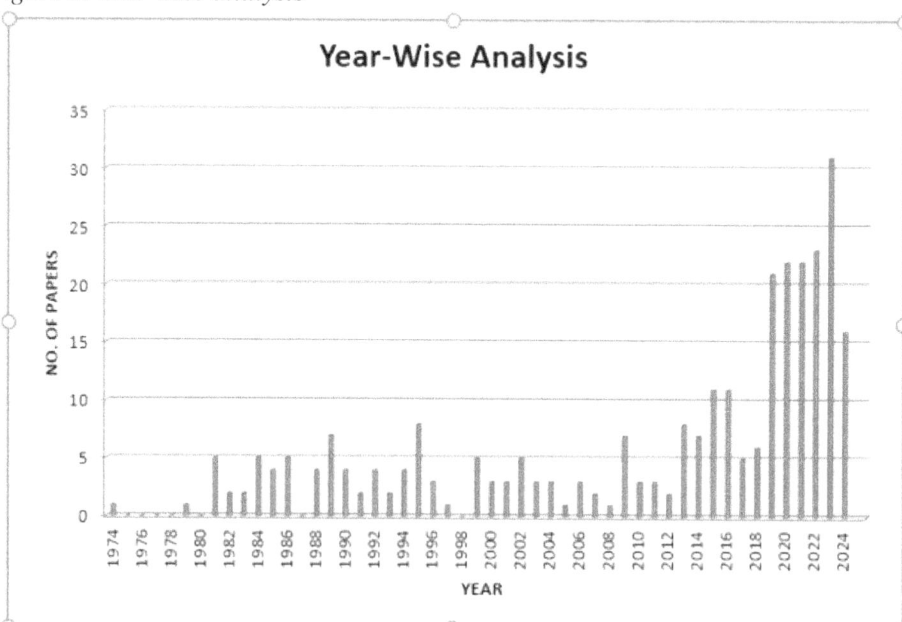

8.2 Document Type Analysis:

The figure illustrates the categorisation of documents analysed, divided into three types: Articles, Books, and Book Chapters, comprised of 291 documents. The articles come on top with 274 hits and are followed by proceedings with 132 hits. This large number supports the importance of peer-reviewed journal articles as a reference information source in scholarly contexts as a result of the academic rigour and the sheer frequency of research result publication through this medium. The least populated is books at 5 entries out of the total. This low count may mean that systematic, monographic research is less frequent in the reviewed field, possibly because of the time-consuming process of book writing or due to traditions in academic networks to produce more but shorter publications. Next in the list, with 12 entries, come Book Chapters, which often present these as parts of the chapter in a coauthored book or an edited volume. Some of these chapters are usually devoted to certain sub-fields of the general fields of the books they are in, and they offer specific information that supports the general fields of knowledge of the books. The sum of 291 documents increases the understanding of the number of sources considered in the scope of this study to stress the comprehensiveness of the reviewed works. A predominance of articles indicates tight adherence to the results of current large-scale studies published in peer-reviewed journals, whereas book and book chapter sources supplement the existing research perspective. The combination of these document types makes the study more stable, allowing for a deep analysis of the academic discourse present in the field.

Figure 3. Document type analysis

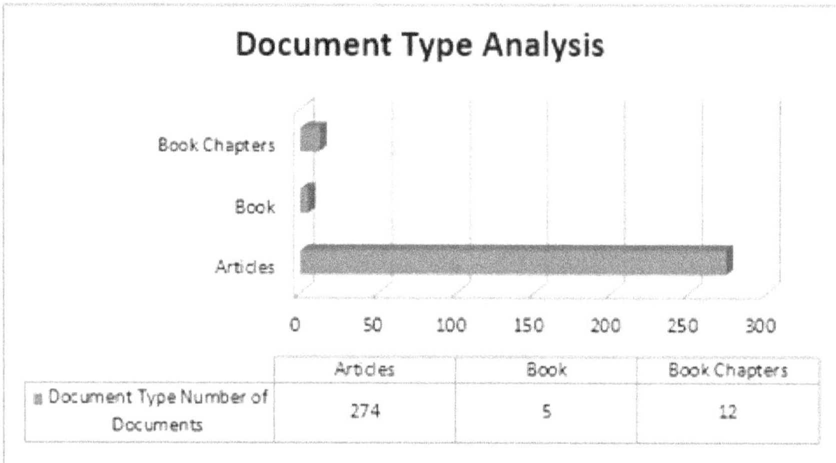

8.3 Source-Wise Analysis:

The following table shows the distribution of papers in terms of the journal in which they were published, as well as an indication of the geographical spread and focus of analysed sources. Most of these journals are not far from each other, with most of them located in the same region, as shown by the Journal of Futures Markets, which published the largest number of papers (41) in the context of the field under study. This concentration seems to indicate a particularly high interest in future markets within the research domain. Other journals that are featured frequently include Research in International Business and Finance, with 9 papers. Applied Economics Letters with 8 papers, Finance Research Letters, International Review of Economics & Finance, Journal of Banking & Finance and Journal of Financial Economics that featured 7 papers each. Together, these journals seem to have an interest in relevant financial and economic work, and they provide information concerning matters of international finance, trading, and markets. Five papers are documented in mid-tier journals such as the Journal of Empirical Finance and the

Journal of Finance. Other journals represented by four papers include Econometric Modelling, International Journal of Finance and Economics, Journal of Forecasting and Physica A-Statistical Mechanics and its Applications based on different categories of quantitative analysis methods. Thereof, 3 articles pertain to several journals that are Emerging Markets Review, Heliyon and Mathematical Finance, meaning they offer fairly unique, although important, research input to some twenty specialisations. In general, the dataset points to the fact that the analysed outputs primarily concern finance and economics, with a special focus on empirical research journals related to futures markets and international trade. This also confirms the interdisciplinary and international focus of the studied field. The diversity of journals discussed in this network analysis offers a more fortified data set when it comes to the literature review, as insights from different perspectives can help substantiate the results found.

Table 2. Journals list

Source Title	Number of Papers
APPLIED ECONOMICS LETTERS	8
APPLIED ECONOMICS	3
ECONOMIC MODELLING	4
EMERGING MARKETS REVIEW	3
EMERGING MARKETS FINANCE AND TRADE	3
FINANCE RESEARCH LETTERS	7
HELIYON	3
INTERNATIONAL JOURNAL OF FINANCE & ECONOMICS	4
INTERNATIONAL JOURNAL OF FORECASTING	3
INTERNATIONAL REVIEW OF ECONOMICS & FINANCE	7
JOURNAL OF BANKING & FINANCE	7
INTERNATIONAL REVIEW OF FINANCIAL ANALYSIS	6
JOURNAL OF BUSINESS	4
JOURNAL OF ECONOMETRICS	3
JOURNAL OF EMPIRICAL FINANCE	5
JOURNAL OF FINANCE	5
JOURNAL OF FINANCIAL ECONOMICS	7
JOURNAL OF FORECASTING	4
JOURNAL OF FUTURES MARKETS	41
JOURNAL OF PORTFOLIO MANAGEMENT	3

continued on following page

Table 2. Continued

Source Title	Number of Papers
JOURNAL OF INTERNATIONAL FINANCIAL MARKETS INSTITUTIONS & MONEY	3
JOURNAL OF RISK AND FINANCIAL MANAGEMENT	3
MATHEMATICAL FINANCE	3
NORTH AMERICAN JOURNAL OF ECONOMICS AND FINANCE	4
PACIFIC-BASIN FINANCE JOURNAL	3
PHYSICA A-STATISTICAL MECHANICS AND ITS APPLICATIONS	4
RESEARCH IN INTERNATIONAL BUSINESS AND FINANCE	9
STOCK MARKET VOLATILITY	5

8.4 Keyword Analysis:

In the context of research, to which specific clusters correspond, as well as the weight of relevance in the field. Algorithmic Trading (-0.2883, -0.3451) is located in the first cluster and shows both the highest relative frequency and the highest absolute link strength (31), which underlines its importance in the present research context. Another term in Cluster 2 with relatively high (\(>\)30) total link strength and 62 appearances is Financial Markets (-0.0759, 0.1862). Still, Cluster 2 is less frequently mentioned (3) and characterised by less connection strength (2) to point up its niche or emerging character, Future Market (-0.294, 0.8493). GARCH Models categorised in Cluster 3, given a couple of frequent words (27 occurrences), a couple of link values (-0.1236) and a total link strength of 22, establish its importance in the volatility of financial data. Investor Sentiment has strong relationships with Clusters 3 and 8, with occurrence 3 and total link strength 2, and Investor Attention is similar to Clusters 1 and 9, with occurrence 4 and total link strength 4. These topics emphasise the behavioural characteristics of market participants, which is an area that has recently received often increasing attention in finance.

Finally, the term Financial Crisis has been located at a low extent with 0.2648 of link functions and -0.6767 of link strength in Cluster 4 and has observed 3 numbers of occurrences having total link strength of 4. It seems to be either a less active or a less focused topic. Thus, the analysis shows that Algorithmic Trading and Financial Markets are leading. Finally, some topics remain underdeveloped or concern specific areas; therefore, more could be explored, such as the future market financial crisis. The clustering also points out the interdisciplinary links between quantitative modelling, behaviours in the markets, and trading structures.

Figure 4. Keywords analysis

9. CONCLUSION:

The systematic literature review on the role of algorithmic trading (AT) in shaping futures market efficiency reveals that AT has become a fundamental component, significantly impacting price discovery, liquidity, and market volatility. Most studies indicate that algorithmic trading enhances market efficiency by enabling faster and more accurate responses to information, reducing bid-ask spreads, and promoting liquidity. However, certain concerns arise, particularly regarding high-frequency trading (HFT) strategies, which can amplify short-term volatility and trigger market destabilisation during stressed conditions. Overall, while AT appears to drive efficiency improvements, its effects vary across markets and conditions, calling for continuous monitoring and contextual assessments (Goodell et al., 2021).

From the analysis, the number of papers published in this area has been on an upward trend across the decades, with marked upticks since 2010 to reach its pinnacle of 31 papers in 2023 in recognition of the dynamism and prognostic significance of the phenomenon. Out of the 291 documents reviewed, primarily peer-reviewed articles (274) contribute to a strengthening of journals' predominance in disseminating knowledge; books (5) and book chapters (12) add further information. Such journals as the Journal of Futures Markets (41 papers) and Research in International Business and Finance (9 papers) are leading, once again, underlining the importance of finance, economics and the markets of the future. Based on clustering analysis, algorithmic trading and financial markets are considered priority research areas due to the revealed link strength and frequency. However, GARCH models and concepts such as investor sentiment and attention are the focus of emerging interest. Pre-developed communities, such as future markets and financial crises, must remain further developed. On balance, the study emphasises quantitative modelling as an interdisciplinary field, the behaviour of markets and trading systems, the interest of which grows globally and in terms of academics.

9.1 Managerial Implications:

It indicates that managers in trading firms, hedge funds, and financial institutions can leverage algorithmic trading (AT) to enhance strategic decision-making. By incorporating AT with predictive analytics, firms can potentially improve trade execution and reduce transaction costs.

The literature highlights that AT provides a sophisticated tool for risk management, allowing for rapid responses to market anomalies. Managers are encouraged to develop and implement robust risk frameworks to mitigate risks associated with algorithmic trades, particularly during periods of low liquidity.

Studies emphasise the importance of compliance with evolving regulatory frameworks. Managers are advised to establish adaptive compliance mechanisms to align with regulations on market transparency, trading limits, and safeguards against market abuse.

9.2 Practical Implications:

Findings from the review underscore the need for substantial investment in advanced computing technology and skilled personnel, which is essential for implementing AT effectively. This investment is also necessary for firms to maintain competitiveness as algorithmic and technological complexities grow.

Literature on AT suggests that enhanced trade execution through predictive analytics can lead to significant cost reductions and improved profitability, making it a valuable operational strategy.

A well-designed risk management framework is recommended to help firms mitigate the stresses and potential risks inherent to AT, especially in low-liquidity situations. This can contribute to more stable operations.

The review supports the importance of developing practical mechanisms for ongoing regulatory monitoring. Firms should have adaptive systems to ensure that AT practices remain transparent and compliant with regulatory standards, fostering market integrity and stability.

9.3 Limitations and Future Directions:

- ✓ The literature shows inconsistent findings on AT's impact on market efficiency, liquidity, and volatility, varying across different markets, asset classes, and trading conditions, complicating generalisation.
- ✓ Many studies encounter data access and quality issues, particularly with proprietary trading data, which limits the depth of analysis and may affect the accuracy of findings, as simulations do not always capture real-time conditions effectively.
- ✓ Research often focuses on developed markets with established infrastructures, creating a gap in understanding AT's effects in emerging or less-regulated markets and limiting the global applicability of findings.
- ✓ Existing studies frequently examine AT's short-term effects, such as immediate changes in liquidity or volatility, but overlook potential long-term impacts on market stability, investor behaviour, and the broader financial ecosystem.
- ✓ Future research could benefit from cross-market studies that assess AT's impact across diverse asset types and regions, including emerging markets, to capture AT's influence in varied market structures, liquidity levels, and regulatory contexts.
- ✓ Further investigation into the long-term impacts of AT on systemic risk, stability, and economic trends would provide a fuller understanding of AT's broader implications.
- ✓ As AI and machine learning become integral to AT, studying their effects on market efficiency and risk management would shed light on the future potential and challenges of AI-enhanced AT strategies.

REFERENCES

Baker, H. K., Kumar, S., & Pandey, N. (2021). Forty years of the Journal of Futures Markets: A bibliometric overview. *Journal of Futures Markets*, 41(7), 1027–1054. DOI: 10.1002/fut.22211

Barro, D., Basso, A., Funari, S., & Visentin, G. A. (2023). A Bilbliometric Analysis of Art in Financial Markets. SSRN *Electronic Journal*. DOI: 10.2139/ssrn.4593365

Carè, R., & Cumming, D. (2024). Technology and automation in financial trading: A bibliometric review. *Research in International Business and Finance*, 71, 102471–102471. DOI: 10.1016/j.ribaf.2024.102471

Dakalbab, F., Manar Abu Talib, Nasir, Q., & Saroufil, T. (2024). Artificial intelligence techniques in financial trading: A systematic literature review. *Journal of King Saud University. Computer and Information Sciences/Ma ala am a Al-Malīk Saud: Ùlm Al- asib Wa Al-Ma lumat, 36*(3), 102015–102015. DOI: 10.1016/j.jksuci.2024.102015

Dao, N. H., Wang ChuanYuan, Suzuki, A., Sudo, H., Ye, L., & Roy, D. (2024). AI in Stock Market Forecasting: A Bibliometric Analysis. *SHS Web of Conferences, 194*, 01003–01003. DOI: 10.1051/shsconf/202419401003

Goodell, J. W., Kumar, S., Lim, W. M., & Pattnaik, D. (2021). Artificial intelligence and machine learning in finance: Identifying foundations, themes, and research clusters from bibliometric analysis. *Journal of Behavioral and Experimental Finance*, 32(1), 100577. DOI: 10.1016/j.jbef.2021.100577

Goyal, P., & Soni, P. (2024). *Stock markets volatility during crises periods: a bibliometric analysis*. Qualitative Research in Financial Markets., DOI: 10.1108/QRFM-06-2023-0143

Handro, P., & Dima, B. (2024). ANALYSING FINANCIAL MARKETS EFFICIENCY: INSIGHTS FROM A BIBLIOMETRIC AND CONTENT REVIEW. *Journal of Financial Studies*, 9(16). Advance online publication. DOI: 10.55654/JFS.2024.9.16.09

Hansen, K. B. (2024). The Stack Inversion: On Algo-Centrism and the Complex Architecture of Automated Financial Securities Trading Systems. *Science, Technology & Human Values*, 01622439241269983. Advance online publication. DOI: 10.1177/01622439241269983

Horobet, A., Boubaker, S., Belascu, L., Negreanu, C. C., & Dinca, Z. (2024). Technology-driven advancements: Mapping the landscape of algorithmic trading literature. *Technological Forecasting and Social Change*, 209, 123746–123746. DOI: 10.1016/j.techfore.2024.123746

Jain, R., & Bagrecha, Dr. C. (2024). Algorithmic Trading And Market Liquidity Dynamics In Indian Energy Futures: A Comprehensive Analysis". *Educational Administration Theory and Practices*. DOI: 10.53555/kuey.v30i6.5735

Joshi, G., & Dash, R. K. (2024). Exchange-traded funds and the future of passive investments: A bibliometric review and future research agenda. *Future Business Journal*, 10(1), 17. Advance online publication. DOI: 10.1186/s43093-024-00306-8

Kou, M., Yang, Y., & Chen, K. (2024). Financial technology research: Past and future trajectories. *International Review of Economics & Finance*, 93, 162–181. Advance online publication. DOI: 10.1016/j.iref.2024.03.032

Kumar, A., Sharma, S., Vashistha, R., Srivastava, V., Tabash, M. I., Munim, Z. H., & Paltrinieri, A. (2022). International Journal of Emerging Markets: a bibliometric review 2006–2020. *International Journal of Emerging Markets*. DOI: 10.1108/IJOEM-05-2021-0668

Kumar Inani, S., Pradhan, H., Kumar, S., & Biswas, B. (2024). Navigating the technical analysis in stock markets: Insights from bibliometric and topic modeling approaches. *Investment Management and Financial Innovations*, 21(1), 275–288. DOI: 10.21511/imfi.21(1).2024.21

Lee, M.-J., & Choi, S.-Y. (2024). Insights into the dynamics of market efficiency spill-over of financial assets in different equity markets. *Physica A*, 641, 129719–129719. DOI: 10.1016/j.physa.2024.129719

Madhava Priya Dananjayan, Sridevi Gopakumar, & Parthasarathi Narayanasamy. (2023). Unleashing the algorithmic frontier: Navigating the impact of algo trading on investor portfolios. *Journal of Information Technology Teaching Cases*. DOI: 10.1177/20438869231189519

Manogna, R. L., & Anand, A. (2023). A bibliometric analysis on the application of deep learning in finance: Status, development and future directions. *Kybernetes*. Advance online publication. DOI: 10.1108/K-04-2023-0637

Moshood Yussuf, Mayowa Timothy AdesinaSunday David EsebreAbdullah Tunde AdewuyiOluwaseun Aaron AdigunTemitope Dickson OlajideComfort Idongesit MichaelDivine ILOH. (2024). Algorithmic trading and machine learning: Advanced techniques for market prediction and strategy development. *World Journal of Advanced Research and Reviews*, 23(2), 979–990. DOI: 10.30574/wjarr.2024.23.2.2405

Nahar, J., Nishat, N., Shoaib, A. S. M., & Hossain, Q. (2024). MARKET EFFICIENCY AND STABILITY IN THE ERA OF HIGH-FREQUENCY TRADING: A COMPREHENSIVE REVIEW. *International Journal of Business and Economics*, 1(3), 1–13. DOI: 10.62304/ijbm.v1i3.166

Ni, Y. (2024). Navigating Energy and Financial Markets: A Review of Technical Analysis Used and Further Investigation from Various Perspectives. *Energies*, 17(12), 2942–2942. DOI: 10.3390/en17122942

Patel, R., Goodell, J. W., Oriani, M. E., Paltrinieri, A., & Yarovaya, L. (2022). A bibliometric review of financial market integration literature. *International Review of Financial Analysis*, 102035, 102035. Advance online publication. DOI: 10.1016/j.irfa.2022.102035

Qudah, H., Baqila, B. K. A., Albadienah, J. M. O., AlQudah, M. Z., Al Qudah, S., Alrahamneh, S., Ababne, A., & Qudah, I. (2024). Using bibliometrics to understand algorithmic finance. *Journal of Applied Econometrics*, 27(1), 2389497. Advance online publication. DOI: 10.1080/15140326.2024.2389497

Sharma, V. K., & Bhatia, S. (2023). Knowledge mapping of studies on implied volatility in equity derivatives markets: A bibliometric approach. *International Journal of Financial Markets and Derivatives*, 9(3), 188–207. DOI: 10.1504/IJFMD.2023.133457

Sukma, N., & Namahoot, C. S. (2024). Enhancing Trading Strategies: A Multi-indicator Analysis for Profitable Algorithmic Trading. *Computational Economics*. Advance online publication. DOI: 10.1007/s10614-024-10669-3

Chapter 10
Cryptocurrency and Future of Money:
Introduction to Cryptocurrency

Syeda Fizza Abbas
Kinnaird College for Women University, Pakistan

Aliza Sajjad
https://orcid.org/0009-0003-6574-5169
Kinnaird College for Women University, Pakistan

Haider Rizavi
University of Central Punjab, Pakistan

Nadia Sadiq
https://orcid.org/0000-0002-6764-2513
Government College University, Faisalabad, Pakistan

ABSTRACT

Cryptocurrency, emerging post-recession, has the potential to reshape the financial landscape. Since Bitcoin's debut in 2009, cryptocurrencies have evolved into advanced assets using blockchain technology. These decentralized digital currencies stand out from traditional money by expanding banking access, cutting transaction costs, and enhancing security. Beyond technology, they shift trust and control in finance away from centralized entities like banks and governments, leveraging blockchain and distributed systems to boost efficiency and promote financial inclusion, especially in developing countries.

DOI: 10.4018/979-8-3693-6386-7.ch010

INTRODUCTION TO CRYPTOCURRENCY

The rise of the digital age has brought about groundbreaking technological advancements (Ndung'u et al., 2016). The emergence of cryptocurrencies in the digital age marks a significant fusion of cryptography and digital assets (Milutinović, 2018). This convergence has led to the creation of decentralized financial systems made possible by blockchain technology. The interplay between cryptography, digital assets, and blockchain technology has the potential to revolutionize traditional finance and introduce new modes of transactions and economic models in the digital realm (Makarov & Schoar, 2022a).

Cryptocurrency is a digital money designed for conducting transactions over the internet. It uses cryptography to ensure the security of transactions and uphold the accuracy of records (Chuen et al., 2017). Cryptocurrency functions autonomously without the need for a central authority or traditional banking institutions.

It can be defined as a maturing subclass of digital or virtual currencies that employs the use of cryptographic techniques to facilitate secure transactions and verify the transfer of assets among the trading parties. Unlike other forms of money, it works on peer-to-peer networks built on principles of blockchain technology which implies that there is no central authority that governs the cryptocurrency network hence resulting in a decentralized operational nature of the network which not only enhances security but also ensures transparency (Nakamoto, 2008).

The term "*cryptocurrency*" is a combination of two words '*crypto-*' which stands for the application of cryptography and '*-currency*' which means it is a medium of exchange. The usufruct of these cryptographic algorithms ensures that the transactions from modifications or counterfeit the digital assets, to maintain the integrity and security. Bitcoin, established in 2009, was the inaugural cryptocurrency and its decentralized character stems from the absence of a centralized structure (Nakamoto, 2009).

Historical Overview

Since the emergence of the econo-physics around a quarter century ago, numerous studies have been carried out to observe the macro and micro financial phenomena ranging from the economic bubble formations, speculative market behaviors, efficacy of the investing strategies, portfolio evaluations and evolutions to the price formation of the assets. This exposed all types of financial markets, be it stock and commodity markets or real -estate and Forex markets under the scrutiny of researchers worldwide in order to minimize the systematic errors, introduce innovation and predict their future behaviors and economic implications.

Similarly, more than a decade ago, (Nakamoto, 2008) established the emerging avenue of a cutting-edge financial market which is the cryptocurrency market which put forth what the existing markets lacked- *decentralization* (Wątorek et al., 2021). The white paper titled as, "Bitcoin: A Peer-to-Peer Electronic Cash System," written by (Nakamoto, 2008) introduced the new digital asset as a form of digital currency which allows P2P transactions through cash transfers without the involvement of third parties. As per the study of (Wątorek et al., 2021), the emergence of Bitcoin-BTC has not been coincidental as it intercedes the peak time of the Global Financial Crisis 2008- the time where people had a shaken trust levels on the central depository authorities and the central banks. Mt. Gox established in February 2011 became the pioneer exchange which facilitated the transaction of BTC-fiat currency, hence indicating the acceptance and promotion of the new cryptocurrency market. Currently, there are more than 3600 different types of cryptocurrencies which are being traded on over three hundred and fifty exchanges, making it the fastest growing financial market (Almeida & Gonçalves, 2023).

Key features of the Cryptocurrencies

According to the work of Kucheryavenko et al (2019) has highlighted the key features of the cryptocurrencies which are quintessential founding elements of a cryptocurrency are discussed as follows:

- **Decentralization**

It is the most basic feature of this technology which distributes the control and fosters the inclusivity in digital transaction management (Atzori, 2015). Decentralization of cryptocurrency network implies that there is no one center which decides but it is made by the nodes in a network. The ledger is maintained and developed by the network participants known as nodes in a decentralized network, which is more of a consensus as compared to the centralized decision of a headquarter (Antal et al., 2021). These leads towards reduced threats or risk where there are one or more central points of failure, increases the transparency and therefore builds confidence among the users.

Regarding cryptocurrencies, decentralization is adopted in various manners, for instance, the consensus protocol, distribution systems, and P2P (Glaser & Bezzenberger, 2015). For example, where the PoW (Proof of Work) is linked to Bitcoins, then the PoW has to render computational complex problems to validate the transactions and create new blocks on the chain. This makes miners to exercise bona fide since they are benefiting out of the process and at the same time act as a guarantor to the network (Steinbock, 2005).

With this being said, not all the cryptocurrencies may be fully decentralized, due to their technical nature, application specifications, and use cases (Kucheryavenko et al., 2019).

- **The openness of the software code**

The cryptography used in the system often relies on the open source software codes which are then used to power the cryptographic networks (Amin et al., 2008). The open code software allows the experts to simultaneously work together to make the cryptocurrency efficient while also ensuring not to grant control in a singular central point (Kucheryavenko et al., 2019).

- **Irreversible nature of transactions**

The transaction carried out using the cryptocurrencies are irreversible which implies that these can not be undone, delayed or frozen under any circumstances of the user being unsatisfied (Sabry, 2021).

- **Exchange rate driven by the demand and supply**

Since the cryptocurrencies are not regulated or governed by any third party and are not backed by some underlying asset, so unlike fiat money, there is no entity to ensure the price formation and liquidity of these digital assets. Consequently, they price or the exchange rate of the cryptocurrencies are set by the market forces of demand and supply, set through the traders of these assets (Girasa, 2018).

- **Open access to transaction information and saving transaction information**

As the records are publicly available through the blockchain technology so they can be checked by everyone and can be used to create new applications by the users (Niranjanamurthy et al., 2019). Additionally, the transaction information is stored until the life of the cryptocurrency network which adds to the element of security of the network (Kucheryavenko et al., 2019).

- **Openness to other payment systems**

Another distinctive feature of the cryptocurrencies is their openness towards exchange over various crypto platforms as well with the traditional electronic and fiat currencies such as dollars, euros, WebMoney etc. This exchange usually takes place on the crypto exchanges however the legislations of these kind of exchanges varies and have gaps from the regulatory perspectives as well (Hairudin et al., 2022; Mikhaylov, 2020).

- **Anonymity**

The maintenance of secrecy is another important characteristic of the system as one doesn't need to share the personal details for transferring the data across the nodes or even for single transaction, a blockchain address would do so (Niranjanamurthy et al., 2019).

- **Transparency**

The public availability of the ledger of the transaction details, makes the system transparent and trustworthy (Menon & Jain, 2021).

- **Cryptography**

Cryptography is very important in determining the security as well as the working of the cryptocurrencies (Ghosh et al., 2020). It entails employing specific mathematical computations or algorithms to implement security and preserve the data's confidentiality, consistency, and genuineness. Several features of the cryptocurrency operations are based on the cryptographic concepts, such as the validation of the transaction, key and network (Delgado-Segura et al., 2018).

CRYPTOCURRENCY FUNDAMENTALS

Blockchain Technology

At the core of cryptocurrencies lies the blockchain which acts as a public ledger, recording and confirming all transactions occurring within the cryptocurrency network (Nakamoto, 2009). The usage of blockchain is prevalent in most cryptocurrencies; although there might be an exception with the utilization of other related technologies in the vast growing cryptocurrency network (Hassani et al., 2018). A blockchain is considered a distributed, decentralized database that is used to store records of activities of particular network, and such records consist of nodes, making the system transparent and ensure integrity. It achieves this by linking transactional data chronologically into blocks secured cryptographically and interlinked (Nakamoto, 2008). Cryptography ensures the security and immutability of cryptocurrencies by utilizing intricate codes to safeguard financial data, protecting it from unauthorized access. Each block contains a unique identifier (hash) of the previous block, forming an unbreakable chain of transactional records (Singhal et al., 2018). This structure makes the blockchain resistant to manipulation and alterations, ensuring the validity and reliability of the recorded transactions.

Consequently, the structure of blockchain increases the system's anti-tampering and anti-fraud capabilities because any alteration of certain elements in a block would impact all subsequent blocks, something that cannot be achieved by numerous networks in terms of computational ability (Zhang et al., 2022). As the system essentially cuts out the middleman, who validates and logs transactions through blockchains since it is on a distributed server. However, to reach consensus over nodes about the state of the ledger, the consensus algorithms such as the Proof of Work (PoW) or Proof of Stake (PoS) are used. It also enhances the security and the generation of trust because nobody and no organization has full control over the blockchain (Bhuvana & Aithal, 2020).

Types of Blockchains Technology

(Niranjanamurthy et al., 2019) highlights three main types of the blockchain, which are discussed as follows:

Public Blockchains

The openness of the network is the key feature of a public blockchain as anyone can check and verify the transaction (Niranjanamurthy et al., 2019). This participation allows anyone to access the transaction data and contribute to the network which ensures the security without having to need a central authority. Additionally, it uses PoW or PoS as the consensus mechanism (Niranjanamurthy et al., 2019). Cryptocurrencies like Bitcoin and Ethereum uses the public blockchain networks (Mohammed et al., 2021; Nakamoto, 2008).

Consortium Blockchains

These blockchain networks allow the authorized participants of the network to access the transaction data, which makes it slightly less transparent than the public blockchain network (Lind et al., 2019). However, this adds a level of further security among the authorized participants by granting a higher control but limiting the element of centralization (Lind et al., 2019). The consensus mechanism used by this network is slightly advanced and efficient like Practical Byzantine Fault Tolerance (PBFT). Examples include R3CEV (Niranjanamurthy et al., 2019).

Private Blockchains

In the private blockchain system, not every node on the network can participate which makes the access to the system limited (Niranjanamurthy et al., 2019). Centralized authorities manage the access and interaction with the data, which makes sure that only the authorized participant are engaged. The examples of private blockchain would include enterprise blockchains like IBM Blockchain (Bhuvana & Aithal, 2020).

The way blockchain operates

Table 1. Step by step illustration of how the blockchain system operates

Step	Description
1. Transaction Request	- Transaction is initiated through the record of data or execution of a smart contract. - The initiated transaction is presented to a P2P network consisting of computers known as nodes.
2. Validation	- The nodular network validates the transaction and the status through the computer algorithms. - This process endures that the sender has enough funds and that if the conditions of the smart contract are fulfilled.
3. Verification and Inclusion	- After the transaction is validated, it becomes part of a block. - A verified transaction can include cryptocurrency, smart contracts, records, or any other relevant information.
4. Block Creation	- All the transactions which are verified, are then grouped together to make a new block of data for the public ledger. - Each block contains a cryptographic hash of the previous block, creating a chain of blocks.
5. Adding to the Blockchain	- The new block, which includes validated operations, is added to the current blockchain. This act of stapling guarantees that the blockchain expands in an ordered and chronological manner.
6. Permanence and Immutability	- Once a transaction is uploaded to the blockchain, it becomes an immutable and unchangeable entry in the ledger.
7. Transaction Completion	- The procedure is finalized after the transaction is recorded on the blockchain.

Types of cryptocurrencies

Cryptocurrencies have moved a notch higher since the emergence of the most famous digital asset, bitcoin in 2009. Modern cryptocurrencies mean a wide spectrum of assets that differ from each other in various parameters and functions. Following are the types of cryptocurrencies discussed by (CFI):

Payment Cryptocurrency

The first major type of cryptocurrency is payment cryptocurrencies which means these digital assets are designed in a way that they can facilitate the medium of exchange on a P2P platform. Such cryptocurrencies have their own blockchain and do not have decentralized applications or smart contracts as their underlying technology (Sukarno, 2020). Furthermore, these digital assets are limited in number of coins available, which makes their nature inflationary as their price would appreciate with an increase in the demand of the currency (Nicholas Taleb, 2021).

Bitcoin (BTC) is the oldest and probably the most popular payment cryptocurrency that people also called digital gold because of its characteristics (Popper, 2015). Bitcoin, created by Satoshi Nakamoto in 2008, is a decentralized peer-to-peer payment system that uses the blockchain technology system (Nakamoto, 2008). Fundamentally, bitcoin is used as digital money to pay for goods and services and as a store of value, bouncing fiat money. Another of the characteristics of bitcoins is that their number is strictly limited – 21 million – so consumers who invest in bitcoins are actually using it as an anti-inflation tool. Also, its decentralized ledger and security aroused its appeal of a remittance tool, a cross-border payments instrument and an investment asset.

Similarly, Litecoin (LTC) which was launched in 2011 by Charlie Lee is emerging as the silver to Bitcoin's gold. It is almost similar to Bitcoin but they included some modifications to enhance on the speed of transactions and less charges (Jumaili & Karim, 2021). Litecoin utilizes the Scrypt hashing algorithm and its blocks can be generated at quicker rates and for cheaper than in Bitcoin (Hameed & Farooq, 2017).

However, the main utilization of Litecoin is in the role of a digital currency as an exchange mean of payments especially when the speed of transactions and their cost is of essence. Their block times are shorter, therefore, are more convenient for daily and small buy – sell transactions (Jumaili & Karim, 2021). Further examples of such payment cryptocurrencies would include Dogecoin, and Monero etc.

Utility Tokens

Utility tokens are the second major types of cryptocurrencies which operate over another blockchain. Vitalik Buterin, the creator of Ethereum was the first one to introduce these as it was an open access program-based system which uses smart contracts (Buterin, 2016). In contrast to the payment cryptocurrencies, these tokens do not have a limited supply which eliminates deflationary element from them. This means that alike the fiat currency, the increased supply of these tokens in the market would put a downward pressure on their price (Georgeson, 2018). The primary purpose of these tokens is to make a specific service or application accessible on a blockchain.

Such tokens are usually introduced through the ICO (Initial Coin Offerings) hence enabling financing the early stages of the projects or they may grant discounted trading fees on the platforms such as the Binance Coin (Boreiko, 2024a). Such tokens may also be representative of ownership and then be known as security tokens. Else they can also facilitate the financial activities of lending, crowd funding and betting to be classified as the financial tokens (Ante et al., 2018). The examples of utility tokens include Ether token of Ethereum, Binance Coin (BNB) etc (Guseva, 2020).

Stable coins

Stable coins are another subcategory in which a cryptocurrency, which cater the volatile nature of the cryptocurrency by anchoring it to a stable item such as fiat money or commodity (Ólafsson, 2014). Hence the primary use case of such digital assets is store of value and smoothen out the volatile nature of the asset (Azar et al., 2022). Additionally, this characteristic makes them more suitable for actual usage and as a means of payment. Furthermore, they maintain their value because despite of being built on a blockchain, the company which pegs them against an asset maintains the reserve which ensures the value of the cryptocurrency is maintained (Rossi, 2022).

Tether-USDT, which is pegged with the US dollar and is the third largest cryptocurrency by capitalization, is an example of such fiat-backed stable coins. Basically, every Tether token is equivalent to a specified lawful money kept in Tether Treasury to prevent market fluctuations (Tether, 2020). The utility of Tether is to offer a stable value of the money market, which can be used by traders to transact through exchanges without influence from the digital currencies' price swings (Rossi, 2022).

MakerDAO is yet another project, and DAI is the stable coin that it fosters, similar to the Tether. However, unlike the fiat base-stable coins, the DAI is anchored to the USD through smart contracts and CDPs on the Ethereum platform (Schär, 2021). DAI can be created by locking up the Ethereum or other supported assets as collateral providing a mechanism for its creation. Due to DAI's decentralized nature and complete transparency it is being applied to as collateral, medium of exchange and has been used as store of value in various DeFi protocols (Schär, 2021).

Central Bank Digital Currencies (CBDC)

CBDC are digital currencies which are issued by the central banks of multiple countries and are pegged to the currency of the issuing bank (Náñez Alonso et al., 2021). Furthermore, as these are issued by the central banks, hence they have full control over their regulation. The main purpose of these cryptocurrencies is to improve the payment efficiency and decreased transaction costs. Furthermore, these cryptocurrencies create 'paper trail' of all the transactions so that it can be monitored by the governments and authorities for the taxation and legality purposes (Fink, 2018).

Legal and regulatory challenges

The legalities and regulation around the cryptocurrencies landscape has been incredibly contentious (Whitford & Anderson, 2021). Despite the advantages that these cryptocurrencies offer, many governments and central banks around the world are reluctant to accept them under full force, concerning the issue of their stability to be incorporated in the financial system, and the risk associated with fraudulent and illegal activities through them such as money laundering (Azarenkova et al., 2018). Even today the legal uncertainties surrounding cryptocurrency still have a larger impact on the global landscape of cryptocurrency adoption with real life case studies from China, the United States and El Salvador show how different approaches are applied towards this case (Miato, 2023).

Major economies like China has boldly resisted the incorporation of cryptocurrencies in the financial system, by first dissuading the People's Bank of China (PBoC) from conducting any cryptocurrency transactions and mining-related activity (Kwok & Zhang, 2024). The Chinese government has risen up against crypto for the reason of ruining a financial stability as well as capital flight (Michelsen, 2021).

On one hand, regulators of the United States and Europe have been more calculated in creating legal frameworks preventing exploitive nature of cryptocurrencies rather than banning them (Ibrahim, 2024). For example, the U.S. Securities and Exchange Commission (SEC) has been actively at work to classify many cryptocurrencies, including Initial Coin Offering (ICO) as some form of securities under existing securities laws (Goforth, 2024). At the same time, the European Union's Markets in Crypto Assets (MiCA) regulation, inclusive of 2024, aims at the converge cryptocurrency regulation between its member states (Wronka, 2024). This will contribute to the creation of a standardized legal framework aimed to respond to important concerns such as investor protection, market integrity and financial stability (Marcacci, 2018).

One real world example of challenges in cryptocurrencies is the virtual currency used by El Salvador in legal tender in 2021 (Alvarez et al., 2023). The move was praised by cryptocurrency advocates for its innovation, but it also highlighted big regulatory and economic issues. International Monetary Fund (IMF) warned against abuse of Bitcoin, and opined that its use by El Salvador may limit it to macroeconomic risks, such as volatility in exchange rates and risk of money laundering (McCarthy-Jones & Turner, 2024). This underscores the broader issue that many countries face the challenge of achieving the innovative potential of cryptocurrencies while ensuring robust regulatory frameworks that safeguard economies and the public from all the potential risks inherent in the assets (Xiong & Luo, 2024).

Finally, the regulatory challenges around cryptocurrencies are complex and multi-dimensional (Silva & Mira da Silva, 2022). Some countries have gone totally bans on the cryptocurrencies, while others are trying to find ways in whom to regulate and integrate the cryptocurrencies into their financial systems (Girasa, 2018).

One of the biggest issues is that cryptocurrency regulations enjoy extremely broad variation across different jurisdictions, resulting in what is commonly referred to as regulatory arbitrage (Chiu, 2023). The crypto industry moves operations to places that have less stringent oversight and stricter regulation in most cases because cryptocurrency companies and exchanges are escaping as they relocate, this is the case (Mokhtarian & Lindgren, 2018). For reference, Binance has moved the base of its operations from one country to another multiple times owing to regulatory crackdown. Online exchanges which facilitate such trade, owing to the legal challenges in the USA, Japan and the UK prefer shifting their headquarters in more crypto friendly countries like Malta, which at some point had a good regulatory environment for digital assets (Hays & Kirilenko, 2021).

Additionally, the bankruptcy of FTX in 2022 showed tens of thousands of investors who were not prepared for such a financial loss, and prompted an urgent questions of whether the sector needed more controls (De Blasis et al., 2024). The U.S. SEC with other global regulators have sharply ramped up scrutiny of cryptocurrency exchanges and digital assets in response to the events, and are taking further steps to introduce additional investor protections (Allen, 2022). Even with these efforts, however, enforcement is difficult. Because cryptocurrency transactions on decentralized exchanges (DEX) happen without a central authority, many of these are complicate to deal with in enforcing regulations such as AML and KYC (Moreno et al., 2021). Privacy coins like Monero and Zcash add to a problem since they're created to conceal transactions and make it even harder for regulators to trace who arranged transactions and imposed the laws against any illicit activity (Richardson, 2024).

While summing up, it is noteworthy that the legal and regulatory challenges around multiple aspects of the use cases of cryptocurrency for retail and commercial purposes are only intensifying as governments, financial institutions and business continue to adopt and use them around the world (Girasa, 2018). The supporters emphasize the advantages it can gauge presses over the regulating these digital assets by optimizing trust to ensure technological innovation without losing financial safety (Lorenz, 2024). However, the proliferation of decentralized technologies and privacy focused cryptocurrencies continues to indicate that the regulatory environment will be forever fluid and complicated (Johnson, 2020).

Cryptographic Principles

Public-Private Key Cryptography

Public-private key cryptography, or asymmetric cryptography, is one of the basic components of cryptocurrency security (Aydar et al., 2019). It involves the use of two cryptographic keys (Aydar et al., 2019). Firstly, the one that is made available and second is the other that is kept very secure and only known by the owner, and are known as the public key and the private key respectively. When a user begins a transaction, it is secured with the receiver's public key and can only be opened with the receiver's private key. This makes it possible for only the intended recipient to transact on the funds, giving the transaction the much needed confidentiality and/or security (Aydar et al., 2019).

Also, the public and the private keys are employed in the digital signatures that ensure the credibility and the validity of the transactions conducted (Brands, 2000). The data is encrypted by the user or the sender when they sign a transaction with their private key and other parties can decrypt it using the public key hence one can confirm that the transaction has not been tampered with whether it came from the right sender (Jiménez-Serranía et al., 2021).

Hash Algorithms

Hash functions are encrypted operations which take an input data and produce an output data in the form of a chain of characters which qualitatively resembles random (Fuller et al., 2017). These algorithms are used in certifying the authenticity of transactions while at the same time protecting the data. Applicable also in the context of cryptocurrencies, hash algorithms help to create cryptographic hashes for the transactional data and any change made to the data would lead to a considerably different hash tag (Dong et al., 2024).

For instance, the application of the SHA-256 (Secure Hash Algorithm 256-bit) coding function in securing the Bitcoin block chain (Santos Jr et al., 2024). Every block has a record of previous block's hash code which joins all the blocks in a single chain through reciprocal hash codes. This means that for efficiency purposes, each block in the blockchain can never be altered as this would mean that the identity of following blocks will also need to change since the hash code of a block is connected to the previous block's hash code therefore making it nearly impossible for most networks (Bruce, 2014).

CRYPTOCURRENCY ECOSYSTEM

Cryptocurrency Exchanges

The cryptocurrency environment is vast and consists of a large number of elements that are necessary for the functioning, trading, and use of cryptocurrencies. In this case, cryptocurrency exchanges occupy a central position since they provide consumers with the opportunity to purchase, sell, and exchange cryptocurrencies. There are two primary types of exchanges: which are centralized exchanges (CEXs) and decentralized exchanges (DEXs). Each type of exchange has unique features, benefits, and drawbacks.

Centralized Cryptocurrency Exchanges (CEXs)

CEX refers to a type of trading platforms that is organized and managed by a single central body or an organization (Wu et al., 2024). These are organizations which help to connect buyers and sellers by offering interfaces and several types of transactions. These exchanges are similar to stock exchanges, but for cryptocurrencies (Pandey, 2022). It works like this; users sign up, they have their money stored in financial baskets owned by the exchange. The exchange records buy and sell offers in the order book and directly trades on behalf of the users (Wu et al., 2024). Examples of such popular centralized exchanges include; Binance, Coinbase, and Kraken.

The advantage of using a CEXs is that they are usually more liquid as compared to decentralized exchanges. This leads to higher speed of the trade and lower bid-ask spread which is good for the traders out there (Wu et al., 2024). Additionally, CEXs are easy to use and offer additional trading tools including the margin trade, futures contract, and different types of order which makes them preferable by new and professional traders (Schär, 2021).

However, the centralized nature of the CEXs is a drawback as a malicious attack on the central point would disrupt operations at macro level (Pandey, 2022). Some of the heists, like the Mt. Gox hack in 2014, have led to loss of huge amounts of users' money, which has raised questions on the security of the money stored in these places (Cheung et al., 2015). Additionally, users face a lack of control over their funds in CEX because the private keys are kept by the exchange contradicting the decentralized exchange systems which advocates the full authority of the user on the assets (Wu et al., 2024). Furthermore, as the centralized exchanges are obliged to follow the Anti-Money Laundering policies and the Know-Your Customer policy, hence resulting in compromised user privacy and it has been observed that this could limit the access of the users in some jurisdictions (Fuller et al., 2017).

Decentralized Cryptocurrency Exchanges (DEXs)

DEX work decentralized, which means the control is not at a single focal point but is spread throughout the network. This means that the exchange is carried out directly between the users without the intermediation of a central hub. These trades use blockchain and smart contracts to perform trades in a self-executing and decentralized manner (Wu et al., 2024).

These exchanges work based on the smart contract system by which the trading process is completely handled by computers. Clients assuage overall control of their money and perform every transaction independently from their pockets. Order matching and trade execution are done through an exchange's protocol. The examples of such DEXs are Uniswap, SushiSwap, and PancakeSwap etc (Xu et al., 2023).

DEXs cannot be easily hacked and are not regularly at risk of large scale hacking as CEXs are due to their decentralized nature as the control is not exercised at a central point (Azar et al., 2022). One of the significant drawbacks of CEX is that they usually demand personal data from the users, DEX caters this issue as it does not infringe on the user's right to privacy or anonymity. In addition to this, the DEXs are based on the distributed networks, and governments cannot block them or limit the usage in a short time. This fully corresponds to the principles of blockchain and the freedom of finance (Náñez Alonso et al., 2021).

On the other hand, the DEXs have been observed with lower liquidity compared to CEXs leading to higher slippage and less favorable conditions for trading, particularly for large orders (Glaser & Bezzenberger, 2015). Moreover, the designs of DEXs may be less friendly, and sometimes more complicated than the CEXs especially for first-time users (Pandey, 2022). Also, other features including options for sophisticated trading and customer services are usually restrained.

While concluding, it is important to understand that the issue of using centralized and decentralized exchanges relates to several factors such as the attitudes of the users, security aspects, and legal measures that have to be taken into consideration. Analyzing the differences between centralized an decentralized exchanges, it is possible to define that both have benefits, which make them useful for the functioning of cryptocurrencies and their users. CEXs provide better order depth, and traders' interactions, and services, which is preferable for experienced traders and those who value comfort. But they entail inherent security vulnerability concerns and regulatory compliance application issues. (Pandey, 2022)

On the other hand, decentralized exchanges focus on the security, privacy, and censorship issues that are considered to be highly important among the representatives of the cryptocurrency world. Nevertheless, there are some disadvantages which include; liquidity issue, user interface, and scalability (Xu et al., 2023). Therefore, as the environment of the cryptosystems is developing, the further development and implementation of the combined models can be observed, which will contain the best features of both the centralized and decentralized exchanges (Xu et al., 2023).

Wallets

Wallets are an example of the usage of cryptocurrencies, which allow an individual to store, send and receive cryptocurrencies safely (Suratkar et al., 2020). These wallets are of different types with each of them with their own characteristics of operational mechanism and protection from unauthorized access. Thus, it is essential to get acquainted with various kinds of wallets and their capabilities to make the right choice for protection of assets (Allen et al., 2020). The following paragraphs discusses at the various types of wallets, how they work, and the supporting technology in consultation with literature.

Depending on their connection to the internet, the classifications of the cryptocurrency wallets is done, which are elaborated as follows:

Hot Wallets

Hot wallets can be described as the wallets which are are actively connected to the internet and thus while they are easy to use in accordance with the frequent transactions they are also vulnerable to breaches and hacks (Castonguay & Stein Smith, 2020). Furthermore, there are software wallets which have the measures of safety like the encryptions of the private keys, meaning that even if the device they are stored in is hacked, the keys cannot be accessed. In addition to this, they utilize specialized hardware cards which contain secure elements to store information. Such measures guarantee that none other than the concerned parties will be allowed to manipulate the information or physically tamper with it, which results in added security (Thota et al., 2020).

The application wallets are those which can be installed on electronic or computerized devices and hence can be further divided into desktop, mobile and web-based wallets. The desktop-based model enables maximum control over the private keys of the users as they are installed in the personal computer of the user, and provide a good level of security except when the whole computer system is bounded under hacking (Plotkin, 2020). These mobile software wallets are installed on a smartphone to facilitate on the go spending. They can also have options like, for instance, the possibility to pay with the help of a QR code scanner. However, they are risky to be lost or stolen if the gadget is not well protected judiciously or prudently. Finally, web wallets are hosted on the internet and can be accessed from anywhere with internet connectivity and any internet-connected devise, however, the management of private keys is done by the service providers, which is worrying as it highlights issues of centralization and hacking (Thota et al., 2020).

Cold Wallets

Cold wallets are those ground pockets that are more secure than the online wallets because the key is never on the internet (Fritsche, 2018). Thus, they are suitable for long-term storage of large amounts of cryptocurrency as they provide a safeguard against threats inherent to the online domain due to their offline oriented functionality (Fritsche, 2018). Users can never begin mining and at the same time expose their private keys to the internet as there is no single point of contact for this activity. Hardware wallets are the physical devices designed to store private keys and keep them safe from any influence of the online world. It is regarded as one of the safest ways of storing cryptocurrencies because it cannot be invaded by hackers. The data can be signed without using private keys, which eliminates additional risks, such as leaving the keys on the Web (Mahnamfar et al., 2024). A paper wallet is an extract of a couple of public/private keys usually in the form of QR codes. Whereas, paper wallets are purely offline hence such dangers or threats are incomprehensible for penetrating through the paper wallets. However, they are physically tackled and erasable and the users are expected to be careful when handling and storing them (Benmalek, 2024). In essence, cryptocurrency wallets are utilized for the storage of actual or virtual keys, transmitting of coins, and identification of users.

Mining and Consensus Mechanisms

Mining and consensus mechanisms used in blockchain networks are core fundamental facets of a blockchain as they make up the protocols of the decentralized systems (Hossan et al., 2024). It single-handedly controls the industry and is subcategorized into two types of mechanisms, PoW and PoS that work differently at the operational level while having some exclusive benefits and drawbacks. Both Proof of Work and Proof of Stake can be regarded as major styles that have their pros and cons. In future due to difference in functions of the PoW and PoS more powerful and effective consensus models may be introduced which can be the combination of PoW and PoS. However, further work is needed to overcome the challenges of these mechanisms and improve the possibilities for blockchain solutions' wide implementation, security, and accessibility (Hossan et al., 2024).

The discussion as follows focuses on outlining these mechanisms to demonstrate their feasibility and impact on the environment and securities by defining the interpretation of the use of the literature in the current academic setting.

Proof of Work (PoW)

A consensus method primarily adopted by the pioneers of the first online currency is Proof of Work. It requires the miners to solve complex numerical problems to validate transactions as well as uphold the platform. In a PoW system miners, participate in solving complicated mathematical problems. When the first participant is successful in giving the solution, then he is able to add the subsequent block to the chain and is rewarded making him the bona fide to the system (Alharby et al., 2024).

The idea of PoW is quite secure because a sufficient amount of computational power is required to make changes on the blockchain. Since to perform a 51% attack, a party needs to control a majority of the network's hash rate which requires tremendous computing power, and it is practically impossible (Hossan et al., 2024). Moreover, the more than a decade long history of the Bitcoin itself is the evidence of the efficiency of the consensus mechanism as there hasn't been a single report of a double-spending attack until now (Alharby et al., 2024). Bitcoin's ten years history, which did not experience a double-spending attack, prove the efficiency of PoW (JOURJON).

However, with all these advantages, there are some disadvantages to the system as well as it utilizes a staggering amount of electricity which makes it non-eco-friendly. For example, Bitcoin uses as much energy annually as some countries, which has drawn criticism concerning the overall cryptocurrency's sustainability. Furthermore, the usage of specialized mining hardware (ASICs) hinders on the entry of normal users into mining (Hossan et al., 2024).

Proof of Stake (PoS)

Proof of Stake is another consensus method that is considered as the improvement over PoW, mainly to counter of the high-power consumption (Jain et al., 2024). It uses validators that have to lock up their coins to be able to contribute to PoS network consensus. Every validator is selected to create new blocks and approve transactions depending on the coins owned and the number of coins the holder is ready to risk – staking. The process of selection can use various techniques such as randomization and many others with the aim of being fair. As for the incentives, validators receive transaction fees and, in some systems, – newly mined coins (Jain et al., 2024).

Although PoS is not free from flaws, the efficiency of this consensus algorithm is far greater than that of PoW since it does not require resource-intensive mining (Deval et al., 2024). Moreover, accessibility is another advantage of PoS which means that more people can be involved in the consensus process because it does not require the hard ware expenses of mining. This can extend resultant layouts to the network decentralization (Abellán Álvarez et al., 2024).

On the contrary, it was pointed out that, PoS can cause centralization of wealth since those with more coins control the network. This can also worsen somehow the income inequality within the system as pointed by (Saleh, 2021). Furthermore, PoS is in theory prone to some issues, for example, nothing at stake, which is when the validators are interested in validating as many conflicting chains as possible. Additionally, PoS mechanisms might be rather complicated to be implemented and realized as compared to PoW what can lead to errors in implementation and, therefore, lead to security threats.

Thus, PoW and PoS have certain advantages and disadvantages, as well as serve different functions and are preferred by different users in the world of cryptocurrencies (Al Ahmad et al., 2018). In the aspect of security infrastructure, PoW is coupled with issues of high energy consumption, impacting the environment and mainly focused on hardware (Saleh, 2021). On the other hand, PoS has the advantages of energy efficiency and accessibility but is also associated with such problems as the concentration of wealth and theoretical threats to the security of the protocol (Al Ahmad et al., 2018).

ECONOMIC IMPLICATIONS OF CRYPTOCURRENCY

Cryptocurrencies have brought revolution in the financial technology industry essentially through the transformation it brought for the economic and hence enjoy a great impact especially (Machkour & Abriane, 2020). Alongside transforming the features of the core financial institution, while at the same time imposing transformative changes to their general business models and juridical notion. This section lays emphasis on the effects that cryptocurrencies have on the banking institutions, payment structures and financial services sectors.

Disintermediation

Amongst the most profound effects of cryptocurrencies as an external variable, is their factor of disintermediation, posing it as a threat to the traditional financial infrastructure (Gomaa, 2018). Cryptocurrencies are digital currencies which can be used to buy other commodities as well as services, direct from the users without involving the services of a third party for instance, the banks. The elimination of the intermediary possesses the capability of reducing the transaction cost and the time taken in the transactions consequently increasing the financial inclusion through extension of banking services to the under banked (Donovan, 2012).

Impact on Payment Systems

The impact of cryptocurrencies on the traditional payment systems is also noteworthy as these offer media of exchange with comparatively lower transactional costs and considerably lesser settlement time per transaction (Makarov & Schoar, 2022b). Credit card systems and money wiring service providers move to development of payment systems through the use of cryptocurrencies due to the increased shift of consumer preferences (Geng, 2017).

As these are cheaper to use, are faster when it comes to the processing period and so are preferred for cross border transactions. Additionally, the P2P factor of transaction helps to facilitate payment without having to engage an intermediary which bypasses the process of screening of funds and the declaration of their sources (Bank, 2024). For instance, Bitcoin and all the other online virtual currencies can significantly reduce the expenses of time and money in the remittance process (CFI).

Banking Services and Innovation

Additionally, the impact of the cryptocurrencies on the banking industry can be measured through the fact that the central banks of many countries have introduced their digital currencies which are pegged to their home currencies, and incorporate the block chain technology (Fung & Halaburda, 2016). The development of the CBDC or incorporating blockchain into the works such as in cross-border payments' clearance and settlement, trade finance, and KYC verification (Minesso et al., 2022). These changes are centralizing banking operation into digital innovation.

Investment Opportunities

The exponential growth of these digital currencies also demonstrated that it is possible to make good money with cryptocurrencies as the high risk element of these assets is adherent to the higher return possibilities as well (Corbet et al., 2019). Investments in bitcoins, Ethereum, and all the other cryptocurrencies have seen their investments grow in geometric progression which attract investors across the world to seek profit making out of them (Mikhaylov, 2020). For example, the pioneer cryptocurrency, Bitcoin has an impressive growth rate, with its price of around $0.09 in 2010 to $73,794 in 2024 (Teo, 2024). However, it is important to notice that with the high return yield, there is high possibility of losses due to the volatile nature of these assets. Furthermore, the factor of volatility also contributes to the speculative bubble formation, which may result in allocation of the resources from a potentially better investment opportunity hence being an obstacle to the economic growth in a longer run (Tang, 2024).

Moreover, cryptocurrencies are proved to be an instrument for investing that can expand the portfolios based on traditional financial tools (Chernova et al., 2024). These can be useful in portfolio diversification since the exposure to the market has different risk-reward profiles as compared to the other asset classes available in the financial markets (Kajtazi & Moro, 2017). In addition to this, they enhance the financial inclusion by providing access to finance to those who may have been rejected by the traditional financial institutions. For example, the ICO and STO offer chances of investing in early-stage undertakings of DLT-based ventures (Romero-Castro et al., 2022). These mechanisms enable the investors to back unproven technologies and possibly gain huge returns.

However, there is little doubt that cryptocurrencies are highly volatile especially on the issue of price. Fear and panic, technical signals, regulation news and among others constrain can cause large fluctuations in the prices, which can prove very risky for investors (Siegel, 2021). Additionally, the cryptocurrencies are yet to find stable regulatory status. Fluctuations in the regulation greatly influence the market by having legal restrictions or other limitations on what is considered to be a digital asset.

Furthermore, there are potentials of hacking, and there was a prevalent fraud associated with digital currencies. Exchange hacks and scams have led to investor's losses in large numbers and of high-profile cases, which has resulted in loss of investor confidence (Boreiko, 2024b). As it has been utterly pointed out, cryptocurrencies do not have previous typical approaches to value determination which makes it difficult for investors to evaluate their intrinsic value hence making it difficult to make the right decisions when investing (Boreiko, 2024b).

Role of the Governments

Financial technology, including cryptocurrency, is still largely influenced by governments since they engage in the regulation of such technologies. This section aims at presenting the legal regimes that have emerged to regulate their activities in response to the emergence of digital assets as witnessed below.

The main interest of political authorities is connected with the risks connected with the usage of cryptocurrencies in criminal purposes including money laundering and financing of terrorism (Oh & Nguyen, 2018). A number of countries have introduced, or are discussing, legislation to compel crypto exchanges and the firms they work with to observe anti-money laundering (AML) as well as know your customer (KYC) laws. Another problem derived from regulators' noninterventionist approach in the cryptocurrency market is the absence of protection of consumers. The authorities do seek to regulate the problem of fake ICO, frauds, scams, and market manipulation and at the same time promote innovation (Zabchuk & Pashchuk, 2020).

In addition to this, governments and tax collection agencies are trying to decide on how to implement taxes for cryptocurrency transactions and for holding. This characteristic makes it difficult to enforce regulations and collect taxes because of the anonymity that comes with the decentralized system of cryptocurrencies (Oh & Nguyen, 2018). Governments and financial regulatory agencies continuously focus on the influence cryptocurrencies have on the stability of the financial system. This is just as the price values of the digital assets remain highly unstable and as the use of stable coins and Defi platforms become more apparent (Azar et al., 2022).

The positive role of the government is observed with a number of states have an approval and positive attitude towards cryptocurrencies since they may become a driving force for innovations in the field of fintech and economic development (Gohwong, 2019). For example, Switzerland with its significant efforts at giving legal contours to the trading of cryptocurrencies, and dedicates itself in making a competitive blockchain environment of the country (Braun-Dubler et al., 2020). Alongside this, some have resorted to regulation in an effort to control for risks but enable innovation at the same time in a bid to avoid any related catastrophes. For example, the United States has established a dynamic of federal and state regulations that could accommodate both consumer protectionism and the market formation (Koopman et al., 2014). Adding to these points, certain governments have opted to regulate them by putting covert measures that will narrow the flow of cryptocurrencies and trading. China for instance has suppressed cryptocurrency exchanges and initial coin offerings on anti-cryptocurrency fraud grounds (Broadhurst et al., 2018). However, it is also working on the creation of the CBDC of its own, central bank digital currency. It is noteworthy that some countries, however, have outright banned cryptocurrencies with some countries extending the ban to blockchain technology

(Fung & Halaburda, 2016). Such measures are used with reference to financial risks, capital regulation, and possible invocations of criminality. Some examples related to the current study are Algeria, Bolivia, and Morocco (Taskinsoy, 2022).

While concluding, one must understand that the consequences of cryptocurrencies cover the impact upon traditional banking, development of new investment possibilities and threats, and variable governmental actions. Of course, it is crucial for the counterparts to be aware of such dynamics as the market of cryptocurrencies is still developing (Wątorek et al., 2021). The governments are then put in a middle of trying to encourage innovation while at the same time tending to the internal issues of stability of fund, and the rights of consumers. The investing public and the finance industry must shift focus and continue to leverage the opportunities that come with digital assets while at the same time having to deal with the risks that accompany them (Castonguay & Stein Smith, 2020).

THE SECURITY AND PRIVACY DISCUSSION

Cryptocurrencies can be considered as a new means in global financial activity, providing a decentralized system of P2P transactions (Nabilou, 2019). Nevertheless, the emergence of digital currencies has created numerous problems in the sphere of safety and anonymity. This section covers the various risks associated with cryptocurrency systems including theft and fraud, IT system hacking, and the potential for 51% attacks and anonymity features in cryptocurrencies including zk-SNARKS and coin mixing.

Information Breaching

Information security is an integral component of the cryptocurrency ecosystem. The use of cryptocurrencies is secure due to the strong cryptographic premises; nonetheless, information breaches are still pressing (Weichbroth et al., 2023). They can be at the exchange level, wallet level, and user level devices, For example, at the exchange level, this happens because digital exchanges are considered to be a rich source of digital currencies by hackers since it's the platform where they are majorly stored (Schumacher, 2024). Prior public cases like Mt. Gox hack in the year 2014 where nearly about 850,000 Bitcoins were stolen, show the adverse impacts arising out of security negligence. For all intents and purposes, exchanges continue to be inherently insecure from different forms of assaults, as well as internal and external disruptive events (Caldwell & Williams, 2016). Additionally, even the applications that enable the users to store the private keys are vulnerable to breaches. Malware or phishing attacks are capable to target soft wallets especially those developed to operate on mobile devices (Weichbroth et al., 2023).

As aforementioned, software wallets are less secure as compared to the hardware wallets, but again they are not foolproof and can be vulnerable to physical tampering. Moreover, research indicates that it was discovered, the users have inadequate perception when it comes to protecting their keys and other personnel information. Ineffective security measures that include the use of low quality, easily guessable passwords or failure to turn on two factor authentication leaves the application open to theft (Weichbroth et al., 2023).

Another challenge that is ascertainable is fraud which is literally described as immoral practices that seek to swindle users. Frauds pose threat to the security of the cryptocurrency systems in a multifold manner. Firstly, Phishing scams is a common profound phenomenon in this arena. It tricks individuals in giving out their own critical details or log in information. This can be through fake websites, emails or messages in what seems to be send by a genuine firm

In addition to this, the investors in this market are not adequately protected especially due to its newness as compared to other markets, and pertaining Ponzi schemes such as fraudulent ICOs (Tiwari et al., 2020). By the startling growth of these assets, it is evident that the investors are attracted by high anticipated returns (Weichbroth et al., 2023). Consequently, they may be trapped by the Initial Coin Offering with highly promised returns and while to their surprise the operators disappear with investors' money leaving the investors with heavy losses (Boreiko, 2024b).

Moreover, ransomware is again another example of a malware that locks computers or specific files on the computers and provides the decryption to the affected files for some coins (Liska & Gallo, 2016). These activities put the participants at the mercy of such schemes since the utilization of digital currencies entail anonymity

Smart Contract

Smart contract, which is an automated execution of computer code for carrying out the provisions of a contract, is widely used in most of the cryptocurrencies; self-executing applications of smart contracts are popular. However, they are not free from threats and drawbacks.

Initiating with the code vulnerabilities, which is, if there are errors in the program, this would result in errors of the smart contract and would be rather more expensive (Boreiko, 2024b). The risk of smart contracts not working as intended is seen, for instance, in the popular 2016 DAO hack in which $50 million of Ether were lost due to the code vulnerabilities of the smart contract (Gerard, 2017). Next, Oracle Manipulation is again a threat for the users of the cryptocurrencies. This is because it is the most popular form of operation of smart contracts that are deployed in the contemporary sector. For cases where they may get corrupted or get into the wrong hands, then the respective contracts are carried out inefficiently or even harm the owner. Lastly, the reentrancy attacks pose major challenges for the security of system, as they occur when a hacker's contract repeatedly points to the targeted vulnerable contract that results in embezzlement (Lee, 2019).

Sybil Attacks

A Sybil attack can be described as the one that involves the creation of multiple fake identities by one node in a network just to amass substantive control (Boreiko, 2024b). In consensus mechanisms within the blockchain of cryptocurrencies, sybil attacks distort consensus mechanism by causing network interrupts, or manipulation of the voting that is normally done in governance of decentralized platforms (Hameed et al., 2022). Some of the measures that can be used to prevent Sybil attacks are inclusive of the aof the proof-of-work (PoW) or proof-of-stake (PoS) schemes which are quite expensive, hence making the creation of multiple fake identities to be costly itself (Akbar et al., 2021).

51% Attack

Specifically, a 51% attack takes place when an individual or a group of individuals control more than 51% of the network's mining hash rate, in order to conduct a detrimental action on the blockchain. This control allows the attacker to perform reverse transaction, multiple spending of the same coins, and the inability to confirm new transactions (Boreiko, 2024b). In theory, 51% attacks are very difficult to perform; however, they have been performed in practice. Smaller form of coins with less rates of hash are highly victimized under such cases resulting in technical and financial losses. This is one of the most dangerous issues because it makes people doubt the stability of a cryptocurrency (Ametrano, 2016). In extreme cases, it results in extreme financial losses, users' distrust, and negative effects on market value of the problematic currency which not only distorts the currency but also disrupts the market trust in the security system of the cryptocurrencies.

However, there are several suggested measures for avoiding the 51% attacks and they involve increasing the network hash rates, complication of the presently existing consensus type and decentralizing the mining activities.

PRIVACY-ENHANCING TECHNOLOGIES

Due to the security and privacy issues, the community of cryptocurrencies has developed several methods to enhance privacy. These technologies are designed for preserving users' identities and details of the transactions made, thus guaranteeing that there is privacy while at the same time there is security in the transactions (Bernabe et al., 2019).

Zero-Knowledge Proofs

ZKPs are a set of digital methods that allow one party to convince the other party of the veracity of matters without relaying additional information to the second party aside from the statement factually (Bamberger et al., 2022). The usage of ZKPs can be considered in the case when transactions take place in crypt forms and such information as the amount of the transaction, or identities of the counterparts, should remain confidential. For example, Zcash, a popular cryptocurrency makes use of the zk-SNARKs (Zero-Knowledge Succinct Non-Interactive Arguments of Knowledge) for the purpose of its improvement (Chen et al., 2022). This method of cryptography allows both the parties to be involved in a certain transaction to be assured that the specific transaction has taken place without actually issuing the details of that transaction (Pinto, 2020).

Through the ZKPs, the record contains transactions that are opaque and illicit to third parties. This is particularly important to prevent the owners of the system and other third parties from identifying the users of the system, while keeping the financial details a closely guarded secret. However, they bring some disadvantages; for instance, some of them are computationally expensive which can slow down the occurrence of transactions. Furthermore, the general structure of ZKPs may not be easy to implement, and hence designed flaws may be present if this is done wrongly

Coin Mixing

It is a process that is used to mask some parts of the given route of some other cryptocurrencies in the context of enhancing the aspect of privacy (Zaghloul et al., 2020). A coin mixing service or simply a tumbler essentially merges many users' transactions and then return the money to more new addresses. Some of the digital currencies like Monero and Dash have the inherent features of mixing to enhance anonymity. Although it proves helpful in enhancing anonymity, coin mixing is employed in unlawful activities such as money laundering (Teichmann & Falker, 2020).

Ring Signatures

Ring signatures can take place wherever there exist keys for every member of users and all of them can performance the ring signatures. Its format does not allow the identification of the specific member who contributed the signature. For instance, in Monero, ring signatures are used to protect the anonymity of the transaction. Technically, when a transaction occurs, the sender's details are combined with other potential signers, hence it is almost impossible to determine the true sender of the transaction (Teichmann & Falker, 2020).

Among the pros of using the ring signature, ring signatures have better anonymity than normal signatures and do not require the services of a third party. Moreover, they are very helpful where identity has to be protected. Although, there are some cons to the situation as well, which is the first major problem associated with application of ring signatures, is the problem of increasing computational load and transaction size, which has impact on the performance and general scalability of the cryptocurrency.

Stealth Addresses

Stealth addresses make it possible for a sender to come up with a new address for every transaction, but only the recipient has the capability to steal it to retrieve the cash back. To identify a specific transaction, the sender indeed creates a new address once for each transaction with the recipient's public key (Wronka, 2022). The recipient can later on use the private key to unlock the funds sent to these stealth addresses They optimize on privacy since addresses used in different transactions are not the same and hence it becomes extremely hard for the third party to track down the activity of that specific address. The main disadvantage of stealth addresses can be the fact that they can complicate the given cryptocurrency's protocol and also make transactions larger (Teichmann & Falker, 2020).

Summarizing the security of the cryptocurrency ecosystems, it is noteworthy that two very important issues related to cryptocurrencies still need to be addressed before the cryptocurrencies can stand the test of time and be embraced; which are security and privacy. Credibility threats that include information security threats, fraud, 51% attack pose an invasive threat in the cryptocurrency setting are some of the major withstanding challenges (Bhat et al., 2020). In addition, other things being equal; the weakness in smart contracts, and the prospects of Sybil attack creating more problems brings more worries to the security bash. Such methods as zero-knowledge proofs, coin mixing, the ring signatures, the stealth address, and confidential transactions may be considered pointing at satisfactory solutions for maintaining users' anonymity and transactions' shielded character (Noether &

Mackenzie, 2016). The findings demonstrate that because the form of payment with the help of cryptocurrency is still considered to be rather fresh, and still evolving, more attempts must be made to eliminate these issues and enhance consumers' and the digital monetary system's protection.

FUTURE TRENDS IN CRYPTOCURRENCY

Cryptocurrencies are among the most revolutionary phenomena in the field of financial markets with the usage of decentralized, secure, and transparent money systems. As an emerging type of asset class, cryptocurrency is still very active in its evolution as a form of innovation in the financial structure that opens up new doors (Dupuis & Gleason, 2020). Thus, it is significant for various interested parties, starting from a sole trader and leading up to a large institutions and different public authorities, to possessing the knowledge of the further tendencies in this sphere.

First of all, Decentralized Finance also commonly referred to as DeFi is a concept that is that introduces decentralization and the exclusion of middlemen. In its simplest form, DeFi endeavors to use existing frameworks like loans, insurance policies, and trading without intermediaries (Schär, 2021).

On the DeFi platforms, the solution known as smart contract is employed to execute and perform financial operations accurately (Makarov & Schoar, 2022b). These smart contracts reduce the roles of middlemen and thus a transaction is cheaper and can be come in effect within a shorter period of time. Moreover, the decentralization makes the level of security and privacy better, but it finds some problems in liquidity and usability (Schär, 2021). Aave and Compound and similar platforms are examples of such Defi systems which are used for lending and borrowing coins and tokens, and to earn interest on coins or getting a loan without credit check. Most of these protocols rely on collateral which allows their risk management as well (Makarov & Schoar, 2022b).

However, there are some challenges to the system as well. For instance, the DeFi having been the hope when it comes to decentralization, but the one thing that still persists is the issue of insecurity. Exploitation along with the vulnerabilities present in smart contracts have caused huge fund loss (Geng, 2017). For instance, the recent hack in the 2020 that affected the DeFi protocol, had the impact which was felt with an amount lost being over $8 million.

The current status of the regulation of DeFi is another challenge as it is still rather open-ended. At the same time, global financial legislation raises concerns on the effectiveness of the regulation of these decentralized platforms and the basic requirement concepts such as consumer protection and systemic risk. Moreover, the development of the DeFi platforms has highlighted the issues with their scalability as well. This can be attributed to the rising transaction fees and network overload when using the Ethereum platform common for hosting many DeFi projects (Mohammed et al., 2021).

Secondly, the NFTs are another emerging trend in the digital assets that are not interoperable with other similar assets and are affiliated with blockchain. While emerging as decentralized digital assets stores like Bitcoin, NFTs are configured in non-divisible nature and thus to be found application in referencing exclusive digital art, collectibles, and other similar objects (Abellán Álvarez et al., 2024).

The application of these NFTs are profound in the realm of the digital art and the collectibles. Artists are now able to find business models through which they can sell the various art masterpieces that they produce (Kucheryavenko et al., 2019). Marketplaces such as *OpenSea* and *Rarible* allow the buying and selling of digital art as well as secondary sales through auction that reverts royalties back to the artists. Moreover, gaming is another arena where the increased adoption of NFTs is observed. Players are interested in NFTs due to their ability to purchase true ownership of virtual assets found in video games. For virtual goods, the players are allowed to buy, sell, and exchange them across the available games, thus developing the gaming economy or secondary market economy. Additionally, they have opened up a new arena of digital real estate with website such as *Decentraland* and the *Sandbox* enables users to buy, develop and sell the real estate in form of plot of land in the form of NFT. This type of market is however relatively new akin to the real estate market, but is an online market (Kucheryavenko et al., 2019).

In contrast to this, they have some challenges and criticism as well. Starting with their environmental impact, because of the huge computational power that is required to generate a NFT and conduct a transaction on a public ledger like Ethereum, such procedures are expensive in terms of energy and have raised many questions about their sustainability (Braun-Dubler et al., 2020). However, attempts have been made to move to better consensus algorithms although these attempts have not yet materialized. Additionally, at this moment, there are conflicts that arise as market speculation and the build-up of bubbles due to the increasing trend of using NFTs. Sales instances like *Beeple's NFT* art at $69 million put a lot of paint into the market as highly speculative; and that maneuver cannot be sustainable in the long run. Furthermore, the NFTs stimulate some creative and complex discourses about the protection of copyright. The parties to an object or rights to access the same can at times be closely competed especially in as much as creators of exclusive content do not receive adequate payments (Hameed & Farooq, 2017).

Another emerging trend for the future of cryptocurrencies is the development of the CBDCs mean a fiat currency of a country that is created in electronic and digital form offered by a country's Central Bank. CBDCs are the digital counterparts of fiat currencies backed by the state and in essence, contain all attributes of digital currencies along with the backing of the conventional financial institutions (Fung & Halaburda, 2016).

Therefore, CBDCs can facilitate digital finance, which seems to be beyond the reach of several people who do not have a bank account at the moment (Schumacher, 2024). Therefore, the possibility to conduct operations with CBDCs using a mobile application can significantly enhance the access to financial services. It enhances the payment efficiency that this is because they remove the middlemen and therefore can assist in cutting down time and costs within the payment systems. It can accelerate the processes of cross-border activities and enable organizations to reduce the reliance on intermediaries (Náñez Alonso et al., 2021). Moreover, the CBDCs can be useful for effectuating monetary policy to central banks as provided through direct distribution can help in the regulating of the money supply and the rate of interest.

Alike with other emerging trends, it too faces some challenges and risks. To some extent, it is worth stating that introducing CBDCs presents a great threat to privacy (Allen et al., 2020). Due to its centralized nature, the system can gather a large amount of information as well as observe the citizens eroding their privacy right (Oh & Nguyen, 2018). In addition to this, it possesses some technical risks as well as the CBDC's infrastructure with the required security and solidity is difficult to build and develop with the help of technology. Initially contemplated issues are to ward off hacker dangers and shield the general steadiness (Náñez Alonso et al., 2021). It is highly significant to notice that the threats that CBDC point out to the local banking systems as well. For example, the central banks may therefore be perceived as competitors of banks which may lead to a wholesale shift in the position of the latter in credit creation and in terms of the agency they perform as financial intermediation brokers (Minesso et al., 2022).

CONCLUSION

In turn, all these tendencies stand in a continuum with the subjects that exist in the financial realm and affect the trends in this domain in some manner. However, it is quintessential for these technologies to cater quite a number of challenges some of which include the security risks, resolving the scalability problems, and sustainable policies. NFTs, although, are the ambassador of a novel form of ownership and value in the digital world affecting art, gaming, and even virtual real estate. Still, the use of NFTs has some risks and drawbacks, including environmental impacts and threats formation of speculative bubbles. CBDCs, on the other hand, possess the potential for improving financial inclusion and optimizing the payment system; however, they have certain problems linked with privacy concerns, technologically secured centralized bases, and sociopolitical challenges that can jeopardize the monopolistic banking system's current positions.

The incorporation of these trends into the broader financial ecosystem has several adamant implications both at macro and micro levels of the economy. Thus, such technologies contribute to bettering the position of individuals and increasing the efficiency of financial systems. In addition to this, at the heart of these trends, blockchain technology will enable more effectiveness and streamlined clarity of the financial activity. The effective utility of the smart contracts and decentralized protocols can help in saving transaction costs and increase the speed of the transaction, besides bringing in transparency and immutability. Lastly, these technologies have evolved with exponential progression, hence leaving consumers and systems very exposed to risks that require sound regulation.

REFERENCES

Abellán Álvarez, I., Gramlich, V., & Sedlmeir, J. (2024). Unsealing the secrets of blockchain consensus: A systematic comparison of the formal security of proof-of-work and proof-of-stake. Proceedings of the 39th ACM/SIGAPP Symposium on Applied Computing, Akbar, N. A., Muneer, A., ElHakim, N., & Fati, S. M. (2021). Distributed hybrid double-spending attack prevention mechanism for proof-of-work and proof-of-stake blockchain consensuses. *Future Internet*, 13(11), 285.

Al Ahmad, M. A., Al-Saleh, A., & Al Masoud, F. A. (2018). Comparison between pow and pos systems of cryptocurrency. *Indonesian Journal of Electrical Engineering and Computer Science*, 10(3), 1251–1256. DOI: 10.11591/ijeecs.v10.i3.pp1251-1256

Alharby, M., Alssaiari, A., Alateef, S., Thomas, N., & Moorsel, A. (2024). A quantitative analysis of the security of PoW-based blockchains. *Cluster Computing*, 27(10), 1–18. DOI: 10.1007/s10586-024-04645-7

Allen, H. J. (2022). Testimony of Hilary J. Allen, US Senate Committee on Banking, Housing, and Urban Affairs Hearing on'Crypto Crash: Why the FTX Bubble Burst and the Harm to Consumers'. *Allen, US Senate Committee on Banking, Housing, and Urban Affairs Hearing on'Crypto Crash: Why the FTX Bubble Burst and the Harm to Consumers'(December 14, 2022)*.

Allen, S., Čapkun, S., Eyal, I., Fanti, G., Ford, B. A., Grimmelmann, J., Juels, A., Kostiainen, K., Meiklejohn, S., & Miller, A. (2020). *Design choices for central bank digital currency: Policy and technical considerations*.

Almeida, J., & Gonçalves, T. C. (2023). A decade of cryptocurrency investment literature: A cluster-based systematic analysis. *International Journal of Financial Studies*, 11(2), 71. DOI: 10.3390/ijfs11020071

Alvarez, F., Argente, D., & Van Patten, D. (2023). Are cryptocurrencies currencies? Bitcoin as legal tender in El Salvador. *Science*, 382(6677), eadd2844. DOI: 10.1126/science.add2844 PMID: 38127756

Ametrano, F. M. (2016). Hayek money: The cryptocurrency price stability solution. *Available atSSRN* 2425270.

Amin, F., Jahangir, A., & Rasifard, H. (2008). Analysis of public-key cryptography for wireless sensor networks security. *International Journal of Computer and Information Engineering*, 2(5), 1448–1453.

Antal, C., Cioara, T., Anghel, I., Antal, M., & Salomie, I. (2021). Distributed ledger technology review and decentralized applications development guidelines. *Future Internet*, 13(3), 62. DOI: 10.3390/fi13030062

Ante, L., Sandner, P., & Fiedler, I. (2018). Blockchain-based ICOs: Pure hype or the dawn of a new era of startup financing? *Journal of Risk and Financial Management*, 11(4), 80. DOI: 10.3390/jrfm11040080

Atzori, M. (2015). Blockchain technology and decentralized governance: Is the state still necessary? *Available atSSRN* 2709713. DOI: 10.2139/ssrn.2709713

Aydar, M., Cetin, S. C., Ayvaz, S., & Aygun, B. (2019). Private key encryption and recovery in blockchain. *arXiv preprint arXiv:1907.04156.*

Azar, P. D., Baughman, G., Carapella, F., Gerszten, J., Lubis, A., Perez-Sangimino, J. P., Scotti, C., Swem, N., Vardoulakis, A., & Rappoport W, D. E. (2022). The financial stability implications of digital assets. *FRB of New York Staff Report*(1034).

Azarenkova, G., Shkodina, I., Samorodov, B., Babenko, M., & Onishchenko, I. (2018). The influence of financial technologies on the global financial system stability. *Investment Management & Financial Innovations*, 15(4), 229–238. DOI: 10.21511/imfi.15(4).2018.19

Bamberger, K. A., Canetti, R., Goldwasser, S., Wexler, R., & Zimmerman, E. J. (2022). Verification dilemmas in law and the promise of zero-knowledge proofs. *Berkeley Technology Law Journal*, 37, 1.

Bank, N. R. (2024). CONSULTATIVE DOCUMENT ON PEER-TO-PEER LENDING AND CROWDFUNDING.

Benmalek, M. (2024). Ransomware on cyber-physical systems: Taxonomies, case studies, security gaps, and open challenges. *Internet of Things and Cyber-Physical Systems*.

Bernabe, J. B., Canovas, J. L., Hernandez-Ramos, J. L., Moreno, R. T., & Skarmeta, A. (2019). Privacy-preserving solutions for blockchain: Review and challenges. *IEEE Access : Practical Innovations, Open Solutions*, 7, 164908–164940. DOI: 10.1109/ACCESS.2019.2950872

Bhat, S. A., Sofi, I. B., & Chi, C.-Y. (2020). Edge computing and its convergence with blockchain in 5G and beyond: Security, challenges, and opportunities. *IEEE Access : Practical Innovations, Open Solutions*, 8, 205340–205373. DOI: 10.1109/ACCESS.2020.3037108

Bhuvana, R., & Aithal, P. (2020). Blockchain based service: A case study on IBM blockchain services & hyperledger fabric. [IJCSBE]. *International Journal of Case Studies in Business, IT, and Education*, 4(1), 94–102.

Boreiko, D. (2024a). Economics of Initial Coin Offerings. In *Understanding Initial Coin Offerings* (pp. 67–106). Edward Elgar Publishing. DOI: 10.4337/9781803921587.00010

Boreiko, D. (2024b). Initial Coin Offerings pitfalls: Scams, flops, and security breaches. In *Understanding Initial Coin Offerings* (pp. 176–200). Edward Elgar Publishing. DOI: 10.4337/9781803921587.00014

Brands, S. (2000). *Rethinking public key infrastructures and digital certificates: building in privacy*. Mit Press. DOI: 10.7551/mitpress/5931.001.0001

Braun-Dubler, N., Gier, H.-P., Bulatnikova, T., Langhart, M., Merki, M., Roth, F., Burret, A., & Perdrisat, S. (2020). *Blockchain: Capabilities, economic viability, and the socio-technical environment* (Vol. 73). vdf Hochschulverlag AG.

Broadhurst, R., Lord, D., Maxim, D., Woodford-Smith, H., Johnston, C., Chung, H. W., Carroll, S., Trivedi, H., & Sabol, B. (2018). Malware trends on 'darknet' crypto-markets: Research review. *Available atSSRN* 3226758.

Bruce, J. (2014). The mini-blockchain scheme. *White paper, 1*, 1-10.

Buterin, V. (2016). Ethereum: platform review. *Opportunities and challenges for private and consortium blockchains, 45*, 1-45.

Caldwell, D., & Williams, R. E. (2016). *Seeking security in an insecure world*. Rowman & Littlefield.

Castonguay, J. J., & Stein Smith, S. (2020). Digital assets and blockchain: Hackable, fraudulent, or just misunderstood? *Accounting Perspectives*, 19(4), 363–387. DOI: 10.1111/1911-3838.12242

CFI. *What are the Main Types of Cryptocurrencies* Corporate Finance Institute Retrieved 1st August from https://corporatefinanceinstitute.com/resources/cryptocurrency/types-of-cryptocurrency/

Chen, T., Lu, H., Kunpittaya, T., & Luo, A. (2022). A review of zk-SNARKs. *arXiv preprint arXiv:2202.06877.*

Chernova, N., Serhiienko, O., Bril, M., Bilotserkivskyi, O., & Kochorba, V. (2024). Investigation of modern investment opportunities with cryptocurrency market: Optimization approach. *Intellectual Economics*, 18(1), 80–105.

Cheung, A., Roca, E., & Su, J.-J. (2015). Crypto-currency bubbles: An application of the Phillips–Shi–Yu (2013) methodology on Mt. Gox bitcoin prices. *Applied Economics*, 47(23), 2348–2358. DOI: 10.1080/00036846.2015.1005827

Chiu, I. H. (2023). An institutional account of responsiveness in financial regulation-Examining the fallacy and limits of 'same activity, same risks, same rules' as the answer to financial innovation and regulatory arbitrage. *Computer Law & Security Report*, 51, 105868. DOI: 10.1016/j.clsr.2023.105868

Chuen, D. L. K., Guo, L., & Wang, Y. (2017). Cryptocurrency: A new investment opportunity? *Journal of Alternative Investments*, 20(3), 16–40. DOI: 10.3905/jai.2018.20.3.016

Corbet, S., Lucey, B., Urquhart, A., & Yarovaya, L. (2019). Cryptocurrencies as a financial asset: A systematic analysis. *International Review of Financial Analysis*, 62, 182–199. DOI: 10.1016/j.irfa.2018.09.003

De Blasis, R., Galati, L., Grassi, R., & Rizzini, G. (2024). Information Flow in the FTX Bankruptcy: A Network Approach. *arXiv preprint arXiv:2407.12683*.

Delgado-Segura, S., Pérez-Solà, C., Herrera-Joancomartí, J., Navarro-Arribas, G., & Borrell, J. (2018). Cryptocurrency networks: A new P2P paradigm. *Mobile Information Systems*, 2018(1), 2159082.

Deval, V., Dwivedi, V. K., Dixit, A., Norta, A., Shah, S. A., Sharma, R., & Draheim, D. (2024). Mobile Smart Contracts: Exploring Scalability Challenges and Consensus Mechanisms. *IEEE Access : Practical Innovations, Open Solutions*, 12, 34265–34288. DOI: 10.1109/ACCESS.2024.3371901

Dong, C., Wang, F., & Feng, D. (2024). DxHash: A Memory-saving Consistent Hashing Algorithm. *ACM Transactions on Internet Technology*, 24(1), 1–22. DOI: 10.1145/3631708

Donovan, K. (2012). Mobile money for financial inclusion. *Information and Communications for development, 61*(1), 61-73.

Dupuis, D., & Gleason, K. (2020). Money laundering with cryptocurrency: Open doors and the regulatory dialectic. *Journal of Financial Crime*, 28(1), 60–74. DOI: 10.1108/JFC-06-2020-0113

Fink, A. S. (2018). *Can cryptocurrency be audited to Bank Secrecy Act and anti-money laundering regulations and normalized in the United States*. Utica College.

Fritsche, R. V. (2018). Recommendations for implementing a Bitcoin wallet using smart card.

Fuller, B., Varia, M., Yerukhimovich, A., Shen, E., Hamlin, A., Gadepally, V., Shay, R., Mitchell, J. D., & Cunningham, R. K. (2017). Sok: Cryptographically protected database search. 2017 IEEE Symposium on Security and Privacy (SP), Fung, B. S., & Halaburda, H. (2016). Central bank digital currencies: a framework for assessing why and how. *Available at SSRN 2994052*.

Geng, D. (2017). How technology Is reshaping financial services: Essays on consumer behavior in card, channel and cryptocurrency services.

Georgeson, D. A. (2018). Cryptocurrencies as an Alternative to Fiat Monetary Systems.

Gerard, D. (2017). *Attack of the 50 foot blockchain: Bitcoin, blockchain, Ethereum & smart contracts*. David Gerard.

Ghosh, A., Gupta, S., Dua, A., & Kumar, N. (2020). Security of Cryptocurrencies in blockchain technology: State-of-art, challenges and future prospects. *Journal of Network and Computer Applications*, 163, 102635. DOI: 10.1016/j.jnca.2020.102635

Girasa, R. (2018). Regulation of cryptocurrencies and blockchain technologies. *National and International Perspectives. Suiza: Palgrave Macmillan*.

Glaser, F., & Bezzenberger, L. (2015). Beyond cryptocurrencies-a taxonomy of decentralized consensus systems. 23rd European conference on information systems (ECIS), Münster, Germany, Goforth, C. (2024). THE SECURITIES AND EXCHANGE COMMISSION AND CRYPTOASSETS: A STUDY IN IRONY. *Albany Law Review*, 87(1), 55–106.

Gohwong, S. G. (2019). Government-based Cryptocurrencies. *Asian Political Science Review, 3*(2).

Gomaa, A. (2018). *The creation of a cryptocurrency to support disintermediation*. NeilsonJournals Publishing. DOI: 10.4135/9781529733846

Guseva, Y. (2020). A conceptual framework for digital-asset securities: Tokens and coins as debt and equity. *Md. L. Rev.*, 80, 166.

Hairudin, A., Sifat, I. M., Mohamad, A., & Yusof, Y. (2022). Cryptocurrencies: A survey on acceptance, governance and market dynamics. *International Journal of Finance & Economics*, 27(4), 4633–4659. DOI: 10.1002/ijfe.2392

Hameed, K., Barika, M., Garg, S., Amin, M. B., & Kang, B. (2022). A taxonomy study on securing Blockchain-based Industrial applications: An overview, application perspectives, requirements, attacks, countermeasures, and open issues. *Journal of Industrial Information Integration*, 26, 100312. DOI: 10.1016/j.jii.2021.100312

Hameed, S., & Farooq, S. (2017). The art of crypto currencies: A comprehensive analysis of popular crypto currencies. *arXiv preprint arXiv:1711.11073.*

Hassani, H., Huang, X., & Silva, E. (2018). Big-crypto: Big data, blockchain and cryptocurrency. *Big Data and Cognitive Computing*, 2(4), 34. DOI: 10.3390/bdcc2040034

Hays, D., & Kirilenko, A. (2021). Cryptocurrency regulation and enforcement in the US and Europe. *Fostering FinTech for Financial Transformation*, 26.

Hossan, M. R., Nirob, F. A., Islam, A., Rakin, T. M., & Al-Amin, M. (2024). A Comprehensive Analysis of Blockchain Technology and Consensus Protocols Across Multilayered Framework. *IEEE Access : Practical Innovations, Open Solutions.*

Ibrahim, O. (2024). Cryptocurrency; the new unleashed financial instrument, should it be regulated. *Humanities Journal of University of Zakho*, 12(2), 303–317. DOI: 10.26436/hjuoz.2024.12.2.1272

Jain, A. K., Gupta, N., & Gupta, B. B. (2024). A Survey on Scalable Consensus Algorithms for Blockchain Technology. *Cyber Security and Applications*, 100065.

Jiménez-Serranía, V., Parra-Domínguez, J., De La Prieta, F., & Corchado, J. M. (2021). Cryptocurrencies impact on financial markets: Some insights on its regulation and economic and accounting implications. International Congress on Blockchain and Applications, Johnson, K. N. (2020). Decentralized finance: Regulating cryptocurrency exchanges. *Wm. & Mary L. Rev., 62*, 1911. JOURJON, G. Blockchain Double Spending With Low Mining Power and Network Delays.

Jumaili, M. L. F., & Karim, S. M. (2021). Comparison of tow two cryptocurrencies: Bitcoin and Litecoin. Journal of Physics: Conference Series, Kajtazi, A., & Moro, A. (2017). Bitcoin, portfolio diversification and Chinese financial Markets. *Available atSSRN* 3062064.

Koopman, C., Mitchell, M., & Thierer, A. (2014). The sharing economy and consumer protection regulation: The case for policy change. *SSRN*, 8, 529. DOI: 10.2139/ssrn.2535345

Kucheryavenko, M., Dmytryk, O., & Golovashevych, O. (2019). Cryptocurrencies: development, features and classification. *Financial and credit activity problems of theory and practice, 3*(30), 371-374.

Kwok, S., & Zhang, X. (2024). Deployment of Blockchain Technology on the Banking Industry in China: A Policy Review Study. *European Academic Journal-II CHINA, 1*(1).

Lee, J. H. (2019). *Systematic approach to analyzing security and vulnerabilities of blockchain systems*. Massachusetts Institute of Technology.

Lind, J., Naor, O., Eyal, I., Kelbert, F., Sirer, E. G., & Pietzuch, P. (2019). Teechain: a secure payment network with asynchronous blockchain access. Proceedings of the 27th ACM Symposium on Operating Systems Principles, Liska, A., & Gallo, T. (2016). *Ransomware: Defending against digital extortion*. " O'Reilly Media, Inc.". DOI: 10.1145/3341301.3359627

Lorenz, G. (2024). Regulating Decentralized Financial Technology: A Qualitative Study on the Challenges of Regulating DeFi with a Focus on Embedded Supervision. *Stan. J. Blockchain L. & Pol'y*, 7, 136.

Machkour, B., & Abriane, A. (2020). Industry 4.0 and its Implications for the Financial Sector. *Procedia Computer Science*, 177, 496–502. DOI: 10.1016/j.procs.2020.10.068

Mahnamfar, A., Bicakci, K., & Uzunay, Y. (2024). ROSTAM: A passwordless web single sign-on solution mitigating server breaches and integrating credential manager and federated identity systems. *Computers & Security*, 139, 103739. DOI: 10.1016/j.cose.2024.103739

Makarov, I., & Schoar, A. (2022a). *Cryptocurrencies and decentralized finance*. DeFi. DOI: 10.3386/w30006

Makarov, I., & Schoar, A. (2022b). Cryptocurrencies and decentralized finance (DeFi). *Brookings Papers on Economic Activity*, 2022(1), 141–215. DOI: 10.1353/eca.2022.0014

Marcacci, A. (2018). *Regulating Investor Protection under EU Law*. Springer. DOI: 10.1007/978-3-319-90297-5

McCarthy-Jones, A., & Turner, M. (2024). *Illicit Business*. Taylor & Francis. DOI: 10.4324/9781003293620

Menon, S., & Jain, K. (2021). Blockchain technology for transparency in agri-food supply chain: Use cases, limitations, and future directions. *IEEE Transactions on Engineering Management*.

Miato, A. (2023). The adoption of bitcoin by third world countries: how to beat dependency theory? Michelsen, B. (2021). China's Moonshot: How the Introduction of the Digital Renminbi Furthers China's Societal Grip and Threatens the Future of Digital Currencies. *U. St. Thomas JL & Pub. Pol'y*, 15, 813.

Mikhaylov, A. (2020). Cryptocurrency market analysis from the open innovation perspective. *Journal of Open Innovation*, 6(4), 197. DOI: 10.3390/joitmc6040197

Milutinović, M. (2018). Cryptocurrency. *Економика-Часопис за економску теорију и праксу и друштвена питања*(1), 105-122.

Minesso, M. F., Mehl, A., & Stracca, L. (2022). Central bank digital currency in an open economy. *Journal of Monetary Economics*, 127, 54–68. DOI: 10.1016/j.jmoneco.2022.02.001

Mohammed, A. H., Abdulateef, A. A., & Abdulateef, I. A. (2021). Hyperledger, Ethereum and blockchain technology: a short overview. 2021 3rd International Congress on Human-Computer Interaction, Optimization and Robotic Applications (HORA), Mokhtarian, E., & Lindgren, A. (2018). Rise of the crypto hedge fund: Operational issues and best practices for an emergent investment industry. *Stan. JL Bus. & Fin., 23*, 112.

Moreno, S. M., Seigneur, J.-M., & Gotzev, G. (2021). A survey of KYC/AML for cryptocurrencies transactions. In *Handbook of Research on Cyber Crime and Information Privacy* (pp. 21–42). IGI Global.

Nabilou, H. (2019). How to regulate bitcoin? Decentralized regulation for a decentralized cryptocurrency. *International Journal of Law and Information Technology*, 27(3), 266–291. DOI: 10.1093/ijlit/eaz008

Nakamoto, S. (2008). Bitcoin: A peer-to-peer electronic cash system.

Nakamoto, S. (2009). Bitcoin. *A peer-to-peer electronic cash system, 21260.*

Náñez Alonso, S. L., Jorge-Vazquez, J., & Reier Forradellas, R. F. (2021). Central banks digital currency: Detection of optimal countries for the implementation of a CBDC and the implication for payment industry open innovation. *Journal of Open Innovation*, 7(1), 72. DOI: 10.3390/joitmc7010072

Ndung'u, N., Morales, A., & Ndirangu, L. (2016). Digital Revolution. *Growth's Ups and Downs*, 14.

Nicholas Taleb, N. (2021). Bitcoin, currencies, and fragility. *Quantitative Finance*, 21(8), 1249–1255. DOI: 10.1080/14697688.2021.1952702

Niranjanamurthy, M., Nithya, B., & Jagannatha, S. (2019). Analysis of Blockchain technology: Pros, cons and SWOT. *Cluster Computing*, 22(S6), 14743–14757. DOI: 10.1007/s10586-018-2387-5

Noether, S., Mackenzie, A., & Research Lab, T. M. (2016). Ring confidential transactions. *Ledger*, 1, 1–18. DOI: 10.5195/ledger.2016.34

Oh, J. H., & Nguyen, K. (2018). The growing role of cryptocurrency: What does it mean for central banks and governments. *International Telecommunications Policy Review*, 251, 33–55.

Ólafsson, Í. A. (2014). *Is Bitcoin money? An analysis from the Austrian school of economic thought*. Citeseer.

Pandey, D. (2022). *Decentralized Exchanges: A Qualitative Comparison Against Centralized Exchanges*. NTNU.

Pinto, A. M. (2020). An introduction to the use of zk-SNARKs in blockchains. Mathematical Research for Blockchain Economy: 1st International Conference MARBLE 2019, Santorini, Greece, Plotkin, R. (2020). *Privacy, Security, and Cyberspace*. Infobase Holdings, Inc. DOI: 10.1007/978-3-030-37110-4_16

Popper, N. (2015). Digital gold: Bitcoin and the inside story of the misfits and millionaires trying to reinvent money.

Richardson, M. (2024). *Blockchain Technology: Learn Step by Step Smart Contracts, Monero, Blockchain Wallet, Bitcoin, Zcash, Ethereum, Ripple, Dash, Mining, Litecoin, IOTA*. Mike Richardson.

Romero-Castro, N., Pérez-Pico, A. M., & Ulrich, K. (2022). ICOs, IEOs and STOs: Token sales as innovative formulas for financing start-ups. In *Financing startups: Understanding strategic risks, funding sources, and the impact of emerging technologies* (pp. 117–147). Springer. DOI: 10.1007/978-3-030-94058-4_8

Rossi, F. (2022). Stablecoins in Three Dimensions: Foundations of Value in the Crypto-economy. *Available atSSRN* 4123691. DOI: 10.2139/ssrn.4123691

Sabry, F. (2021). *Digital Currency: While All Cryptocurrencies Can Be Termed as Digital Currencies, the Reverse Is Not True* (Vol. 2). One Billion Knowledgeable.

Saleh, F. (2021). Blockchain without waste: Proof-of-stake. *Review of Financial Studies*, 34(3), 1156–1190. DOI: 10.1093/rfs/hhaa075

Santos, C. E.Jr, Silva, L. M., Torquato, M. F., Silva, S. N., & Fernandes, M. A. (2024). SHA-256 Hardware Proposal for IoT Devices in the Blockchain Context. *Sensors (Basel)*, 24(12), 3908. DOI: 10.3390/s24123908 PMID: 38931692

Schär, F. (2021). Decentralized finance: On blockchain-and smart contract-based financial markets. *FRB of St. Louis Review*.

Schumacher, L. V. (2024). Architecting a Retail CBDC. In *Decoding Digital Assets: Distinguishing the Dream from the Dystopia in Stablecoins, Tokenized Deposits, and Central Bank Digital Currencies* (pp. 245-311). Springer. DOI: 10.1007/978-3-031-54601-3_15

Siegel, J. J. (2021). *Stocks for the long run: The definitive guide to financial market returns & long-term investment strategies*. McGraw-Hill Education.

Silva, E. C., & Mira da Silva, M. (2022). Research contributions and challenges in DLT-based cryptocurrency regulation: A systematic mapping study. *Journal of Banking and Financial Technology*, 6(1), 63–82. DOI: 10.1007/s42786-021-00037-2

Singhal, B., Dhameja, G., Panda, P. S., Singhal, B., Dhameja, G., & Panda, P. S. (2018). How blockchain works. *Beginning Blockchain: A Beginner's Guide to Building Blockchain Solutions*, 31-148.

Steinbock, D. J. (2005). Data matching, data mining, and due process. *Ga. L. Rev.*, 40, 1.

Sukarno, K. S. (2020). The use of cryptocurrency as a Payment Instrument. 3rd International Conference on Law and Governance (ICLAVE 2019), Suratkar, S., Shirole, M., & Bhirud, S. (2020). Cryptocurrency wallet: A review. 2020 4th international conference on computer, communication and signal processing (ICCCSP), Tang, Z. (2024). *The emergence of asset price bubbles and debt overhang* University of Glasgow].

Taskinsoy, J. (2022). The Great Silent Crash of the 21st Century. *Available atSSRN* 4274584. DOI: 10.2139/ssrn.4274584

Teichmann, F., & Falker, M.-C. (2020). Money laundering through cryptocurrencies. Artificial Intelligence: Anthropogenic Nature vs. Social Origin, Teo, E. G. (2024). Emergence, growth, and sustainability of bitcoin: the network economics perspective. In *Handbook of digital currency* (pp. 185-194). Elsevier. DOI: 10.1007/978-3-030-39319-9_57

Thota, A. R., Upadhyay, P., Kulkarni, S., Selvam, P., & Viswanathan, B. (2020). Software wallet based secure participation in hyperledger fabric networks. 2020 International Conference on COMmunication Systems & NETworkS (COMSNETS), Tiwari, M., Gepp, A., & Kumar, K. (2020). The future of raising finance-a new opportunity to commit fraud: A review of initial coin offering (ICOs) scams. *Crime, Law, and Social Change*, 73, 417–441.

Wątorek, M., Drożdż, S., Kwapień, J., Minati, L., Oświęcimka, P., & Stanuszek, M. (2021). Multiscale characteristics of the emerging global cryptocurrency market. *Physics Reports*, 901, 1–82. DOI: 10.1016/j.physrep.2020.10.005

Weichbroth, P., Wereszko, K., Anacka, H., & Kowal, J. (2023). Security of cryptocurrencies: A view on the state-of-the-art research and current developments. *Sensors (Basel)*, 23(6), 3155. DOI: 10.3390/s23063155 PMID: 36991866

Whitford, A. B., & Anderson, D. (2021). Governance landscapes for emerging technologies: The case of cryptocurrencies. *Regulation & Governance*, 15(4), 1053–1070. DOI: 10.1111/rego.12366

Wronka, C. (2022). Money laundering through cryptocurrencies-analysis of the phenomenon and appropriate prevention measures. *Journal of Money Laundering Control*, 25(1), 79–94. DOI: 10.1108/JMLC-02-2021-0017

Wronka, C. (2024). Crypto-asset activities and markets in the European Union: Issues, challenges and considerations for regulation, supervision and oversight. *Journal of Banking Regulation*, 25(1), 84–93. DOI: 10.1057/s41261-023-00217-8

Wu, X., Deng, W., Quan, Y., & Zhang, L. (2024). Trust Dynamics and Market Behavior in Cryptocurrency: A Comparative Study of Centralized and Decentralized Exchanges. *arXiv preprint arXiv:2404.17227.*

Xiong, X., & Luo, J. (2024). Global Trends in Cryptocurrency Regulation: An Overview. *arXiv preprint arXiv:2404.15895*. DOI: 10.1007/978-3-031-68974-1_4

Xu, J., Paruch, K., Cousaert, S., & Feng, Y. (2023). Sok: Decentralized exchanges (dex) with automated market maker (amm) protocols. *ACM Computing Surveys*, 55(11), 1–50. DOI: 10.1145/3570639

Zabchuk, H., & Pashchuk, I. (2020). THE ROLE OF CRYPTOCURRENCY IN ECONOMIC DEVELOPMENT. *The Institute of Accounting. Control and Analysis in the Globalization Circumstances*, (3-4), 113–119.

Zaghloul, E., Li, T., Mutka, M. W., & Ren, J. (2020). Bitcoin and blockchain: Security and privacy. *IEEE Internet of Things Journal*, 7(10), 10288–10313. DOI: 10.1109/JIOT.2020.3004273

Zhang, G., Zhang, X., Bilal, M., Dou, W., Xu, X., & Rodrigues, J. J. (2022). Identifying fraud in medical insurance based on blockchain and deep learning. *Future Generation Computer Systems*, 130, 140–154. DOI: 10.1016/j.future.2021.12.006

Chapter 11
Decoding Initial Coin Offerings (ICOs):
Comprehensive Review Insights Into Regulatory Challenges, Success Factors, and Market Dynamics

S. Baranidharan
https://orcid.org/0000-0002-7780-4045
Christ University, India

Priya Vinod
Christ University, India

Chippy Mohan
https://orcid.org/0000-0001-8589-4944
Christ University, India

ABSTRACT

This study provides a comprehensive review of the current literature on Initial Coin Offerings (ICOs), focusing on their regulatory challenges, success factors, investor behavior, technological innovations, and market dynamics. Drawing from a diverse range of scholarly articles, the review synthesizes key findings to offer a holistic understanding of ICOs and their impact on the digital economy. The research highlights the critical importance of regulatory clarity and investor protection measures in fostering ICO success and mitigating risks. Identified success factors include team expertise, project transparency, and adherence to regulatory compliance. Additionally, the study underscores the influence of investor behav-

DOI: 10.4018/979-8-3693-6386-7.ch011

ior and sentiment analysis on ICO outcomes, the role of social media and public perception. Technological advancements such as decentralized finance (DeFi) and security tokens are explored for their potential to transform traditional financial systems. The study concludes with a targeted regulatory interventions to ensure the sustainable growth of the ICO ecosystem.

INTRODUCTION

Initial Coin Offerings have become basically a path towards raising funds in the digital era, going through blockchain technology to eliminate the need for any financial intermediaries and thus make it more accessible. The ICO has been started back in 2013, and until now, it has been widely acclaimed by entrepreneurs, investors, regulators, and researchers. ICOs allow startups to raise capital by issuing digital tokens. It will not only give an entirely new paradigm to venture financing but also promises efficiency, transparency, and inclusivity. Recently, Initial Coin Offerings (ICOs) have proven to be upending the entire character of the financial world regarding a new way of fundraising and investing by means of blockchain technology. Issuing digital tokens to investors is a new kind of paradigm in which startups and entrepreneurs go ahead with raising investments by cutting the traditional intermediaries where such procedures would have fallen under some regulatory frameworks. This has attracted attention from all sides, drawing in the curiosity of both academia and the practical side of this process: the debate on its chances and challenges will shape this new fundraising mechanism. The rapid increase in ICOs has revealed several challenges and risks. There is uncertainty everywhere concerning fraud schemes and volatility from which investor confidence is threatened, and so is the market's integrity due to a lack of supervening regulatory frameworks. The recent spurt of ICOs has brought to the forefront a lot of challenges and risks. The absence of a regulatory framework or lack of oversight has created a conundrum of uncertainty around which fraud schemes and market volatility everyday erode investor confidence and undermine the integrity of the market (Ahern, 2021). Some of the critical factors such as project viability, team competence, regulatory compliance, and investor sentiment make the ecosystem complex (Xu et al., 2021; Gan et al., 2023).

This ICO is a system where fundraising by means of decentralized innovation, democratizing finance, utilizing its potential to transform the digital economy. Its emergence is an affect in favor of ICO as an increasingly popular practice-the call that indeed will accentuate the amount of money that projects could possibly raise because of the proliferation of blockchain-started projects, not limited to the different types of industries serviced, startups as well as decentralized applications

(DApps) (Naik & Oza, 2023). ICO is crowdfunded through digital tokens offered to the investor in return for cryptocurrency or fiat currency. ICOs result in new crowdfunding means that bypass traditional intermediaries such as venture capitalists and investment banks. Indeed, in today's world, the most booming topic is the boom of ICOs. So far, their outstanding theories have attracted the attention of many scholars, practitioners, and regulators alike. The studies conducted include a wide variety of aspects related to ICOs-such as their technological foundations, regulatory implications, market dynamics, and investor behaviour. The facts behind ICO success have been researched in studies that identify characteristics of the project, team expertise, and regulatory environment and market conditions (Ahmad et al., 2023; Chitsazan et al., 2022; Xu et al., 2021). Among others, researchers have analyzed how informed the investment perception and outcome of fundraising are impacted by white papers from ICOs, social media metrics, and corporate social responsibility (CSR) initiatives (Thewissen et al., 2023; Chursook et al., 2022; Zhao et al., 2023).

There are still substantial gaps in the cohesive synthesis and analysis of the literature on ICOs, which make participants at all levels want to learn about the fundraising phenomenon. The research thus proposes systematic literature review work covering recent research on ICOs to help fill this gap. Drawing from a diverse range of studies, the review seeks to contribute toward a holistic understanding of both opportunities and challenges inherent in ICOs along with future research avenues in this rapidly developing area. A structured analysis of articles, conference papers, and book chapters will create a broad scope for the review in examining key themes and findings in the area of ICOs within the academic literature. Topics of interest include technological innovations, regulatory frameworks, success factors, investor behaviour, market trends, and international implications. The current research will contribute by critically evaluating existing research work in this area to provide valuable insights to the academics, practitioners, policymakers, and entrepreneurs who navigate the complex world of blockchain-based fundraising and decentralized finance.

LITERATURE REVIEW ON INITIAL COIN OFFERINGS (ICOS)

Naik and Oza (2023) demonstrated the possible application of blockchain technology in the building of solid crowdfunding applications. The power of blockchain to enhance transparency, security, and efficiency in crowdfunding processes is one of the outcomes of their research. They advocated that any form of fraud would be avoided, and trust among parties would be guaranteed due to blockchain. This could promise more robust crowdfunding platforms. Pande et al. (2022) introduced Bitland, a totally decentralized platform where all real estate commercial activities take place. The authors ' research report was largely technical: how to blockchain real estate and base everything on decentralization, transparency, and immutability of property records. The importance of this research rested on demonstrated ability by the existing property transaction processes to revolutionize real estate practice by eliminating intermediaries and their associated costs of transaction. Ahmad et al. (2023) undertook a cross-country analysis of the factors that may associate with the success of initial coin offerings (ICOs). Results showed that the regulatory environment, market conditions, as well as project characteristics are important to the outcome of ICOs. They stressed the importance of regulatory clarity and investor protection measures towards supporting ICO success across different jurisdictions.

According to Thewissen et al. (2023), the linguistic errors in the ICO white papers are an object of the research influence of the linguistic errors in ICO white papers on investment decisions. It was found that the linguistic errors reflected by the quality of white papers negatively correlated with investor confidence. They also stress the need for clear, professional communication in the documentation for ICOs used to attract investments from the public. Regulatory challenges have come in the way of adoption of FinTech innovations, according to Ahern (2021), particularly with the concepts of regulatory sandboxes. Highlighted in the study were the factors that inhibited development in FinTech but were suggested as ways of regulatory adaptation regarding upcoming technologies such as blockchain and ICOs. According to Chitsazan et al. (2022), systematic scrutiny is the study of the empirical literature on success factors in ICOs. Their study synthesized earlier findings to conceptualize the ICO success phenomenon and listed various theoretical frameworks that can help in the understanding of this phenomenon. They stressed the need for an all-embracing empirical study that will validate theoretical constructs in order to inform about practical strategies for the launching of successful ICOs.

Chursook et al. (2022) researched the relationship between sentiment found on Twitter and expert ratings for ICO fundraising in the markets of Australia and Singapore. As per their findings, a high positive sentiment related to that of an expert's evaluation mostly suggested that online discourse had a role to play in influencing the investor's sentiments towards fundraising results. Their study also found that a predictive model for ICO success was based on team expertise and expert evaluations presented by Xu et al. (2021). This revealed how significant team composition was and project evaluation criteria in forecasting the performance of the ICO. They recommended mixed quantitative and qualitative criteria in the assessment of viability and attractiveness for the potential investor interested in ICO. Gan et al. (2023) discussed a governance and tokenomics design principle exploring decentralized platforms with ICOs as the specific example. The study clarified how the governance mechanism and token economics promote participant incentives and sustained decentralized ecosystems. They also provided insight int defining the “fair” design for an ICO to instill community engagement and platform growth. Rajput et al. (2023) revealed research into international business, identifying the opportunities and challenges presented for global expansion for blockchain-based organizations. The chapter examines the impact of regulatory frameworks, market dynamics, and technology innovations in blockchain startups' internationalization strategies. Regulatory underpinnings are necessary for innovation, so there should be regulations like those instituted by Chiu (2023). This perspective emphasizes the institutional viewpoint on the response of financial regulation to technological innovation and regulatory arbitrage. It uses a case study to discuss the limits of conventional regulatory techniques in addressing the challenges posed by financial innovation and a resulting requirement for adaptive regulatory frameworks enabling innovation while curbing risks. One of the comprehensive reviews of the literature on ICOs, covering all dimensions- technology applications, regulatory challenges, success factors, investor behaviour, as well as international implications- will contribute to understanding ICOs as increasingly becoming important in the finance-technology landscape.

Different prediction models such as Ridge regression, Artificial Neural Network (ANN), Random Forest regression, and hybrid ANN-Ridge have been compared by Tran et al. (2023) for performance prediction of ICOs. The study provided many insights into the efficacy of varying ML techniques put in place for predicting ICO outcomes, effectively affirming the model selection and finest working feature engineering as critical for predictive analytics of ICOs. Theorizing a network scam in the 2017 blockchain ICO bubble, Swartz (2022) tried to slice through socio-technical dynamics causing the speculative frenzy. The analysis presented in the study was focused on investigating the extent to which social networks, media hype, and psychology of investors fueled the ICO bubble, exposing such fundraising systems to a lot of market manipulation and irrational exuberance vulnerabilities. Current trends and future research directions in ICOs are presented by Wats et al. (2023) summarizing this with insights from the literature published recently. Emerging themes discovered by the review were regulatory developments, innovations in technology, investor behavior, and market dynamics, thereby paving a path for future research agendas in an ever-changing ICO landscape.

Corporate social responsibility (CSR) initiatives have been investigated by Zhao et al. (2023) regarding their signalling effects in the global ICO market. They asserted that CSR actions correlate positively with perceptions of legitimacy and credibility for investors. CSR incorporation, along with other effective ICO marketing measures, substantially enhances investor confidence and project success, which is very functional to the strategic consideration in marketing ICOs. Alshater et al. (2023) performed a hybrid empirical review in ICO literature that baselines qualitative studies with quantitative ones. Their review narrated and excavated most aspects of

ICOs, including success factors, regulatory challenges, market trends, and investor behavior, thus giving an objective understanding of the ICO phenomenon and its implications for entrepreneurship and finance. Risius et al. (2023) investigated the performance of blockchain-based token offerings within electronic markets. Their research presented an assessment of the factors influencing token valuation, market liquidity, and investor participation in blockchain token sales. They are insights into how token economies function and how decentralized financial ecosystems evolve with time. For instance, security tokens were discussed by Momtaz (2023) concerning investment opportunities and challenges in crypto assets. This chapter looks at the regulatory environment for security tokens, market dynamics, and innovative technologies shaping the security token landscape. It integrates traditional finance with blockchain-based capital markets while addressing investor protection and regulatory compliance concerns.

This information is derived from the work done by Tao et al. in 2023, who proposed an ideal ICO prototype under the speculative token trading condition. His study involves the use of mathematical optimization techniques to find the best token issuance strategy considering the market dynamics and investor behaviour. The approach suggests practical advice for ICO project teams in maximizing fundraising results and token value during price fluctuations.Kumar et al. (2022) have used fuzzy Interpretive Structural Modeling (ISM) to analyze the factors affecting the growth of ICOs. Their research identified those key drivers and related them through different mutual relationships among the factors such as regulatory environment, market conditions, technology application, and investor sentiment. They constructed a framework to understand the complicated dynamics of the ICO ecosystem. Jangjarat et al. (2023) studied the adoption of ICOs for investment in a developing economy context. The authors investigated the factors affecting investor perception and intention towards ICOs in emerging markets by stating different factors like regulatory environment, investor education, and market infrastructure, which are important in shaping ICO adoption dynamics. Pandian et al. (2023) explored the notion of decentralized finance (DeFi) and its potential to resonate with the financial sector. According to their chapter, DeFi applications on the blockchain, such as decentralized exchanges, lending platforms, etc. asset management protocols, can be provisions for revolutionizing traditional financial services and democratizing access to financial products.

The research by Chou et al. (2023) reviewed the quality parameter of ICO white papers and how it relates to the disability in fundraising performance, with the benchmarking by using security token offerings (STO) white papers. The study found the positive correlation that clearer, more complete, and more professional white papers made investors more confident. The authors stressed, therefore, the need for making them opening and credible documentation for winning the interest of investors and thus the success of fundraising. Sivarajah & Ahangama (2023) had reviewed the impact of social media on ICOs; they investigated how online discussion or participation and sentiment analysis influence the outcome of ICO fundraising. The study addressed how social media serves as a marketing channel and dissemination means for ICO projects, stressing the need for strong social media strategies to successful crowdfunding campaigns. Thus, recent literature on ICO goes around a diverse range of subjects; they cover from technological advancements to market conditions, through regulatory challenges, and further down to investor behaviour. Collectively, these studies further an understanding of threats and opportunities of ICOs regarding future evolution toward understanding the landscape of blockchain-based fundraising and decentralized finance.

STATEMENT OF PROBLEM

There is an unprecedented proliferation of ICOs in recent years with no little resulting stampede, much interest, and argumentative disputes attracting attention from scholars, practitioners, and regulators. ICOs are a new fundraising and innovation mechanism that could potentially disrupt established mechanisms. There are quite a few challenges and risks that these digital economic stakeholders face in pursuing such goals. The primary concern that the ICO ecosystem must deal with is regulatory ambiguity and oversight, leading to investor concerns related to protection, market integrity, and financial stability (Ahern, 2021). Because no regulatory framework has been created with supporting enforcement mechanisms, this has proven to be an excellent breeding ground for fraudulent activity, scams, and market manipulation, thus breaking the trust and confidence of ICO projects as well as the blockchain ecosystem as a whole.

Such an ICO landscape is characterized by a high degree of volatility, uncertainty, and speculation driven by ongoing technological innovation, changes in market sentiment, and regulatory activities (Swartz, 2022). However, it is an even greater challenge for the budding young entrepreneurs, the investors, and policy makers, as complications have emerged in fundraising and decentralized finance on the blockchain. Another main issue concerns the evaluation and assessment of ICO projects, as many of the investors face an uphill battle in terms of judging project viability, team experience, market potential, and compliance (Xu et al., 2021). Growth in the number of ICOs has also stimulated a rise in the number of white papers, marketing materials, and promotional press releases, thereby making it really hard for the investors to differentiate legit projects from fraud. In addition, it is ever changing, with the introduction of new trends, technologies, and market dynamics that shape the future of the ICO landscape (Wats et al., 2023). The ICO landscape is changing continuously with new innovations and transformations, from the face of security tokens and decentralized finance (DeFi) normalizing, to social media sentiment analysis and integrating into initiatives of corporate social responsibility (CSR).

RESEARCH METHODOLOGY

This study employed articles from the year 2021 to 2023, the date range for article references for the study on Initial Coin Offerings (ICOs) and related issues. The search used a plethora of academic databases: Scopus, Google Scholar, ProQuest, and many others. These databases have been carefully selected for coverage of most disciplines, such as business, economics, finance, and computer science. Keywords and key terms focused on ICOs, its surrounding areas such as blockchain technology, crowdfunding, decentralized finance (DeFi), cryptocurrency, token offerings, and many similar themes, constituted the search strategy. References considered within this study dealt with topics ranging from ICOs, blockchain technology, and token offerings, to crowdfunding and associated regulatory aspects, investor behaviour, market dynamics, or technological innovations concerning decentralized finance. Articles published between 2021 and 2023 were preferred to ensure that recently produced literature gets considered. Preference would be given to peer-reviewed journal articles, conference papers, and book chapters from reputable publishers and scholarly conferences. Criteria for selection included representation of the widest possible range of viewpoints, methodologies, and theoretical frameworks while reflecting the multidisciplinary nature of research into ICOs.

REGULATORY CHALLENGES

Ahern (2021) discussed the notions of regulatory lag, friction, and transitions as barriers to FinTech, particularly when looking at the EU regulatory sandbox phenomenon. Chiu (2023) evaluated the limitations of the "same activity, same risks, same rules" approach in financial regulation, arguing that it was not captured in terms of financial innovation and regulatory arbitrage realities. Ahern in 2021 discussed Regulatory lag is where there comes a time lag between the introduction of new financial technologies and the corresponding regulation. Such delays bring uncertainty and risks to the innovators and investors. Regulatory friction refers to the impediments that arise through existing regulatory frameworks that are not particularly suited to new technologies, resulting in inefficiencies and increased compliance costs. Regulatory transition thus refers to that period during which regulatory institutions make necessary adjustments to align their frameworks to developing technologies. Regulatory Lag- Delays in relating the regulations sometimes discourage innovations and expose investors to unregulated risks. Regulatory Friction - Old regulations and new technologies sometimes do not fit together and create compliance difficulties and also operational inefficiencies. Regulatory Transition- The process of updating regulations is often slow and complex because it requires a balance between fostering innovation and ensuring investor protection.

Chiu (2023) offers a critical perspective on the principle of ""same activity, same risks, same rules,"" which indicates that similar financial activities should apply similar regulatory requirements, irrespective of the technology used. This principle has governed financial regulation over the years, but it proves not effective concerning the rapidly changing landscape of financial innovation such as ICOs and other blockchain-related technologies. Inadequate for Innovation- Such traditional regulatory regimes always do not capture those characteristics and risks of financial technologies that are new. Regulatory Arbitrage- Innovators exploit the regulatory gaps by moving to other jurisdictions with more lenient regulations, where they can effectively carry out their businesses. Need for Tailored Approaches-: Regulating innovations in the financial sector effectively entails different regulatory regimes specific to the risks and benefits of the introduced technology.

The regulatory environment varies from country to country, which complicates the ICO landscape for issuers and investors much more. The research by Ahmad et al. (2023) characterized varied success factors determining ICOs depending on the countries involved, which meant that regulatory environments affected much in the ICO project outcomes. Decentralized Finance (DeFi) and Regulatory Oversight- Pandian et al. (2023) discussed the larger implications of decentralized finance and the purported challenges for regulators in overseeing the innovative systems of finance. Ahern (2021) and Chiu (2023) emphasized the need for adaptive and forward-looking regulatory frameworks that can keep pace with technological advancements. Some of the key recommendations include: - Proactive regulatory engagement- Regulators must proactively engage with innovators to understand emerging technologies and their risk-benefit profiles. Sandbox environments- A regulatory sandbox for innovators to trial a new product under regulatory surveillance could be the perfect way to strike the right balance between facilitating innovations and protecting investors. International coordination is harmonizing regulatory approaches across jurisdictions that could reduce regulatory arbitrage and provide even clearer guidelines for global operations.

SUCCESS FACTORS

Many factors have been established successfully to predict success and failure in ICO studies. Among them, for instance, Ahmad et al. (2023) discussed the country-specific factors impacting ICO success and noticed the differences in impact across regions. Alshater et al. (2023), meanwhile, discussed an empirical review of ICOs with an emphasis on, rather than one or the other, indicative of a hybrid approach to understanding their success. Chitsazan et al. (2022) provided a guarantee for systematic analyses of empirical studies to conceptualize ICO success factors. The research by Chou et al. (2023) indicates that the quality of white papers affects the success of fundraising. According to Chursook et al. (2022), Twitter mood and expert ratings are related to the ICO fundraising performance.

MARKET DYNAMICS

Sufficient study has been conducted on the dynamic nature of ICO markets. Gan et al. (2023) provided the foundation in decentralizing platforms through governance, tokenomics, and ICO design.

Jangjarat et al. (2023) investigated the propensity to use ICOs in developing economies to mobilize funds. Kumar et al. (2022) discussed the identification of fuzzy ISM factors for ICO growth. Momtaz (2021a, b) examined what entrepreneurial finance and moral hazard mean in addition to that new security token market. Naik and Oza (2023) portrayed the role that blockchain technologies play in creating resilient crowdfunding solutions. Additional studies discuss the wider implications of ICOs and their impact on blockchain technology. Pandian et al. (2023) dealt with decentralized finance, while Rajput et al. (2023) are studying global entrepreneurial ventures through blockchain applications. Risius et al. (2023) examined the performance of token offerings based on blockchain technology. Sivarajah and Ahangama (2023) had the opportunity to address the influence of social media on ICOs, whereas Swartz (2022) found that in 2017 the blockchain ICO mania was a net scam.

Tao et al. (2023) construed optimal ICO strategies in speculative trading conditions. The research work related to ICOs also addresses unique aspects such as linguistic inaccuracies in white papers influencing investment decisions (Thewissen et al., 2023) and prediction models for ICO success (Tran, 2023; Xu et al., 2021). Finally, Zhao et al. (2023) conceptualize the signaling effect of social responsibility applied to global ICO markets.

DISCUSSION

The discussion synthesized important findings and insights relating to articles regarding different aspects of Initial Coin Offering (ICOs)-blockchain technology, decentralized finance (DeFi) and others.

4.1 Regulatory Environment And Compliance

Many authors have studied the regulatory issues and compliance concerns relating to ICOs. As Ahmad et al. (2023) concluded in their piece published on the subject, regulatory clarity and measures to protect investors will significantly enhance the capacity of an ICO to be successful across different federal jurisdictions. Ahern (2021) examined regulatory lag and friction as a barrier to FinTech innovations while advocating for dynamic regulatory frameworks to accommodate the change in emerging technologies including blockchains and ICOs. Chitsazan et al. (2022) also explained how these factors regulatory in nature affect the success of ICOs, with attention being paid to the importance of the regulatory environment on perception and outcome of fundraising by investors.

4.2 Success Factors And Performance

Several scholars have investigated aspects, with respect to success and performance of initial coin offerings. Xu et al. (2021) presented a predictive model concerning ICO success through team experience and evaluation of experts, thus suggesting the factor of team composition as well as project evaluation criteria. Gan et al. (2023) tackled the issue of giving the governance mechanisms and token economics in decentralized platforms; thereby laying out ICO design principles and strategies for community engagement. Risius et al. (2023) evaluated the performance of blockchain-based token offerings, focusing on the factors influencing token valuations and market liquidity.

4.3 Investor Behaviour And Sentiment Analysis

Research identified investor behavior and sentiment evaluation specific to ICOs. Chursook et al. (2022) examined the correlation between Twitter-based sentiment analysis and expert ratings on ICO fundraising amounts, emphasizing the contribution of the social media discourse about investments. Thewissen et al. (2023) investigated how linguistic errors in ICO white papers deter potential investment decisions, underscoring the importance of good communication and professionalism in all ICO documentation.

4.4 Technological Innovations And Trends

An inquiry was made into technological innovations and new trends in ICOs and blockchain-financed. The researchers here are Pande et al. (2022), who discussed Bitland, which generally was a decentralized platform developed for commercial real estate transactions, and proved what impact blockchain could bring to traditional industries. Tao et al. presented (2023) an optimal ICO model under conditions of speculative token trading to guide the ICO project teams in fundraising optimization.

4.5 Social Responsibility And Csr Initiatives

Researchers analyzed the signaling effects of corporate social responsibility (CSR) initiatives in the international ICO market. Zhao et al. (2023) studied CSR's association with investors' legitimacy and credibility perceptions of projects, stressing the strategic significance of integrating social and environmental goals into ICO campaigns.

4.6 Market Dynamics And International Implications

Furthermore, a market discussion will also include international business ramifications and future research avenues. Rajput et al. (2023) covered international business and blockchain ventures intersecting and set the grounds for opportunities and challenges that would have attracted global expansion from such blockchain-based entities. In such a scenario, Wats et al. (2023) detailed present-day trends and future research directions regarding ICOs, which, apart from throwing light on regulatory developments and technological innovations, encroach upon such market dynamics that, in many ways, shape the ICO surrounding. The multifaceted nature of ICOs, ways through which ICOs change the digital economy, and the opportunities and challenges they pose to stakeholders in this fast-developing ecosystem are summarized in the report. By collating and analyzing disparate insights from diversified perspectives and methodologies, this study contributes to a more coherent understanding of ICOs and their future shaping in both the financial and technological realms.

5. IMPLICATIONS

5.1 Social Implications

There are numerous social implications of research on ICOs. First is that ICOs can democratize access to capital. Individuals and small businesses can raise funds across borders without facing the traditional barriers. This would greatly enhance economic inclusion and empowerment in areas that do not have access to traditional spaces of financing. On a different level, ICOs are decentralizing innovation. They give entrepreneurs and developers a facility through which they can fund projects without falling into the constraints of the ordinary financial systems. This stimulates much creativity and diversity in the development of technologies, yielding innovative solutions to societal challenges. The same ICOs have their share of social risks, including the possibility of cheating and loses to investors. ICOs can as well become fertile ground for scams and Ponzi schemes without any proper regulation and monitoring. Trust is then lost in the broader blockchain space with negative impacts on unsuspecting investors.

5.2 Research Implications

Research into ICOs opens up numerous possibilities for future research avenues. As case studies with their respective methodologies and bigger data sets unfold, they shall look into what may influence successful ICOs, such as team composition, project characteristics, and the legal environment. Moreover, one could conduct longitudinal studies to track how ICO projects perform over the long run and how sustainable they are in terms of developing an impact. In addition to such research, there is a clear requirement for interdisciplinary research that integrates finance, economics, computer science, law, and other fields so that a much more holistic picture can be presented about ICOs and their implications. This would go a long way toward spelling out synergies and trade-offs among various aspects of ICOs and would inform policy formulation and strategies at a business level.

5.3 Practical Implications

Practically speaking, the study of ICOs will lend basic data for all those entrepreneurs, investors, policy-makers, and regulators. The entrepreneurs who want to launch ICOs can understand most of the key success factors from the studies and literature, which include transparent communication, regulatory compliance, and community involvement. Investors would also have to put their research on ICOs into perspective before investing, with the findings seeking to mitigate the risks associated with ICO investments. Conducting thorough due diligence and determining project fundamentals allows investors to value the viability and chance of return from ICO projects, thus minimizing exposure to scam projects and failures. The research on ICOs can also be useful to the policymakers and regulators who want to come up with sound regulators for their jurisdictions. Understanding the mode of operation of ICO markets and the threats they pose allows regulators to position sharper interventions towards encouraging market integrity, confidence among investors, and innovation while reducing possible harms.

6. CONCLUSION

In-depth literature review on Initial Coin Offerings, or ICOs, will do much learning to regard blockchains and decentralized finance in their multi-faceted ways. From various studies, researchers have considered aspects such as the regulatory environment, the success factors determining whether an ICO succeeds or fails, investor flows such as motivations for investing, emerging technological innovations, and the market dynamics shaping the ICO landscape itself. The research provides successful ICO attributes, including regulatory clarity, investor protection measures, and/or adaptive frameworks to support ICOs while mitigating potential risks, within the regulatory viewpoint. Major success factors have been identified by several authors to include team skills, project characteristics, and compliance with regulations, as ways to really guide entrepreneurs and investors through the complexities of ICOs. Therein, investor behavior, sentiment analysis, social responsibility initiatives, and other similar concepts are also included among those to predict ICOs as well as market perceptions thereof. It is stated that by understanding how investors think and feel about projects tied to social and environmental aspects in their ICO campaigns, entrepreneurs may enhance legitimacy and credibility related to projects that improve the chances of attracting more interest or investment. On top of this, technological innovations such as decentralized platforms, security tokens, and decentralized finance (DeFi) continue to create a different paradigm for the financial landscape and exciting opportunities for innovative disruption. Researchers have also looked into how the use of blockchain technology could help transform not just industries but also real estate, crowdfunding, or international business, paving the way for more economic inclusion and empowerment.

Even though his research highlights some of the challenges as well as risks associated with ICOs such regulatory uncertainties fraud or fraudulent activity, as well as volatility within the market it must also be understood that without well-organized oversight, ICOs might serve as a breeding ground for improper schemes like ponzi schemes, giving rise to mistrust within the blockchain ecosystem at large and exposing unsuspecting investors to heavy losses. This makes the literature of ICOs very helpful to scholars, practitioners, policy makers, and regulators interested in understanding these new opportunities and challenges for blockchain-based fundraising. Thus, this study will go on to add towards understanding ICOs better in consideration of future finance, technology, or societal aspects since it studies across perspectives and methodologies. Researchers have to fill gaps or cognitions that may remain without closure as the landscape of ICOs keeps evolving to ensure the sustainability of decentralized finance development.

REFERENCES

Ahern, D. (2021). Regulatory lag, regulatory friction and regulatory transition as FinTech disenablers- Calibrating an EU response to the regulatory sandbox phenomenon. *European Business Organization Law Review, 22*(3), 395–432. doi-10.1007/s40804-021-00217-z

Ahmad, M. F., Kowalewski, O., & Pisany, P. (2023). What determines initial coin offering success- a cross-country study. *Economics of Innovation and New Technology, 32*(5), 622–645. doi-10.1080/10438599.2021.1982712

Alshater, M. M., Joshipura, M., Khoury, R. E., & Nasrallah, N. (2023). Initial coin offerings- A hybrid empirical review. *Small Business Economics*. doi-10.1007/s11187-022-00726-2

Chitsazan, H., Bagheri, A., & Tajeddin, M. (2022). Initial coin offerings (ICOs) success- Conceptualization, theories and systematic analysis of empirical studies. *Technological Forecasting and Social Change*, 180, 121729. DOI: 10.1016/j.techfore.2022.121729

Chiu, -Y. (2023). An institutional account of responsiveness in financial regulation- Examining the fallacy and limits of "same activity, same risks, same rules" as the answer to financial innovation and regulatory arbitrage. *Comput. Law Secur. Rep, 51*(105868).

Chou, S.-C., Li, Z.-A., Wang, T., & Yen, J.-C. (2023). How the quality of initial coin offering white papers influences fundraising- Using security token offerings white papers as a benchmark. *Intelligent Systems in Accounting Finance & Management, 30*(1), 3–18. doi-10.1002/isaf.1527

Chursook, A., Yahya Dawod, A., Chanaim, S., Naktnasukanjn, N., & Chakpitak, N. (2022). Twitter sentiment analysis and Expert Ratings of Initial Coin Offering fundraising- Evidence from Australia and Singapore markets. *TEM Journal*, 44–55. doi-10.18421/tem111-06

Gan, J., Tsoukalas, G., & Netessine, S. (2023). Decentralized platforms- Governance, tokenomics, and ICO design. *Management Science*, 69(11), 6667–6683. DOI: 10.1287/mnsc.2021.02076

Jangjarat, K., Kraiwanit, T., Thanawiwat, T., & Chutipat, V. (2023). Acceptance of an initial coin offering for investment in a developing economy. *Corporate and Business Strategy Review*, 4(2), 29–36. DOI: 10.22495/cbsrv4i2art3

Kumar, S., Janu, N., Raja, L., & Kumar, A. (2022). A fuzzy ISM analysis of factors in growth of initial coin offerings (ICOs). *Journal of Interdisciplinary Mathematics*, 25(3), 815–825. DOI: 10.1080/09720502.2021.2015099

Momtaz, P. P. (2021a). Entrepreneurial finance and moral hazard- Evidence from token offerings. *Journal of Business Venturing, 36*(5), 106001. doi-10.1016/j.jbusvent.2020.106001

Momtaz, P. P. (2021b). Security tokens. SSRN *Electronic Journal*. doi-10.2139/ssrn.3865233

Naik, D. P. G., & Oza, D. K. S. (2023). Leveraging the power of blockchain technology for building a resilient crowdfunding solution. *Procedia Computer Science, 230*, 11–20. doi-10.1016/j.procs.2023.12.056

Pande, S. S., Mandolikar, S., & Shitole, S. (2022, December 8). Bitland-A decentralized commercial real estate platform. *2022 IEEE Bombay Section Signature Conference (IBSSC)*. Presented at the 2022 IEEE Bombay Section Signature Conference (IBSSC), Mumbai, India. doi-10.1109/ibssc56953.2022.10037494 DOI: 10.1109/IBSSC56953.2022.10037494

Pandian, K., Pfeiffer, D., & Qian, S. (2023). Decentralized Finance. In *The Emerald Handbook on Cryptoassets- Investment Opportunities and Challenges* (pp. 141–156). DOI: 10.1108/978-1-80455-320-620221010

Rajput, N., Garg, V., Alaverdov, E., & Varmani, S. G. (2023). *International Business and Block-Chain Ventures* (pp. 69–83). Singapore; Singapore- Springer Nature.

Risius, M., Breidbach, C. F., Chanson, M., Krannichfeldt, R. V., & Wortmann, F. (2023). On the performance of blockchain-based token offerings. *Electronic Markets*, 33(1), 1. DOI: 10.1007/s12525-023-00652-5

Sivarajah, S., & Ahangama, S. (2023). Review of social media's impact on initial coin offerings. In *3rd International Conference on Advanced Research in Computing (ICARC). Presented at the 2023 3rd International Conference on Advanced Research in Computing (ICARC)*. Belihuloya, Sri Lanka. DOI: 10.1109/ICARC57651.2023.10145746

Swartz, L. (2022). Theorizing the 2017 blockchain ICO bubble as a network scam. *New Media & Society, 24*(7), 1695–1713. doi-10.1177/14614448221099224

Tao, Z., Peng, B., & Ma, L. (2023). Optimal initial coin offering under speculative token trading. *European Journal of Operational Research*, 306(2), 632–644. DOI: 10.1016/j.ejor.2022.07.023

Thewissen, J., Thewissen, J., Torsin, W., & Arslan-Ayaydin, Ö. (2023). Linguistic errors and investment decisions- the case of ICO white papers. *European Journal of Finance, 29*(7), 826–868. doi-10.1080/1351847x.2022.2075780

Tran, T. K., Senkerik, R., Vo, H. T. X., Vo, H. M., Ulrich, A., Musil, M., & Zelinka, I. (2023). Initial Coin Offering prediction comparison using Ridge regression, Artificial neural network, Random forest regression, and hybrid ANN-Ridge. *Mendel*, 29(2), 283–294. DOI: 10.13164/mendel.2023.2.283

Wats, S., Joshi, M., & Singh, S. (2024). Initial coin offerings- current trends and future research directions. *Quality & Quantity, 58*(2), 1361–1387. doi-10.1007/s11135-023-01701-z

Xu, W., Wang, T., Chen, R., & Zhao, J. L. (2021). Prediction of initial coin offering success based on team knowledge and expert evaluation. *Decision Support Systems, 147*(113574), 113574. doi-10.1016/j.dss.2021.113574

Zhao, R., Hou, W., Kumar, V., & Kumar, A. (2023). Signalling effects of doing good in global ICO markets. *Journal of Business Research*, 168, 114224. DOI: 10.1016/j.jbusres.2023.114224

KEY TERMS WITH DEFINITION

Blockchain Technology: A decentralized digital ledger that records transactions across many computers in such a way that the registered transactions cannot be altered retroactively. This technology underpins cryptocurrencies and ICOs, ensuring transparency and security.

Decentralized Finance (DeFi): An emerging financial technology based on secure distributed ledgers similar to those used by cryptocurrencies. DeFi aims to democratize finance by eliminating intermediaries and providing financial services through decentralized applications (dApps).

Initial Coin Offerings (ICOs): A fundraising mechanism where new projects sell their underlying cryptocurrency tokens in exchange for fiat currency or established cryptocurrencies. This method is often used by startups to bypass the rigorous and regulated capital-raising process required by venture capitalists or banks.

Investor Behavior: The study of how investors make decisions about buying, holding, and selling financial assets, influenced by factors such as market sentiment, information asymmetry, and psychological biases.

Regulatory Environment: The set of laws, regulations, and guidelines that govern financial markets and institutions, particularly relevant to ICOs where regulatory clarity and compliance are crucial for success and investor protection.

Security Tokens: Digital assets that represent ownership or a stake in an external asset or enterprise, regulated under securities laws. They offer a new way to raise capital by providing investors with legal rights and protections similar to traditional securities.

Sentiment Analysis: The process of using natural language processing, text analysis, and computational linguistics to identify and extract subjective information from source materials. In the context of ICOs, sentiment analysis often involves assessing social media discourse to gauge investor sentiment and predict market trends.

Chapter 12

Digital Finance, Financial Inclusion, and Economic Growth:
Evidence From Bangladesh

Sheikh Abu Taher
https://orcid.org/0000-0001-7827-5459
Jahangirnagar University, Bangladesh

ABSTRACT

It is essential for an economy to have well and developed financial system for its population since access to formal finance reduces poverty and increases economic growth. This chapter, therefore, empirically investigates the link between the various channels of digital finance, financial inclusion (FI) and its impact on economic growth in Bangladesh. Secondary data is collected from World Bank and International Monetary Fund (IMF). To formulate an econometric model, autoregressive distributed lag (ARDL) model and error correction (ECM) model are performed. Besides, to check the data order Augmented Dicky Fuller (ADF) and Philipe-Perron tests are implemented. Empirical results disclose interesting findings that a good number of digital finance and FI indicators have positive association with economic development both for short and long-run in Bangladesh. As more FI encourages people to become financially educate and thereby promote sound financial infrastructure of an economy, the results suggest deepening of financial structure through promotion of nationwide financial services.

DOI: 10.4018/979-8-3693-6386-7.ch012

1. INTRODUCTION

A strong financial system is essential to improve health of an economy (Burton and Brown, 2014; Asanović, 2020; Emara and El Said, 2021; Adedokun and Ağa, 2023). A well operating financial system confirms to deliver funds from savers; the group who have available funds, to those who have shortage and to the potential investors (Mayer, 1988). Therefore, financial literacy along with adequate FI is extensively needed (Santos, 2017; Raza et al., 2023; Reddy et al., 2024). But few numbers of banked population in developing countries like Bangladesh hinder this potentiality of growth to some extent. However, due to the expansion of Information and Communication Technology (ICT), specially from the year 2000 and a good number of populations to have cheap accessibility to mobile phones, the number of unbanked populations is declining. This trend certainly has positive effect on the economic growth of Bangladesh since more financial exclusion deteriorates the financial structure thereby reduce economic efficiency.

In recent years, inclusive finance becomes a key concern for sustainable development and economic growth for many countries, especially in the developing economies (Anakpo et al., 2023; Hussain et al., 2023). Policy makers and regulators put emphasize to spread FI so that people can access to the financial system at affordable cost without having much tension to provide line of documents. This makes easy access to formal financial systems, such as to deposits, remittances, lending/borrowing, savings, insurance or even payment options. While reduced costs to access to finance is a major attention for policy makers and many financial stakeholders, technological innovation in financial systems or FinTech plays essential roles (Ediagbonya and Tioluwani, 2023). Therefore, more innovation on financial products and services makes people life easy and comfortable (Dahiya and Kumar, 2020; Hasan et al., 2022). Besides, FI in many ways, increase financial network, improves people life standard, relieve poverty and confirms economic growth and development (Van et al., 2021; Shili and Panjwani, 2022; Lee et al., 2023). Countries adopted strategies and policies to promote FI through easy accessibility and low charges. The country-wide implementation of digital finance, for example, a key tool to provide formal financial access for many emerging countries in the world while the access has increased from 25% in 2011 to 50% in the globe (Demirguc-Kunt *et al.* 2018).

In many ways, availability of financial services engineer development. First, the financial sector spreads economic growth by offering a wide variety of facilities to small households, enterprises and governments which ultimately promotes economic growth (Australian Financial Center Forum, 2009). Second, poor or illiterate people in many countries lack financial services, such as bank accounts or payment services, can be facilitated through digital financial services which narrow gaps of financial exclusion and promote economic growth in that region. Therefore, promotion of formal financial services is a key priority for many economies into their national agenda. Third, policy makers have observed that a wide spread of FI help people to escape poverty and derives economic growth (Levine, 2005; Beck et. al., 2007; Sharma, 2016; Demirguc-Kunt et al., 2018; Kim et al., 2018; Dahiya and Kumar, 2020; Sikarwar et al., 2020, Singh and Stakić, 2021; Boachie et al., 2023).

Still, much of the research is centered on developed countries instead of developing economies. There is a need for research to document how FI impacts economic growth since many of the developing countries key agenda to enhance FI for the marginalized groups (Ofoeda et al., 2024). Besides, there is limited research on the effect of digital finance on economic growth, despite the fact that most people in developing economies access to formal finance via digital platforms (Ediagbonya and Tioluwani, 2023). Therefore, in the research, we aim to explore the association between digital finance, FI and economic growth in an emerging economy like Bangladesh. We select the sample on data availability and under the emergency of financial access. We develop hypotheses to capture the relationship, construct an effective time series model from World Bank, IMF and GSMA data, over the period from 2004 to 2020. Both the short and long-run relationships are observed though the analysis.

Our study begins by as follows; section two discusses the current state of FI, section three reviews past literatures. In section four, data and methodology for the study is explained. Section five, outlines the different analysis and interpret the results. In section six, conclusion and recommendations are drawn for policy analysis and strategic decision formulation for FI in emerging economies.

2. CURRENT STATE OF FINANCIAL INCLUSION IN BANGLADESH

FI becomes a key challenge for the world now (Atkinson and Messy, 2013; Chen and Sivakumar, 2021; Ozturk and Ullah, 2022; Chowdhury and Chowdhury, 2024). Through this challenge, the global financial exclusion has declined from 2.5 billion in the year 2011 to 1.7 billion in the year 2017 (Demirguc-Kunt et al., 2018). Access to formal finance is a key concern for Bangladesh government with the aim to meet the sustainable development goal. With this aim, there are a number of policies have undertaken since the early 2010 to provide affordable financial services to the marginal people. Among the policies, eKYC (electronic know your customer) which minimizes the hassle to open an account digitally with formal financial system and to promote agent banking in the rural area, are some notable examples. These policies have direct impact on FI in which bKash (a prominent mobile financial service provider) alone has confirmed more than 60 million account holders in Bangladesh.

The Global Findex data (World Bank) and the IMF have stated the situation of FI in their report. The World Bank investigated the global state of FI in the year 2011, 2014 and 2017, respectively and the IMF surveyed availability of financial access in 2020. The position of FI of Bangladesh in respect to emerging Asian economies are illustrated in Figure 1, 2, 3 and 4, respectively.

Figure 1. Number of Banks in 2019 (World Bank)

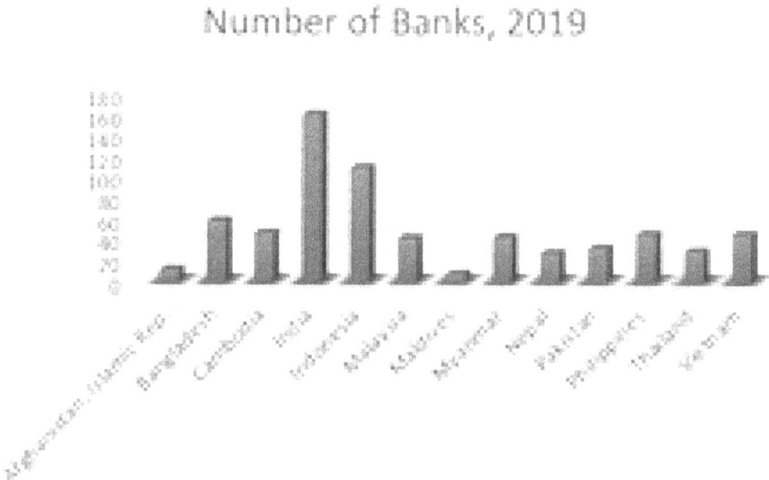

Figure 2. Number of ATMs per 100,000 adults (World Bank)

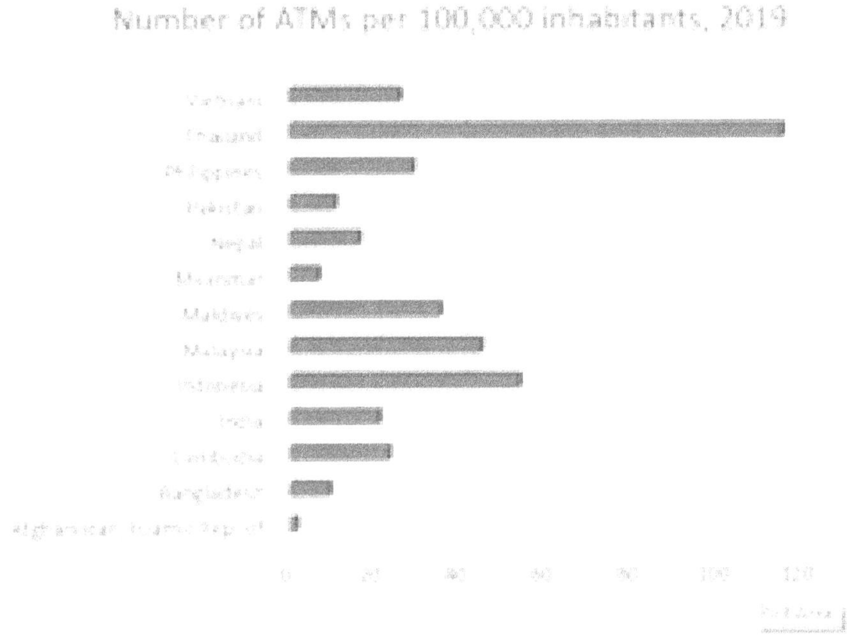

Figure 3. Number of Debit and credit cards per 100,000 adults (World Bank)

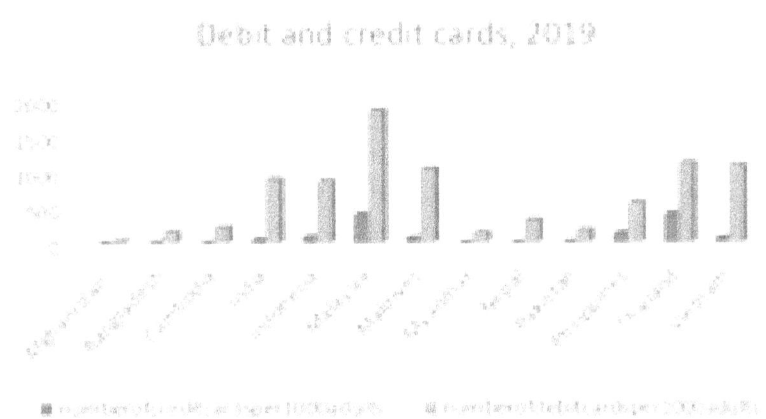

Figure 4. Bank branches (World Bank)

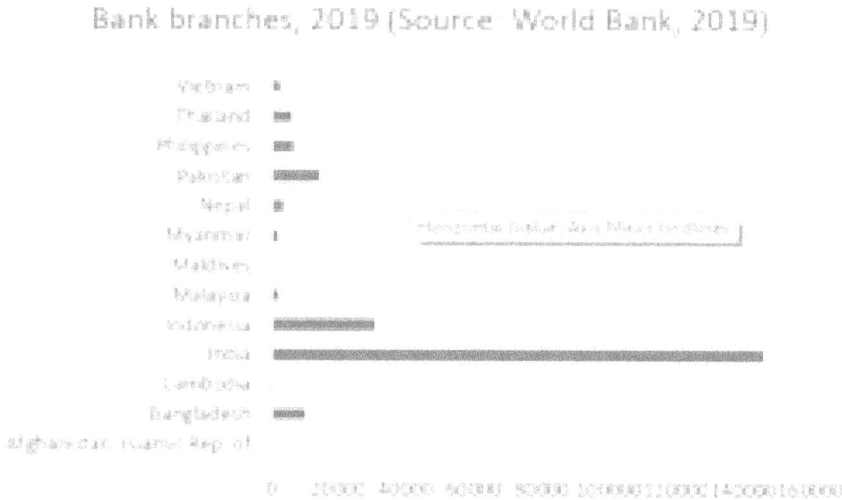

In Bangladesh, still many people depend on traditional financial system. Most of the financial transactions are done through banking channels or non-bank financial institutions (Taher and Uddin, 2018). For the purpose of developing a more dynamic financial sector, regulator's role is essential. The financial system is still underdeveloped in contrast with global market (Taher and Tsuji, 2022). This sector has three main parts; such as formal, semi-formal and informal, respectively. The categorization is done with a view to the degree of regulation. There are 59 scheduled and 5 non-scheduled banks, 34 non-bank financial institutions (NBFIs), 62 insurance companies, and 599 micro finance institutions (MFIs) are consisted to formal sector and are regulated by the Bangladesh Bank (BB), Insurance Development & Regulatory Authority, Bangladesh Security and Exchange Commission (BSEC), and Microcredit Regulatory Authority.

In the research, we employ financial access data over the period from 2004 to 2020. In every aspect, the positive growth of FI is seen. The access, usage and penetration of financial services are shown in Figure 5 and 6 below.

Figure 5. Total number of commercial bank branches and ATMs (World Bank, IMF)

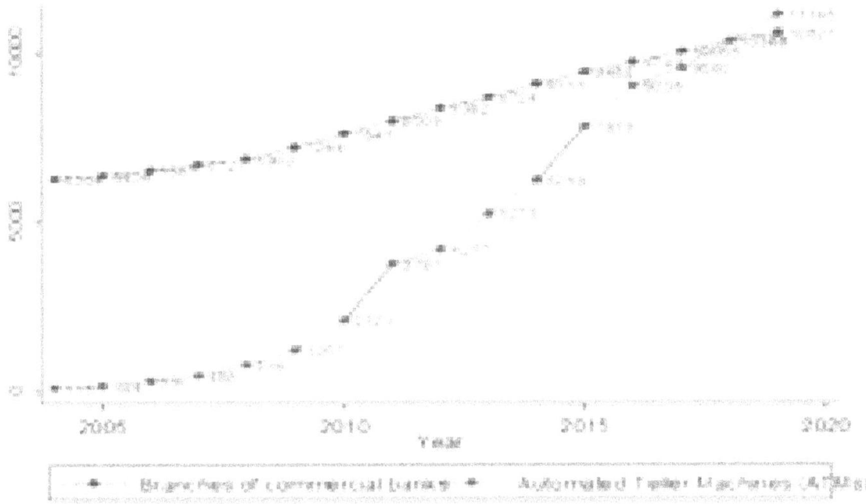

Figure 6. Number of Insurance companies and commercial banks (World Bank, IMF)

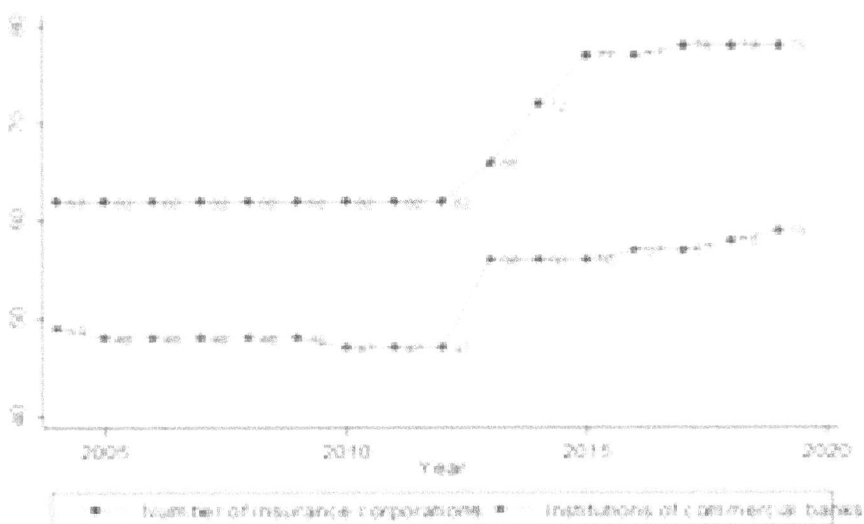

In fFigure 5, the extent to access to commercial bank branches and ATM services are almost similar level. Although the penetration of bank branches and ATM services are observed a positive trend but in early 2018 the number of ATM services surpassed bank branches. The positive growth of ATM offers many banking services such as withdraw or deposit cash in many aspects which minimizes time, cost and distance (Fabris, 2019; Iqbal and Kassim, 2023). Besides, a sharp rise of number of commercial banks and FIs are observed from Figure 6.

The overall discussion of FI provides a brief understanding of formal financial access and a trend of Bangladesh from the year 2004 to 2020. This will critically employ in the following section to demonstrate the link between financial access and economic growth of Bangladesh.

3. LITERATURE REVIEW

Previous studies investigated single indicators or set of indicators to observe the nexus between FI and economic growth. Such as, Schumpeter (1912) attempted to highlight the effective role of banking system on economic development in many countries. Channeling well-organized funds from banks to public networks lead to innovation and financial development are investigated by (Goldsmith, 1969; McKinnon, 1973; Shaw, 1973; King and Levine, 1993). A robust financial system is essential for financial access to any economy. When people can access to all financial needs, such as deposit or savings, withdraw, remittance, lend/borrow or even advise to investment, this may positively affect on their economic development (Sethi and Acharya, 2018; Ahmad *et al.* 2021; Shen, Hu and Hueng, 2021; Van *et al.* 2021; Singh and Stakic; 2021).

Research on FI has paid much attention since the year 1990s (Kim et al., 2018) as much concern has been given to the people who are socially or financially excluded ((Leyshon and Thrift, 1993, 1994, 1995; Collard, 2007). Few studies focus on early 2000s since emerging economies financial exclusion was high during that time.

An association between per capita GDP growth, capital stock growth and total productivity growth on financial depth is investigated by Kind and Levine (1993a). An empirical model is constructed using a panel of 77 economies over the thirty years period from 1960 to 1989. This massive study suggests that there is a positive relationship between financial depth and three types of growth mentioned in the literature. In line with Schumpeter (1912) study, the finance and growth are once studied and found positive relationship (Kind and Levine, 1993b). For 10 developing countries, Christopoulos and Tsionas (2004) develop econometric model to verify the relationship between financial depth, growth and other ancillary variables. Six factors, such as, monetary sector and monetary policy development, bank and non-bank sector development, supervision and regulation, trade openness, and institutional quality, are explored on MENA region and find the variations of regulatory and supervisory discrepancy among countries on financial development (Creane et al., 2004). The decision of savings and investment in order to the financial system of any country and their role on economic growth is investigated by Levine (2005). This comprehensive study investigates and include the role of ex-ante information on investments, investment and corporate governance, trading, portfolio and risk management, savings mobilization and mobilization of goods and services and concludes that these factors contribute to economic growth. Stock markets and banking development and their role on economic development is studied by Naceur and Samir (2007). An unbalanced panel data from 11 countries of Middle East and North Africa (MENA) region are included in the study and recommended that a well-functioning financial market is necessary to impetus economic development. In the study of Bhattacharya and Wolde (2010) includes the importance of access to credit and its impact on economic growth for MENA and other regions. Lack of access to credit is one of the essential factors that backward economic prosperity of the region. Smooth functioning of banks, equity markets and bond markets channels fund efficiently and help the users of financial systems which ultimately increase economywide productivity (Estrada et al., 2010; Sethi and Acharya, 2018; Van et al., 2021; Singh and Stakic, 2021; He and Wei, 2023). Therefore, various level of FI and financial system development facilitates and develops socio-economy and people at large providing access to formal financial access to the marginals (Sharma, 2016; Behera and Behera, 2018; Zhang and Wei, 2023).

The importance of banking institutions as a proxy of FI are given importance in the study of Bruhn and Love (2014). Their research investigates the necessity of opening bank branches for betterment of labor market activity and easy access for finance for low-income inhabitants in Mexico. To challenge poverty and income inequality on economic expansion of Asia and the Pacific Park and Mercado (2015) examines the role of FI and assumes this as one of the most important economic agents to make long-term consumption and investment decisions for 37 selected Asian emerging economies. Various macroeconomic variables and country-specific factors are given importance in the study too.

A study conducted by Kim et al., (2018) on 55 OIC (Organization of Islamic Cooperation) countries to assess the relationship between FI and economic growth applying dynamic panel analysis. The study incorporates per capital GDP as a proxy of economic growth and a set of independent variables as a proxy of FI, such as inflation, population growth rate, primary school enrollment, unemployment rate, trade percentage, ATM (automated teller machines) per 100000 adults, commercial bank branches per 100000 adults, deposit accounts with commercial banks per 1,000 adults, borrowers from commercial banks per 1000 adults and life insurance volume to GDP. This comprehensive study is modeled and tested using sophisticated econometric model and concludes that though FI and economic growth have mutual causalities with each other according to Granger causality tests but this two are positively related. The study of Ali et al., (2020) examines the effect of FI index as a proxy of FI on 45 IsDB (Islamic Development Bank) member states over the period from 2000 to 2016. A dynamic panel model, 2SLS (two-stage least squares), VAR (vector autoregressive) and Granger causality tests are exploited to assess the relationship between FI and economic growth in the IsDB member countries. Sethi and Acharya (2018) considers 31 developed and developing countries in the world. The study emphasizes the effect of policy formulation on FI and long-run relationship of FI and economic growth in the region.

After the wide spread of mobile phones in the world, mobile money, a disruptive innovation in finance, give rise to formal financial access for poor. As mobile phones diffusion has reached to 100 percent level in many parts in the world, therefore, people get access to mobile financial services through their phones. The effect of mobile money and socio-economic development are studies by many researchers. Nan (2019) examines the role of mobile money on socio-economic development on Sub-Saharan Africa and concludes that these two variables ae positively associated. Agrawal (2016) assumes mobile money as an engine of FI for bottom of pyramid and last-mile people. The study reveals that mobile money plays essential role for FI and has positive effect on socio-economic development. The impact of fixed and mobile phones (as a proxy of ICT) and mobile money on economic growth and FI is studied by (Ahmad et al., 2023). Their study covers 22 years panel data of 146 countries and documents that mobile money plays significant role on economic growth through direct and indirect channels.

Besides, the impact of digital finance on economic growth is explored by several studies. The study by (Ahmad et al., 2021) explores the role of digital financial inclusion and human capital on China's provincial economic growth. They found positive association between digital financial inclusion and human capital on economic growth of China's province. Digital inclusive finance, growth and innovative development is studied by (Wang et al., 2023). Their study concludes with interesting findings that digital inclusive finance impacts positively on economic growth and innovative development.

The comprehensive study reveals that digital finance, FI and economic growth are studied by several researchers but the research in this field in Bangladesh are absent. Hence, the study is of Bangladesh, we aim to explore the effect of digital finance, FI and economic growth using time series data from 2004 to 2020. The study uses a set of variables as proxy of FI and constructs an econometric model to test the hypotheses.

4. RESEARCH METHOD

The effect of FI and economic growth has been investigated in panel of countries in Africa, IsDB or OIC and found positive relationship between FI and economic growth in the region (Kim et al., 2018; Sethi and Acharya, 2018; Ali et al., 2020; Ozili et al., 2023) or single country such in India (Sharma, 2016) and in Saudi Arabia (Tarchoun and Ghraieb, 2022). Yet, the research on digital finance, FI and economic growth in Bangladesh is absent. Therefore, in this research, we aim to explore the association between digital finance, FI and economic growth in Bangladesh. The time series data over the period from 2004 to 2020 is used from World Bank and IMF. We select the sample period because FI becomes a great concern for policy makers in many emerging economies during that time. Besides, the World Bank and IMF have surveyed globally to assess the FI during the same period.

The research assumes that digital finance, FI spurs economic growth in Bangladesh, thus, the growth rate of annual GDP is considered as a proxy of economic growth and as dependent variable (*Lgdpg*) for the econometric model while a set of indicators are used as a proxy of digital finance, FI and independent variables. In the model, number of ATMs (automated teller machine) per 0.1 million adults (*lnATMs*100000), number of commercial bank branches (*lnBCB*), deposit taking financial institutions (*Depo*1000) per one thousand inhabitants, number of insurance companies (*lnIns*), number of total banks (*lnBanks*) and inflation (*INF*) are considered as independent variables. In all forms, we use natural logarithm to produce appropriate result from the analysis.

4.1 Econometric model

As the research intend to explore the association between digital finance, FI and economic growth, the following equation can be proposed as

$$Y_t = \alpha_0 + \alpha_1 F_t + u_t \quad (1)$$

In the model, Y_t reports economic growth at time t while F_t as FI variables and u_t as disturbance term. More specifically,

$$Lgdpg = \beta_0 + \beta_1 \ln ATMs100000 + \beta_2 \ln BCB + \beta_3 Depo1000 + \beta_4 \ln Ins + \beta_5 \ln Banks + INF + u_t \quad (2)$$

In the equation, *Lgdpg* is dependent variable and is used as a proxy of economic growth.

$\ln ATMs100000, \ln BCB, \ln Depo1000, \ln Ins, \ln Banks$ and INF are respective independent variables and are used as proxy of digital finance and FI while β_i (1, 2, ……..5) are coefficient parameters.

4.1.1 ARDL and ECM models

The ARDL model is exploited in order to the unit root test which is implemented and modelled by (Pesaran et al.; 2001). In time series analysis ARDL model is widely used while the order of data is mixed (i.e., a combination of stationary and non-stationary) order and addresses autocorrelation and endogeneity (Shumway et al., 2000; Pesaran et al., 2001; Shrestha and Bhatta, 2018; Boţoroga et al., 2022). Besides, ARDL specifically delivers the parameters for short and long run simultaneously. The model (short-run) can be demonstrated as follows:

$$\Delta Lgdpg = \beta_0 + \sum \beta_{1t} \Delta Lgdpg_{t-1} + \sum \beta_{2t} \Delta \ln ATMs100000_{t-1} + \sum \beta_{3t} \Delta \ln BCB_{t-1} + \sum \beta_{4t} \Delta \ln Depo1000_{t-1} + \sum \beta_{5t} \Delta \ln INS_{t-1} + \sum \beta_{6t} \Delta \ln Banks_{t-1} + \beta_{7t} INF_{t-1} + u_t$$

(3)

In the model (equation 3), Δ indicates first difference operators, $\beta_1 - \beta_6$ are long-run coefficient parameters representing short-run dynamics of the model with $\sum$ sign. The Wald test (F-statistic) is used to test for cointegration in ARDL and explores the lower bound and upper bound. Besides, we hypothesize as there is no cointegration among the coefficient parameters $(\beta_1 - \beta_6)$ as null hypothesis (H_0) and there is cointegration as alternative hypothesis (H_a). The long-run ARDL equation and the ECM can be stated as follows (equation 4 and 5):

$$Lgdpg = \beta_0 + \beta_1 \Delta Lgdpg_{t-1} + \beta_{2t} \Delta \ln ATMs10000_{t-1} + \beta_{3t} \Delta \ln BCB_{t-1} + \beta_{4t} \Delta \ln Depo1000_{t-1} + \beta_{5t} \Delta \ln Banks_{t-1} + \beta_{7t} INF_{t-1} + u_t$$
(4)

$$\Delta Lgdpg_t = \beta_0 + \sum \beta_{1t} \Delta Lgdpg_{t-1} + \sum \beta_{2t} \Delta \ln ATMs100000_{t-1} + \sum \beta_{3t} \Delta \ln BCB_{t-1} + \sum \beta_{4t} \Delta \ln Depo1000_{t-1} + \sum \beta_{5t} \Delta \ln INS_{t-1} + \sum \beta_{6t} \Delta \ln Banks_{t-1} + \beta_{7t} INF_{t-1} + \lambda ECT_{t-1} + u_t$$
(5)

The ECM is used when first; the time series variables are non-stationary and second; bound testing approach defines cointegration among the variables. The adjustment of speed after a short-run shock is measured by λECT_{t-1}.

5. RESULTS ANALYSIS AND INTERPRETATION

In the section, we aim to explore the empirical results with proper econometric modelling and to assess the assortation between digital finance, FI and economic growth of Bangladesh. The summary statistics of the variables are illustrated in Table 1.

Table 1. Summary statistics

Variable	Mean	Std. Dev.	Minimum	Maximum
Lgdpg	1.865	0.133	1.618	2.098
LnATMs_100000	3.071	0.092	1.956	5.197
LnBCB	9.004	0.182	8.749	9.271
LnDepo_1000	6.298	0.332	5.862	6.832
LnINS	4.211	0.106	4.127	4.357
LnBanks	3.944	0.092	3.850	4.078
inflation	7.103	1.653	5.420	11.400

Source: Author calculation

Unit root tests are explored to test whether the variables are stationary or non-stationary. Two types of tests, namely, Augmented Dicky Fuller (ADF) test and Phillips-Perron tests (Dickey and Fuller, 1979; Phillips and Perron, 1988) are explored in the research. The both tests' results are stated in Table 2 and 3, respectively.

Table 2. Augmented Dicky – Fuller test

	At level		At difference	
	t statistics	p -value	t statistics	p - value
Lgdpg	-1.568	0.4995	-1.463	0.5517
LnATMs_100000	0.247	0.7340	-1.972	0.2991
LnBCB	0.276	0.9762	-1.848	0.3568
LnDepo_1000	0.806	0.9917	0.326	0.9785
LnINS	0.116	0.9671	-1.127	0.7040
LnBanks	-0.444	0.9025	-0.453	0.9009
INF	-2.935	0.0414	-2.194	0.2086

Source: Author calculation

Table 3. Phillip-Perron unit root test

		At level		At difference	
	t statistics	**p -value**		**t statistics**	**p - value**
Lgdpg	-1.568	0.4995		-1.819	0.3713
LnATMs_100000	0.243	0.7820		0.147	0.7504
LnBCB	0.276	0.9762		0.158	0.9698
LnDepo_1000	0.806	0.9917		0.736	0.9905
LnINS	0.116	0.9671		-0.177	0.9413
LnBanks	-0.444	0.9025		-0.422	0.9064
INF	-2.935	0.0414		-2.943	0.0406

Source: Author calculation

The unit root test and data stationary graphs (Figure 7) disclose the variables have both stationary and non-stationary in nature and suggests us to explore ARDL model for our hypothesis to check the association between digital finance, FI and economic growth.

Figure 7. Data stationary (dependent and independent variables) (Author calculation)

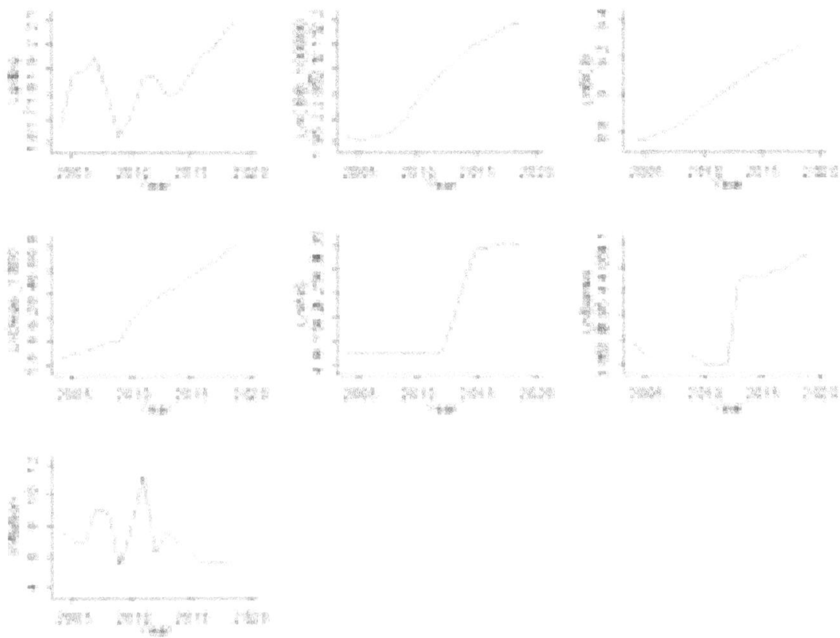

Table 4. ARDL bounds test

Test statistics	**Value**	**Critical value**					
		1% level		**5% level**		**10% level**	
		I(0)	I(1)	I(0)	I(1)	I(0)	I(1)
F -statistics	8.445	3.15	4.43	2.45	3.61	2.12	3.23
t- statistics	-1.975	-3.43	-4.99	-2.86	-4.38	-2.57	-4.04

Source: Author calculation

Table 5. Estimation results (ARDL long-run, short-run and ECM)

	(1)	(2)	(3)
VARIABLES	ADJ	LR	SR
L.LnATMs_100000		7.30**	
		(4.53)	
L.LnBCB		-16.25	
		(10.83)	
L.LnDepo_1000		5.477*	
		(2.566)	
L.LnINS		3.822	
		(2.392)	
L.LnBanks		-2.383	
		(2.023)	
L.inflation		0.0134	
		(0.0302)	
L.Lgdpg	-0.392*		
	(0.198)		
D.LnATMs_100000			5.348*
			(3.033)
D.LnBCB			-6.367***
			(1.519)
D.LnDepo_1000			2.146***
			(0.503)
D.LnINS			1.497**
			(0.434)
D.LnBanks			-0.933*
			(0.465)
D.inflation			0.00524
			(0.0107)
Constant			32.92***
			(7.852)
R-squared	0.894	0.894	0.894

Standard errors in parentheses
*** p<0.01, ** p<0.05, * p<0.1

ARDL bounds test (Table 4) shows F-statistics 8.445 which is higher than critical value of all level 1%, 5%, and 10%, respectively. Besides, the value from t-statistics is also greater than the critical value of all levels of upper and lower bounds. This evidence confirms and suggests the long-run association between digital finance, financial inclusion and economic growth. Thus, the cointegration is confirmed for ARDL bounds test and needs to be estimated the long-run and short-run relationship using ARDL and ECM model as illustrated in equation 4 and 5. The results of the ARDL long-run and short-run model is demonstrated in Table 5.

In the long-run (LR) association, LnATMs_1000 finds 5% significant level while the LnDepo-1000 finds significant at 1% level which suggests that both digital finance and financial inclusion spur economic growth in Bangladesh. Other variable, such as LnBCB and LnBanks show negative relations which is one of the major indicators for financial access but finds insignificant for economic development. This can be explained as more people access to formal financial services through other channels such as mobile financial services (MFS) and the necessity of having a bank account or having more banks may not play effective role for the economy.

Besides, short-run (SR) estimation is conducted through ECM which is shown below the long-run association and confirms that FI has strong association on economic growth. The λECT_{t-1} is found at 10% level ($p<0.10$) and the coefficient is 0.3917 which shows the speed of adjustments and the correction rate from short-run by one yar is almost forty percent.

5.1 Model diagnosis

To validate and to test the appropriateness of the results estimated, model di agnosis and normality tests are performed and illustrated in table 6. In order to the tests, no serial correlation and heteroskedasticity is observed in the model. Besides, the tests confirmed and verified that the model residuals are normally distributed and there are no omitted variables.

Table 6. Model diagnosis and normality tests

Tests	F-stat and P-value	H0	Criteria	Decision
Breusch-Godfrey LM test for autocorrelation	0.142 (0.7065)	No serial correlation	If P<.05, reject H0	Accept H0, no serial correlation
Breusch-Pagan / Cook-Weisberg test for heteroskedasticity	0.25 (0.6182)	No heteroskedasticity	If P<.05, reject H0	Accept H0, no heteroskedasticity
Jarque–Bera test	0.04 (0.9781)	Normal distribution	If P<.05, reject H0	Accept H0, normally distributed
Ramsey Regression Equation Specification Error Test (RESET)	0.61 (0.6327)	No omitted variables	If P<.05, reject H0	Accept H0, no omitted variables

(p-value in the parentheses)

Besides, Cumulative Sum of Recursive Residuals (CUSUM and CUSUMSQ) tests are performed for checking the stability of the model (Brown et al., 1975). The tests also confirm that the model is stable and that falls in between 5% significance level (Figure 8).

Figure 8. Cusum and Cusum squared tests

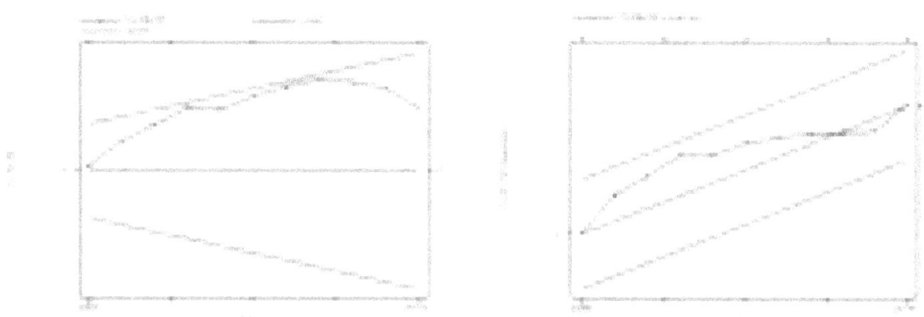

6. CONCLUSION AND RECOMMENDATION

The aim of the research is to identify the association between digital finance, FI and economic growth in an emerging economy like Bangladesh over the period from 2004 to 2020. For this, a detail study is conducted and investigated implementing rigorous econometric models. The research is necessary since financial system in Bangladesh largely depend on banking system and needs to be checked while more exclusion hinder economic growth for the nation.

The study uses ARDL model since the variables are confirmed mixed in order through the Augmented Dicky Fuller and Philip-Perron unit root tests. The model approaches with short and long-run relationships and find a good number of FI variables significant. ECM shows high coefficient which suggests medication speed in equilibrium is reasonable. The study suggests that policy makers should pay effort to reduce financial exclusion through digital finance and promote FI for the marginal groups via appropriate policy guidelines. The gender inequality and regional disparities needs to be reduced through financial literacy, infrastructure development, affordable financial products, mobile banking solutions and different types of promotional activities. There are some recent policies have been introduced to narrow the gap of exclusion, such as eKYC or reduction of the number of documents for opening an account with a formal financial institution. Besides, policies by Central Bank to promote agent banking nationwide is another milestone for reducing the gap. This study has limitations too. The data scarcity and the inclusion of more variables such as the penetration of MFS account or the inclusion of micro-finance intuitions (MFIs) might produce good results. Therefore, the study suggests an avenue for future research in which more accurate results are expected through inclusion of more variables or cross-country study.

REFERENCES

Adedokun, M. W., & Ağa, M. (2023). Financial inclusion: A pathway to economic growth in Sub-Saharan African economies. *International Journal of Finance & Economics*, 28(3), 2712–2728. DOI: 10.1002/ijfe.2559

Agrawal, R. (2016). Mobile Money Empowering People Living at Bottom of Pyramid and Boosting Socio-Economic Development in a Big Way. *Economic Analysis*, 49(1-2), 15–23.

Ahmad, A. H., Green, C. J., Jiang, F., & Murinde, V. (2023). Mobile money, ICT, financial inclusion and growth: How different is Africa? *Economic Modelling*, 121, 106220. DOI: 10.1016/j.econmod.2023.106220

Ahmad, M., Majeed, A., Khan, M. A., Sohaib, M., & Shehzad, K. (2021). Digital financial inclusion and economic growth: Provincial data analysis of China. *China Economic Journal*, 14(3), 291–310. DOI: 10.1080/17538963.2021.1882064

Ali, M., Hashmi, S. H., Nazir, M. R., Bilal, A., & Nazir, M. I. (2021). Does financial inclusion enhance economic growth? Empirical evidence from the IsDB member countries. *International Journal of Finance & Economics*, 26(4), 5235–5258. DOI: 10.1002/ijfe.2063

Anakpo, G., Xhate, Z., & Mishi, S. (2023). The policies, practices, and challenges of digital financial inclusion for sustainable development: The case of the developing economy. *FinTech*, 2(2), 327–343. DOI: 10.3390/fintech2020019

Asanović, Ž. (2020). Essay on finance-Growth nexus. *Journal of Central Banking Theory and Practice*, 1(1), 97–109. DOI: 10.2478/jcbtp-2020-0006

Atkinson, A., & Messy, F. A. (2013). *Promoting financial inclusion through financial education: OECD/INFE evidence, policies and practice*. Retrieved from https://www.oecd-ilibrary.org/finance-and-investment/promoting-financial-inclusion-through-financial-education_5k3xz6m88smp-en

Australian Financial Centre Forum. (2009). *Australia as a Financial Centre Building on our Strengths. Australian Financial Centre Forum*. Retrieved from https://trove.nla.gov.au/work/36802810

Bangladesh Bank. (2020). *Overview of Financial System of Bangladesh*. Retrieved from https://www.bb.org.bd/fnansys/index.php

Beck, T., Demirgüç-Kunt, A., & Levine, R. (2007). Finance, inequality and the poor. *Journal of Economic Growth*, 12(1), 27–49. DOI: 10.1007/s10887-007-9010-6

Bhattacharya, M. R., & Wolde, H. (2010). *Constraints on Growth in the MENA Region. International Monetary Fund.* Retrieved from https://www.researchgate.net/profile/Rina-Bhattacharya/publication/228289502_Constraints_on_Growth_in_the_MENA_Region/links/55ef243508ae199d47bffed0/Constraints-on-Growth-in-the-MENA-Region.pdf

Boachie, R., Aawaar, G., & Domeher, D. (2023). Relationship between financial inclusion, banking stability and economic growth: A dynamic panel approach. *Journal of Economic and Administrative Sciences*, 39(3), 655–670. DOI: 10.1108/JEAS-05-2021-0084

Boţoroga, C. A., Horobeţ, A., Belaşcu, L., Popoviciu, A. S., & Gîrlovan, A. (2022). Assessing the Nexus Between Education, Economic Growth, and Innovation: An Empirical Analysis. *Studies in Business and Economics*, 17(3), 18–34. DOI: 10.2478/sbe-2022-0043

Brown, R. L., Durbin, J., & Evans, J. M. (1975). Techniques for testing the constancy of regression relationships over time. *Journal of the Royal Statistical Society. Series B, Statistical Methodology*, 37(2), 149–163. DOI: 10.1111/j.2517-6161.1975.tb01532.x

Bruhn, M., & Love, I. (2014). The real impact of improved access to finance: Evidence from Mexico. *The Journal of Finance*, 69(3), 1347–1376. DOI: 10.1111/jofi.12091

Burton, M., & Brown, B. (2014). *The financial system and the economy: Principles of money and banking*. Routledge. DOI: 10.4324/9781315699776

Chen, Y., & Sivakumar, V. (2021). Investigation of finance industry on risk awareness model and digital economic growth. *Annals of Operations Research*, •••, 1–22. PMID: 34785834

Chowdhury, E. K., & Chowdhury, R. (2024). Role of financial inclusion in human development: Evidence from Bangladesh, India and Pakistan. *Journal of the Knowledge Economy*, 15(1), 3329–3354. DOI: 10.1007/s13132-023-01366-x

Christopoulos, D. K., & Tsionas, E. G. (2004). Financial development and economic growth: Evidence from panel unit root and cointegration tests. *Journal of Development Economics*, 73(1), 55–74. DOI: 10.1016/j.jdeveco.2003.03.002

Collard, S. (2007). Toward financial inclusion in the UK: Progress and challenges. *Public Money & Management*, 27(1), 13–20. DOI: 10.1111/j.1467-9302.2007.00550.x

Creane, S., Mobarak, A. M., Goyal, R., & Sab, R. (2004). *Financial sector development in the Middle East and North Africa*. Retrieved from https://papers.ssrn.com/sol3/papers.cfm?abstract_id=879026

Dahiya, S., & Kumar, M. (2020). Linkage between Financial Inclusion and Economic Growth: An Empirical Study of the Emerging Indian Economy. *Vision: The Journal of Business Perspective*, 24(2), 184–193. DOI: 10.1177/0972262920923891

Dahiya, S., & Kumar, M. (2020). Linkage between Financial Inclusion and Economic Growth: An Empirical Study of the Emerging Indian Economy. *Vision: The Journal of Business Perspective*, 24(2), 184–193. DOI: 10.1177/0972262920923891

Demirguc-Kunt, A., Klapper, L., Singer, D., & Ansar, S. (2018). *The Global Findex Database 2017: Measuring financial inclusion and the fintech revolution*. World Bank Publications. DOI: 10.1596/978-1-4648-1259-0

Dickey, D. A., & Fuller, W. A. (1979). Distribution of the estimators for autoregressive time series with a unit root. *Journal of the American Statistical Association*, 74(366a), 427–431.

Ediagbonya, V., & Tioluwani, C. (2023). The role of fintech in driving financial inclusion in developing and emerging markets: Issues, challenges and prospects. *Technological Sustainability*, 2(1), 100–119. DOI: 10.1108/TECHS-10-2021-0017

Emara, N., & El Said, A. (2021). Financial inclusion and economic growth: The role of governance in selected MENA countries. *International Review of Economics & Finance*, 75, 34–54. DOI: 10.1016/j.iref.2021.03.014

Estrada, G. B., Park, D., & Ramayandi, A. (2010). *Financial development and economic growth in developing Asia*. Retrieved from https://papers.ssrn.com/sol3/papers.cfm?abstract_id=1751833

Fabris, N. (2019). Cashless society–the future of money or a utopia? *Journal of Central Banking Theory and Practice*, 8(1), 53–66. DOI: 10.2478/jcbtp-2019-0003

Goldsmith, R. (1969). *Financial structure and development*. New Haven Yale University Press.

Hasan, M. M., Yajuan, L., & Khan, S. (2022). Promoting China's inclusive finance through digital financial services. *Global Business Review*, 23(4), 984–1006. DOI: 10.1177/0972150919895348

He, Z., & Wei, W. (2023). China's financial system and economy: A review. *Annual Review of Economics*, 15(1), 451–483. DOI: 10.1146/annurev-economics-072622-095926

Hussain, S., Gul, R., & Ullah, S. (2023). Role of financial inclusion and ICT for sustainable economic development in developing countries. *Technological Forecasting and Social Change*, 194, 122725. DOI: 10.1016/j.techfore.2023.122725

Iqbal, A., & Kassim, A. Z. (2023). Ease of use and standardisation on potential usage of ATMs in Bahrain. *International Journal of Electronic Banking*, 4(1), 1–18. DOI: 10.1504/IJEBANK.2023.134482

Kim, D., Yu, J., & Hassan, M. (2018). Financial inclusion and economic growth in OIC countries. *Research in International Business and Finance*, 43, 1–14. DOI: 10.1016/j.ribaf.2017.07.178

King, R. G., & Levine, R. (1993). Finance, entrepreneurship, and growth: Theory and evidence. *Journal of Monetary Economics*, 32(3), 513–542. DOI: 10.1016/0304-3932(93)90028-E

King, R. G., & Levine, R. (1993). Finance and growth: Schumpeter might be right. *The Quarterly Journal of Economics*, 108(3), 717–737. DOI: 10.2307/2118406

King, R. G., & Levine, R. (1993a). *Financial intermediation and economic development* (Vol. 15689). Cambridge University Press.

Lee, C. C., Lou, R., & Wang, F. (2023). Digital financial inclusion and poverty alleviation: Evidence from the sustainable development of China. *Economic Analysis and Policy*, 77, 418–434. DOI: 10.1016/j.eap.2022.12.004

Levine, R. (2005). Finance and growth: theory and evidence. *Handbook of economic growth, 1*, 865-934.

Leyshon, A., & Thrift, N. (1993). The restructuring of the UK financial services industry in the 1990s: A reversal of fortune? *Journal of Rural Studies*, 9(3), 223–241. DOI: 10.1016/0743-0167(93)90068-U

Leyshon, A., & Thrift, N. (1994). Access to financial services and financial infrastructure withdrawal: Problems and policies. *Area*, 268–275.

Leyshon, A., & Thrift, N. (1995). Geographies of financial exclusion: Financial abandonment in Britain and the United States. *Transactions of the Institute of British Geographers*, 20(3), 312–341. DOI: 10.2307/622654

Mayer, C. (1988). New issues in corporate finance. *European Economic Review*, 32(5), 1167–1183. DOI: 10.1016/0014-2921(88)90077-3

Mckinnon, R. I. (1973). *Money and Capital in Economic Development*. Brookings Institution Press.

Naceur, S. B., & Ghazouani, S. (2007). Stock markets, banks, and economic growth: Empirical evidence from the MENA region. *Research in International Business and Finance*, 21(2), 297–315. DOI: 10.1016/j.ribaf.2006.05.002

Nan, W. V. (2019). Mobile money and socioeconomic development: A cross-country investigation in Sub-Saharan Africa. *Journal of International Technology and Information Management*, 27(4), 36–65. DOI: 10.58729/1941-6679.1392

Ofoeda, I., Amoah, L., Anarfo, E. B., & Abor, J. Y. (2024). Financial inclusion and economic growth: What roles do institutions and financial regulation play? *International Journal of Finance & Economics*, 29(1), 832–848. DOI: 10.1002/ijfe.2709

Ozili, P. K., Ademiju, A., & Rachid, S. (2023). Impact of financial inclusion on economic growth: Review of existing literature and directions for future research. *International Journal of Social Economics*, 50(8), 1105–1122. DOI: 10.1108/IJSE-05-2022-0339

Ozturk, I., & Ullah, S. (2022). Does digital financial inclusion matter for economic growth and environmental sustainability in OBRI economies? An empirical analysis. *Resources, Conservation and Recycling*, 185, 106489. DOI: 10.1016/j.resconrec.2022.106489

Park, C. Y., & Mercado, R. (2015). Financial inclusion, poverty, and income inequality in developing Asia. *Asian Development Bank Economics Working Paper Series*, (426).

Pesaran, M. H., Shin, Y., & Smith, R. J. (2001). Bounds testing approaches to the analysis of level relationships. *Journal of Applied Econometrics*, 16(3), 289–326. DOI: 10.1002/jae.616

Raza, A., Tong, G., Erokhin, V., Bobryshev, A., Chaykovskaya, L., & Malinovskaya, N. (2023). Sustaining Performance of Wheat–Rice Farms in Pakistan: The Effects of Financial Literacy and Financial Inclusion. *Sustainability (Basel)*, 15(9), 7045. DOI: 10.3390/su15097045

Reddy, K., Wallace, D., & Wellalage, N. H. (2024). The impact of financial literacy on financial inclusion. *Australian Journal of Management*, •••, 03128962241270809. DOI: 10.1177/03128962241270809

Santos, A. C. (2017). Cultivating the self-reliant and responsible individual: The material culture of financial literacy. *New Political Economy*, 22(4), 410–422. DOI: 10.1080/13563467.2017.1259302

Schumpeter, J. A. (1912). *Theorie Derwirt-Schaftlichenentwicklung*. Dunker & Humblot.

Sethi, D., & Acharya, D. (2018). Financial inclusion and economic growth linkage: Some cross-country evidence. *Journal of Financial Economic Policy*, 10(3), 369–385. DOI: 10.1108/JFEP-11-2016-0073

Sharma, D. (2016). Nexus between financial inclusion and economic growth: Evidence from the emerging Indian economy. *Journal of Financial Economic Policy*, 8(1), 13–36. DOI: 10.1108/JFEP-01-2015-0004

Shaw, E. S. (1973). *Financial deepening in economic development*. Oxford University Press.

Shen, Y., Hu, W., & Hueng, C. J. (2021). Digital financial inclusion and economic growth: A cross-country study. *Procedia Computer Science*, 187, 218–223. DOI: 10.1016/j.procs.2021.04.054

Shili, N., & Panjwani, K. (2022). Revolution of Financial Inclusion through Fintech in the Digital Age. In *Digitalization and Economic Development* (pp. 141–160). Routledge. DOI: 10.4324/9781003198284-7

Shrestha, M. B., & Bhatta, G. R. (2018). Selecting appropriate methodological framework for time series data analysis. *The Journal of Finance and Data Science*, 4(2), 71–89. DOI: 10.1016/j.jfds.2017.11.001

Sikarwar, T., Goyal, A., & Mathur, H. (2020). Household Debt, Financial Inclusion, and Economic Growth of India: Is it Alarming for India? *Asian Economic and Financial Review*, 10(2), 229–248. DOI: 10.18488/journal.aefr.2020.102.229.248

Singh, D., & Stakic, N. (2021). Financial inclusion and economic growth nexus: Evidence from SAARC countries. *South Asia Research*, 41(2), 238–258. DOI: 10.1177/0262728020964605

Taher, S. A., & Tsuji, M. (2022). An overview of FinTech in Bangladesh: problems and prospects. *FinTech development for financial inclusiveness*, 82-95.

Tarchoun, M., & Ghraieb, I. (2022). Trade openness relationship with macroeconomic factors on Saudi Arabian economy: ARDL application. *International Trade. Politics and Development*, 6(3), 121–129. DOI: 10.1108/ITPD-03-2022-0005

Van, L. T. H., Vo, A. T., Nguyen, N. T., & Vo, D. H. (2021). Financial inclusion and economic growth: An international evidence. *Emerging Markets Finance & Trade*, 57(1), 239–263. DOI: 10.1080/1540496X.2019.1697672

Wang, W., He, T., & Li, Z. (2023). Digital inclusive finance, economic growth and innovative development. *Kybernetes*, 52(9), 3064–3084. DOI: 10.1108/K-09-2021-0866

Zhang, S., & Wei, J. (2023). Can Digital Inclusive Finance better serve the development of the real economy. *Journal of Applied Finance and Banking*, 13(4), 101–123. DOI: 10.47260/jafb/1345

Chapter 13
The Effect of Market Power on Stability and Financial Performance of Islamic and Conventional Banks in Pakistan

Muhammad Ayub Awan
https://orcid.org/0009-0000-0917-0135
International Islamic University, Islamabad, Pakistan

Abdul Rashid
International Islamic University, Islamabad, Pakistan

Muhammad Ali Chohan
https://orcid.org/0000-0002-8860-0603
Guangdong CAS Cogniser Information Technology Co., Ltd., China

Shamaila Butt
https://orcid.org/0000-0003-1411-9590
Sohar University, Oman

Ain Naadia Binti Mazlan
https://orcid.org/0000-0001-5132-146X
University of Technology Malaysia, Malaysia

ABSTRACT

The aim of the study is to explore the impact of market power on the financial stability and financial performance of Islamic banks and their counterparts. In our

DOI: 10.4018/979-8-3693-6386-7.ch013

study the five conventional and five Islamic banks are selected from Pakistan for the period of 2007 to 2016 using Panel data. We have used different techniques to analyze the effect of market power on stability and financial performance. The findings reveal that efficiency of Islamic bank does not depend on the stability. Market share is statistically significant for both Islamic and their counterparts, therefore greater market share leads to increase the financial stability. The asset growth is statistically insignificant in case of both Islamic and their counterparts, therefore asset growth does not have any impact on financial stability. The interest rate spread is statistically significant with conventional banks. The policy makers of the conventional banking sector should work on a tradeoff among the financial performance and financial stability.

1.1. INTRODUCTION

Banks play a vital role in the economy and financial system of the any country. Currently banks have momentous role in society; even without the banking system the imagination of the life is not possible. A bank is a financial organization that licensed to accept the deposits. Banks also provide the financial services. In order to encourage the economy government plays a vital role via banking system through "Monetary Tools". The banks are the group of actors of the financial market as objective is the financial intermediation. Allen and Wood (2015).

Financial performance is defined in the words of FrichKohlar (2015), suggested that performance is the general word which refers to a part or all the activities conducted in the organization for a specific time period. Often though these activities may be related to the past projects, the efficiency of the project costs, and may also include the responsibility or accountability of management in any organization. Financial performance is used for the indication of the success of any organization in different financial activities. It is the process of measuring the firm's policy and also operations in monetary terms (Mayor Roth 2010). It is also used for checking the financial health of the any organization for a specific time periods across the same industry.

Financial stability is the important for the financial system of the any country and for economic development. Furthermore, the financial stability of the banking industry is prerequisite for managers, Regulatory authorities, and as well as for the government officials. Financial stability plays a vital role in the development of any country and important for the policy design and operational frameworks (Schinasi, 2014 and Chant, 2010). Financial stability is the prerequisite for sustainable and essential for the stability of economic growth (Swamy, 2014).

Market power is the capability of the organization to increase the price of market commodities above the marginal cost. The market power is the indicator of the competition; it is significantly affecting the financial performance and efficiency of the banking sectors. The organizations that have the market power may often describe the "Price makers". Financial stability reflects capability of the financial system constantly provides the credit intermediation and disbursement services to the real economy. Financial performance is the measurement of firm basic assets, how to use in the mode of business activity to generate the profit. The intention of the study is to answer the following questions. Firstly, does market power effect financial stability and financial performance of banks in case of Pakistan? Secondly, does the effect of market structure on stability and financial performance determinants differ for both Islamic and conventional banks in case of Pakistan?

The Islamic banking system is different from the conventional banking system from many aspects. As Santos (2000), conventional banks take the deposits from the depositors at a very low interest rate and then allocate these funds at higher interest rate to the firms. Islamic banks are different from the conventional banking system. Islamic banks do not receive the predetermined interest from the borrower, and they do not pay the predetermined interest to depositors. Islamic banking return depends on the profit-sharing agreement with the borrowers and depositors. Islamic banks prohibit Interest (Riba) and interest replaces with profit share. Islamic banks avoid the activities that involve oppressions. However, recent studies suggested that Islamic banks are shown a tendency to mimic the conventional banking sectors.

Now we discuss the variables which we are using in the study with the help of literature.

In order to check the effects of the structure of the market on the financial stability of the banks, the earlier studies by (e.g., Levy Yeyati and Micco, 2007) used the Z-Score model. Z-Score model is defined as the following formula. $Z = \frac{\mu + Cap}{\sigma\mu}$ where μ is the percentage on return on assets, and cap is the equity capital and $\sigma\mu$ is a standard deviation. It also implies that when the Z-score is higher the lower the probability of risk insolvency.

Return on asset is a financial ratio that explores the profit percentage of any company which the company earns from the context of overall resources. Specifically, we can define the net income of the company divided on the total assets of the company. Net Income derived from the company's income statement and net income is the profit after taxes. Return on assets is the indication of the company profits as compared to the company total assets. Return on assets (ROA) gives the idea to the bank managers, Analysts, and investors how to use the assets to get the higher earnings or higher profits.

The market share is the sales of the total markets that earned by a specific organization in a specific time framework. The market share provides the general thought about the size of the any firm as compared to whole market or competitors. Demirguc-Kunt et al. (2004) suggested that the Market share is measured through the sales of the any company in specific time period and then divide it on the total sales of the industry for the same time period.

Market concentration is representing the behavior, which is collusive, that behavior investigate the powers of the firms through getting the higher profit, that is appropriate due to the behavior of oligopolistic. Concentration is the indication of the firm size as compared to whole industry. If the concentration is low the firms have greater competition between the firms exist in the industry. A firm that has 100% concentration that is evident that industry prevails the monopoly.

Interest rate spread is the difference among the bank receives from the loans and bank pays on deposits. This is the key determinant of the profitability of the bank. When the spread is greater, the firm is more profitable. We expect a positive relationship among IRS and profitability. The size of the bank According to Goddard et al (2004b), reported that due to many reasons the bank size can affect the profitability positively.

The capital is the best indicators to check the strength of the bank capital. The banks which are having the more capital, those banks have lower risk of bankruptcy. As, Pasiouras and kosmidon (2007), reported that the banks are safer relatively that are having the liquidation with high equity to assets.

Pasiouras and Kosmidon (2007), we used the cost to income ratio as a measure of efficiency and explain that when changing in cost as compared to change in income. Higher profits are due to minimizing the expanses. The liquidity is defined the ratio of liquid assets by total assets. A negative relationship among the variables and profitability is expected (Bourke, 1989). The effect of yearly growth of total assets on profitability and Bikker and Hu (2012) reported that the bank which is growing faster may earn the higher profit ultimately, they are facing the more risk at the same time.

In this study we are investigating the effect of market power on financial stability and financial performance of banks in Pakistan and to Check the impact of Market Structure on stability and financial performance determinants of both Islamic and Convention Banks in Pakistan. As earlier we have mentioned objectives of the study. We are using the estimation techniques i.e: OLS, Fixed Effect and Random Effect. To check the best model among the fixed effect and Random effect Housman Test is applied. This is justified on the grounds that there is no comprehensive comparative study available on the effect of market power on stability and performance of Islamic and conventional banks in Pakistan. Existing studies only analyzed the comparison between Islamic and conventional bank performance. Several other studies analyze the competition and financial stability. Therefore, we seek to bridge the gap on the effect of market power on stability and financial performance of Islamic and conventional banks in Pakistan. Following are the objectives of the study; a) To examine the impact of market power on stability and financial performance of banks in case of Pakistan. b) To explore the effect of market structure on stability and financial performance determinants of both Islamic and conventional banks. These research objectives are developed to address the following research questions; a) Does market power affect stability and financial performance of banks in case of Pakistan? b) Does the effect of market structure on stability and financial performance determinants differ for both Islamic and conventional banks in Pakistan?

The current chapter includes the following sections after this introduction, section 2 includes the theoretical framework of the study, section 3 will discuss the literature related to the study, section 4 represents the data and methodology used in the study, section 5 is about the empirical and regression result of the study and finally section 6 discussing the conclusion and policy implications of the study.

Theoretical Framework

The recognition of the market concentration levels, and its performance can be endorsed to Bain (1951) who states that a concentrated market structure enhances the oligopolistic performance by competitors. The structure of the related literature is most of the time we are known as the Structure-Conduct-Performance (SCP Hypothesis). SCP basically stated that in the concentrated market the dominant firms have the ability through the collusion to earn the high profits to adjusting the prices. The Structure-conduct-Performance depicts that concentration and performance have positive relationship (Stigler, 1964), i.e., the impact of the market share variable is small, and efficiency as well or insignificant.

Alternatively, the Relative Market power hypothesis (RMP) diagnose that only the firms that have larger market share and well-defined products are able to implement market power to earn abnormal profits (Shepherd, 1982; Rhoades, 1985). Hence, when we measure the Relative Market Power Hypothesis the key variable is the market share. Positive Coefficients for the market share variable support the RMP Hypothesis. This suggests that firm that have relatively greater market power are related to superior prices and profits. Moreover, RMP only holds, the concentration coefficient has to be insignificant, so the variable of efficiency has too relatively unimportant.

The Efficient Structure (ES) Hypothesis is the initiative for challenging description for the positive relationship explained by the RMP Hypothesis. Demsetz (1973, 1974) and many others (Phillips, 1976; Peltzman, 1977; Gale and Branch,1982) recommended that the firm that have specific advantages leads to abnormal profit.

Firms work with lower relative cost are more cost efficient, due to their cost advantage they earn the economic rents. The ES depicts greater efficiency of some firm's leads to concentration of market, which therefore, increase market share and are more beneficial. Those firms want to maximize benefit either by maintaining the current level of price and size of the firms or by minimize price and maximize the size of firm (Lloyd-Williams et al., 1994). In this case, the positive correlation among performance and concentration is spurious, the consequence of efficiency the relationship among market share and financial performance is positive.

The Hypothesis extensively supports the banking literature (Gilbert, 1984; Berger and Hannan, 1989 and 1997; Berger 1995). Many others, Smirlock (1985), Molyneux and Forbes (1995) suggested that concentration and profitability have no relationship among them but among the market share and profitability (used as the proxy for firm's efficiency).

The literature available on the structural approaches investigated that market structure how affects the market competition between firms. Alternatively, non-structural approaches suggest that market structure and concentration may not affect competitive behavior, such as entry/exit barriers and contestability of the market (panzer and Rosse, 1987). The procedure used in the study conducted for different industries, a number of relevant studies (Weiss, 1974; Frech et al., 2000 [Hospitals]; Choi and Weiss, 2005; Pope and Ma, 2008 [Insurance], Kari et al., 2002 [Trucking industry], Perekhozhuk et al. (2023) [Hungarian Dairy products]) or markets (Jenny and Weber, 1976 [France]; Neumann et al., 1985 [Germany]; McDonald, 1999 [Australia]). The general purpose of the above studies was to examine the factors that affect the structure-conduct- performance of the particular industries.

The next section will provide the theoretical model of structure and financial performance.

Theoretical Model of Structure & Financial Performance

Traditionally, the most common way of checking both hypotheses to introduce the concentration and market share as explanatory variables of performance, on the assumption that effect of efficiency reflects the market share. In this case, the effects of market share is positively related to profitability, concentration is insignificant, the efficiency hypothesis do not reject.

To investigate the SCP Hypothesis, the first measure is the static well-known

Herfindahal- Hirschman Concentration index calculated through the market share (qi) of all firms in the market: H= (qi). The benefit of this calculation is to calculate a "number equivalent" of firms (N* =1/H) Where N* is the possible no of firms of the equal size which exist in the market for a given degree of concentration.

As competition increases, the profit of the efficient firm will increase. The hypothesis is same as the Relative profit differences measures by Boone (2008a and 2008b). To check the alternative hypothesis, the second measure is introduced by Kwoka's (1977) Dominance index:

D = [qi-qi +1]2. This highlighting the gap among successive firms when they are ranked by size. The value of this measurement is from 1 to 0, with the previous value signifying a monopolistic market. Conversely, the nearer to zero the result is, the power of the single company is lower.

Earlier studies like Smirlock (1985), Molyneux and Forbes (1995) precise the association with financial performance as follows; Performance $\pi = f$ [CR, MS, Xi] where CR measure the concentration ratio of the market, MS is the Market Share variable (qi) which captures firms greater effectiveness in obtaining big portion of the market, Xi the firm specific variables that affect the effectiveness of the firm. Herfindhal index alternatively used the dominance index as concentration ratio variable.

The market share present in the equation support the Relative market power hypothesis if Market share is significant or support the efficient structure hypothesis. Berger and Hannan argued that the strength of the market shares variable check through the efficiency. On the other hand, concentration ratio supports the structure-conduct-performance hypothesis if concentration ratio is significant.

Thus, in this section firstly review the role of market structure and many other factors affecting the profitability, then after that we look at the studies that are related to the impact of market structure on financial stability.

The Relationship among the Concentration & Profitability

This segment discusses the theoretical and empirical history of the relationship among market power and bank financial performance. According to the available studies, there are three main hypotheses which explore the relationship among market structure and financial performance. The first hypothesis is the structure-conduct-performance (SCP) Hypotheses (Bain, 1956). The SCP paradigm states that on the assumption that due to higher concentration as a result banks earn the abnormal profit that enables banks to collude. The second hypotheses namely we known as the relative-market-power (RMP) Hypotheses. This hypothesis diagnoses that firms that are earning the supernormal profit that is because of the well-differentiated products that will increase the market share and then use their market power in products pricing. The last but not the least hypotheses is the efficient structure hypotheses (Demsetz, 1973) which recommended that due to increase in efficiency firm will earn the supernormal profit due to that reason higher profitability and greater market shares banks will have. The third hypotheses are further divided in to two main hypotheses namely we have known as X-efficiency hypotheses and scale efficiency hypotheses (Berger 1995). Moreover, the empirical and theoretical studies done in US and European countries that explain the relationship among the profit-structure (Goddard et al, 2004 and Vander Vennet, 2002 for the European case, 1995 for the US, among others).

Earlier research related to the determinants of financial performance of banks such as Bourke (1989) and currently Mamatzakis and Remoundos (2003) depend on the structure-conduct-performance hypotheses. The above authors mainly assert that among the concentration market and profitability have the positive empirical relationship. The structure-conduct-performance diagnoses that bank financial performance most of the time depends upon the different factors of market concentration, market structure, number and bank size. When the market is more concentrated, the degree of competition is less then bank is more profitable. (Goddard et al 2004a), stated that among market concentration and profitability have positive relationship. Simirlock (1985), on the other side, Simirlock argue that concentration do not have any significant effect on profitability. However, he reported that market share has significant effect on the profitability, which results that market share positively affect the profitability rather than the concentration of market.

Moreover, according to Goddard et al. (2004b), if there are a large number of banks, there will be no collusion among these banks. They also reported that if the profit is higher in the large number of banks that is ambiguous. However, they are explaining the reasons of high profit that is due to the result of more concentrated market or concentrated market structure and collusion, or that is possible due to the reduction of cost from the management in order to achieve the higher returns. Mamatzakis and Remoundos (2003) argue that there is no significant relationship among the structure of the market and financial performance of the market as a result they reject the structure conduct performance hypotheses. By controversy, the relation among the profitability and concentration is positive reported by Demirguc-Kunt and Huizinga (1999), as well as Athanasoglou et al (2006).

Molyneux and Thornton (1992) also shows the relationship among the concentration ratio and return on equity ratio is significant and positive, these results are consistent with the structure-conduct-performance doctrine and also fallow the results by Bourke (1989) and Short (1979).

Researchers also recommended the many other determinants of bank financial performance other than the market structure. So far, researchers have examined the impact of different variables on the financial performance, relevant to the purpose and nature of the study. Athanasoglou et al. (2008) discussed that bank profitability determinants are most of the time used as the internal and external functions of variables. The variables used as the proxy for microeconomics or determinants which are Bank-specific are internal variables such as the size of the bank, quality of assets, capital adequacy, liquidity ratios, operating ratios, and include the leverage. The external variable determinants reflect (See Rhoades 1985; Bourke 1989; and Damirguc-Kunt and Huizinga 2000; among others).

Especially in the Middle East in case of Islamic banks, a portion of Turk Ariss (2010), also reported that most of the researchers attempt the profitability determinants for Islamic banks and little bit concentrate on the financial performance of Islamic banks. Haron (1996) currently check the profitability determinants for Islamic banks and concluded that profitability is significantly and positively associated with the competition. He used the data for eight Middle Eastern countries from 1993-1998, Bashir (2021) also did work on the profitability determinants for Islamic banks. He recommended that many variables are significantly related to profitability, which includes the structure of the market, capital to asset ratio and loan to asset ratio. Similarly, Hassan and Bashir (2023) inspect a many internal and external banking features as the profitability determinants of Islamic banks. He took the bank data from the period 1994-2001, they argued that the loan to asset ratio and bank size affect the Islamic bank profitability negatively while capital ratio positively affects the profitability of Islamic banks. Furthermore, he reported that per capita gross domestic product and inflation do not have any significant impact on Islamic banks profitability, but the gross domestic product growth significantly affects the profitability or profits. Ben-Khadiri and Ben-Khadiri (2019) investigate the profitability determinants in the MENA region, for Islamic banks from the years 1999-2006. Their conclusion verifies that the bank profitability increases due to bank concentration and the efficiency of management and capitalization boost the financial performance of the bank. He also suggested that the economic growth and inflation is positively associated with bank profitability. Lastly, Al Manaseer (2007) investigates profitability determinants of banks in the four Arab countries include, Jordan, Bahrain, Egypt, and Saudi Arabia from the time period 1996-2003. They commented that Islamic banks and conventional banks have different profitability determinants of banks in those countries. Finally, many researchers have done the investigation on Islamic performance of different features like bank ownership etc. (Sufian et al. 2020).

To Summarize, the available studies on the bank financial determinants and structure of the market provide the extensive knowledge on the effect of bank profitability on internal and external variables for individual country or group of countries. However, in the Islamic banking the structure of the market and financial performance is not properly dealt with.

The Relationship among the Concentration &Stability

The impact of concentration of market on financial stability is important for both aspects such as economic theory and empirical point of view, and this is current discussion on the banking literature. There are two different points of views on the concentration of market and financial stability. The first view is the "concentration-stability" and the second point of view is the "concentration fragility" Therefore there are comprehensive literature that concludes that banks choose the more risky portfolios rationally when the competition will increase (less concentration), but new studies found that the mechanisms of risk incentive show the different direction, which means that when the market more concentrated the banks will take the more risk.

Udhe and Heimeshoff (2019) divided the arguments related the existing two different points of views. According to this division, proponents of the "concentration-stability" view investigate that in concentrated banking sectors the larger banks decrease the financial fragility through the different channels. Firstly, the traditional hypotheses stated that profits increase in the larger banks and therefore bank create high "capital buffer" that allows the less liquidity or overall shocks (Boyd et al. 2004). Secondly, and same as the previous channel, the charter value of the larger banks increase that encourages the bank managers to avoid the behavior of more risk-taking activities (Keeley,1990). The third channel explains that the larger banks have more difficulties towards the financial stability while the fewer banks are easy to monitor, the result will be the effective supervision, and alternatively reduce the possibility of risk (Allen and Gale, 2000). Fourth, channel suggested that greater banks are most of the time subject to credit monitoring services (Boot and Thakor, 2000). And finally, larger banks have the scope of increase the economies of scale and have the ability to manage the risk of loan-portfolio efficiently (Boyd and Prescott, 1986), and also manage the geographically risk through the activities of cross border. (Meon and Will, 2005).

However, the "concentration fragility" view investigate that concentration of market in the larger banks demolish the stability in three different paths (Uhde and Heimeshoff, 2009). Firstly, the banks which are too large subject to "too big to fail" and the institutions that are getting the guarantee from general public, the problem of moral hazard would become more serious (Mishkin, 1999). Second, the banks which are larger they may have change the loan interest rate more frequently due to their higher market power, as a result take the projects from borrowers that are more risky and to compensate high rate, alternatively the default risk of the borrower will increase (Boyd and De Nicolo, 2022).Third the degree of risk diversification reduces due to managerial efficiency, as a result operational risk increase. (Cetorelli et al. 2019).

According to current empirical studies, Beck et al. (2006), used the data for sixty-nine countries from the time period started from 1980-1997, suggested that when the banking system is more concentrated the chance of the financial crisis is less likely to occur. Furthermore, systematic risk is increase when markets are the less contestable. On the same way, Carletti and Vives (2008) argued that market power may effect on bank risk taking activities or incentive. Also, Jimenez et al. (2007) as well as Berger et al. (2009) suggested that market power and overall risk exposure have negative association among them, this is the result from Spanish and twenty-seven developed economies, respectively. In contradictory, Boyd et al. (2006) implemented the stability test (Z-score) he concluded that whether the deposits are concentrated, or loans are concentrated that are correlated with higher probability which increase the risk. Molyneux and Nguyen-Linh (2018) also stated that relationship among the bank risk taking and competition in southeast Asian banking do not increase.

Finally, for the sake of the Islamic banking system stability, Bourkhis and Nabi (2022) analyze the challenges in the recent financial crisis of both Islamic banks and their counterparts. They concluded that in the beginning of the financial crisis, Islamic banks are more flexible and more stable and when the crises pass through the real economy the Islamic banks indeed affected. Comparison of Islamic and conventional banks, Beck et al. (2019) reported that Islamic and conventional banks have significant differences in financial performance of banks including financial stability. In these studies, however, they are not considering the impact of market structure on the financial stability of Islamic banks.

Market Power Hypotheses Vs Efficient Structurc Hypotheses: Emergence of New Theories and Hypotheses

The empirical and theoretical review of the studies explore that a number of serious modellings took the measurement of two versions of efficient structure hypotheses. Shepherd (1986), Schmalensee (1987), Timme and Yang (1991), Sathye (2005), Berger (1995), Weber and Park (2006), Byeongyong and Welss (2008), Chortareaset.Al (2009), Seelanatha, (2010), they observed that the market share most of the time we are using for the proxy for financial performance and reported that financial performance measures directly because the effect of other variables accept financial performance only capture the market share.

Smirlok (2018), also describing the relation of efficiency hypotheses, he also verifies that the market share always used as the proxy for financial performance. Efficiency hypotheses accepted when the positive and significant correlation among the market share and financial performance. The above hypotheses assumed that when the concentration of market is greater that will the reasons of market power.

Shepherds (1986) critically observed this method and suggested that the domination of participants in the individual market is the main and direct source of market power, so the emergence of new hypotheses which is relative market power (RMP) hypotheses. It also reported that the banks are having greater market share and well differentiated products that may be used their market power for getting higher profits through determine the market prices. Alternatively, he argued that market power measures accurately via individual market and also measures the imperfections of the market.

The Relative market power is empirically testified because when we used the explanatory variables or equations of financial performance is insignificant for concentration, conversely price or profitability is positively and significantly correlated to market share. So, when we implemented the structure of market in that kind of equations produce the results which are definite. The bank having a strong hold in the market may reinforce the dominance on the market and get the greater financial performance.

Some of the empirical studies test the profit-concentration relation (market share) through the structure-conduct-performance and relative market power hypotheses, but these studies are not capable to favor one of the hypotheses. The reason of this conclusion is that the effect of the financial performance and market power may be included in the variables describing the structure of the market and they are neutralized with market share. (Concentration Coefficient). The second problem is due to the inconsistency with the theory, negative correlation among the market concentration and financial performance. So as a result, the coefficient of structure of the market is positively and significantly work may be fallacious. The above studies do not confirm the both hypotheses such as RMP and SCP, due to the dual effect of inefficiency and the power of market.

The market power hypotheses mentioned specifically. The Quite Life Hypotheses (Hicks, 1935) explore that the bank management unit which have larger market share are not centered on financial performance allowing to deriving the benefit through the power of market in terms of fixing the price. Furthermore, that will increase the market power which decline financial performance due to that banks are not capable to earn the higher profitability. The quite life hypotheses take the step forward and explain the apparent relation among the structure of the market and financial performance. The works of Berg and Kim (1994), Maudos (1998), Berger (1995), Berger and Hannan (1997), Goldberg and Rai (1996), Papadoplous (2004), Byeongyong (2002), Park and Weber (2016), Samad (2008), Al-Obaidan (2018), Fu and Heffernan (2009), Chortareaset. Al (2019), Al-Muharrami and Matthews (2009), Seelanatha, (2010). Once the efficiency is recognized, the different studies done on the efficiency. Thus, a production technique dimensions include the efficient structure hypotheses, dimension of a production scale and finally dimension of resource allocation.

Berger (1995) introduces the efficiency hypotheses; these hypotheses are divided in to two hypotheses first one is the X-Efficiency hypotheses and second is the Scale-Efficiency hypotheses. A first hypothesis which is X-efficiency reported that the efficient management of the bank will decrease the incurred cost and ultimately higher financial performance. The X-efficiency of the bank is batter, ultimately the market share will be higher and concentration as well. According to the efficiency hypotheses, the financial performance of the two firms are not depends on the differences in management quality but due to the scale efficiency hypotheses. When the banks have lower cost as compare to their competitors as a result financial performance will increase. The banks may want to extend the market shares as a result the concentration of the market will increases.

Regarding the traditional efficiency hypotheses in the review of the above studies, Fiordelisi (2004) represents the three channel of efficiency which is technical, allocate, and scale efficiency respectively. All the measures are used in the Italian manufacturing industry from the period 1993-1997. The Allocate channel is the first contribution of the author and that is more interesting in the wisdom that it allows the new idea of relative market power hypotheses and expanding the efficient structure hypotheses under the shadow of Allocative Efficient structure (AE).

Currently, Al-Obaidan (2008), represented the general composite model. He used the deterministic and stochastic functions' for estimating the technical efficiency and concluded that the efficiency hypotheses in the commercial banking of the Gulf Cooperation Council emerging market from the period (1996-2005). Al-Muharrami and Mattews (2019), found the difference among the country fixed effects and bank fixed effects from the period of 1993-2002, for the Arab bank industry in GCC countries best explained by structure-conduct-performance hypotheses, but they are unable to provide the evidence for the quite life hypotheses. Fu and Heffernan (2019) investigate the Chinese banking sector for the period 1985-2002, the relationship among the structure of the market and financial performance. They are using the random effects estimation technique and used the panel data; the power market hypotheses and efficient structure hypotheses are diagnosed.

The gradual strategy of Chinese banking structure of the market recommended that the new policies enlarge the market shares of banks which are most efficient. Fu and Heffernan (2009) investigate the various applications for the structure of the market (market Share and concentration) and financial performance (Scale efficiency and X-efficiency) which accept or reject the hypotheses. If the correlation among financial performance and market share is positive, then the other structural and financial performance variables are not relevant. Furthermore, we check the relation among the X-efficiency when there is positive correlation exists among scale efficiency and profitability. So the other variables of the structure of the market and financial performance are not relevant. But for the confirmation of the efficiency hypotheses then there should be positive correlation among the structure of the market and financial performance (Berger and Hannan (1997). Same as,

Chortareaset. Al (2009) verifies the efficient structure hypotheses from the periods of 1997-2005 for the Latin Americans countries. The writer investigates mainly the market power hypotheses such as the relative market hypotheses and structure conduct performance, he also discusses the efficient hypotheses such as X-and scale efficiency hypotheses.

Currently, Seelanatha (2020) argued that the overall performance of banking affects the bank financial performance and the structure of the market in the context of effectiveness and the net interest margin through the literature of the structural conduct performance. To summarizing the empirical analysis done on the Srilankan banks from the time period of 1977-2005, and he concluded that banks financial performance does not depend on the market power on the individual bank or the concentration of the market but depend on the level of the financial performance of the different units of banks.

Many previous studies done on the market power for banking sector. The Panzer-Rosse H- statistic used by the different countries and used also for the different regions. For example, Bikker and Groeneveld (2000) measure the competition of the bank for fifteen EU countries from the period 1989-1996. They concluded that most of countries are in the position of monopolistic competition accept Greece and Belgium, they are in the state of perfectly competitive condition. De Bandt and Davis (2000) estimate bank competition in different countries such as Germany, Italy, France, and United States from the time periods 1992-1996. They concluded that the small banks are always in the position of monopoly but on the other hand the larger banks are in the state of monopolistic competition.

Bikker and Haaf (2002) investigated that the competition in the banking industry of twenty-three countries; they recommended that on the results of their sample study the monopolistic competition prevails. Claessens and Laeven (2014) asses the competition of bank for fifty different countries and he concluded that all the countries nearly in the position of monopolistic competition. Perera et al. (2016) examine the bank competition in south Asia from the period of 1995-2003. Their results suggested that interest-based product is having the greater competition in the Bangladesh and Pakistan, alternatively the fee-based products are more competitive in India and Sri-Lanka.

There are large studies that examine the competition in the Chinese banking industry. Yuan (2006) estimate the condition of the competitive structure for the Chinese banks industry from the period 1996-2000. They concluded that the Chinese banking structure is already in the position of perfect competition, but these results are before the foreign banks enter in the Chinese banking sector. Fu 2006 also explores the competitive market condition using a panel data for seventy-six banks from the periods 1997 to 2007. She recommended that monopolistic competition prevails in the Chinese banking sector. She also commented that when the agreement done with WTO, bank lending competition in the market will increase. Masood and Sergi (2019) estimate the competitive market conditions for the sixteen Chinese banks from the period 2004-2007. The discussion of the above studies reported that monopolistically competitive conditions were examined in the Chinese banking sectors.

The different studies found the different competitive market conditions and concluded that the authors have used the different measures for competition. Moreover, the results are related to specific reforms in the banking industry of China. For example, Chinese government established the three policy banks in 1994, for the lending responsibilities previously take the state-owned banks.

The determinants of market power are studied in the different empirical studies for banking industry. Fungacova et al. (2016) used the Lerner index and examine the competitive conditions of the market from the period 2001-2007 for Russian banking industry. They concluded that the competition of the market increase for the period studied. The result suggested that size of the bank and the concentration of the market and risk is significantly and positively affect the market power of the Russian banking industry. Anzoategui et al. (2018) also reported the competition of the Russian bank, the state-owned banks have more market power as compared to other banks. Moreover, competition is negatively related to the concentration of bank, but financial development and economic development effects positively.

Fernandez de Guevera and Maudos (2017) investigated the market power of the Spanish banking Industry from the time period 1986-2002. They also suggested that in the mid-1990s the market power will increase. Moreover, the size of the bank, financial performance, positively and significantly related to the bank market power of the Spanish banking. Fernandez de Guevara et al. (2005) analyzed the market power in the banking sector of European Union. They also investigate that the degree of competition is not increase in the European Union, but the size of the bank, financial performance, risk and economic cycles are significantly and positively affecting the market power of the banks of Europe.

Literature Review

In 1941 Jeo S. Bain firstly studied the structure of the market effects and financial performance and reported that we can measure the profit from monopoly power. Since the number of studies done on the literature related to financial performance and the structure of the market. Earlier studies took the cross-section data for the analysis of the industry, which have mainly checked the effects on the variables of the structure of the market such as, market concentration, firm size and barriers to entry, on financial performance. Recently, the studies done on the international trade variables were given the special attention. The variables which are used in the recent studies are business cycles, Exchange Rate, Imports, and Exports as well. Moreover, the focus is now on firm level analysis and panel data techniques are extensively used to allow the effects for particular firm. Now we show the theoretical as well as empirical results in the shadow of the earlier studies done on the area.

Bain (1951), use the hypotheses to test the relation among profit and the concentration of the industry was taken by the Jeo S. Bain for the US manufacturing. Jeo S. Bain reported the relation of concentration of firm and profit in his research paper and looked the greater detail about the issues regarding the definition of the firm in theoretical context. Bain selected the forty-two firms due to the issues of the theory out of three forty two firms under consideration. He used the various financial variables and concluded that: (1) the relation between profit margins and concentration is not linear (2) average industry profits do not seem to be significantly affected by industry concentration (3) firms having earned more significantly average profits where 70% output control the eight firms. (4) There is no association between absolute firm size and profit margins and (5) Ratio of capital assets, cost ratio of overhead was found not to be associated with profits margins, concentration and size of the firms. He has suggested that concentration and entry barriers together serve to raise the profitability of the large firms.

Preston and Collins (1969) fond the relationship among the structure of the market and financial performance from the period 1958-1963 and used the Ordinary Least Square technique for the estimation, on the assumption that the relationship is linear for US data. Using the difference between gross revenues and direct costs as a measure of price-cost margins, they found that this measure was positive and significantly affected by the market concentration and ratio of capital-output. They also suggested that market concentration for consumer goods firms is particularly strong. Collins reported that when the CR4 concentration lies within 30 to 70 percent, the fifth through eight firm concentrations has negative effects on margins of cost-price. The relationship among margins of cost-price and concentration was found to increase over the study period, particularly in industries in which the level of four-firm concentration was stable or increasing.

Miller (1969) studied the structure performance relation for 106 internal revenue service industries using four-year average data (1958/59 – 1961/62) for the United States. The four-firm concentration ratio was found to have positive effect on profits while the marginal concentration (fifth through eight firm concentrations) had restraining impact on profit. Using advertisement expenditure as proxy for product differentiation, a positive relation was found between profits and product differentiation. The diversity measure had positive and significant effect on profits only when advertisement expenditure also appears as explanatory variable in the regression equation. He also argued that the interpretation of advertisement as proxy for entry barriers in producers' goods industries became questionable because it could better serve as proxy for entry barriers only in consumers goods industries.

Waterson and Cowling (1976) Theoretical model construct for the relationship among financial performance and firm structure, on the assumption that N numbers of firms are producing the homogeneous products and for each firm cost conditions are same, they theoretically investigated that the margin of cost price (Monopoly power measure through Lerner index) and the number of firms in the industry are negatively related, and industry demand of price elasticity. However, relation among margin of cost-price and concentration of firm is observed positively. Then investigate the US data for production industries from the period of 1958-1968 on ninety-four industries, they used the estimation technique, Four- firms concentration ratio and Lerner Index to measure the concentration changes. As a result, Cowling finds the changes among margin of cost-price and concentration ratio are significant. Percentage changes in unemployment and sale were found to have no significant role. The margins of cost-price is significantly related to durable industries and noted that insignificant for the non-durable goods.

Porter (1979) investigates theory for strategic groups from the period 1965 to 1980 for the US thirty-eight industries. Size of the firm is used for the strategic groups. He also measures the determinants of leader (means firms having large size) and followers (means firms having small size) financial performance with the help of econometric technique. The determinants of leaders rate of return was observed the 11.68% as compare to the follower's rate of return was observed 10.81%. The difference among the two rates of returns was observed 0.14. This is surprising that the followers are earning the more profit as compared to leaders in the fifteen industries out of thirty eight industries. Furthermore, his econometric results explore the positive effect on the profits of leader for four firm concentration ratio CR4, while negatively effects the followers. The leaders Relative market shares and numbers of firm to follower do not have any impact on the profits of the leaders, but it is insignificantly and negatively impact on the profit of the followers. The requirement is concern with the requirement of capital and growth do not relate with the profits of the leaders, but effects negatively profit of the followers. Furthermore, he reported that the best measure of the scale economies is interaction of concentration of scale economies and for the structure of the market average-advertise–sale- ratio is best as compared to leaders or followers approach.

Jacquemin (1982) proposed the oligopoly (non-cooperative) model with the assumption that homogeneous goods are producing the N number of firms and each firm assumes that no change occur in the competitors supply in the short run, by the country producers of foreign traders, but the production of its own changes. Furthermore, with the perfectly inelastic supply assumption of imports industry, and mathematically derive the relation among the margins cost price and rate of return and suggested that concentration positively affect the domestic producers and negatively related to demand elasticity of imports. They also concluded that the strong competition in the domestically concentrated industries is observed, and it affects the imports negatively. When the assumption of inelastic import supply is relaxed, and then the imports also interact and reduced the profitability of producers which are working domestically.

Amjad (1982) did research for the west Pakistani manufacturing industries during the period for 1965 to 1970. Price cost margin measures from two different methods and get a positive relation among profit and four firm concentrations CR4. For the sake of measuring the competition used the number of firms available in the industry. The results examine that if increase the number of firms as a result increase competitive behavior as indicated by lower price-cost margins. Amjad argued that the rate of effective protection should not be relied upon to measure the relationship between protection and profitability. When he combined a dummy variable for imports with concentration, he found that imports has restraining effect on profitability, but not as strong as the theory predicts. Capacity utilization was found to have significant positive, while export and advertisement had no significant association with price-cost margins.

Rotemberg and Sloner (1984) concluded, on the basis of Game-Theoretic Model, that implicitly colluding oligopolists had the tendency to unilaterally give up collusion when businesses were booming. On the basis of their model they predicted that optimizing oligopolists reduces their prices when demand is high, resulting in lower profitability.

Schmalensee (1985) study done for the period from 1975-1989 and used the cross section data for US four hundred fifty six manufacturing industry to check the market effect, market share effect and firm effect. His analysis suggested the non-existence of firm effect. The effect of industry exist seventy five percent. The effect of market share is not important but still exists. Furthermore, effect of industry and share of market is negatively associated, implying a negative relationship between industry profitability and concentration.

Domowitz, Hubbard and Petersen (1986) study and criticized the margins of cost-price using the data which is cross section and the market concentration relation because, they argued, it does not capture the intertemporal nature of the relation and its determinants. In particular they have notice that the gap of price-cost margins between the concentrated and non-concentrated manufacturing had dramatically reduced during 1958- 81 periods in US. The result of the above analysis state that the margins of cost-price are strongly procyclical in the more concentrated industries.

Import competition was found to reduce the margins in the concentrated industries but was not as strong as the demand effects were.

Levisohn (1991) in his “imports-as- market- discipline hypothesis” formulated a simple static oligopoly model and tested it for Turkish manufacturing industries using firm level data for 1984 to 1986 period. He applied what is called new approach instead of common. They studied the eleven industries, he suggested that many industries found to be competitive, and in 1984 after trade liberalization many industries decrease the margins of cost-price and protection as well. Alternatively he verified the reported hypotheses empirically.

Hersch, Bhandari and Kemme (1994) investigated the margins of cost-price determinants for private manufacturing sector. (Hungary and Poland) used by the World Bank data collected in 1992 for the different organizations, they used the estimation technique which is fixed effect model. They are unable to collect the data of market revenue, they depend upon the world Bank questionnaire and used three dummies as proxy for market concentration (D1=1 if number of competitor is zero, D2=1 if number of competitor is between 1 and 10, D3=1 if number of competitor is between 11 and 50). Their analysis is just consistent with theory, implying that the coefficient ofD1>D2>D3. Furthermore, the impact of exports on margins of cost price is positively associated, while the impact of imports on margins of cost price is negatively related. As a result impact of explanatory variables has insignificant impact in case of CSFR and Hungary. State competition was significant role even after liberalization in Poland.

Battacharya and Block (1997) took into account the problems of omission of relevant explanatory variables, simultaneity and measurement errors. They regress different explanatory variables through different regression equations, and examined that the magnitude and significant of the positive relation between profit and concentration depend on the set of explanatory variables included in the regression equation. To see the simultaneity problem they also ran IV regression with concentration as the only endogenous variable. The results of OLS and IV were quite similar. In case of two different deflation methods for profit, the R-squared value and import coefficient changes significantly (with import coefficient positive in one case and negative in the other one), showing that measurement error matter a lot for the results. They concluded that if omitted the explanatory variables which are relevant, biased result among the market concentration and profitability would be observed. Therefore, to measure the profitability the choice of correct independent variable is necessary.

Audretsch, Thurik, Prince, (1999) analyzed the 66 Dutch industries which are related to manufacturing sector for the period 1975 to 1986, to check the hypotheses for price setting mechanism and stated that the small firms are following the large firms or work independently or not. The pooled data regression results show that small firm are not following the leader firms, but the margins of cost price of the small firms are independent as compare to margins of cost price of the large firms. Margins of cost price positively affect the market growth, market share of large and small industries. Concentration and small business were found to have negative impacts on the margins for both types of firms. The degree of capital intensity and consumers goods orientation has different implications for the small and large firms.

Feeny (2000) used the sample of 180738 Australian tax entities averaged over 1995-97 periods to study the determinants of profitability. Using simple OLS technique for the cross section of 180738 entities (142 industries), he estimated 142 regression equations and fined that, (1) entity size has positive impact on profits of entities (2) entity gearing has negative but small average effect on profitability's (3) the coefficients of capital intensity were significant for 58% of the industries, about all with positive signs (4) U shaped relation among the share of market and financial performance to be found. (5) Concentration ratio and financial performance have significantly and positively related to 38 industries while negative for 11 industries (6) three proxies, minimum efficient scale, industry capital intensity and industry trademark intensity were used for entry barriers, where only capital intensity was found to behave according to the theory.

Lee (2001) tested, Haltiwanger and Harrington theoretical prediction that for oligopolists, it is difficult to collude in economic slumps so that they price more counter cyclically during recession, for the panel of 180 US manufacturing over 1963-1987. His results confirmed that for firms it is optimal to price counter cyclically in state of high incentives to cheat.

Eriotis, Frangouli and Ventoura-Neokosmides (2002), using firm's level data for the 1995-96, concluded on the basis of profitability concentration analysis, that firms prefer to compete rather than to cooperate with each other. On the basis of debt equity ratio and profitability analysis they found that firms that have used retain profits have earned more than those which prefer borrowed capital for investment activities. Investment levels were found to lead to more profits.

Gallet and Euzent (2002) estimated the demand fluctuations in the US brewing industry and to investigate the competition strength to employ the market demand, supply model. Using annual data over 1964-1992 periods, they concluded that when the demand and expected profits are low then the competition increase in the industry. Furthermore, examine that when the advertisement is more as a result competition is decrease among brewers.

Slade (2003) discuss the models which are related to competition. The structure conduct performance industrial organization model (Harvard approach), the industrial model for market share (Chicago approach). Which reported that due to increase in the financial performance firms always get the greater profits which shows the greater market share as compare to monopoly power, this argument support from the famous model of the financial economics (CAPM Model) which reported that the assets which are having more systematic risk always leads to a more increase in return. The other model (Natural Exhaustible-Resource Model) which also recommended that the exhaustible-resources increase marginally with the passage of time and the structure of the market and profitability of the firm do not have any systematic relationship among both of the variables.

Slade (2008) analyzing the two different sectors, the nonferrous mining and the markets for refining, he used the panel data and component analyses technique from the period 1994-1998, verifies the structural-conduct- performance model strongly. The mentioned studies examine that the profits of the firms, related to the market structure significantly as well as positively. They also recommended that the firm share of the market do not have any impact on the profitability. So the (CAPM Model) supports the results partially, while the Model for Exhaustible-Resource does not have any support.

Li, McCarthy and Urmanbetova (2004) took the different sectors for analyzing the panel data from the period 1970-1997 for US paper, paperboard, pulp industries, to check the concentration and margins for cost-price and concluded that the relation among both variables is strongly impact on the cycles of the business as measured by the current and one period lead the rates of unemployment. In the concentrated industry observed that the margins are increased in the expansion periods. Competition find in the imports sectors shows the lower margins and observed the increase in the margins when the environmental regulations are implemented.

Culha and Yalcin (2005) investigate the margin cost-price determinants for Turkish manufacturing firms, used the panel data and fixed effect model analyses for the period 1995-2003. They recommended that the small and young firms are always work their own way or work in a different way as compare to the firms that are having the larger share in the market. On average the price cost margins are pro-cyclical and responding positively to the market shares as suggested by the theory.

Mulato, Castanedo, Sabido, (2006) studied the impact of concentration, import penetration and capital-output ratio on the price-cost margins for 63 industries in Mexico for 1980- 1998 period. They sub divided the data between 1980-85 and 1986-98 to examine the effects of the trade liberalization measures taken by the Mexican government in 1986.They found that the liberalization has forced the domestic concentrated firms to reduce the margins for the given level of concentration. The import penetration has found to have disciplining effects as the theory suggests and these effects have increased in recessions. Firms are found to charge small margins in booms as compared to recessions. They also found that the margins of cost-price have no impact on concentration especially for non-durable goods but the type of goods did not matter in case of import competition.

Hsu, Tsai, and Yang (2008) studied the impact of the structure of the market on the financial performance for small open economy and construct the simple theoretical model for Taiwan. They reported in their model that N homogenous firms have oligopolistic behavior available in local market, but they are having competitive fringe in the foreign market. Addition to the effect of concentration, elasticity of demand and number of firms, their model suggested that the exchange rates affect the profitability of the firm in a two different ways. The direct affect and the indirect effect, indirect effect shows the positive impact on the financial performance; while the direct effect investigated that the sign is dependent on the orientation of industrial financial performance. They tested their model using 1986, 1991 and 1996 census data on 164 cross section observations. Using the index of effective exposure Goldberg -1990 to check the exchange rate changes in to the profitability through the exposure channel and different econometric techniques such as OLS, within panel estimator, random effect and SUR technique, they found the positive relation of different variables such as concentration and advertising, with the profit margin. Coefficient of advertising was insignificant in some techniques while the capital-sales ratio was insignificant in almost all cases. Export oriented industries were found to have lower profitability which was, according to them, that is due to the reason that the Taiwan's exports more contributed in the small and Medium Enterprises, so they work in the international market as price taker. Exchange rate positively and significantly impact on the exports. They also suggested that the industries that are dependent on the imported inputs effects more when the NT dollar devalued.

Hariprasad, Barua, Chakraborty, (2010) analyzed the data for fourteen different sectors for the period 1990-2008. They showed that although concentration has decreased as a result of liberalization, the price-cost margin increased in general. According to them it may be due to the fact that the cost has decreased more as a compared to market power. The elasticity of demand in equilibrium is inelastic which they deem another reason for the rise in price-cost margins.

From the literature we can conclude that In 1941 Jeo S. Bain studied the structure of the market effects and financial performance and reported that we can measure the profit from monopoly power. Earlier studies took the cross section data for the analysis of the industry, which have mainly checks the effects on the variables of the structure of the market such as, market concentration, firm size and barriers to entry, on financial performance. Bain (1951), use the hypotheses to test the relation among profit and the concentration of the industry was taken by the Jeo S. Bain for the US manufacturing. Jeo S. Bain reported the relation of concentration of firm and profit in his research paper and looked the greater detail about the issues regarding the definition of the firm in theoretical context. Bain selected the forty two firms due to the issues of the theory out of three forty two firms under consideration.

Preston and Collins (1969) fond the relationship among the structure of the market and financial performance from the period 1958-1963, and used the Ordinary Least Square technique for the estimation, on the assumption that the relationship is linear for US data. Miller (1969) studied the structure performance relation for 106 internal revenue service industries using four year average data (1958/59 – 1961/62) for the United States. The four-firm concentration ratio was found to have positive effect on profits while the marginal concentration (fifth through eight firm concentrations) had restraining impact on profit. Waterson and Cowling (1976) Theoretical model construct for the relationship among financial performance and firm structure, on the assumption that N numbers of firms are producing the homogeneous products and for each firm cost conditions are the same, they theoretically investigated that the margi.0n of cost price (Monopoly power measure through Lerner index) and the number of firms in the industry are negatively related, and industry demand of price elasticity. Porter (1979) investigates theory for strategic groups from the period 1965 to 1980 for the US thirty eight industries. Size of the firm is used for the strategic groups. He also measure the determinants of leader (means firms having large size) and followers (means firms having small size) financial performance with the help of econometric technique. Jacquemin (1982) proposed the oligopoly (non-cooperative) model with the assumption that homogeneous goods are producing the N number of firms and each firm assumes that no change occur in the competitors supply in the short run, by the country producers of foreign traders, but the production of its own changes. Amjad (1982) did research for the west Pakistani manufacturing industries during the period for 1965 to 1970. Price cost margin measures from two different methods and get a positive relation among profit and four firm concentrations ratio CR4. Rotemberg and Sloner (1984) concluded, on the basis of Game-Theoretic Model, that implicitly colluding oligopolists had the tendency to unilaterally give up collusion when businesses were booming. On the basis of their model they predicted that optimizing oligopolists reduces their prices when demand is high, resulting in lower profitability. Schmalensee (1985) study done for the period from 1975-1989 and used the cross section data for US four hundred fifty six manufacturing industry to check the market effect, market share effect and firm effect. Hersch, Bhandari and Kemme (1994) investigated the margins of cost-price determinants for private manufacturing sector. (Hungary and Poland) used by the World Bank data collected in 1992 for the different organizations, they used the estimation technique which is fixed effect model. Audretsch, Thurik, Prince, (1999) analyzed the 66 Dutch industries which are related to manufacturing sector for the period 1975 to 1986, to check the hypotheses for price setting mechanism and stated that the small firms are following the large firms or work independently or not. Lee (2001) tested, Haltiwanger and Harrington theoretical prediction that for oligopolists, it is difficult to collude in economic slumps so that they price more counter cyclically during recession, for the panel of 180 US manufacturing over 1963-1987. Eriotis, Frangouli and Ventoura-Neokosmides (2002), using firm's level data for the 1995-96, concluded on the basis of profitability concentration analysis, that firms prefer to compete rather than to cooperate with each other. Gallet and Euzent (2002) estimated the demand fluctuations in the US brewing industry and to investigate the competition strength to employ the market demand, supply model. Slade (2008) analyzing the two different sectors, the nonferrous mining and the markets for refining, he used the panel data and component analyses technique from the period 1994-1998, verifies the structural-conduct- performance model strongly. The mentioned studies examine that the profits of the firms, related to the market structure significantly as well as positively. Culha and Yalcin (2005) investigate the margin cost-price determinants for Turkish manufacturing firms, used the panel data and fixed effect model analyses for the period 1995-2003. Hsu, Tsai, and Yang (2008) studied the impact of the structure market on the financial performance for small open economy and construct the simple model for Taiwan.

Data and Methodology

The Annual data relating the variables is used in this study taken from the State Bank of Pakistan as well as from the respective banks websites. Panel data is used in this study which is the combination of time series and cross section data. Data analyses for the study includes for the period 2007 to 2016. In our study the five conventional and five Islamic banks are mainly focused. The intention of the study is to explore the Impact of Market Power on the Financial Stability as well as the Financial Performance of Islamic Banks and their counterparts in Pakistan. We have used different techniques for the panel data, such as the descriptive statistics, Ordinary Least Square Analysis. To check the appropriation of the model between the common effect model and fixed effect model, F-statistic test is used, and to diagnose the best model with in the random effect model and fixed effect model, Housman technique is implemented. We have used the Z-score model for the measurement of bank's financial stability. To check the financial performance we are using the return on asset as the proxy for measuring the financial performance. To check the market power we used the market structure variables which include Market share and concentration ratio, we are also using the Bank specific variables which include the bank size, efficiency, capital adequacy, market growth, interest rate spread.

The panel data models are used in this study. We are investigating the financial performance of the conventional and Islamic banks through the structure of the market. The structure of the market includes the two basic variables; such variables are Market share and concentration ratio. The market share is the sales of the total markets that earned by a specific organization in a specific time framework. The market share provide the general thought about the size of the any firm as compare to whole market or competitors. Market concentration is represents the behavior which is collusive, that behavior investigate the powers of the firms through getting the higher profit, that is appropriate due to the behavior of oligopolistic. We are checking the health of the banking system through the financial performance of the bank, which is measured through the risk and return of the bank. We are focusing on the earlier models to develop our own models. The following model is recognized by Dianna and Douglas (1988) and Smirlock (1985).

$$\pi_{it} = \alpha_{0+\alpha_1} MS_{it} + \alpha_2 CR_{4it} + \sum_{j=1}^{j} 1 \beta_j X_{jit+\sum_{m=1}^{M} x} + \varepsilon_{it} \quad (1)$$

Where π measures the financial performance, MS measures the market share, CR4 measures the concentration ratio. A combination of coefficient of $\alpha 1 = 0$ and $\alpha 2 > 0$ verify that the firm that have the higher market share are earn the more profit and more efficient than their competitors. These coefficients are supporting the relative market theory (RMP) theory; the basic element of the structure of the market in this theory is the market share. Alternatively, the combination of coefficient of $\alpha 1 = 0$ and $\alpha 2 > 0$ verify the structure-conduct -performance traditional theory (SCP). In this model Xj is used for the specific variables of the bank and Xm is used for the specific variables for the country, and ε_{it} is the disturbance term or error term.

In order to investigate the financial performance and financial stability of the banking sector in Pakistan, the two models are developing which are as follows:

In order to check the effects of the structure of the market on the financial performance of the banks, the two indicators are used in the earlier studies (e.g. Pasiouras and Kosmidou 2007) for investigating the financial performance or profitability, Return on Average Assets (ROAA), return on Average Equity (ROAE).

Model 1: To measure the financial performance of the banks.

$$ROA_{it=}\beta_0 + \beta_1 MS_{it} + \beta_2 CR_{4it} + \beta_3 Size_{it} + \beta_4 Efficiency_{it} + \beta_5 Liquidity_{it} + \beta_6 CaptialAdequacy_{it} + \beta_7 MarketGrowth_{it} + \beta_8 Interestratespread_{it} + \mu_{it}$$

In order to check the effects of the structure of the market on the financial stability of the banks, the earlier studies by (e.g. Levy Yeyati and Micco, 2007) used the Z-Score model. Z-Score model is defined as the following formula. $Z = \frac{\mu + Cap}{\sigma\mu}$ Wwhere μ is the percentage on return on assets, and cap is the equity capital and $\sigma\mu$ is a standard deviation. It also implies that when the Z-score is higher the lower the probability of risk insolvency.

Model 2: To measure the financial stability of the banks.

$$ZScore_{it} = \beta_0 + \beta_1 MS_{it} + \beta_2 CR_{4it} + \beta_3 Size_{it} + \beta_4 Efficiency_{it} + \beta_5 Liquidity_{it} + \beta_6 CaptialAdequacy_{it} + \beta_7 MarketGrowth_{it} + \beta_8 Interestratespread_{it} + \mu_{it}$$

The Definitions of the Variables

This study includes the different variables which we are using in our regression models, we are using the two dependent variables such as, Z-Score which is used for financial stability and Return on Assets (ROA) is used for financial performance, we are also using the several independent variables such as, Market share, Concentration Ratio, Efficiency, Capital Adequacy, Size, Liquidity Ratio, Market growth, and Interest Rate Spread.

Dependent variables

We are using the two dependent variables in our study such as Z-Score and Return on Assets (ROA), we are using the Return on Assets (ROA) as proxy for measuring the financial performance and Z-Score model is used for the financial stability. Now we discuss the first dependent variable Return on Asset (ROA) and then define the second variables Z-Score.

Return on Assets (ROA)

Return on asset is a financial ratio that explores the profit percentage of any company which the company earns from the context of overall resources. Specifically we can define the net income of the company divided on the total assets of the company. Net Income derived from the company's income statement and net income is the profit after taxes. Return on assets is the indication of the company profits as compare to the company total assets. Return on assets (ROA) gives the idea to the bank managers, Analysts, and investors how to use the assets to get the higher earnings or higher profits.

Z-Score Model

Z-Score model is developed by the Altman. He was the professor in the New York University. Z-Score is the statistical tool that used for the measurement of likelihood that may be company go bankrupt. Although Altman developed the Z-Score in 1960s but still this is reliable for the financial stability of the banking sectors. Earlier literature suggested that the different measures of financial stability of bank are used: Z-Score model (1968) and ZETA (1977) model. Z-score is mostly used for the banking sector stability and this measure is accepted worldwide to check the stability of overall banking. This also explaining by the literature by (Srairi, 2013; Blasko and Sinkey, 2006; Boyd and Graham, 1986; Angkinand& Wihlborg, 2010; Beny*et al.* 2011; demirgiic-kunt and huizing 2013; leaven and Levine 2009). Thus, a higher the Z-Score value, the lower the risk so as a result bank is more stable position. Z-Score model is defined as the following formula. $Z = \frac{\mu + Cap}{\sigma\mu}$ where μ is the percentage on return on assets, and cap is the equity capital and $\sigma\mu$ is a standard deviation. It also implies that when the Z-score is higher the lower the probability of risk insolvency.

Independent Variables

The Market Share

The market share is the sales of the total markets that earned by a specific organization in a specific time framework. The market share provides the general thought about the size of the any firm as compare to whole market or competitors. Market share is measured through the sales of the any company in specific time period and then divide it on the total sales of the industry for the same time period.

The Concentration Ratio

Market concentration is representing the behavior which is collusive, that behavior investigate the powers of the firms through getting the higher profit, that is appropriate due to the behavior of oligopolistic. Concentration is the indication of the firm size as compared to whole industry. If the concentration is low the firms have greater competition between the firms exist in the industry. A firm that has 100% concentration that is evident that industry prevails the monopoly.

Bank-specific Variables

- SIZE= Size of the bank is measure as the natural logarithm of total assets.
- Efficiency (EFF) = cost by income ratio.
- Liquidity (L) = the ratio of liquid assets by total assets.
- Capital adequacy (CA) = the ratio of equity by total assets.
- Year (YR) =Period selected for collecting data.
- Market growth (MG) = the growth of the total assets.

- Interest rate spread (IRS) = difference between the average yield a bank receives from loan and other interest-accruing activities and the rate it pays on deposits and borrowings.

β_1, β_2, β3, β4, β5, β6, β7 and β8, are the respective co-efficient terms and B_0 is the intercept. We use "t" for time period and "i" for cross-recessional unit. Here "t" (2007 to 2016) is the time period and "i" (10 banks) is the cross section units

Estimation Techniques

We have used different techniques for the panel data, such as the descriptive statistics, Ordinary Least Square Analysis. To check the appropriation of the model between the common effect model and fixed effect model, F-statistic test is used and to diagnose the best model with in the random effect model and fixed effect model, Housman technique is implemented.

The panel data analysis is used to derive the results for the methodology chosen. Panel data is also known as the longitudinal or cross-sectional time series data, in which we observe the behavior of the different entities across time. We can use and analyze the panel data from two techniques, fixed effects, Random effects, and to check which the best technique is, Hauseman Test is implemented.

Fixed effects model

The fixed effect model we can use, when we are only interesting to analyze the impact of variable that change over time. Fixed effect model explains the relationship among predictor and outcome variables within an entity. Every entity includes the individual characteristics that may be effect or may not be affect the predictor variable. When we are using the fixed effects, we take the assumption that something with in the individual may impact we need to control it. This is the reasons behind the assumption of the Correlation among the predictor and error term. Fixed effect removes the effect of those time invariant characteristics. So due to that we assess the net effect of predictor on the variable outcome.

Another important assumption of the fixed effects model is that the time invariant characteristics are unique to the Individual, and there should not be correlated with another individual characteristic. The entity error term and constant should not be correlated with the others. If error terms are correlated than fixed effect is not suitable. So, this the main reason to apply the Hauseman Test.

Random Effects model

The wisdom behind the random effects model is that the variation among entities is assumed to be random rather than fixed and uncorrelated with the predictor or independent variables including in the models.

If the differences among the entities have some effect on the dependent variables so we used the Random Effect. The advantage of random effect is that we can include the variables which are time invariant. Random effect assumes that entity error term is not correlated with the independent variable which allows the time invariant variables to play a role as explanatory variables.

If Random effect, we need to specify those individual characteristics that may or may not affect the predictor variables. The problem is sometime is that some variables are not available, so therefore omitted the variables bias in the model.

Fixed Effects Model or Random Effects Model. (Hauseman Test)

The Houseman test is established to check the choice among the Fixed effects and Random effects techniques. In 1978 Hauseman developed a hypothesis to investigate among the estimators, Fixed effects, and Random effects, which is the more efficient estimators. Hauseman assumed that the two estimators β_0 and β_1 of the vector β parameter and he developed the two-hypothesis testing procedure.

Table 1.

	H_0 is true	H_1 is true
b_1 (RE Estimator)	Consistent Efficient	Inconsistent
b_0 (FE Estimator)	Consistent Inefficient	Consistent Efficient

If H_0 is true, both RE and FE are consistent, but only RE is preferred due to higher efficiency. If H_1 is true, FE is at least consistent and RE is not so FE is preferred. After performing Hausman test we will employ FE/RE estimator to estimate the two equations.

Result and Discussion of the Study

Panel data is used in this study which is the combination of time series and cross section data. Data analyses for the study includes for the period 2007 to 2016. In our study the five conventional and five Islamic banks are mainly focused. The intention of the study is to explore the Impact of Market Power on the Financial Stability as well as the Financial Performance of Islamic Banks and their counterparts in Pakistan. We have used different techniques for the panel data, such as the descriptive statistics, Ordinary Least Square Analysis. To check the appropriation of the model between the common effect model and fixed effect model, F-statistic test is used and to diagnose the best model within the random effect model and fixed effect model, Housman technique is implemented. We have used the Z-score model for the measurement of bank's financial stability. To check the financial performance, we are using the return on asset as the proxy for measuring the financial performance. To check the market power, we used the market structure variables which include Market share and concentration ratio, we are also using the Bank specific variables which include the bank size, efficiency, capital adequacy, market growth, interest rate spread.

Table 2. Descriptive statistics of Z-score

Bank Sample	All banks	Islamic banks	Conventional banks
Mean	0.1835	0.1254	0.2045
Maximum	8.0505	1.1019	8.0505
Minimum	-0.0382	-0.0382	-0.0382
St.dev	0.7526	0.1668	0.8541
Observations	220	50	170

The Empirical Results of the Z-Score Model

We are performing our empirical analyses for both Islamic and Conventional Banks for the time period of 2007-2016. We are measuring the Z-Score model to check the financial stability of the Islamic and Conventional banks in Pakistan. The results are given in Table 2. The purposes of the comparison of the different values of standard deviation, maximum, mean minimum value of Z-score is to measure the stability for all banks, Islamic banks, and conventional banks which are included in our sample respectively.

This is observed from the Z-Score Table that the Z-score average value of all banks is 0.1835 and all banks having a standard deviation is 0.7526. So, in the same way Z-Score average values of Islamic bank is 0.1254 and have a standard deviation is 0.1668. In the same way the

Z-score Average value for conventional banks is 0.2045 having a standard deviation which is 0.8541. The results of the above Table suggested that the Z-Score value of conventional banks is comparatively high as compared to Z-score average value of Islamic banks. The results also recommended that the value of Z-Score of Islamic banks is not only lower from Z-Score from the conventional banks but also lower from the Z-score of all banks.

The Z-score minimum value for conventional banks is -0.0382 and Z-score maximum value for conventional banks is 8.0505. In the same way the Z-score maximum and minimum value for Islamic bank lies between -0.0382 to 1.1019. The Z-score minimum and maximum value for all banks lies within the range from -0.0382 to 8.0505. The Z-score standard deviation for all banks is 0.7526 and Z-score for Islamic banks observed is 0.1668 and Z-score observed for the conventional banks is 0.8541. The comparisons of the standard deviation for all, Islamic and conventional banks respectively show the result that the standard deviation of conventional banks is higher as compared to Islamic banks. The standard deviation of Islamic banks in not only lower from the conventional banks but it also lowers from the overall sample of the banks. The Z-score average value of Islamic banks is lower from both conventional, and from the sample of overall banks.

The Z-score average value of conventional banks is greater than the Z-score average for Islamic banks, so this comparison recommended that the conventional banks in our country are the more stable as compared to Islamic banks and as well as batter from the overall sample of the banks. So as a result, the Z-score average value is greater for conventional banks which also interpreted that the conventional banks have less chance for the risk of default, alternatively conventional banks are more stable than the both Islamic and overall sample of the banks.

Table 2 explain that the stability of the banks depends on the Z-score average value. The comparison shows in Table 2 that the conventional banks are having the more financial stability than the Islamic and overall baking sample. Therefore, Srairi (2008) also investigated that conventional banks are more financial stability as compared to Islamic banks. So the results of Srairi are consistent with our findings. They also commented that the banks are having the differences among because of the specific variables of the banks.

Table 3. Descriptive statistics of ROA

Bank sample	All banks	Islamic banks	Conventional banks
Mean	0.1463	0.1400	0.1430
Maximum	0.8416	0.8416	0.8416
Minimum	0.0076	0.1398	0.0139
St.dev	0.0812	0.1364	0.0869
Observations	220	50	170

The Empirical Results of the Return on Asset (ROA) Model

We are performing our empirical analyses for both Islamic and Conventional Banks for the time period of 2007-2016. We are measuring the Return on Asset (ROA) model to check the financial performance of the Islamic and Conventional banks in Pakistan. The results are given in Table 3. The purposes of the comparison of the different values of standard deviation, maximum, mean minimum value of Return on Asset (ROA) is to measure the financial performance for all banks, Islamic banks, and conventional banks which are included in our sample respectively.

This is observed from the Return on Asset (ROA) Table that the Return on Asset (ROA) average value of all banks is 0.1463 and all banks having a standard deviation is 0.0812. So, in the same way Return on Asset (ROA) average values of Islamic bank is 0.1400 and have a standard deviation is 0.1364. In the same way the Return on Asset (ROA) Average value for conventional banks is 0.1430 having a standard deviation which is 0.0869. The results of the above Table suggested that the Return on Asset (ROA) value of conventional banks is comparatively high as compared to Return on Asset (ROA) average value of Islamic banks. The results also recommended that the value of Return on Asset (ROA) of Islamic banks is not only lower from Return on Asset (ROA) from the conventional banks but also lower from the Return on Asset (ROA) of all banks.

The Return on Asset (ROA) minimum value for conventional banks is 0.0139 and Return on Asset (ROA) maximum value for conventional banks is 0.8416. In the same way the Return on Asset (ROA) maximum and minimum value for Islamic bank lies between 0.1398 to 0. 8416. The Return on Asset (ROA) minimum and maximum value for all banks lies within the range from 0.0076 to 0.8416. The Return on Asset (ROA) standard deviation for all banks is 0.0812 and Return on Asset (ROA) for Islamic banks observed is 0.1364 and Return on Asset (ROA) observed for the conventional banks is 0.0869. The comparisons of the standard deviation for all, Islamic and conventional banks respectively show the result that the standard deviation of Islamic banks is higher as compared to Conventional banks. The standard deviation of the Conventional banks is lower from the standard deviation of the Islamic banks. The results also shows that the standard deviation of the Islamic banks is not only higher from the conventional banks but also from the overall sample of the banks The average value of Return on Asset (ROA) for Islamic banks is lower from both conventional, and from the sample of overall banks.

The Return on Asset (ROA) average value of conventional banks is greater than the Return on Asset (ROA) average for Islamic banks, so this comparison recommended that the financial performance of the conventional banks in our country is more batter as compare to the financial performance of the Islamic banks and the results of the overall sample of the banks recommended that the financial performance of the overall banks is batter from the financial performance of both Islamic and conventional banks. So as a result, the Return on Asset (ROA) average value is greater for conventional banks which also interpreted that the conventional banks have greater or batter quality of Assets as compared to Islamic Banks. So, the financial performance of the conventional banks is better than the Islamic banks suggested that the conventional banks have more opportunity of solvency as compare to Islamic banks.

Table 3 explain that the financial performance of the banks depends on the Return on Asset (ROA) average value. The comparison shows in Table 3 that the conventional banks are having the more financial performance than the Islamic baking sample. Therefore, Pasiouras and Kosmidou (2007) also investigated that conventional banks have the greater assets quality due to the structure of the market and concentration; financial performance of conventional banks is batter as compared to Islamic banks. So, the results of Pasiouras and Kosmidou are consistent with our findings.

Table 4. Descriptive statistics of independent variables

Bank's sample	Summary Statistics	All banks	Conventional Banks	Islamic banks
MS	Mean	0.0181	0.0230	0.0003
	Max	1.6936	1.6936	0.1067
	Man	-0.0724	-0.0724	-0.0541
	St.dev	0.1607	0.1823	0.0243
CR	Mean	0.1335	0.1297	0.1392
	Max	0.6305	0.6305	0.5156
	Man	0.0002	0.0002	0.0008
	St.dev	0.1096	0.1163	0.1330

continued on following page

Table 4. Continued

Bank's sample	Summary Statistics	All banks	Conventional Banks	Islamic banks
SIZE	Mean	18.7273	18.6653	17.6580
	Max	21.2628	21.2628	19.9730
	Man	14.7109	14.7109	14.7109
	St.dev	1.3127	1.3574	1.2690
EFY	Mean	0.6535	0.6567	0.6760
	Max	2.4782	2.4782	1.7191
	Man	0.1299	0.1299	0.1299
	St.dev	0.2570	0.2799	0.3428
LIQ	Mean	0.0119	0.0148	0.0185
	Max	0.1938	0.9138	0.5679
	Man	-0.0183	-0.0183	-0.0183
	St.dev	0.0809	0.0918	0.0863
CA	Mean	0.0039	0.0045	0.0046
	Max	0.2541	0.2541	0.1066
	Man	-0.0099	-0.0099	-0.0099
	St.dev	0.01969	0.0222	0.0162
MG	Mean	0.0455	0.0492	0.0382
	Max	1.4536	1.4536	0.2683
	Man	0.0043	0.0043	0.0052
	St.dev	0.1335	0.1516	0.0460
IRS	Mean	-0.0988	-0.1227	-0.60298
	Max	4.1457	4.1457	0.5069
	Man	-0.8685	0.8685	-0.8685
	St.dev	0.8613	0.8362	0.3262

Empirical Results of the Independent Variables

Table 4 includes the empirical results of the independent variables such as market share, size of the bank, efficiency, capital adequacy, liquidity and market growth and interest rate spread. We are using the independent variables for Islamic and Conventional banks, and Table 4 shows the values of mean, maximum, minimum and standard deviation for independent variables. The results shows that the average means values of market share stated that the market share of the conventional banks 0.0230 is greater than the market share of the Islamic banks which is 0.0003. In the case of concentration ratio, the concentration ratio of the Islamic banks is 0.1392 which is greater than the conventional banks concentration ratio which is 0.1297. The mean values of the size of the bank reported that the size of the conventional bank is better than the Islamic banks. The mean value of the efficiency of the banks stated that the efficiency of the Islamic banks is greater than the efficiency of the conventional banks. The results also concluded that the mean values of liquidity, and capital adequacy ratio is greater in case of Islamic banks as compared to the conventional banks while the mean values of market growth rate is batter for the conventional banks as compare to Islamic banks and interest rate spread is batter in case of Islamic banks as compare to conventional banks. The results investigated that the value of asset growth of conventional banks is higher while for the Islamic banks concentration ratio is higher which means that the growth of asset is higher in the conventional banking sector, but the concentration ratio is higher for Islamic banks. The average mean values of the Market share, Size of the bank, and market growth are higher for the conventional banks while the average mean values of concentration ratio, efficiency of the bank, liquidity ratio, capital adequacy and interest rate spread are higher for the Islamic banks. The conclusion of the above the discussion reported that the conventional banks are performing better than Islamic banks so that therefore conventional banks are having more solvent or credit and profitable than Islamic banks.

MODEL 01 for Financial Stability

Table 5. Regression results for baseline model; Random effect, 2007-2016 (Dependent variable: Z-score)

Coefficients		All banks	Conventional Banks	Islamic banks
MS		**3.8079*** (0.000)**	**3.8644*** (0.000)**	**4.3587*** (0.000)**
CR		0.2189*** (0.003)	0.2789*** (0.000)	0.3347** (0.054)
Size		-0.0869*** (0.000)	-0.0726*** (0.000)	-0.1242 (0.639)
EFY		0.0250 (0.382)	0.0160 (0.596)	-0.0552 (0.413)
LIQ		-0.0888 (0.251)	-0.0534 (0.487)	-0.0069 (0.974)
CA		-0.064 (0.984)	-0.0187 (0.953)	-0.1362 (0.884)

continued on following page

Table 5. Continued

Coefficients	All banks	Conventional Banks	Islamic banks
MS	**3.8079*** (0.000)**	**3.8644*** (0.000)**	**4.3587*** (0.000)**
MG	0.8993*** (0.000)	0.8775*** (0.000)	1.8811*** (0.000)
IRS	0.0287* (0.078)	0.0276** (0.144)	-0.1821* (0.060)
Constant	1.6598 (0.000)	1.3866 (0.000)	0.1529 (0.777)
No.of.obs	220	170	50
R-squared	0.9888	0.9916	0.6427
Porb> chi	0.0000	0.0000	0.0000

Note:"*" indicates significance of 10%," **" indicates significance of 5%," ***" indicates Significance of 1% level, respectively. The value of dummy is 1 for Conventional banks and 0 for the Islamic banks. The () shows the P- values.

The Regression results of the Random effect Model for all banks by

Using Z-Score Model (Explanatory Variables)

Table 5 shows the regression results for overall sample of the banks, conventional banks and Islamic banks respectively. To investigate the discrepancy among the Islamic and conventional banks overall financial stability, we are using the random effect technique for the estimation of specific models. To check the effect of market power of Islamic and Conventional banks on the financial stability, the one dummy used in our models. The dummy is most of the time used for the bank nature, Dummy used for the Islamic banks is 1 and for conventional banks is 0. We check the financial stability of both banks through differential effect for the variables.

The result of Table 5 recommended that significantly affect the specific bank variables on the Z-score for conventional and Islamic banks. The Table 5 concluded that the market shares, concentration ratio, efficiency, market growth and interest rate spread are significantly related to the Z-Score of the banks, but on the other hand the Size of the bank, liquidity ratio, capital adequacy ratio are insignificantly related to the Z-Score solvency of the banks. Z-Score for the conventional banks is significantly related to the efficiency and interest rate spread while Z-score is insignificantly related to Islamic Banks.

The relationships among the above variables are explained through the different studies:

The result of the 5th Table reported that the average mean value of ownership concentration which is observed 62% for Pakistan which is higher from the other countries. If we take the example of US (Lehn and Demsetz, 1985). The concentration is significantly differing for both Islamic and conventional banks. In our model, we are using the coefficient concentration with the bank's specific variables. The objective of including the coefficient concentration in our model is to investigate the impact of concentration behavior on the financial stability and financial performance of the banking sector. The result reported that the concentration affects the financial stability, positively and significantly by the banking sector of Pakistan.

Furthermore, our finds investigated that when the competition is more in the banking sector its leads the financial system positively. The result which shows that the concentration affects the financial stability of Pakistani banking sector significantly and our results are consistent with the studies (Matinez and Ramirez, 2011; Saunders, Strock and travlos, 1990; Sullivan and Spong, 2007) also depicted that the well-functioning of the banks depends on the significance of the concentration. The results are also significant and consistent with the studies of

(Shehzad et al, 2010; Vishny and Shleifer, 1986) suggested that improving the quality of governance with the help of block holder. The value of the coefficient of concentration for all banks is reported as 0.2189 and having the probability value is 0.000, which states that is lower from the conventional and Islamic banks.

The most banks are controlled by the big companies; this is the result on the behalf of observed Table 5 which reports the nature of the owners of the banks. The is also observed from the Table that the conventional banks are having the higher equity percentage and ultimately the Islamic banks are having the less equity percentage, this difference exist due to the 50% share of the government in conventional banking sectors. In this regard we observed the ownership of state on the bank's solvency with respect to financial stability, we find the significant and positive relation for the coefficient of state-owned bank variables for Z-score Model. So, the result confirms that the conventional banks are more financially stability proportion as compare to Islamic banks. The studies (e.g., Nocera & Sironi, 2007; Iannotta, Khaksari & Tehranian, 2010; Guo, Cornett; Klapper, &Udell, 2005; Clarke, Cull, Berger). The above all studies investigated that the ownership of government in the banking sector and risk are significantly and positively related. The comparison among the Islamic and conventional banks shows from the Table 5 that the overall results of the specific variables of the banks concluded for the Islamic and Conventional banks are positive and significantly related to the Z-Score model. Finally, the results concluded that the Islamic banks are less stable as compare to the Conventional banks because the conventional banks have the greater value than the Islamic and overall value of the banks.

When we investigate the results of banks assets size on the financial stability, it investigated that the size of the bank coefficient is negative and insignificant at 1% significance level. Which states the coefficient of the size of the banks is not important or any impact on the financial stability of the banks. Our result is also consistent with the study of Turk Ariss (2010) who investigate the relationship among the size of the bank and financial stability is negative, although the result is insignificant statistically. In our results the value of the size of the bank for all banks assets size which is observed from the Table 5 is -0.0869 and the P-value is 0.000, shows no effect of size of the bank on financial stability of the banking sectors.

The efficiency coefficient is statistically significant and positive relationship with Z-score for the conventional banks, but negative for the Islamic banks and statistically insignificant relationship with Z-Score. So, results show the financial stability of the conventional banks depends upon the efficiency but the financial stability of Islamic banks does not depend upon the efficiency. Therefore, the coefficient of the liquidity ratio is statistically insignificant and negatively related with the Z-Score model for all banks, Islamic banks, and Conventional Banks respectively.

The coefficient of capital adequacy is defined as the equity ratio to total assets is also measured. The capital adequacy is used to check the strength of the bank capital. So, the banks have more capital face the less funding cost and as a result bankruptcy risk is lower. We expect equity to asset relation is negatively related and the risk of bankruptcy. So, the coefficient of capital adequacy is statistically insignificant and negatively related with the Z-Score, hence the capital adequacy is no impacts on banks financial stability. Our results are consistent with the study of Abedifaret al. (2013); found the negative and insignificant relation among the capital adequacy and financial stability. The coefficient of Asset growth or market share is statistically insignificant and negative relation among the growth of assets or market share with Z-Score model. The growth of assets variables is included in our regression model to check the growth strategy of banks. The value of coefficient of asset growth for all banks is statistically insignificant in our model.

The Regression results of the Random effect Model for Islamic and Conventional banks by using Z-Score Model (Explanatory Variables).

The concentration ratio is positive for Islamic and conventional banks as well as statistically significant. The bank that has the higher concentration ratio that leads the higher Z-score it means that the bank which have the higher Z-Score that increase the financial stability of the bank. The positive value of the coefficient of concentration ratio is observed for the conventional banks from Table 5 are 0.2789 and the P-value is 0.000. we can interpret the above result in this way, concentration increase the one unit of conventional banks it brings 0.2789% increase the financial stability of the banks (Z-Score) other thing remaining the same. The positive value of the coefficient of concentration ratio is observed for the Islamic banks from Table 5 are 0.3347 and the P-value is 0.054. we can interpret the above result in this way, concentration increase the one unit of Islamic banks it brings 0.3347% increase the financial stability of the banks (Z-Score) other thing remaining the same. As a result, the conventional banks have the higher concentration that shows the higher financial stability or (Z-Score). It is observed that when the concentration is increased the probability of insolvency is decreased. Furthermore, our results are consistent with the study of Amjad (2014) who suggested that the concentration is positive and statistically significant with the banks financial stability.

The coefficient of size of the bank is insignificant statistically at the 1% significance level and negatively related to the conventional banks as well as for the Islamic banks with Z-Score model. So the financial stability of the both banks does not depend on the bank size. Our results are inconsistent with (Srari 2014) he investigated that the financial stability depends upon the size of the bank and significantly and positively related to financial stability of the banking sectors.

The market share is positive for Islamic and conventional banks as well as statistically significant. The bank that has the higher market share that leads the higher Z-score it means that the bank which have the higher Z-Score that increase the financial stability of the bank. The positive value of the coefficient of market share is observed for the conventional banks from Table 5 are 3.8644 and the P-value is 0.000. we can interpret the above result in this way, market share increases the one unit of conventional banks it brings 3.8644% increase the financial stability of the banks (Z-Score) other thing remaining the same. The positive value of the coefficient of market share is observed for the Islamic banks from Table 5 are 4.3587 and the P-value is 0.000. we can interpret the above result in this way, market share increases the one unit of conventional banks it brings 4.3587% increase the financial stability of the banks (Z-Score) other thing remaining the same. The above results states that when the market share is increased the probability of insolvency is decreased. Our results are the consistent with the study of Berger (2015) who suggested that the market share is positive and statistically significant with the banks financial stability.

The coefficient of income to cost (efficiency) is significant statistically at 5% significance level and Z-score model is positively related to conventional banks and negatively related to Islamic banks. The coefficient of efficiency is observed for the conventional banks from the Table is 0.0160 and having a P-value 0.596 and the coefficient of efficiency is observed for the Islamic banks from the Table is -0.0552 and having a P-value 0.413. We can interpret the above result in this way, efficiency of the bank increases the one unit of conventional banks it brings 0.0160% increase the financial stability of the banks (Z-Score) other thing remaining the same. While the financial stability of the Islamic banks does not depend upon the efficiency of the bank. As a result, conventional banks are more financial stability because of the higher Z-Score value as compare to Islamic banks. The above results states that when the efficiency of the banking sector is increased the probability of insolvency is decreased.

The coefficient of growth of the assets is negative for Islamic and conventional banks as well as statistically insignificant. Therefore, the financial stability of banking sector in Pakistan is not depending upon the growth of Assets. Our results are consistent with the Srairi (2013) he reported that financial stability of banking sector is insignificantly and negatively related to the growth of assets.

The coefficient of interest rate spread is positive for conventional banks as well as significant statistically while negative for Islamic banks as well as insignificant statistically. The banks have the higher Z-score value means that the banks higher the financial stability. Our results suggested that the conventional banks have the higher interest rate spread value as compared to Islamic banks which reported that conventional banks are more stable than their counterparts.

MODEL 02 for Financial Performance

Table 6. Regression results for baseline model; fixed effect, 2007-2016 (Dependent variable: ROA)

Coefficient		All banks	Conventional Banks	Islamic banks
MS		**-0.3974** (0.010)**	**-0.3850* (0.025)**	**-1.9052* (0.000)**
CR		-0.1196* (0.057)	-0.1022 (0.137)	-0.3074** (0.015)
Size		0.0331*** (0.003)	-0.0478*** (0.000)	-0.0567** (0.030)
EFY		0.0315 (0.197)	0.0204 (0.446)	-0.0694 (0.169)
LIQ		0.3045*** (0.000)	0.2878*** (0.000)	0.7649*** (0.000)
CA		-0.1412 (0.605)	-0.1081 (0.704)	-0.3590 (0.559)
MG		0.4947** (0.011)	0.4491** (0.036)	1.1995* (0.006)

continued on following page

Table 6. Continued

Coefficient		All banks	Conventional Banks	Islamic banks
MS		**-0.3974** **(0.010)**	**-0.3850*** **(0.025)**	**-1.9052*** **(0.000)**
IRS		0.0314** (0.024)	0.3753** (0.026)	0.2463*** (0.008)
Constant		0.7464 (0.000)	1.0235 (0.000)	1.3232 (0.012)
No.of.obs		220	170	50
R-squared		0.3127	0.9916	0.8334
Porb> chi		0.0000	0.0000	0.0000

Note:"*" indicates significance of 10%," **" indicates significance of 5%," ***" indicates Significance of 1% level, respectively. The value of dummy is 1 for Conventional banks and 0 for the Islamic banks. The () shows the P- Values.

Table 6 shows the regression results for overall sample of the banks, conventional banks, and Islamic banks respectively. To investigate the discrepancy among the Islamic and conventional banks overall financial performance, we are using the fixed effect technique for the estimation of specific models. To check the effect of market power of Islamic and Conventional banks on the financial performance, the one dummy used in our models. The dummy is most of the time used for the bank nature, Dummy used for the Islamic banks is 1 and for conventional banks is 0. We check the financial performance of both banks through differential effect for the variables.

The result of Table 6 recommended that significantly affect the specific bank variables on the Return on Assets (ROA) for conventional and Islamic banks. Table 6 concluded that the efficiency, liquidity ratio, market growth and interest rate spread are significantly and positively related to the Return on Assets (ROA) of the banks, but on the other hand the Size of the bank, concentration ratio, market share, capital adequacy are negatively and insignificantly related to the Return on Asset (ROA) solvency and financial performance of all the banks.

The relationships among the above variables are explained through different studies:

The value of the coefficient of concentration observed from Table 6 suggested that the concentration ratio is insignificant statistically and negatively related. The results shows that the concentration is high degree states that the return on Asset (ROA) decrease further for Islamic as well as for the conventional banks tend to quality of batter assets. The negative relation among the concentration and Return on Assets (ROA) verifies our results. Saunders at el. (1990) and Turk Ariss (2012) investigated that the managers of the conventional banks are taking the risk which is calculated which is due to the batter monitoring and guidelines or supervisions. The coefficient of the size of the bank is negative for Islamic and conventional banks as well as insignificant statistically for Return on Assets (ROA).

The Regression results of the Fixed effect Model for Islamic and Conventional banks by

Using Return on Assets (ROA) Model (Explanatory Variables)

The value of the concentration observed from Table 6 suggested that the concentration ratio is insignificant statistically and negatively related to Return on Assets (ROA). The value of coefficient of concentration for conventional banks is negative -0.1022 and having a P value is 0.137.

The coefficient of the size of the bank is insignificant statistically at the 1% significance level and negatively related to the Islamic banks. The coefficient of the size of the bank is insignificant statistically at the 10% significance level and negatively related to the conventional banks. The value of coefficient of the size of the bank for Islamic banks is negative -0.0567 and having a P value is 0.000. As a result, the Return on Assets (ROA) or financial performance of the banks in Pakistan does not depend upon the size of the bank.

The coefficient of income to cost (efficiency) is significant statistically with the Return on assets (ROA) model is positively related to conventional banks and negatively related to Islamic banks. This is suggested that the solvency of the banking sector is not significantly depends upon the efficiency ratio in case of Islamic banks.

The coefficient of market share for the Return on Assets (ROA) is negative for Islamic and conventional banks as well as statistically insignificant. The value of the coefficient of market share is observed from Table 6 are -0.3850 for the conventional banks and for the Islamic banks is -1.9052. As a result, the market share has no significant impact on the financial performance of the Islamic as well as conventional banks in Pakistan.

The coefficient of liquidity ratio for both Islamic banks as well as for conventional banks is significant statistically at 1% significance level and positively related. The coefficient of liquidity ratio is observed for the Islamic banks from Table 6 is 0.7649 and having a P-value 0.000. We can interpret the above result in this way, liquidity ratio of the bank increase the one unit of Islamic banks it brings 0.7649% increase the financial performance of the banks (ROA) other thing remaining the same. The increase in the value of liquidity ratio of the Islamic banks ultimately increases the Return on Assets (ROA) or increase the financial performance of the Islamic banking sector in Pakistan.

The coefficient of market growth ratio for both Islamic banks as well as for conventional banks is significant statistically at 1% significance level and positively related. The coefficient of market growth ratio is observed for the Islamic banks from Table 6 are 1.1995 and having a P-value 0.006. We can interpret the above result in this way, market growth ratio increases the one unit of Islamic banks it brings 1.1995% increase the financial performance of the banks (ROA) other thing remaining the same. The coefficient of market growth ratio is observed for the conventional banks from Table 6 are 0.4491 and having a P-value 0.000. We can interpret the above result in this way, market growth ratio increase the one unit of Conventional banks it brings 0.4491% increase the financial performance of the banks (ROA) other thing remaining the same. The increase in the value of market growth ratio of the Islamic banks ultimately increases the Return on Assets (ROA) or increase the financial performance of the Islamic banking sector in Pakistan.

The coefficient of Interest rate spread for both Islamic banks as well as for conventional banks is significant statistically at 1% significance level and positively related. The coefficient of Interest rate spread is observed for the Islamic banks from Table 6 are 0.2463 and having a P-value 0.008. We can interpret the above result in this way, Interest rate spread increase the one unit of Islamic banks it brings 0.2463% increase the financial performance of the banks (ROA) other thing remaining the same. The coefficient of Interest rate spread is observed for the conventional banks from Table 6 are 0.3753 and having a P-value 0.000. We can interpret the above result in this way, Interest rate spread increase the one unit of Conventional banks it brings 0.3753% increase the financial performance of the banks (ROA) other thing remaining the same. The increase in the value of Interest rate spread of the Conventional banks ultimately increases the Return on Assets (ROA) or increase the financial performance of the Islamic banking sector in Pakistan.

CONCLUSION

Panel data is used in this study which is the combination of time series and cross section data. Data analyses for the study includes for the period 2007 to 2016. In our study the five conventional and five Islamic banks are mainly focused. The intention of the study is to explore the Impact of Market Power on the Financial Stability as well as the Financial Performance of Islamic Banks and their counterparts in Pakistan. We have used different techniques for the panel data, such as the descriptive statistics, Ordinary Least Square Analysis. To check the appropriation of the model between the common effect model and fixed effect model, F-statistic test is used and to diagnose the best model within the random effect model and fixed effect model, Housman technique is implemented. We have used the Z-score model for the measurement of bank's financial stability. To check the financial performance, we are using the return on asset as the proxy for measuring the financial performance. To check the market power, we used the market structure variables which include Market share and concentration ratio, we are also using the Bank specific variables which include the bank size, efficiency, capital adequacy, market growth, interest rate spread.

Key Findings of the Study

Our empirical results suggest that the average Z-score is higher in case of conventional banks as compared to their counterparts. So, its means that the conventional banks are more stable than their counterparts and results also depict that the conventional banks are away from default. The average Return on asset is slightly greater than the conventional banks as compared to their counterparts, so these results suggest that conventional banks have batter quality of assts (loans) than Islamic banks. High average value of ROA in the conventional banks suggested that they have more chances of solvency than Islamic banks. Descriptive results of the independent variables suggested that Mean value of market share, concentration ratio, and size of banks, capital adequacy, market growth and Interest rate spread are greater for conventional banks as compared to their counterparts but the mean value of liquidity ratio, efficiency ratio are slightly batter in case of Islamic banks. Therefore, Conventional banks are more solvent and profitable than Islamic banks.

To analyze the regression esults of random effect model for independent variables for Z-Score suggest that size of bank has no impact on banking stability. Efficiency of Islamic banks does not depend on the stability while the conventional banks have. Market share is statistically significant for both Islamic and their counterparts, therefore greater market share leads to increase the financial stability. The asset growth is statistically insignificant in case of both Islamic and their counterparts, therefore asset growth does not have any impact on financial stability. The interest rate spread is statistically significant with conventional banks and insignificant in case of Islamic banks.

To examine the regression results of fixed effect model for independent variable for ROA which is used as proxy for financial performance suggested that concentration ratio, Market share, and bank size is statistically insignificant which depict that they have no impact on financial performance of Islamic and their counterparts. But the efficiency liquidity and market growth, interest rate spread are the statistically significant and have positive impact on financial performance.

Policy Implications and Recommendation

The policy implication of our result is that the regulators of the banking sector should take in notice the different aspects of systematic stability for the future criterion to remove the retractions of entry and disappointment of the process of merger and acquisitions within the Islamic banking sectors. Alternatively, the policy makers of the conventional banking sector should bear in their minds a possible trade off among the financial performance and financial stability.

REFERENCES

Amjad, M., Akhtar, J., Anwar-ul-Haq, M., Yang, A., Akhtar, S. S., & Jacobsen, S.-E. (2014). Integrating role of ethylene and ABA in tomato plants' adaptation to salt stress. *Scientia Horticulturae*, 178, 49–61. DOI: 10.1016/j.scienta.2014.03.024

Amjad, R., & Mahmood, K. (1982). Industrial relations and the political process in Pakistan 1947–1977. *Munich Personal RePEc Archive*.

As Santos, N. C., Israelian, G., & Mayor, M. (2004). Spectroscopic analysis of 98 stars with planetary companions: Metallicity and the probability of planet formation. *Astronomy & Astrophysics*, 415(3), 1153–1166. DOI: 10.1051/0004-6361:20034469

Bain, J. S. (1951). Relation of profit rate to industry concentration: American manufacturing, 1936–1940. *The Quarterly Journal of Economics*, 65(3), 293–324. DOI: 10.2307/1882217

Bain, J. S. (1956). *Barriers to new competition: Their character and consequences in manufacturing industries*. Harvard University Press. DOI: 10.4159/harvard.9780674188037

Bashir, M. R., Alkhouri, N., & Labriola, D. (2023). Resmetirom for nonalcoholic fatty liver disease: A randomized, double-blind, placebo-controlled phase 3 trial. *Nature Medicine*. PMID: 37845512

Bashir, S., Hussain, A., Hussain, S. J., Wani, O. A., Zahid Nabi, S., Dar, N. A., Baloch, F. S., & Mansoor, S. (2021). Plant drought stress tolerance: Understanding its physiological, biochemical, and molecular mechanisms. *Biotechnology, Biotechnological Equipment*, 35(1), 92–112. DOI: 10.1080/13102818.2021.2020161

Berger, A. N., & Bouwman, C. H. S. (2015). *Bank Liquidity Creation and Financial Crises*. Academic Press. Google Books

Berger, A. N., Herring, R. J., & Szegö, G. P. (1995). The role of capital in financial institutions. *Journal of Banking & Finance*, 19(3–4), 393–430. DOI: 10.1016/0378-4266(95)00002-X

Berger, A. N., & Mester, L. J. (1997). Inside the black box: What explains differences in the efficiencies of financial institutions? *Journal of Banking & Finance*, 21(7), 895–947. DOI: 10.1016/S0378-4266(97)00010-1

Block, R. A., & Zakay, D. (1997). Prospective and retrospective duration judgments: A meta-analytic review. *Psychonomic Bulletin & Review*, 4(2), 184–197. DOI: 10.3758/BF03209393 PMID: 21331825

Boone, J. P., Khurana, I. K., & Raman, K. K. (2008). Audit firm tenure and the equity risk premium. *Journal of Accounting, Auditing & Finance*, 23(1), 115–140. DOI: 10.1177/0148558X0802300107

Bourke, P. (1989). Concentration and other determinants of bank profitability in Europe, North America, and Australia. *Journal of Banking & Finance*, 13(1), 65–79. DOI: 10.1016/0378-4266(89)90020-4

Byeongyong, P., & DongRo, C. (2002). An unrecorded species of *Pratylenchus loosi* Loof (Tylenchida: Pratylenchidae) from tea in Korea. *CABI Digital Library*.

Chant, S., & Evans, A. (2010). Gendered poverty across space and time: Introduction and overview. [SAGE Journals]. *Environment and Urbanization*, 22(2), 371–391.

Collins, A. M., & Quillian, M. R. (1969). Retrieval time from semantic memory. *Journal of Verbal Learning and Verbal Behavior*, 8(2), 240–247. DOI: 10.1016/S0022-5371(69)80069-1

Cowling, K. (1976). On the theoretical specification of industrial structure-performance relationships. *European Economic Review*, 8(1), 1–14. DOI: 10.1016/0014-2921(76)90038-6

Demsetz, H. (1973). Industry structure, market rivalry, and public policy. *The Journal of Law & Economics*, 16(1), 1–9. DOI: 10.1086/466752

Demsetz, H., & Lehn, K. (1985). The structure of corporate ownership: Causes and consequences. *Journal of Political Economy*, 93(6), 1155–1177. DOI: 10.1086/261354

Douglas, R. J., Martin, K. A. C., & Whitteridge, D. (1988). Selective responses of visual cortical cells do not depend on shunting inhibition. *Nature*, 332(6165), 642–644. DOI: 10.1038/332642a0 PMID: 3357519

Euzent, P. J., & Gallet, C. A. (2002). The business cycle and competition in the US brewing industry. *Journal of Applied Business Research*.

Feeny, N. C., Zoellner, L. A., Fitzgibbons, L. A., & Foa, E. B. (2000). Exploring the roles of emotional numbing, depression, and dissociation in PTSD. *Journal of Traumatic Stress*, 13(3), 489–498. DOI: 10.1023/A:1007789409330 PMID: 10948488

Fiordelisi, F., & Molyneux, P. (2004). Shareholder value efficiency in European banking. *Journal of Banking & Finance*, 31(7), 2151–2161. DOI: 10.1016/j.jbankfin.2006.10.021

Fiordelisi, F., & Ricci, O. (2004). Measuring risk in European banking. *Risk Management Journal*, 6(2), 112–127.

Forbes, J. M., Hagan, M. E., Miyahara, S., Vial, F., Manson, A. H., Meek, C. E., & Portnyagin, Y. I. (1995). Quasi-16-day oscillation in the mesosphere and lower thermosphere. *Journal of Geophysical Research*, 100(D5, A5), 9149–9156. DOI: 10.1029/94JD02157

Fu, Q., Johanson, C. M., Wallace, J. M., & Reichler, T. (2006). Enhanced mid-latitude tropospheric warming in satellite measurements. *Science*, 311(5765), 1160–1163. DOI: 10.1126/science.1125566 PMID: 16728633

Gale, D., & Allen, F. (2000). Financial contagion. *Journal of Political Economy*, 108(1), 1–33. DOI: 10.1086/262109

Gilbert, R. A. (1984). Bank market structure and competition: A survey. *Journal of Money, Credit and Banking*, 16(4), 617–645. DOI: 10.2307/1992096

Graham, B. (1986). *The Intelligent Investor: A Book of Practical Counsel*. Harper Business Essentials.

Groeneveld, J. M., & Bikker, J. A. (2000). Competition and concentration in the EU banking industry. *Credit and Capital Markets*, 33(1), 62–77. DOI: 10.3790/ccm.33.1.62

Haaf, K., & Bikker, J. A. (2002). Measures of competition and concentration in the banking industry: A review of the literature. *Economic & Financial Modelling*, 9(1), 53–70.

Hannan, T. H. (1997). Market share inequality, the number of competitors, and the HHI: An examination of bank pricing. *Review of Industrial Organization*, 12(1), 23–35. DOI: 10.1023/A:1007744119377

Hannan, T. H., & Berger, A. N. (1989). The price-concentration relationship in banking. *The Review of Economics and Statistics*, 71(2), 291–299. DOI: 10.2307/1926975

Haron, S. (1996). Competition and other external determinants of the profitability of Islamic banks. *Islamic Economic Studies*, 4(2), 49–64.

Heffernan, S., & Fu, X. (2009). The effects of reform on China's bank structure and performance. *Journal of Banking & Finance*, 33(1), 39–52. DOI: 10.1016/j.jbankfin.2006.11.023

Heffernan, T., & McKay, A. (2019). The academic exodus: The role of institutional support in academics leaving universities and the academy. *Professional Development in Education*, 45(3), 255–273. DOI: 10.1080/19415257.2018.1474491

Hicks, J. R. (1935). Annual survey of economic theory: The theory of monopoly. *Econometrica*, 3(1), 1–20. DOI: 10.2307/1907343

Hu, Z., & Tang, L. (2012). Income inequality and environmental quality in developing countries. *Ecological Economics*, 75, 12–21.

Huizinga, H., & Demirgüç-Kunt, A. (1999). Determinants of commercial bank interest margins and profitability: Some international evidence. *The World Bank Economic Review*, 13(2), 379–408. DOI: 10.1093/wber/13.2.379

Huizinga, H., & Demirgüç-Kunt, A. (2000). Financial structure and bank profitability. *World Bank Policy Research Working Paper No. 2430*. World Bank

Jacquemin, A. (1982). Imperfect market structure and international trade: Some recent research. *Kyklos*, 35(1), 135–152. DOI: 10.1111/j.1467-6435.1982.tb01216.x

Jacquemin, A., & de Jong, H. (1982). Price dispersion and oligopolistic price leadership. [JSTOR]. *The Review of Economics and Statistics*, 64(3), 497–503.

Kemme, P. A., Jongbloed, A. W., & Mroz, Z. (1994). Apparent digestibility and retention of nutrients bound to phytate complexes as influenced by microbial phytase and feeding regimen in pigs. *Journal of Animal Science*, 72(1), 126–135. DOI: 10.2527/1994.721126x PMID: 8138479

Kim, C. J. (1994). Dynamic linear models with Markov-switching. *Journal of Econometrics*, 60(1), 135–160.

Kosmidou, K., Pasiouras, F., & Tsaklanganos, A. (2007). Domestic and multinational determinants of foreign bank profits: The case of Greek banks operating abroad. *Journal of Multinational Financial Management*, 17(1), 1–15. DOI: 10.1016/j.mulfin.2006.02.002

Laeven, L., Ratnovski, M., & Tong, M. H. (2014). Bank size and systemic risk. *IMF Economic Review*, 61(2), 225–270. DOI: 10.1057/imfer.2013.12

Lee, J., & Layne, K. (2001). Developing fully functional E-government: A four-stage model. *Government Information Quarterly*, 18(2), 122–136. DOI: 10.1016/S0740-624X(01)00066-1

Levine, L., Ratnovski, M., & Tong, M. H. (2009). Bank governance, regulation, and risk-taking. *Journal of Financial Economics*, 93(2), 259–275. DOI: 10.1016/j.jfineco.2008.09.003

Levisohn, J. A., & Isacson, O. (1991). Excitotoxic lesions of the rat entorhinal cortex: Effects of selective neuronal damage on acquisition and retention of a non-spatial reference memory task. *Brain Research*, 568(1), 113–122. DOI: 10.1016/0006-8993(91)91458-D PMID: 1810624

Linh, T. H. (2018). Analysis of income inequality determinants in developing countries. *Development Policy Review*, 36(5), 623–640.

Ma, J., & Zhao, L. (2008). An analysis of the Chinese housing market bubble. *China Economic Review*, 19(4), 539–552.

Matthews, K. (2009). Credit crunch and financial instability: A UK perspective. [Emerald Insight]. *Journal of Financial Regulation and Compliance*, 17(1), 19–34.

Matthews, K., & Thompson, J. (2019). *The Economics of Banking* (4th ed.). Wiley-Blackwell.

Maudos, J. (2017). Financial structure and growth: Empirical evidence for Spain. *Economic Modelling*, 60, 107–120.

Maudos, J., & de Guevara, J. F. (1998). Explaining interest margins in the Spanish banking sector. *Review of European Economic Policy*, 33(3), 123–135.

Micco, A., & Panizza, U. (2007). Bank ownership and lending behavior. *Economics Letters*, 93(2), 248–254. DOI: 10.1016/j.econlet.2006.05.009

Micco, A., Panizza, U., & Yañez, M. (2007). Bank ownership and performance. Does politics matter? *Journal of Banking & Finance*, 31(1), 219–241. DOI: 10.1016/j.jbankfin.2006.02.007

Mishkin, F. S. (1999). Lessons from the Asian crisis. *Journal of International Money and Finance*, 18(4), 709–723. DOI: 10.1016/S0261-5606(99)00020-0

Papadopoulos, G., & Pentzaropoulos, G. C. (2004). Market structure, innovation, and productivity in European telecommunications. *Telecommunications Policy*, 28(9–10), 715–728.

Peltzman, S. (1977). The gains and losses from industrial concentration. [University of Chicago Press]. *The Journal of Law & Economics*, 20(2), 229–263. DOI: 10.1086/466902

Phillips, A. W. (1976). The Phillips curve and labor market dynamics. [AEA Web]. *The Journal of Economic Perspectives*, 2(2), 15–30.

Phillips, A. W. (1976). Stabilization policy and unemployment. [AEA Web]. *The Journal of Economic Perspectives*, 2(1), 19–33.

Porter, M. E. (1979). The structure within industries and companies' performance. [JSTOR]. *The Review of Economics and Statistics*, 61(2), 214–227. DOI: 10.2307/1924589

Porter, M. E. (1979). How competitive forces shape strategy. *Harvard Business Review*, 57(2), 137–145. PMID: 18271320

Prescott, E. C. (1986). Theory ahead of business-cycle measurement. *Carnegie-Rochester Conference Series on Public Policy*, 25, 11–44. DOI: 10.1016/0167-2231(86)90035-7

Rai, A. (1996). The effect of credit constraints on financial inclusion. *Development Economics Review*, 9(3), 77–98. PMID: 10158737

Ramirez, M. D. (2011). Banking and economic growth: A reassessment for Latin America and the Caribbean. *The Quarterly Review of Economics and Finance*, 51(1), 92–109.

Rosse, J. N., & Panzar, J. C. (1987). Testing for monopoly equilibrium. *The Journal of Industrial Economics*, 35(4), 443–456. DOI: 10.2307/2098582

Samad, A. (2008). Efficiency of conventional versus Islamic banks in Malaysia: Comparative analysis. [Emerald Insight]. *International Journal of Islamic and Middle Eastern Finance and Management*, 1(2), 191–209.

Samad, A. (2008). Efficiency and performance analysis of conventional and Islamic banks in Malaysia. *Journal of Islamic Finance*, 4(1), 23–39.

Schinasi, G. J. (2014). *Safeguarding financial stability: A macroprudential perspective. International Monetary Fund*. IMF.

Schmalensee, R. (1985). Do markets differ much? [JSTOR]. *The American Economic Review*, 75(3), 341–351.

Short, J. (1979). The concept of time in social systems. *The Sociological Review*, 27(1), 87–111.

Smirlock, M. (1985). Evidence on the (non) relationship between concentration and profitability in banking. [JSTOR]. *Journal of Money, Credit and Banking*, 17(1), 69–83. DOI: 10.2307/1992507

Srairi, S. (2008). Costs and efficiency in GCC banking: Impacts of scale economies, competition, and strategic behavior. *Journal of Banking Regulation*, 10(3), 200–210.

Srairi, S. (2013). Ownership structure, risk, and performance in MENA banks: A comparative analysis. [Emerald Insight]. *Journal of Financial Economic Policy*, 5(3), 252–274.

Stigler, G. J. (1964). A theory of oligopoly. [University of Chicago Press]. *Journal of Political Economy*, 72(1), 44–61. DOI: 10.1086/258853

Stigler, G. J. (1964). A theory of oligopoly. [University of Chicago Press]. *Journal of Political Economy*, 72(1), 44–61. DOI: 10.1086/258853

Swamy, V., & Dharani, M. (2014). Financial inclusion and growth: A cross-country analysis. *Economic Modelling*, 47, 279–293.

Tehranian, H., & Cornett, M. M. (2010). The financial crisis and its consequences for investment banks. *Journal of Applied Corporate Finance*, 22(3), 56–69.

Tehranian, H., & Cornett, M. M. (2010). Investment banking crises: A global perspective. *Global Finance Journal*, 21(3), 223–245.

Thornton, J. (1992). Co-integration, error correction, and the demand for money in Singapore. [Taylor & Francis]. *Applied Economics Letters*, 12(2), 123–129.

Turk Ariss, R. (2010). Competitive behavior in Middle East and North Africa banking systems. *The Quarterly Review of Economics and Finance*, 50(2), 180–191.

Udell, G. F. (2005). Financial innovation, regulation, and competition in bank lending to small- and medium-sized enterprises. *Journal of Banking & Finance*, 30(11), 2945–2966.

Uhde, A., & Heimeshoff, U. (2009). Consolidation in banking and financial stability in Europe: Empirical evidence. *Journal of Banking & Finance*, 33(7), 1299–1311. DOI: 10.1016/j.jbankfin.2009.01.006

Vander Vennet, R. (2002). Cost and profit efficiency of financial conglomerates and universal banks in Europe. [JSTOR]. *Journal of Money, Credit and Banking*, 34(1), 254–282. DOI: 10.1353/mcb.2002.0036

Vives, X. (2008). Innovation and competitive pressure. *The RAND Journal of Economics*, 39(2), 294–309.

Weber, W. E. (2016). Efficiency in central bank digital currency: The next frontier. [IMF]. *IMF Working Paper*, 11(3), 45–56.

Weiss, L. W. (1974). The concentration-profits relationship and antitrust. *Industrial Organization Review*, 32(1), 18–27.

Wihlborg, C. (2010). Capital adequacy and international banking. *Journal of Banking & Finance*, 34(6), 1161–1172.

Wihlborg, C., & Scholtens, B. (2010). Financial stability and systemic risk: An institutional perspective. *Journal of Financial Regulation*, 22(1), 117–132.

Will, G. (2005). Risk management in financial institutions: Theory and practice. *Journal of Risk Management in Financial Institutions*, 2(3), 211–229.

Will, P. (2005). Financial globalization and risk management. *Finance Research Letters*, 12(1), 47–55.

Wood, P. (2015). Financing low-carbon innovation: Implications for policy and regulation. *Energy Policy*, 83, 158–167.

Yalcin, T. (2005). Capital structure and the cost of capital in European banking. *Financial Markets, Institutions and Instruments*, 14(4), 183–223.

Yang, B., & Zhou, Y. (2008). The rise of Chinese enterprise innovation: Paths, strategies, and implications. *Technovation*, 29(4), 195–204.

Yang, C., & Ma, F. (1991). Structural changes in banking efficiency in China: An empirical investigation. *China Economic Review*, 3(1), 45–72.

Yang, J., & Zhou, Y. (1991). Economic reforms and industrial productivity in China. *China Economic Review*, 3(2), 83–101.

Yuan, S., & Liu, Y. (2006). Exchange rate regimes and macroeconomic performance in developing countries. [University of Chicago Press]. *Economic Development and Cultural Change*, 55(1), 101–123.

Zhao, J., & Ma, X. (2018). Environmental sustainability practices and their performance impact: Evidence from the textile industry. *Journal of Cleaner Production*, 190, 134–147.

Chapter 14
Impact of Green Banking Practices on Sustainable Performance of Banks Through Analysis of the Mediating Effect of Green Finance

Shamaila Butt
https://orcid.org/0000-0003-1411-9590
Sohar University, Oman

Muhammad Ashfaq
https://orcid.org/0009-0000-1497-5595
University of Sialkot, Pakistan

Muhammad Ali Chohan
https://orcid.org/0000-0002-8860-0603
Research and Innovation Centre, Sohar University, Oman

Resham Iftikhar
https://orcid.org/0009-0008-1778-5541
University of Sialkot, Pakistan

Muhammad Ayub Awan
https://orcid.org/0009-0000-0917-0135
International Institute of Islamic Economics, Pakistan

Ain Naadia Binti Mazlan
https://orcid.org/0000-0001-5132-146X
Universiti Teknologi Malaysia, Malaysia

Tariq Mahmood
University of Sialkot, Pakistan

ABSTRACT

This research paper explores the impact of green banking practices on the sustainable performance through analysis of the mediating effect of green financing and

DOI: 10.4018/979-8-3693-6386-7.ch014

moderating effect of green leadership. The data were collected from 250 employees of the banking sector through a self-administered questionnaire and online questionnaire made in google forms. The analysis was conducted through Smart PLS-4 and SEM model was used. The study's findings demonstrate that, in contrast to bank customer-related GB practices, which were not statistically significant; people, normal business operations, and policy-related GB practices have significant positive effects on green financing. Banks' environmental performance was significantly and favorably affected by the financing of green initiatives. Also, it was found that in contrast to employee and customer-related GB activities, banks' ordinary business operations and policy-related practices significantly affect their environmental performances. Green banking practices can have a significant impact on the sustainable performance of the banks

1- INTRODUCTION

Sustainability is an emerging trend globally, with major corporations integrating it into business practices. Industrialization has disrupted ecological balance, often at the community's expense, sparking social concerns over environmental issues. As a result, many industries are embracing environmental responsibility as part of their corporate social responsibility (CSR). The banking sector, crucial for sustainable development, has seen the concept of "green banking" gain traction. Banks now play a significant role in addressing climate risks, promoting economic recovery, and lowering climate vulnerability through ethical financing practices (Lymperopoulos, 2012). Globally, banks are investing heavily in green initiatives to reduce carbon emissions and build a green brand image (Skouloudis, 2009; Green Finance Development in Bangladesh, 2018). Studies have found a positive association between CSR and green marketing, which in turn enhances banks' green reputation (Amoah, 2022).

Banks play an important role in the sustainable development of a country and the term "green banking" has gained prominence in recent years. Financial, economic, and environmental changes are causing the financial services sector to adapt, and banking operations are now fully integrating ethical principles and ideals (Lymperopoulos, A model of green bank marketing, 2012). (Lymperopoulos C. a., 2012).The banking sector supports environmental adaptation by allocating finance to climate-vulnerable industries, lowering climate risks, and supporting economic recovery. Sustainability is now synonymous with environmental and green banking (Bowman, 2010). The banks are broadcasting corporate social responsibility (CSR) activities (Kiliç, 2016).

Banks all around the world are investing a lot in green initiatives to present a green image (Skouloudis, 2009); (Green Finance Development in Bangladesh:, 2018) progressively reducing carbon emissions through bank greening. Several significant studies have previously been conducted on green banking. Scholtens claims that the larger CSR notion encompasses green bank marketing. (Gonenc, Responsibility and performance relationship in the banking industry, 2019). (Grove, 1996) outlined the connection (Jha, 2013) (Khan, 2015) (Kärnä, Business responses to climate change: Identifying emergent strategies, 2003) (Kumar, 2018) (Lymperopoulos, A model of green bank marketing, 2012) (Park, 2020) (Scholtens, Corporate social responsibility in the international insurance industry, 2011) (Zhixia, 2018) (Amacanin, 2005) (Hossain, 2020) on between CSR and green marketing in the non-banking sector. (Amoah, 2022) looked at the benefits of green bank marketing and green image, (Al Amin, 2023) whereas (Skouloudis, Sustainability reporting in Greece: are we there yet?, 2009) focused on the creation of green services. Implementing sustainable banking practices can operate as a potent accelerator for sustainable development, claim (Dar, 2018). Additionally, they draw attention to the paucity of sustainable banking research in Indian institutions. Although they have been ignored by developing countries, green banking has attracted significant research in rich countries, including India (Khan H. Z., 2021). A relatively recent subject of research is green banking (Kumar K. &., 2020). The majority of research done in India focuses on CSR, environmental management, and green banking techniques (Biswas, 2016). Equator Principles (EPs), United Nations Environmental Protection Finance Initiative (UNEPF1), and other organizations promote sustainable development through financial institutions (Sharma, 2022). It has been embraced by more than 200 member nations, and India, a member nation, is abiding by (RBI) Reserve Bank of India, 2017 (Pandey, 2019). Unfortunately, despite the vigorous measures taken by the Indian government, the average citizen has yet to experience sustainability. For a variety of reasons, including a communication gap between the different stakeholders, a lack of awareness, a negative image of the bank's commitment to the environment, and a lack of trust, the results of the banks' green outreach have not been as successful as intended. (Lymperopoulos C. C., 2012) provided empirical support for their claim that green bank marketing improves the bank's positive green reputation.

Green Leadership refers to the behaviors of leaders who encourage their followers to accomplish environmental goals and inspire them to perform beyond anticipated levels of environmental effectiveness. The green leader is a visionary with an aptitude for understanding systems and concepts to lead for meeting workplace goals. He uses true colors personality typology. This temperament manages with rationality, objectivity, and logic. People with the green temperament have a flair for innovation and analyzing systems and processes for improvement and change.

The following are some ways that this study adds to the body of knowledge already on green banking, green finance, and banks' environmental performance:

This study aims to contribute to the literature on green banking, green finance, and environmental performance by filling the following gaps: (1) empirically examining green banking practices in the context of bankers' industry knowledge, (2) employing structural equation modeling (SEM) to measure the impact of these practices, a method previously underused in this field, and (3) analyzing primary data from bank employees to understand the link between green banking practices and green finance. The findings will inform private commercial bankers, especially in developing countries, on integrating sustainable practices.

The current study begins by examining the research gap by theoretically and empirically investigating the various green banking practices based on bankers' knowledge of the banking industry. Second, structural equation modeling (SEM) is used in the study to quantify the impact of green banking practices on banks' environmental performance. This is because previous research primarily relied on descriptive statistics and multiple regression analysis to establish relationships between study variables. Lastly, this is a ground-breaking study that uses primary data collected from bank workers to assess the connection between different green banking practices and the banks' sources of green funding. As far as the researcher is aware, no study has yet looked into this issue globally, even in developing nations. Thus, we focus on private commercial bankers who are well-versed in green banking operations, green finance, and internal environmental management of banks.

2- LITERATURE REVIEW

2.1 Green Banking Practices and Banks' Environmental Performance

Green banking practices are not only promoted at the company level, but also at policy level, via green project funding, in order to ensure environmental sustainability (Rehman et al., 2021). Banks, being one of the key funding sources for many industries and companies, are expose to tremendous liability and responsibility, as they could indirectly contribute to environmental contamination if they fail to exercise strict environmental protection measures on industries and enterprises before they are financed. On the one hand, banking institutions have also been criticized for being one of the major factors directly and indirectly affecting global climate change, resulting in the introduction of the green banking approach in the last decade to reduce the adverse impact of banks on the healthy environment (Rehman, 2021). On the other hand, banks are generally regarded as eco-friendly in terms of carbon emissions and environmental degradations, as they represent a key component of the economy and are closely linked to society (Jayarathne, 2020). Therefore, banks should be constructive in obliging industries to invest in climate protection and the use of suitable technology and management structures for mandated investment (Aktar, 2014).This helps banks to contribute to the improvement of the overall climate, quality of life, the performance of the material and energy usage, service quality and goods, despite environmental conservation not being their primary objective.

(De Vass, 2018) studied the factors influencing the environmental performance of the banking sector in Bangladesh using multiple regression analysis based on secondary information. They observed that credit-rating scores had a positive effect on banks' environmental performance, in contrast to bank's longevity in service. The study also reported that highly profitable banks are more concerned with environmental issues. More recently, (Rehman, Analyzing the relationship between green innovation and environmental performance in large manufacturing firms, 2021) studied the association between GB practices and their impact on banks' environmental performances, based on socially responsible investment (SRI) theory.

The findings indicated that there is a strong positive relationship among policy-related practices, daily operations practices and green investments of GB in Pakistan. Additionally, the study also highlighted that the effect of green initiatives on policy decisions and investments in green infrastructure has become more prominent in fostering a green climate. Similarly, Shaumya and Arulrajah (2017) studied the impact of GB practices impact on banks' environmental performance in Sri lanka. The study found that GB practices had a positive and significant effect on banks' environmental performance.

Similarly, (Risal, 2018) studied the impact of GB practices on banks' environmental performance in Nepal using multiple regression analysis. The study concluded that environmental training, banks' green policy and energy-efficient equipment significantly influenced the environmental performance of banks, contrary to the customer-related practices' (green financing and green projects), the effects of which were statistically insignificant.

Hence, any organization's environmental performance can be measured by a number of metrics, including low environmental emissions, pollution control, waste reduction and recycling (Risal, Measuring green banking practices on bank's environmental performance: Empirical evidence from Kathmandu valley, 2018). The environmental issues of banks, on the other hand, are primarily expressed in their initiatives, e.g., green finance, paperless banking, solar panel construction, recycling activities, maximum daily light usage, reduced use of gas and petroleum, investment in ecofriendly projects and marketing, climate risk-fund budgeting and the environmental risk assessment of projects (Shee, 2018). In another study by (Jha N. &., 2013), it was identified that the major GB strategies, which support the achievement of sustainable economic development in a country, include online banking, use of green checking accounts, saving paper, green loans for home improvement, green policy, green credit cards, use of solar energy and green products and services (Parveen, 2018). Therefore, it can be concluded that GB represents a means by which banks can reduce emissions and protect their environment in a bid to boost their environmental efficiency, and, consequently, raise their reputation as good corporate citizens towards the achievement of sustainable economic development in a region.

Green banking (GB) practices promote sustainability at both the company and policy levels through green project funding (Rehman et al., 2021). Banks, given their funding roles, are increasingly accountable for environmental practices. In Pakistan, GB policies significantly influence banks' environmental performance, promoting investments in green infrastructure and green policies (Rehman, 2021; Shaumya & Arulrajah, 2017).

For a holistic understanding, this study examines several environmental performance metrics, including emission reductions, recycling, and eco-friendly banking initiatives, such as paperless banking, solar power adoption, and risk assessments of environmental projects (Jha & Kumar, 2013). Consequently, this leads to the formulation of the following hypothesis:

Hypothesis 1 (H1):*Green Banking Practices significantly influence Banks' environmental performance.*

2.2 Green Banking Practices and Banks' Sources of Green Financing

Green finance (GF) blends social and environmental objectives with economic gains (Wang, 2016). It includes loans for eco-friendly projects, waste management, and renewable energy (Khairunnessa, 2021). Studies show GB enhances environmental performance by reducing banks' carbon footprints (Chen, 2022).

Green finance can be defined as a modern financial event that blends social and economic gains with environmental improvement (Wang, 2016). Similarly, green finance represents a new growth of and engine for sustainable economic development, with social responsibility and environmental protection at its core (Friedlingstein, 2020). Thus, green finance is aimed at harmonizing monetary improvement, environmental stability, ecological security and achievement of the country's sustainable economic development (Ni, 2020). In addition, banks' overall internal carbon footprint and external carbon production can be minimized via the green financing of GB activities (Zheng, 2021).

Furthermore, (Chen, 2022) indicated that GB is one of the factors influencing the improvement of sustainable economic growth in emerging economies, while (Ning, 2023) also noted that green finance, as a part of GB, is considered an important monetary tool for the sustainable economic growth of any country. Such banks mainly provide loans for various green financing projects, such as waste (solid and liquid) management, green establishment, green brick manufacturing (fire-burnt and non-fire block), industrial safety and security, clean energy, energy consumption, green tourism and alternative energy (Khairunnessa, 2021).

More recently, (Zheng G. W., 2021) studied the role of PCBs in the development of green finance in Bangladesh and identified the four major sources of green financing, based on banker's perceptions. The sources include investment in waste management, green establishment, green brick manufacturing recycling and recyclable product, all of which are instrumental to the environmental improvement by banks and the sustainable economic development of the country. In another study, (Chen, The effect of green banking practices on banks' environmental performance and green financing: An empirical study, 2022) showed that a positive relationship exists between the GB practices (operations and policy-related practices) and bank's green projects.

Moreover, GB practices in banks resulted in the improvement of banks' environmental performances via the reduction of the negative environmental impacts resulting from daily operations, such as cutting paper use and reducing energy consumption, fuel consumption and emissions (Arulrajah, 2020). Banks also exert a positive effect on the environment by promoting proper GB activities in banks, such as the enhancement of environmental training and staff awareness, development of green buildings, provision of loans for green projects and the use of solar and wind energy (Ahmad, Factors behind the adoption of green banking by Bangladeshi commercial banks, 2013). Therefore, it can be said that the GB activities are essential for the improvement of banks' green financing and environmental performance towards (Scholtens, 2011) attaining sustainable economic development in a country. Based on the aforementioned argument, the following research hypotheses are proposed:

Hypothesis 2 (H2): *Green Banking practices significantly influence the sources of green financing.*

2.3 Green Finance and Environmental Performance

According to (Sinha, 2023), GF mechanisms may demonstrate a progressive detrimental influence on environmental and social responsibility. Besides, GF and CSR are forms of corporate accountability to stakeholders (the public, shareholders, investors, customers, and other groups) that assist organizations in the achievement of financial and sustainable successes while avoiding legitimacy gap so social and environmental conflicts (Indriastuti, 2021). According to (Indriastuti, The role of green investment and corporate social responsibility investment on sustainable performance., 2021), green finance may enhance the corporate sustainability of organizations via the financing of numerous eco-friendly projects, which will significantly result in EP (Chen Z. L., 2022).

(Wahba, 2015), on the other hand, stated that investments in CSR have the potential to significantly contribute to the improvement of society and businesses, consequently improving the company's financial and sustainability performance (Friedlingstein P. J., 2022) and EP (Kraus, 2020). Researchers have recently demonstrated that GF significantly improves the EP of banking institutions (Lymperopoulos A. R., 2012) (Park, 2020) (Zheng G. W., 2021). Therefore, it can be concluded that investing in various eco-friendly projects may improve the organizations' corporate accountability and EP. Green finance has a direct, positive impact on environmental performance (Sinha, 2023; Wahba, 2015). Investments in CSR enhance a company's sustainability, benefiting both environmental and financial performance (Kraus, 2020). The following research hypothesis is thus formulated:

Hypothesis 3 (H3):*GF has a significant positive impact on the EP of banking institutions.*

2.4 Mediation of Green Finance between Green Banking practices and the Banks' Environmental Performance

Green banking activities are supported not only at firm level but also at policy level through the financing of green projects to ensure environmental sustainability. Thus, GB practices contribute to banks' environmental performance by cutting down on activities with negative impacts on the environment (e.g., reduction of paper use, fuel consumption, and carbon emissions) and promoting environmental benefits (e.g., improvement of employee environmental training and understanding, green infrastructure, and the use of solar and wind power). On the other hand, green finance can be characterized as a modern financial event, which considers environmental improvement for social and economic rewards. Similarly, green finance provides a new engine for sustainable economic development, with a focus on social responsibility and environmental conservation.

In addition, banks' overall internal carbon footprint and external carbon production can be reduced via the green financing of GB activities. Thus, the purpose of green finance is to harmonize monetary progress, environmental stability, ecological security, and sustainable economic development of a country. Although the environmental performance of a company can be measured through its activities and products, the best way to assess the environmental efficiency of businesses remains the effective use of the material, as stated by Tung et al. It is noteworthy that environmental performance is not organizational protection of the environment; rather, it involves constructive and consistent administration of activities to achieve well-defined and long-term goals of natural resources conservation and business productivity.

Furthermore, the emission intensity was applied to estimate the environmental performance of the firm, and the study stated that the firm's environmental impact can be calculated by using different indexes, rankings, or environmental scores. Therefore, it can be concluded that the activities of GB are essential to the improvement of banks' green financing and environmental performance, towards the attainment of a sustainable economic development.

More recently, Zheng et al. studied the role of PCBs in the development of green finance in Bangladesh and identified the four major sources of green financing based on the bankers' perception. The sources include investment in waste management, green establishment, green brick manufacturing recycling, and recyclable products, all of which are instrumental to the environmental improvement of banks and the sustainable economic development of a country. In another study, Rehman et al. highlighted a positive relationship between GB practices (operations and policy-related practices) and banks' green financing. Furthermore, the GB activities in banks resulted in the improvement of their environmental performance by minimizing daily activities with negative environmental impact, such as cutting down on paper use, reducing energy conservation, financing ecofriendly projects, lowering fuel consumption, and minimizing carbon emissions.

Banks also exert a positive effect on the environment through the promotion of proper GB activities via the enhancement of environmental training and staff awareness, development of green buildings, provision of loans for green projects, and the use of solar and wind energy. Miah et al. studied the factors influencing the environmental performance of the banking sector in Bangladesh using a multiple regression analysis based on secondary information. They observed that the credit-rating score had a positive effect on banks' environmental performance, as opposed to bank's longevity in service.

More recently, (Salah, 2019) studied the association between GB activities and its impact on banks' environmental performance based on the Socially Responsible Investment (SRI) theory. The findings indicate that a strong positive relationship exists among policy-related practices, daily operations practice, and green financing activities of GB in Pakistan. Similarly, (TILAHUN, 2023), studied the impact of GB practices on banks' environmental performance in Sri Lanka. The study discovered that GB practices had a positive and significant effect on the banks' environmental performance. In addition, the study also revealed that staff, day-to-day activities, and policy-related practices had a positive effect on banks' overall environmental performance change, while banks' customer-related practices of GB were statistically insignificant on their environmental performance.

Another study conducted by (Oyedele, 2023) identified the various green initiatives integrated by banking institutions to improve their environmental performance. The GB activities include environmental training of employees, energy-efficient practices, green financing, green projects, and green policies. The study further revealed that GB activities positively influenced banks' environmental performance in Coimbatore city of India. Similarly, (Risal, Measuring green banking practices on bank's environmental performance: Empirical evidence from Kathmandu valley, 2018) studied the impact of GB activities on banks' environmental performance in Nepal using a multiple regression analysis. The study concluded that environmental training, banks' green policies, and the availability of energy-efficient equipment significantly affected the environmental performance of banks, contrary to customer-related practices (green financing and green projects) whose effects were discovered to be statistically insignificant. Therefore, it can be said that the involvement of businesses in GB activities and banks' financing of eco-friendly projects are means by which banks can reduce carbon emissions, improve their environmental performance, enhance their business reputation, and ultimately achieve sustainable economic development.

Green banking activities reduce environmental impacts, such as paper use and carbon emissions, while promoting green practices. Green finance harmonizes monetary progress with environmental goals, thus enhancing environmental performance through sustainable financing practices (Tung et al., 2023).

Based on the above discussion, two key research variables and one mediating variable were identified and include green banking practices as independent variables, sources of green financing as a mediating variable, and banks' environmental performance as a dependent variable. As a result, the current study adds to the existing literature on the GB and green funding, as well as organizational environmental management. Besides, this is recognized as one of the earliest studies to investigate the role of green financing in mediating the relationship between GB activities and bank environmental performance in emerging economies such as Bangladesh. Therefore, the following research hypothesis is provided in view of the theoretical background and review of the previous literature:

Hypothesis 4 (H4). *Green Finance mediates the relationship between Green Banking practices and the Banks' Environmental performance.*

2.5 Moderation of Green Leadership between Green Banking Practices and the Banks' Environmental Performance through mediating effect of green finance.

Green leaders have an influence on organizational performance in a variety of ways, including employee behavior and attitude, employee engagement, and economic health, green performance and psychological performance (Ramus, 2000). (Cuyvers, 2021) found that green leadership positively affects green work engagement, ultimately affecting environmental performance.

According to (Sunarsi, 2020) the leadership style will determine the company's response to its environment. The leadership style shows a different attitude of environmental concern. According to (Sutiah, 2020) transformational leader who has green values, then he will have an influence on the green behavior of his subordinates, where he will motivate subordinates to overcome obstacles by paying more attention to things that are beneficial to the organizational environment, thinking about sustainable organizational development, and solving problems. environment in more innovative ways. In addition, it also increases the subordinates' concerns about environmental issues by building good relationships with them and then increasing the green values of their subordinates.

The role of the business 's green leadership in the formation of an environmentally cultured school, namely: (1) educator; (2) manager; (3) innovators; (4) motivator; and (5) figures. Leadership role green school principal as educator, indicated by the process of providing value education environmental care, which is carried out through three models, namely: (a) awareness (through socialization and posters with the theme of environment and health); (b) habituation (through the application of school culture steadily to form a habit in students); and (c) strengthening (through giving oral and written appreciation).

According to (Sartika, 2021) and (Bernarto, 2020) the green leadership role of the principal as manager is shown in the form of: (a) environmentally friendly school policy formulation; (b) student empowerment to become environmental cadres as well as some school personnel to oversee the policy; and (c) delegated the task of making an MoU on cross-sectoral cooperation to several business personnel. According to (Soelton, 2020); (Putri, 2020) and (Bernarto, 2020) the role of the principal's green leadership as an innovator is manifested in form creation of innovative environmentally friendly supporting facilities. The green leadership role of the principal as a motivator, indicated by the provision of motivation to school members to actively implementing environment-based school activities and maintaining a school-based culture environment. Meanwhile, the role of the principal's green leadership as a figure is indicated by There is an exemplary attitude of caring for the environment, so that the principal is imprinted as a role model business for cultured environment.

Green leadership significantly influences environmental performance by promoting eco-friendly behaviors among employees and fostering a sustainable culture within the organization (Sunarsi, 2020). Leaders with green values motivate employees towards sustainable development and environmentally responsible behaviors. Hence, based on the literature, we formulated the following hypothesis.

Hypothesis 5 (H5). *Green Leadership moderates the relationship between Green Banking Practices and the Banks' Environmental Performance through mediating effect of green finance.*

Conceptual Framework

The hypothesized conceptual framework of the study is shown in figure. the conceptual research model is designed based on the theoretical foundation and review of the recent literature on green banking practices, green leadership, green finance, as well as the environmental performance of organizations.

Figure 1. Research model

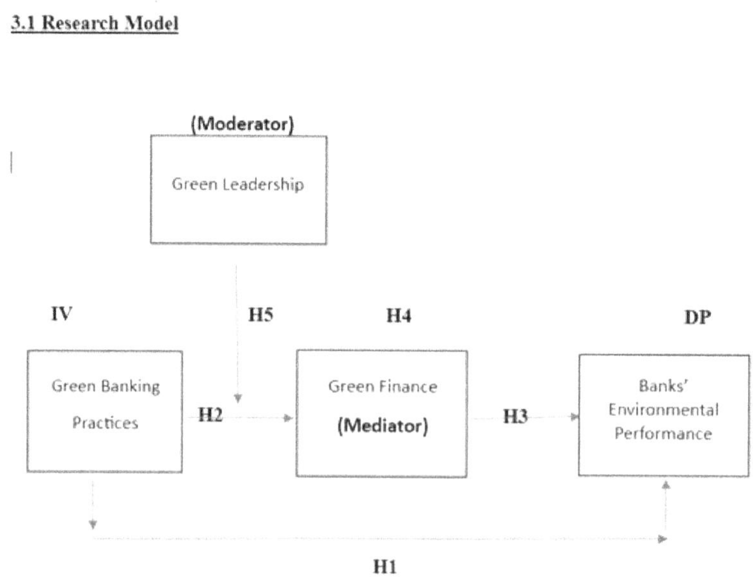

Hypotheses:

The following research hypotheses are proposed:

Hypothesis 1 (H1). Green Banking practices significantly influence banks' environmental performance.

Hypothesis 2 (H2). Green Banking practices significantly influence the sources of green finance.

Hypothesis 3 (H3). Banks' sources of green financing significantly influence the environmental

performance of the bank.

Hypothesis 4 (H4). Green Finance mediates the relationship between Green Banking practices and the Banks' Environmental performance.

Hypothesis 5 (H5). Green Leadership moderates the relationship between Green Banking Practices and the Banks' Environmental Performance through mediating effect of green finance.

3- MATERIALS AND METHODS

This study used a survey research design with a questionnaire to gather data that would be subject to PLS-SEM analysis. This study uses a survey research design with a sample of 250 employees from the Pakistani banking sector. A non-probability sampling technique was employed due to time constraints and exploratory objectives. Data collection spanned July to August 2023. The demographic breakdown includes gender, age, education level, and employment level. The population of the study was the employees of banking sector. The scientific table by (Krejcie, 1970) was used to calculate the study's sample size, which was 250. Data for the study were gathered from the sample of 250 employees. Furthermore, data for the study were gathered using a non-probability sampling technique. Non probability sampling was used since it was to get participants from the large banking sector, there was a shortage of time and an exploratory approach was required. This approach made it easier to get information from banking sector employees. A sample of 250 employees were selected from banking sector of Pakistan. An online survey questionnaire was used and distributed by using URL through online medium like e-mail, WhatsApp, Instagram and Facebook to target sample. Time period for data collection was two months i.e., from July to August 2023. 250 responses were received out of 270 and used for final analysis. The demographic information includes gender, qualification, age, working experience and employment level. From 250 respondents 176 (70.04%) were male and 74 (29.6) were female. 33 respondents fall in the age of 20-25 years, 69 were from the group 26-31 years, 75 were from the group 32-37 years, 74 were from 38 and above. The qualification level was considered 14 years, 16 years, 18 years and 18 years above. 30% (75) respondents having 14 years of education, 26.4o% (66) have 16 years, 44.8% (112) have 18 years and 1% (3) have 18 years above education. The employment level was considered junior, middle and senior. 17.6% (44) respondents were junior, 36% (90) were middle level of employment and 47.6% (119) were senior level of employment. Further, 44 (17.6%) respondents fall in 0-2 years of experience, 70 (28%) respondents have 3-5 years of experience, 65 (26%) respondents have 6-8 years of experience, 71 (28.4%) respondents have 9 years and more experience.

Figure 2.

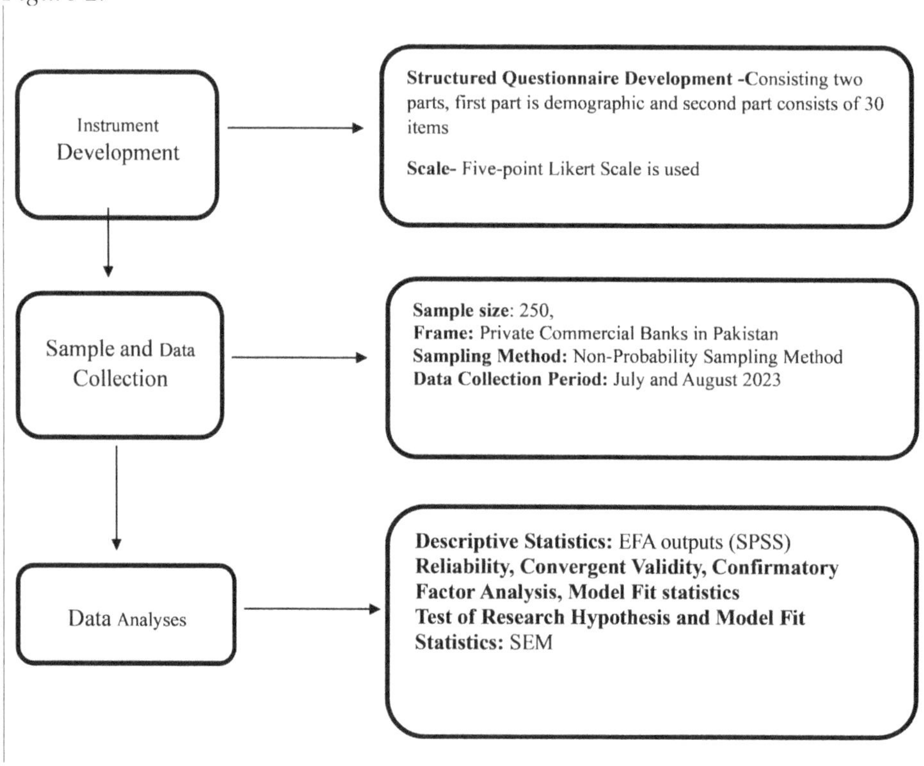

The questionnaire based on two parts. First part is used to get demographic data related to gender, age, qualification, working experience and employment level. Second part dealt with the questionnaire for the study based on literature review consisted of four sections. First section dealt with twelve questions for green banking practices adapted from the items based on the major functions of green banking practices. Second section adapted Six questions for green finance. Third section consist of four items for banks' environmental performance. Fourth section consist of eight questions of green leadership. Five Point Likert Scale is used having 1-5 options of strongly disagree, disagree, neutral, agree and strongly agree.

To test the hypothetical model of this study, Structural Equation Modeling (SEM) has been used which is a second-generation data analysis technique. For descriptive statistics, SPSS 25 has been used. As the current study is using both mediator and moderator, PLS-SEM (SMART-PLS 4) is used to analyze the mediation effect and stats Packages Tools (Star wiki Tools) has been used to check the moderation effect. The results of mediation effect were also checked by using SPSS Process Macro 4.2.

4- RESULTS AND DISCUSION

Conformity factor analysis was used to check the reliability and validity of construct and for checking the internal consistency and reliability Cronbach Alpha has been used, the composite reliability of construct must be more than 0.40 (Brown, 1980; Hair et al., 2017). The composite reliability of all constructs is more than 0.40 mentioned in Table 1.

Table 1.

Sr #	Construct Items in Details		Factor Loading
1.	**BERP1**	**My bank ensures the provision of environment-related training and education.**	**.853**
2.	BERP2	My bank provides a sustainable performance evaluation system.	.525
3.	BERP3	Green reward facilities are available in my bank.	.725
4.	BORP1	My bank focuses on the reduction of paper usage.	.730
5.	BORP2	My bank has introduced energy-efficient equipment, such as ATMs and online banking.	.831
6.	BORP3	My bank provides eco-friendly banking services.	.703
7.	BCRP1	The bank provides loan for eco-friendly projects.	.491
8.	BCRP2	The bank provides online banking services (i.e., online bills payment, acceptance of remote deposit, and provision of e-statements).	.577

continued on following page

Table 1. Continued

Sr #		Construct Items in Details	Factor Loading
1.	**BERP1**	**My bank ensures the provision of environment-related training and education.**	**.853**
9.	BCRP3	The bank ensures the assessment of clients' environmental risks.	.574
10.	BPRP1	The bank plans the establishment of more green branches.	.626
11.	BPRP2	The bank has implemented a green policy.	.517
12.	BPRP3	The bank ensures the Promotion of green partnerships among suppliers and investors.	.451
13.	GF1	The bank has increased the amount invested in eco-friendly projects.	.569
14.	GF2	The bank has increased the resources invested in recycling and recyclable products.	.734
15.	GF3	The bank has increased the amount invested in waste management and green brick manufacturing.	.550
16.	GF4	The bank has increased the amount invested in energy efficiency projects.	.720
17.	GF5	The bank has increased the amount invested in green industry development.	.797
18.	GF6	The bank has increased the amount invested in green marketing and others.	.584
19.	BEP1	The bank ensures the reduction of energy consumption from banking activities.	.628
20.	BEP2	The bank ensures the minimization of carbon emissions from banking activities.	1.012
21.	BEP3	The bank focuses on improving banks compliance with environmental standards.	.554
22.	BEP4	The bank ensures the Provision of training on environmental protection and energy savings to the staff.	1.067
23.	GL1	I recognize each person's ability to effectively allocate money to help the organization's environmental performance.	.928
24.	GL2	I show a commitment to the natural environment.	.901
25.	GL3	I am optimistic that I must help to improve the organization's environmental performance.	.914
26.	GL4	I encourage actions that should benefit the organization's environmental performance.	.894
27.	GL5	I urge people to think creatively about the environmental performance and development portion of the budget.	.979
28.	GL6	I demonstrate that each individual's suggestion for the organization's environmental performance is important.	.913
29.	GL7	I show that he/she valued the environment.	.858
30.	GL8	I challenge myself to think about the organization's environmental performance in a different way.	.594

Further, the composite reliability is considerable if more than 0.50 (Rafi et al., 2022). Table 2 showed the significance of relationship among the variables. The Cronbach Alpha (α) is 0.846. The correlation analysis shows that there is a significance relationship among GBP and BEP (0.559**), among GF with BEP (0.544**), significant relationship exists between GF with GBP and BEP (0.731**) and (0.737**). Similarly, GF has a significant relation with BEP (0.07**).

Table 2. Correlation analysis for variable

	bp	GF	BEP	GL
bp	1	-	-	-
GF	.559**	1	-	-
BEP	.544**	.248**	1	-
GL	.731**	.173**	.732**	1

**. Correlation is significant at the 0.01 level (2-tailed).

Structural Model

PLS-SEM was used to check the model fitness. The threshold for the value of SRMR is considered small ≥ 0.2, medium ≥ 0.0 and large ≥ 0.0. here the value is 0.168. According to the Figure 3 Green banking practices are positively related with banks' environmental performance (r=0.374, $p < 0.01$). positive re1ation also exists between GBP and source of green finance (r=0.805, $p < 0.01$), positive relation exists between sources of green finance and banks' environmental performance (r=0.174, $p < 0.01$) for analyzing the mediation effect, the values of analysis using SPSS Process Macro *4*.

The SEM results indicate significant relationships across green banking practices, green finance, and environmental performance. To improve construct validity, indicators with factor loadings below 0.60 were omitted. Key findings are presented in Table 2, showing path coefficients and p-values to clarify these relationships.

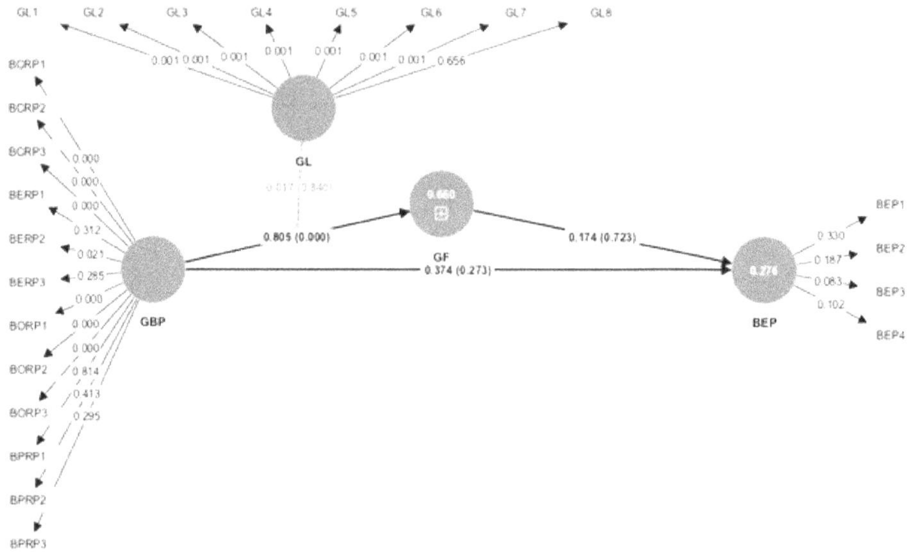

Green leadership moderates the relationship between green banking practices and banks' environmental performance through mediation of green finance. The value of r-square (R^2) for green banking practices, green finance, and banks' environmental performance is 0.656 which is significant and that mediation has a positive effect of the sustainable performance of the banks. The moderation effect of the green leadership on the relation of' GBP and banks' environmental performance also shows significance. The regression co-efficient for GBP and banks' environmental and sources of green finance is 0.017 which is mentioned in Table 3.

Table 3. Unstandardized regression co-efficient

Green banking practices Banks' environmental performance	**1.108**
Green Leadership Green Finance	.544
Green banking practices Green leadership Banks' environmental performance	.017

From the analysis of using different statistical tools, the results support the hypothesis H1 that GBP is positively related to Banks' environmental perfo1mance with the co-efficient path b=0.374, $P < 0.O1$. with the use of good green banking practices, the banks can achieve sustainable performance. H2 is accepted with the path co-efficient b=0.805, $p < 0.01$ which showed that there is a positive relation of GBP with green finance. H3 hypothesized that GF has positive impact on banks' environmental performance and is accepted with the path co-efficient b=0.174. p <

0.01. Similarly: H4 Proposed that there exists a mediation effect of green finance on the relation of GBP and banks' environmental performance, which is also accepted ($b=0.660$, $p < 0.01$). Green finance increases the banks' environmental performance with the help of green banking practices. H5 proposed that there is a moderating effect of green leadership on the GBP and banks' environmental performance which is also accepted ($b=0.017$, $p < 0.01$). Perceived organizational support along with e-leadership enhances the performance of the employees and make their performance sustainable.

Table 4. Hypothesis summary

Sr No	Hypothesis	Path Coefficient	Significance	Results
1	(H1). Green Banking practices significantly influence banks' environmental performance.	0.374	$p < 0.01$	Accepted
2	(H2). Green Banking practices significantly influence the sources of green finance.	0.805	$p < 0.01$	Accepted
3	(H3). Banks' sources of green financing significantly influence the environmental performance of the bank.	0.174	$p < 0.01$	Accepted
4	(H4). Green Finance mediates the relationship between Green Banking practices and the Banks' Environmental performance.	0.660	$p < 0.01$	Accepted
5	(H5). Green Leadership moderates the relationship between Green Banking Practices and the Banks' Environmental Performance through mediating effect of green finance	0.017	$p < 0.01$	Accepted

5- CONCLUSION AND IMPLICATIONS

Current study focuses of the sustainable performance of the banks. There exists a vital role of green leadership towards environmental performance of the banking institutions. This study admits and acknowledges the efforts done by previous literature. The goal of the study to investigate the relationship of green banking practices with the sustainable performance of the banks. Current study tried to place a contribution. Further, in order to address the gap, current study has explored the mediating effect of green finance and moderating effect of green leadership upon the relation of green banking practices and banks' sustainable performance. The findings of the study showed that banks performed extraordinarily if green banking practices are adopted in the presence of green leadership. To get the collective advantage, digitalization plays a vital role especially of software development companies (Luo et al., 2023). Considering the sources of green finance as mediator and green leadership as moderator the banks' environmental performance increases when green banking practices are adopted. Organizations are trying to achieve maximum performance and success and are focusing on the green banking practices by providing green leadership support and foster positive effects of green financing which plays a vital role for achieving organizational goals. The results also support the theory implication.

This study concludes that green leadership and green finance significantly enhance banks' environmental performance. Green banking, supported by digitalization and structured leadership, is essential for banks aiming for sustainable development. For policymakers, this study highlights the necessity of regulatory support for green banking initiatives. Future research should examine green banking across different economic contexts and include qualitative approaches to validate the proposed framework.

The current study contributed to the knowledge that how these factors interact and have an impact on each other. This study contributes specially in the field of green banking and green leadership working in remote technology-based organizations. It also shows the importance of green leadership by supporting the performance of the banks in the presence of green finance facilities. The banks should adopt green banking practices by providing finances to the green projects to enhance the banks' environmental performance. The banks should focus on adopting the green banking practices by investing in green finance projects. The training of the bankers regarding green banking practices and green finances should be arranged. The banks should develop a structure which promote the green activities to obtain sustainable development goals. They should focus on supporting and investing in the environment protection activities. The proposed relationship in this quantitative study can be further validated qualitatively, and the impact of demographics on it can also be investigated. The study has been conducted in Pakistan, and an exhaustive study in different countries at different stages of development can provide valuable insight. The proposed framework can also be studied from the point of view of other stakeholders apart from bank employees. The study has explained how the use of green initiatives by banks can enhance green brand image and solidify trust with stakeholders. The research results provide relevant and divergent insights into government, strategist and academician to chalk out effective green banking strategies for "green economy". The State of Green Bank Report (2020) also declares that for a sustainable economic recovery during the global COVID 19 crises as well as for reducing emission before 2050 "climate-resilient green banks" are the need of the hour.

REFERENCES

Ahmad, F. Z. (2013). Factors behind the adoption of green banking by Bangladeshi commercial banks. *ASA University Review*, 7(2).

Aktar, S. (2014). Reasons to Create Intention of Entrepreneurship among University Students: A Study on Bangladesh. *Journal of Entrepreneurship and Management*, 3(2).

Al Amin, M. A., Ahad Mia, M. A., Bala, T., Iqbal, M. M., & Alam, M. S. (2023). Green finance continuance behavior: The role of satisfaction, social supports, environmental consciousness, green bank marketing initiatives and psychological reactance. *Management of Environmental Quality*, 34(5), 1269–1294. DOI: 10.1108/MEQ-09-2022-0257

Amacanin, M. C. (2005). The strategic implications of corporate responsibility and sustainability in the UK banking sector. *Doctoral dissertation, University of Nottingham, UK.*

Amoah, L. D. (2022). Sustainable finance and banking in Africa. In *The Economics of Banking and Finance in Africa* (pp. 405–429). Developments in Africa's Financial Systems. DOI: 10.1007/978-3-031-04162-4_12

Arulrajah, A. (2020). Mediating role of employee green behaviour towards sustainability performance of banks. *Journal of Governance & Regulation*, 9(2), 92–102. DOI: 10.22495/jgrv9i2art7

Bernarto, I. B. (2020). Effect of transformational leadership, perceived organizational support, job satisfaction toward life satisfaction. *Evidences from indonesian teachers.*

Biswas, U. A., Garg, S., & Singh, A. (2016). The need for regulatory intervention in corporate social responsibility in India: Evidence from corporate social disclosures. *International Journal of Indian Culture and Business Management*, 12(3), 293–317. DOI: 10.1504/IJICBM.2016.075534

Bowman, M. (2010). The role of the banking industry in facilitating climate change mitigation and the transition to a low-carbon global economy. *Environment and Planning Law Journal*, 27, 448.

Chen, J. S., Siddik, A., Zheng, G.-W., Masukujjaman, M., & Bekhzod, S. (2022). The effect of green banking practices on banks' environmental performance and green financing: An empirical study. *Energies*, 15(4), 1292. DOI: 10.3390/en15041292

Chen, Z. L., Lv, H., Zhang, Q., Wang, H., & Chen, G. (2022). Construction of a cement–rebar nanoarchitecture for a solution-processed and flexible film of a Bi_2Te_3/CNT hybrid toward low thermal conductivity and high thermoelectric performance. *Carbon Energy*, 4(1), 115–128. DOI: 10.1002/cey2.161

Cuyvers, S. H., Haq, B., Op de Beeck, C., Poelman, S., Hermans, A., Wang, Z., Gocalinska, A., Pelucchi, E., Corbett, B., Roelkens, G., Van Gasse, K., & Kuyken, B. (2021). Low Noise Heterogeneous III-V-on-Silicon-Nitride Mode-Locked Comb Laser. *Laser & Photonics Reviews*, 15(8), 2000485. DOI: 10.1002/lpor.202000485

Dar, M. Z., Deepika, K., Jan, K., Swer, T. L., Kumar, P., Verma, R., Verma, K., Prakash, K. S., Jan, S., & Bashir, K. (2018). Modification of structure and physicochemical properties of buckwheat and oat starch by γ-irradiation. *International Journal of Biological Macromolecules*, 108, 1. DOI: 10.1016/j.ijbiomac.2017.11.067 PMID: 29133096

De Vass, T. S. (2018). The effect of "Internet of Things" on supply chain integration and performance: An organisational capability perspective. *Australasian Journal of Information Systems*, 22. et al, N. (2019). The impact of social and environmental sustainability on financial performance. *Journal of Multinational Financial Management*, 49, 35-53.

Friedlingstein, P. J., Jones, M. W., O'Sullivan, M., Andrew, R. M., Bakker, D. C. E., Hauck, J., Le Quéré, C., Peters, G. P., Peters, W., Pongratz, J., Sitch, S., Canadell, J. G., Ciais, P., Jackson, R. B., Alin, S. R., Anthoni, P., Bates, N. R., Becker, M., Bellouin, N., & Zeng, J. (2022). Global carbon budget 2021. *Earth System Science Data*, 14(4), 1917–2005. DOI: 10.5194/essd-14-1917-2022

Friedlingstein, P. O. (2020). Global carbon budget 2020. *Earth System Science Data Discussions*, 2020, 1–3.

Gonenc, H., & Scholtens, B. (2019). Responsibility and performance relationship in the banking industry. *Sustainability (Basel)*, 11(12), 3329. DOI: 10.3390/su11123329

Green Finance Development in Bangladesh: . (2018). *The Role of private commercial banks.*

Grove, R. H. (1996). Green imperialism: colonial expansion, tropical island Edens and the origins of environmentalism. *Cambridge University Press*, 1600-1860.

Hossain, M. (2020). The effects of green banking practices on financial performance of listed banking companies in Bangladesh. *Canadian Journal of Business and Information Studies*, 020, 01200128.

Indriastuti, M., & Chariri, A. (2021). The role of green investment and corporate social responsibility investment on sustainable performance. *Cogent Business & Management*, 8(1), 1960120. DOI: 10.1080/23311975.2021.1960120

Jayarathne, P. G. (2020). The Impact of Employee Green Behavior on Green Banking Performance of Select Private Sector Banks in Sri Lanka. *IUP Journal of Bank Management,*, 19(2).

Jha, D. &. (2013). A study of green banking trends in India. *International Monthly Refereed Journal Of Research In Management And Technology*, 127–132.

Jha, N. (2013). A study of green banking trends in India. *International Monthly Referred Journal of Research in Management and Technology*, 2, 127–132.

Kärnä, K. A. (2003). Business responses to climate change: Identifying emergent strategies. *California Management Review*, 47(3), 6–20.

Khairunnessa, F. V.-B., Vazquez-Brust, D. A., & Yakovleva, N. (2021). A review of the recent developments of green banking in Bangladesh. *Sustainability (Basel)*, 13(4), 1904. DOI: 10.3390/su13041904

Khan, H. Z., Bose, S., Sheehy, B., & Quazi, A. (2021). Green banking disclosure, firm value and the moderating role of a contextual factor: Evidence from a distinctive regulatory setting. *Business Strategy and the Environment*, 30(8), 3651–3670. DOI: 10.1002/bse.2832

Khan, M. K. (2015). The Role of Financial institutions and the Economic Growth: A Literature Review. *European Journal of Business and Management*, 7(1), 95–99.

Kiliç, M. (2016). Online corporate social responsibility (CSR) disclosure in the banking industry: Evidence from Turkey. *International Journal of Bank Marketing*, 34(4), 550–569. DOI: 10.1108/IJBM-04-2015-0060

Kraus, S. R., Rehman, S. U., & García, F. J. S. (2020). Corporate social responsibility and environmental performance: The mediating role of environmental strategy and green innovation. *Technological Forecasting and Social Change*, 160, 120262. DOI: 10.1016/j.techfore.2020.120262

Krejcie, R. V., & Morgan, D. W. (1970). Determining sample size for research activities. *Educational and Psychological Measurement*, 30(3), 607–610. DOI: 10.1177/001316447003000308

Kumar, K., & Prakash, A. (2018). Developing a framework for assessing sustainable banking performance of the Indian banking sector. *Social Responsibility Journal*, 15(5), 689–709. DOI: 10.1108/SRJ-07-2018-0162

Kumar, K., & Prakash, A. (2020). Managing sustainability in banking: Extent of sustainable banking adaptations of banking sector in India. *Environment, Development and Sustainability*, 22(6), 5199–5217. DOI: 10.1007/s10668-019-00421-5

Lymperopoulos, A. R. (2012). GRK2 inhibition in heart failure. *something old, something new.Current Pharmaceutical Design*, 18(2), 186–191. DOI: 10.2174/138161212799040510 PMID: 22229578

Lymperopoulos, C., Chaniotakis, I. E., & Soureli, M. (2012). A model of green bank marketing. *Journal of Financial Services Marketing*, 17(2), 177–186. DOI: 10.1057/fsm.2012.10

Lymperopoulos, C. C., Chaniotakis, I. E., & Soureli, M. (2012). A model of green bank marketing. *Journal of Financial Services Marketing*, 17(2), 177–186. DOI: 10.1057/fsm.2012.10

Ni, L. Y., Ye, F., Cheng, M.-L., Feng, Y., Deng, Y.-Q., Zhao, H., Wei, P., Ge, J., Gou, M., Li, X., Sun, L., Cao, T., Wang, P., Zhou, C., Zhang, R., Liang, P., Guo, H., Wang, X., Qin, C.-F., & Dong, C. (2020). Detection of SARS-CoV-2-specific humoral and cellular immunity in COVID-19 convalescent individuals. *Immunity*, 52(6), 971–977. DOI: 10.1016/j.immuni.2020.04.023 PMID: 32413330

Ning, Y. C.-O.-U.-D., Cherian, J., Sial, M. S., Álvarez-Otero, S., Comite, U., & Zia-Ud-Din, M. (2023). Green bond as a new determinant of sustainable green financing, energy efficiency investment, and economic growth: A global perspective. *Environmental Science and Pollution Research International*, 30(22), 61324–61339. DOI: 10.1007/s11356-021-18454-7 PMID: 34993809

Oyedele, O. O. (2023). Does green finance affect environmental performance?. *International Journal of Business Innovation*, e27631-e27631.

Park, H. &. (2020). Transition towards green banking: role of financial regulators and financial institutions. *Asian Journal of Sustainability and Social Responsibility*, .DOI: 10.1186/s41180-020-00034-3

Parveen, S. N., Nasreen, S., Allen, J. V., Kamm, K. B., Khan, S., Akter, S., Lopa, T. M., Zaman, K., El Arifeen, S., Luby, S. P., & Ram, P. K. (2018). Barriers to and motivators of handwashing behavior among mothers of neonates in rural Bangladesh. *BMC Public Health*, 18(1), 1–13. DOI: 10.1186/s12889-018-5365-1 PMID: 29642885

Putri, R. S. (2020). Impact of the COVID-19 pandemic on online home learning: An explorative study of primary schools in Indonesia. *International journal of advanced science and technology*, 29(5), 4809-4818.

Ramus, C. A., & Steger, U. (2000). The roles of supervisory support behaviors and environmental policy in employee "Ecoinitiatives" at leading-edge European companies. *Academy of Management Journal*, 43(4), 605–626. DOI: 10.2307/1556357

Rehman, S. U., Kraus, S., Shah, S. A., Khanin, D., & Mahto, R. V. (2021). Analyzing the relationship between green innovation and environmental performance in large manufacturing firms. *Technological Forecasting and Social Change*, 163, 120481. DOI: 10.1016/j.techfore.2020.120481

Rehman, S. U., Kraus, S., Shah, S. A., Khanin, D., & Mahto, R. V. (2021). Analyzing the relationship between green innovation and environmental performance in large manufacturing firms. *Technological Forecasting and Social Change*, 163, 120481. DOI: 10.1016/j.techfore.2020.120481

Risal, N., & Joshi, S. K. (2018). Measuring green banking practices on bank's environmental performance: Empirical evidence from Kathmandu valley. *Journal of Business and Social Sciences*, 2(1), 44–56. DOI: 10.3126/jbss.v2i1.22827

Salah, K. R.-F., Rehman, M. H. U., Nizamuddin, N., & Al-Fuqaha, A. (2019). Blockchain for AI: Review and open research challenges. *IEEE Access : Practical Innovations, Open Solutions*, 7, 10127–10149. DOI: 10.1109/ACCESS.2018.2890507

Sartika, S. H. (2021). Motivasi Belajar dan Regulasi Diri Mahasiswa Selama Pandemi Covid-19. Edunesia. *Jurnal Ilmiah Pendidikan*, 2(1), 260–271.

Scholtens, B. (2011). Corporate social responsibility in the international insurance industry. *Sustainable Development (Bradford)*, 19(2), 143–156. DOI: 10.1002/sd.513

Sharma, M., & Choubey, A. (2022). Green banking initiatives: A qualitative study on Indian banking sector. *Environment, Development and Sustainability*, 24(1), 293–319. DOI: 10.1007/s10668-021-01426-9 PMID: 33967597

Shee, H. M. (2018). The impact of cloud-enabled process integration on supply chain performance and firm sustainability: the moderating role of top management. *Supply Chain Management: An International Journal*, 23(6. Sinha, A. G. (2023). Green financing of renewable energy generation: Capturing the role of exogenous moderation for ensuring sustainable development. *Energy Economics*, 126, 107021.

Skouloudis, A. &. (2009). Environmental Quality Management. *Sustainability reporting in Greece: are we there yet?*, 19(1), 43-60.

Skouloudis, A., & Evangelinos, K. I. (2009). Sustainability reporting in Greece: Are we there yet? *Environmental Quality Management*, 19(1), 43–60. DOI: 10.1002/tqem.20235

Soelton, M. N. (2020). Recognizing the Role of Job Satisfaction in Predicting the Relationship Between Political Organization, Organizational Climate, and Organizational Culture on Organizational Citizenship Behaviour on Liquor Distributor Companies in Indonesia. *European Journal of Business and Management*, 12(13), 2222–1905.

Sunarsi, D. R. (2020). Effect of e-leadership style, organizational commitment and service quality towards indonesian school performance. *Systematic Reviews in Pharmacy*, 11, 472–481.

Sustainability reporting in Greece: are we there yet? (n.d.). *Skouloudis, A., & Evangelinos, K. I. (2009) Environmental Quality Management*, 19(1), 43-60.

Sutiah, S. S., Slamet, S., Shafqat, A., & Supriyono, S. (2020). Implementation of distance learning during the covid-19 pandemic in faculty of education and teacher training. *Cypriot Journal of Educational Science*, 15(1), 1204–1214. DOI: 10.18844/cjes.v15i5.5151

TILAHUN. L. B. (2023). THE EFFECT OF GREEN BANKING PRACTICES ON BANKS'ENVIRONMENTAL PERFORMANCE: THE CASE OF COOPERATIVE BANK OF OROMIA HAWASSA CITY BRANCHES. *Doctoral dissertation.*

Wahba, H., & Elsayed, K. (2015). The mediating effect of financial performance on the relationship between social responsibility and ownership structure. *Future Business Journal*, 1(1-2), 1–12. DOI: 10.1016/j.fbj.2015.02.001

Wang, Y., & Zhi, Q. (2016). The role of green finance in environmental protection: Two aspects of market mechanism and policies. *Energy Procedia*, 104, 311–316. DOI: 10.1016/j.egypro.2016.12.053

Zheng, G. W., Siddik, A. B., Masukujjaman, M., Fatema, N., & Alam, S. S. (2021). Green finance development in Bangladesh: The role of private commercial banks (PCBs). *Sustainability (Basel)*, 13(2), 795. DOI: 10.3390/su13020795

Zheng, S. L. (2021). Rethinking semantic segmentation from a sequence-to-sequence perspective with transformers. *In Proceedings of the IEEE/CVF conference on computer vision and pattern recognition*, pp. 6881-6890.

Zhixia, C. H., Hossen, M. M., Muzafary, S. S., & Begum, M. (2018). Green Banking for Environmental Sustainability-Present Status and Future Agenda: Experience from Bangladesh. *Asian Economic and Financial Review*, 8(5), 571–585. DOI: 10.18488/journal.aefr.2018.85.571.585

Chapter 15

A Bibliometric Analysis of Green Human Resource Management Practices

Shamaila Butt
https://orcid.org/0000-0003-1411-9590
Sohar University, Oman

Ibtisam Khalid
https://orcid.org/0009-0005-7317-636X
University of Sialkot, Pakistan

Muhammad Usman
https://orcid.org/0009-0009-4457-4210
University of Sialkot, Pakistan

Muhammad Farrukh Shahzad
https://orcid.org/0000-0002-6578-4139
Beijing University of Technology, China

Muhammad Ali Chohan
https://orcid.org/0000-0002-8860-0603
Research and Innovation Centre, Sohar University, Oman

Ain Naadia Binti Mazlan
https://orcid.org/0000-0001-5132-146X
University of Technology Malaysia, Malaysia

Tariq Mahmood
University of Sialkot, Pakistan

ABSTRACT

Green human resource management (GHRM) has been receiving more attention recently, although the discipline is still very new, and conceptual clarity has not yet been established. The VOSviewer software application was used to analyse a bibliometric evaluation of GHRM from 1913 to 2022 on Scopus and 574 papers on GHRM were examined. The goal of this study was to evaluate the GHRM field's volume, expanding tendency, global distribution, important journals, trailblazing authors, dominant nations, and dominant industries. In this work, word combinations were combined using logical operators, TITLE-ABS-KEY ("Green human resource management" OR "GHRM" OR "green HRM" OR "green HR" OR "Environmental

DOI: 10.4018/979-8-3693-6386-7.ch015

Human Resource" OR "eco-friendly Practices" OR "Environmental Training" OR "Green Training") AND (EXCLUDE (OA, "all")) AND (EXCLUDE (PUBYEAR, 2023)) AND (LIMIT-TO (LANGUAGE, "English")), thus expanding the gap. The review revealed that the GHRM is still a developing idea which aims to assist modern scholars.

1. INTRODUCTION

Over the past 20 years, green human resource management has received a lot of attention. Practices of Green human Resource are made with the achievement of sustainability of social and economic balance which remain consistent with organizational goals Dumont et al. (2017). The need of natural concerns to adhere to key norms and expectations through human asset management is highlighted by practices of GHRM. The increased adoption of green human resource strategies has brought attention to how multilayered this framework is (Tang et al., 2018). The practice of recruitment, hiring, assigning, and managing personnel is known as human resource management (HRM). Generally, HR is used for HRM. HRM practices are used to enforce the sustainable environmental practices and raise the level of commitment of employees. Organizations' HR department is usually responsible for the development, implementation, and monitoring the policies and their interaction with the (Yulianty & Senen, 2023). The phrase "human resources" was initially used to refer to all of the employees of an organisation in the early 1900s, and it became more popular in the 1960s. The HRM practices has the responsibility to manage workforce for the accomplishment of organizational objectives. The study conducted by Chowdhury et al. (2023), based on the literature review, there are different aspect to focus on for GHRM and previously this holistic approach was missing in this context.

The word green is used to refer environment in green human resource management in academics Oyewale (2019). According to Opatha (2014), GHRM practices are the strategies that aims to transform the work environment supportive for the organizations' sustainable objectives. Rana & Jain (2014) Describe GHRM as an employment model that aids business professionals in preserving, remembering, and retaining the talent they require to achieve their long-term objectives. Over the past two decades, environmental challenges have drawn more attention on a global scale. It is becoming more and more crucial to do study on the ways that diverse businesses contribute to the achievement of environmental goals as the global green movement gains popularity. The industrial sector must use environmentally friendly techniques in order to achieve the environmentally friendly Goals, according to Dissanayake, et. al, (2019). A green economy that is advantageous to the entire community could result from this. This project included human resource management, which is important for developing corporate culture in long term Sharma & Gupta (2015). Ecologically sound HR practices and the conservation of intellectual capital are two essential facets of (GHRM), both of which assist businesses in lowering their carbon footprints by enhancing productivity and cutting costs while also enhancing employee engagement and retention. The GHRM practice embrace the achievement of sustainable development goals by building green competence, employee involvement, better environment performance, and developing eco-friendly environment (Tahir et al., 2024; Alnajdawi, 2024)

Current study gives a complete insight about the role of green human resource management practices to boost the eco-friendly environment and behavior by the employees which increases the performance of environment. Further, organizations should adopt the major green human resource practices like enhancement of motivation, employee involvement, and green competence building for better performance. Therefore, organization can retain eco-friendly and committed employees who show ecological values and their objectives are compatible with the organization.

In relation to human resource management, being green means protecting and maintaining the environment, preventing or reducing environmental contamination, and creating spaces that mimic natural settings. As a result, if a person follows these principles, they are referred to as "green employees." Haden and Saeed claimed that although though GHRM incorporates several practices, such as HRM, it advances since it is more focused on sustainability and waste minimization. Systems, practices, and policies which make the employees of the organization to adopt green Policies, practices, and systems that make green employees which benefit he organization and businesses. According to Ren (, HRM is referred to be "Green Human Resource Management" when it implements various environmental protection measures. Renwick examined the literature that is currently accessible and focused on the Ability-Motivation-Opportunity (AMO) theory's function people management process of GHRM. The GHRM practices are related to three factors: inspiring green personnel, fostering green talent, and offering green chances.

The expansion of the global economy over the past two centuries has been a sign of human affluence and longevity. However, it is becoming more obvious how different industrial practices affect the environment, as seen by pollution and the buildup of waste and residues Jackson et al. 2011). Every country and region in the world are using mixture of HR practices and by adopting GHRM they respond to influence the multilevel ways (Malik et al., 2022; Raut et al., 2020)). In view of the conclusions of past literature on convergence and divergence, this research offers a viewpoint that in the region of Asia, there is a mixture of unique business systems which respond by the various HR practices

Indirectly through attempts to reduce carbon emissions at the global level and directly by addressing the untidiness of the effects of extreme weather events, climate change provides a new set of difficulties (IPCC 2018). It is vital for society to get ready for and adapt to new eventualities as a result of climate change since it will cause socioeconomic systems to undergo previously unheard-of transformations Winn et al. (2011). The case study conducted by (Sujata et al., 2024; Al-Alawneh et al., 2024) showed that green training and development and HR practices showed a positive relation with sustainability, commitment with top management, and organizational performance and further give a holistic approach and new ways how to implement the GHRM practices in different sectors.

HRM may be act as the tool of organization that incorporates people into the sustainability of the environment dealing with the bundle of activities. These are based on the social resources of the functions of organization (Martínez- del-Río et al. 2012; Renwick et al. 2013). Recent studies describe that for fostering green innovation can face difficulties but those organizations adopting sustainability with green expertise, are using AI and digital platforms (Saddar 2023). This is implied from recruiting through termination throughout the employee life cycle (Benn et al. 2015; Jabbour et al. 2010; Zibarras and Coan 2015).

Current research uses a bibliometric analysis which provide the evolution of GHRM from 2010-2022 taking into account the growing relevance and attention towards the achievement of GHRM. Using statistical tools to analyze scientific output quantitatively is known as "bibliometric analysis (Ellegaard and Wallin 2015). They bring a quantifiable rigour to the particular evaluation of the literature by focusing on several areas of awareness that donate to the description in research, such as journals, publications, languages, nations, and organizations (Ellegaard and Wallin 2015; Zupic and Cˇ ater 2015). Due to development of new measures in the contemporary digital age, scientific work can be analyzed according to variety of ways (Ellegaard and Wallin 2015). These bibliometric techniques could make evaluations more thorough by introducing a methodical, transparent, and repeatable review procedure. By directing the researcher to the most important publications and outlining the research area which is helpful tool in reviewing the literature, mitigating the subjective bias. Additionally, they enable researchers to draw conclusions from combined the data of bibliographic generated through some other researchers through collaboration, citation, or writing (Zupic and Cater 2015). Researchers can examine the field's structure, social networks, and key issues by analyzing this aggregate data (Zupic and Cater 2015). The VOS viewer software package will support the bibliometric analysis in current research. The objectives of this study are to: (1) classify research reviews; (2) plot the considered subjects; (3) detect with analyzing the sequential development of the concept; and (4) use of construct as useful tool instead just using it as academic tool for bibliometric studies.

The procedures required to collect the data and later its analysis are comprehensive in process section of this research. The material gathered from the search of keyword and the mapping of bibliometric which is then separated in the section of result that showing both techniques in results. Lastly the goals of the paper are described in conclusion, its key findings, limitations, and it makes suggestions for further GHRM research.

Table 1.

Authors	Database	Duration	Paper Type	Themes	Document Analyzed	No. of Documents	Future research Agendas
Jéssica Fachada, Teresa Rebelo, Paulo Lourenço, Isabel Dimas and Helena Martins	Web of Science	2010-2020	Bibliometric Analysis	Green Human Resource Management	Article	143	analysis of the relationship among GHRM practices and other features of organization, such as GSC and environmental certification systems, also an important way forward
Muhammad Hamza Khan & Syaharizatul Noorizwan Muktar	Scopus	2008-2020	Bibliometric Analysis	Green Human Resource Management	Articles, conference papers, review papers, book, conference review, other sources	147	bibliometric analysis using other databases like google scholar and Web of Science which will add more information regarding this field

2. METHODOLOGY

A bibliometric analysis study builds its understanding of worldwide research trends in a particular topic on the outputs of academic literature databases. Bibliometric analysis papers differ from review papers in this way (Wang & Zhi, Energy Proc, 2016), which focus on a specific issue's most recent developments, challenges, and potential future paths (Wang & Zhi, 2016; vsky and Raghavan, 2018).

2.1. Search Strategy and Source of Data:

A sample of papers from the Scopus database that were published between 1913 and 2022 is utilized to ensure that the goals are met. The Scopus was chosen because it collects the publications with the greatest influence in the social sciences. A expressive analysis of Scopus papers from 1913 to 2022 made up the first stage. The search terms "Green human resource management" OR "GHRM" OR "green HRM" OR "green HR" OR "Environmental Human Resource" OR "eco-friendly Practices" OR "Environmental Training" OR "Green Training" focus on the entire subject area. The entirety of the textual information on green human resource management has been provided. Data has only been available for articles. The year (2023) was specifically excluded under the exclusion criteria. The only language chosen for use when working on green human resource management is English. The variables were chosen from the methodology, abstract, title, and keywords. The search term and list have been preserved in the Scopus database. The VOS viewer afterwards exported two files in bibtex and CSV. There are 574 articles available for search in the Scopus database. VOS viewer, a completely free computer programme for bibliometric mapping, is chosen for visualization. It pays particular attention to how maps are represented graphically.

2.2. Flow Chart

Scopus which is the largest citation and abstract database of academic literature that has passed peer review, Scopus, was used to select the sample for this study. Around 84% of the literature is the same in both the Scopus and Web of Science databases. With regard to the current research topic, the selected database aids in both identifying the significant work completed throughout time and having a better understanding of the historical development of Green HRM.

utilizing related keywords, facts collection, data cleaning and data formatting, and data analysis utilizing relevant technology are all steps in the current review's data collection process. 574 published papers that were carefully and methodically included and removed from the data set that formed the basis of the study. The study employed the same methodology as the bibliometric analysis of Green HRM.

To ensure that only peer reviewed articles, journal articles and review papers were taken depending on the kind of document. In the end, each article was examined separately, and any that didn't apply were withdrew. After reviewing the abstracts, papers were removed. Research that did not fall under the study's purview were excluded. The flowchart below describes the structure for data collection.

Figure 1. Research process adapted in the study (Author's compilation)

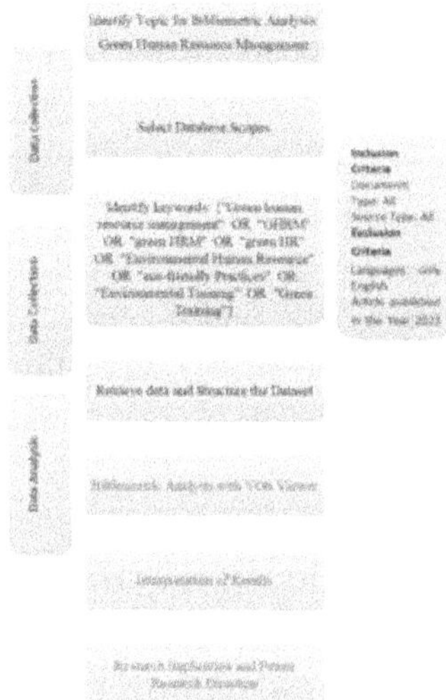

2.3. Data Analysis

Figure 2. Articles publications

There was a total of 574 articles published throughout the course of 110 years. The initial article was released in 1913. According to the following graph, the majority of the articles were published between 2019 and 2022. There have reportedly been publications in Green HRM every year since 1913, however a few years, specifically 2018, 2019, 2020, 2021, and 2022, obviously showed tremendous growth.

After applying the criteria of inclusion and exclusion, further analysis is carried out using a dataset of 594 out of 650 articles. Bibliometric analysis is carried out using the statistical program Bibliometric, which is accessible through both VOS

Viewer and R-Studio. These tools enable the retrieval of applicable bibliometric material, such as the most popular authors, search terms, and countries. The research is done from 1913 until 2022. The extended time frame makes it simpler to study the development of the concept. With the VOS viewer, the dataset may be graphically represented, which also makes it easy to comprehend huge data sets. The bibliometric maps are simple to look at and comprehend thanks to its robust user interface.

The analysis of the 574-record dataset highlights the evolution of the research literature, current trends of research, and potential areas of future investigation. Consequently, the data in the following section includes information on the trends of publication, subject matters, related sources, subject matters, author data, and data thematic organization.

2.4. Main information, publication trend and sources

The major data on publication trends is shown in Table 2, which shows that over the course of research period, gradual growth has been observed in the number of publications, participation of nations, and collaboration of author.

Table 2. Main information

Description	Results
MAIN INFORMATION ABOUT DATA	
Timespan	1913:2022
Sources (Journals, Books, etc)	335
Documents	581
Annual Growth Rate %	4.74
Document Average Age	6.92
Average citations per doc	21.64
References	30189
DOCUMENT CONTENTS	
Keywords Plus (ID)	2002
Author's Keywords (DE)	1495
AUTHORS	
Authors	1447
Authors of single-authored docs	84
AUTHORS COLLABORATION	
Single-authored docs	94
Co-Authors per Doc	3.01

continued on following page

Table 2. Continued

Description	Results
International co-authorships %	27.88
DOCUMENT TYPES	
Article	446
Book	4
book chapter	32
conference paper	76
conference review	1
Editorial	1
Note	1
Retracted	1
Review	18

The selected articles span the years 1913–2022. Research on Green HRM grew starting in 2014. This indicates that beginning in the 2014-time frame, the publication numbers also began to progressively and reliably rise, as shown in the accompanying graph. The growth in research in this area may be related to the rise in measures done on a global scale to adapt to and mitigate climate change. Additionally, since 2017, academics and other global stakeholders have started to pay closer attention to sustainability and its components. The findings also indicate a dearth of early 2013–2010 articles.

2.5. Three-Field Plot

Figure 3. Plot

2.6. Most Relevant Source

Figure 4. Most relevant source

The graph above demonstrates that the journal of cleaner production has published the most articles, with 38; the international journal of manpower has published the second-highest number of articles, with 23; and corporate social responsibility and the environment published 14, the third highest number of articles.

2.7. Annual Scientific Production

According to the graph above, article manufacture began in 1918 at a relatively slow rate but abruptly picked up in 2020. The journal with the most article publications is highlighted in various colors as seen above.

Figure 5. Affiliations production over time

2.8. Most Relevant Affiliations

Table 3. Most relevant affiliations

Affiliation	Articles
UNIVERSITI SAINS MALAYSIA	15
UNIVERSITY OF THE PUNJAB	13
UNIVERSITI MALAYSIA TERENGGANU	12
XI'AN JIAOTONG UNIVERSITY	12
MONTPELLIER BUSINESS SCHOOL	9
EASTERN MEDITERRANEAN UNIVERSITY	8
UNIVERSITY OF TEHRAN	8
SUAN SUNANDHA RAJABHAT UNIVERSITY	7
ABU DHABI UNIVERSITY	6
AMITY UNIVERSITY	6

The aforementioned graph reveals that Universiti Sains Malaysia has the most publications (15), followed by University of the Punjab with 13 and Universiti Malaysia Terengganu and Xi'an Jiaotong University with 12 respectively.

2.9. Average Citation per Year

Figure 6. Average citations per year

The figure above shows the average citation per year which reaches a maximum at 9.

2.10. Most Relevant Authors

Figure 7. Most relevant authors

The above data reveals that the authors Jabbour CJC and Yusliza My have the most articles, totaling 13, while Ramayah T comes in second with 8. After them, HO TH and Yong JY are third with 06, and so on.

2.11. Co-occurrence

Figure 8. Co-occurrence

The normal VOSViewer criterion, in which repeated keywords are chosen at least six times, lead to in 42 of the 1492 keywords discovered being exhibited (see Figure). The analysis includes keywords and the option of VOS Viewer for including terms that often appears in the title of bibliographic reference. The decision was made because the bibliographic map comprises additional information and enables more investigation of sample.

2.12. Co-Authors

Figure 9. Co-authors

The co-authors' VOSViewer visualization reveals that Pakistan, China, Malaysia, and Australia have the highest densities.

3. RESULTS AND DISCUSSION

Current research investigated by performing bibliometric mapping related to the development of GHRM practices during 1913s converging primarily on the exploring the literature and the most recurrent topics, by performing keyword search bibliometric mapping.

Following a discussion of the primary contributions made by the keyword search and VOSviewer, the stage of GHRM's evolution will be identified.

The construct's recent flow, which began in 2018, may be identified through keyword search. Investigating from variety of other fields (such as psychology, management, and environmental engineering) are playing a vital role for the devotion of GHRM. It is widely known as EM. However, there is no broadly known description of GHRM. (Benevene and Buonomo 2020; Ren et al. 2018). Though more analysis is considerable in other sustainability aspects like circular economy, additional explanation that put more weight on the environmental factor (Ren et al. 2018).

Current research focuses on the fact that the bibliographic coupling map of references signifies flawless circular figure when it comes to the findings of the analyses performed in VOSviewer. This shows that GHRM is a heterogeneous topic of the stud and that the streams of literature are not yet totally separate and well-defined. However, four groups of things that were connected to one another emerged from the studies, in accordance with the software's assumption of a similarity criterion (Van Eck and Waltman 2010, 2014). Four clusters, blue (application of GHRM as an aspect of EM), red (repercussions on employees), green (repercussions at the structural / organizational level), and yellow (first do reviews, models, and then measures)—could be distinguished by a distinctive theme. All clusters do, however, contain some publications that stray from their primary subject, it should be emphasized. For illustration, the article by Moktadir et al. (2019), related to green cluster and focuses mostly on the effects of GHRM at the organizational level while also examining the origins of GHRM. This may be explained by the fact that the literature on GHRM still lacks a representative representation of the research of antecedents; in contrast, the GHRM study effects at organizational level and dominates (Benevene and Buonomo 2020). The yellow cluster is particularly misleading, despite the fact that all clusters exhibit considerable overlap. While it brings together literature reviews on the one hand (Jackson et al. 2011; Ren et al. 2018; Renwick et al. 2013; Tariq et al. 2016) and theoretical developments (Renwick et al. 2016), However, it also incorporates empirical investigations that are either quantitative or qualitative. The validity of HRM measurement scale is important (Tang et al. 2018) on the evaluation of adopted green practices (Masri and Jaaron 2017) and on environmentally friendly actions taken at work (Rayner and Morgan, 2018) or away from work (Bombiak and Marciniuk-Kluska 2018).

Compared to blue and yellow clusters, the articles mentioning the red and most recent clusters are red and green, according to the temporal evolution maps. Although there isn't a very clear temporal transition revealed by the keyword map, it does show that recent articles have a tendency to concentrate on the attitudinal measurement, while the previous terminologies (such as implementation, EM, and sustainable operations) show a real GHRM concept, which is more limited to its execution in organizations as a management system or tool for environment. The literature on GHRM was dominated by writers like Jabbour, Renwick, and Teixeira by the middle of the decade, and they saw it as an instrument for the achievement of sustainable environment. As a result, the efforts put forward were primarily directed at studying and analyzing the advantages of GHRM practices in regard to environmental performance. On the other hand, writers who have lately made a name for themselves are part of a research stream that views GHRM as a goal in and of itself, able to influence attitudes and behaviors that have an impact on organizational performance. The fact that the majority of empirical investigations are carried out in developing nations like Malaysia and India is another important consideration. As a result, GHRM appears to play prominent part in these scenarios because of the large industries that predominates in these nations and its significant demand for natural resources and CO2 emissions. The introduction of GHRM will aid in the preservation of natural resources and a decrease in greenhouse (Yong et al. 2019a).

Ren et al.'s (2018), the definition of GHRM helped to define the boundaries of the concept in respect to other practices of HRM specialties by reinforcing HRM as a expressive phenomenon to comprehend the linkages among the impact of environment of organizational activities and systems of HRM. One of these is sustainable human resource management (HRM), which refers to the triple bottom line strategy and eliminates the environmental component (Ahmad 2015).

Future study appears to be relevant in the delineation of boundaries in connection to other HRM specialties, such as Sustainable HRM. In this regard, it is clear that the diversity of HRM measurements reflects the absence of a shared definition of the term. For instance, we observe authors that use tactical HRM measuring tools (Paillé et al. 2014). Let's take note of Tang et al.'s (2018) scale contribution, which emphasized the ecological aspect of HRM practices in this context. In the future, it will be crucial to validate the instrument outside of the Chinese environment.

In each cluster, we could see from our study that there is no shared definition, but there is a significant tendency to include GA in the definition. Particularly in the red cluster, clusters typically utilize the definition proposed by Renwick et al. (2013) (Dumont et al. 2017; Kim et al. 2019; Pham et al. 2019b, 2020; Saeed et al. 2019; Singh et al. 2020). However, this definition is also used to the yellow (Roscoe et al. 2019; Tang et al. 2018), blue (Obeidat et al. 2020; Yu et al. 2020), and green (Longoni et al. 2018) clusters. Based on our research, we were unable to draw the conclusion that a specific cluster is the only one having GHRM practices. For instance, the yellow cluster (Masri and Jaaron 2017; Tang et al. 2018; Ren et al. 2018; Renwick et al. 2016; Roscoe et al. 2019) and blue cluster (Guerci et al., 2016) both contain green recruitment and selection practices. The various clusters also include additional practices including employee empowerment, performance reviews, incentive and pay, and green training and development. We focus on what appears to be the primary differentiator of these clusters the study of the impact of organizational antecedents and consequents on green practices and GHRM implementation rather than the green practices connected to particular clusters. In terms of the methodologies, empirical publications are primarily found in the blue, red, and green clusters, with quantitative research outpacing qualitative studies. Data from questionnaires and interviews are combined in mixed-method articles like Paillé et al. (2014) from the yellow cluster, Pham et al. (2019b) from the red cluster, and Yu et al. (2020) from the blue cluster. Regarding review publications, only one bibliometric analysis study on GHRM was discovered based on our literature review (Khan and Muktar 2020), and it also employs VOSviewer bibliometric maps.

CONCLUSIONS AND FUTURE DIRECTIONS

The significance of GHRM practices in recent times in developing areas is emphasized by the bibliometric study of published literature between 2013 and 2023, from the last half of the decade. The main objective of GHRM practices is to effectively contribute to the development of environment-friendly paths and to solve ecological and environmental challenges from the perspective of an organization, among the significant threats that mankind is facing is covered by SHRM specially. This section of the chapter highlights the main contribution by synthesizing the main points. Further, the discussion reinforces the value for both practitioners as well as for academics. It also recommends the practical application of the results. This literature will provide readers with a satisfying closure and practical implication of findings and further the utility and relevance in guiding the practices of GHRM.

The goals of this paper have been achieved with the identification of stages of development of the construct and mapping up the available literature streams for implementing GHRM practices, As a strand of EM, its outcomes at the employee level and organizational level, mapping the contributions of GHRM during current decade. The findings revealed that adoption of green practices by organizations there is a significant decrease in environmental pollution and water contamination. Despite the focus on the effects of GHRM at work, due to the transferability of green environmental concerns, it is extended beyond the workplace settings used for personal life and vice versa. The fact that the construct has evolved beyond a concept that was solely focused on EM shows that personnel who are endowed with distinctive strategic value and their crucial role in organizational sustainability are taken into consideration. This is where the resource-based view (Barney, 1991) provides a theoretical contribution (Yusliza et al. 2017).

Despite the contributions made by this work, it is vital to draw attention to several shortcomings and efforts made to address them. The information we extrapolated might be biased because we were only able to access a small portion of the literature on GHRM by using one database, the WOS. The work of Khan and Muktar (2020), which employed the Scopus database, produced results that are converging with ours, a finding that confirms the reliability of the results obtained. However, in the category of bibliometric reviews. Additionally, we believe that the current bibliometric review advances the work of Khan and Muktar (2020) insofar as it crosses two similarity maps that enable the mapping of GHRM research lines and the identification of the topics that comprise them, as it also seeks to determine the stage of the construct's evolution.

We found that significant research potential is untapped for GHRM regardless of the increasing interest of researchers on the subject. We therefore offer some suggestions for further research based on the discussion of the results. It's crucial to arrive at a more universal definition of GHRM (Ari et al. 2020) and to create a clearer, more universal vocabulary for the build. Therefore, the researcher is focusing on the need for research that how GHRM practices are related to other concepts in the same area, with various methodologies being put out for a better understanding of the differences and similarities of various constructs. the many methodologies that have been put out to better understand the similarities and differences between the various constructions. As we know Renwick et al. (2013; Bahuguna et al., 2023)

, known as the first creator of a systematic review of concepts had made it already. He has pointed to GHRM as a methodology that enables moving beyond the narrow perception of the economic side and places the well-being of all stakeholders as the prime objective of the HRM. t will be easier to define, conceptualize, and measure GHRM by drawing boundaries with other HRM disciplines. On the other hand, it is pertinent to emphasize the importance of further research on the contextualization of GHRM because multiple stakeholders can influence it. Such as municipal corporations, regulatory authorities and legislators that can impose restrictions and demands regarding the implementation of GHRM (Ren et al. 2018:). The leaders and employees are also included in these stakeholders who are most influential organizational actors. We also draw attention to the need to delve further into GHRM's antecedents, particularly those at the employee level (Obeidat et al. 2020). As developed countries are not much focused in recent research, most of the work is focused on emerging nations. It is need of time to study the GHRM practices in developed countries too.

A crucial next step is to continue the analysis of the connections between GHRM and other organizational components like GSC and environmental certification systems. Organizational practices have to be forecasted on the complex agendas of performance goals beyond the goals of HRM. Similarly, knowing how Green HRM practices has interaction with and impact on other facets of the institution helps to analyze the impacts of specific practices of managing human resources of organization in real life. Finally, we draw attention to the fact that big data and artificial intelligence have increasingly dominated how we work and that exploring the benefits of their interaction with GHRM is an exciting new area of research.

REFERENCES

Aggarwal, S., & Kumar, A. (2022). Dealing with a New Normal 'E-leadership': A Study Using Bibliometric Analysis and Content Analysis. *Vision (Basel)*, •••, 09722629221130592. DOI: 10.1177/09722629221130592

Alnajdawi, S. M. (2024, January). The Impact of GHRM Practices on Sustainable Development Goals. In *2024 ASU International Conference in Emerging Technologies for Sustainability and Intelligent Systems (ICETSIS)* (pp. 165-170). IEEE. DOI: 10.1109/ICETSIS61505.2024.10459585

Ari, E., Karatepe, O. M., Rezapouraghdam, H., & Avci, T. (2020). A Conceptual Model for Green Human Resource Management: Indicators, Differential Pathways, and Multiple Pro-Environmental Outcomes. *Sustainability (Basel)*, 12(17), 7089. DOI: 10.3390/su12177089

Bahuguna, P. C., Srivastava, R., & Tiwari, S. (2023). Two-decade journey of green human resource management research: A bibliometric analysis. *Benchmarking*, 30(2), 585–602. DOI: 10.1108/BIJ-10-2021-0619

Barney, J. B. (1991). Firm Resources and Sustained Competitive Advantage. *Journal of Management*, 17(1), 99–120. DOI: 10.1177/014920639101700108

Bombiak, E., & Marciniuk-Kluska, A. (2018). Green Human Resource Management as a Tool for the Sustainable Development of Enterprises: Polish Young Company Experience. *Sustainability (Basel)*, 10(6), 1739. DOI: 10.3390/su10061739

Chowdhury, S. R., Mendy, J., & Rahman, M. (2023). A systematic literature review of GHRM: Organizational sustainable performance reimagined using a new holistic framework. *Sustainability (Basel)*, 15(9), 7513. DOI: 10.3390/su15097513

Dumont, J., Shen, J., & Deng, X. (2017). Effects of Green HRM Practices on Employee Workplace Green Behavior: The Role of Psychological Green Climate and Employee Green Values: Effect of Green HRM on Employee Workplace Green Behavior. *Human Resource Management*, 56(4), 613–627. DOI: 10.1002/hrm.21792

Guerci, M., Montanari, F., Scapolan, A., & Epifanio, A. (2016). Green and Nongreen Recruitment Practices for Attracting Job Applicants: Exploring Independent and Interactive Effects. *International Journal of Human Resource Management*, 27(2), 129–150. DOI: 10.1080/09585192.2015.1062040

Jabbour, C. J. C., Fernando, C. A. S., & Nagano, M. S. (2010). Contributions of HRM throughout the Stages of Environmental Management: Methodological Triangulation Applied to Companies in Brazil. *International Journal of Human Resource Management*, 21(7), 1049–1089. DOI: 10.1080/09585191003783512

Jackson, S. E., Renwick, D. W. S., Charbel, J. C. J., & Muller-Camen, M. (2011). State-of-the-Art and Future Directions for Green Human Resource Management: Introduction to the Special Issue. *German Journal of Human Resource Management: Zeitschrift Für Personalforschung*, 25(2), 99–116. DOI: 10.1177/239700221102500203

Khan, M. H., & Muktar, S. N. (2020). A Bibliometric Analysis of Green Human Resource Manage- ment Based on Scopus Platform. *Cogent Business & Management*, 7(1), 1831165. DOI: 10.1080/23311975.2020.1831165

Kim, Y. J., Kim, W. G., Choi, H.-M., & Phetvaroon, K. (2019). The Effect of Green Human Resource Management on Hotel Employees' Eco-Friendly Behavior and Environmental Performance. *International Journal of Hospitality Management*, 76, 83–93. DOI: 10.1016/j.ijhm.2018.04.007

Longoni, A., Luzzini, D., & Guerci, M. (2018). Deploying Environmental Management Across Functions: The Relationship Between Green Human Resource Management and Green Supply Chain Management. *Journal of Business Ethics*, 151(4), 1081–1095. DOI: 10.1007/s10551-016-3228-1

Malik, A., Pereira, V., Budhwar, P., Froese, F. J., Minbaeva, D., Sun, J., Nguyen, A. T., & Xue, S. (2022). Multilevel relational influences on HRM practices: A cross-country comparative reflective review of HRM practices in Asia. *Asian Business & Management*, 21(5), 745–779. DOI: 10.1057/s41291-022-00208-z

Martínez-del-Río, J., Céspedes-Lorente, J., & Carmona-Moreno, E. (2012). High-Involvement Work Practices and Environmen- tal Capabilities: How HIWPS Create Environmentally Based Sustainable Competitive Advantages. *Human Resource Management*, 51(6), 827–850. DOI: 10.1002/hrm.21505

Masri, H. A., & Jaaron, A. A. M. (2017). Assessing Green Human Resources Management Practices in Palestinian Manufacturing Context: An Empirical Study. *Journal of Cleaner Production*, 143, 474–489. DOI: 10.1016/j.jclepro.2016.12.087

Moktadir, M., Dwivedi, A., Ali, S. M., Paul, S. K., Kabir, G., & Madaan, J. (2019). Antecedents for Greening the Workforce: Implications for Green Human Resource Management. *International Journal of Manpower*, 41(7), 1135–1153. DOI: 10.1108/IJM-07-2019-0354

Opatha, H., & Anton Arulrajah, A. (2014). Green Human Resource Management: Simplified General Reflections. *International Business Research*, 7(8), 101. DOI: 10.5539/ibr.v7n8p101

Paillé, P., Chen, Y., Boiral, O., & Jin, J. (2014). The Impact of Human Resource Management on Environmental Performance: An Employee-Level Study. *Journal of Business Ethics*, 121(3), 451–466. DOI: 10.1007/s10551-013-1732-0

Pham, N. T., Hoang, H. T., & Quyen, P. T. P. (2019a). Green Human Resource Management: A Comprehensive Review and Future Research Agenda. *International Journal of Manpower*, 41(7), 845–878. DOI: 10.1108/IJM-07-2019-0350

Pham, N. T., & Thanh, T. V. (2020). The Role of Green Human Resource Management in Driving Hotel's Environmental Performance: Interaction and Mediation Analysis. *International Journal of Hospitality Management*, 88, 102392. DOI: 10.1016/j.ijhm.2019.102392

Pham, N. T., Tučková, Z., & Chiappetta Jabbour, C. J. (2019b). Greening the Hospitality Industry: How Do Green Human Resource Management Practices Influence Organizational Citizenship Behavior in Hotels? A Mixed-Methods Study. *Tourism Management*, 72, 386–399. DOI: 10.1016/j.tourman.2018.12.008

Raut, R. D., Gardas, B., Luthra, S., Narkhede, B., & Kumar Mangla, S. (2020). Analysing green human resource management indicators of automotive service sector. *International Journal of Manpower*, 41(7), 925–944. DOI: 10.1108/IJM-09-2019-0435

Ren, S., Tang, G., & Jackson, S. E. (2018). Green Human Resource Management Research in Emergence: A Review and Future Directions. *Asia Pacific Journal of Management*, 35, 769–803. DOI: 10.1007/s10490-017-9532-1

Renwick, D. W. S., Charbel, J. C. J., Muller-Camen, M., Redman, T., & Wilkinson, A. (2016). Contemporary Developments in Green (Environmental) HRM Scholarship. *International Journal of Human Resource Management*, 27(2), 114–128. DOI: 10.1080/09585192.2015.1105844

Renwick, D. W. S., Redman, T., & Maguire, S. (2013). Green Human Resource Management: A Review and Research Agenda*: Green Human Resource Management. *International Journal of Management Reviews*, 15(1), 1–14. DOI: 10.1111/j.1468-2370.2011.00328.x

Saddar, N. (2023).. . *Exploring the Role of Artificial Intelligence and Big Data in the Human Resource Management Process: An Overview of Benefits, Risks, and Ethical Implications.*, 5(1), 12–27.

Saeed, B. B., Afsar, B., Hafeez, S., Khan, I., Tahir, M., & Afridi, M. A. (2019). Promoting Employee's Proenvironmental Behavior through Green Human Resource Management Practices. *Corporate Social Responsibility and Environmental Management*, 26(2), 424–438. DOI: 10.1002/csr.1694

Singh, S. K., Del Giudice, M., Chierici, R., & Graziano, D. (2020). Green Innovation and Environmental Performance: The Role of Green Transformational Leadership and Green Human Resource Management. *Technological Forecasting and Social Change*, 150, 119762. DOI: 10.1016/j.techfore.2019.119762

Tahir, A. H., Umer, M., Nauman, S., Abbass, K., & Song, H. (2024). Sustainable development goals and green human resource management: A comprehensive review of environmental performance. *Journal of Environmental Management*, 370, 122495. DOI: 10.1016/j.jenvman.2024.122495 PMID: 39332294

Tang, G., Chen, Y., Jiang, Y., Paillé, P., & Jia, J. (2018). Green Human Resource Management Practices: Scale Development and Validity. *Asia Pacific Journal of Human Resources*, 56(1), 31–55. DOI: 10.1111/1744-7941.12147

Teixeira, A. A., Jose Chiappetta Jabbour, C., Beatriz Lopes de Sousa Jabbour, A., Latan, H., & Henrique Caldeira de Oliveira, J. (2016). Green Training and Green Supply Chain Management: Evidence from Brazilian Firms. *Journal of Cleaner Production*, 116, 170–176. DOI: 10.1016/j.jclepro.2015.12.061

Van Eck, N. J., & Waltman, L. (2014). Visualizing Bibliometric Networks. In Ding, Y., Rousseau, R., & Wolfram, D. (Eds.), *Measuring Scholarly Impact* (pp. 285–320). Springer International Publishing. DOI: 10.1007/978-3-319-10377-8_13

Winn, M., Kirchgeorg, M., Griffiths, A., Linnenluecke, M. K., & Günther, E. (2011). Impacts from Climate Change on Organizations: A Conceptual Foundation. *Business Strategy and the Environment*, 20(3), 157–173. DOI: 10.1002/bse.679

Yong, J. Y., Yusliza, M.-Y., & Fawehinmi, O. O. (2019a). Green Human Resource Management: A Systematic Literature Review from 2007 to 2019. *Benchmarking*, 27(7), 2005–2027. DOI: 10.1108/BIJ-12-2018-0438

Yu, W., Chavez, R., Feng, M., Wong, C. Y., & Fynes, B. (2020). Green Human Resource Management and Environmental Cooperation: An Ability-Motivation-Opportunity and Contingency Perspective. *International Journal of Production Economics*, 219, 224–235. DOI: 10.1016/j.ijpe.2019.06.013

Yulianty, P. D., & Senen, S. H. (2023). Analysis Systematic Literature Review: The Study of HRM Transformation Into Digital-Based GHRM Future Research Agenda. *West Science Business and Management*, 1(05), 553–561. DOI: 10.58812/wsbm.v1i05.517

Yusliza, M.-Y., Othman, N. Z., & Charbel, J. C. J. (2017). Deciphering the Implementation of Green Human Resource Management in an Emerging Economy. *Journal of Management Development*, 36(10), 1230–1246. DOI: 10.1108/JMD-01-2017-0027

Compilation of References

Awotunde, J. B., Adeniyi, E. A., Ogundokun, R. O., & Ayo, F. E. (2021). Application of big data with Fintech in financial services. *Fintech with Artificial Intelligence, Big Data, and Blockchain*, 107–132. DOI: 10.1007/978-981-33-6137-9_3

Gera, R., Chadha, P., Saxena, A., & Dixit, S. (2023). A scientometric and bibliometric review of impacts and application of artificial intelligence and Fintech for Financial Inclusion. *Artificial Intelligence, Fintech, and Financial Inclusion*, 82–111. DOI: 10.1201/9781003125204-7

Makhija, P., Chacko, E., & Sinha, M. (2021). Transforming Financial Sector Through Financial Literacy and Fintech Revolution. *Financial Inclusion in Emerging Markets*, 239–255.

Makina, D. (2019). The potential of FinTech in enabling financial inclusion. *Extending Financial Inclusion in Africa*, 299–318

Orogun, A., & Onyekwelu, B. (2019). Predicting consumer behaviour in digital market: a machine learning approach.

Ray, S., Paul, S., & Miglani, S. (2023). Exploring the regulatory contexts of Fintech innovation for Financial Inclusion. *Artificial Intelligence, Fintech, and Financial Inclusion*, 39–51.

Sahid, A., & Maleh, Y. (2024). Emerging Fintech and Digital Money. *Advances in Emerging Financial Technology and Digital Money*, 1–24.

Yanting, Z., & Ali, M. (2023). Artificial Intelligence, Digital Finance, and Financial Inclusion: A conceptual framework. *Financial Inclusion Across Asia: Bringing Opportunities for Businesses*, 77–85.

Abbasi, K., Alam, A., Brohi, N. A., Brohi, I. A., & Nasim, S. J. E. L. (2021). P2P lending Fintechs and SMEs' access to finance. *204*, 109890.

Abellán Álvarez, I., Gramlich, V., & Sedlmeir, J. (2024). Unsealing the secrets of blockchain consensus: A systematic comparison of the formal security of proof-of-work and proof-of-stake. Proceedings of the 39th ACM/SIGAPP Symposium on Applied Computing, Akbar, N. A., Muneer, A., ElHakim, N., & Fati, S. M. (2021). Distributed hybrid double-spending attack prevention mechanism for proof-of-work and proof-of-stake blockchain consensuses. *Future Internet*, 13(11), 285.

Abu Jamie, N. H., Abu-Jamie, T. N., & Al-Absy, M. S. (2024). Advances in AI and their effects on Finance and Economic Analysis. *The AI Revolution: Driving Business Innovation and Research*, 507–523

Adedokun, M. W., & Ağa, M. (2023). Financial inclusion: A pathway to economic growth in Sub-Saharan African economies. *International Journal of Finance & Economics*, 28(3), 2712–2728. DOI: 10.1002/ijfe.2559

Adi, E., Anwar, A., Baig, Z., & Zeadally, S. (2020). Machine learning and data analytics for the IoT. *Neural Computing & Applications*, 32(20), 16205–16233. DOI: 10.1007/s00521-020-04874-y

Afjal, M. (2023). Bridging the financial divide: A Bibliometric analysis on the role of digital financial services within FinTech in enhancing financial inclusion and economic development. *Humanities & Social Sciences Communications*, 10(1), 645. DOI: 10.1057/s41599-023-02086-y

Afshan, S., Leong, K. Y., Najmi, A., Razi, U., Lelchumanan, B., & Cheong, C. W. H. (2024). Fintech advancements for financial resilience: Analysing exchange rates and digital currencies during oil and financial risk. *Resources Policy*, 88, 104432. DOI: 10.1016/j.resourpol.2023.104432

Agarwal, S., & Zhang, J. (2020). FinTech, Lending and Payment Innovation: A Review. *Asia-Pacific Journal of Financial Studies*, 49(3), 353–367. DOI: 10.1111/ajfs.12294

Agency, A. Z. D. (Producer). (2022). nepad.org. Retrieved from https://www.nepad.org/blog/unlocking-potential-of-africas-smes-using-emerging-technologies-africa

Aggarwal, S., & Kumar, A. (2022). Dealing with a New Normal 'E-leadership': A Study Using Bibliometric Analysis and Content Analysis. *Vision (Basel)*, •••, 09722629221130592. DOI: 10.1177/09722629221130592

Agrawal, R. (2016). Mobile Money Empowering People Living at Bottom of Pyramid and Boosting Socio-Economic Development in a Big Way. *Economic Analysis*, 49(1-2), 15–23.

Ahern, D. (2021). Regulatory lag, regulatory friction and regulatory transition as FinTech disenablers- Calibrating an EU response to the regulatory sandbox phenomenon. *European Business Organization Law Review, 22*(3), 395–432. doi-10.1007/s40804-021-00217-z

Ahlers, G., Cumming, D. J., Guenther, C., & Schweizer, D. (2015, February 12). *Signaling in Equity Crowdfunding*. Social Science Research Network. https://papers.ssrn.com/sol3/papers.cfm?abstract_id=2564121

Ahlström, H., & Monciardini, D. (2021). The regulatory dynamics of sustainable finance: Paradoxical success and limitations of EU reforms. *Journal of Business Ethics*, •••, 1–20. PMID: 33642657

Ahmad, F. Z. (2013). Factors behind the adoption of green banking by Bangladeshi commercial banks. *ASA University Review*, 7(2).

Ahmad, I., Ghani, M. U., Anwar, S., Butt, F. K. J. E. o. R. A., Government Packages,, & Policies. (2022). SME sector in Pakistan: mapping the policy framework, opportunities and constraints. *145*.

Ahmad, M. F., Kowalewski, O., & Pisany, P. (2023). What determines initial coin offering success- a cross-country study. *Economics of Innovation and New Technology, 32*(5), 622–645. doi-10.1080/10438599.2021.1982712

Ahmad, A. H., Green, C. J., Jiang, F., & Murinde, V. (2023). Mobile money, ICT, financial inclusion and growth: How different is Africa? *Economic Modelling*, 121, 106220. DOI: 10.1016/j.econmod.2023.106220

Ahmadi, S. (2024). A comprehensive study on integration of big data and AI in financial industry and its effect on present and future opportunities. *International Journal of Current Science Research and Review*, 7(01), 66–74. DOI: 10.47191/ijcsrr/V7-i1-07

Ahmad, M., Majeed, A., Khan, M. A., Sohaib, M., & Shehzad, K. (2021). Digital financial inclusion and economic growth: Provincial data analysis of China. *China Economic Journal*, 14(3), 291–310. DOI: 10.1080/17538963.2021.1882064

Ahmed, S., Alshater, M. M., El Ammari, A., & Hammami, H. (2022). Artificial intelligence and machine learning in finance: A bibliometric review. *Research in International Business and Finance*, 61, 101646. DOI: 10.1016/j.ribaf.2022.101646

Aithal, P. S. (2023). How to Create Business Value Through Technological Innovations Using ICCT Underlying Technologies. [IJAEML]. *International Journal of Applied Engineering and Management Letters*, 7(2), 232–292. DOI: 10.47992/IJAEML.2581.7000.0184

Akanfe, O., Valecha, R., & Rao, H. R. (2020). Design of a compliance index for privacy policies: A study of mobile wallet and remittance services. *IEEE Transactions on Engineering Management*, 70(3), 864–876. DOI: 10.1109/TEM.2020.3015222

Akhtar, N. (2023). *Who Benefits from Digital Technologies in Large Corporates of Pakistan?* [online] www.linkedin.com. Available at: https://www.linkedin.com/pulse/who-benefits-from-digital-technologies-large-pakistan-naghman-akhtar

Aktar, S. (2014). Reasons to Create Intention of Entrepreneurship among University Students: A Study on Bangladesh. *Journal of Entrepreneurship and Management*, 3(2).

Al Ahmad, M. A., Al-Saleh, A., & Al Masoud, F. A. (2018). Comparison between pow and pos systems of cryptocurrency. *Indonesian Journal of Electrical Engineering and Computer Science*, 10(3), 1251–1256. DOI: 10.11591/ijeecs.v10.i3.pp1251-1256

Al Amin, M. A., Ahad Mia, M. A., Bala, T., Iqbal, M. M., & Alam, M. S. (2023). Green finance continuance behavior: The role of satisfaction, social supports, environmental consciousness, green bank marketing initiatives and psychological reactance. *Management of Environmental Quality*, 34(5), 1269–1294. DOI: 10.1108/MEQ-09-2022-0257

Alam, S., Hussain, T., & Rahman, M. (2022). Fintech and SME financing: Opportunities and challenges. *Journal of Financial Innovation*, 12(3), 143–157.

Aldboush, H. H., & Ferdous, M. J. I. J. o. F. S. (2023). Building trust in fintech: an analysis of ethical and privacy considerations in the intersection of big data, AI, and customer trust. *11*(3), 90.

Aldridge, I., & Krawciw, S. (2017). *Real-time risk: What investors should know about FinTech, high-frequency trading, and flash crashes*. John Wiley & Sons. DOI: 10.1002/9781119319030

Alexander, K., & Fisher, P. (2018). Banking regulation and sustainability. Available at *SSRN* 3299351.

Alghazo, J. M., Kazmi, Z., & Latif, G. (2017). *Cyber security analysis of internet banking in emerging countries: User and bank perspectives.* Paper presented at the 2017 4th IEEE international conference on engineering technologies and applied sciences (ICETAS). DOI: 10.1109/ICETAS.2017.8277910

Alharby, M., Alssaiari, A., Alateef, S., Thomas, N., & Moorsel, A. (2024). A quantitative analysis of the security of PoW-based blockchains. *Cluster Computing*, 27(10), 1–18. DOI: 10.1007/s10586-024-04645-7

Ali, K. (2022, August 29). *Cyber security deficiency led to data theft at SECP, report finds*. Retrieved from DAWN: https://www.dawn.com/news/1707294

Ali, M., Hashmi, S. H., Nazir, M. R., Bilal, A., & Nazir, M. I. (2021). Does financial inclusion enhance economic growth? Empirical evidence from the IsDB member countries. *International Journal of Finance & Economics*, 26(4), 5235–5258. DOI: 10.1002/ijfe.2063

Allen, F., Gu, X., & Jagtiani, J. J. R. o. C. F. (2021). A survey of fintech research and policy discussion. *1*, 259-339.

Allen, H. J. (2022). Testimony of Hilary J. Allen, US Senate Committee on Banking, Housing, and Urban Affairs Hearing on'Crypto Crash: Why the FTX Bubble Burst and the Harm to Consumers'. *Allen, US Senate Committee on Banking, Housing, and Urban Affairs Hearing on'Crypto Crash: Why the FTX Bubble Burst and the Harm to Consumers'(December 14, 2022)*.

Allen, S., Čapkun, S., Eyal, I., Fanti, G., Ford, B. A., Grimmelmann, J., Juels, A., Kostiainen, K., Meiklejohn, S., & Miller, A. (2020). *Design choices for central bank digital currency: Policy and technical considerations*.

Alliance, N. C. (2022, May 8). *National Cyber Security Alliance Statement Regarding Incorrect Small Business Statistic*. National Cybersecurity Alliance. https://staysafeonline.org/news-press/national-cyber-security-alliance-statement-regarding-incorrect-small-business-statistic/

Almeida, J., & Gonçalves, T. C. (2023). A decade of cryptocurrency investment literature: A cluster-based systematic analysis. *International Journal of Financial Studies*, 11(2), 71. DOI: 10.3390/ijfs11020071

Alnajdawi, S. M. (2024, January). The Impact of GHRM Practices on Sustainable Development Goals. In *2024 ASU International Conference in Emerging Technologies for Sustainability and Intelligent Systems (ICETSIS)* (pp. 165-170). IEEE. DOI: 10.1109/ICETSIS61505.2024.10459585

Al-Okaily, M., Alkhwaldi, A. F., Abdulmuhsin, A. A., Alqudah, H., & Al-Okaily, A. (2022). Cloud-based accounting information systems usage and its impact on Jordanian SMEs' performance: The post-COVID-19 perspective. *Journal of Financial Reporting and Accounting*, 21(1), 126–155. Advance online publication. DOI: 10.1108/JFRA-12-2021-0476

Alshater, M. M., Joshipura, M., Khoury, R. E., & Nasrallah, N. (2023). Initial coin offerings- A hybrid empirical review. *Small Business Economics*. doi-10.1007/s11187-022-00726-2

Alt, R., Beck, R., & Smits, M. T. (2018). FinTech and the transformation of the financial industry. *Electronic Markets*, 28(3), 235–243. DOI: 10.1007/s12525-018-0310-9

Alvarez, F., Argente, D., & Van Patten, D. (2023). Are cryptocurrencies currencies? Bitcoin as legal tender in El Salvador. *Science*, 382(6677), eadd2844. DOI: 10.1126/science.add2844 PMID: 38127756

Amacanin, M. C. (2005). The strategic implications of corporate responsibility and sustainability in the UK banking sector. *Doctoral dissertation, University of Nottingham, UK.*

American Psychological Association. (2017). *Publication Manual of the American Psychological Association* (7th ed.). American Psychological Association.

Ametrano, F. M. (2016). Hayek money: The cryptocurrency price stability solution. *Available atSSRN* 2425270.

Amin, F., Jahangir, A., & Rasifard, H. (2008). Analysis of public-key cryptography for wireless sensor networks security. *International Journal of Computer and Information Engineering*, 2(5), 1448–1453.

Amjad, R., & Mahmood, K. (1982). Industrial relations and the political process in Pakistan 1947–1977. *Munich Personal RePEc Archive.*

Amjad, M., Akhtar, J., Anwar-ul-Haq, M., Yang, A., Akhtar, S. S., & Jacobsen, S.-E. (2014). Integrating role of ethylene and ABA in tomato plants' adaptation to salt stress. *Scientia Horticulturae*, 178, 49–61. DOI: 10.1016/j.scienta.2014.03.024

Amnas, M. B., Selvam, M., & Parayitam, S. (2024). FinTech and Financial Inclusion: Exploring the mediating role of Digital Financial Literacy and the moderating influence of perceived regulatory support. *Journal of Risk and Financial Management*, 17(3), 108. DOI: 10.3390/jrfm17030108

Amoah, L. D. (2022). Sustainable finance and banking in Africa. In *The Economics of Banking and Finance in Africa* (pp. 405–429). Developments in Africa's Financial Systems. DOI: 10.1007/978-3-031-04162-4_12

Anagnostopoulos, I. (2018). Fintech and regtech: Impact on regulators and banks. *Journal of Economics and Business*, 100(1), 7–25. https://www.sciencedirect.com/science/article/abs/pii/S014861951730142X. DOI: 10.1016/j.jeconbus.2018.07.003

Anakpo, G., Xhate, Z., & Mishi, S. (2023). The policies, practices, and challenges of digital financial inclusion for sustainable development: The case of the developing economy. *FinTech*, 2(2), 327–343. DOI: 10.3390/fintech2020019

Andreoni, A., Mondliwa, P., Roberts, S., & Tregenna, F. (2021). Towards a new industrial policy for structural transformation. Structural transformation in South Africa: The challenges of inclusive industrial development in a middle-income country, 337-361.

Anifa, M., Ramakrishnan, S., Joghee, S., Kabiraj, S., & Bishnoi, M. M. (2022). Fintech innovations in the financial service industry. *Journal of Risk and Financial Management*, 15(7), 287. DOI: 10.3390/jrfm15070287

Antal, C., Cioara, T., Anghel, I., Antal, M., & Salomie, I. (2021). Distributed ledger technology review and decentralized applications development guidelines. *Future Internet*, 13(3), 62. DOI: 10.3390/fi13030062

Ante, L., Sandner, P., & Fiedler, I. (2018). Blockchain-based ICOs: Pure hype or the dawn of a new era of startup financing? *Journal of Risk and Financial Management*, 11(4), 80. DOI: 10.3390/jrfm11040080

Anwar, M. W. (2020, December). Cyber Security in Pakistan: Regulations, Gaps and Way Forward. *ResearchGate*. Retrieved from https://www.researchgate.net/publication/349097228_Cyber_Security_in_Pakistan_Regulations_Gaps_and_Way_Forward

Argyroudis, S. A., Mitoulis, S. A., Chatzi, E., Baker, J. W., Brilakis, I., Gkoumas, K., Vousdoukas, M., Hynes, W., Carluccio, S., Keou, O., Frangopol, D. M., & Linkov, I. (2022). Digital technologies can enhance climate resilience of critical infrastructure. *Climate Risk Management*, 35, 100387. DOI: 10.1016/j.crm.2021.100387

Ari, E., Karatepe, O. M., Rezapouraghdam, H., & Avci, T. (2020). A Conceptual Model for Green Human Resource Management: Indicators, Differential Pathways, and Multiple Pro-Environmental Outcomes. *Sustainability (Basel)*, 12(17), 7089. DOI: 10.3390/su12177089

Arner, D. W., Barberis, J. N., Walker, J., Buckley, R. P., Dahdal, A. M., & Zetzsche, D. A. (2020). Digital finance & the COVID-19 crisis. University of Hong Kong Faculty of Law Research Paper, (2020/017).

Arner, D. W., Barberis, J. N., & Buckley, R. P. (2015, October 1). *The Evolution of Fintech: A New Post-Crisis Paradigm?* Papers.*ssrn*.com. https://papers.ssrn.com/sol3/papers.cfm?abstract_id=2676553 DOI: 10.2139/ssrn.2676553

Arner, D. W., Barberis, J., & Buckey, R. P. (2016). FinTech, RegTech, and the re-conceptualization of financial regulation. *Nw. J. Int'l L. & Bus.*, 37, 371.

Arulrajah, A. (2020). Mediating role of employee green behaviour towards sustainability performance of banks. *Journal of Governance & Regulation*, 9(2), 92–102. DOI: 10.22495/jgrv9i2art7

As Santos, N. C., Israelian, G., & Mayor, M. (2004). Spectroscopic analysis of 98 stars with planetary companions: Metallicity and the probability of planet formation. *Astronomy & Astrophysics*, 415(3), 1153–1166. DOI: 10.1051/0004-6361:20034469

Asanović, Ž. (2020). Essay on finance-Growth nexus. *Journal of Central Banking Theory and Practice*, 1(1), 97–109. DOI: 10.2478/jcbtp-2020-0006

Asebedo, S., & Payne, P. (2019). Market volatility and financial satisfaction: The role of financial self-efficacy. *Journal of Behavioral Finance*, 20(1), 42–52. DOI: 10.1080/15427560.2018.1434655

Ashraf, M. (2019, december 31). *Cyber threats to Digital Pakistan*. Retrieved from The Nation: https://www.nation.com.pk/31-Dec-2019/cyber-threats-to-digital-pakistan

Asif, S. (2023). *The Importance of Digital Transformation for Businesses in Pakistan*. [online] Entrepreneurs Of Pakistan. Available at: https://entrepreneursofpakistan.com/the-importance-of-digital-transformation-for-businesses-in-pakistan/

Asif, M., Khan, M. N., Tiwari, S., Wani, S. K., & Alam, F. (2023). The impact of Fintech and digital financial services on financial inclusion in India. *Journal of Risk and Financial Management*, 16(2), 122. DOI: 10.3390/jrfm16020122

Atkinson, A., & Messy, F. A. (2013). *Promoting financial inclusion through financial education: OECD/INFE evidence, policies and practice*. Retrieved from https://www.oecd-ilibrary.org/finance-and-investment/promoting-financial-inclusion-through-financial-education_5k3xz6m88smp-en

Attaran, M., & Woods, J. (2019). Cloud computing technology: improving small business performance using the Internet. *Journal of Small Business & Entrepreneurship, 31*(6), 495–519. Tandfonline. DOI: 10.1080/08276331.2018.1466850

Atzori, M. (2015). Blockchain technology and decentralized governance: Is the state still necessary? *Available atSSRN* 2709713. DOI: 10.2139/ssrn.2709713

Atz, U., Van Holt, T., Liu, Z. Z., & Bruno, C. C. (2023). Does sustainability generate better financial performance? review, meta-analysis, and propositions. *Journal of Sustainable Finance & Investment*, 13(1), 802–825. DOI: 10.1080/20430795.2022.2106934

Australian Financial Centre Forum. (2009). *Australia as a Financial Centre Building on our Strengths. Australian Financial Centre Forum*. Retrieved from https://trove.nla.gov.au/work/36802810

Aydar, M., Cetin, S. C., Ayvaz, S., & Aygun, B. (2019). Private key encryption and recovery in blockchain. *arXiv preprint arXiv:1907.04156*.

Azar, P. D., Baughman, G., Carapella, F., Gerszten, J., Lubis, A., Perez-Sangimino, J. P., Scotti, C., Swem, N., Vardoulakis, A., & Rappoport W, D. E. (2022). The financial stability implications of digital assets. *FRB of New York Staff Report*(1034).

Azarenkova, G., Shkodina, I., Samorodov, B., Babenko, M., & Onishchenko, I. (2018). The influence of financial technologies on the global financial system stability. *Investment Management & Financial Innovations*, 15(4), 229–238. DOI: 10.21511/imfi.15(4).2018.19

Babilla, T. U. K. J. E. M. (2023). Digital innovation and financial access for small and medium-sized enterprises in a currency union. *120*, 106182.

Baesens, B. (2014). *Analytics in a big data world: The essential guide to data science and its applications*. John Wiley & Sons.

Bagale, G. S., Vandadi, V. R., Singh, D., Sharma, D. K., Garlapati, D. V. K., Bommisetti, R. K., & Sengan, S. (2021). *Small and medium-sized enterprises' contribution in digital technology*. Petra Christian University, Balboa, E., Ladesma, M., & Manguerra, A. N. J. J. J. I. e. d. m. (2024). *Digital Financing Innovations and Their Impact on the Financial Performance of SMEs in the Digital Economy Era.*, 11(1), 88–98.

Bahuguna, P. C., Srivastava, R., & Tiwari, S. (2023). Two-decade journey of green human resource management research: A bibliometric analysis. *Benchmarking*, 30(2), 585–602. DOI: 10.1108/BIJ-10-2021-0619

Bai, C., Quayson, M., & Sarkis, J. (2021). COVID-19 pandemic digitization lessons for sustainable development of micro-and small-enterprises. *Sustainable Production and Consumption*, 27, 1989–2001. DOI: 10.1016/j.spc.2021.04.035 PMID: 34722843

Bain, J. S. (1951). Relation of profit rate to industry concentration: American manufacturing, 1936–1940. *The Quarterly Journal of Economics*, 65(3), 293–324. DOI: 10.2307/1882217

Bain, J. S. (1956). *Barriers to new competition: Their character and consequences in manufacturing industries*. Harvard University Press. DOI: 10.4159/harvard.9780674188037

Baker, H. K., Kumar, S., & Pandey, N. (2021). Forty years of the Journal of Futures Markets: A bibliometric overview. *Journal of Futures Markets*, 41(7), 1027–1054. DOI: 10.1002/fut.22211

Ballestar, M. T., Grau-Carles, P., & Sainz, J. (2019). Predicting customer quality in e-commerce social networks: A machine learning approach. *Review of Managerial Science*, 13(3), 589–603. DOI: 10.1007/s11846-018-0316-x

Balyuk, T. (2016). Financial Innovation and Borrowers: Evidence from Peer-to-Peer Lending. SSRN Electronic Journal. https://doi.org/DOI: 10.2139/ssrn.2802220

Bamberger, K. A., Canetti, R., Goldwasser, S., Wexler, R., & Zimmerman, E. J. (2022). Verification dilemmas in law and the promise of zero-knowledge proofs. *Berkeley Technology Law Journal*, 37, 1.

Bangladesh Bank. (2020). *Overview of Financial System of Bangladesh*. Retrieved from https://www.bb.org.bd/fnansys/index.php

Bank, N. R. (2024). CONSULTATIVE DOCUMENT ON PEER-TO-PEER LENDING AND CROWDFUNDING.

Bank, W. "Pakistan Economic Policy for Export Competitiveness, Digital Pakistan: A Business and Trade Assessment." Worldbank.org, 2020, documents1.worldbank.org/curated/en/894921591073694322/Digital-Pakistan-Economic-Policy-for-Export-Competitiveness-A-Business-and-Trade-Assessment.docx

Bank, W. J. S., & FINANCE, M. E. (2023). Improving SMEs access to finance and finding innovative solutions to unlock sources of capital.

Barney, J. B. (1991). Firm Resources and Sustained Competitive Advantage. *Journal of Management*, 17(1), 99–120. DOI: 10.1177/014920639101700108

Barro, D., Basso, A., Funari, S., & Visentin, G. A. (2023). A Bilbliometric Analysis of Art in Financial Markets. SSRN *Electronic Journal*. DOI: 10.2139/ssrn.4593365

Basel Committee on Banking Supervision (BCBS). (2021). Principles for Operational Resilience. Retrieved from Bank for International Settlements. https://www.bis.org/bcbs/publ/d516.htm

Bashir, M. R., Alkhouri, N., & Labriola, D. (2023). Resmetirom for nonalcoholic fatty liver disease: A randomized, double-blind, placebo-controlled phase 3 trial. *Nature Medicine*. PMID: 37845512

Bashir, S., Hussain, A., Hussain, S. J., Wani, O. A., Zahid Nabi, S., Dar, N. A., Baloch, F. S., & Mansoor, S. (2021). Plant drought stress tolerance: Understanding its physiological, biochemical, and molecular mechanisms. *Biotechnology, Biotechnological Equipment*, 35(1), 92–112. DOI: 10.1080/13102818.2021.2020161

Battisto, J., Lieberman, S., Mills, C. K., Wiersch, A. M., & de Zeeuw, M. (2019). 2019 Report on Employer Firms. *Small Business Credit Survey*, 20190416. Advance online publication. DOI: 10.55350/sbcs

Bazarbash, M. (2019, May 17). *FinTech in Financial Inclusion: Machine Learning Applications in Assessing Credit Risk*. IMF. https://www.imf.org/en/Publications/WP/Issues/2019/05/17/FinTech-in-Financial-Inclusion-Machine-Learning-Applications-in-Assessing-Credit-Risk-46883

Bazarbash, M., Malatesta, L., & Parisi, F. (2020). The future of SME lending in a fintech world. *International Monetary Fund Working Paper, 21*(2), 89-106.

BBVA OpenMind. (n.d.). *10 Examples of How AI Is Already Used in Our Day-to-Day Life*.

Beck, T., & Demirguc-Kunt, A. (2006). Small and medium-size ises: Access to finance as a growth constraint. *Journal of Banking & Finance*, 30(11), 2931–2943. DOI: 10.1016/j.jbankfin.2006.05.009

Beck, T., Demirgüç-Kunt, A., & Levine, R. (2007). Finance, inequality and the poor. *Journal of Economic Growth*, 12(1), 27–49. DOI: 10.1007/s10887-007-9010-6

Belleflamme, P., Lambert, T., & Schwienbacher, A. (2014). Crowdfunding: Tapping the Right Crowd. *Journal of Business Venturing*, 29(5), 585–609. DOI: 10.1016/j.jbusvent.2013.07.003

Benmalek, M. (2024). Ransomware on cyber-physical systems: Taxonomies, case studies, security gaps, and open challenges. *Internet of Things and Cyber-Physical Systems*.

Berger, A. N., & Bouwman, C. H. S. (2015). *Bank Liquidity Creation and Financial Crises*. Academic Press. Google Books

Berger, A. N., Herring, R. J., & Szegö, G. P. (1995). The role of capital in financial institutions. *Journal of Banking & Finance*, 19(3–4), 393–430. DOI: 10.1016/0378-4266(95)00002-X

Berger, A. N., & Mester, L. J. (1997). Inside the black box: What explains differences in the efficiencies of financial institutions? *Journal of Banking & Finance*, 21(7), 895–947. DOI: 10.1016/S0378-4266(97)00010-1

Berger, A. N., & Udell, G. F. (2006). A more complete conceptual framework for SME finance. *Journal of Banking & Finance*, 30(11), 2945–2966. DOI: 10.1016/j.jbankfin.2006.05.008

Bernabe, J. B., Canovas, J. L., Hernandez-Ramos, J. L., Moreno, R. T., & Skarmeta, A. (2019). Privacy-preserving solutions for blockchain: Review and challenges. *IEEE Access : Practical Innovations, Open Solutions*, 7, 164908–164940. DOI: 10.1109/ACCESS.2019.2950872

Bernarto, I. B. (2020). Effect of transformational leadership, perceived organizational support, job satisfaction toward life satisfaction. *Evidences from indonesian teachers.*

Bharathi, S. V., Perdana, A., & Kulkarni, M. S. (2023). Exploring the synergy between financial technologies and financial inclusion: What we know and where we should be heading? *Pacific Asia Journal of the Association for Information Systems*, 15, 87–126. DOI: 10.17705/1pais.15104

Bhaskar, R., Hunjra, A. I., Bansal, S., & Pandey, D. K. (2022). Central bank digital currencies: Agendas for future research. *Research in International Business and Finance*, 62, 101737. DOI: 10.1016/j.ribaf.2022.101737

Bhat, S. A., Sofi, I. B., & Chi, C.-Y. (2020). Edge computing and its convergence with blockchain in 5G and beyond: Security, challenges, and opportunities. *IEEE Access : Practical Innovations, Open Solutions*, 8, 205340–205373. DOI: 10.1109/ACCESS.2020.3037108

Bhattacharya, M. R., & Wolde, H. (2010). *Constraints on Growth in the MENA Region. International Monetary Fund.* Retrieved from https://www.researchgate.net/profile/Rina-Bhattacharya/publication/228289502_Constraints_on_Growth_in_the_MENA_Region/links/55ef243508ae199d47bffed0/Constraints-on-Growth-in-the-MENA-Region.pdf

Bhuvana, R., & Aithal, P. (2020). Blockchain based service: A case study on IBM blockchain services & hyperledger fabric. [IJCSBE]. *International Journal of Case Studies in Business, IT, and Education*, 4(1), 94–102.

Bisogno, M., Cuadrado-Ballesteros, B., Manes-Rossi, F., & Peña-Miguel, N. (2024). Financial Sustainability and Sustainable Development in Local Governments: Empirical Insights. *Public Performance & Management Review*, 47(3), 1–28. DOI: 10.1080/15309576.2024.2340116

Biswas, U. A., Garg, S., & Singh, A. (2016). The need for regulatory intervention in corporate social responsibility in India: Evidence from corporate social disclosures. *International Journal of Indian Culture and Business Management*, 12(3), 293–317. DOI: 10.1504/IJICBM.2016.075534

Block, J. H., Colombo, M. G., Cumming, D. J., & Vismara, S. (2018). New players in entrepreneurial finance and why they are there. *Small Business Economics, 50*(2), 239–250. springer. DOI: 10.1007/s11187-016-9826-6

Block, R. A., & Zakay, D. (1997). Prospective and retrospective duration judgments: A meta-analytic review. *Psychonomic Bulletin & Review*, 4(2), 184–197. DOI: 10.3758/BF03209393 PMID: 21331825

Boachie, R., Aawaar, G., & Domeher, D. (2023). Relationship between financial inclusion, banking stability and economic growth: A dynamic panel approach. *Journal of Economic and Administrative Sciences*, 39(3), 655–670. DOI: 10.1108/JEAS-05-2021-0084

Board, F. S. (2018). Crypto-assets: report to the G20 on the work of the FSB and standardsetting bodies. Basel, Switzerland: Financial Stability Board, 16.

Board, F. S. (2020). Effective practices for cyber incident response and recovery. Financial Stability Board, Consultative Document.

Bombiak, E., & Marciniuk-Kluska, A. (2018). Green Human Resource Management as a Tool for the Sustainable Development of Enterprises: Polish Young Company Experience. *Sustainability (Basel)*, 10(6), 1739. DOI: 10.3390/su10061739

Boone, J. P., Khurana, I. K., & Raman, K. K. (2008). Audit firm tenure and the equity risk premium. *Journal of Accounting, Auditing & Finance*, 23(1), 115–140. DOI: 10.1177/0148558X0802300107

Bordo, M. D., & Levin, A. T. (2017). *Central bank digital currency and the future of monetary policy (No. w23711)*. National Bureau of Economic Research. DOI: 10.3386/w23711

Boreiko, D. (2024a). Economics of Initial Coin Offerings. In *Understanding Initial Coin Offerings* (pp. 67–106). Edward Elgar Publishing. DOI: 10.4337/9781803921587.00010

Borenstein, M., Hedges, L. V., Higgins, J. P., & Rothstein, H. R. (2011). *Introduction to Meta-Analysis*. John Wiley & Sons. [Book]

Boţoroga, C. A., Horobeţ, A., Belaşcu, L., Popoviciu, A. S., & Gîrlovan, A. (2022). Assessing the Nexus Between Education, Economic Growth, and Innovation: An Empirical Analysis. *Studies in Business and Economics*, 17(3), 18–34. DOI: 10.2478/sbe-2022-0043

Bourke, P. (1989). Concentration and other determinants of bank profitability in Europe, North America, and Australia. *Journal of Banking & Finance*, 13(1), 65–79. DOI: 10.1016/0378-4266(89)90020-4

Bouveret, A. (2018). *Cyber risk for the financial sector: A framework for quantitative assessment*. International Monetary Fund.

Bowman, M. (2010). The role of the banking industry in facilitating climate change mitigation and the transition to a low-carbon global economy. *Environment and Planning Law Journal*, 27, 448.

Boyes, H., Hallaq, B., Cunningham, J., & Watson, T. (2018). The industrial internet of things (IIoT): An analysis framework. *Computers in Industry*, 101, 1–12. DOI: 10.1016/j.compind.2018.04.015

Brands, S. (2000). *Rethinking public key infrastructures and digital certificates: building in privacy*. Mit Press. DOI: 10.7551/mitpress/5931.001.0001

Braun-Dubler, N., Gier, H.-P., Bulatnikova, T., Langhart, M., Merki, M., Roth, F., Burret, A., & Perdrisat, S. (2020). *Blockchain: Capabilities, economic viability, and the socio-technical environment* (Vol. 73). vdf Hochschulverlag AG.

BrewDog. (2020). *Equity for Punks - Benefits T&Cs | BrewDog*. Www.brewdog .com. https://www.brewdog.com/uk/equityforpunks/benefits

Brimble, M., Stewart, J., & de Zwaan, L. (2010). Climate change and financial regulation: Challenges for the financial sector following the global financial crisis. *Griffith Law Review*, 19(1), 71–85. DOI: 10.1080/10854669.2010.10854669

Broadhurst, R., Lord, D., Maxim, D., Woodford-Smith, H., Johnston, C., Chung, H. W., Carroll, S., Trivedi, H., & Sabol, B. (2018). Malware trends on 'darknet' crypto-markets: Research review. *Available atSSRN* 3226758.

Brooks, C. (2022) Alarming Cyber Statistics For Mid-Year 2022 That You Need To Know, Global Thought Leader in Cybersecurity and Emerging Tech. Available on https://www.forbes.com/sites/chuckbrooks/2022/06/03/alarming-cyber-statistics -for-mid-year-2022-that-you-need-to-know/?sh=79b43a37864a

Brown, R. L., Durbin, J., & Evans, J. M. (1975). Techniques for testing the constancy of regression relationships over time. *Journal of the Royal Statistical Society. Series B, Statistical Methodology*, 37(2), 149–163. DOI: 10.1111/j.2517-6161.1975.tb01532.x

Bruce, J. (2014). The mini-blockchain scheme. *White paper, 1*, 1-10.

Bruckner, M. A. (n.d.). preventing predation & encouraging innovation in fintech lending. Retrieved June 21, 2021, from https://www.dfs.ny.gov/reportpub/online _lending_survey_rpt_

Bruhn, M., & Love, I. (2014). The real impact of improved access to finance: Evidence from Mexico. *The Journal of Finance*, 69(3), 1347–1376. DOI: 10.1111/jofi.12091

Brunnermeier, M. K., James, H., & Landau, J. P. (2019). *The digitalization of money (No. w26300)*. National Bureau of Economic Research. DOI: 10.3386/w26300

Bryman, A. (2016). *Social Research Methods*. Oxford University Press.

Bryman, A., & Bell, E. (2019). *Business Research Methods*. Oxford University Press.

Brynjolfsson, E., & McAfee, A. (2014). *The second machine age: Work, progress, and prosperity in a time of brilliant technologies*. W. W. Norton & Company.

Buchanan, B. G., & Wright, D. (2021). The impact of machine learning on UK financial services. *Oxford Review of Economic Policy*, 37(3), 537–563. DOI: 10.1093/oxrep/grab016 PMID: 34642572

Buckley, R. P., & Webster, S. J. J. o. F. T. (2016). FinTech in developing countries: charting new customer journeys. *44*.

Burtch, G., Ghose, A., & Wattal, S. (2012). An Empirical Examination of the Antecedents and Consequences of Investment Patterns in Crowd-Funded Markets. SSRN *Electronic Journal*. DOI: 10.2139/ssrn.1928168

Burton, M., & Brown, B. (2014). *The financial system and the economy: Principles of money and banking*. Routledge. DOI: 10.4324/9781315699776

Buterin, V. (2014). A next-generation smart contract and decentralized application platform. white paper, 3(37), 2-1.

Buterin, V. (2016). Ethereum: platform review. *Opportunities and challenges for private and consortium blockchains, 45*, 1-45.

Byeongyong, P., & DongRo, C. (2002). An unrecorded species of *Pratylenchus loosi* Loof (Tylenchida: Pratylenchidae) from tea in Korea. *CABI Digital Library*.

Caldwell, D., & Williams, R. E. (2016). *Seeking security in an insecure world*. Rowman & Littlefield.

Cambridge Centre for Alternative Finance. (2020). *In partnership with: With support of: Global Alternative Finance Market Benchmarking The Report Trends, Opportunities and Challenges for Lending, Equity, and Non-Investment Alternative Finance Models*. https://www.jbs.cam.ac.uk/wp-content/uploads/2020/08/2020-04-22-ccaf-global-alternative-finance-market-benchmarking-report.pdf

Candra, S., Nuruttarwiyah, F., & Hapsari, I. H. (2020). Revisited the Technology Acceptance Model with E-Trust for Peer-to-Peer Lending in Indonesia (Perspective from Fintech Users). *International Journal of Technology*, 11(4), 710–721. DOI: 10.14716/ijtech.v11i4.4032

Capital, L. (2024, May 13). *How Revenue-Based Financing and Venture Capital Work Together*. Lighter Capital; Lighter Capital. https://www.lightercapital.com/blog/how-revenue-based-financing-venture-capital-funding-work-together

Carè, R., & Cumming, D. (2024). Technology and automation in financial trading: A bibliometric review. *Research in International Business and Finance*, 71, 102471–102471. DOI: 10.1016/j.ribaf.2024.102471

Carter, W. A. (2017). *Forces shaping the cyber threat landscape for financial institutions*. SWIFT Institute.

Castonguay, J. J., & Stein Smith, S. (2020). Digital assets and blockchain: Hackable, fraudulent, or just misunderstood? *Accounting Perspectives*, 19(4), 363–387. DOI: 10.1111/1911-3838.12242

CFI. *What are the Main Types of Cryptocurrencies* Corporate Finance Institute Retrieved 1st August from https://corporatefinanceinstitute.com/resources/cryptocurrency/types-of-cryptocurrency/

Chang, V., Baudier, P., Zhang, H., Xu, Q., Zhang, J., & Arami, M. (2020). How Blockchain can impact financial services–The overview, challenges and recommendations from expert interviewees. *Technological Forecasting and Social Change*, 158, 120166. DOI: 10.1016/j.techfore.2020.120166 PMID: 32834134

Chant, S., & Evans, A. (2010). Gendered poverty across space and time: Introduction and overview. [SAGE Journals]. *Environment and Urbanization*, 22(2), 371–391.

Chen, T., Lu, H., Kunpittaya, T., & Luo, A. (2022). A review of zk-SNARKs. *arXiv preprint arXiv:2202.06877*.

Chen, H., Chiang, R. H., & Storey, V. C. (2012). Business intelligence and analytics: From big data to big impact. *Management Information Systems Quarterly*, 36(4), 1165–1188. DOI: 10.2307/41703503

Chen, H., Liu, X., & Shen, Y. (2022). Fintech and financial inclusion: Evidence from mobile banking adoption. *Economic Journal of Developing Economies*, 17(1), 45–65.

Chen, J. S., Siddik, A., Zheng, G.-W., Masukujjaman, M., & Bekhzod, S. (2022). The effect of green banking practices on banks' environmental performance and green financing: An empirical study. *Energies*, 15(4), 1292. DOI: 10.3390/en15041292

Chen, Y., & Sivakumar, V. (2021). Investigation of finance industry on risk awareness model and digital economic growth. *Annals of Operations Research*, •••, 1–22. PMID: 34785834

Chen, Z. L., Lv, H., Zhang, Q., Wang, H., & Chen, G. (2022). Construction of a cement–rebar nanoarchitecture for a solution-processed and flexible film of a Bi_2Te_3/CNT hybrid toward low thermal conductivity and high thermoelectric performance. *Carbon Energy*, 4(1), 115–128. DOI: 10.1002/cey2.161

Chernova, N., Serhiienko, O., Bril, M., Bilotserkivskyi, O., & Kochorba, V. (2024). Investigation of modern investment opportunities with cryptocurrency market: Optimization approach. *Intellectual Economics*, 18(1), 80–105.

Cheung, A., Roca, E., & Su, J.-J. (2015). Crypto-currency bubbles: An application of the Phillips–Shi–Yu (2013) methodology on Mt. Gox bitcoin prices. *Applied Economics*, 47(23), 2348–2358. DOI: 10.1080/00036846.2015.1005827

Chitsazan, H., Bagheri, A., & Tajeddin, M. (2022). Initial coin offerings (ICOs) success- Conceptualization, theories and systematic analysis of empirical studies. *Technological Forecasting and Social Change*, 180, 121729. DOI: 10.1016/j.techfore.2022.121729

Chiu, -Y. (2023). An institutional account of responsiveness in financial regulation-Examining the fallacy and limits of "same activity, same risks, same rules" as the answer to financial innovation and regulatory arbitrage. *Comput. Law Secur. Rep, 51*(105868).

Chiu, I. H. (2023). An institutional account of responsiveness in financial regulation-Examining the fallacy and limits of 'same activity, same risks, same rules' as the answer to financial innovation and regulatory arbitrage. *Computer Law & Security Report*, 51, 105868. DOI: 10.1016/j.clsr.2023.105868

Chou, S.-C., Li, Z.-A., Wang, T., & Yen, J.-C. (2023). How the quality of initial coin offering white papers influences fundraising- Using security token offerings white papers as a benchmark. *Intelligent Systems in Accounting Finance & Management, 30*(1), 3–18. doi-10.1002/isaf.1527

Chowdhury, E. K., & Chowdhury, R. (2024). Role of financial inclusion in human development: Evidence from Bangladesh, India and Pakistan. *Journal of the Knowledge Economy*, 15(1), 3329–3354. DOI: 10.1007/s13132-023-01366-x

Chowdhury, S. R., Mendy, J., & Rahman, M. (2023). A systematic literature review of GHRM: Organizational sustainable performance reimagined using a new holistic framework. *Sustainability (Basel)*, 15(9), 7513. DOI: 10.3390/su15097513

Christopoulos, D. K., & Tsionas, E. G. (2004). Financial development and economic growth: Evidence from panel unit root and cointegration tests. *Journal of Development Economics*, 73(1), 55–74. DOI: 10.1016/j.jdeveco.2003.03.002

Chueca Vergara, C., & Ferruz Agudo, L. (2021). Fintech and sustainability: Do they affect each other? *Sustainability (Basel)*, 13(13), 7012. DOI: 10.3390/su13137012

Chuen, D. L. K., Guo, L., & Wang, Y. (2017). Cryptocurrency: A new investment opportunity? *Journal of Alternative Investments*, 20(3), 16–40. DOI: 10.3905/jai.2018.20.3.016

Chursook, A., Yahya Dawod, A., Chanaim, S., Naktnasukanjn, N., & Chakpitak, N. (2022). Twitter sentiment analysis and Expert Ratings of Initial Coin Offering fundraising- Evidence from Australia and Singapore markets. *TEM Journal*, 44–55. doi-10.18421/tem111-06

Claessens, S., Frost, J., Turner, G., & Zhu, F. (2018). Fintech credit markets around the world: size, drivers and policy issues. Www.bis.org. https://www.bis.org/publ/qtrpdf/r_qt1809e.htm

Claessens, M. S., & Kose, M. A. (2013). *Financial crises explanations, types, and implications*. International Monetary Fund. DOI: 10.2139/ssrn.2295201

Claessens, S. (2017). *Regulation and structural change in financial systems*. Centre for Economic Policy Research.

Colaert, V. (2022). The changing nature of financial regulation: Sustainable finance as a new EU policy objective. *Common Market Law Review*, 59(6), 1669–1710. DOI: 10.54648/COLA2022115

Collard, S. (2007). Toward financial inclusion in the UK: Progress and challenges. *Public Money & Management*, 27(1), 13–20. DOI: 10.1111/j.1467-9302.2007.00550.x

Collins, A. M., & Quillian, M. R. (1969). Retrieval time from semantic memory. *Journal of Verbal Learning and Verbal Behavior*, 8(2), 240–247. DOI: 10.1016/S0022-5371(69)80069-1

Corbet, S., Lucey, B., Urquhart, A., & Yarovaya, L. (2019). Cryptocurrencies as a financial asset: A systematic analysis. *International Review of Financial Analysis*, 62, 182–199. DOI: 10.1016/j.irfa.2018.09.003

Cordova Paredes, M. J., Calabuig Moreno, F., & Alonso Dos Santos, M. (2019). Key determinants on non-governmental organization's financial sustainability: A case study that examines 2018 fifa foundation social festival selected participants. *Sustainability (Basel)*, 11(5), 1411. DOI: 10.3390/su11051411

Cowling, K. (1976). On the theoretical specification of industrial structure-performance relationships. *European Economic Review*, 8(1), 1–14. DOI: 10.1016/0014-2921(76)90038-6

Cox, J., Nguyen, T. J. J. o. S. B., & Development, E. (2018). Does the crowd mean business? An analysis of rewards-based crowdfunding as a source of finance for start-ups and small businesses. *25*(1), 147-162.

Creane, S., Mobarak, A. M., Goyal, R., & Sab, R. (2004). *Financial sector development in the Middle East and North Africa*. Retrieved from https://papers.ssrn.com/sol3/papers.cfm?abstract_id=879026

Crowdcube. (2019, July 4). *Crowdcube success story | Monzo*. Crowdcube | Funding the Wonderful. https://www.crowdcube.com/explore/raising/success-stories/monzo

Cumming, D., Johan, S., & Reardon, R. J. M. B. R. (2023). Global fintech trends and their impact on international business: a review. *31*(3), 413-436.

Cumming, D., & Hornuf, L. (2018). *The Economics of Crowdfunding*. Springer International Publishing., DOI: 10.1007/978 3-319-66119-3

Cunha, P. R., Melo, P., & Sebastião, H. (2021). From bitcoin to central bank digital currencies: Making sense of the digital money revolution. *Future Internet*, 13(7), 165. DOI: 10.3390/fi13070165

Currie, W. L., & Seddon, J. J. (2022). Exploring technological instantiation of regulatory practices in entangled financial markets. *Journal of Information Technology*, 37(1), 31–50. DOI: 10.1177/02683962211027308

Cuyvers, S. H., Haq, B., Op de Beeck, C., Poelman, S., Hermans, A., Wang, Z., Gocalinska, A., Pelucchi, E., Corbett, B., Roelkens, G., Van Gasse, K., & Kuyken, B. (2021). Low Noise Heterogeneous III-V-on-Silicon-Nitride Mode-Locked Comb Laser. *Laser & Photonics Reviews*, 15(8), 2000485. DOI: 10.1002/lpor.202000485

Cyber Readiness Institute. (2023). *You are being redirected...* Www.juniperresearch.com. https://www.juniperresearch.com/press/ai-enabled-financial-fraud-detection-spend/

Cyber Readiness Institute. (2024, January 8). *Cyber Readiness Institute*. Cyber Readiness Institute. https://cyberreadinessinstitute.org/news-and-events/cyber-readiness-institute-survey-highlights-critical-gaps-in-mfa-implementation-among-u-s-SBs/

D'Silva, D., Filková, Z., Packer, F., & Tiwari, S. (2019). The design of digital financial infrastructure: lessons from India. BIS Paper, (106).

da Silva Etges, A. P. B., & Cortimiglia, M. N. (2019). A systematic review of risk management in innovation-oriented firms. *Journal of Risk Research*, 22(3), 364–381. DOI: 10.1080/13669877.2017.1382558

Dahiya, S., & Kumar, M. (2020). Linkage between Financial Inclusion and Economic Growth: An Empirical Study of the Emerging Indian Economy. *Vision: The Journal of Business Perspective*, 24(2), 184–193. DOI: 10.1177/0972262920923891

Dahlberg, T., Guo, J., & Ondrus, J. (2015). A critical review of mobile payment research. *Electronic Commerce Research and Applications*, 14(5), 265–284. DOI: 10.1016/j.elerap.2015.07.006

Dakalbab, F., Manar Abu Talib, Nasir, Q., & Saroufil, T. (2024). Artificial intelligence techniques in financial trading: A systematic literature review. *Journal of King Saud University. Computer and Information Sciences/Ma ala am a Al-Malīk Saud: Ùlm Al- asib Wa Al-Ma lumat, 36*(3), 102015–102015. DOI: 10.1016/j.jksuci.2024.102015

Dananjayan, M. P., Gopakumar, S., & Narayanasamy, P. (2023). Money in the age of bits and bytes: Technology in reshaping finance. Journal of Information Technology Teaching Cases, 20438869231178845.

Danladi, S., Prasad, M., Modibbo, U. M., Ahmadi, S. A., & Ghasemi, P. J. S. (2023). Attaining sustainable development goals through financial inclusion: exploring collaborative approaches to Fintech adoption in developing economies. *15*(17), 13039.

Dao, N. H., Wang ChuanYuan, Suzuki, A., Sudo, H., Ye, L., & Roy, D. (2024). AI in Stock Market Forecasting: A Bibliometric Analysis. *SHS Web of Conferences, 194*, 01003–01003. DOI: 10.1051/shsconf/202419401003

Dapp, F. T. (2015)Deutsche bank report: Digital economy and structural change FinTech reloaded-Traditional banks as digital ecosystems. Available on https://www.deutschebank.nl/nl/docs/Fintech_reloaded_Traditional_banks_as_ecosystems.pdf

Daraz. (2022). *Daraz Breaks Records with Over $1 Billion in GMV in 2022.*

Dar, M. Z., Deepika, K., Jan, K., Swer, T. L., Kumar, P., Verma, R., Verma, K., Prakash, K. S., Jan, S., & Bashir, K. (2018). Modification of structure and physicochemical properties of buckwheat and oat starch by γ-irradiation. *International Journal of Biological Macromolecules*, 108, 1. DOI: 10.1016/j.ijbiomac.2017.11.067 PMID: 29133096

Davenport, T. H., & Kirby, J. (2016). Just how smart are smart machines? *Harvard Business Review, 94*(5), 90–100.

De Blasis, R., Galati, L., Grassi, R., & Rizzini, G. (2024). Information Flow in the FTX Bankruptcy: A Network Approach. *arXiv preprint arXiv:2407.12683.*

De Vass, T. S. (2018). The effect of "Internet of Things" on supply chain integration and performance: An organisational capability perspective. *Australasian Journal of Information Systems*, 22. et al, N. (2019). The impact of social and environmental sustainability on financial performance. *Journal of Multinational Financial Management*, 49, 35-53.

Del Giudice, M., Campanella, F., & Dezi, L. (2016). The bank of things: An empirical investigation on the profitability of the financial services of the future. *Business Process Management Journal*, 22(2), 324–340. DOI: 10.1108/BPMJ-10-2015-0139

Delgado-Segura, S., Pérez-Solà, C., Herrera-Joancomartí, J., Navarro-Arribas, G., & Borrell, J. (2018). Cryptocurrency networks: A new P2P paradigm. *Mobile Information Systems*, 2018(1), 2159082.

Dell Inc. (2019). *Thought Leadership Perspectives.* https://www.dell.com/en-us/perspectives/a-positive-look-at-gdpr-a-year-in/

Deloitte. (2016). *Marketplace lending A temporary phenomenon?*https://www2.deloitte.com/content/dam/Deloitte/de/Documents/financial-services/deloitte-uk-fs-marketplace-lending.pdf

Deloitte. (2017), "Fintech and Regulatory Compliance", Available on http://www2.delitte.com/cntent/dam/Deloitte/us/Documents/regulatory/us-regulatory-future-of-finTechs-risk-and-regulatory-compliance.pdf

Deloitte. (2022). *2021 banking and capital markets outlook Strengthening resilience, accelerating transformation A Deloitte Center of Financial Services report.* https://www2.deloitte.com/content/dam/Deloitte/tw/Documents/financial-services/pr210330-2021-banking-and-capital-markets-outlook-strengthening-resilience-accelerating-transformation.pdf

Deloitte. (2023). *How Artificial Intelligence Is Transforming the Financial Services Industry*. Www.deloitte.com. https://www.deloitte.com/ng/en/services/risk-advisory/services/how-artificial-intelligence-is-transforming-the-financial-services-industry.html

Deloitte. M. (2020). Internet of Medical Things (2018) https://www2. deloitte.com/content/dam/Deloitte/global/Documents/Life-Sciences-Health-Care/gx-lshc-medtech-iomt-brochure. pdf

Demirguc-Kunt, A., Klapper, L., Singer, D., & Ansar, S. (2018). *The Global Findex Database 2017: Measuring financial inclusion and the fintech revolution*. World Bank Publications. DOI: 10.1596/978-1-4648-1259-0

Demsetz, H. (1973). Industry structure, market rivalry, and public policy. *The Journal of Law & Economics*, 16(1), 1–9. DOI: 10.1086/466752

Demsetz, H., & Lehn, K. (1985). The structure of corporate ownership: Causes and consequences. *Journal of Political Economy*, 93(6), 1155–1177. DOI: 10.1086/261354

Deval, V., Dwivedi, V. K., Dixit, A., Norta, A., Shah, S. A., Sharma, R., & Draheim, D. (2024). Mobile Smart Contracts: Exploring Scalability Challenges and Consensus Mechanisms. *IEEE Access : Practical Innovations, Open Solutions*, 12, 34265–34288. DOI: 10.1109/ACCESS.2024.3371901

Dhakal, C. P. (2017). Dealing with outliers and influential points while fitting regression. *Journal of Institute of Science and Technology*, 22(1), 61–65. DOI: 10.3126/jist.v22i1.17741

Dhiaf, M. M., Khakan, N., Atayah, O. F., Marashdeh, H., & El Khoury, R. J. J. o. D. S. (2024). The role of FinTech for manufacturing efficiency and financial performance: in the era of industry 4.0. *33*(2), 220-241.

Dhingra, D., Ashok, S., & Kumar, U. (2021). Demystifying global cybersecurity threats in financial services. In Handbook of Research on Advancing Cybersecurity for Digital Transformation (pp. 181-202). IGI Global. Digital transformation in banking: the evolution of financial services Can digital transformation in finance be simplified by adopting tools like XCALLY? https://www.xcally.com/news/digital-transformation-in-banking-the-evolution-of-financial-services/

Dickey, D. A., & Fuller, W. A. (1979). Distribution of the estimators for autoregressive time series with a unit root. *Journal of the American Statistical Association*, 74(366a), 427–431.

Dong, C., Wang, F., & Feng, D. (2024). DxHash: A Memory-saving Consistent Hashing Algorithm. *ACM Transactions on Internet Technology*, 24(1), 1–22. DOI: 10.1145/3631708

Donovan, K. (2012). Mobile money for financial inclusion. *Information and Communications for development, 61*(1), 61-73.

Dorfleitner, G., & Hornuf, L. Schmitt, M., & Weber, M. (2017). FinTech in Germany. In *Springer eBooks*. Springer Nature. DOI: 10.1007/978-3-319-54666-7

Douglas, R. J., Martin, K. A. C., & Whitteridge, D. (1988). Selective responses of visual cortical cells do not depend on shunting inhibition. *Nature*, 332(6165), 642–644. DOI: 10.1038/332642a0 PMID: 3357519

Dumont, J., Shen, J., & Deng, X. (2017). Effects of Green HRM Practices on Employee Workplace Green Behavior: The Role of Psychological Green Climate and Employee Green Values: Effect of Green HRM on Employee Workplace Green Behavior. *Human Resource Management*, 56(4), 613–627. DOI: 10.1002/hrm.21792

Dupuis, D., & Gleason, K. (2020). Money laundering with cryptocurrency: Open doors and the regulatory dialectic. *Journal of Financial Crime*, 28(1), 60–74. DOI: 10.1108/JFC-06-2020-0113

Dutta, K. D., & Saha, M. (2023). Role of governance in the nexus between financial development and sustainable development. *Journal of International Development*, 35(6), 1181–1215. DOI: 10.1002/jid.3724

Economics, O. (2019, April 29). *The Big Business of Small Business*. Oxford Economics. https://www.oxfordeconomics.com/resource/the-big-business-of-small-business/

Ediagbonya, V., & Tioluwani, C. J. T. S. (2023). The role of fintech in driving financial inclusion in developing and emerging markets: issues, challenges and prospects. *2*(1), 100-119.

Ediagbonya, V., & Tioluwani, C. (2023). The role of fintech in driving financial inclusion in developing and emerging markets: Issues, challenges and prospects. *Technological Sustainability*, 2(1), 100–119. DOI: 10.1108/TECHS-10-2021-0017

Edu, A. S., Agoyi, M., & Agozie, D. (2021). Digital security vulnerabilities and threats implications for financial institutions deploying digital technology platforms and application: FMEA and FTOPSIS analysis. *PeerJ. Computer Science*, 7, e658. DOI: 10.7717/peerj-cs.658 PMID: 34435101

Efijemue, O., Obunadike, C., Taiwo, E., Kizor, S., Olisah, S., Odooh, C., & Ejimofor, I. (2023). Cybersecurity strategies for safeguarding customers data and preventing financial fraud in the United States financial sectors. *International Journal of Soft Computing*, 14(3), 10–5121.

Egger, M., Smith, G. D., Schneider, M., & Minder, C. (1997). Bias in meta-analysis detected by a simple, graphical test. [DOI]. *BMJ (Clinical Research Ed.)*, 315(7109), 629–634. DOI: 10.1136/bmj.315.7109.629 PMID: 9310563

El Hajj, M., & Hammoud, J. (2023). Unveiling the influence of artificial intelligence and machine learning on financial markets: A comprehensive analysis of AI applications in trading, risk management, and financial operations. *Journal of Risk and Financial Management*, 16(10), 434. DOI: 10.3390/jrfm16100434

Emara, N., & El Said, A. (2021). Financial inclusion and economic growth: The role of governance in selected MENA countries. *International Review of Economics & Finance*, 75, 34–54. DOI: 10.1016/j.iref.2021.03.014

Escobar, J. J., Rodríguez, F., Prieto, B., Kimovski, D., Ortiz, A., & Damas, M. (2023). A distributed and energy-efficient KNN for EEG classification with dynamic money-saving policy in heterogeneous clusters. *Computing*, 105(11), 2487–2510. DOI: 10.1007/s00607-023-01193-7

Estrada, G. B., Park, D., & Ramayandi, A. (2010). *Financial development and economic growth in developing Asia*. Retrieved from https://papers.ssrn.com/sol3/papers.cfm?abstract_id=1751833

European Banking Authority (EBA), (2022). EBA Financial Education Repository 2021/2022

European Commission. (2021). *Digital skills initiatives | Shaping Europe's digital future*. Digital-Strategy.ec.europa.eu. https://digital-strategy.ec.europa.eu/en/policies/digital-skills-initiatives

European Commission. (2022). *EDIHs | Shaping Europe's digital future*. Digital-Strategy.ec.europa.eu. https://digital-strategy.ec.europa.eu/en/activities/edihs

European Commission. (2023). The GDPR: New Opportunities, New Obligations. Retrieved from European Commission. https://eur-lex.europa.eu/legal-content/EN/TXT/?uri=CELEX:32023R0363

Euzent, P. J., & Gallet, C. A. (2002). The business cycle and competition in the US brewing industry. *Journal of Applied Business Research*.

Executive Agency for Small and Medium-sized Enterprises. (2016). *FINANCE - Understanding... Crowdfunding*. Europa.eu. https://ec.europa.eu/newsroom/fisma/redirection/item/31532

Fabris, N. (2019). Cashless society–the future of money or a utopia? *Journal of Central Banking Theory and Practice*, 8(1), 53–66. DOI: 10.2478/jcbtp-2019-0003

Fawzy, D., Moussa, S. M., & Badr, N. L. (2022). The internet of things and architectures of big data analytics: Challenges of intersection at different domains. *IEEE Access : Practical Innovations, Open Solutions*, 10, 4969–4992. DOI: 10.1109/ACCESS.2022.3140409

Fed Small Business. (2021). *Small Business Credit Survey*. Www.fedsmallbusiness.org. https://www.fedsmallbusiness.org/reports/survey

Feeny, N. C., Zoellner, L. A., Fitzgibbons, L. A., & Foa, E. B. (2000). Exploring the roles of emotional numbing, depression, and dissociation in PTSD. *Journal of Traumatic Stress*, 13(3), 489–498. DOI: 10.1023/A:1007789409330 PMID: 10948488

Felix, A., & Rembulan, G. D. (2023). Digital Transformation and The Customer Experience: Enhancing Engagement and Loyalty. Entrepreneur: Jurnal Bisnis Manajemen dan Kewirausahaan, 4(03), 228-240.

Ferilli, G. B., Palmieri, E., Miani, S., & Stefanelli, V. (2024). The impact of FinTech innovation on digital financial literacy in Europe: Insights from the banking industry. *Research in International Business and Finance*, 69, 102218. DOI: 10.1016/j.ribaf.2024.102218

Fingerprint. (2022). *The Definitive Guide to the Real Cost of Online Fraud*. Fingerprint. https://fingerprint.com/blog/definitive-guide-real-cost-online-fraud/

Fink, A. S. (2018). *Can cryptocurrency be audited to Bank Secrecy Act and anti-money laundering regulations and normalized in the United States*. Utica College.

Fiordelisi, F., & Molyneux, P. (2004). Shareholder value efficiency in European banking. *Journal of Banking & Finance*, 31(7), 2151–2161. DOI: 10.1016/j.jbankfin.2006.10.021

Fiordelisi, F., & Ricci, O. (2004). Measuring risk in European banking. *Risk Management Journal*, 6(2), 112–127.

Forbes, J. M., Hagan, M. E., Miyahara, S., Vial, F., Manson, A. H., Meek, C. E., & Portnyagin, Y. I. (1995). Quasi-16-day oscillation in the mesosphere and lower thermosphere. *Journal of Geophysical Research*, 100(D5, A5), 9149–9156. DOI: 10.1029/94JD02157

Friedlingstein, P. J., Jones, M. W., O'Sullivan, M., Andrew, R. M., Bakker, D. C. E., Hauck, J., Le Quéré, C., Peters, G. P., Peters, W., Pongratz, J., Sitch, S., Canadell, J. G., Ciais, P., Jackson, R. B., Alin, S. R., Anthoni, P., Bates, N. R., Becker, M., Bellouin, N., & Zeng, J. (2022). Global carbon budget 2021. *Earth System Science Data*, 14(4), 1917–2005. DOI: 10.5194/essd-14-1917-2022

Friedlingstein, P. O. (2020). Global carbon budget 2020. *Earth System Science Data Discussions*, 2020, 1–3.

Fritsche, R. V. (2018). Recommendations for implementing a Bitcoin wallet using smart card.

Frost, J., Gambacorta, L., Huang, Y., Shin, H., & Zbinden, P. (2019). *BigTech and the changing structure of financial intermediation*. https://www.bis.org/publ/work779.pdf

Fuller, B., Varia, M., Yerukhimovich, A., Shen, E., Hamlin, A., Gadepally, V., Shay, R., Mitchell, J. D., & Cunningham, R. K. (2017). Sok: Cryptographically protected database search. 2017 IEEE Symposium on Security and Privacy (SP), Fung, B. S., & Halaburda, H. (2016). Central bank digital currencies: a framework for assessing why and how. *Available at SSRN 2994052*.

Fu, Q., Johanson, C. M., Wallace, J. M., & Reichler, T. (2006). Enhanced mid-latitude tropospheric warming in satellite measurements. *Science*, 311(5765), 1160–1163. DOI: 10.1126/science.1125566 PMID: 16728633

Fuster, A., Goldsmith-Pinkham, P., Ramadorai, T., & Walther, A. J. T. J. o. F. (2022). Predictably unequal? The effects of machine learning on credit markets. *77*(1), 5-47.

Fuster, A., Plosser, M., Schnabl, P., & Vickery, J. (2019). The Role of Technology in Mortgage Lending. *Review of Financial Studies*, 32(5), 1854–1899. DOI: 10.1093/rfs/hhz018

Gale, D., & Allen, F. (2000). Financial contagion. *Journal of Political Economy*, 108(1), 1–33. DOI: 10.1086/262109

Gan, J., Tsoukalas, G., & Netessine, S. (2023). Decentralized platforms- Governance, tokenomics, and ICO design. *Management Science*, 69(11), 6667–6683. DOI: 10.1287/mnsc.2021.02076

Gas, S. (2017). Mobile money, cashless society and financial inclusion: case study on somalia and kenya. Cashless Society and Financial Inclusion: Case Study on Somalia and Kenya (July 15, 2017).

Gąsiorkiewicz, L., Monkiewicz, J., & Monkiewicz, M. (2020). Technology-driven innovations in financial services: The rise of alternative finance. *Foundations of Management*, 12(1), 137–150. DOI: 10.2478/fman-2020-0011

Ge, D., Gu, J., Chang, S., & Cai, J. (2020, April). Credit card fraud detection using lightgbm model. In *2020 international conference on E-commerce and internet technology (ECIT)* (pp. 232-236). IEEE. DOI: 10.1109/ECIT50008.2020.00060

Geng, D. (2017). How technology Is reshaping financial services: Essays on consumer behavior in card, channel and cryptocurrency services.

Georgeson, D. A. (2018). Cryptocurrencies as an Alternative to Fiat Monetary Systems.

Gerard, D. (2017). *Attack of the 50 foot blockchain: Bitcoin, blockchain, Ethereum & smart contracts*. David Gerard.

Ghasemaghaei, M., & Calic, G. (2020). Assessing the impact of big data on firm innovation performance: Big data is not always better data. *Journal of Business Research*, 108, 147–162. DOI: 10.1016/j.jbusres.2019.09.062

Ghosh, A., Gupta, S., Dua, A., & Kumar, N. (2020). Security of Cryptocurrencies in blockchain technology: State-of-art, challenges and future prospects. *Journal of Network and Computer Applications*, 163, 102635. DOI: 10.1016/j.jnca.2020.102635

Gilbert, R. A. (1984). Bank market structure and competition: A survey. *Journal of Money, Credit and Banking*, 16(4), 617–645. DOI: 10.2307/1992096

Girasa, R. (2018). Regulation of cryptocurrencies and blockchain technologies. *National and International Perspectives. Suiza: Palgrave Macmillan.*

Glaser, F., & Bezzenberger, L. (2015). Beyond cryptocurrencies-a taxonomy of decentralized consensus systems. 23rd European conference on information systems (ECIS), Münster, Germany, Goforth, C. (2024). THE SECURITIES AND EXCHANGE COMMISSION AND CRYPTOASSETS: A STUDY IN IRONY. *Albany Law Review*, 87(1), 55–106.

Gohwong, S. G. (2019). Government-based Cryptocurrencies. *Asian Political Science Review, 3*(2).

Goldman Sachs. (2020). Marcus by Goldman Sachs reaches $60 billion in deposits. Retrieved from Goldman Sachs website

Goldsmith, R. (1969). *Financial structure and development.* New Haven Yale University Press.

Gomaa, A. (2018). *The creation of a cryptocurrency to support disintermediation*. NeilsonJournals Publishing. DOI: 10.4135/9781529733846

Gomber, P., Koch, J. A., & Siering, M. (2017). Digital Finance and FinTech: Current research and future research directions. *Journal of Business Economics*, 87(5), 537–580. DOI: 10.1007/s11573-017-0852-x

Gomber, P., & Koch, J. J. J. B. R. (2017). M. Siering."Digital Finance and FinTech. *Current Research and Future Research Directions*, (79), 1–8.

Gonenc, H., & Scholtens, B. (2019). Responsibility and performance relationship in the banking industry. *Sustainability (Basel)*, 11(12), 3329. DOI: 10.3390/su11123329

Goodell, J. W., Kumar, S., Lim, W. M., Pattnaik, D. J. J. o. B., & Finance, E. (2021). Artificial intelligence and machine learning in finance: Identifying foundations, themes, and research clusters from bibliometric analysis. *32*, 100577.

Goodell, J. W., Kumar, S., Lim, W. M., & Pattnaik, D. (2021). Artificial intelligence and machine learning in finance: Identifying foundations, themes, and research clusters from bibliometric analysis. *Journal of Behavioral and Experimental Finance*, 32, 100577. DOI: 10.1016/j.jbef.2021.100577

Google. (2019, May 9). *Grow with Google: ten million people trained, here's what's next*. Google. https://blog.google/around-the-globe/google-europe/grow-google-ten-million-people-trained-heres-whats-next/

Gopal, M., & Schnabl, P. (2020). The Rise of Finance Companies and FinTech Lenders in Small Business Lending. SSRN Electronic Journal. https://doi.org/DOI: 10.2139/ssrn.3600068

Gopal, S., Gupta, P., & Minocha, A. (2023, May). Advancements in Fin-Tech and Security Challenges of Banking Industry. In 2023 4th International Conference on Intelligent Engineering and Management (ICIEM) (pp. 1-6). IEEE. DOI: 10.1109/ICIEM59379.2023.10165876

GOV.UK. (2019). *Completed acquisition by PayPal Holdings, Inc. of iZettle AB Final report*. https://assets.publishing.service.gov.uk/media/5cffa74440f0b609601d0ffc/PP_iZ_final_report.pdf

Government of Pakistan, of (2020). *Pakistan Economic Survey 2018-2019*. [online] Available at: https://www.finance.gov.pk/survey/chapters_19/Economic_Survey_2018_19.pdf

Goyal, P., & Soni, P. (2024). *Stock markets volatility during crises periods: a bibliometric analysis*. Qualitative Research in Financial Markets., DOI: 10.1108/QRFM-06-2023-0143

Graham, B. (1986). *The Intelligent Investor: A Book of Practical Counsel*. Harper Business Essentials.

Green Finance Development in Bangladesh: . (2018). *The Role of private commercial banks*.

Groeneveld, J. M., & Bikker, J. A. (2000). Competition and concentration in the EU banking industry. *Credit and Capital Markets*, 33(1), 62–77. DOI: 10.3790/ccm.33.1.62

Grove, R. H. (1996). Green imperialism: colonial expansion, tropical island Edens and the origins of environmentalism. *Cambridge University Press*, 1600-1860.

Guerci, M., Montanari, F., Scapolan, A., & Epifanio, A. (2016). Green and Nongreen Recruitment Practices for Attracting Job Applicants: Exploring Independent and Interactive Effects. *International Journal of Human Resource Management*, 27(2), 129–150. DOI: 10.1080/09585192.2015.1062040

Guo, J. (2013, February 2). *Analyzing the business model for mobile payment from banks' perspective: An empirical study*. 24th European Regional ITS Conference, Florence 2013; International Telecommunications Society (ITS). https://ideas.repec.org/p/zbw/itse13/88483.html

Guo, Y., & Liang, C. (2016). Blockchain Application and Outlook in the Banking Industry. *Financial Innovation*, 2(1), 24. Advance online publication. DOI: 10.1186/s40854-016-0034-9

Gupta, M., & Sharma, A. (2022). Enhance Customer Engagement via Facebook Fanpage for Increased Purchase Intentions: Case of eWallet. In *Research Anthology on Social Media Advertising and Building Consumer Relationships* (pp. 1117–1134). IGI Global. DOI: 10.4018/978-1-6684-6287-4.ch060

Guseva, Y. (2020). A conceptual framework for digital-asset securities: Tokens and coins as debt and equity. *Md. L. Rev.*, 80, 166.

Haaf, K., & Bikker, J. A. (2002). Measures of competition and concentration in the banking industry: A review of the literature. *Economic & Financial Modelling*, 9(1), 53–70.

Haddad, C., & Hornuf, L. (2019). The emergence of the global fintech market: Economic and technological determinants. *Small Business Economics*, 53(1), 81–105. DOI: 10.1007/s11187-018-9991-x

Hairudin, A., Sifat, I. M., Mohamad, A., & Yusof, Y. (2022). Cryptocurrencies: A survey on acceptance, governance and market dynamics. *International Journal of Finance & Economics*, 27(4), 4633–4659. DOI: 10.1002/ijfe.2392

Hall, M. A. (1999). *Correlation-based feature selection for machine learning* (Doctoral dissertation, The University of Waikato).

Hameed, S., & Farooq, S. (2017). The art of crypto currencies: A comprehensive analysis of popular crypto currencies. *arXiv preprint arXiv:1711.11073.*

Hameed, K., Barika, M., Garg, S., Amin, M. B., & Kang, B. (2022). A taxonomy study on securing Blockchain-based Industrial applications: An overview, application perspectives, requirements, attacks, countermeasures, and open issues. *Journal of Industrial Information Integration*, 26, 100312. DOI: 10.1016/j.jii.2021.100312

Handro, P., & Dima, B. (2024). ANALYSING FINANCIAL MARKETS EFFICIENCY: INSIGHTS FROM A BIBLIOMETRIC AND CONTENT REVIEW. *Journal of Financial Studies*, 9(16). Advance online publication. DOI: 10.55654/JFS.2024.9.16.09

Hannan, T. H. (1997). Market share inequality, the number of competitors, and the HHI: An examination of bank pricing. *Review of Industrial Organization*, 12(1), 23–35. DOI: 10.1023/A:1007744119377

Hannan, T. H., & Berger, A. N. (1989). The price-concentration relationship in banking. *The Review of Economics and Statistics*, 71(2), 291–299. DOI: 10.2307/1926975

Hansen, K. B. (2024). The Stack Inversion: On Algo-Centrism and the Complex Architecture of Automated Financial Securities Trading Systems. *Science, Technology & Human Values*, 01622439241269983. Advance online publication. DOI: 10.1177/01622439241269983

Haq, R. (2021). Digital Transformation: Pakistan Is Now Online! [online] South Asia Investor. Available at: https://www.southasiainvestor.com/2021/08/digital-transformation-pakistan-is-now.html

Haron, S. (1996). Competition and other external determinants of the profitability of Islamic banks. *Islamic Economic Studies*, 4(2), 49–64.

Hasan, M., Hoque, A., & Le, T. (2023). Big Data-Driven Banking Operations: Opportunities, Challenges, and Data Security Perspectives. *FinTech, 2*(3), 484–509. MDPI. DOI: 10.3390/fintech2030028

Hasan, M. M., Yajuan, L., & Khan, S. (2022). Promoting China's inclusive finance through digital financial services. *Global Business Review*, 23(4), 984–1006. DOI: 10.1177/0972150919895348

Hassani, H., Huang, X., & Silva, E. (2018). Big-crypto: Big data, blockchain and cryptocurrency. *Big Data and Cognitive Computing*, 2(4), 34. DOI: 10.3390/bdcc2040034

Hayat, A. (2023). *How digital transformation impacts businesses?* [online] The Express Tribune. Available at: https://tribune.com.pk/story/2444919/how-digital-transformation-impacts-businesses

Hayder, I. M., Al Ali, G. A. N., & Younis, H. A. (2023). Predicting reaction based on customer's transaction using machine learning approaches. *Iranian Journal of Electrical and Computer Engineering*, 13(1), 1086. DOI: 10.11591/ijece.v13i1.pp1086-1096

Hays, D., & Kirilenko, A. (2021). Cryptocurrency regulation and enforcement in the US and Europe. *Fostering FinTech for Financial Transformation*, 26.

Heaton, J. B., Polson, N. G., & Witte, J. H. (2017). Deep learning for finance: Deep portfolios. *Applied Stochastic Models in Business and Industry*, 33(1), 3–12. DOI: 10.1002/asmb.2209

Heffernan, S., & Fu, X. (2009). The effects of reform on China's bank structure and performance. *Journal of Banking & Finance*, 33(1), 39–52. DOI: 10.1016/j.jbankfin.2006.11.023

Heffernan, T., & McKay, A. (2019). The academic exodus: The role of institutional support in academics leaving universities and the academy. *Professional Development in Education*, 45(3), 255–273. DOI: 10.1080/19415257.2018.1474491

Hendrikse, R., Van Meeteren, M., Bassens, D. J. E., Economy, P. A., & Space. (2020). Strategic coupling between finance, technology and the state: Cultivating a Fintech ecosystem for incumbent finance. *52*(8), 1516-1538.

Herdinata, C., Pranatasari, F. D., & Santoso, W. (2023). Factors affecting financial performance in companies based on big data analytics.

Hernandez, A., & Xu, W. (2023). Cybersecurity challenges in fintech for small businesses. *Cybersecurity Review*, 19(4), 212–230.

He, Z., & Wei, W. (2023). China's financial system and economy: A review. *Annual Review of Economics*, 15(1), 451–483. DOI: 10.1146/annurev-economics-072622-095926

Hicks, J. R. (1935). Annual survey of economic theory: The theory of monopoly. *Econometrica*, 3(1), 1–20. DOI: 10.2307/1907343

Hidayat-ur-Rehman, I., Alsolamy, M. J. J. o. O. I. T., Market,, & Complexity. (2023). A SEM-ANN analysis to examine sustainable performance in SMEs: The moderating role of transformational leadership. *9*(4), 100166.

Hochstein, A., Horn, E., & Palomino, M. (2015, June). Intelligent pipeline solution: leveraging breakthrough industrial internet technologies and Big data analytics for safer, more efficient oil and gas pipeline operations. In 10th Pipeline Technology Conference 2015. EITEP Institute.

Hollanders, M. J. J. o. p. s., & systems. (2020). FinTech and financial inclusion: Opportunities and challenges. *14*(4), 315-325.

Hollebeek, L. D., & Macky, K. (2019). Digital content marketing's role in fostering consumer engagement, trust, and value: Framework, fundamental propositions, and implications. *Journal of Interactive Marketing*, 45(1), 27–41. DOI: 10.1016/j.intmar.2018.07.003

Horobet, A., Boubaker, S., Belascu, L., Negreanu, C. C., & Dinca, Z. (2024). Technology-driven advancements: Mapping the landscape of algorithmic trading literature. *Technological Forecasting and Social Change*, 209, 123746–123746. DOI: 10.1016/j.techfore.2024.123746

Hossain, M. (2020). The effects of green banking practices on financial performance of listed banking companies in Bangladesh. *Canadian Journal of Business and Information Studies*, 020, 01200128.

Hossan, M. R., Nirob, F. A., Islam, A., Rakin, T. M., & Al-Amin, M. (2024). A Comprehensive Analysis of Blockchain Technology and Consensus Protocols Across Multilayered Framework. *IEEE Access : Practical Innovations, Open Solutions*.

Hsueh, S.-C., & Kuo, C.-H. (2017). *Effective matching forP2Plending by mining strong association rules.* Paper presented at the Proceedings of the 3rd International Conference on Industrial and Business Engineering.

Huang, K. (2020, November). An optimized LightGBM model for fraud detection. [). IOP Publishing.]. *Journal of Physics: Conference Series*, 1651(1), 012111. DOI: 10.1088/1742-6596/1651/1/012111

Hua, X., & Huang, Y. (2020). Understanding China's fintech sector: Development, impacts and risks. *European Journal of Finance*, 27(4–5), 321–333.

Huizinga, H., & Demirgüç-Kunt, A. (2000). Financial structure and bank profitability. *World Bank Policy Research Working Paper No. 2430*. World Bank

Huizinga, H., & Demirgüç-Kunt, A. (1999). Determinants of commercial bank interest margins and profitability: Some international evidence. *The World Bank Economic Review*, 13(2), 379–408. DOI: 10.1093/wber/13.2.379

Hu, J., Shi, Y., & Xu, L. (2022). Fintech response to COVID-19: Implications for small business financing. *Journal of Pandemic Economics*, 14(3), 101–115.

Hussain, M., Ameen, Z., & Rasool, N. (2023). Roshan Digital Account: A Digital Innovation in Pakistan and Its Impact on Customers' Satisfaction. *Journal of Development and Social Sciences*, 4(I). Advance online publication. DOI: 10.47205/jdss.2023(4-I)04

Hussain, M., & Papastathopoulos, A. (2022). Organizational readiness for digital financial innovation and financial resilience. *International Journal of Production Economics*, 243, 108326. DOI: 10.1016/j.ijpe.2021.108326

Hussain, S., Gul, R., & Ullah, S. (2023). Role of financial inclusion and ICT for sustainable economic development in developing countries. *Technological Forecasting and Social Change*, 194, 122725. DOI: 10.1016/j.techfore.2023.122725

Hu, Z., & Tang, L. (2012). Income inequality and environmental quality in developing countries. *Ecological Economics*, 75, 12–21.

IBM. (2023). *Cost of a Data Breach 2023*. IBM. https://www.ibm.com/reports/data-breach

Ibrahim, O. (2024). Cryptocurrency; the new unleashed financial instrument, should it be regulated. *Humanities Journal of University of Zakho*, 12(2), 303–317. DOI: 10.26436/hjuoz.2024.12.2.1272

Iman, N. (2018). Is mobile payment still relevant in the fintech era? *Electronic Commerce Research and Applications*, 30, 72–82. DOI: 10.1016/j.elerap.2018.05.009

Indriastuti, M., & Chariri, A. (2021). The role of green investment and corporate social responsibility investment on sustainable performance. *Cogent Business & Management*, 8(1), 1960120. DOI: 10.1080/23311975.2021.1960120

Ingraham, N. (2012, May 10). *The Pebble smartwatch: a record-breaking Kickstarter success story*. The Verge. https://www.theverge.com/2012/5/10/3011651/pebble-smartwatch-kickstarter-project

International Finance Corporation. (2017). *ASSESSMENT OF THE SHORTFALLS AND OPPORTUNITIES IN FINANCING MICRO, SMALL AND MEDIUM ENTERPRISES IN EMERGING MARKETS MSME FINANCE GAP Public Disclosure Authorized Public Disclosure Authorized Public Disclosure Authorized Public Disclosure Authorized.* https://documents1.worldbank.org/curated/en/653831510568517947/pdf/121264-WP-PUBLIC-MSMEReportFINAL.pdf

International Monetary Fund. (2020). "Digital Money Across Borders: Macro-Financial Implications." Retrieved from IMF website. https://www.imf.org/en/Publications/Policy-Papers/Issues/2020/10/17/Digital-Money-Across-Borders-Macro-Financial-Implications-49823

Intuit. (2021). *Small business e-commerce survey: Moving online in 2021 | QuickBooks*. Quickbooks.intuit.com. https://quickbooks.intuit.com/r/inspiration/small-business-ecommerce-survey/

Iqbal, A., & Kassim, A. Z. (2023). Ease of use and standardisation on potential usage of ATMs in Bahrain. *International Journal of Electronic Banking*, 4(1), 1–18. DOI: 10.1504/IJEBANK.2023.134482

Islam, J. U., & Rahman, Z. (2016). Linking customer engagement to trust and word-of-mouth on Facebook brand communities: An empirical study. *Journal of Internet Commerce*, 15(1), 40–58. DOI: 10.1080/15332861.2015.1124008

Jabbour, C. J. C., Fernando, C. A. S., & Nagano, M. S. (2010). Contributions of HRM throughout the Stages of Environmental Management: Methodological Triangulation Applied to Companies in Brazil. *International Journal of Human Resource Management*, 21(7), 1049–1089. DOI: 10.1080/09585191003783512

Jackson, S. E., Renwick, D. W. S., Charbel, J. C. J., & Muller-Camen, M. (2011). State-of-the-Art and Future Directions for Green Human Resource Management: Introduction to the Special Issue. *German Journal of Human Resource Management: Zeitschrift Für Personalforschung*, 25(2), 99–116. DOI: 10.1177/239700221102500203

Jacquemin, A. (1982). Imperfect market structure and international trade: Some recent research. *Kyklos*, 35(1), 135–152. DOI: 10.1111/j.1467-6435.1982.tb01216.x

Jacquemin, A., & de Jong, H. (1982). Price dispersion and oligopolistic price leadership. [JSTOR]. *The Review of Economics and Statistics*, 64(3), 497–503.

Jagtiani, J., & Lemieux, C. (2018). Do fintech lenders penetrate areas that are underserved by traditional banks? *Journal of Economics and Business*, 100, 43–54. DOI: 10.1016/j.jeconbus.2018.03.001

Jagtiani, J., & Lemieux, C. (2019). The roles of alternative data and machine learning in fintech lending: Evidence from the LendingClub consumer platform. *Financial Management*, 48(4), 1009–1029. DOI: 10.1111/fima.12295

Jain, A. K., Gupta, N., & Gupta, B. B. (2024). A Survey on Scalable Consensus Algorithms for Blockchain Technology. *Cyber Security and Applications*, 100065.

Jain, R., & Bagrecha, Dr. C. (2024). Algorithmic Trading And Market Liquidity Dynamics In Indian Energy Futures: A Comprehensive Analysis". *Educational Administration Theory and Practices*. DOI: 10.53555/kuey.v30i6.5735

Jain, R., Prajapati, D., & Dangi, A. (2023). Transforming the financial sector: A review of recent advancements in FinTech. Available at *SSRN* 4380348.

Jangjarat, K., Kraiwanit, T., Thanawiwat, T., & Chutipat, V. (2023). Acceptance of an initial coin offering for investment in a developing economy. *Corporate and Business Strategy Review*, 4(2), 29–36. DOI: 10.22495/cbsrv4i2art3

Jarvis, R., & Han, H. (2021). FinTech innovation: Review and future research directions. International Journal of Banking. *Finance and Insurance Technologies*, 1(1), 79–102.

Javelin Strategy & Research. (2020). *2020 Identity Fraud Study: Genesis of the Identity Fraud Crisis*. Javelin. https://javelinstrategy.com/research/2020-identity-fraud-study-genesis-identity-fraud-crisis

Jayarathne, P. G. (2020). The Impact of Employee Green Behavior on Green Banking Performance of Select Private Sector Banks in Sri Lanka. *IUP Journal of Bank Management*,, 19(2).

Jayasekara, S. D. (2021). Deficient regimes of anti-money laundering and countering the financing of terrorism: Agenda of digital banking and financial inclusion. *Journal of Money Laundering Control*, 24(1), 150–162. DOI: 10.1108/JMLC-04-2020-0035

Jejeniwa, T. O., Mhlongo, N. Z., & Jejeniwa, T. O.Temitayo Oluwaseun JejeniwaNoluthando Zamanjomane MhlongoTitilola Olaide Jejeniwa. (2024). AI solutions for Developmental Economics: Opportunities and challenges in financial inclusion and poverty alleviation. *International Journal of Advanced Economics*, 6(4), 108–123. DOI: 10.51594/ijae.v6i4.1073

Jejeniwa, T. O., Mhlongo, N. Z., & Jejeniwa, T. O.Temitayo Oluwaseun Jejeniwa-Noluthando Zamanjomane MhlongoTitilola Olaide Jejeniwa. (2024). Theoretical perspectives on digital transformation in financial services: Insights from case studies in Africa and the United States. *Finance & Accounting Research Journal*, 6(4), 674–683. DOI: 10.51594/farj.v6i4.1068

Jeong, H., Shin, K., Kim, E., & Kim, S. (2020). Does open innovation enhance a large firm's financial sustainability? A case of the Korean food industry. *Journal of Open Innovation*, 6(4), 101. DOI: 10.3390/joitmc6040101

Jha, D. &. (2013). A study of green banking trends in India. *International Monthly Refereed Journal Of Research In Management And Technology*, 127–132.

Jha, N. (2013). A study of green banking trends in India. *International Monthly Referred Journal of Research in Management and Technology*, 2, 127–132.

Jiménez-Serranía, V., Parra-Domínguez, J., De La Prieta, F., & Corchado, J. M. (2021). Cryptocurrencies impact on financial markets: Some insights on its regulation and economic and accounting implications. International Congress on Blockchain and Applications, Johnson, K. N. (2020). Decentralized finance: Regulating cryptocurrency exchanges. *Wm. & Mary L. Rev., 62*, 1911. JOURJON, G. Blockchain Double Spending With Low Mining Power and Network Delays.

Jordan, M. (2018). *European Economic and Social Committee*. https://www.eesc.europa.eu/sites/default/files/files/qe-01-18-515-en-n.pdf

Joshi, G., & Dash, R. K. (2024). Exchange-traded funds and the future of passive investments: A bibliometric review and future research agenda. *Future Business Journal*, 10(1), 17. Advance online publication. DOI: 10.1186/s43093-024-00306-8

Joshi, R., Gupte, R., & Saravanan, P. (2018). A random forest approach for predicting online buying behavior of Indian customers. *Theoretical Economics Letters*, 8(03), 448–475. DOI: 10.4236/tel.2018.83032

Judijanto, L., Fildansyah, R., Sudarmanto, E., Harsono, I., & Afandy, C. (2024). Bibliometric Analysis of the Application of Internet of Things (IoT) in Financial Services. *West Science Interdisciplinary Studies*, 2(02), 398–405. DOI: 10.58812/wsis.v2i02.664

Judijanto, L., Mokodenseho, S., Mokodompit, A. T., Mamonto, M., & Lantong, S. M. (2024). Trends in Sustainable Banking Practices: A Bibliometric Review of Green Financial Services and Risk Management Strategies. *Jurnal Multidisiplin West Science*, 3(03), 305–313. DOI: 10.58812/jmws.v3i03.1049

Jumaili, M. L. F., & Karim, S. M. (2021). Comparison of tow two cryptocurrencies: Bitcoin and Litecoin. Journal of Physics: Conference Series, Kajtazi, A., & Moro, A. (2017). Bitcoin, portfolio diversification and Chinese financial Markets. *Available atSSRN* 3062064.

Jussila, A. (2015). Mobile money as an enabler for entrepreneurship: case Eastern Africa.

Kaivo-oja, J. R. L., & Lauraeus, I. T. (2018). The VUCA approach as a solution concept to corporate foresight challenges and global technological disruption. foresight, 20(1), 27-49.

Kajol, K., Singh, R., & Paul, J. (2022). Adoption of digital financial transactions: A review of literature and future research agenda. *Technological Forecasting and Social Change*, 184, 121991. DOI: 10.1016/j.techfore.2022.121991

Kandpal, V., & Mehrotra, R. (2019). Financial inclusion: The role of fintech and digital financial services in India. *Indian Journal of Economics and Business*, 18(1), 95–104.

Karim, S., Naz, F., Naeem, M. A., Vigne, S. A. J. E. A., & Policy. (2022). Is FinTech providing effective solutions to Small and Medium Enterprises (SMEs) in ASEAN countries?, *75*, 335-344.

Karim, M., Qureshi, I., & Haider, S. (2021). Financial inclusion through fintech in emerging markets. *Journal of Finance and Development*, 15(2), 58–74.

Kärnä, K. A. (2003). Business responses to climate change: Identifying emergent strategies. *California Management Review*, 47(3), 6–20.

Kass-Hanna, J., Lyons, A. C., & Liu, F. (2022). Building financial resilience through financial and digital literacy in South Asia and Sub-Saharan Africa. *Emerging Markets Review*, 51, 100846. DOI: 10.1016/j.ememar.2021.100846

Kemme, P. A., Jongbloed, A. W., & Mroz, Z. (1994). Apparent digestibility and retention of nutrients bound to phytate complexes as influenced by microbial phytase and feeding regimen in pigs. *Journal of Animal Science*, 72(1), 126–135. DOI: 10.2527/1994.721126x PMID: 8138479

KEMP. S. (February, 16 2022). *DIGITAL 2022: PAKISTAN*. Retrieved from DATA REPORTAL: https://datareportal.com/reports/digital-2022-pakistan

Kergroach, S. (2021). SMEs Going Digital: Policy challenges and recommendations. Www.oecd-Ilibrary.org. DOI: 10.1787/ec5958b3-en

Khairunnessa, F. V.-B., Vazquez-Brust, D. A., & Yakovleva, N. (2021). A review of the recent developments of green banking in Bangladesh. *Sustainability (Basel)*, 13(4), 1904. DOI: 10.3390/su13041904

Khalid, M., Abbas, S., & Rizvi, S. K. A. (2018). Exploring the Impact of Digitalization on Business: A Case Study of Pakistan. *Pakistan Journal of Commerce and Social Sciences*, 12(2), 472–492.

Khan, H. Z., Bose, S., Sheehy, B., & Quazi, A. (2021). Green banking disclosure, firm value and the moderating role of a contextual factor: Evidence from a distinctive regulatory setting. *Business Strategy and the Environment*, 30(8), 3651–3670. DOI: 10.1002/bse.2832

Khan, M. H., & Muktar, S. N. (2020). A Bibliometric Analysis of Green Human Resource Manage- ment Based on Scopus Platform. *Cogent Business & Management*, 7(1), 1831165. DOI: 10.1080/23311975.2020.1831165

Khan, M. K. (2015). The Role of Financial institutions and the Economic Growth: A Literature Review. *European Journal of Business and Management*, 7(1), 95–99.

Khanom, T. (2017). Cloud Accounting: A Theoretical Overview. *IOSR Journal of Business and Management*, 19(06), 31–38. DOI: 10.9790/487X-1906053138

Khilji, U. (2021, August 21). *Cybersecurity policy*. Retrieved from DAWN: https://www.dawn.com/news/1641754

Kiliç, M. (2016). Online corporate social responsibility (CSR) disclosure in the banking industry: Evidence from Turkey. *International Journal of Bank Marketing*, 34(4), 550–569. DOI: 10.1108/IJBM-04-2015-0060

Kim, K., & Hann, I.-H. (2013). Does Crowdfunding Democratize Access to Capital? A Geographical Analysis. SSRN *Electronic Journal*. DOI: 10.2139/ssrn.2334590

Kim, C. J. (1994). Dynamic linear models with Markov-switching. *Journal of Econometrics*, 60(1), 135–160.

Kim, D., Yu, J., & Hassan, M. (2018). Financial inclusion and economic growth in OIC countries. *Research in International Business and Finance*, 43, 1–14. DOI: 10.1016/j.ribaf.2017.07.178

Kim, S., Lee, M., & Park, J. (2021). The digital divide in fintech: Urban and rural disparities. *Technology in Finance Journal*, 10(2), 98–110.

Kim, Y. J., Kim, W. G., Choi, H.-M., & Phetvaroon, K. (2019). The Effect of Green Human Resource Management on Hotel Employees' Eco-Friendly Behavior and Environmental Performance. *International Journal of Hospitality Management*, 76, 83–93. DOI: 10.1016/j.ijhm.2018.04.007

King, R. G., & Levine, R. (1993). Finance and growth: Schumpeter might be right. *The Quarterly Journal of Economics*, 108(3), 717–737. DOI: 10.2307/2118406

King, R. G., & Levine, R. (1993). Finance, entrepreneurship, and growth: Theory and evidence. *Journal of Monetary Economics*, 32(3), 513–542. DOI: 10.1016/0304-3932(93)90028-E

King, R. G., & Levine, R. (1993a). *Financial intermediation and economic development* (Vol. 15689). Cambridge University Press.

Koh, L., Dolgui, A., & Sarkis, J. (2020). Blockchain in transport and logistics–paradigms and transitions. *International Journal of Production Research*, 58(7), 2054–2062. DOI: 10.1080/00207543.2020.1736428

Koopman, C., Mitchell, M., & Thierer, A. (2014). The sharing economy and consumer protection regulation: The case for policy change. *SSRN*, 8, 529. DOI: 10.2139/ssrn.2535345

Kosmidou, K., Pasiouras, F., & Tsaklanganos, A. (2007). Domestic and multinational determinants of foreign bank profits: The case of Greek banks operating abroad. *Journal of Multinational Financial Management*, 17(1), 1–15. DOI: 10.1016/j.mulfin.2006.02.002

Kou, M., Yang, Y., & Chen, K. (2024). Financial technology research: Past and future trajectories. *International Review of Economics & Finance*, 93, 162–181. Advance online publication. DOI: 10.1016/j.iref.2024.03.032

Kowalewski, O., & Pisany, P. J. T. (2023). The rise of fintech: a cross-country perspective. *122*, 102642.

KPMG. (2019). *Courage to change*. https://assets.kpmg.com/content/dam/kpmg/dk/pdf/dk-2020/01/KPMG_2019_annual_report_web.pdf

KPMG. (2020, February 3). *Pulse of Fintech archive*. KPMG; KPMG. https://kpmg.com/xx/en/home/insights/2020/02/pulse-of-fintech-archive.html

Kraus, S. R., Rehman, S. U., & García, F. J. S. (2020). Corporate social responsibility and environmental performance: The mediating role of environmental strategy and green innovation. *Technological Forecasting and Social Change*, 160, 120262. DOI: 10.1016/j.techfore.2020.120262

Krejcie, R. V., & Morgan, D. W. (1970). Determining sample size for research activities. *Educational and Psychological Measurement*, 30(3), 607–610. DOI: 10.1177/001316447003000308

Kucheryavenko, M., Dmytryk, O., & Golovashevych, O. (2019). Cryptocurrencies: development, features and classification. *Financial and credit activity problems of theory and practice, 3*(30), 371-374.

Kumar Inani, S., Pradhan, H., Kumar, S., & Biswas, B. (2024). Navigating the technical analysis in stock markets: Insights from bibliometric and topic modeling approaches. *Investment Management and Financial Innovations*, 21(1), 275–288. DOI: 10.21511/imfi.21(1).2024.21

Kumar, A., Sharma, S., Vashistha, R., Srivastava, V., Tabash, M. I., Munim, Z. H., & Paltrinieri, A. (2022). International Journal of Emerging Markets: a bibliometric review 2006–2020. *International Journal of Emerging Markets*. DOI: 10.1108/IJOEM-05-2021-0668

Kumar, A., & Jain, P. (2020). Digital Transformation and Its Impact on Business Performance. *Journal of Management Information and Decision Sciences*, 23(3), 311–328.

Kumar, K., & Prakash, A. (2018). Developing a framework for assessing sustainable banking performance of the Indian banking sector. *Social Responsibility Journal*, 15(5), 689–709. DOI: 10.1108/SRJ-07-2018-0162

Kumar, K., & Prakash, A. (2020). Managing sustainability in banking: Extent of sustainable banking adaptations of banking sector in India. *Environment, Development and Sustainability*, 22(6), 5199–5217. DOI: 10.1007/s10668-019-00421-5

Kumar, S., Janu, N., Raja, L., & Kumar, A. (2022). A fuzzy ISM analysis of factors in growth of initial coin offerings (ICOs). *Journal of Interdisciplinary Mathematics*, 25(3), 815–825. DOI: 10.1080/09720502.2021.2015099

Kumar, V., & Pansari, A. (2016). Competitive advantage through engagement. *JMR, Journal of Marketing Research*, 53(4), 497–514. DOI: 10.1509/jmr.15.0044

Kumar, V., Ramachandran, D., & Kumar, B. (2021). Influence of new-age technologies on marketing: A research agenda. *Journal of Business Research*, 125, 864–877. DOI: 10.1016/j.jbusres.2020.01.007

Kurt, S., Heitz, J., Bundi, N., & Breymann, W. (2018). Large-scale data-driven financial risk modeling using big data technology. In 2018 IEEE/ACM 5th International Conference on Big Data Computing Applications and Technologies (BDCAT) (pp. 206-207). IEEE. DOI: 10.1109/BDCAT.2018.00033

Kwok, S., & Zhang, X. (2024). Deployment of Blockchain Technology on the Banking Industry in China: A Policy Review Study. *European Academic Journal-II CHINA, 1*(1).

La Torre, M., & Chiappini, H. (2020). Sustainable finance: Trends, opportunities and risks. Contemporary Issues in Sustainable Finance: Creating an Efficient Market through Innovative Policies and Instruments, 281-287.

Laeven, L., Ratnovski, M., & Tong, M. H. (2014). Bank size and systemic risk. *IMF Economic Review*, 61(2), 225–270. DOI: 10.1057/imfer.2013.12

Laghari, F., & Ahmed, F. (2023). Cash flow management and its effect on firm performance: Empirical evidence on non-financial firms of China. *PLoS ONE, 18*(6). ncbi. DOI: 10.1371/journal.pone.0287135

Lahmadi, A., Bertin, E., & Li, R. (2022). BRAINS 2020 special issue: Blockchain research and applications for innovative networks and services. *International Journal of Network Management*, 32(2), e2189. DOI: 10.1002/nem.2189

Lähteenmäki, I., Nätti, S., & Saraniemi, S. J. J. o. b. r. (2022). Digitalization-enabled evolution of customer value creation: An executive view in financial services. *146*, 504-517.

Larivière, B., & Van den Poel, D. (2005). Predicting customer retention and profitability by using random forests and regression forests techniques. *Expert Systems with Applications*, 29(2), 472–484. DOI: 10.1016/j.eswa.2005.04.043

Lebedev, V. V., Deberdeeva, N. A., Farkova, N. A., & Korobeinikova, L. S. (2022). Systemic Risk Management of Investments in Innovation Based on CSR. *Risks*, 10(5), 87. DOI: 10.3390/risks10050087

Lee, C. C., Lou, R., & Wang, F. (2023). Digital financial inclusion and poverty alleviation: Evidence from the sustainable development of China. *Economic Analysis and Policy*, 77, 418–434. DOI: 10.1016/j.eap.2022.12.004

Lee, C. L., Ahmad, R., Lee, W. S., Khalid, N., & Karim, Z. A. (2022). The financial sustainability of state-owned enterprises in an emerging economy. *Economies*, 10(10), 233. DOI: 10.3390/economies10100233

Lee, I., & Shin, Y. J. (2018). Fintech: Ecosystem, business models, investment decisions, and challenges. *Business Horizons*, 61(1), 35–46. DOI: 10.1016/j.bushor.2017.09.003

Lee, J. H. (2019). *Systematic approach to analyzing security and vulnerabilities of blockchain systems*. Massachusetts Institute of Technology.

Lee, J., & Layne, K. (2001). Developing fully functional E-government: A four-stage model. *Government Information Quarterly*, 18(2), 122–136. DOI: 10.1016/S0740-624X(01)00066-1

Lee, J., & Yoon, K. (2023). The role of fintech in SME growth: A review of digital solutions. *Financial Management Quarterly*, 32(1), 50–65.

Lee, M. T., & Raschke, R. L. (2020). Innovative sustainability and stakeholders' shared understanding: The secret sauce to "performance with a purpose". *Journal of Business Research*, 108, 20–28. DOI: 10.1016/j.jbusres.2019.10.020

Lee, M.-J., & Choi, S.-Y. (2024). Insights into the dynamics of market efficiency spill-over of financial assets in different equity markets. *Physica A*, 641, 129719–129719. DOI: 10.1016/j.physa.2024.129719

Lendio. (2024). *Lendio Surpasses $1.5 Billion in Small Business Loans Facilitated.* SME Finance Forum. https://smefinanceforum.org/post/lendio-surpasses-15-billion-in-small-business-loans-facilitated?page=120

Levine, R. (2005). Finance and growth: theory and evidence. *Handbook of economic growth, 1*, 865-934.

Levine, L., Ratnovski, M., & Tong, M. H. (2009). Bank governance, regulation, and risk-taking. *Journal of Financial Economics*, 93(2), 259–275. DOI: 10.1016/j.jfineco.2008.09.003

Levisohn, J. A., & Isacson, O. (1991). Excitotoxic lesions of the rat entorhinal cortex: Effects of selective neuronal damage on acquisition and retention of a non-spatial reference memory task. *Brain Research*, 568(1), 113–122. DOI: 10.1016/0006-8993(91)91458-D PMID: 1810624

Leyshon, A., & Thrift, N. (1993). The restructuring of the UK financial services industry in the 1990s: A reversal of fortune? *Journal of Rural Studies*, 9(3), 223–241. DOI: 10.1016/0743-0167(93)90068-U

Leyshon, A., & Thrift, N. (1994). Access to financial services and financial infrastructure withdrawal: Problems and policies. *Area*, •••, 268–275.

Leyshon, A., & Thrift, N. (1995). Geographies of financial exclusion: Financial abandonment in Britain and the United States. *Transactions of the Institute of British Geographers*, 20(3), 312–341. DOI: 10.2307/622654

Li, E. Y., & Zafar, U. (2023). Fostering Fintech adoption in growing economies: Opportunities, challenges, and strategies.

Li, H., Lu, Z., & Yin, Q. J. S. (2023). The development of Fintech and SME innovation: Empirical evidence from China. *15*(3), 2541.

Lim, W. M., Gupta, S., Aggarwal, A., Paul, J., & Sadhna, P. J. J. o. S. M. (2021). How do digital natives perceive and react toward online advertising? Implications for SMEs. 1-35.

Lind, J., Naor, O., Eyal, I., Kelbert, F., Sirer, E. G., & Pietzuch, P. (2019). Teechain: a secure payment network with asynchronous blockchain access. Proceedings of the 27th ACM Symposium on Operating Systems Principles, Liska, A., & Gallo, T. (2016). *Ransomware: Defending against digital extortion.* " O'Reilly Media, Inc.". DOI: 10.1145/3341301.3359627

Linh, T. H. (2018). Analysis of income inequality determinants in developing countries. *Development Policy Review*, 36(5), 623–640.

Liu, J., Li, Z., & Hu, X. (2023). A Study of the Impact of Mobile Payment on the Enhancement of Consumption Structure and Pattern of Chinese Rural Households. *Agriculture*, 13(11), 2082. DOI: 10.3390/agriculture13112082

Liu, Q., Chan, K.-C., & Chimhundu, R. (2024). Fintech research: Systematic mapping, classification, and Future Directions. *Financial Innovation*, 10(1), 24. DOI: 10.1186/s40854-023-00524-z

Li, X., Sigov, A., Ratkin, L., Ivanov, L. A., & Li, L. (2023). Artificial intelligence applications in finance: A survey. *Journal of Management Analytics*, 10(4), 676–692. DOI: 10.1080/23270012.2023.2244503

Longoni, A., Luzzini, D., & Guerci, M. (2018). Deploying Environmental Management Across Functions: The Relationship Between Green Human Resource Management and Green Supply Chain Management. *Journal of Business Ethics*, 151(4), 1081–1095. DOI: 10.1007/s10551-016-3228-1

Lopez Subires, M. D., Alcaide Munoz, L., Navarro Galera, A., & Rodriguez Bolivar, M. P. (2019). The influence of socio-demographic factors on financial sustainability of public services: A comparative analysis in regional governments and local governments. *Sustainability (Basel)*, 11(21), 6008. DOI: 10.3390/su11216008

Lorenz, E., Pommet, S. J. I., & Innovation. (2021). Mobile money, inclusive finance and enterprise innovativeness: An analysis of East African nations. *28*(2), 136-159.

Lorenz, G. (2024). Regulating Decentralized Financial Technology: A Qualitative Study on the Challenges of Regulating DeFi with a Focus on Embedded Supervision. *Stan. J. Blockchain L. & Pol'y*, 7, 136.

Loshin, D. (2013). *Big data analytics: from strategic planning to enterprise integration with tools, techniques, NoSQL, and graph.* Elsevier.

Lu, Y., Tian, T., & Ge, C. J. R. P. (2023). Asymmetric effects of renewable energy, fintech development, natural resources, and environmental regulations on the climate change in the post-covid era. *85*, 103902.

Lukkarinen, A., Teich, J. E., Wallenius, H., & Wallenius, J. (2016). Success drivers of online equity crowdfunding campaigns. *Decision Support Systems*, 87, 26–38. DOI: 10.1016/j.dss.2016.04.006

Lymperopoulos, A. R. (2012). GRK2 inhibition in heart failure. *something old, something new.Current Pharmaceutical Design*, 18(2), 186–191. DOI: 10.2174/138161212799040510 PMID: 22229578

Lymperopoulos, C., Chaniotakis, I. E., & Soureli, M. (2012). A model of green bank marketing. *Journal of Financial Services Marketing*, 17(2), 177–186. DOI: 10.1057/fsm.2012.10

Lyons, A., & Kass-Hanna, J. (2019). *THE FUTURE OF WORK AND EDUCATION FOR THE DIGITAL AGE Leaving No One Behind: Measuring the Multidimensionality of Digital Literacy in the Age of AI and other Transformative Technologies*. https://t20japan.org/wp-content/uploads/2019/03/t20-japan-tf7-10-multidimensionality-digital-literacy.pdf

Machkour, B., & Abriane, A. (2020). Industry 4.0 and its Implications for the Financial Sector. *Procedia Computer Science*, 177, 496–502. DOI: 10.1016/j.procs.2020.10.068

MacKenzie, I., Meyer, C., & Noble, S. (2019, October 1). *How retailers can keep up with consumers*. McKinsey & Company. https://www.mckinsey.com/industries/retail/our-insights/how-retailers-can-keep-up-with-consumers

Madhava Priya Dananjayan, Sridevi Gopakumar, & Parthasarathi Narayanasamy. (2023). Unleashing the algorithmic frontier: Navigating the impact of algo trading on investor portfolios. *Journal of Information Technology Teaching Cases*. DOI: 10.1177/20438869231189519

Mahnamfar, A., Bicakci, K., & Uzunay, Y. (2024). ROSTAM: A passwordless web single sign-on solution mitigating server breaches and integrating credential manager and federated identity systems. *Computers & Security*, 139, 103739. DOI: 10.1016/j.cose.2024.103739

Maiti, M., & Ghosh, U. (2021). Next-generation internet of things in fintech ecosystem. *IEEE Internet of Things Journal*, 10(3), 2104–2111. DOI: 10.1109/JIOT.2021.3063494

Ma, J., & Zhao, L. (2008). An analysis of the Chinese housing market bubble. *China Economic Review*, 19(4), 539–552.

Makarov, I., & Schoar, A. (2022a). *Cryptocurrencies and decentralized finance*. DeFi. DOI: 10.3386/w30006

Makarov, I., & Schoar, A. (2022b). Cryptocurrencies and decentralized finance (DeFi). *Brookings Papers on Economic Activity*, 2022(1), 141–215. DOI: 10.1353/eca.2022.0014

Malik, A., Pereira, V., Budhwar, P., Froese, F. J., Minbaeva, D., Sun, J., Nguyen, A. T., & Xue, S. (2022). Multilevel relational influences on HRM practices: A cross-country comparative reflective review of HRM practices in Asia. *Asian Business & Management*, 21(5), 745–779. DOI: 10.1057/s41291-022-00208-z

Manogna, R. L., & Anand, A. (2023). A bibliometric analysis on the application of deep learning in finance: Status, development and future directions. *Kybernetes*. Advance online publication. DOI: 10.1108/K-04-2023-0637

Marcacci, A. (2018). *Regulating Investor Protection under EU Law*. Springer. DOI: 10.1007/978-3-319-90297-5

MarketsandMarkets. (2023). *FinTech Blockchain Market Size, Share and Global Market Forecast to 2023 | MarketsandMarkets*. Www.marketsandmarkets.com. https://www.marketsandmarkets.com/Market-Reports/fintech-blockchain-market-38566589.html

Martínez-del-Río, J., Céspedes-Lorente, J., & Carmona-Moreno, E. (2012). High-Involvement Work Practices and Environmen- tal Capabilities: How HIWPS Create Environmentally Based Sustainable Competitive Advantages. *Human Resource Management*, 51(6), 827–850. DOI: 10.1002/hrm.21505

Masood, T., & Sonntag, P. J. C. i. i. (2020). Industry 4.0: Adoption challenges and benefits for SMEs. *121*, 103261.

Masri, H. A., & Jaaron, A. A. M. (2017). Assessing Green Human Resources Management Practices in Palestinian Manufacturing Context: An Empirical Study. *Journal of Cleaner Production*, 143, 474–489. DOI: 10.1016/j.jclepro.2016.12.087

Mastercard. (2024, May 24). *Mastercard accelerates commitment to digital transformation in Africa*. Mastercard.com. https://www.mastercard.com/news/press/2024/may/mastercard-accelerates-commitment-to-digital-transformation-in-africa/

Matthews, K. (2009). Credit crunch and financial instability: A UK perspective. [Emerald Insight]. *Journal of Financial Regulation and Compliance*, 17(1), 19–34.

Matthews, K., & Thompson, J. (2019). *The Economics of Banking* (4th ed.). Wiley-Blackwell.

Maudos, J. (2017). Financial structure and growth: Empirical evidence for Spain. *Economic Modelling*, 60, 107–120.

Maudos, J., & de Guevara, J. F. (1998). Explaining interest margins in the Spanish banking sector. *Review of European Economic Policy*, 33(3), 123–135.

Mavlutova, I., Spilbergs, A., Verdenhofs, A., Natrins, A., Arefjevs, I., & Volkova, T. (2022). Digital Transformation as a driver of the Financial Sector Sustainable Development: An impact on financial inclusion and operational efficiency. *Sustainability (Basel)*, 15(1), 207. DOI: 10.3390/su15010207

Mayer, C. (1988). New issues in corporate finance. *European Economic Review*, 32(5), 1167–1183. DOI: 10.1016/0014-2921(88)90077-3

Mbama, C. I., & Ezepue, P. O. (2018). Digital banking, customer experience and bank financial performance: UK customers' perceptions. *International Journal of Bank Marketing*, 36(2), 230–255. DOI: 10.1108/IJBM-11-2016-0181

Mbiti, I., & Weil, D. N. (2015). Mobile Banking: The Impact of M-Pesa in Kenya. *NBER Chapters*, 247–293. https://ideas.repec.org/h/nbr/nberch/13367.html

Mbogo, M. (2010). The impact of mobile payments on the success and growth of micro-business: The case of M-Pesa in Kenya. Journal of language, technology & entrepreneurship in Africa, 2(1), 182-203.

McCarthy-Jones, A., & Turner, M. (2024). *Illicit Business*. Taylor & Francis. DOI: 10.4324/9781003293620

Mccorquodale, R. (2016, August 11). *6 years of small business stories | Funding Circle UK*. Funding Circle UK. https://www.fundingcircle.com/uk/resources/news/supporting-small-businesses/funding-stories/6yearsofsmallbusinessstories/

Mckinnon, R. I. (1973). *Money and Capital in Economic Development*. Brookings Institution Press.

McKinsey & Company. (2021). The state of AI in 2021. Retrieved from https://www.mckinsey.com

McKinsey & Company. (n.d.). *How Cybersecurity Can Accelerate Your Digital Transformation*. Available at: Digital Transformation Challenges.

Mehrban, S., Nadeem, M. W., Hussain, M., Ahmed, M. M., Hakeem, O., Saqib, S., & Khan, M. A. (2020). Towards secure FinTech: A survey, taxonomy, and open research challenges. *IEEE Access : Practical Innovations, Open Solutions*, 8, 23391–23406. DOI: 10.1109/ACCESS.2020.2970430

Mehrotra, A. (2022). FinTech driven financial inclusion - the hype and the reality of missed targets. *International Journal of Public Sector Performance Management*, 9(3), 1. DOI: 10.1504/IJPSPM.2022.10038076

Menon, S., & Jain, K. (2021). Blockchain technology for transparency in agri-food supply chain: Use cases, limitations, and future directions. *IEEE Transactions on Engineering Management*.

Meyer, L., Burt, T., Romero, S., Weinert, A., Bertoli, G., & Ferres, J. (2019). *How effective is multifactor authentication at deterring cyberattacks?*https://query.prod.cms.rt.microsoft.com/cms/api/am/binary/RW166lD?culture=en-us&country=us

Mhlanga, D. (2021). Financial inclusion in emerging economies: The application of machine learning and artificial intelligence in credit risk assessment. International journal of financial studies, 9(3), 39.

Mhlanga, D. (2020). Industry 4.0 in finance: The impact of artificial intelligence (AI) on Digital Financial Inclusion. *International Journal of Financial Studies*, 8(3), 45. DOI: 10.3390/ijfs8030045

Miato, A. (2023). The adoption of bitcoin by third world countries: how to beat dependency theory? Michelsen, B. (2021). China's Moonshot: How the Introduction of the Digital Renminbi Furthers China's Societal Grip and Threatens the Future of Digital Currencies. *U. St. Thomas JL & Pub. Pol'y*, 15, 813.

Micco, A., & Panizza, U. (2007). Bank ownership and lending behavior. *Economics Letters*, 93(2), 248–254. DOI: 10.1016/j.econlet.2006.05.009

Micco, A., Panizza, U., & Yañez, M. (2007). Bank ownership and performance. Does politics matter? *Journal of Banking & Finance*, 31(1), 219–241. DOI: 10.1016/j.jbankfin.2006.02.007

Mikalef, P., Krogstie, J., Pappas, I. O., & Pavlou, P. (2020). Exploring the relationship between big data analytics capability and competitive performance: The mediating roles of dynamic and operational capabilities. *Information & Management, 57*(2). ScienceDirect. https://www.sciencedirect.com/science/article/pii/S0378720618301022

Mikhaylov, A. (2020). Cryptocurrency market analysis from the open innovation perspective. *Journal of Open Innovation*, 6(4), 197. DOI: 10.3390/joitmc6040197

Mills, K. (2016). The State of Small Business Lending: Innovation and Technology and the Implications for Regulation. SSRN *Electronic Journal*. DOI: 10.2139/ssrn.2877201

Milojević, N., & Redzepagic, S. (2021). Prospects of artificial intelligence and machine learning application in banking risk management. *Journal of Central Banking Theory and Practice*, 10(3), 41–57. DOI: 10.2478/jcbtp-2021-0023

Milutinović, M. (2018). Cryptocurrency. *Економика-Часопис за економску теорију и праксу и друштвена питања*(1), 105-122.

Minesso, M. F., Mehl, A., & Stracca, L. (2022). Central bank digital currency in an open economy. *Journal of Monetary Economics*, 127, 54–68. DOI: 10.1016/j.jmoneco.2022.02.001

Mishkin, F. S. (1999). Lessons from the Asian crisis. *Journal of International Money and Finance*, 18(4), 709–723. DOI: 10.1016/S0261-5606(99)00020-0

Mohammed, A. H., Abdulateef, A. A., & Abdulateef, I. A. (2021). Hyperledger, Ethereum and blockchain technology: a short overview. 2021 3rd International Congress on Human-Computer Interaction, Optimization and Robotic Applications (HORA), Mokhtarian, E., & Lindgren, A. (2018). Rise of the crypto hedge fund: Operational issues and best practices for an emergent investment industry. *Stan. JL Bus. & Fin., 23*, 112.

Moktadir, M., Dwivedi, A., Ali, S. M., Paul, S. K., Kabir, G., & Madaan, J. (2019). Antecedents for Greening the Workforce: Implications for Green Human Resource Management. *International Journal of Manpower*, 41(7), 1135–1153. DOI: 10.1108/IJM-07-2019-0354

Moldow, C. (2015). *A Trillion Dollar Market By the People, For the People How Marketplace Lending Will Remake Banking As We Know It*. https://foundationcapital.com/wp-content/uploads/2020/04/FC_CharlesMoldow_TrillionDollarMarket.pdf

Molina, F., Patel, V., & Zhou, X. (2023). The impact of fintech on small business competition: An urban-rural analysis. *Journal of Business Economics*, 29(1), 89–108.

Momtaz, P. P. (2021a). Entrepreneurial finance and moral hazard- Evidence from token offerings. *Journal of Business Venturing, 36*(5), 106001. doi-10.1016/j.jbusvent.2020.106001

Momtaz, P. P. (2021b). Security tokens. SSRN *Electronic Journal*. doi-10.2139/ssrn.3865233

Mondal, A., & Singh, A. (2018). Emerging technologies and opportunities for innovation in financial data analytics: a perspective. In Big Data Analytics: 6th International Conference, BDA 2018, Warangal, India, December 18–21, 2018 [Springer International Publishing.]. *Proceedings*, 6, 126–136.

Moreno, S. M., Seigneur, J.-M., & Gotzev, G. (2021). A survey of KYC/AML for cryptocurrencies transactions. In *Handbook of Research on Cyber Crime and Information Privacy* (pp. 21–42). IGI Global.

Moscato, V., Picariello, A., & Sperlí, G. J. E. S. w. A. (2021). A benchmark of machine learning approaches for credit score prediction. *165*, 113986.

Moshood Yussuf, Mayowa Timothy AdesinaSunday David EsebreAbdullah Tunde AdewuyiOluwaseun Aaron AdigunTemitope Dickson OlajideComfort Idongesit MichaelDivine ILOH. (2024). Algorithmic trading and machine learning: Advanced techniques for market prediction and strategy development. *World Journal of Advanced Research and Reviews*, 23(2), 979–990. DOI: 10.30574/wjarr.2024.23.2.2405

Mosteanu, N. R., & Faccia, A. (2021). Fintech frontiers in quantum computing, fractals, and blockchain distributed ledger: Paradigm shifts and open innovation. *Journal of Open Innovation*, 7(1), 19. DOI: 10.3390/joitmc7010019

Mushtaq, R., Gull, A. A., & Usman, M. J. T. P. (2022). ICT adoption, innovation, and SMEs' access to finance. *46*(3), 102275.

Nabilou, H. (2019). How to regulate bitcoin? Decentralized regulation for a decentralized cryptocurrency. *International Journal of Law and Information Technology*, 27(3), 266–291. DOI: 10.1093/ijlit/eaz008

Naceur, S. B., & Ghazouani, S. (2007). Stock markets, banks, and economic growth: Empirical evidence from the MENA region. *Research in International Business and Finance*, 21(2), 297–315. DOI: 10.1016/j.ribaf.2006.05.002

Nahar, J., Nishat, N., Shoaib, A. S. M., & Hossain, Q. (2024). MARKET EFFICIENCY AND STABILITY IN THE ERA OF HIGH-FREQUENCY TRADING: A COMPREHENSIVE REVIEW. *International Journal of Business and Economics*, 1(3), 1–13. DOI. 10.62304/ijbm.v1i3.166

Naik, D. P. G., & Oza, D. K. S. (2023). Leveraging the power of blockchain technology for building a resilient crowdfunding solution. *Procedia Computer Science, 230*, 11–20. doi-10.1016/j.procs.2023.12.056

Nakamoto, S. (2008). Bitcoin: A peer-to-peer electronic cash system.

Nakamoto, S. (2008). Bitcoin: A Peer-to-Peer Electronic Cash System. Retrieved from https://bitcoin.org/bitcoin.pdf

Nakamoto, S. (2009). Bitcoin. *A peer-to-peer electronic cash system, 21260.*

Náñez Alonso, S. L., Jorge-Vazquez, J., & Reier Forradellas, R. F. (2021). Central banks digital currency: Detection of optimal countries for the implementation of a CBDC and the implication for payment industry open innovation. *Journal of Open Innovation*, 7(1), 72. DOI: 10.3390/joitmc7010072

Nan, W. V. (2019). Mobile money and socioeconomic development: A cross-country investigation in Sub-Saharan Africa. *Journal of International Technology and Information Management*, 27(4), 36–65. DOI: 10.58729/1941-6679.1392

Naughton, J. M., & Brady, A. K. (2022). Building resilience to crisis through digital financial services with a gender lens. *Enterprise Development & Microfinance*, (1), 28–44. DOI: 10.3362/1755-1986.21-00035

NCSI. (2022). *National Cyber Security Index.* Retrieved from https://ncsi.ega.ee/ncsi-index/?order=-rank

Ndung'u, N., Morales, A., & Ndirangu, L. (2016). Digital Revolution. *Growth's Ups and Downs*, 14.

Nejad, M. (2016). Research on financial services innovations: A quantitative review and future research directions. *International Journal of Bank Marketing*, 34(7), 1042–1068. DOI: 10.1108/IJBM-08-2015-0129

Nejad, M. G. (2022). Research on financial innovations: An interdisciplinary review. *International Journal of Bank Marketing*, 40(3), 578–612. DOI: 10.1108/IJBM-07-2021-0305

Nguyen, N., Duong, T., Chau, T., Nguyen, V. H., Trinh, T., Tran, D., & Ho, T. (2022). A proposed model for card fraud detection based on Catboost and deep neural network. *IEEE Access : Practical Innovations, Open Solutions*, 10, 96852–96861. DOI: 10.1109/ACCESS.2022.3205416

Nicholas Taleb, N. (2021). Bitcoin, currencies, and fragility. *Quantitative Finance*, 21(8), 1249–1255. DOI: 10.1080/14697688.2021.1952702

Nidugondi, S., & Bhargava, M. (2019). Mobile money: Creating a cash-light Africa to solve the financial inclusion problem. The PayTech book: The payment technology handbook for investors, entrepreneurs and FinTech visionaries, 217-221.

Nie, G., Rowe, W., Zhang, L., Tian, Y., & Shi, Y. (2011). Credit card churn forecasting by logistic regression and decision tree. *Expert Systems with Applications*, 38(12), 15273–15285. DOI: 10.1016/j.eswa.2011.06.028

Ni, L. Y., Ye, F., Cheng, M.-L., Feng, Y., Deng, Y.-Q., Zhao, H., Wei, P., Ge, J., Gou, M., Li, X., Sun, L., Cao, T., Wang, P., Zhou, C., Zhang, R., Liang, P., Guo, H., Wang, X., Qin, C.-F., & Dong, C. (2020). Detection of SARS-CoV-2-specific humoral and cellular immunity in COVID-19 convalescent individuals. *Immunity*, 52(6), 971–977. DOI: 10.1016/j.immuni.2020.04.023 PMID: 32413330

Ning, Y. C.-O.-U.-D., Cherian, J., Sial, M. S., Álvarez-Otero, S., Comite, U., & Zia-Ud-Din, M. (2023). Green bond as a new determinant of sustainable green financing, energy efficiency investment, and economic growth: A global perspective. *Environmental Science and Pollution Research International*, 30(22), 61324–61339. DOI: 10.1007/s11356-021-18454-7 PMID: 34993809

Niranjanamurthy, M., Nithya, B., & Jagannatha, S. (2019). Analysis of Blockchain technology: Pros, cons and SWOT. *Cluster Computing*, 22(S6), 14743–14757. DOI: 10.1007/s10586-018-2387-5

Ni, Y. (2024). Navigating Energy and Financial Markets: A Review of Technical Analysis Used and Further Investigation from Various Perspectives. *Energies*, 17(12), 2942–2942. DOI: 10.3390/en17122942

Noether, S., Mackenzie, A., & Research Lab, T. M. (2016). Ring confidential transactions. *Ledger*, 1, 1–18. DOI: 10.5195/ledger.2016.34

Nzioka, D. K. (2010). Impact of mobile banking on microfinance institutions: a case study of Small and Micro Enterprise Program (SMEP), Kenya (Doctoral dissertation, Southern New Hampshire University).

Ochuba, N. A., Amoo, O. O., Okafor, E. S., Akinrinola, O., & Usman, F. O. (2024). Strategies for leveraging big data and analytics for business development: A comprehensive review across sectors. *Computer Science & IT Research Journal*, 5(3), 562–575. DOI: 10.51594/csitrj.v5i3.861

OE, M., & OI, M. As of October 2023, 130 countries, representing 98 percent of global GDP, were exploring the potential use of a CBDC (Kosse and Mattei 2022). 2, 3 A survey of IMF country teams representing 31 Middle East and Central Asia (ME&CA) economies4 finds that 19 countries are considering or exploring a CBDC. This is consistent with information from country authorities' public statements (Figure 3). Most ME&CA countries interested.

oecd-ilibrary. (2024). Retrieved from https://www.oecd-ilibrary.org/industry-and-services/financing-smes-and-entrepreneurs-2022_3bc2915c-en

Ofoeda, I., Amoah, L., Anarfo, E. B., & Abor, J. Y. (2024). Financial inclusion and economic growth: What roles do institutions and financial regulation play? *International Journal of Finance & Economics*, 29(1), 832–848. DOI: 10.1002/ijfe.2709

Oh, J. H., & Nguyen, K. (2018). The growing role of cryptocurrency: What does it mean for central banks and governments. *International Telecommunications Policy Review*, 251, 33–55.

Ohlhorst, F. J. (2012). *Big data analytics: turning big data into big money* (Vol. 65). John Wiley & Sons. DOI: 10.1002/9781119205005

Okoye, C. C., Nwankwo, E. E., Usman, F. O., Mhlongo, N. Z., Odeyemi, O., Ike, C. U. J. I. J. o. S., & Archive, R. (2024). Accelerating SME growth in the African context: Harnessing FinTech, AI, and cybersecurity for economic prosperity. *11*(1), 2477-2486.

Okoye, C. C., Nwankwo, E. E., Usman, F. O., Mhlongo, N. Z., Odeyemi, O., & Ike, C. U. (2024). Securing financial data storage: A review of cybersecurity challenges and solutions. *International Journal of Science and Research Archive*, 11(1), 1968–1983. DOI: 10.30574/ijsra.2024.11.1.0267

Ólafsson, Í. A. (2014). *Is Bitcoin money? An analysis from the Austrian school of economic thought*. Citeseer.

Oliveira, T., Thomas, M., Baptista, G., & Campos, F. (2016). Mobile payment: Understanding the determinants of customer adoption and intention to recommend the technology. *Computers in Human Behavior*, 61, 404–414. DOI: 10.1016/j.chb.2016.03.030

Ololade, Y. J. J. F., & Journal, A. R. (2024). Conceptualizing fintech innovations and financial inclusion: comparative analysis of African and US initiatives. *6*(4), 546-555.

OnDeck. (2024, May 30). *Small Business Cash Flow Trend Report | OnDeck*. OnDeck. https://www.ondeck.com/small-business-trends

Oosthoek, K., & Doerr, C. (2020). Cyber security threats to Bitcoin exchanges: Adversary exploitation and laundering techniques. *IEEE Transactions on Network and Service Management*, 18(2), 1616–1628. DOI: 10.1109/TNSM.2020.3046145

Opatha, H., & Anton Arulrajah, A. (2014). Green Human Resource Management: Simplified General Reflections. *International Business Research*, 7(8), 101. DOI: 10.5539/ibr.v7n8p101

Othman, A. A. E., & Hussein, R. M. (2023). Innovation management framework for achieving sustainability through managing risks of innovative solutions during the design process. Journal of Engineering, Design and Technology.

Oyedele, O. O. (2023). Does green finance affect environmental performance?. *International Journal of Business Innovation*, e27631-e27631.

Ozili, P. K. (2020, January 1). *Financial Inclusion Research Around the World: A Review*. Papers.*ssrn*.com. https://papers.ssrn.com/sol3/papers.cfm?abstract_id=3515515 DOI: 10.2139/ssrn.3515515

Ozili, P. K., Ademiju, A., & Rachid, S. (2023). Impact of financial inclusion on economic growth: Review of existing literature and directions for future research. *International Journal of Social Economics*, 50(8), 1105–1122. DOI: 10.1108/IJSE-05-2022-0339

Ozturk, I., & Ullah, S. (2022). Does digital financial inclusion matter for economic growth and environmental sustainability in OBRI economies? An empirical analysis. *Resources, Conservation and Recycling*, 185, 106489. DOI: 10.1016/j.resconrec.2022.106489

PAGE. (2021). *Digital transformation in customer service*. [online] Pakistan & Gulf Economist. Available at: https://www.pakistangulfeconomist.com/2021/08/23/digital-transformation-in-customer-service/

Paillé, P., Chen, Y., Boiral, O., & Jin, J. (2014). The Impact of Human Resource Management on Environmental Performance: An Employee-Level Study. *Journal of Business Ethics*, 121(3), 451–466. DOI: 10.1007/s10551-013-1732-0

Pakistan Bureau of Statistics 2022, Economic Survey of Pakistan.

Pakistan Telecommunication Authority. (n.d.). Reports and Publications.

Palmié, M., Wincent, J., Parida, V., & Caglar, U. (2019). The Evolution of the Financial Technology ecosystem: An Introduction and Agenda for Future Research on Disruptive Innovations in Ecosystems. *Technological Forecasting and Social Change*, 151(1), 119779. DOI: 10.1016/j.techfore.2019.119779

Pan, Y. (2016). Sustainability trends in financial services sector: Evidence from Europe and North America. In 2016 13th International Conference on Service Systems and Service Management (ICSSSM) (pp. 1-6). IEEE.

Pande, S. S., Mandolikar, S., & Shitole, S. (2022, December 8). Bitland-A decentralized commercial real estate platform. *2022 IEEE Bombay Section Signature Conference (IBSSC)*. Presented at the 2022 IEEE Bombay Section Signature Conference (IBSSC), Mumbai, India. doi-10.1109/ibssc56953.2022.10037494 DOI: 10.1109/IBSSC56953.2022.10037494

Pandey, D. (2022). *Decentralized Exchanges: A Qualitative Comparison Against Centralized Exchanges*. NTNU.

Pandian, K., Pfeiffer, D., & Qian, S. (2023). Decentralized Finance. In *The Emerald Handbook on Cryptoassets- Investment Opportunities and Challenges* (pp. 141–156). DOI: 10.1108/978-1-80455-320-620221010

Panduman, Y. Y. F., Funabiki, N., Fajrianti, E. D., Fang, S., & Sukaridhoto, S. (2024). A Survey of AI Techniques in IoT Applications with Use Case Investigations in the Smart Environmental Monitoring and Analytics in Real-Time IoT Platform. *Information (Basel)*, 15(3), 153. DOI: 10.3390/info15030153

Papadopoulos, G., & Pentzaropoulos, G. C. (2004). Market structure, innovation, and productivity in European telecommunications. *Telecommunications Policy*, 28(9–10), 715–728.

Parashar, B., Sharma, R., Rana, G., & Balaji, R. (2023). Foundation concepts for industry 4.0. In *New Horizons for Industry 4.0 in Modern Business* (pp. 51–68). Springer. DOI: 10.1007/978-3-031-20443-2_3

Parate, S., Josyula, H. P., & Reddi, L. T. (2023). Digital identity verification: Transforming KYC processes in banking through advanced technology and enhanced security measures. *International Research Journal of Modernization in Engineering Technology and Science*, 5(9), 128–137.

Park, C. Y., & Mercado, R. (2015). Financial inclusion, poverty, and income inequality in developing Asia. *Asian Development Bank Economics Working Paper Series*, (426).

Park, H. &. (2020). Transition towards green banking: role of financial regulators and financial institutions. *Asian Journal of Sustainability and Social Responsibility*, .DOI: 10.1186/s41180-020-00034-3

Park, H., & Cho, S. (2024). Artificial intelligence in fintech: Opportunities for small business financial management. *Journal of Financial Technology*, 11(2), 233–250.

Park, S. K. (2023). Sustainable finance in global capital markets. In *Research Handbook on Global Capital Markets Law* (pp. 236–250). Edward Elgar Publishing. DOI: 10.4337/9781800379305.00024

Parveen, S. N., Nasreen, S., Allen, J. V., Kamm, K. B., Khan, S., Akter, S., Lopa, T. M., Zaman, K., El Arifeen, S., Luby, S. P., & Ram, P. K. (2018). Barriers to and motivators of handwashing behavior among mothers of neonates in rural Bangladesh. *BMC Public Health*, 18(1), 1–13. DOI: 10.1186/s12889-018-5365-1 PMID: 29642885

Patel, R., Goodell, J. W., Oriani, M. E., Paltrinieri, A., & Yarovaya, L. (2022). A bibliometric review of financial market integration literature. *International Review of Financial Analysis*, 102035, 102035. Advance online publication. DOI: 10.1016/j.irfa.2022.102035

Patel, R., Migliavacca, M., & Oriani, M. (2022). Blockchain in Banking and Finance: Is the best yet to come. A bibliometric review. *Research in International Business and Finance*, 62, 101718. DOI: 10.1016/j.ribaf.2022.101718

Paul, L. R., & Sadath, L. (2021). *A systematic analysis on fintech and its applications.* Paper presented at the 2021 International Conference on Innovative Practices in Technology and Management (ICIPTM). DOI: 10.1109/ICIPTM52218.2021.9388371

Pazarbasioglu, C., Mora, A., Uttamchandani, M., Natarajan, H., Feyen, E., & Saal, M. (2020). *Digital Financial Services.* https://pubdocs.worldbank.org/en/230281588169110691/Digital-Financial-Services.pdf

Pazowski, P., & Czudec, W. (2014). *Economic prospects and conditions of crowdfunding.* Paper presented at the Management Knowledge and Learning International Conference.

Peltzman, S. (1977). The gains and losses from industrial concentration. [University of Chicago Press]. *The Journal of Law & Economics*, 20(2), 229–263. DOI: 10.1086/466902

Pesaran, M. H., Shin, Y., & Smith, R. J. (2001). Bounds testing approaches to the analysis of level relationships. *Journal of Applied Econometrics*, 16(3), 289–326. DOI: 10.1002/jae.616

Pham, N. T., Hoang, H. T., & Quyen, P. T. P. (2019a). Green Human Resource Management: A Comprehensive Review and Future Research Agenda. *International Journal of Manpower*, 41(7), 845–878. DOI: 10.1108/IJM-07-2019-0350

Pham, N. T., & Thanh, T. V. (2020). The Role of Green Human Resource Management in Driving Hotel's Environmental Performance: Interaction and Mediation Analysis. *International Journal of Hospitality Management*, 88, 102392. DOI: 10.1016/j.ijhm.2019.102392

Pham, N. T., Tučková, Z., & Chiappetta Jabbour, C. J. (2019b). Greening the Hospitality Industry: How Do Green Human Resource Management Practices Influence Organizational Citizenship Behavior in Hotels? A Mixed-Methods Study. *Tourism Management*, 72, 386–399. DOI: 10.1016/j.tourman.2018.12.008

Phillips, A. W. (1976). Stabilization policy and unemployment. [AEA Web]. *The Journal of Economic Perspectives*, 2(1), 19–33.

Phillips, A. W. (1976). The Phillips curve and labor market dynamics. [AEA Web]. *The Journal of Economic Perspectives*, 2(2), 15–30.

Pinto, A. M. (2020). An introduction to the use of zk-SNARKs in blockchains. Mathematical Research for Blockchain Economy: 1st International Conference MARBLE 2019, Santorini, Greece, Plotkin, R. (2020). *Privacy, Security, and Cyberspace*. Infobase Holdings, Inc. DOI: 10.1007/978-3-030-37110-4_16

Plus, I. A. S. (2023). *Reducing financial reporting risk It's more than fixing financial controls*. https://www.iasplus.com/en/binary/dttpubs/1002reducingrisk.pdf

Popescu, A. D. (2021). Central Banks Digital Currency-Opportunities and Innovation. Ovidius University Annals, Series Economic Sciences, 21(1).

Popper, N. (2015). Digital gold: Bitcoin and the inside story of the misfits and millionaires trying to reinvent money.

Porter, M. E., & Heppelmann, J. E. (2015). How smart, connected products are transforming companies. *Harvard Business Review, 93*(10), 96–114.

Porter, M. E. (1979). How competitive forces shape strategy. *Harvard Business Review*, 57(2), 137–145. PMID: 18271320

Porter, M. E. (1979). The structure within industries and companies' performance. [JSTOR]. *The Review of Economics and Statistics*, 61(2), 214–227. DOI: 10.2307/1924589

Post, F. H., Nielson, G., & Bonneau, G. P. (Eds.). (2002). Data visualization: The state of the art.

Pranata, N., & Ray Farandy, A. (2016). Big Data-Based Peer-to-Peer Lending Fintech: Surveillance System through the Utilization of a Google Play Review. Tokyo: Asian Development Bank Institute (ADBI). https://www.adb.org/publications/big-data-based-peer-peer-lending-fintech

Prescott, E. C. (1986). Theory ahead of business-cycle measurement. *Carnegie-Rochester Conference Series on Public Policy*, 25, 11–44. DOI: 10.1016/0167-2231(86)90035-7

Puschmann, T. (2017). Fintech. *Business & Information Systems Engineering*, 59(1), 69–76. DOI: 10.1007/s12599-017-0464-6

Puschmann, T. J. B., & Engineering, I. S. (2017).. . *Fintech.*, 59, 69–76.

Putri, R. S. (2020). Impact of the COVID-19 pandemic on online home learning: An explorative study of primary schools in Indonesia. *International journal of advanced science and technology*, 29(5), 4809-4818.

Qadeer, N. (2023). *Digital Transformation – Are Pakistani Businesses Ready For It?* [online] Nabeel Qadeer. Available at: https://nabeel.pk/portfolio-item/digital-transformation-are-pakistani-businesses-ready-for-it/

Qudah, H., Baqila, B. K. A., Albadienah, J. M. O., AlQudah, M. Z., Al Qudah, S., Alrahamneh, S., Ababne, A., & Qudah, I. (2024). Using bibliometrics to understand algorithmic finance. *Journal of Applied Econometrics*, 27(1), 2389497. Advance online publication. DOI: 10.1080/15140326.2024.2389497

Qudah, H., Malahim, S., Airout, R., Alomari, M., Hamour, A. A., & Alqudah, M. (2023). Islamic finance in the era of financial technology: A bibliometric review of future trends. *International Journal of Financial Studies*, 11(2), 76. DOI: 10.3390/ijfs11020076

Rahid, A. O. J. I. J. S., & Enterprises, M. (2023). SME FINANCING OF COMMERCIAL BANKS IN BANGLADESH. *POLICY DIRECTIONS BASED ON SME LOAN BORROWERS'VIEW*, 6(1), 1–8.

Rahm, E., & Do, H. H. (2000). Data cleaning: Problems and current approaches. *IEEE Data Eng. Bull.*, 23(4), 3–13.

Rai, A. (1996). The effect of credit constraints on financial inclusion. *Development Economics Review*, 9(3), 77–98. PMID: 10158737

Rajput, N., Garg, V., Alaverdov, E., & Varmani, S. G. (2023). *International Business and Block-Chain Ventures* (pp. 69–83). Singapore; Singapore- Springer Nature.

Ramirez, M. D. (2011). Banking and economic growth: A reassessment for Latin America and the Caribbean. *The Quarterly Review of Economics and Finance*, 51(1), 92–109.

Ramus, C. A., & Steger, U. (2000). The roles of supervisory support behaviors and environmental policy in employee "Ecoinitiatives" at leading-edge European companies. *Academy of Management Journal*, 43(4), 605–626. DOI: 10.2307/1556357

Ransbotham, S., Kiron, D., & Prentice, P. (2019). The Digital Dividend: First Mover Advantage. *MIT Sloan Management Review*, 60(3), 1–5.

Raskin, M., & Yermack, D. (2018). Digital currencies, decentralized ledgers and the future of central banking. In *Research handbook on central banking* (pp. 474–486). Edward Elgar Publishing. DOI: 10.4337/9781784719227.00028

Raut, R. D., Gardas, B., Luthra, S., Narkhede, B., & Kumar Mangla, S. (2020). Analysing green human resource management indicators of automotive service sector. *International Journal of Manpower*, 41(7), 925–944. DOI: 10.1108/IJM-09-2019-0435

Ravi, V., & Kamaruddin, S. (2017). Big data analytics enabled smart financial services: opportunities and challenges. In Big Data Analytics: 5th International Conference, BDA 2017, Hyderabad, India, December 12-15, 2017 [Springer International Publishing.]. *Proceedings*, 5, 15–39.

Raza, S. I. (2022, September 26). *Leaks reveal massive breach in security at PM Office*. Retrieved from DAWN: https://www.dawn.com/news/1712044

Raza, A., Tong, G., Erokhin, V., Bobryshev, A., Chaykovskaya, L., & Malinovskaya, N. (2023). Sustaining Performance of Wheat–Rice Farms in Pakistan: The Effects of Financial Literacy and Financial Inclusion. *Sustainability (Basel)*, 15(9), 7045. DOI: 10.3390/su15097045

Reddy, K., Wallace, D., & Wellalage, N. H. (2024). The impact of financial literacy on financial inclusion. *Australian Journal of Management*, •••, 03128962241270809. DOI: 10.1177/03128962241270809

Rehman, S. U., Al-Shaikh, M., Washington, P. B., Lee, E., Song, Z., Abu-AlSondos, I. A., . . . Allahham, M. J. E. (2023). FinTech adoption in SMEs and bank credit supplies: a study on manufacturing SMEs. *11*(8), 213.

Rehman, S. U., Kraus, S., Shah, S. A., Khanin, D., & Mahto, R. V. (2021). Analyzing the relationship between green innovation and environmental performance in large manufacturing firms. *Technological Forecasting and Social Change*, 163, 120481. DOI: 10.1016/j.techfore.2020.120481

Renduchintala, T., Alfauri, H., Yang, Z., Pietro, R. D., & Jain, R. (2022). A survey of blockchain applications in the fintech sector. *Journal of Open Innovation*, 8(4), 185. DOI: 10.3390/joitmc8040185

Ren, S., Tang, G., & Jackson, S. E. (2018). Green Human Resource Management Research in Emergence: A Review and Future Directions. *Asia Pacific Journal of Management*, 35, 769–803. DOI: 10.1007/s10490-017-9532-1

Renwick, D. W. S., Charbel, J. C. J., Muller-Camen, M., Redman, T., & Wilkinson, A. (2016). Contemporary Developments in Green (Environmental) HRM Scholarship. *International Journal of Human Resource Management*, 27(2), 114–128. DOI: 10.1080/09585192.2015.1105844

Renwick, D. W. S., Redman, T., & Maguire, S. (2013). Green Human Resource Management: A Review and Research Agenda*: Green Human Resource Management. *International Journal of Management Reviews*, 15(1), 1–14. DOI: 10.1111/j.1468-2370.2011.00328.x

Resnik, D. B. (2011). What is Ethics in Research & Why is it Important? [URL]

Richardson, M. (2024). *Blockchain Technology: Learn Step by Step Smart Contracts, Monero, Blockchain Wallet, Bitcoin, Zcash, Ethereum, Ripple, Dash, Mining, Litecoin, IOTA*. Mike Richardson.

Riesener, M., Kuhn, M., Schümmelfeder, S., & Schuh, G. (2023). Business Model Research in the Age of Digitalization—A Systematic Literature Research for the Derivation of a Taxonomy of Business Models in the Manufacturing Industry. *Journal of Economics. Business and Management*, 11(4), 157–168. DOI: 10.18178/joebm.2023.11.4.754

Risal, N., & Joshi, S. K. (2018). Measuring green banking practices on bank's environmental performance: Empirical evidence from Kathmandu valley. *Journal of Business and Social Sciences*, 2(1), 44–56. DOI: 10.3126/jbss.v2i1.22827

Risius, M., Breidbach, C. F., Chanson, M., Krannichfeldt, R. V., & Wortmann, F. (2023). On the performance of blockchain-based token offerings. *Electronic Markets*, 33(1), 1. DOI: 10.1007/s12525-023-00652-5

Rizvi, S. K., Rahat, B., Naqvi, B., & Umar, M. (2024). Revolutionizing finance: The Synergy of Fintech, digital adoption, and Innovation. *Technological Forecasting and Social Change*, 200, 123112. DOI: 10.1016/j.techfore.2023.123112

Rogers, D. L. (2016). *The Digital Transformation Playbook: Rethink Your Business for the Digital Age*. Columbia University Press. DOI: 10.7312/roge17544

Rogulenko, T., Orlov, E. V., Smolyakov, O. A., Bodiako, A. V., & Ponomareva, S. V. (2021). Analytical methods to assess financial capacity in face of innovation projects risks. *Risks*, 9(9), 171. DOI: 10.3390/risks9090171

Romānova, I., & Kudinska, M. (2016). Banking and Fintech: A Challenge or Opportunity? *Contemporary Studies in Economic and Financial Analysis*, 98, 21–35. DOI: 10.1108/S1569-375920160000098002

Romero-Castro, N., Pérez-Pico, A. M., & Ulrich, K. (2022). ICOs, IEOs and STOs: Token sales as innovative formulas for financing start-ups. In *Financing startups: Understanding strategic risks, funding sources, and the impact of emerging technologies* (pp. 117–147). Springer. DOI: 10.1007/978-3-030-94058-4_8

Rosavina, M., Rahadi, R. A., Kitri, M. L., Nuraeni, S., & Mayangsari, L. J. Q. R. i. F. M. (2019). P2P lending adoption by SMEs in Indonesia. *11*(2), 260-279.

Rosse, J. N., & Panzar, J. C. (1987). Testing for monopoly equilibrium. *The Journal of Industrial Economics*, 35(4), 443–456. DOI: 10.2307/2098582

Rossi, A., Vanacker, T. R., & Vismara, S. J. A. a. S. (2020). Equity crowdfunding: New evidence from US and UK markets.

Rossi, E. (2022). Stablecoins in Three Dimensions: Foundations of Value in the Crypto-economy. *Available atSSRN* 4123691. DOI: 10.2139/ssrn.4123691

Russell, S., & Norvig, P. (2021). *Artificial Intelligence: A Modern Approach*. Pearson Education. (Russell & Norvig, 2021)

Sabbeh, S. F. (2018). Machine-learning techniques for customer retention: A comparative study. *International Journal of Advanced Computer Science and Applications*, 9(2).

Sabry, F. (2021). *Digital Currency: While All Cryptocurrencies Can Be Termed as Digital Currencies, the Reverse Is Not True* (Vol. 2). One Billion Knowledgeable.

Sachin Kumar Sharma, P. (2023). Small businesses and FinTech: A systematic review and future directions. *Electronic Commerce Research*, 24(1), 535–575. Advance online publication. DOI: 10.1007/s10660-023-09705-5

Saddar, N. (2023).. . *Exploring the Role of Artificial Intelligence and Big Data in the Human Resource Management Process: An Overview of Benefits, Risks, and Ethical Implications.*, 5(1), 12–27.

Saeed, B. B., Afsar, B., Hafeez, S., Khan, I., Tahir, M., & Afridi, M. A. (2019). Promoting Employee's Proenvironmental Behavior through Green Human Resource Management Practices. *Corporate Social Responsibility and Environmental Management*, 26(2), 424–438. DOI: 10.1002/csr.1694

Sage. (2020). *The Practice of Now 2020 Insight and practical advice for today's accountants and bookkeepers based on the latest independent research.* https://www.sage.com/en-gb/blog/wp-content/uploads/sites/10/2020/07/The-Practice-Of-Now-2020.pdf

Sahabuddin, M., Sakib, M. N., Rahman, M. M., Jibir, A., Fahlevi, M., Aljuaid, M., & Grabowska, S. J. S. (2023). The evolution of FinTech in scientific research: a bibliometric analysis. *15*(9), 7176.

Salah, K. R.-F., Rehman, M. H. U., Nizamuddin, N., & Al-Fuqaha, A. (2019). Blockchain for AI: Review and open research challenges. *IEEE Access : Practical Innovations, Open Solutions*, 7, 10127–10149. DOI: 10.1109/ACCESS.2018.2890507

Saleh, F. (2021). Blockchain without waste: Proof-of-stake. *Review of Financial Studies*, 34(3), 1156–1190. DOI: 10.1093/rfs/hhaa075

Samad, A. (2008). Efficiency and performance analysis of conventional and Islamic banks in Malaysia. *Journal of Islamic Finance*, 4(1), 23–39.

Samad, A. (2008). Efficiency of conventional versus Islamic banks in Malaysia: Comparative analysis. [Emerald Insight]. *International Journal of Islamic and Middle Eastern Finance and Management*, 1(2), 191–209.

Sampat, B., Mogaji, E., & Nguyen, N. P. (2023). The Dark Side of Fintech in financial services: A qualitative enquiry into Fintech developers' perspective. *International Journal of Bank Marketing*, 42(1), 38–65. DOI: 10.1108/IJBM-07-2022-0328

Sanga, B., & Aziakpono, M. J. D. B. (2023). FinTech and SMEs financing: A systematic literature review and bibliometric analysis. 100067.

Sanga, B., & Aziakpono, M. J. J. o. E. i. E. E. (2024). FinTech developments and their heterogeneous effect on digital finance for SMEs and entrepreneurship: evidence from 47 African countries.

Santos, A. C. (2017). Cultivating the self-reliant and responsible individual: The material culture of financial literacy. *New Political Economy*, 22(4), 410–422. DOI: 10.1080/13563467.2017.1259302

Santos, C. E.Jr, Silva, L. M., Torquato, M. F., Silva, S. N., & Fernandes, M. A. (2024). SHA-256 Hardware Proposal for IoT Devices in the Blockchain Context. *Sensors (Basel)*, 24(12), 3908. DOI: 10.3390/s24123908 PMID: 38931692

Sarraf, S. (2023). Formulating A Strategic Plan Based On Statistical Analyses And Applications For Financial Companies Through A Real-World Use Case. arXiv preprint arXiv:2307.04778.

Sartika, S. H. (2021). Motivasi Belajar dan Regulasi Diri Mahasiswa Selama Pandemi Covid-19. Edunesia. *Jurnal Ilmiah Pendidikan*, 2(1), 260–271.

Savin-Baden, M., & Major, C. H. (2013). *Qualitative Research: The Essential Guide to Theory and Practice*. Routledge.

SBP. (2018). *State Bank of Pakistan Annual Report*.

SBP. (2019). *Third Quarter Review 2018-19*.

Schaeffer, S. E., & Sanchez, S. V. R. (2020). Forecasting client retention—A machine-learning approach. *Journal of Retailing and Consumer Services*, 52, 101918. DOI: 10.1016/j.jretconser.2019.101918

Schär, F. (2021). Decentralized finance: On blockchain-and smart contract-based financial markets. *FRB of St. Louis Review*.

Schinasi, G. J. (2014). *Safeguarding financial stability: A macroprudential perspective. International Monetary Fund*. IMF.

Schmalensee, R. (1985). Do markets differ much? [JSTOR]. *The American Economic Review*, 75(3), 341–351.

Scholtens, B. (2011). Corporate social responsibility in the international insurance industry. *Sustainable Development (Bradford)*, 19(2), 143–156. DOI: 10.1002/sd.513

Schulte, J., & Hallstedt, S. I. (2018). Company risk management in light of the sustainability transition. *Sustainability (Basel)*, 10(11), 4137. DOI: 10.3390/su10114137

Schumacher, L. V. (2024). Architecting a Retail CBDC. In *Decoding Digital Assets: Distinguishing the Dream from the Dystopia in Stablecoins, Tokenized Deposits, and Central Bank Digital Currencies* (pp. 245-311). Springer. DOI: 10.1007/978-3-031-54601-3_15

Schumpeter, J. A. (1912). *Theorie Derwirt-Schaftlichenentwicklung*. Dunker & Humblot.

Scoreboard, F. S. E. A. O. (Producer). (2024). Oecdilibrary. Retrieved from https://www.oecd-ilibrary.org/sites/13753156-en/index.html?itemId=/content/component/13753156-en

Sempere-Ripoll, F., Estelles-Miguel, S., Rojas-Alvarado, R., & Hervas-Oliver, J. L. (2020). Does technological innovation drive corporate sustainability? Empirical evidence for the European financial industry in catching-up and central and eastern Europe countries. *Sustainability (Basel)*, 12(6), 2261. DOI: 10.3390/su12062261

Senyo, P., Karanasios, S., Gozman, D., & Baba, M. J. E. J. o. I. S. (2022). FinTech ecosystem practices shaping financial inclusion: The case of mobile money in Ghana. *31*(1), 112-127.

Senyo, P. K., Karanasios, S., Gozman, D., & Baba, M. (2021). FinTech ecosystem practices shaping financial inclusion: The case of mobile money in Ghana. *European Journal of Information Systems*, 31(1), 112–127. DOI: 10.1080/0960085X.2021.1978342

Sesini, G., Castiglioni, C., & Lozza, E. (2020). New trends and patterns in sustainable consumption: A systematic review and research agenda. *Sustainability (Basel)*, 12(15), 5935. DOI: 10.3390/su12155935

Sestino, A., Prete, M. I., Piper, L., & Guido, G. (2020). Internet of Things and Big Data as enablers for business digitalization strategies. *Technovation*, 98, 102173. DOI: 10.1016/j.technovation.2020.102173

Sethi, D., & Acharya, D. (2018). Financial inclusion and economic growth linkage: Some cross-country evidence. *Journal of Financial Economic Policy*, 10(3), 369–385. DOI: 10.1108/JFEP-11-2016-0073

Sharma, S. K., Ilavarasan, P. V., & Karanasios, S. J. E. C. R. (2024). Small businesses and FinTech: a systematic review and future directions. *24*(1), 535-575.

Sharma, A., & Adhikary, S. (2021). "Digitalization and Business Performance: The Mediating Role of Innovation." International Journal of Information Management, 61, 102382. McAfee, A., & Brynjolfsson, E. (2012). Big Data: The Management Revolution. *Harvard Business Review*.

Sharma, D. (2016). Nexus between financial inclusion and economic growth: Evidence from the emerging Indian economy. *Journal of Financial Economic Policy*, 8(1), 13–36. DOI: 10.1108/JFEP-01-2015-0004

Sharma, M., & Choubey, A. (2022). Green banking initiatives: A qualitative study on Indian banking sector. *Environment, Development and Sustainability*, 24(1), 293–319. DOI: 10.1007/s10668-021-01426-9 PMID: 33967597

Sharma, V. K., & Bhatia, S. (2023). Knowledge mapping of studies on implied volatility in equity derivatives markets: A bibliometric approach. *International Journal of Financial Markets and Derivatives*, 9(3), 188–207. DOI: 10.1504/IJFMD.2023.133457

Shava, E. (2021). Financial sustainability of NGOs in rural development programmes. *Development in Practice*, 31(3), 393–403. DOI: 10.1080/09614524.2020.1853059

Shaw, E. S. (1973). *Financial deepening in economic development*. Oxford University Press.

Shee, H. M. (2018). The impact of cloud-enabled process integration on supply chain performance and firm sustainability: the moderating role of top management. *Supply Chain Management: An International Journal*, 23(6. Sinha, A. G. (2023). Green financing of renewable energy generation: Capturing the role of exogenous moderation for ensuring sustainable development. *Energy Economics*, 126, 107021.

Shen, Y., Hu, W., & Hueng, C. J. (2021). Digital financial inclusion and economic growth: A cross-country study. *Procedia Computer Science*, 187, 218–223. DOI: 10.1016/j.procs.2021.04.054

Shili, N., & Panjwani, K. (2022). Revolution of Financial Inclusion through Fintech in the Digital Age. In *Digitalization and Economic Development* (pp. 141–160). Routledge. DOI: 10.4324/9781003198284-7

Shi, Q., & Sun, X. (2020). A scientometric review of digital currency and electronic payment research: A network perspective. *Complexity*, 2020(1), 8876017. DOI: 10.1155/2020/8876017

Short, J. (1979). The concept of time in social systems. *The Sociological Review*, 27(1), 87–111.

Shrestha, M. B., & Bhatta, G. R. (2018). Selecting appropriate methodological framework for time series data analysis. *The Journal of Finance and Data Science*, 4(2), 71–89. DOI: 10.1016/j.jfds.2017.11.001

Siegel, J. J. (2021). *Stocks for the long run: The definitive guide to financial market returns & long-term investment strategies*. McGraw-Hill Education.

Siew, E. G., & Farouk, F. M. (2023). Big data analytics implementation issues: A case study of a large bank in Malaysia. Journal of Information Technology Teaching Cases, 20438869231176836.

Sikarwar, T., Goyal, A., & Mathur, H. (2020). Household Debt, Financial Inclusion, and Economic Growth of India: Is it Alarming for India? *Asian Economic and Financial Review*, 10(2), 229–248. DOI: 10.18488/journal.aefr.2020.102.229.248

Silva, E. C., & Mira da Silva, M. (2022). Research contributions and challenges in DLT-based cryptocurrency regulation: A systematic mapping study. *Journal of Banking and Financial Technology*, 6(1), 63–82. DOI: 10.1007/s42786-021-00037-2

Simonsen, J., & Richardson, K. (2017). *The Ethical Decision-Making Manual for Helping Professionals*. Pearson.

Singhal, B., Dhameja, G., Panda, P. S., Singhal, B., Dhameja, G., & Panda, P. S. (2018). How blockchain works. *Beginning Blockchain: A Beginner's Guide to Building Blockchain Solutions*, 31-148.

Singh, D., & Stakic, N. (2021). Financial inclusion and economic growth nexus: Evidence from SAARC countries. *South Asia Research*, 41(2), 238–258. DOI: 10.1177/0262728020964605

Singh, S. K., Del Giudice, M., Chierici, R., & Graziano, D. (2020). Green Innovation and Environmental Performance: The Role of Green Transformational Leadership and Green Human Resource Management. *Technological Forecasting and Social Change*, 150, 119762. DOI: 10.1016/j.techfore.2019.119762

Singhvi, S., & Dadhich, M. (2023). FinTech revolution and future of sustainable banking: Opportunities and risks analysis. *International Journal of Management and Development Studies*, 12(04), 12–21. DOI: 10.53983/ijmds.v12n04.003

Sivarajah, S., & Ahangama, S. (2023). Review of social media's impact on initial coin offerings. In *3rd International Conference on Advanced Research in Computing (ICARC). Presented at the 2023 3rd International Conference on Advanced Research in Computing (ICARC)*. Belihuloya, Sri Lanka. DOI: 10.1109/ICARC57651.2023.10145746

Skouloudis, A. &. (2009). Environmental Quality Management. *Sustainability reporting in Greece: are we there yet?*, 19(1), 43-60.

Skouloudis, A., & Evangelinos, K. I. (2009). Sustainability reporting in Greece: Are we there yet? *Environmental Quality Management*, 19(1), 43–60. DOI: 10.1002/tqem.20235

Small, U. S. Business Administration. (2019, January 30). *Small Businesses Generate 44 Percent of U.S. Economic Activity*. SBA's Office of Advocacy. https://advocacy.sba.gov/2019/01/30/small-businesses-generate-44-percent-of-u-s-economic-activity/

Smirlock, M. (1985). Evidence on the (non) relationship between concentration and profitability in banking. [JSTOR]. *Journal of Money, Credit and Banking*, 17(1), 69–83. DOI: 10.2307/1992507

Soelton, M. N. (2020). Recognizing the Role of Job Satisfaction in Predicting the Relationship Between Political Organization, Organizational Climate, and Organizational Culture on Organizational Citizenship Behaviour on Liquor Distributor Companies in Indonesia. *European Journal of Business and Management*, 12(13), 2222–1905.

SoftCon. (2021). *Sofcom Management Tools & Solutions for Company*. [online] sofcom.net. Available at: https://sofcom.net/blog-digitalization-of-hr-in-pakistan [Accessed 14 Nov. 2023].

Soni, G., Kumar, S., Mahto, R. V., Mangla, S. K., Mittal, M., Lim, W. M. J. T. F., & Change, S. (2022). A decision-making framework for Industry 4.0 technology implementation: The case of FinTech and sustainable supply chain finance for SMEs. *180*, 121686.

Sonkavde, G., Dharrao, D. S., Bongale, A. M., Deokate, S. T., Doreswamy, D., & Bhat, S. K. (2023). Forecasting stock market prices using machine learning and deep learning models: A systematic review, performance analysis and discussion of implications. *International Journal of Financial Studies*, 11(3), 94. DOI: 10.3390/ijfs11030094

Spyropoulos, A. Z., Bratsas, C., Makris, G. C., Garoufallou, E., & Tsiantos, V. (2023). Interoperability-Enhanced Knowledge Management in Law Enforcement: An Integrated Data-Driven Forensic Ontological Approach to Crime Scene Analysis. *Information (Basel)*, 14(11), 607. DOI: 10.3390/info14110607

Srairi, S. (2008). Costs and efficiency in GCC banking: Impacts of scale economies, competition, and strategic behavior. *Journal of Banking Regulation*, 10(3), 200–210.

Srairi, S. (2013). Ownership structure, risk, and performance in MENA banks: A comparative analysis. [Emerald Insight]. *Journal of Financial Economic Policy*, 5(3), 252–274.

Srivastava, K., & Dhamija, S. (2022). Fintech: Application of Artificial Intelligence in indian banking. *Proceedings of International Conference on Communication and Artificial Intelligence*, 601–613. DOI: 10.1007/978-981-19-0976-4_50

Stanko, M. A., & Henard, D. H. (2017). Toward a better understanding of crowd-funding, openness and the consequences for innovation. *Research Policy*, 46(4), 784–798. DOI: 10.1016/j.respol.2017.02.003

State Bank of Pakistan. (2018). Digialization of Services in Pakistan. [online] pp.87–8*. Available at: https://www.sbp.org.pk/reports/annual/arFY18/Chapter-07.pdf

State Bank of Pakistan. (2021). Annual Performance Review 2020.

Statista. (2019). *Crowdfunding - Worldwide | Statista Market Forecast*. Statista. https://www.statista.com/outlook/dmo/fintech/digital-capital-raising/crowdfunding/worldwide

Statista. (2021). *Crowdfunding - Worldwide | Statista Market Forecast*. Statista. https://www.statista.com/outlook/dmo/fintech/digital-capital-raising/crowdfunding/worldwide

Steinbock, D. J. (2005). Data matching, data mining, and due process. *Ga. L. Rev.*, 40, 1.

Stigler, G. J. (1964). A theory of oligopoly. [University of Chicago Press]. *Journal of Political Economy*, 72(1), 44–61. DOI: 10.1086/258853

Stiglitz, J. E., & Weiss, A. J. T. A. e. r. (1981). Credit rationing in markets with imperfect information. *71*(3), 393-410.

Sukarno, K. S. (2020). The use of cryptocurrency as a Payment Instrument. 3rd International Conference on Law and Governance (ICLAVE 2019), Suratkar, S., Shirole, M., & Bhirud, S. (2020). Cryptocurrency wallet: A review. 2020 4th international conference on computer, communication and signal processing (ICCCSP), Tang, Z. (2024). *The emergence of asset price bubbles and debt overhang* University of Glasgow].

Sukma, N., & Namahoot, C. S. (2024). Enhancing Trading Strategies: A Multi-indicator Analysis for Profitable Algorithmic Trading. *Computational Economics*. Advance online publication. DOI: 10.1007/s10614-024-10669-3

Sunarsi, D. R. (2020). Effect of e-leadership style, organizational commitment and service quality towards indonesian school performance. *Systematic Reviews in Pharmacy*, 11, 472–481.

Sundmaeker, H., Guillemin, P., Friess, P., & Woelfflé, S. (2010). Vision and challenges for realising the Internet of Things. Cluster of European research projects on the internet of things. *European Commision*, 3(3), 34–36.

Sunhare, P., Chowdhary, R. R., & Chattopadhyay, M. K. (2022). Internet of things and data mining: An application oriented survey. *Journal of King Saud University. Computer and Information Sciences*, 34(6), 3569–3590. DOI: 10.1016/j.jksuci.2020.07.002

Suryono, R. R., Budi, I., & Purwandari, B. (2020). Challenges and trends of Financial Technology (Fintech): A systematic literature review. *Information (Basel)*, 11(12), 590. DOI: 10.3390/info11120590

Sustainability reporting in Greece: are we there yet? (n.d.). *Skouloudis, A., & Evangelinos, K. I. (2009) Environmental Quality Management*, 19(1), 43-60.

Sutiah, S. S., Slamet, S., Shafqat, A., & Supriyono, S. (2020). Implementation of distance learning during the covid-19 pandemic in faculty of education and teacher training. *Cypriot Journal of Educational Science*, 15(1), 1204–1214. DOI: 10.18844/cjes.v15i5.5151

Swamy, V., & Dharani, M. (2014). Financial inclusion and growth: A cross-country analysis. *Economic Modelling*, 47, 279–293.

Swartz, L. (2022). Theorizing the 2017 blockchain ICO bubble as a network scam. *New Media & Society, 24*(7), 1695–1713. doi-10.1177/14614448221099224

Taher, S. A., & Tsuji, M. (2022). An overview of FinTech in Bangladesh: problems and prospects. *FinTech development for financial inclusiveness*, 82-95.

Tahir, A. H., Umer, M., Nauman, S., Abbass, K., & Song, H. (2024). Sustainable development goals and green human resource management: A comprehensive review of environmental performance. *Journal of Environmental Management*, 370, 122495. DOI: 10.1016/j.jenvman.2024.122495 PMID: 39332294

Tang, G., Chen, Y., Jiang, Y., Paillé, P., & Jia, J. (2018). Green Human Resource Management Practices: Scale Development and Validity. *Asia Pacific Journal of Human Resources*, 56(1), 31–55. DOI: 10.1111/1744-7941.12147

Tao, Z., Peng, B., & Ma, L. (2023). Optimal initial coin offering under speculative token trading. *European Journal of Operational Research*, 306(2), 632–644. DOI: 10.1016/j.ejor.2022.07.023

Tapscott, D., & Tapscott, A. (2016). *Blockchain revolution: how the technology behind bitcoin is changing money, business, and the world*. Penguin.

Tarchoun, M., & Ghraieb, I. (2022). Trade openness relationship with macroeconomic factors on Saudi Arabian economy: ARDL application. *International Trade. Politics and Development*, 6(3), 121–129. DOI: 10.1108/ITPD-03-2022-0005

Tashakkori, A., & Creswell, J. W. (2007). Exploring the Nature of Research Questions in Mixed Methods Research. *Journal of Mixed Methods Research*, 1(3), 207–211. DOI: 10.1177/1558689807302814

Taskinsoy, J. (2022). The Great Silent Crash of the 21st Century. *Available atSSRN* 4274584. DOI: 10.2139/ssrn.4274584

Tehranian, H., & Cornett, M. M. (2010). Investment banking crises: A global perspective. *Global Finance Journal*, 21(3), 223–245.

Tehranian, H., & Cornett, M. M. (2010). The financial crisis and its consequences for investment banks. *Journal of Applied Corporate Finance*, 22(3), 56–69.

Teichmann, F., & Falker, M.-C. (2020). Money laundering through cryptocurrencies. Artificial Intelligence: Anthropogenic Nature vs. Social Origin, Teo, E. G. (2024). Emergence, growth, and sustainability of bitcoin: the network economics perspective. In *Handbook of digital currency* (pp. 185-194). Elsevier. DOI: 10.1007/978-3-030-39319-9_57

Teixeira, A. A., Jose Chiappetta Jabbour, C., Beatriz Lopes de Sousa Jabbour, A., Latan, H., & Henrique Caldeira de Oliveira, J. (2016). Green Training and Green Supply Chain Management: Evidence from Brazilian Firms. *Journal of Cleaner Production*, 116, 170–176. DOI: 10.1016/j.jclepro.2015.12.061

Temelkov, Z., Gogova Samonikov, M. J. I. J. o. I., Business, & Management. (2018). The need for fintech companies as non-bank financing alternatives for sme in developing economies. *10*(3), 25-33.

Thales Group. (2021, October 27). *Majority of businesses don't protect their sensitive data in the cloud, finds Thales*. Thales Group. https://www.thalesgroup.com/en/poland/press_release/majority-businesses-protect-their-sensitive-data-cloud-finds-thales

Thewissen, J., Thewissen, J., Torsin, W., & Arslan-Ayaydin, Ö. (2023). Linguistic errors and investment decisions- the case of ICO white papers. *European Journal of Finance, 29*(7), 826–868. doi-10.1080/1351847x.2022.2075780

Thommandru, A., & Chakka, B. (2023). Recalibrating the banking sector with blockchain technology for effective anti-money laundering compliances by banks. *Sustainable Futures : An Applied Journal of Technology, Environment and Society*, 5, 100107. DOI: 10.1016/j.sftr.2023.100107

Thornton, J. (1992). Co-integration, error correction, and the demand for money in Singapore. [Taylor & Francis]. *Applied Economics Letters*, 12(2), 123–129.

Thota, A. R., Upadhyay, P., Kulkarni, S., Selvam, P., & Viswanathan, B. (2020). Software wallet based secure participation in hyperledger fabric networks. 2020 International Conference on COMmunication Systems & NETworkS (COMSNETS), Tiwari, M., Gepp, A., & Kumar, K. (2020). The future of raising finance-a new opportunity to commit fraud: A review of initial coin offering (ICOs) scams. *Crime, Law, and Social Change*, 73, 417–441.

Tian, L., & Kling, G. (2021). Financial Inclusion and financial technology: Finance for everyone? *European Journal of Finance*, 28(1), 1–2. DOI: 10.1080/1351847X.2021.1981418

TILAHUN. L. B. (2023). THE EFFECT OF GREEN BANKING PRACTICES ON BANKS'ENVIRONMENTAL PERFORMANCE: THE CASE OF COOPERATIVE BANK OF OROMIA HAWASSA CITY BRANCHES. *Doctoral dissertation*.

Timmers, P. (2018). *Business Ecosystems: How to Leverage Business Ecosystems for Digital Transformation and Growth*. CreateSpace Independent Publishing Platform.

Trabulsi, R. U. (2018). The Impact of Accounting Information Systems on Organizational Performance: The Context of Saudi's SMEs. *International Review of Management and Marketing*, 8(2), 69–73. https://www.econjournals.com/index.php/irmm/article/view/6221

Tranfield, D., Denyer, D., & Smart, P. (2003). Towards a methodology for developing evidence-informed management knowledge by means of systematic review. [DOI]. *British Journal of Management*, 14(3), 207–222. DOI: 10.1111/1467-8551.00375

Tran, T. K., Senkerik, R., Vo, H. T. X., Vo, H. M., Ulrich, A., Musil, M., & Zelinka, I. (2023). Initial Coin Offering prediction comparison using Ridge regression, Artificial neural network, Random forest regression, and hybrid ANN-Ridge. *Mendel*, 29(2), 283–294. DOI: 10.13164/mendel.2023.2.283

Treleaven, P., Brown, R. G., & Yang, D. (2017). Blockchain technology in finance. *Computer*, 50(9), 14–17. DOI: 10.1109/MC.2017.3571047

Trotta, A., Rania, F., & Strano, E. (2024). Exploring the linkages between Fintech and ESG: A bibliometric perspective. *Research in International Business and Finance*, 69, 102200. DOI: 10.1016/j.ribaf.2023.102200

Tsindeliani, I., Kot, S., Vasilyeva, E., & Narinyan, L. (2019). Tax system of the Russian Federation: Current state and steps towards financial sustainability. *Sustainability (Basel)*, 11(24), 6994. DOI: 10.3390/su11246994

Turk Ariss, R. (2010). Competitive behavior in Middle East and North Africa banking systems. *The Quarterly Review of Economics and Finance*, 50(2), 180–191.

Tuyon, J., Onyia, O. P., Ahmi, A., & Huang, C. H. (2023). Sustainable financial services: Reflection and future perspectives. *Journal of Financial Services Marketing*, 28(4), 664–690. DOI: 10.1057/s41264-022-00187-4

Txend. (2023, November 7). *The Role of AI and Machine Learning In FinTech - Txend*. Txend. https://txend.com/ai-and-machine-learning-in-fintech/

Tyagi, S. K. S., & Boyang, Q. (2021). An intelligent internet-of-things-aided financial crisis prediction model in fintech. *IEEE Internet of Things Journal*, 10(3), 2183–2193. DOI: 10.1109/JIOT.2021.3088753

Udell, G. F. (2005). Financial innovation, regulation, and competition in bank lending to small- and medium-sized enterprises. *Journal of Banking & Finance*, 30(11), 2945–2966.

Uhde, A., & Heimeshoff, U. (2009). Consolidation in banking and financial stability in Europe: Empirical evidence. *Journal of Banking & Finance*, 33(7), 1299–1311. DOI: 10.1016/j.jbankfin.2009.01.006

Ullah, F., Degong, M., Anwar, M., Hussain, S., & Ullah, R. (2021). Supportive tactics for innovative and sustainability performance in emerging SMEs. *Financial Innovation*, 7(1), 1–31. DOI: 10.1186/s40854-021-00284-8

Umar, M., Rizvi, S. K. A., & Naqvi, B. (2021). Dance with the devil? The nexus of fourth industrial revolution, technological financial products and volatility spillovers in global financial system. *Technological Forecasting and Social Change*, 163, 120450. DOI: 10.1016/j.techfore.2020.120450

Umoga, U. J., Sodiya, E. O., Amoo, O. O., & Atadoga, A. (2024). A critical review of emerging cybersecurity threats in financial technologies. *International Journal of Science and Research Archive*, 11(1), 1810–1817. DOI: 10.30574/ijsra.2024.11.1.0284

UNCTAD. (2020). *E-commerce and the Digital Economy.*

Usanti, T. P., Setiawati, A. P., & Nugraheni, N. (2020). The Legal Principle of Collateral in Fintech Lending. *Hang Tuah Law Journal*, 3(2), 158. DOI: 10.30649/htlj.v3i2.137

Van Eck, N. J., & Waltman, L. (2014). Visualizing Bibliometric Networks. In Ding, Y., Rousseau, R., & Wolfram, D. (Eds.), *Measuring Scholarly Impact* (pp. 285–320). Springer International Publishing. DOI: 10.1007/978-3-319-10377-8_13

Vander Vennet, R. (2002). Cost and profit efficiency of financial conglomerates and universal banks in Europe. [JSTOR]. *Journal of Money, Credit and Banking*, 34(1), 254–282. DOI: 10.1353/mcb.2002.0036

Van, L. T. H., Vo, A. T., Nguyen, N. T., & Vo, D. H. (2021). Financial inclusion and economic growth: An international evidence. *Emerging Markets Finance & Trade*, 57(1), 239–263. DOI: 10.1080/1540496X.2019.1697672

Varga, D. (2017). Fintech, the new era of financial services. Vezetéstudomány / Budapest. *Management Review*, 48(11), 22–32. DOI: 10.14267/VEZTUD.2017.11.03

Verizon. (2020). *Small business cyber security and data breaches.* Verizon Enterprise. https://www.verizon.com/business/resources/articles/small-business-cyber-security-and-data-breaches/

Vives, A. (2022). Social and environmental responsibility in small and medium enterprises in Latin America. In *Corporate Citizenship in Latin America: New Challenges for Business* (pp. 39-50): Routledge. DOI: 10.4324/9781351288484-6

Vives, X. (2008). Innovation and competitive pressure. *The RAND Journal of Economics*, 39(2), 294–309.

Vives, X. (2019). Digital disruption in banking. *Annual Review of Financial Economics*, 11(1), 243–272. DOI: 10.1146/annurev-financial-100719-120854

Vodafone. (2021). M-Pesa celebrates 40 million active customers across Africa. Retrieved from Vodafone website

Voigt, P., & Von dem Bussche, A. (2017). The eu general data protection regulation (gdpr). A Practical Guide, 1st Ed., Cham: Springer International Publishing, 10(3152676), 10-5555.

Vorecol. (2019). *Data Privacy and Security in HR Systems*. Vorecol.com. https://vorecol.com/blogs/blog-data-privacy-and-security-in-hr-systems-10476

Wahba, H., & Elsayed, K. (2015). The mediating effect of financial performance on the relationship between social responsibility and ownership structure. *Future Business Journal*, 1(1-2), 1–12. DOI: 10.1016/j.fbj.2015.02.001

Wang, L., & Liu, Z. (2023). Fintech adoption and its implications for small business efficiency. *Management Review*, 27(4), 187–203.

Wang, W., He, T., & Li, Z. (2023). Digital inclusive finance, economic growth and innovative development. *Kybernetes*, 52(9), 3064–3084. DOI: 10.1108/K-09-2021-0866

Wang, Y., & Zhi, Q. (2016). The role of green finance in environmental protection: Two aspects of market mechanism and policies. *Energy Procedia*, 104, 311–316. DOI: 10.1016/j.egypro.2016.12.053

Wątorek, M., Drożdż, S., Kwapień, J., Minati, L., Oświęcimka, P., & Stanuszek, M. (2021). Multiscale characteristics of the emerging global cryptocurrency market. *Physics Reports*, 901, 1–82. DOI: 10.1016/j.physrep.2020.10.005

Wats, S., Joshi, M., & Singh, S. (2024). Initial coin offerings- current trends and future research directions. *Quality & Quantity, 58*(2), 1361–1387. doi-10.1007/s11135-023-01701-z

Weber, W. E. (2016). Efficiency in central bank digital currency: The next frontier. [IMF]. *IMF Working Paper*, 11(3), 45–56.

Weichbroth, P., Wereszko, K., Anacka, H., & Kowal, J. (2023). Security of cryptocurrencies: A view on the state-of-the-art research and current developments. *Sensors (Basel)*, 23(6), 3155. DOI: 10.3390/s23063155 PMID: 36991866

Weiss, L. W. (1974). The concentration-profits relationship and antitrust. *Industrial Organization Review*, 32(1), 18–27.

Westerman, G., Bonnet, D., & McAfee, A. (2014). *Leading Digital: Turning Technology into Business Transformation*. Harvard Business Review Press.

Whitford, A. B., & Anderson, D. (2021). Governance landscapes for emerging technologies: The case of cryptocurrencies. *Regulation & Governance*, 15(4), 1053–1070. DOI: 10.1111/rego.12366

Wihlborg, C. (2010). Capital adequacy and international banking. *Journal of Banking & Finance*, 34(6), 1161–1172.

Wihlborg, C., & Scholtens, B. (2010). Financial stability and systemic risk: An institutional perspective. *Journal of Financial Regulation*, 22(1), 117–132.

Will, G. (2005). Risk management in financial institutions: Theory and practice. *Journal of Risk Management in Financial Institutions*, 2(3), 211–229.

Will, P. (2005). Financial globalization and risk management. *Finance Research Letters*, 12(1), 47–55.

Winn, J. K. (2016). Mobile payments and financial inclusion: Kenya, Brazil, and India as case studies. In Research handbook on electronic commerce law (pp. 62-88). Edward Elgar Publishing.

Winn, M., Kirchgeorg, M., Griffiths, A., Linnenluecke, M. K., & Günther, E. (2011). Impacts from Climate Change on Organizations: A Conceptual Foundation. *Business Strategy and the Environment*, 20(3), 157–173. DOI: 10.1002/bse.679

Wood, P. (2015). Financing low-carbon innovation: Implications for policy and regulation. *Energy Policy*, 83, 158–167.

World Bank. (2020). *Small and Medium Enterprises (SMEs) Finance*. World Bank; www.worldbank.org. https://www.worldbank.org/en/topic/smefinance

Wronka, C. (2022). Money laundering through cryptocurrencies-analysis of the phenomenon and appropriate prevention measures. *Journal of Money Laundering Control*, 25(1), 79–94. DOI: 10.1108/JMLC-02-2021-0017

Wronka, C. (2023). Financial crime in the decentralized finance ecosystem: New challenges for compliance. *Journal of Financial Crime*, 30(1), 97–113. DOI: 10.1108/JFC-09-2021-0218

Wronka, C. (2024). Crypto-asset activities and markets in the European Union: Issues, challenges and considerations for regulation, supervision and oversight. *Journal of Banking Regulation*, 25(1), 84–93. DOI: 10.1057/s41261-023-00217-8

Wu, X., Deng, W., Quan, Y., & Zhang, L. (2024). Trust Dynamics and Market Behavior in Cryptocurrency: A Comparative Study of Centralized and Decentralized Exchanges. *arXiv preprint arXiv:2404.17227.*

Wu, Y., & Huang, S. J. E. E. (2022). The effects of digital finance and financial constraint on financial performance: Firm-level evidence from China's new energy enterprises. *112*, 106158.

Xiong, X., & Luo, J. (2024). Global Trends in Cryptocurrency Regulation: An Overview. *arXiv preprint arXiv:2404.15895*. DOI: 10.1007/978-3-031-68974-1_4

Xu, W., Wang, T., Chen, R., & Zhao, J. L. (2021). Prediction of initial coin offering success based on team knowledge and expert evaluation. *Decision Support Systems, 147*(113574), 113574. doi-10.1016/j.dss.2021.113574

Xu, X., & Xiao, Y. (2020). Integrating blockchain and IoT in digital ecosystems. *Information Systems Frontiers, 22*(5), 1011–1022. (Xu & Xiao, 2020)

Xu, J., Paruch, K., Cousaert, S., & Feng, Y. (2023). Sok: Decentralized exchanges (dex) with automated market maker (amm) protocols. *ACM Computing Surveys*, 55(11), 1–50. DOI: 10.1145/3570639

Yadav, S., & Verma, A. (2023). Harmonizing fintech regulations for SMEs: A policy perspective. *Global Financial Regulations Review*, 8(2), 132–154.

Yalcin, T. (2005). Capital structure and the cost of capital in European banking. *Financial Markets, Institutions and Instruments*, 14(4), 183–223.

Yang, B., & Zhou, Y. (2008). The rise of Chinese enterprise innovation: Paths, strategies, and implications. *Technovation*, 29(4), 195–204.

Yang, C., & Ma, F. (1991). Structural changes in banking efficiency in China: An empirical investigation. *China Economic Review*, 3(1), 45–72.

Yang, J., & Zhou, Y. (1991). Economic reforms and industrial productivity in China. *China Economic Review*, 3(2), 83–101.

Yasir, A., Ahmad, A., Abbas, S., Inairat, M., Al-Kassem, A. H., & Rasool, A. (2022). How artificial intelligence is promoting financial inclusion? A study on barriers of financial inclusion. *2022 International Conference on Business Analytics for Technology and Security (ICBATS)*. DOI: 10.1109/ICBATS54253.2022.9759038

Yawalkar, P. M., Paithankar, D. N., Pabale, A. R., Kolhe, R. V., & William, P. (2023). Integrated identity and auditing management using blockchain mechanism. *Measurement. Sensors*, 27, 100732. DOI: 10.1016/j.measen.2023.100732

Yong, J. Y., Yusliza, M.-Y., & Fawehinmi, O. O. (2019a). Green Human Resource Management: A Systematic Literature Review from 2007 to 2019. *Benchmarking*, 27(7), 2005–2027. DOI: 10.1108/BIJ-12-2018-0438

Yourstory.com: Opinion – FinTech startups are India's new hope forfull financial inclusion - Anand Tandon (2018) Available Athttps://yourstory.com/2018/08/FinTech -financial-inclusion/ (Lastaccessed on 25.12.2018)

Yuan, S., & Liu, Y. (2006). Exchange rate regimes and macroeconomic performance in developing countries. [University of Chicago Press]. *Economic Development and Cultural Change*, 55(1), 101–123.

Yulianty, P. D., & Senen, S. H. (2023). Analysis Systematic Literature Review: The Study of HRM Transformation Into Digital-Based GHRM Future Research Agenda. *West Science Business and Management*, 1(05), 553–561. DOI: 10.58812/wsbm.v1i05.517

Yuniarti, S., & Rasyid, A. (2020). Consumer Protection in Lending Fintech Transaction in Indonesia: Opportunities and Challenges. *Journal of Physics: Conference Series*, 1477(5), 52016. DOI: 10.1088/1742-6596/1477/5/052016

Yusliza, M.-Y., Othman, N. Z., & Charbel, J. C. J. (2017). Deciphering the Implementation of Green Human Resource Management in an Emerging Economy. *Journal of Management Development*, 36(10), 1230–1246. DOI: 10.1108/JMD-01-2017-0027

Yu, W., Chavez, R., Feng, M., Wong, C. Y., & Fynes, B. (2020). Green Human Resource Management and Environmental Cooperation: An Ability-Motivation-Opportunity and Contingency Perspective. *International Journal of Production Economics*, 219, 224–235. DOI: 10.1016/j.ijpe.2019.06.013

Zabchuk, H., & Pashchuk, I. (2020). THE ROLE OF CRYPTOCURRENCY IN ECONOMIC DEVELOPMENT. *The Institute of Accounting. Control and Analysis in the Globalization Circumstances*, (3-4), 113–119.

Zaghloul, E., Li, T., Mutka, M. W., & Ren, J. (2020). Bitcoin and blockchain: Security and privacy. *IEEE Internet of Things Journal*, 7(10), 10288–10313. DOI: 10.1109/JIOT.2020.3004273

Zaidi, H. B. (2016, February 7). *Clinton emails suggest US examines Pakistani media closely*. Retrieved from DAWN: https://www.dawn.com/news/1237963

Zalan, T., & Toufaily, E. (2017, December 31). *The Promise of Fintech in Emerging Markets: Not as Disruptive*. Papers.*ssrn*.com. https://papers.ssrn.com/sol3/papers.cfm?abstract_id=3200954

Zetsche, D. A., Buckley, R. P., Arner, D. W., & Barberis, J. N. (2017). From FinTech to TechFin: The regulatory challenges of data-driven finance. *NYUJL & Bus.*, 14, 393.

Zhang, & Juhlin. (2018). *Proceedings of the 17th International Conference on Mobile and Ubiquitous Multimedia*. https://doi.org/DOI: 10.1145/3282894

Zhang, Y., Wang, Z., & Chen, L. (2020). Data-driven decision-making in the digital age. *Journal of Information Systems, 34*(1), 24–32. (Zhang, Wang, & Chen, 2020)

Zhang, G., Zhang, X., Bilal, M., Dou, W., Xu, X., & Rodrigues, J. J. (2022). Identifying fraud in medical insurance based on blockchain and deep learning. *Future Generation Computer Systems*, 130, 140–154. DOI: 10.1016/j.future.2021.12.006

Zhang, S., & Wei, J. (2023). Can Digital Inclusive Finance better serve the development of the real economy. *Journal of Applied Finance and Banking*, 13(4), 101–123. DOI: 10.47260/jafb/1345

Zhang, Y., Tong, J., Wang, Z., & Gao, F. (2020, March). Customer transaction fraud detection using xgboost model. In *2020 International Conference on Computer Engineering and Application (ICCEA)* (pp. 554-558). IEEE. DOI: 10.1109/ICCEA50009.2020.00122

Zhao, J., & Ma, X. (2018). Environmental sustainability practices and their performance impact: Evidence from the textile industry. *Journal of Cleaner Production*, 190, 134–147.

Zhao, R., Hou, W., Kumar, V., & Kumar, A. (2023). Signalling effects of doing good in global ICO markets. *Journal of Business Research*, 168, 114224. DOI: 10.1016/j.jbusres.2023.114224

Zheng, S. L. (2021). Rethinking semantic segmentation from a sequence-to-sequence perspective with transformers. *In Proceedings of the IEEE/CVF conference on computer vision and pattern recognition*, pp. 6881-6890.

Zheng, G. W., Siddik, A. B., Masukujjaman, M., Fatema, N., & Alam, S. S. (2021). Green finance development in Bangladesh: The role of private commercial banks (PCBs). *Sustainability (Basel)*, 13(2), 795. DOI: 10.3390/su13020795

Zhixia, C. H., Hossen, M. M., Muzafary, S. S., & Begum, M. (2018). Green Banking for Environmental Sustainability-Present Status and Future Agenda: Experience from Bangladesh. *Asian Economic and Financial Review*, 8(5), 571–585. DOI: 10.18488/journal.aefr.2018.85.571.585

Zhu, M., & Zhang, T. (2021). Alternative financing options for SMEs in the fintech era. *Small Business Finance Journal*, 5(3), 73–90.

Ziegler, T., Shneor, R., Garvey, K., Wenzlaff, K., Yerolemou, N., Hao, R., & Zhang, B. (2017). Expanding horizons: The 3rd European alternative finance industry report. *Unit.no*. http://hdl.handle.net/11250/2479028

Ziolo, M., Filipiak, B. Z., Bąk, I., & Cheba, K. (2019). How to design more sustainable financial systems: The roles of environmental, social, and governance factors in the decision-making process. *Sustainability (Basel)*, 11(20), 5604. DOI: 10.3390/su11205604

Поляцкий, Д. J. П. п. (2023). Современные тенденции развития малого и среднего бизнеса. *16*(4), 31-34.

About the Contributors

Hamad Raza holds a PhD degree from Universiti Teknologi Malaysia (UTM) and currently serving as Assistant Professor at Lyallpur Business School (LBS), Government College University Faisalabad, Pakistan. He has received Certificate of Excellence for his PhD Thesis and also completed his MBA with commendation from University of Bedforshire, UK. He has more than 12 years of teaching and research experience in the field of Accounting and Finance. Dr. Raza has made significant contributions to academia through his various research articles published in Web of Science, Scopus and HEC 'X & Y' indexed journals. He has also authored many book chapters and won research project. He has participated as a session chair and keynote guest speaker in national and international conferences / symposiums. He is Managing Editor of Journal of Marketing and Information Systems (JMIS). He is also reviewer of many reputable journals i.e. Foresight, Applied Economics, Sustainability, Frontiers in Sustainability, Inderscience, Estudios de Economiìa Aplicada, Pakistan Journal of Multidisciplinary Research and Reader Insight journals. Moreover, He is editorial board member of Journal of Excellence in Management Sciences, Journal of Economic Info (JEI) and Journal of Management Info (JMI). Dr Raza is a founding member of Connecting ASIA and TheAPRA research network. He plays a vital role in fostering global connections and supporting educational opportunities. He has conducted several training workshops and has been a member of Scientific Committee as well as Organising Committee of various International Conferences. He is expert in Quantitative Analysis and also Professional Trainer of STATA, VOS Viewer, EndNote as well as Gretl Softwares. Dr. Raza's exceptional accomplishments in both teaching and research have established him as a respected figure in the field of Accounting and Finance. His dedication and expertise continue to inspire and contribute to the academic community.

Ahsan Riaz graduated from the Asia Pacific University of Technology & Innovation, Malaysia, with a Ph.D. in corporate finance with a merit award. Dr.

Ahsan Riaz is an Assistant Professor at Lyallpur Business School GC University Faisalabad, Pakistan. He has vast teaching and research experience of more than 14 years in Accounting and Finance. He has authored many research articles and is an editorial board member of the Asian Institute of Research for the journal Economics and Business Quarterly Reviews. He is also a reviewer of many reputable journals like Sustainability (MDPI), Sustainability Accounting, Management and Policy Journal (Emerald) Asian Social Science, International Business Research, and the International Journal of Economics and Finance of the Canadian Center of Science and Education (CCSE). He is an expert in quantitative analysis and a professional Eviews, Gretl, Jamovi and Vos-Viewer trainer.

Nimra Riaz is a Ph.D. scholar who completed her MS (MPhil) Finance degree at Lyallpur Business School at GC University Faisalabad, Pakistan. She is a Lecturer at the National Business School at the University of Faisalabad, Pakistan. She has more than five years of teaching and research experience in accounting and finance. She has authored ten research articles and three book chapters.

Suresh Ramakrishnan has several years of teaching, research, and practical experience in various capacities in Malaysia. He is currently working as an Associate Professor in Faculty of Management, Universiti Teknologi Malaysia. He has also additional duties of Associate Director Global Strategy & Engagement at UTM International. He has published more than 100 research articles in indexed journals. He has led and collaborated on various national and international research projects, especially from the industries in Malaysia, International grants, University fund and the Malaysian Ministry of Higher Education. He has supervised 52 PhD students and 5 Masters students after his doctoral degree. He was appointed as the Expert Panel for Research and Development Grants by the Kementerian Sains, Teknologi dan Inovasi (MOSTI) - Ministry of Science, Technology, and Innovation, Malaysia. He holds a Ph.D. in Finance from Deakin University Australia.

***

Alhamzah F. Abbas is a senior lecturer at the Faculty of Management, University Technology of Malaysia (UTM), and his research interests are digital marketing, information technology, consumer behavior, tourism marketing, entrepreneurship, and Technology Acceptance Model (TAM). With a focus on emerging trends, he has made significant contributions published in high-index journals, particularly in the fields of digital marketing, tourism marketing, and entrepreneurship. Actively engaged in conferences and collaborative initiatives, his multifaceted roles as an educator and researcher continue to shape the discourse, emphasizing his commitment to academic excellence in the dynamic and interconnected realms of digital marketing, information technology, tourism, entrepreneurship, and TAM.

Syeda Fizza Abbas is a distinguished academician with an illustrious career spanning over 18 years in higher education, specializing in accounting and finance. Currently serving as the Head of Department (Accounting and Finance) at Kinnaird College for Women, Lahore, Pakistan, Syeda Fizza Abbas has been a pivotal member of the institution since 2006. Apart from teaching, Syeda Fizza Abbas contributes significantly to academic leadership through research supervision and curriculum development, shaping the educational landscape in their field. With a robust academic background, Syeda Fizza Abbas holds an MPhil in Commerce from the University of Central Punjab, Lahore, where she achieved a remarkable CGPA of 3.85/4.00, alongside earning a Gold Medal in MSc Banking & Finance from Government College University, Lahore. Syeda Fizza Abbas is renowned for her research prowess, with 18 publications in esteemed journals and presentations at 22 international conferences. Notably, her research on derivatives in Pakistani banks earned acclaim as a Co-Principal Investigator in a HEC SRGP Project in 2019. Awarded for her scholarly contributions, Syeda Fizza Abbas received the Best Paper Awards at prestigious international conferences, underscoring her expertise in analyzing capital structure dynamics in emerging market economies amidst political instability and exchange rate volatility.

Sheikh Abu Taher is currently a professor at the department of Finance and Banking, Jahangirngar University, Bangladesh. He completed BS in Finance from University of Dhaka, Bangladesh and MS and PhD from University of Hyogo, Japan (with Japanese Government Scholarship recipient). His research interest mainly focuses on digital economy, ICT and innovation, digital finance and modeling of future finance industry. He publishes papers in Telematics and Informatics (Elsevier), International Journal of Innovation in the Digital Economy (IGI Global), International Journal Applied Behavioral Economics (IGI Global), Informatica Economica, Springer Medical Lecture Series and so on. He has been nominated for several best papers award namely, O.S. Braunstein Best Student Paper Award (Pacific Telecommunication Council, USA) and International Telecommunication Society Best Student Paper Award (ITS Biennial Conference, Japan).

HumaraAhmad is a distinguished academic and the current Business Head at Ivy College of Business Management. With a prolific academic career, she has published 13 research articles in various renowned journals. In addition to her publications, Dr. Humaira plays a vital role in the academic community as an editor and reviewer for multiple journals. Her leadership extends to organizing and chairing sessions at Connecting Asia, where she contributes to fostering academic collaboration and knowledge exchange. Beyond her administrative and editorial roles, Dr. Humaira is dedicated to mentoring and guiding students in the field of business management. Her expertise and contributions have made her a respected figure in academia.

Areeba Rahat Alvi is a Tax Financial Officer at Vivo Electric, specializing in Finance with a focus on macroeconomic factors, institutional quality, and stock market volatility. Areeba holds an MS in Business Administration from GCUF and is dedicated to exploring and addressing financial dynamics in various contexts.

Muhammad Ashfaq is a dedicated Ph.D. scholar at the Faculty of Management and Administrative Sciences, University of Sialkot, where he focuses on advancing research in green financing and climate change. With a robust industrial background and a keen interest in innovative solutions, Ashfaq brings a wealth of knowledge to his scholarly pursuits. In addition to his academic endeavors, Ashfaq is a seasoned banking professional, serving as a Manager at MCB Bank Limited in Mandi Bahauddin. His role at the bank involves strategic management, customer relations, and operational excellence, showcasing his versatility and commitment to both academic and professional excellence. Ashfaq's dual expertise in academia and banking uniquely positions him to bridge the gap between theoretical research and practical application, making significant contributions to both fields.

Hafiz Muhammad Ayub Awan is a Ph.D. scholar specializing in Islamic Banking & Finance at the International Institute of Islamic Economics, International Islamic University Islamabad. His research focuses on advancing the principles and practices of Islamic finance. Ayub is dedicated to contributing to the development and understanding of ethical financial systems within the Islamic framework.Author also have good knowledge and skills of Economics and Finance.

Shamaila Butt is a highly accomplished professional with a robust academic background and diverse experience. Having earned her Ph.D. in Management specializing in Finance from Universiti Teknologi Malaysia (UTM) in 2020, she demonstrates a commitment to continuous learning. Her extensive educational foundation equips her with strong theoretical knowledge and analytical skills. In her academic journey, Dr. Butt has showcased notable research prowess with a focus on financial complexities, evident in publications such as the "Hybrid model of exchange rate determinants in Malaysia." Transitioning from academia to leadership, she served as the Head of Department of Commerce at the University of Sialkot, Pakistan, showcasing strong organizational acumen. She worked as post doctoral researcher and Director of Research and Innovation at Guangdong CAS Cogniser, Information Technology, Guangzhou, Guangdong, China.

Muhammad Ali Chohan, a PhD graduate from Universiti Teknologi Malaysia, Malaysia, conducted a Sectorial analysis on dividend policy across non-financial Pakistani listed firms. Collaborating with academic leaders, including Prof Dr. Nur Naha and Dr. Suresh Ramakrishnan, he contributed to Malaysia's Higher Education Action Plan. Currently a Postdoctoral Researcher at Guangzhou Nansha Information Technology Park and Director of Research and Innovation, Guangdong CAS Cogniser, Information Technology, he focuses on enterprise risk management using deep learning, fostering academia-industry collaboration through a holistic approach.

Lakshmi D is presently designated as a Senior Associate Professor in the School of Computing Science Engineering and Artificial Intelligence and Assistant Director, at the Centre for Innovation in Teaching & Learning (CITL) at VIT Bhopal. From 2016 to 2021 served as an Educational Research Officer, at Vishnu Educational Development and Innovation Centre (VEDIC) Shri Vishnu Educational Society, Hyderabad She has 26 years of teaching experience. She has addressed innumerable guest lectures, acted as a session chair, and was invited as a keynote speaker at several international conferences. She has conducted FDPs that cover approximately ~1,00,000 plus faculty members including JNTU, TEQIP, SERB, SWAYAM, DST, AICTE, MHRD, ATAL, ISTE, Madhya Pradesh Government-sponsored, MALVIYA MISSION TEACHER TRAINING, Central University of Gujarat and self-financed workshops across India as well as Misamis University, Philipines on Artificial Intelligence in Education: The Future and Futuristic Perspectives both theory and practical sessions. The other titles such as Modern Tools and Software in Teaching Learning Practices, Outcome Based Education, Scientific Educational Practices, Flipped Learning, Blended Learning, Activity Based Learning, Marching towards Quality and Excellence in Higher Educational Institutions, NEP 2022, Emotional Intelligence, Python Essential, Data Analytics, IoT, Machine Learning, Deep Learning, Cyber Security, AR/VR in Medicine, Architecture and Military Applications Instructional Strategies, Assessment techniques, Research Writing, etc. She has 20 international conference presentations, and 90 international journal papers and book chapters inclusive of SCOPUS & SCI. A total of 20 SCOPUS-indexed book chapters. A total of 24 patents are in various stages and 18 patents have been granted at both national and international levels. She was appointed as an external examiner for several Ph.D candidates at reputed universities. Under her supervision, one scholar has completed a Ph.D. at Annamalai University. One scholar is pursuing a Ph.D. right now at VIT Bhopal University. She has won three Best Paper awards at international conferences, one at the IEEE conference and another one at EAMMIS 2021 (First European, Asian, Middle Eastern North African Conference on Management & Information Systems). She received two awards in the year 2022 on the eve of Teacher's Day 1. Kamal Sharma Award of Academic Excellence - 2022 from Lexicon Group of Institutions, Pune for the Engaged Pedagogies. from the virtual ceremony. 2. Bharat Academic Excellence "UttamaAdyapika" Award from Braino Vision. She published a book on "Theory of Computation" in 2003, "Leading Education in the Age of Disruption" in 2021, and "Smart Cities: Disruptive Technologies Driving the Force", in 2023. In the last three editions, she acted as a SPOC for KAVACH and the Smart India Hackathon. She has created 15 hours of the high-quality "Python Essentials" online course at VITyarthi Online Learning Platform. She has 11 SCOPUS Indexed book edits with three CRS Press, Taylor, and Francis, four IGI Global, and two IEEE Rivers.Dr. Lakshmi D is presently designated as a Senior Associate Professor in the School of Computing Science Engineering and Artificial Intelligence and Assistant Director, at the Centre for Innovation in Teaching & Learning (CITL) at VIT Bhopal. From 2016 to 2021 served as an Educational Research Officer, at Vishnu Educational Development and Innovation Centre (VEDIC) Shri Vishnu Educational Society, Hyderabad She has 26 years of teaching experience. She has addressed innumerable guest lectures, acted as a session chair, and was invited as a keynote speaker at several international conferences. She has conducted FDPs that cover approximately ~1,00,000 plus faculty members including JNTU, TEQIP, SERB, SWAYAM, DST, AICTE, MHRD, ATAL, ISTE, Madhya Pradesh Government-sponsored, MALVIYA MISSION TEACHER TRAINING, Central University of Gujarat and self-financed workshops across India as well as Misamis University, Philipines on Artificial Intelligence in Education: The Future and Futuristic Perspectives both theory and practical sessions. The other titles such as Modern Tools and Software in Teaching Learning Practices, Outcome Based Education, Scientific Educational Practices, Flipped Learning, Blended Learning, Activity Based Learning, Marching towards Quality and Excellence in Higher Educational Institutions, NEP 2022, Emotional Intelligence, Python Essential, Data Analytics, IoT, Machine Learning, Deep Learning, Cyber Security, AR/VR in Medicine, Architecture and Military Applications Instructional Strategies, Assessment techniques, Research Writing, etc. She has 20 international conference presentations, and 90 international journal papers and book chapters inclusive of SCOPUS & SCI. A total of 20 SCOPUS-indexed book chapters. A total of 24 patents are in various stages and 18 patents have been granted at both national and international levels. She was appointed as an external examiner for several Ph.D candidates at reputed universities. Under her supervision, one scholar has completed a Ph.D. at Annamalai University. One scholar is pursuing a Ph.D. right now at VIT Bhopal University. She has won three Best Paper awards at international conferences, one at the IEEE conference and another one at

EAMMIS 2021 (First European, Asian, Middle Eastern North African Conference on Management & Information Systems). She received two awards in the year 2022 on the eve of Teacher's Day 1. Kamal Sharma Award of Academic Excellence - 2022 from Lexicon Group of Institutions, Pune for the Engaged Pedagogies. from the virtual ceremony. 2. Bharat Academic Excellence “UttamaAdyapika” Award from Braino Vision. She published a book on “Theory of Computation“ in 2003, “Leading Education in the Age of Disruption” in 2021, and “Smart Cities: Disruptive Technologies Driving the Force”, in 2023. In the last three editions, she acted as a SPOC for KAVACH and the Smart India Hackathon. She has created 15 hours of the high-quality “Python Essentials” online course at VITyarthi Online Learning Platform. She has 11 SCOPUS Indexed book edits with three CRS Press, Taylor, and Francis, four IGI Global, and two IEEE Rivers.

Syed Ahmad Gillani, a distinguished scholar, obtained his PhD degree in corporate finance with honors from University Technology Malaysia (UTM). Currently, he is serving Assistant Professor at Lyallpur Business School, GC University Faisalabad, Pakistan. With over 16 years of extensive experience in the field of Accounting and Finance, Dr. Gillani is a renowned educator and researcher. Dr. Gillani has made significant contributions to academia through his numerous research articles and book chapters. His expertise has earned him the role of Guest Editor for the prestigious Studies of Applied Economics. Additionally, he serves as an esteemed member of the editorial boards for the Journal of Economic Info and the Journal of Management Info. His proficiency is acknowledged by renowned journals, including the Journal of Sustainability, Foresight Journal, Inderscience, Journal of Applied Economics, and Reader Insight, where he actively participates as a reviewer. As a founding member of Connecting ASIA and the head of international grants and scholarships at APRA, Dr. Gillani plays a vital role in fostering global connections and supporting educational opportunities. His expertise in quantitative analysis is widely recognized, and he is also regarded as a professional STATA and SPSS trainer. Dr. Syed Ahmad Gillani's exceptional accomplishments in both teaching and research have established him as a respected figure in the field of Accounting and Finance. His dedication and expertise continue to inspire and contribute to the academic community.

Resham Iftikhar is a dedicated Ph.D. scholar at the University of Sialkot, specializing in business administration. Her research focuses on finance and economics. Resham is committed to bridging the gap between academic theory and real-world applications and making significant contributions to both fields.

Shriya. K holds a bachelor's degree in commerce from SDNB Vaishnav college for women, Chennai, Tamil Nādu, India. She holds a master's in business administration from SRM Institute of Science and Technology, Chennai, Tamil Nādu, India. she is currently pursuing a full-time Ph.D. in the field of management-finance on the topic of investor perception and sentiment analysis in portfolio management from srm institute of science and technology, Chennai, Tamil Nādu, India. Her main research interest falls under banking, financial services, and investment portfolio management. Her perseverance toward research started during her master's when she presented a research paper at Bharathidasan university and a business plan at IIM Udaipur. while she holds pride in presenting her research articles at prestigious institutions like IIM Bodhgaya, IIM Nagpur, and Loyola college. She holds the credit of publishing her articles in UGC care journals and book chapters.

Ibtisam Khalid is a PhD Scholar in the Faculty of Management and Administrative Science at the University of Sialkot, Pakistan. Her research focuses on advancing management practices by bridging theoretical knowledge with practical application. Committed to academic excellence, Ibtisam actively participates in research projects and academic conferences, contributing valuable insights to the field of management science.

Saleh F. A. Khatib is a senior lecturer in Accounting and Finance at the Faculty of Management, Universiti Teknologi Malaysia (UTM), Malaysia. He has been awarded a Ph.D. in Finance from UTM in 2022. His exceptional work and dedication to the field also earned him the Chancellor Award and Best Postgraduate Student Award. Throughout his academic career, Dr. Khatib has conducted extensive research on various functional domains, including Corporate Governance, Auditing, Corporate Finance, Corporate Social Responsibility, and Sustainability Disclosure. Dr. Khatib's articles are published in top-tier academic journals, including theBusiness Strategy and The Environment, Management Review Quarterly, Journal of Financial Reporting and Accounting, Global Business Review, Corporate Governance, Meditarian Accountancy Research, and Environmental Science and Pollution Research, among others.

Manjit Kour is working as Professor at University Business School at Chandigarh University. She holds a PhD in Business Management from IK Gujral Punjab Technical University, India. She has a good research record with several research papers published in reputed journals. She is an editorial board member and reviewer of many reputed journals including Scopus and ABDC-indexed journals. Her areas of interest include sustainability, green practices, Fintech, online marketing trends and business ethics.

Tariq Mahmood is a Government Officer working with the Punjab Police, Pakistan. In addition to his professional responsibilities, he has recently completely his MS in Finance from the Faculty of Management and Administrative Sciences at the University of Sialkot. His dual role as a government officer and a scholar reflects a deep commitment to both his country and the pursuit of higher education. Mr. Tariq Mahmood is focused on expanding his expertise in management and administrative sciences, especially in Finance.

Ain Naadia Mazlan is a senior lecturer in the Faculty of Civil Engineering at Universiti Teknologi Malaysia and manages International Alliances at UTM International. She specialises in economics in construction, risk management, and value engineering. She is an associate fellow at the Construction Research Centre, the Institute for Smart Infrastructure and Innovative Construction, and a former residential fellow at Rahman Putra College. She has a 7 on the H-index and has authored and co-authored more than ten publications. In addition to her research, she is actively involved in community social engagement and participates in international collaborations.

Chippy Mohan having 8 years of teaching experience and research experience. she has published 11 books and International & National 10 articles

Zubair Mustafa stands as a distinguished figure in the field of finance, wielding a Ph.D. and an expansive repertoire of multidimensional expertise that enriches the financial landscape. His illustrious career seamlessly intertwines academia, research, and practical projects, reflecting a profound commitment to advancing financial knowledge. With a strategic focus on shareholders' wealth, corporate sustainability, and the principles of good corporate governance, Zubair has emerged as a thought leader, shaping the discourse in these pivotal areas. His impactful research, prominently featured in reputable journals, has not only expanded the boundaries of financial understanding but has also earned him commendable reviews, solidifying his reputation as a scholar of merit. Beyond the confines of academia, Zubair actively applies his wealth of knowledge to diverse real-world projects, addressing challenges with a seasoned perspective.

Abdul Rashid is an HEC Approved Supervisor and currently serves as a Professor, Director General (DG), and Chairman of Research. He earned his Ph.D. from the University of Sheffield, United Kingdom. He holds an M.Phil. in Financial Economics from the Institute of Business Management, Karachi, Pakistan, an M.A. in Economics, and a B.A. from Bahauddin Zakariya University, Multan, Pakistan. His areas of specialization include Capital Structure and Capital Markets. Dr.

Rashid's research interests focus on Behavioral Finance, International Finance, and Applied Econometrics.

Hamad Raza holds a PhD degree from Universiti Teknologi Malaysia (UTM) and currently serving as Assistant Professor at Lyallpur Business School (LBS), Government College University Faisalabad, Pakistan. He has received Certificate of Excellence for his PhD Thesis and also completed his MBA with commendation from University of Bedforshire, UK. He has more than 12 years of teaching and research experience in the field of Accounting and Finance. Dr. Raza has made significant contributions to academia through his various research articles published in Web of Science, Scopus and HEC 'X & Y' indexed journals. He has also authored many book chapters and won research project. He has participated as a session chair and keynote guest speaker in national and international conferences / symposiums. He is Managing Editor of Journal of Marketing and Information Systems (JMIS). He is also reviewer of many reputable journals i.e. Foresight, Applied Economics, Sustainability, Frontiers in Sustainability, Inderscience, Estudios de Economía Aplicada, Pakistan Journal of Multidisciplinary Research and Reader Insight journals. Moreover, He is editorial board member of Journal of Economic Info (JEI) and Journal of Management Info (JMI). Dr Raza is a founding member of Connecting ASIA and TheAPRA research network. He plays a vital role in fostering global connections and supporting educational opportunities. He has conducted several training workshops and has been a member of Scientific Committee as well as Organising Committee of various International Conferences. He is expert in Quantitative Analysis and also Professional Trainer of STATA, VOS Viewer as well as Gretl Softwares. Dr. Raza's exceptional accomplishments in both teaching and research have established him as a respected figure in the field of Accounting and Finance. His dedication and expertise continue to inspire and contribute to the academic community.

Baranidharan S, specialized in Finance Economics and Econometrics. Having 5 years research experience, 2 years of Industrial experience and 6 years of teaching experience. Published 6 patent, 45 research articles in international and national journal which are indexed in Scopus, WoS, Proquest, ABDC, etc.,

Nadia Sadiq is serving as a Lecturer in Economics on the disposal of the Punjab government in Pakistan. She has teaching and research experience consisting of more than 12 years in the field of Economics and Commerce.

Muhammad Farrukh Shahzad is a PhD researcher in the School of Economics and Management, Beijing University of Technology, majoring in Management Sciences and Engineering. His area of interest is technology management, artificial intelligence, risk Management, technology adoption and innovation. He is a young, emerging researcher who has published several papers in Scopus and WOS reviewed international journals. His contributions have not only advanced academic understanding but have also provided practical insights for policymakers and industry stakeholders aiming to promote sustainable development and environmental protection.

Yasir Tanveer, is currently working as an assistant professor at Lyallpur Business School, GC University Faisalabad, Pakistan. He obtained his PhD in Management Science and Engineering from Beijing University of Posts and Telecommunications, China. His area of interest includes leadership, conflict management and emotional intelligence.

Muhammad Usman is a PhD researcher in the Faculty of Management and Administrative Sciences, Department of Business Administration, University of Sialkot, Pakistan.

T. Velmurugan is an assistant professor in finance in the college of management at srm institute of science and technology, Chennai, Tamil Nādu, India with over the experience of more than 20 years in the field of teaching. He holds a Doctorate degree from Bharathiar university, Coimbatore, Tamil Nādu, India. He holds a master's degree in philosophy in finance from Annamalai university and a master's in business administration in finance from Bharathidasan University and a bachelor's degree in business administration from Bharathidasan University, Trichy, Tamil Nādu, India. He qualified in SET in the year 2016. His keen interest in research developed in his initial days of education which fulfilled his dream of achieving in publishing and presenting more than 20 research articles in his expertise domain of finance. His achievements have proven his potential and keen interest in the future of research in various areas including financial management, portfolio management, and financial services

Index

K

M

N

P

R

S

V

www.ingramcontent.com/pod-product-compliance
Lightning Source LLC
LaVergne TN
LVHW080350011026
849161LV00009B/2248
* 9 7 9 8 3 6 9 3 6 3 8 6 7 *